CONVOY

CONVOY

The Defence of Sea Trade
1890–1990

JOHN WINTON

LONDON
MICHAEL JOSEPH

First published in Great Britain by Michael Joseph Ltd
44 Bedford Square, London WC1
1983

ISBN 0 7181 2163 5

Typeset by Rowland Phototypesetting Ltd, Bury St Edmunds
Printed in Great Britain by Hollen Street Press, Slough,
and bound by Dorstel Press, Harlow

List of Illustrations

Second World War air cover from MAC and Fighter Catapult ships (*Fleet Air Arm Museum and Imperial War Museum*)
Air cover for the 1980s
HMS *Arrow* helicopter (*John Winton*)
HMS *Invincible* (*HMS* Invincible *Photographic Section*)

Chapter One

On the afternoon of Saturday 5 September 1914, the 2940-ton light cruiser HMS *Pathfinder* was off the approaches to the Firth of Forth, carrying out an anti-submarine patrol on a line from St Abb's Head to May Island to Bass Rock. Commanded by Captain Francis Martin-Leake, *Pathfinder* was leader of the 8th Flotilla, of about twenty 30-knot destroyers, and twelve torpedo-boats (known as 'oily wads' because they burnt oil fuel instead of coal). *Pathfinder* was steaming at an economical 6 knots, to save coal. She had to patrol five days a week, had a small coal-bunker capacity, was long out of dock, and still had to have full speed available at ten minutes' notice.

It was a fine sunny afternoon, with good visibility all round. At about half past three, *Pathfinder* was sighted through the periscope of U-21, commanded by Leutnant Otto Hersing. Hersing had seen *Pathfinder* earlier in the day but had been unable to get close enough to fire. Now, *Pathfinder* was returning on her patrol beat and Hersing was able to attack. At about 3.45 p.m. U-21 fired one 19.69-inch Type 'G' (Whitehead) torpedo. Its track was actually sighted from *Pathfinder*'s bridge, on the starboard bow, range between two and three thousand yards, but before any avoiding action could be taken the torpedo hit *Pathfinder* on the starboard side, just below the bridge.

The explosion countermined the ammunition in the forward magazine and the front half of the ship virtually disintegrated. The fo'c'sle forward of the bridge was blown completely off. The foremast and the forward funnel were blasted over the side. The ship lost way at once and was soon motionless, lying under a vast billowing pall of thick black smoke. She settled very quickly until water began flooding over her upper deck.

Most of *Pathfinder*'s people must have been killed at once, but there were survivors. 'It must have been about five minutes after we were hit that the bulkheads down below carried away,' said one of her Engineer Officers, Lieut (E) Stallybrass. 'The ship gave a heavy lurch forward, and took an angle of about 40 degrees down by the bow. Water came swirling up to the searchlight platform, and the Captain said, "Jump you devils, jump!" All except two of us jumped. The Captain stayed with his ship until she sank and the Captain's Secretary stopped to unlace his boots. Both were saved.'

The explosion was so violent it was felt in a trawler 10 miles away. The great mass of smoke was sighted from the land. Trawlers, motor fishing-boats, destroyers and 'oily wads' were soon on the spot. They found the surface of the sea strewn with a great trail of sad debris, of seamen's caps, and jerseys, boots, letters, photographs, furniture, smashed boats, books, planks, life-jackets and men's corpses, stretching for over a mile. Some fifty-eight officers and men, many of them very badly wounded and burned, were rescued. Four died on their way to the mainland, and more later. The final toll was 259 men lost.

The sinking of *Pathfinder*, an incident in the naval war now almost totally forgotten, was the very first time in naval history that a warship had been sunk by a self-propelled torpedo fired from a genuine submarine in the open sea.

Pathfinder's fate was completely eclipsed on 20 September in the 'Broad Fourteens' off the Dutch coast, where three elderly British cruisers, *Aboukir*, *Cressy* and *Hogue*, nicknamed with somewhat macabre humour the 'Livebait Squadron', were patrolling in support of the destroyer flotillas based at Harwich. Bad weather had forced the destroyers to return to base and the three ancients were quite alone when, at 6.30 a.m. that morning, U-9 (Leutnant Otto Weddigen) fired a single torpedo at *Aboukir*.

One torpedo hit was enough. *Aboukir* listed heavily to starboard and, some twenty-five minutes later, turned right over, floated bottom upwards for a time, and then sank. Meanwhile her companions believed *Aboukir* had struck a mine, and *Hogue* had actually stopped to pick up *Aboukir*'s survivors when she herself was hit by two torpedoes and sank within ten minutes. *Cressy* had also lowered her boats for *Aboukir*'s people, and she did not abandon them now. The result was that U-9 had time to reload and shortly after 7 a.m. Weddigen hit *Cressy* with two more torpedoes. A quarter of an hour later, she rolled over and sank. Nearly 1400 officers and men, most of them naval reservists who had only just joined up, were lost.

In October, Weddigen followed up this tremendous success with another. On the 15th he boldly attacked the 10th Cruiser Squadron off the east coast of Scotland and, although the ships were cruising in dispersed formation specifically to minimize the risk of submarine attack, Weddigen hit and sank the cruiser *Hawke*. Only one boat got safely away from the ship, with three officers and forty-six men in it. The rest of *Hawke*'s company, nearly 500 men, were all lost.

The Germans were also using other unusual weapons. Fields of mines had been discovered, of a type and in locations illegal under international law, which had been sown in the very first days of the war. The cruiser *Amphion* was an early victim, mined and sunk on 6 August 1914 – only two days after Britain declared war on Germany – with the loss of 171 lives (including, ironically, twenty prisoners from the German mine-layer *Königin Luise* which had actually laid the mines).

Although U-boats were proving themselves capable of inflicting stunning blows, there was at first no undue alarm in the Admiralty. No particular interest was shown in another sinking, five days after *Hawke*, on 20 October. No lives were lost, but the incident had the most ominous overtones for the future. It was in the North Sea, on a calm, slightly misty day. The small 866-ton British steamer SS *Glitra* was following the approved Admiralty route, making about 8 knots, bound from Grangemouth to Stavanger with a cargo of coal, coke, iron plates and oil. At about noon she was some 14 miles WSW of Skudesnaes on the Norwegian coast and hoisted the signal for a pilot.

The pilot boat was on its way out to *Glitra* when a 'low, long object' was sighted about three miles to the seaward. It was actually U-17 (Oberleutnant zur Sëë Feldkirchner) returning to Germany after an uneventful patrol. The pilot boat, obviously fearing trouble, returned to shore but *Glitra*'s master, Mr L. A. Johnston, altered course to the north, to put more distance between himself and the submarine.

The U-boat was some 5 knots faster than *Glitra* and followed her. It made a complete circle round her and then fired one round from a gun abaft the conning tower. Mr Johnston took the hint and stopped. The U-boat came within a ship's length and launched a collapsible boat, with one officer and two men, all armed.

Mr Johnston was ordered off his bridge, at pistol point. The Germans, evidently in a highly excitable state, tore down *Glitra*'s ensign and, as variously reported, stamped and spat on it. Mr Johnston and his crew of seventeen were hustled down into the lifeboat without time to collect their belongings. *Glitra*'s charts and papers were taken back to the U-boat, while she was scuttled by opening the sea-cocks. U-17 then towed the lifeboat towards the Norwegian coast for about a quarter of an hour before casting it loose. Johnston was told to row for the shore. He and his crew were later picked up by the pilot boat, and all of them survived.

Glitra was thus the first merchant ship to be sunk by a U-boat, albeit she was scuttled and not torpedoed. Whatever Feldkirchner's boarding party may have done, he himself had behaved perfectly properly. German Naval Prize Regulations allowed an enemy ship to be destroyed if 'it seems inexpedient or unsafe' to bring her in. But before destruction all persons on board were to be placed in safety, with their goods and chattels, if possible. Under international law, ship's boats were not places of safety, unless land was close and the weather was good. U-17 had therefore towed the boat some way towards shore.

As the U-boat war developed, it was clear that the niceties and legal definitions of international law and prize regulations were very much matters of personal interpretation. In the end, it all depended on how the individual

U-boat captain saw the situation through his periscope. The first incident to cause anything of a public outcry occurred six days after *Glitra*'s sinking, when U-24 encountered the French steamer SS *Amiral Ganteaume* in the Channel.

The ship was bound from Calais to Le Havre with some 2400 Belgian refugees, men, women and children. U-24's commander, Leutnant Schneider was less scrupulous than Feldkirchner. The English Channel was a busy waterway. Surfacing the U-boat would put her at risk. By international law Schneider was only entitled to sink a merchantman, with her passengers and crew still on board, if she had persistently refused to stop on being summoned, or if her crew had actively resisted an attempt to board or search. Neither of these conditions obtained, but Schneider fired one torpedo, without surfacing or giving any warning. The ship was badly damaged but eventually reached Le Havre, although some thirty people were killed. The U-boat Captain was accused of breaching international law. It was claimed that he must have seen that some of the people on board were women and children. Schneider is supposed to have replied that he did indeed see people on board but the ship appeared to him to be a troopship.

These first U-boat attacks, in 1914 and the first part of 1915, in no way amounted to a U-boat 'campaign'. They were not directed by any central strategy, except that U-boat commanders were briefed to attack targets of opportunity. The manner and place and the targets of the attacks were left entirely to the U-boat commanders, and they remained sporadic and uncoordinated for most of the first year of the war. It was as though the Imperial German Navy had found its opponent's wind-pipe purely by accident and, after some experimental and tentative squeezes, had let it go again.

In fact, with the sinkings of *Pathfinder*, the 'Livebait Squadron', *Hawke* and *Glitra*, a pre-war age of illusion about submarines, a naive innocence about the true and savage nature of submarine warfare, had begun to pass away. All the pre-war discussion about its ethics, and the likely course such warfare would take, began to seem increasingly academic, although lawyers and naval historians continued to argue whether such-and-such a U-boat had contravened such-and-such an article of international law by such-and-such an action for many years after the war. But, from 1914 onwards, in practical terms the U-boat became its own arbiter.

The likely course of events was accurately forecast by Lord Fisher before the war, at a time when many people found it literally unthinkable that a U-boat would simply sink its prey rather than capture it. They could not shake their minds free of the traditional *guerre de course* image of the privateer capturing his prize and then, in his own interests as well as his country's, bringing it triumphantly back into harbour.

'There is nothing else the submarine can do except sink her capture,' Fisher wrote, in a Memorandum on 'The Submarine and Commerce' in 1913:

and it must therefore be admitted that (provided it is done, and however inhuman and barbarous it may appear) this submarine menace is a truly terrible one for British commerce and Great Britain alike, for no means can be suggested at present of meeting it except by reprisals. . . . It has been suggested that it should be obligatory for a submarine to fire a warning gun, but is such a proceeding practical? We must bear in mind that modern submarines are faster on the surface than the majority of merchantmen, and will not necessarily need to dive at all. Therefore, as the submarine would in most cases be sighted, and as she has no prize crew to put on board, the warning gun is useless, as the only thing the submarine could do would be to sink the enemy; also the apparently harmless merchant vessel may be armed, in which case the submarine may have given herself away if she did not sink her. . . .

Moreover [Fisher went on] . . . under numerous circumstances can a submarine allow a merchant ship to pass unmolested? Harmless trader in appearance, in reality she may be one of the numerous fleet auxiliaries, a mine-layer, or carrying troops, and so on. Can the submarine come to the surface to inquire and lose all chance of attack if the vessel should prove to be faster than she is?

What can be the answer to all the foregoing but that (barbarous and inhuman as, we again repeat, it may appear), if the submarine is used at all against commerce, she must sink her captures?

Two world wars later, Fisher's argument now seems so inescapable as to be hardly worth disputing. But other politicians and naval officers of his day found it impossible to accept. Churchill, First Lord of the Admiralty at the time, 'read and re-read . . . the brilliant and valuable paper on Submarines' but said there were a few points on which he was not convinced. 'Of these the greatest is the question of the use of submarines to sink merchant vessels. I do not believe this would ever be done by a civilized Power.'

Churchill had just as good a command of the English language as Fisher and, after making several hair-raising comparisons of such outrages with the deliberate spreading of pestilence and the assassination of individuals, he concluded that these were 'frankly unthinkable propositions, and the excellence of your paper is, to some extent, marred by the prominence assigned to them'.

The First Sea Lord, Prince Louis of Battenberg, agreed with Churchill that Fisher's 'brilliant paper was marred by this suggestion'. Commodore Roger Keyes, then Commodore of Submarines, said later 'we all discarded' this possible behaviour by submarines as 'impossible and unthinkable'.

Fisher correctly described the progress of events, as though giving an accurate prognosis of a disease, but, ironically, he neglected to provide a remedy. Having prophesied what submarines would do, he did not provide the Navy with the suitable ships and weapons to hunt them down and destroy them. Thus, soon after the war began, fishing vessels, trawlers, motor-boats, yachts, small craft of all kinds, had to be pressed into service to form an improvised Auxiliary Patrol, as it was called, with zones of operation which eventually covered the whole of the waters around the United Kingdom. At the same time, destroyers had to be diverted from what was regarded as their main purpose, of escorting the fleet, to hunt for submarines.

Every sighting of a submarine, or even the suspicion of a submarine, caused alarms and excursions and diversions of ships. One supposed penetration of Scapa Flow by a submarine on 1 September 1914 produced, as Admiral Bacon described it, 'the same sort of excitement as would a cobra in a drawing-room' and such was the resulting *furore* it was sardonically nicknamed the 'battle of Scapa'. There were several other submarine alarums, which forced the Grand Fleet temporarily to abandon Scapa as a base until its submarine defences had been improved.

Anti-submarine weapons had also to be improvised. For years there was no underwater listening device or effective depth-charge, although a special form of sweep was soon developed, fitted with explosive devices designed to detonate in contact with a U-boat's hull, which two trawlers could tow between them. Extensive mine and net barriers were laid, one eventually stretching across the Dover Straits. The tops of barriers were sometimes fitted with indicator buoys, to betray the disturbance of the submarine's entry. The first decoy or 'Q' ship, *Victoria*, was fitted out in November 1914, as a counter to submarines which shelled their targets on the surface.

But for a long time, the main defence against submarines was the human eye. Escorting craft were supposed to sight their quarry, like nautical gaze-hounds, and then to run it down, attacking it if possible with gunfire or ramming, and persistence. These methods did occasionally succeed. On 10 March 1915, off Fife Ness on the east coast of Scotland, U-12 was sunk by ramming and gunfire after a hunt which lasted nearly four days and in which shore signal stations cooperated usefully with the hunters afloat. Eight days later, off the Pentland Firth, Otto Weddigen (then commanding U-29) was lost with all his crew when their U-boat was rammed and sunk by the battleship *Dreadnought*.

In November 1914 Leutnant Hersing was at sea again, in the English Channel. On the 23rd he stopped the small 718-ton British steamer SS *Malachite*, on passage from Liverpool to Le Havre, off the very mouth of the port. U-21 shelled the steamer for about half an hour, in sight of a patrol boat. *Malachite* stayed afloat for another twenty-four hours but no attempt was made to salvage the ship and she sank next day. Meanwhile French escorts hunted U-21, some of them diligently, some desultorily, for the next three days but on the 26th, off Cap d'Antifer, Hersing caught and sank the British collier *Primo* by gunfire, and again got away.

The way in which Hersing had operated off British and French coast-lines and in the presence of several escorts with apparent impunity had very grave implications for the future. The British and French were already beginning to understand the possibilities. So, too, were the Germans. After U-21's activities there was a lull, but it was only temporary. Many German naval officers and some sectors of German public opinion were already objecting to the policy of restricting submarine warfare to attacks on warships and ships carrying troops. With larger, faster, longer-ranged and better-armed U-boats being built, an unrestricted assault on British commerce seemed more and more attractive, especially as German ships were being intercepted by the British blockade and their cargoes being taken to British ports. In an interview to an American journalist published in December 1914, the German Minister of Marine, von Tirpitz himself more than hinted at an increased submarine campaign in the near future.

Nevertheless, the New Year of 1915 began comparatively quietly. A U-boat was sighted off Vickers shipbuilding yard at Barrow in Furness in January. Actually, it was U-21, with Hersing again, who sank three ships off Liverpool on the 30th. The steamer *Oriole* disappeared, believed torpedoed, with all hands in the Channel on the 29th – the first British merchant seamen to be lost in the war. The hospital ship *Asturias* was narrowly missed by a torpedo, also in the Channel, on 1 February.

On 4 February 1915 there was a much more ominous development. The German Admiralty announced that Great Britain had contravened international law by not observing the distinction between conditional and absolute contraband, and, by seeking to paralyse all neutral trade in and out of the continent of Europe, was trying to strike at German economic life as well as her military strength; accordingly all the waters surrounding Great Britain and Ireland, including the whole of the English Channel, were declared to be a war zone. From 18 February onwards, every merchant vessel found within this war zone would be destroyed 'without it always being possible to avoid danger to the crews and passengers'. Also, the statement warned that neutral ships would be exposed to danger in the war zone because of the 'misuse of neutral flags' ordered on 31 January by the British government. The Admiralty did regard neutral flags as a legitimate *ruse de guerre*; the liner *Lusitania* had, in fact, already docked in Liverpool in January wearing the American flag.

By February 1915 Germany had lost seven of the twenty-eight U-boats with which it had entered the war. By then, U-boats had sunk ten British merchantmen of 20,000 tons aggregate, which was less than 10 per cent of the total tonnage lost from all causes in the first six months of the war. To February 1915, surface raiders had sunk fifty-one vessels of 215,000 tons, while fourteen merchantships of 37,000 tons had been sunk by mines.

But by April 1915, all the German surface raiders had been sunk or accounted for and the U-boats had sunk another thirty-eight merchant ships of 105,000 tons since February. The pattern of sinkings for the future had been set. Losses to U-boats far outweighed losses to any other weapon.

In the first year of the war the most effective remaining restraint to a steady expansion of the U-boat war was less and less the German political and national conscience and more and more German fear of neutral, and especially American, opinion. Thus the only real checks in the U-boat campaign came after incidents which outraged international opinion, causing the Germans temporarily to desist.

On 7 May 1915, off Kinsale Head, southern Ireland, the great liner *Lusitania* was torpedoed by U-20 (Kapitan-Leutnant Schwieger) and sank in twenty minutes. Although rescue vessels were at the spot soon after her first call for help, 1198 of the 2000 people on board were lost. The German government had already threatened to sink the ship. Warnings had been issued to passengers embarking in New York. But apparently nobody believed the threat, or if they did, no extra precautions were taken except to give her captain special warning when his ship entered the danger zone of the Western Approaches.

After the sinking of *Lusitania* there was a great shudder of international outrage. But the German government justified their action on the ground that she was carrying arms (which, technically, she was: 5500 cases of small arms ammunition and shrapnel, amounting to 173 tons). But reaction to the *Lusitania* sinking had little or no effect on the German U-boat offensive. The Germans took much more notice of the after-effects of the sinking of the British liner SS *Arabic*, off Ireland, by U-24 on 19 August 1915. Of the forty people lost, three were American. After a very sharp protest from the US government, the Germans abandoned unrestricted U-boat warfare on 30 August. U-boat captains were ordered not to sink passenger steamers, even British ones, without giving prior warning and making attempts to save the lives of passengers and crew.

This restriction, which was almost impracticable for a U-boat to obey, and a further decision of 18 September to withdraw all U-boats from the English Channel and the Western Approaches, where American ships were most concentrated, virtually ended all U-boat activities in home waters for the rest of 1915.

The U-boats then turned their attentions to the Mediterranean, where there were many fewer American ships. Thus, the first victory over the U-boat in the Atlantic and home waters, in which they were successfully deflected from attacking British shipping, was a political and propaganda one. However, by the end of 1915 U-boats had sunk 748,000 tons of British shipping, of the total of 855,000 tons lost. Mines had accounted for 77,000 tons, cruisers and other surface craft for 29,000 tons. New construction more than made up those losses. The U-boats had once again taken a light stranglehold, but verbal threats had made them let it go.

Twenty U-boats were sunk in 1915, making twenty-five since the beginning of the war. But another sixty-one boats had been built and, tactically, the U-boat remained undefeated at sea. For a long time the Admiralty's most potent weapon was ashore, in the form of propaganda. U-boat crews were referred to as 'pirates'. When U-8 was sunk off Dover in March 1915, her captain Stoch, his three officers and twenty-four ship's company who were all picked up after surrendering, were segregated in detention barracks and treated, not as prisoners-of-war, but as pirates awaiting trial on criminal charges. But, after German reprisals on British prisoners-of-war, this attitude was dropped.

But U-boat personnel were still given 'differential treatment' in prisoner-of-war camps. Nobody quite specified what this meant, but clearly life was to be made especially disagreeable for them. King George V himself heard of this and made his own protest to the Prime Minister. In the King's opinion, we would extend 'generous and magnanimous' consideration to our prisoners-of-war.

Clearly, charges of piracy could not be sustained. On a purely practical point, a U-boat with a small crew crowded into a cramped space, could not possibly commit the essence of piracy, which surely was to board a prey, carry off its cargo and capture the vessel herself. U-boats had no hands to spare for prize crews and not much space for extra cargo or prisoners on board.

Much of the wartime and post-war debate on whether, and by how much, U-boats transgressed against international maritime law now seems un-realistic against the perspective of the First World War as a whole. Both sides accused the other of waging war, not just against the other's armed forces, but against the other's whole economic system. Both sides were, of course, correct.

Nevertheless, some U-boat captains did seriously breach the ethics of their times, and caused genuine outrage by their excesses. These were a very fruitful source of propaganda for the British government. For their part, the U-boat captains could argue that the most they could do was to give the crew of a ship time to take to the lifeboats. But this meant surfacing, and if this risked the U-boat herself, then some captains felt fully justified in sinking their targets without warning. U-boat captains could use this argument even more convincingly when the targets themselves were armed, as more and more merchantmen became as the war went on. A surfaced U-boat was obviously extremely vulnerable to shell-fire.

Much was made of the fact that merchantmen were 'defenceless'. So they might be, but they carried food, oil, steel, coal, and all the other stuffs of war. Their safe passage enabled a country to go on fighting. In other words, the merchantmen themselves might be inoffensive, but they provided the means to make war. They might be defenceless, but they were not harmless.

The fact that British merchantmen were 'defenceless' was entirely the Admiralty's own fault. The best method of defending merchant shipping at sea – by convoy – was well-known and well-documented. It had been a traditional cornerstone of naval tactics for hundreds of years. The shelves of every library in the land held books explaining in detail how it had been done. But by the outbreak of the First World War, convoy had fallen into disrepute in the Navy. In the long years of the Pax Britannica, convoy had never been needed. Several generations of naval officers had never had to practise it and therefore came to ignore it. Much was talked in the Navy of the need, the overriding naval *duty*, to 'guard the sea-lanes on which the nation depended'. The Royal Navy of 1914 had lost sight of the vital truth that it was not the sea-lanes which needed to be guarded but the *ships* which used them and the best, indeed the only effective, way to do that was to accompany the ships on their voyages – in convoy.

Ironically (in view of what was to come) convoy was in use from the first days of the war. So-called 'important' shipping, meaning troopships, was almost always escorted. As the Empire rallied to arms in the first days of the war, vast numbers of troops were transported for long distances, unmolested by the enemy. The British Expeditionary Force had been taken safely across to France by 20 August 1914 and a further reinforcement of the IVth Division was also carried across by the 23rd.

At the same time, regular troops were brought home from their stations overseas and were replaced by territorials. Four battalions of infantry with accompanying artillery returned from India, to be replaced by the Wessex Territorial Division. The East Lancashire Territorial Division went to Alexandria, while the Egyptian Army of Occupation was brought home.

There was a steady flow of troops across to France in 1915. The Midland Division crossed in the last week of February, in ten troopers and several transports and storeships, escorted by destroyers. Although U-boats were active in the Channel, the convoys crossed without loss. The South Midland Territorial Division crossed through Boulogne and Le Havre, also without loss, in March. In April, three more Territorial Divisions (the West Riding, the Northumbrian and the Highland), in May three new Divisions (the IXth Scottish, the XIVth and XIIth), some 100,000 men in all, with their stores and equipment, crossed to France without any mishaps, in small fast steamers by night, or by escorted convoys by day. Apart from these major troop movements, extra drafts, reinforcements and stores constantly crossed the Channel under escort.

The largest convoy of all brought the Canadian troop contingent to the United Kingdom in October 1914. The 'Canadian Convoy', as it was in fact called, was originally to have sailed in September with fourteen ships. Admiral Wemyss, with four light cruisers, *Charybdis*, *Diana*, *Eclipse* and *Talbot*, were sent across to the St Lawrence to escort them. But the convoy, when it did sail in October, was much larger than had been expected and consisted of thirty-one ships, with two more, one with the Newfoundland contingent, and another with the 2nd Battalion the Lincolnshire Regiment, due to join off Cape Race.

Very careful arrangements were made on both sides of the Atlantic to escort the convoy. There were only two possible dangers. The first, the German High Seas Fleet at its home bases in Germany, was guarded by the

Grand Fleet at Scapa Flow. A secondary danger, German liners in New York and other ports, who might have sortied out, were watched by the North American Squadron under Admiral Hornby. In addition to the close escort of four light cruisers, 'deep-field' cover was to be provided by the battleships *Glory*, from Hornby's North American Squadron, and *Majestic*, detached from Admiral Bethell's 7th Battle Squadron of the Western Patrol.

Even so, the Canadian government still complained that the cover provided was inadequate. They did not know, because it was thought inadvisable to tell them, that the convoy would also be escorted by the new battle cruiser *Princess Royal*, specially detached from the Grand Fleet. The war in Europe seemed a long way away to Canadians. Security in Canada was almost non-existent. Whilst the Canadian government complained about safeguarding Canadian troops, full details of the convoy and its forces were, with criminal stupidity, actually published in Canadian newspapers. Therefore the Admiralty decided to add *Princess Royal* to the escort, say nothing publicly, and simply endure Canadian complaints.

The convoy sailed on 3 October, escorted by Wemyss's cruisers and by Hornby himself in the cruiser *Lancaster*, to follow a secret diversionary route across the Atlantic. *Glory*, the Newfoundlanders and the Lincolns duly joined on the 5th, while *Majestic* and *Princess Royal* waited at a secret rendezvous, joining on the 10th.

The Canadians had been due to disembark at Southampton, but a U-boat was sighted off the Isle of Wight on 13 October and the convoy was diverted to Plymouth. Wemyss organized his ships into three batches, each with its own escort, to enter harbour separately. The first transports arrived in Plymouth Sound on 14 October and troops began disembarking later that day. Not a ship or a man had been lost.

There were several features to be noted about the Canadian Convoy: above all, the success of the convoy system itself, with its close and deep-field escorts; but also, the need for a secret, diversionary convoy route and the absolute necessity for strict security in the port of embarkation; the advantages of a flexible choice of final destination, enabling the convoy escort commander to change his plan, as Wemyss had done, as soon as any new threat had been reported in the path of the convoy. These were, in fact, the ordinary common benefits of convoy, which would have been thought so well-known as not to be worth comment by naval officers of past generations.

Although Wemyss had done so well with his convoy, he himself completely misunderstood the reasons why he had done so well. Ironically, he thought the Admiralty had been taking too many risks by sending such a convoy: 'A fast enemy's cruiser – and it should be remembered that there were still then several loose and unlocated – well and daringly handled could have created an enormous amount of damage. There really was nothing to prevent such a ship if she had once sighted the convoy from getting ahead of it during the daytime and getting right into the middle of it during the night.'

There would then, Wemyss prophesied, have been a catastrophe which would have had, in his view, 'a deplorable effect' upon Canada and all the Dominions which were gallantly pouring troops into the war theatre. The day after he arrived, Wemyss hurried up to London to see Churchill, the First Lord, who merely smiled and said, 'Oh you must take risks in war-time.' 'Only justifiable risks,' Wemyss replied, 'and I consider that under the circumstances the risks were *not* justifiable.' Wemyss preferred a version of the old theory of 'guarding the sea routes', which was to cost thousands of lives and many ships before the war was over: 'it would have been a better plan to sail each transport separately, causing her to pass through stated rendezvous with ships guarding the route'. So Wemyss believed, with many of his naval generation, in the theory that convoy was inherently risky, to be carried out on occasion, when the risk was justified, but not as a general mode of warfare.

Thus, in 1914, the classical lessons of convoy warfare were ignored, or discounted. It was not thought necessary to provide for the ordinary ocean-going merchantman the same protection which was given as a matter of course to troopships. Convoying was considered, if anything, to be *dangerous* for merchantmen. Merchantmen were safer, it was confidently believed, if they were dispersed over a wide area. To assemble them in convoy would make their enemy's task easier, as herding a flock of sheep together made it easier for the wolf to attack them.

This view of convoy went in defiance of all the Navy's previous history (it was also contrary to normal sheep-rearing practice, as any shepherd would have confirmed). Convoy was the Navy's oldest activity. The Navy had indeed been first formed specifically for convoy protection. The nation's prosperity and security had depended upon the safe passage of ships carrying troops and merchandise, in convoy, ever since the Middle Ages.

At the end of the twelfth century, much of western France was still under English rule. But in 1204 King John lost the Duchy of Normandy to King Philip Augustus of France. From that time onwards, the only direct communication between England and the English empire in southern and western France was by ship, around the politically and navigationally hostile coasts of Normandy and Brittany.

England's main export was wool, through Calais in the north, and the main import was wine, from Bordeaux in the south-west. The convoys were mostly seasonal. But wool convoys sailed regularly, under the command of an official with the ancient title of Wafter of the Wool Fleet. The wine convoys, generally of 200 to 300 ships, sailed to Bordeaux in December, loaded the season's wines, and returned in January or February.

The English kings used convoy as a matter of course. Without considering why, they knew that the larger the convoy, the better. Some of the medieval troop convoys had huge numbers of ships by modern standards. King John sent an army to Flanders in 500 ships in 1215. In 1346, King Edward III had a convoy of 1600 ships to take 32,000 troops from Southampton to France for the campaign leading to the victory at Crecy. In 1415, Henry V had another 1600-ship convoy to take the army which won the battle of Agincourt from Southampton to Le Havre. Two years later, he mounted a convoy of 1500 ships to carry 16,400 soldiers and over 1000 workmen to Harfleur, which enabled him to capture Paris.

Contrary to the consensus of opinion in the pre-1914 Royal Navy, there was nothing new, or revolutionary, or risky about convoy, nor did it impose impossible administrative demands. Naval officers of the thirteenth, fourteenth and fifteenth centuries solved several complicated problems of convoy organization. They arranged assembly ports, at both ends of the voyage. They manned, victualled and armed hundreds of ships. They laid down rules for station-keeping and formulated convoy escort tactics. They frequently joined up two halves of a convoy successfully before departure. Similarly, the medieval state was quite capable of carrying out measures which seemed unthinkable to Asquith's government, introducing acts to make convoy compulsory, imposing penalties on shipmasters who broke away from convoy.

In the sixteenth century, the Spanish kings were well aware of the value of convoy. In the 1520s, squadrons of Spanish ships cruised off Cape St Vincent, the usual landfall of the treasure ships returning from the West Indies, and from Cape St Vincent down to the Azores. This was an attempt to provide 'safe zones' and 'safe routes' by patrolling, much as the Royal Navy of 1914–16 did. But it was quickly found that the only efficient way to protect ships was to accompany them throughout their passages. From 1526, Spanish ships were forbidden to proceed alone.

By 1550 the convoy system for the treasure fleet, or '*flota*', was firmly established. Whenever it was temporarily abandoned, commercial and business interests in Spain soon petitioned for it to be brought back. The *flota* usually sailed twice a year, and consisted of some thirty or forty merchant ships with a dozen or so escorting warships. Later, support groups of warships met the returning convoy at sea. It was just such a convoy support force that Sir Richard Grenville attacked in *Revenge* in 1589. His action was tactically unreasonable and stood no chance whatsoever of success (even his kinsman, Sir Walter Ralegh, thought it very rash: 'but the other course might have been the better', he wrote). Grenville's fate demonstrated what many twentieth-century submarine commanders were to discover at the cost of their lives: an attack upon a defended convoy is one of the most difficult and dangerous enterprises any naval commander can attempt.

From about 1585 until the end of the century, English ships regularly attacked the incoming Spanish treasure *flota*, and regularly they failed. The great Spanish Armada of 1588 was itself a most successful convoy. The three actions fought by the English on the way up Channel were indecisive, and the

Armada was still intact and still just as formidable when it reached Calais. It was the fireships which first cracked its defences and the bad weather of the North Sea which finally and fatally broke it up and destroyed it.

It was not a coincidence that Spanish warships were stationed at the point where the treasure fleet was likely to make its landfall. Convoy landfalls were very often the key to maritime operations in the days of sail. Because of the lack of accurate chronometers, longitude could not be measured precisely. Convoys therefore had to sail along known latitudes towards a known landfall, which they hoped to reach in daylight. Approaching Europe from the Atlantic, Cape St Vincent, Ushant, the Lizard, Finisterre, and the Rock of Lisbon were all recognized landfalls. Knowing this, naval commanders therefore knew where they were likely to find their enemy's convoys, and where also their own convoys were most likely to find attackers lying in wait.

In the heyday of fighting sail, from the Dutch wars of the mid seventeenth century to the end of the great French wars at the beginning of the nineteenth century, convoy was both the central naval strategy and the principle naval tactic. Many of the most famous naval engagements, from the action between the English and the Dutch off the Kentish Knock in September 1652, to Admiral Howe's Glorious First of June of 1794, were convoy actions.

Convoy was nothing less than an arm of the state, introduced on the very first day of hostilities, and sometimes even earlier, and implemented by Convoy Acts, as in the Middle Ages. Insurance rates for convoyed ships were often as much as two-thirds lower than for ships sailing independently. Many merchant-ship masters tried to have the best of both worlds by sailing with a convoy for most of the passage and then 'running', by leaving the convoy early and reaching harbour before the rest to obtain the best market prices for the cargo. So penalties were imposed by the Acts, for joining a convoy late, or leaving it early. Naturally some merchant-ship masters objected to the discipline. Many men-of-war were actually fired upon by the disgruntled merchantmen they were trying to protect.

In all the naval wars under sail (there were ten major wars between 1659 and 1815, with innumerable other alarms, emergencies and skirmishes) convoy was the one crucial doctrine of naval warfare, on which all else turned. Generations of British naval officers were brought up in the convoy tradition. To them, convoy was as natural and as obvious a tactic as, say, gaining and keeping the weather gauge. Convoy was the one sure and proved defence against an organized attack on commerce, the *guerre de course* as it was called, employed by enemies, and especially by the French and the Dutch, over and over again through the centuries. Nelson himself believed that all ships, fast or slow, big or small, should always sail in convoy. In 1805 he earned the thanks of the City of London for saving a 200-ship sugar convoy, the richest ever, worth some ten million pounds, from capture in the West Indies. 'I consider the protection of trade,' he once wrote, 'the essential service that can be performed.'

Convoys were coastal and domestic as well as ocean-going and international. For England, at a time when roads were very poor and there were no railways, coast-wise shipping was vitally important. Ships bringing coal down to the Thames from the sea-ports of Northumberland, and the coastal traffic along the south coast to Southampton, to the Bristol Channel and up the Irish Sea, were always put under convoy in time of war.

In 1650, Cromwell introduced the first Navigation Act, as a protective measure against the activities of the country's greatest trading rivals, the Dutch. Successive Acts laid down that all British imports were to be carried in British ships, with British masters and largely British crews, or in ships belonging to the country of origin of the imports. Under these protected circumstances, the British merchant marine grew to some 3000 ships by 1700, and to some 16,000 ships by 1793.

To implement the Navigation Acts, governments had to involve themselves closely in the control of merchant shipping movements and in the destinations and quantities of imports. In practice, this meant that governments had to set up extensive bureaucratic machinery which, in time of war, enabled them to impose convoy easily, efficiently, and at once. If necessary, total embargoes were placed on ships' movements until escorts and support forces could be provided.

Under the umbrella of the Navigation Acts, British trade thrived and expanded enormously. In war-time this trade had to be protected, requiring a convoy organization as complicated and spread world-wide as anything achieved in the twentieth century. Ships carrying sugar, tobacco and rum from the West Indies, hides and furs from Canada, timber and grain from the Baltic, fruit, marble and wine from the Mediterranean, spices from the Far East, all had to be assembled, mustered, organized and dispatched in convoys. Assembly and dispersal arrangements were set up at Malta, Elsinore, Archangel, St John's, Halifax, New York, Charleston (South Carolina), Barbados, Jamaica, St Helena, Cape Town, Gibraltar and Minorca.

Outward convoys were also most carefully assembled and routed. Ships for the Western Trade, for Portugal, the Mediterranean, the West Indies and North America would assemble, four, five and even six hundred of them, off St Helen's, Isle of Wight, and would sail together under strong escort down Channel as far as 'soundings', the 100-fathom line. There, depending upon the likelihood of attack, the support force (which sometimes included ships of the line and was strong enough to be called a fleet) would turn over the charge of the convoy to the passage escorts. The convoy itself would split up into its various components, each depending upon its final destination. Each part would take its departure, each with its own escort.

In the Napoleonic wars there was an extensive 'timetable' of convoys. Coastal convoys to and from the Thames and Southampton, up the North

Sea, to Ireland or the Channel Islands, sailed at least weekly and generally more often. Convoys to the Baltic sailed every fourteen or twenty-one days, with the occasional convoy to Greenland and the Davis Strait fisheries. Monthly convoys sailed to North America, Newfoundland and Quebec; to the West Indies and Guiana; to South America; to the East Indies, the Cape of Good Hope, St Helena, China and the Great South Seas; to Portugal and to Spain. The great fleet victory off Trafalgar removed only the threat of invasion. The convoy war went on. The Navy was running convoys as far as China as late as 1815.

The Navy of Nelson's day had no sophisticated statistical analyses or formulae evolved by operational research to prove convoy's effectiveness. They only knew convoy worked. They had seen it working. Time after time, in engagement after engagement, convoy imposed its own tactical geometry on the situation, bringing enemy ships to decisive action, while at the same time making it more difficult for the enemy to attack one's own shipping. Convoy made a direct contribution to the destruction of an enemy's force, whilst helping to preserve one's own. It was not just a means of defence. On the contrary, it was often the best method of offence. Convoy, in short, combined the best defence with the most effective attack.

Yet, astoundingly, *incredibly*, by the end of the nineteenth century this priceless piece of naval knowledge had been lost by the Royal Navy.

Chapter Two

How did such priceless naval knowledge come to be lost? How did the oldest and best navy in the world come to abandon its oldest and best practice? It was not that convoy was ignored or forgotten. On the contrary, the subject of trade defence was central to naval strategy, and convoy as one means of defending trade was frequently and keenly debated. The debate was carried on, not just by professional naval officers, but by naval historians, a new kind of scholar who emerged in the latter half of the nineteenth century. The general consensus of opinion was that convoy was inappropriate and impracticable, and might even be dangerous. How did so many able, intelligent and thoughtful men, who had spent their working lives in the naval service, or who had made a special professional study of naval history, how did they *all* come to make such a colossal collective blunder?

The solution lay in the late-nineteenth-century and early-twentieth century preoccupation, which amounted almost to an obsession, with 'sea-lanes' or 'sea routes' or 'sea ways' as they were variously called. The parts of the sea along which merchant ships most frequently passed were vested with an almost physical presence, as though they were visibly marked on the surface of the sea. This image was often represented pictorially by drawing on charts thick, solid, unbroken lines connecting various ports. These were 'sea routes' and the points where they crossed were 'vital focal areas'. It was as though people actually believed that if they took a boat out to the line of one of these 'sea routes' they would be able to see its trace, like a Roman road in the sea. These sea routes, and especially the vital focal areas where they crossed, had to be protected by a sort of nautical foot patrol.

This view was officially expressed in an Admiralty memo on the provision to be made for the protection of trade, published in December 1874. It was the War Plan of Admiral Sir Alexander Milne, who was then First Sea Lord, a crucial document which set out the official policy of guarding sea areas and patrolling sea routes. It remained the foundation of naval planning until the end of the century, having a decisive effect on the design, purpose, range and armament of new warships. In practice, it meant that while the armaments of ships increased in range and firepower, the operational range of the ships themselves did not. Victorian ironclads began to resemble ferocious beasts of prey tethered at the ends of short lengths of chain.

Along with a preoccupation with sea 'routes' arose the belief that the purpose of a navy was to crush its opponent's navy and that the attack on trade was secondary. Alfred Mahan, the great American naval historian and arguably the most influential writer on naval affairs of the late nineteenth century, wrote that interference with commerce was 'a secondary operation of naval war ... but regarded as a primary and fundamental measure, sufficient in itself to crush an enemy, it is probably a delusion, and a most dangerous delusion when presented in the fascinating garb of cheapness to the representatives of the people'.

This view was forcibly expressed nearer home in a paper called 'Naval Intelligence and Protection of Commerce in War', read to the Royal United Services Institution on Friday 13 May 1881 by Captain John Colomb RMA. Commerce, in his opinion, was a peaceful object, which defied the controls of ministers and war policies. Its only rules were the 'eternal laws' of supply and demand. The Navy's task was to defend the 'Imperial sea-roads'. Once a government started to interfere with the movements of shipping in order to run convoys, it would be virtually admitting defeat and making an invasion unnecessary. In other words, a nation that had to resort to convoy was already beat.

Early in 1885, there was one of the periodic 'scares' which were such a feature of Victorian life. In this one, called the 'Penjdeh Incident', there seemed at one time to be a real danger of war between Great Britain and Russia. Ships were commissioned, a Particular Service Squadron was formed under Admiral Sir Geoffrey Phipps Hornby, deserters were offered a bounty if they rejoined the colours, and politicians, press and populace prepared for war. It all blew over, as the 'scares' always did, but had one result; it caused the Admiralty to consider again the question of protecting commerce. A special committee, the Foreign Intelligence Committee, produced their report, 'The protection of commerce by patrolling the ocean highways and by convoy' in May 1885.

The title was a misnomer. Convoy was not given any proper appraisal. The Committee merely confirmed the policies of 1874, recommending that trade should be defended by blockading enemy warships in their base ports, patrolling the areas where sea 'highways' crossed and the highways themselves, and, wherever possible, hunting down enemy raiders at sea.

The Committee mentioned convoy only to condemn it. Convoying fast steamers, such as 'those on the Transatlantic routes or on the principal ocean mail routes, by men-of-war, is out of the question, for the simple reason that the British Navy contains no vessel at the present time capable of keeping pace with them from one of their coaling ports to the next'. This was almost arguing to the point of absurdity, concluding that the Navy had no need for vessels to do a particular job because it had no vessels capable of doing that particular job.

As for convoying slower vessels, the Committee decided that any attempt to do so would so restrict the country's commerce – by delays, by knowledge of the convoy's assembly and passage becoming known to the enemy, and by the impossibility of providing convoy for individual vessels – that all our trade would quickly be transferred to neutral bottoms. As for sailing ships, the Committee had been told by the owners that on the outbreak of war they would at once lay their ships up and their work would then be done by steamers. The only solutions, the Committee repeated, were close blockade of enemy warships, and patrolling the 'sea routes'.

These arguments have a quaint ring to them now, but they had a tremendous effect in their day. When the great upsurge in naval building began in 1889, new ships were designed to carry out these very purposes: close blockade, and patrolling sea routes, using a chain of defended coaling stations stretched across the world.

'Convoys: are they any longer possible?' was the title of a paper read to the Royal United Service Institution in March 1887 by Captain Philip Colomb RN, a Gold Medallist of the Institution and a man who, like his brother John, was gaining a reputation as a naval historian and scholar of naval affairs. Colomb argued on commercial considerations, looking at convoy in the light of pressures commercial interests could bring to bear upon a government to protect trade in time of war.

Here, insurance companies played a crucial part. In fact, the question of whether or not a ship was legally in convoy, as defined, decided whether or not the underwriters met her loss. According to Colomb, for a convoy to be 'legal', it had to be 'regular', under an Officer properly appointed by the government. It must sail from a rendezvous appointed by the government. It must be a convoy 'for the voyage'. Ship's masters must have proper convoy or sailing instructions, and must do and obtain everything that the instructions laid down they must do or obtain. Finally, the ship must stay with the convoy until the end of the voyage.

Taking his examples from past actions in the days of sail, and explaining how ships could legally be in convoy although they had not actually joined, and that a convoy could legally exist even though there was no armed escort, Colomb could see no reason why convoy should not be continued in the age of steam. From the point of view of ship sailings, convoy assembly and station-keeping, steam was 'in every way in favour of a revival of convoy and if nothing else prevented such revival but the change in the mechanical condition of trading ships, convoy in the next naval war might be expected to revive'.

But Colomb did not expect it to revive. Although he had, apparently without realizing the significance of what he was saying, explained and forecast so many aspects of convoy as it would actually be practised in the Second World War, Colomb was looking back to 'convoy on the old system' which was 'dead beyond recall' because of 'changes in the course of trade and in the course of opinion'. Trade had changed because so much cargo was now carried in faster ships which would do better to sail independently and to show a pursuer a clean pair of heels (with perhaps a couple of quick-firing guns mounted aft, to act as extra insurance) rather than run the risk of capture as 'part of a fleet of merchant ships trusting to the slender guard of a naval force absolutely incompetent to meet the concentrated attack of the enemy which such a prize [the convoy] would invite'.

In Colomb's opinion, the best defence of trade lay in maintaining a chain of naval bases world-wide, with ample strength in cruisers, covered by battleships. Convoy might be revived for the slowest steamships, and would be continued for troopships, but 'the course of trade now, in peace-time, is such as to make the idea of convoy abhorrent'.

Summing up, Colomb said that it

> would be opinion rather than impractability which would forbid the revival of convoy in modern naval war. If opinion demanded it, the government could employ numbers of fast steamers which it is proposed to take up and arm in war, by way of convoy to the unarmed trade. There might easily be fortnightly or monthly sailing of convoy from the Thames, the Mersey and the Clyde. The delays would not be so great, the dates of sailing would not be so irregular as they were, now that steam has the mastery of the elements. A steam fleet would be much more easily and safely conducted across the ocean than a fleet of even the most modern type of sailing vessel.

Neither the speaker nor his distinguished audience of naval and army officers, with representatives from the colonies (in London for a conference), seemed aware that he was making out an excellent case *for* convoy whilst at the same time insisting that convoy was impossible, because *opinion* was against it. The discussion which followed was studied with innocently significant remarks. Captain W. H. Henderson RN said, 'As things are, at present, in any maritime war our naval strength will be *frittered* away in trying to protect our commerce instead of *striking effective blows* against the enemy.' Here, enshrined in one lapidary sentence, was the nineteenth-century doctrine of sea power which was to cost so many twentieth-century sailors their lives.

There were several Lloyds underwriters in Colomb's audience, as though to emphasize the historically close links between convoy and marine insurance. One of them, a Mr Heath, said that 'as far as I can see the opinion (of underwriters) is greatly in favour of convoys for slow steamers – steamers carrying coal and grain and such like. As for the fast steamers which carry the mails and perishables, they can look after themselves.' Mr Heath said he had done some research about premiums and although many records, including Lloyds' own, had been destroyed, it seemed that in the French wars 'premium without convoy was four times that charged with convoy'.

Another underwriter, Mr J. W. Janson, said he thought it 'quite impossible that they [ships] should wait about for convoy'. However, he pointed to the example of the *Alabama* which had raided Federal shipping in the American Civil War. Many present-day warships, Mr Janson said, were heavily armed but were too slow and had too short a coal endurance to catch a modern raider. Mr Janson admitted he was a layman in naval matters; as he said himself, with a charming bow to his glittering audience, he 'really came here for instruction'. Yet he had, all unaware, put his finger on one of the crucial deficiencies of Victorian warships.

There was some discussion about whether a merchantman who armed herself ran the risk of being considered, under current international law, a pirate herself. Mr George Baden-Powell MP thought she would. The rest of the meeting thought not. Captain John Colomb said the 'Navy exists for the protection of British trade, of the trade of all British subjects, and all British communities, whether here or abroad'. But when it came to examine the complexity, the 'ever-varying conditions and the diverse forms' of British trade, 'it is a human impossibility to put that commerce without paralysing it into a position applicable to the conditions of convoy'.

The chairman, Sir Donald Currie, founder of the Union-Castle Line, drew attention to the 'inadequate' British Navy at that moment. He thought that the 'statesmanlike' view was that convoy 'which means the power of conveying that which we are to live upon – *food*' depended like all other naval questions, on whether we were prepared to pay for it. In Sir Donald's opinion, the Navy had made no arrangements for protecting merchant shipping, had taken up many of the most unsuitable ships as 'cruizers' during the last Russian 'scare' (of 1885). 'So I venture to say in regard to this convoy question,' he ended, 'if the mercantile marine is to be of some use it is the duty of all who are interested in the protection of trade and commerce to impress upon those in authority to be in time with their preparations and to have those preparations adequate.' After which swingeing peroration, Admiral Sir Edward Fanshawe got up and cautiously proposed the meeting's 'best and warmest thanks to Sir Donald'.

The paper and the discussion were admirable resumés of late Victorian thinking in its various shades. The speakers were expressing widely held opinions about convoy. Only a few days later, Sir Henry Holland's opening address to the conference of colonial ministers and administrators declared, 'in the present circumstances of trade, merchant ships could not be adequately protected by convoy, even if ships of war could be spared for the purpose. They must rely, therefore, for security upon such general protection as the Navy may be able to afford.'

The only dissenter of any real influence was Admiral of the Fleet Sir Geoffrey Phipps Hornby, the ablest naval officer of his day and arguably the best admiral of the Victorian era. In a speech to the Chamber of Commerce in 1888 he demolished the argument that it was not possible to plan ahead for the protection of sea-borne trade. He was uneasy, he said, about the vagueness and indecision of current naval thinking, and about the shortage of small escort craft. He suggested light convoys in the Mediterranean and on trans-ocean routes but, all the same, he preferred the main defence at sea to be provided by patrolling warships. Even Phipps Hornby had this fatal fondness for 'cruising squadrons' in 'focal areas'. He said the Admiralty should provide 186 cruisers for the protection of the country's merchant fleet, which then numbered 36,700 ships, totaling more than ten million tons.

The point about numbers of small escort craft was taken up by Professor J. K. Laughton, another very distinguished naval historian, writing in *Brassey's Annual* for 1894. 'Numbers, not strength, are what is wanted,' he wrote. He advocated a 'cloud of small cruisers, gunboats, torpedo boats', anything in fact big enough to mount a small gun, to provide saturation cover of danger areas like the English Channel. But even Laughton succumbed to the lure of cruisers patrolling trade routes, with larger men of war stationed at bases, ready to go in support.

Laughton did not rule out convoy entirely. He thought slower vessels, of speeds between 8 and 10 knots, might well need it, but faster vessels would not. Ships would run independently, or in convoy, along patrolled routes just as, he said, 'a London policeman may be daily seen convoying a bevy of lone females from pavement to refuge, and from refuge to pavement'.

Laughton believed that, as always, insurance premiums would play an important part. Shipowners' opinions on convoy would depend upon the underwriters' view of premiums and *that* would be influenced by the Admiralty. In other words, if the Admiralty decided that convoy was not necessary (and at that time there was every reason to believe that they would so decide in a future war) then the underwriters would also decide that convoy was not necessary and adjust their premiums to suit. This was a neat reversal of the usual historical process, in which it was the *success* of convoy which affected insurance premiums.

A solution to this question of insurance in war-time was suggested in a very interesting and forward-looking joint paper on 'Suggested Lines of Convoy in War-time with a Scheme of Commerce Protection' read to the Royal United Services Institution by Lieut W. C. Crutchley RNR, and H. L. Swinburne Esq., in June 1895. Crutchley proposed that the government should guarantee trade in time of war. Our trade, he argued, *must* go on. The money did not matter. If we won, the additional premiums could be recovered from the losers, in extra war indemnities. And if we lost – why then it would not matter anyway.

Crutchley thought that 'fast trade' above 14 knots (a genuine, *proven*, 14 knots he insisted) did not need convoy. The 'slow trade' would. Presupposing that the Suez Canal would soon be closed in war-time, Crutchley proposed convoy routes across the Atlantic and round Capes Horn and Good Hope, with coaling stations at vital intervals.

Swinburne developed the theme further. He worked out in detail how many warships would be required to escort the convoys and concluded that they could be provided without seriously weakening the fleet in home waters. In a most thoughtful paper, which took into account published figures of warships' coal-bunker capacity, Swinburne argued that convoy was possible and feasible over the great ocean trade routes. 'Our commerce is enormous,' he said, 'its continuance vital to our empire, and its protection is one of the causes which have made our glorious Navy what it is and for which it exists.'

However, during the later discussion, the Old Navy reared its reactionary head, in the shape of one Commander L. G. Tippinge RN, who took exception to Mr Swinburne's proposal to use obsolete battleships as convoy escorts:

> I think they will be much more needed in *actual fighting*. After our main fleets and first-class ironclads have had a large battle, rendering them *hors de combat* for a considerable time, I think that these obsolete ironclads and armoured ships will be the next that decide the war; and if they are all over the world, employed on commerce protection, they will not be available for that which is, I think, the principal part of their duty – to meet the enemy and *fight* him wherever it is.

Mr Swinburne replied

> you must take some portion of your naval force solely and wholly for this duty of commerce protection, for upon the proper fulfilment of this duty the whole of the trade and industry of our country will have to depend. If you cannot use the old-type battleships, then you must use your modern cruisers, and I think Commander Tippinge will agree with me that our cruisers will be urgently required for other purposes under war conditions.

Nevertheless, at the end of the nineteenth century, the views of Commander Tippinge held sway to such an extent that many shipowners and underwriters at Lloyd's had become seriously alarmed at what they thought was an inadequate naval policy for commerce protection. It was all very well for naval officers to talk about *actual fighting* and large battles between ironclads. Meanwhile, what was to happen to the unarmed merchantmen?

The Secretary of Lloyds, Colonel Sir H. M. Hozier, said that convoy was 'absolutely necessary' for all merchantmen under 14 knots. The Colonel gave several lectures to the Royal Naval College, Greenwich, in 1901 and again in 1904, which Lloyd's subsequently printed in pamphlet form. 'It is doubtful,' said the Colonel in January 1904, 'whether the system of convoy will ever

again be practised on a large scale. It certainly saved various valuable vessels
from capture on well-known occasions; but it often enabled the enemy to
make large hauls, which might otherwise have partly escaped from the nets
which the fleets and the cruisers had drawn.'

Colonel Hozier pointed out that the Navy was not able at that time to
defend commerce. Yet the country depended absolutely upon its commerce.
Therefore if hostilities did break out the government would have to give this
very careful consideration. A tone of voice is difficult to recapture from the
printed page. In spite of these remarks, it does seem that Hozier was arguing
from the point of view, not that convoy was unnecessary, but that the Navy, as
it stood then, was unable to carry it out.

Whatever his precise tone of voice, the Colonel was swiftly and dis-
missively answered by Commander Carlyon Bellairs MP, in the 1904 *Brassey's
Annual*:

> The convoy system is at best a distasteful system of dragooning commerce and
> under the above [Hozier's] proposal could apply to 80 per cent of British
> shipping. I do not think Sir H. M. Hozier took sufficiently into account the
> *waste* of naval force defending the convoys, and the operations of torpedo craft
> against them. If merchant ships place themselves under the protection of a
> military force they become part of that force and can be fired at. The safety of
> commerce is in the superiority of our fighting force in the face of the enemy's
> force.

This view was put with even more cogency and fluency by a most respected
figure, James R. Thursfield, of *The Times*, in an article entitled 'The attack
and defence of commerce' in the 1906 *Naval Annual*. He discussed the
lessons to be drawn from the writings of Mahan and concluded that it 'was
time the *Alabama* myth was exploded' because 'even the *Alabama* is probably
played out'. Thursfield said that 'privateering was a thing of the past'. This
country had 'ample cruisers' to defend shipping against raiders. An enemy,
in Thursfield's opinion, would be foolish to disperse his forces to attack
commerce, and so weaken his main force, which might be needed at any time
to fight the one major and decisive naval action. 'There is no little wisdom,'
he wrote, 'in leaving commerce to take care of itself until attacked.'

Thursfield quoted the Admiralty's two broad general principles, as
deduced from the teaching of naval history: '1. That the command of the sea
is essential to the successful attack or defence of commerce, and should
therefore be the primary aim. 2. That the attack or defence of commerce is
best effected by concentration of force, and that a dispersion of force for
either of those objects is the strategy of the weak, and cannot materially
influence the ultimate result of the war.'

Thursfield stressed this doctrine, that the defence of commerce 'is merely
a secondary object' and 'the command of the sea is always the primary
object'. In a long and closely-argued article, Thursfield did not mention

submarines -- which was understandable. He did not once mention the word convoy – which was almost incredible.

The brothers Colomb, Professor Laughton, Commander Bellairs, James Thursfield and others who thought and wrote as they did, were by no means isolated and eccentric voices crying in the wilderness. On the contrary, they thought deeply about the Navy and its problems, wrote copiously and were read and respected widely. Their writings greatly influenced the climate of opinion of the time.

By the beginning of the twentieth century, the Navy had seemingly turned its back on the lessons of its history. Convoy, the lynch-pin of so many past campaigns, was evidently to have no place in the future. Images of the strength, speed, size and hitting power of the ironclads and dreadnoughts obscured the great truth beyond. The tremendous technological advances of the nineteenth century led naval officers to believe that the rules of the past were obsolete. Every naval generation tends to delude itself that its own advances in weapons and technologies make it immune to the lessons and penalties of earlier generations.

The Victorians took this self-confidence to an extraordinary level. They forgot that technical developments were vital for a Navy's growth but they were not in themselves enough to guarantee a Navy's efficiency in war. They firmly believed that steam had not only abolished sail, it had also abolished the relevance of warfare under sail. The past, it seemed, offered only an inspiring record of naval success and gallantry, providing the Navy only with a tradition of patriotism and inspiration.

Paradoxically, the very success of naval technology reduced the intensity of overall thought about the way in which the new ships and weapons would be fought in wartime. The new historians had made the study of naval history into a respectable academic discipline. It was all the more unfortunate that, having achieved so much, they should come to conclusions about the defence of trade which were almost all wrong.

So it came about that at the very time when advancing technology offered warships the chance of greater mobility, naval strategy became ever more static in its thinking. At the very time when the introduction of steam made convoy easier for merchant ships, convoy was thought inadvisable or impossible. The next war would be decided in terms of clashes between fleets of ironclads which the Royal Navy, having the larger fleets of the most powerful ironclads, would necessarily win. The strategy was to maintain a close blockade around the ports of an enemy, and to patrol specific areas and routes with large numbers of powerful cruisers, supported by battleships. Short-ranged naval forces would operate from a world-wide chain of naval bases and coaling stations linked to each other and to the ships at sea by telegraphs. Warships would have heavy armaments and short ranges. The design of longer-ranged, sea-keeping ships for convoy escort duties was completely neglected.

The 'offensive' was the key and the watchword. Naval forces were intended to take the *offensive* and force an action with the enemy's battle fleet at the earliest possible moment. Nobody gave a thought to the possibility that the enemy's battle fleet might refuse battle, might remain in harbour, a fleet in being, and a constant threat, whilst another wide-ranging, oceanic running battle, the classical *guerre de course* of the French wars, was conducted against merchant shipping using some other weapon such as the submarine. To use a land analogy: the strategy was that of posting heavily-armed knights on short-winded horses at all the important cross-roads, there to stand ready to engage and defeat marauding enemy knights in short, sharp combat. Once the enemy knights had been overcome, the trading traffic, the pack-wagons, and drovers' herds, the 'bevy of lone females' in Laughton's phrase, could once more go about their lawful businesses. Nobody considered the possibility that the enemy knights might stay in their castles whilst footpads ambushed travellers and then disappeared back into the undergrowth before anybody could detect or prevent them.

This view of naval strategy in the next war may appear faintly absurd now, but there were plenty of apparent justifications for it at the time. By 1900 the Royal Navy had not fought a major action since Trafalgar, 95 years before, or a fleet engagement of any kind since Navarino in October 1827. Only one important convoy had sailed in nearly a hundred years, taking Allied troops in French warships escorted by British men-of-war across the Black Sea from Varna to the Crimea in 1854. Thereafter the Allies in front of Sebastopol had to be supplied through the Mediterranean, and their supply route would have been very vulnerable to a *guerre de course*. Some form of convoy would almost certainly have had to be introduced (although such was the complacency and inefficiency of both services at that time that nothing could be confidently forecast). In the event, the Russian navy shut itself up in Sebastopol harbour at the opening of the war, sank blockships across the harbour entrance, and took no further part except for the occasional shelling of Allied troops in the nearest trenches on the heights above the city.

The Navy saw no action afloat for the rest of the century except for brief interludes such as *Shah*'s engagement with *Huascar* in 1876 and the bombardment of Alexandria in 1882. The action was otherwise invariably ashore, with the Naval Brigades: the Zulus, the Ashante, the Burmese, the Chinese, the Maoris, the Afghans, the Sikhs, the Boers and the Soudanese, though all redoubtable opponents on land, had no navies. The prevailing image of the Victorian Navy therefore came to be that of bluejackets ashore hauling guns up to the front to fire against the fuzzy-wuzzies, whilst a frieze of formidable but statuesque ironclads lined the horizon behind them. The image was emphatically *not* of small, storm-tossed, battered but sea-keeping ships convoying merchantmen far out into the oceans.

There were important political changes in attitudes towards merchant shipping in the nineteenth century. Successive governments became more and more interested in the details of the ships and men, whilst less and less concerned with the trade they carried out. There were very few years between 1850 and 1900 when some Act of Parliament was not being prepared or passing through the House on some aspect of merchant ships, their design, their loading, their manning, on their masters' and mates' quali- fications (culminating in the titanic Merchant Shipping Act of 1894 – still the longest Act on the Statute Book).

All the same, and perhaps paradoxically, it was an age of free trade. The old Navigation Acts had been successively repealed from 1822 to 1849, leaving the carriage of British trade to all comers. The resulting free trade did not cause wholesale destruction of the British mercantile marine, as some of those most closely concerned had gloomily forecast. In fact, there was a boom in shipping.

But it was a boom which led to increased independence by shipowners who, as the years passed, suffered less and less interference from the government. Just as the Navy was arranging to operate its warships indepen- dently of merchant shipping, leaving raiders to attack shipping at will, so the government abandoned the habit of imposing controls on ship movements and on imports in time of war, and dismantled the bureaucratic machinery and the expertise which the old Navigation Acts had obliged governments to have. The Navy and the government both, so to speak, turned away from the merchant navy. Although the most enlightened shipowners such as Sir Donald Currie continued to urge closer links between the Navy and the merchant service, the Navy stuck to the policy that 'there was no little wisdom in leaving commerce to take care of itself until attacked'.

With the turn of the century and the dawning of the Fisher era in the Navy, the vision of a great apocalyptic clash between dreadnought fleets became even more deeply imbued in naval thinking. The central belief in naval planning was that on the outbreak of a major war, a naval engagement would follow within days, and certainly within weeks. The Royal Navy, which under Fisher led the world in battleship design and building, would win decisively against a main opponent who, as the opening years of the century rolled by, became more and more clearly identified as Germany. But Fisher, whilst he reduced the numbers of small ships, bringing home and paying off scores of ships which, as he said, were too weak to fight and too slow to run away, made almost no plans for providing anti-submarine escorts. New destroyer con- struction was for fleet work, not for convoy defence. In the event, the Navy could have done with some of those contemptuously dismissed little ships.

Meanwhile the pre-1914 view of naval strategy, with the overwhelming priority given to the destruction of an enemy's battle fleet over the protection of one's own commerce, was perfectly demonstrated in the annual naval manoeuvres of 1906. These now stand, like a song by Marie Lloyd, like the rotund figure of King Edward VII himself, as a perfect period piece.

For exercise purposes, it was assumed that war had broken out between a
stronger naval power (Red) and a weaker but still formidable naval power
(Blue). The Red Fleet commander was Admiral Sir Arthur Knyvet Wilson,
commanding the Channel Fleet Battle Squadron, cruisers and destroyers, at
Milford Haven, and supported by the Mediterranean Fleet under Admiral
Lord Charles Beresford, at Gibraltar. The Blue Fleet was led by Vice
Admiral Sir William H. May, a much-underrated officer, with a battle
squadron, cruisers and destroyers, at Berehaven in southern Ireland.

The exercise rules virtually restricted Blue to an attack on merchant
shipping on passage from the British Isles to the South Atlantic and the
Mediterranean. Several shipping companies (though not as many as had
been hoped) agreed to co-operate in the exercise and lend their ships. But,
where necessary, merchant-ship numbers were made up with warships.
There was no mention of 'convoy' as such, but the exercise accounts do refer
to merchant ships sailing 'in groups'.

The main exercise began on Sunday 14 June 1906, and by the 27th Admiral
May had his forces in position off the Portuguese coast. He disposed his
battleships and cruisers 30 miles apart in three great lines 150 miles apart, off
Cape St Vincent, Lisbon and to the north. Stretching some 200 miles out
into the Atlantic, May's ships formed a huge net through which no merchant
shipping could pass undetected.

This 'ill-fated disposition', as Thursfield called it (he was with the Red
Fleet for *The Times*, and later wrote up the exercises in *Brassey's* 1907),
exposed May's ships to attack by Wilson coming down from the north and by
Beresford from the south. The Blues suffered several casualties. But in spite
of these, May's ships eventually arrived in strength in the English Channel
and sent an ultimatum to the King, the Prime Minister, the Admiralty,
Commanders-in-Chief and mayors of seaport towns, demanding an in-
demnity on pain of instant bombardment of undefended seaside towns.

These demands Arthur Knyvet Wilson loftily ignored. He was backed up
by the Chief Umpire and the Admiralty, who both generally commended
Wilson's decision to attack the Blue battle fleet rather than pay attention to
the defence of merchant shipping. This decision, they all said, 'should
appeal to the Naval and Mercantile mind'.

However, for those with the eyes to see and the wit to understand, there
were several very disquieting aspects of the exercises, quite apart from the
implications of May's impertinent sortie into the Channel. May's cruisers
had conducted a short but extremely effective *guerre de course* in the eight or
nine days of the exercise, when some 400 ships (that is, merchant ships or
warships acting as merchant ships) passed through the exercise areas. Of
those, ninety-four were liable to attack. Of those, fifty-two, or more than
half, were adjudged sunk. Two cruisers, *Sappho* and *Scylla*, operating
independently, captured ten vessels between them. Twelve more ships were
accounted for by a few destroyers, operating in pairs or in small groups.

These 'insignificant vessels', as Thursfield called them in *Brassey's*, accounted for 40 per cent of the captures.

'These figures,' Thursfield wrote, 'might at first be taken to imply that the *guerre de course* is still best conducted in this way, and that the comparatively slow, weak, unarmoured cruiser may still, as Admiral Custance the distinguished author of "Naval Policy" contends, have an important function to discharge in war'. Only a year earlier Thursfield's article in the *Naval Annual* had conclusively proved that the days of the *Alabama* were over and that the life of a commerce raider was likely to be short, sharp and brutish. Now he consoled himself with the Chief Umpire's dictum that 'it is practically certain that the commencement of the third week of the war would have seen all commerce-destroying ships either captured or blockaded in their defended ports'. The rate of capture maintained in those early days, the Chief Umpire thought, 'must in a few days longer have fallen to zero'.

Thursfield summed it up by saying that 'the Red commander-in-chief very properly made it his chief and primary business to seek out and engage the main body of the Blue fleet, well knowing that, as Nelson said, if the trunk were destroyed the branches would perish with it'. The Admiralty Remarks stated that May had been 'directed to carry out a plan of campaign [the attack on merchant shipping] which is generally allowed to be strategically unsound. . . .' The Chief Umpire wrote that 'on the outbreak of war, shipowners would prefer to be left with a free hand as to the action of their vessels as regards routes, times of sailing etc. . . . , but it is absolutely necessary that a limited control should be exercised by the Admiralty over the floating trade'.

In other words, the Navy had imposed its own theories on the exercise, by putting one admiral into such a position that he had to attack trade, and then all the observers without exception ignored or glossed over the results of that attack. Everybody believed that an attack on an enemy's main fleet was the soundest strategy. Everybody then manipulated the exercise evidence to support that belief.

Every year, exercises and naval manoeuvres seemed to confirm that the defence of trade was merely secondary to the activities of the main fleet. At the annual Royal Academy banquet on 3 May 1912 Winston Churchill, as First Lord of the Admiralty, defined the sole aim of naval policy as 'the development of the maximum war power at a given moment, and at a particular point. Everything in the naval world is directed to the manifestation at a particular place during the compass of a few minutes of a shattering, blasting, overbearing force.'

An attack on trade might be 'strategically unsound', as the 1906 Admiralty Remarks said, but it still continued to receive an uneasily inordinate amount of attention, for such a discredited policy. The Gold Medal (Naval) Prize Essay subject for the Royal United Services Institution in that same year of 1912 was, 'What is the influence of oversea commerce on the operations of war? How did it affect our naval policy in the past and how does it in the

present day?' The winning essay, by Commander K. C. B. Dewar RN, and
the runner-up, by Commander E. V. F. R. Dugmore RN, were both published in the *Journal* the following year.

In a wide-ranging, deeply researched, and closely argued article, Dewar
discussed the principles and doctrines of commerce warfare; stressed the
necessity of knowing one's opponent and the greater importance still of
realizing one's own strengths and weaknesses; explained the influence of
finance and insurance on sea-going trade; and reviewed the history of
commerce warfare, from the First Dutch War to the Russo-Japanese War,
the most recent major naval conflict available to historians.

From official publications Dewar gathered statistics to show just how
dependent upon imported food and materials nearly a century of free trade
had made Great Britain. The country imported 80 per cent of its wheat and
50 per cent of its meat. The people's daily bread came from abroad, in
exchange for manufactured goods made in factories manned by workers who
had left the land. The textile industry, as an example, employed well over a
million workers. All the cotton, and 80 per cent of the wool, was imported.
About 50 per cent of the pig iron produced was smelted from imported ore.
The Navy's own warships were already beginning to turn from coal,
produced in abundance at home, to oil, all of it imported.

Dewar defined the 'principal responsibility of the fleet at the beginning of
the war' as 'the protection of our trade and the throttling of the enemy's'.
Reading his carefully thought-out sentences and his masterly assembly of
facts, the reader fully expects Dewar to conclude with an unanswerable call
for convoy. In fact, he writes, 'the destruction of the enemy's naval forces is,
of course, the most effectual method of protecting the trade'. The fleet, he
said, 'must then be preserved for the day on which the enemy decides to
fight. . . .' Intent upon propagating this old heresy, Dewar scarcely mentioned convoy.

Dewar's final chapter, 'Application and conclusions' was not published in
the *Journal*, but printed for private circulation amongst members of the
Naval Society in the *Naval Review* for 1914. The published essay had left the
options of the likeliest opponent open. In private, the enemy was clearly
assumed to be Germany. Dewar recommended a blockage in the North Sea,
a Northern Force powerful enough to 'ensure a superiority in every type of
vessel which the assumed opponent is likely to bring into that area' (the
Grand Fleet, as it became, based at Scapa Flow) and 'the focal and terminal
areas of British trade to be controlled by cruisers with armed merchantmen
on the trade routes'. Here, once again, was the old theory of 'routes' more
forcibly, and convincingly, and more intelligently argued than ever before.

Dugmore, winning the second prize, had much more to say about convoy,
almost all of it derogatory. He thought there would only be a limited number
of commerce destroyers, and modern conditions would enable a large
proportion of trading vessels 'to escape their unwelcome notice'. 'There will

be no convoy system to attract indiscriminate crippling and capture,' he wrote. Steamers, not being bound by the wind as of old, could escape in any direction. Their masters, Dugmore said, would 'have a more intelligent grasp of the situation'. Wireless telegraphy would give accurate knowledge of what was happening on the trade routes, and all hostile ships would be located.

Dugmore foresaw the same difficulties in the path of commerce raiders as Thursfield had: constant concern about coal supplies; inability to engage equal force for fear of damage; lack of recent, accurate intelligence; shortage of manpower, especially of engine-room personnel, to take prizes; and so on. In Dugmore's opinion, shipowners preferred the risks of independent sailing to the delays of convoy. Thus 'we are justified in believing convoy, as a regular system, obsolete'.

In March 1913 Churchill announced that the Admiralty intended to lend guns and ammunition for British merchantmen to defend themselves if attacked. This was a very ancient naval practice but in the context of the 1914–18 war it aroused a great deal of debate as to whether merchant ships which armed themselves were more liable to legitimate attack. Arming merchant ships had in fact been considered on two or three occasions in the nineteenth century, once particularly during the Russian 'scare' of 1885, but nothing had been done. Nor did Churchill's announcement mean much in practice. A number of ships, mostly trading to South America, were armed with guns but none carried ammunition because of the difficulties anticipated with the authorities in foreign ports. In the event, no objection was raised by any of the countries visited. But much more important for the future, the beginnings of an organization for arming merchant ships was laid down in the Admiralty, which was to be activated on the outbreak of war.

Had the Germans carried on the war against commerce entirely with surface warships then, just conceivably, the confident pre-war forecasts and opinions about the impracticability and undesirability of convoy might have seemed nearer the truth. It might, just, have been possible to 'guard the sea-lanes' against surface raiders (although later experience with *Wolf* and *Mowe* demonstrated how much damage these single raiders could do, and how very difficult it was, and how expensive in time and ships, to catch them). But the submarine gave commerce raiding, literally, another dimension.

Chapter Three

The Royal Navy was not nearly so obtuse about the dangers of submarines to surface warships as has often been supposed. There certainly was a body of opinion which believed the submarines to be an underhand weapon, not to be employed by any Christian navy, and manned only by those with the morals of pirates. Nevertheless, exercises between submarines and surface ships quickly showed the Navy that here was a new weapon which turned the old rules upside down. As early as December 1903 the Commander-in-Chief Portsmouth was writing to the Admiralty to suggest an investigation into means of destroying submarines, or at least of frustrating their attacks. A pre-war Submarine Committee carried out many trials and accumulated a great deal of information.

Some of the earliest trials in 1910 were carried out against obsolete Holland and 'A' Class target submarines. They were fumbling affairs, involving charges – 18½-pound tins of gun cotton with Bickford fuses – grapnels, and ropes, and nets, to catch or lasso a submarine, as though it were a giant salmon. A double-looped wire sweep, with a charge detonated by electricity whenever the captain of the towing destroyer estimated he was in the right position, was tried out with some success in the summer of that year.

It had already been conceded that any attempts to hood or catch a submarine's periscope and mask it with a sack or container was like trying to 'catch birds by putting salt on their tails'. But submarine catching did lead to some splendid flights of fancy. In April 1911, trials were carried out with a shell filled with liquid tar, which was supposed to spread over the surface of the water when the shell exploded and obscure a periscope glass. The substance worked perfectly in the lecture room and failed utterly at sea.

That same month a 6-inch gun was fired at the submerged *Holland 2*, at a range of 1900 yards. Eventually the submarine did sink to the bottom, because her observation-glass scuttles had been broken and she filled with

water. In July the destroyer *Crusader* had promising results with a towed
hydroplane, like a surf-board planing along the surface, from which was
suspended a kite or underwater sled containing the explosive, detonated
from the towing ship. In August, rifle grenades containing 9½ ounces of
explosive were fired at the long-suffering *Holland 2* (which had been raised
and pumped out). Some of the grenades did not explode and many had an
unpredictable flight.

In 1912 trials were carried out with aeroplanes and the submarine c.12 at
Harwich. The submarine was almost impossible to spot from the air, unless
the aircraft came down as low as 300 feet, while the submarine herself had to
be shallow and painted a light colour. In June, a modified sweep with nine
explosive charges and twelve supporting floats was tried out. This seemed a
promising device and with practise destroyers could stream the sweep in
three or four minutes and at speeds of up to 12 or 15 knots.

Meanwhile, there was a continuing discussion about submarines and their
potential in war. Much of the argument was closely reasoned projection of
experience, or intelligent and informed guesswork, although it all suffered
from the same disability as had struck Churchill and Battenberg when
reading Fisher's paper, of being simply unable to visualize submarines
sinking their targets without warning and without surfacing.

On 5 June 1914 a letter appeared in *The Times* from Admiral Sir Percy
Scott, the peppery arch-apostle of naval gunnery who, with Fisher and
Jellicoe, had done more than anybody else to drag the Royal Navy's gunnery
into the twentieth century. Sir Percy said he thought the country already had
enough battleships but had not nearly enough submarines or aircraft. He
recommended that the country should stop building battleships and start
building submarines and aircraft, because these two weapons had rev-
olutionized naval warfare. In war, battleships would now have to be locked up
in a safe harbour. The enemy would have to do the same with his battleships.
No fleet could hide from aircraft, and submarines could attack even in broad
daylight. In other words, and not to put too fine a point upon it, the whole
purpose of the battleship had gone.

For Percy Scott, the Master Gunner himself, the great advocate of the big
gun, to write in this vein was like the Archbishop of Canterbury renouncing
the Holy Ghost. There was an answering storm of violently hostile criticism
which called Scott's letter everything from a 'mischievous scare' (Admiral
Sir Edmund Fremantle) to 'premature, ill-advised and calculated to do
serious harm to the cause of the maintenance of British supremacy at sea'
(Mr Hannon, Secretary of the Navy League). 'We have yet to hear of a case
in which a submarine has made a hit from an underwater shot in any
colourable reproduction of war conditions,' wrote 'RN'. 'The submarine is a
craft which can operate by daylight only. It must come to the surface often,
and when it does is visible for some miles. The torpedo, its only weapon of
defence, has no flexibility of aim.'

'RN' was in fact quite wrong. A great many exercises had been held reproducing war conditions as closely as possible, and it was these which had prompted the great range of trials of anti-submarine weapons. But, by the outbreak of the war, the single sweep and the modified multi-charge sweep were the only anti-submarine weapons which had been fitted in ships to any extent, or which had demonstrated any success at all against submarines.

The Submarine Committee, which became the Submarine Attack Committee, exerted itself to find more weapons. Hydrophones for detecting underwater sounds were under consideration in November 1914. Microphones were laid in the Firth of Forth and off Dover in March 1915, and were supplied to anti-submarine trawlers and drifters in April. A depth-charge was suggested in December 1914, and aerial bombs, with hydrostatic fuses, were ordered in January 1915. The first depth-charge was a 'cruiser mine', a converted Mark II mine set to detonate automatically at 45 feet. In June 1915 the torpedo and anti-submarine establishment at HMS *Vernon* announced that a design had been settled for a Type D depth-charge with 300 pounds of TNT or amatol. The distribution of these Type Ds began in January 1916. They were stowed on the quarterdecks of escorts and rolled down specially constructed chutes.

The search for an effective anti-submarine weapon appealed to the British sporting instinct for invention. Percy Scott himself suggested an electromagnet mine, which did seem promising but was not developed in the end. The Jeffrey's Travelling Mine, named after its inventor, was towed behind the escort until the grapnel on the end of a line snagged on a submarine. The line was led to a winch with two drums of different diameters, so that, as the grapnel line was drawn taut, a second line pulled a charge down towards the submarine. A plunger was activated on impact and the charge exploded. But this too was not developed.

Brock's, the fireworks people, produced a smoke-generating apparatus. There were kites, and bomb-throwers, and howitzers, and bomb-lances thrown by hand, and 'astigmatic' binoculars to make submerged submarines more visible, and 'walking mines' with trailing mooring ropes, designed to drift inshore towards an enemy coast. Strong swimmers were to be armed with sharp pointed hammers, to puncture a submarine's hull at one blow. There was a magnetic detector, which oscillated wildly at the movement of the carrying launch but remained absolutely passive when it passed over a real submerged submarine. In June 1916, a Mr Percy Ashcroft claimed to be able to detect submerged oil, rather like a water dowser, by divining with a special rod. In tests off Horsea Island, Mr Ashcroft's rod dipped often violently but always unpredictably and remained motionless over a real drum of petroleum on the bottom.

Such was the hectic activity of the trials – the drama and spectacle of all the explosions and spouts of water, the exciting furore, with hopes being raised and dashed almost daily – that it was quite easy for even the most experienced observers to lose sight of the fact that the country really had no proven anti-submarine weapon at all except harrying a U-boat to the surface and then ramming it. The war against commerce began to cover such large distances, to involve so many men and ships and amounts of materials, to have such frightening implications for the rest of the war, that it tended to stun the normal reasoning processes. Any politician or naval officer could believe what he wanted to believe and could frequently find statistics and opinions to support his beliefs.

There never was a sharper critic of the naval scene than Winston Churchill, nor a man with more vision and enthusiasm for naval affairs, a leader quicker to grasp essentials and with more energy to put solutions into effect. But even he succeeded in convincing himself at the time, and remained convinced for years afterwards, that the U-boats had already been defeated by the time he left the Admiralty in May 1915. His own account, in *The World Crisis*, gives a completely misleading view.

Churchill claimed that by the end of February 1915, the first month of the first unrestricted U-boat campaign against shipping, some 6000 vessels reached British ports, or sailed from them, of which only twenty-one, totalling 65,000 tons, were sunk. This is perfectly true but only so far as it went. Of those 6000 sailings, the great majority were of small ships, coastal traders, or cross-channel steamers and others. Of *ocean-going* ships, the total was only 800.

Churchill also claimed that the 'premature and feeble campaign' of the U-boats had been completely broken by May 1915. This was quite untrue. The enormous 'mosquito fleet' of small vessels which he thought so dangerous to U-boats was actually ineffective. Some twenty U-boats had been sunk in the first years of the war, almost all by ramming or mines or by accident (although two had been destroyed by gunfire from Q ships, and one by torpedo from a decoy submarine). In August 1915, U-boats sank 165,000 tons of shipping in the month and only desisted after yet another diplomatic incident, the sinking of the liner *Arabic* by U-24 off Ireland on the 19th, with the loss of some forty lives, three of them American. The sharp American protest caused the abandonment of unrestricted U-boat warfare on the 30th. U-boat commanders were ordered not to sink passenger steamers, not even obviously British ones, without first giving warning and saving passengers and crew. This once again made U-boats surface and reveal themselves, a very dangerous proceeding. After the sinking of one more liner, *Urbino*, on 24 September, the U-boat offensive died away. By the end of 1915, U-boats had sunk 748,000 tons of British merchant shipping, from a total of 855,000 sunk through enemy action.

This 'victory' over the U-boats was thus only a lull, and the lull only lasted until the end of the year. By then, the German High Command saw a good chance of knocking France out of the war with the new offensive planned to begin at Verdun. But Great Britain, who could only effectively be attacked through the Navy, would still remain. On 7 January 1916, the Chief of Naval Staff, Admiral von Holtzendorff, gave an ominous assurance that if the economic war by submarines was begun again 'with every means available and without restrictions . . . British resistance will be broken in six months at the outside'.

The U-boat offensive began again in March 1916, with a series of attacks south of Ireland, the first ship being sunk on the 4th. But just as the campaign was gathering way, a U-boat captain precipitated another diplomatic incident. At about 3 p.m. on 24 March, the 1350-ton steam ferry *Sussex*, owned by French State Railways but operated by the London, Brighton and South Coast Railway, was in the Channel between Dungeness and Boulogne, plying her usual packet service between Folkestone and Dieppe, when she was attacked by UB-29 of the Flanders Flotilla. *Sussex* was carrying some 380 passengers. It was a bright spring afternoon, with good visibility. The U-boat captain, Leutnant Pustkuchen, afterwards said he could see through his periscope people moving about on deck and so concluded that the vessel was a troopship.

One torpedo hit *Sussex* in the bows and blew them off. *Sussex* did not sink, but nearly eighty people were killed or injured. Two hours later another ship SS *Salybia*, homeward bound from the West Indies, was also torpedoed. Meanwhile the destroyer *Afridi* and a French trawler found *Sussex* and took off her survivors; about 250 of them landed at Boulogne and another 120 at Dover. *Sussex* was eventually beached.

Unfortunately for Germany, twenty-five of the dead were American citizens and two were Spanish, so there was an immediate reaction in both countries. Count Bernstorff, the German Ambassador in the United States, claimed that the *Sussex* explosion was due to a mine. But it was clear from *Salybia*'s sinking that a U-boat must have been operating in the area and this weak excuse only made matters worse.

But the American government did not protest at once, and the U-boat offensive went on. In the first five months of 1916, 131 ships of 442,000 tons were lost. In April alone, thirty-seven ships of 126,000 tons were sunk by submarines and another six by mines, giving a monthly total of 141,000 tons lost. Seven U-boats were destroyed in the same period. But another thirty-four U-boats were completed. On these figures, the U-boat war was once again going dramatically against the Allies.

The American government at last replied on 20 April 1916. Its Note concluded:

> . . . Unless the Imperial Government should now immediately declare and effect an abandonment of its present methods of submarine warfare against passenger and freight-carrying vessels, the Government of the United States can have no choice but to sever diplomatic relations with the German Empire altogether.

The Germans replied with their own statement:

> In self defence against the illegal conduct of British warfare, while fighting in a
> bitter struggle for national existence, Germany had to resort to the hard but
> effective weapon of submarine warfare. As matters stand, the German
> Government cannot but reiterate its regret that sentiments of humanity, which
> the Government of the United States extends with such fervour to the
> unhappy victims of submarine warfare, have not been extended with the same
> feeling to the many millions of women and children, who, according to the
> avowed intention of the British Government, are to be starved, and who by
> suffering are to force the victorious armies of the Central Powers into an
> ignominious capitulation.

Here, in a paragraph, was the German justification. Since the Allies lacked
an effective weapon at sea, the struggle with the U-boats was in a curious way
decided for the time being by public opinion, in Germany and in America. In
America, there was general criticism of German brutality. In Germany, there
was a storm of anti-American sentiment in the press, accusing the American
government of hypocrisy. The wonder is that diplomatic relations were not
broken off there and then.

That they were not broken off was very largely due to the German
government's decision, taken in the face of fierce opposition from the Chief
of Naval Staff, to demur to American objections. On 24 April U-boats were
restricted once more and ordered to return to the principles of prize rules, of
stopping and searching targets before sinking them. The German government replied formally on 4 May, accepting the United States Government's
conditions.

Admiral Scheer, who had just been appointed C-in-C of the High Seas
Fleet, was bitterly critical of this decision. He recalled the U-boats on 25 April
and discontinued the campaign. Ironically, Scheer's position was weakened
by his own success in the raids on Yarmouth and Lowestoft, which seemed to
show that the Royal Navy was not paramount in the North Sea after all. The
U-boats temporarily abandoned commerce raiding and were prepared
instead to play their roles in company with the High Seas Fleet, which
included the great fleet action at Jutland. Sinkings by U-boats therefore
dropped away practically to nothing in home waters in May, June and July
1916, although U-boats still operated in the Mediterranean. The total loss of
shipping in all areas from all causes was twenty ships of 64,000 tons in May,
and only sixteen ships of 36,000 tons in June. It had been another diplomatic
victory over the U-boats. However, the German Navy remained extremely
restive under the new restrictions and was determined to resume a full
U-boat offensive at the first opportunity.

During this summer lull of 1916, convoy was actually introduced on one
particularly vulnerable sea crossing, between England and Holland. This
was an important route for intelligence purposes and for carrying foodstuffs,

especially margarine. In June 1916 the British government concluded an agreement with the Dutch to divert a great quantity of food from Germany to the British Isles.

At first, ships on the Dutch crossing were covered by the Harwich Force, sailings being arranged to take place whilst the Harwich Force was operating in the southern part of the North Sea. In June 1916 the Great Eastern Railway Company's steamer *Brussels* was captured by German destroyers from the Flanders Flotilla, with unfortunate consequences for her Master, Captain Fryatt. On 28 March 1915 in the same ship, he had steered straight for U-33, causing her to dive and foiling her attack. When he was captured Fryatt was taken to Bruges and on 27 July court-martialled, on the grounds that his action of the previous year came within the terms of a German proclamation that 'All persons, not being members of the enemy forces, including civil servants of the enemy government, render themselves liable to the death penalty if they undertake to advantage the enemy state or to do injury to Germany or her allies.' After a travesty of a trial, Captain Fryatt was executed by shooting the same evening.

After a second ship, *Lestris*, had been captured in July, a system of convoys was started, crossing by night, at first in loose formation, with ships of various speeds straggling sometimes as much as twenty miles apart from each other. The first eastbound convoy of three ships, and the first westbound, of ten ships, sailed on 16 July 1916. The convoys had a surface escort of destroyers or sloops and, from April 1917, flying boats based at Felixstowe flew over the convoy route before sailing and gave air escort on passage. In June 1917, the decision was taken to sail the Dutch convoys in closer formation and to maintain if possible a constant convoy speed. On average, a convoy sailed every six or seven days until the end of the war.

Between July 1916 and Armistice Day 1918 a total of 131 Dutch convoys sailed, making 1861 individual ship passages (with a brief interlude of 'patrolled routes' for one month only in November 1916). Six ships were lost, none after the decision to keep close order in June 1917. Escort losses were comparatively heavy: the destroyers *Surprise*, *Torrent* and *Tornado* were all lost, probably mined, in December 1917, and *Ulleswater* and *Scott* from causes unknown but also probably due to mines, in August 1918. Six ships sunk from a total of 1861 is a staggeringly low loss percentage of 0.32 per cent, a figure which alone demonstrated convoy's effectiveness. Yet this astounding but unobtrusive success appeared to pass totally unnoticed in the Admiralty.

The German Navy had been increasingly exasperated by what they considered to be the politically artificial restrictions applied to the U-boats. After an abortive sortie by the High Seas Fleet in August 1916, when only a series of pure chances saved it from a serious battering equivalent to Jutland, it came to be realized that great fleet actions were becoming increasingly irrelevant, that it was no longer possible to destroy the Grand Fleet piecemeal, by luring portions of it to sea. The navy's best way to help the

N

SHETLAND Is.

Lerwick

ORKNEY Is.

Scapa Flow

Little Minch *North Minch* *Loch Ewe*

Invergordon

Aberdeen

Oban

Methil

Glasgow Rosyth *Firth of Forth*

Greenock

Firth of Clyde

Overaay *NORTH CHANNEL*

Buncrana

Londonderry

Newcastle

Hull

Dun Laoghaire (Kingstown) Holyhead Liverpool *Ship Canal* Manchester Grimsby

Rosslare

Lowestoft

Cork Queenstown Fishguard

ST. GEORGE'S CHANNEL

Swansea Avonmouth

London *North Hinder Light Vessel*

Chatham

Dover

Southampton Dunkirk

Newhaven *Cap Griz Nez* Calais

Portsmouth Boulogne

Land's End Falmouth

Penzance

ENGLISH CHANNEL

Dieppe

Cherbourg

Le Havre

U.K. merchant and R.N. ports in the First World War

army was to strangle the United Kingdom through the U-boat blockade.

Late in August 1916 the U-boats were ordered to resume their offensive. From here onwards, the picture of the war at sea began to darken for the Allies. U-boats built in 1915 were now being completed for sea. Fresh numbers of U-boats were becoming available and the campaign was taken up where it had been left off. In September 1916 the U-boat flotilla at Zeebrugge alone sank nearly 50,000 tons of shipping in the Channel, without any hindrance from patrol vessels.

It was soon clear that existing methods of combating submarines simply were not working. For example, in one week of September 1916 three U-boats operated in the Channel between Beachy Head and the Eddystone Light, an area patrolled by forty-nine destroyers, forty-eight torpedo boats, seven Q-ships, and 468 armed auxiliaries – some 572 anti-submarine vessels in all, not counting aircraft. Shipping in the Channel was held up or diverted. The U-boats were hunted. They sank thirty ships, and were entirely unscathed themselves.

U-boat commanders were ordered to regard defensively armed merchant-men as warships. In October 1916, the sinking rate rose to 300,000 tons, ominously close to the rates earlier in the year. But merchant vessels continued to be routed independently. Only the Dutch trade and troopships were convoyed. Admiralty colliers were also escorted through danger zones, often *one at a time*.

Some officers, noticeably those closest to the U-boat war, strongly recommended convoy. For example, Captain H. H. Smith in the armed merchant cruiser HMS *Alsatia*, wrote on 21 October 1916 that 'the present enemy submarine campaign would be considerably reduced if merchant ships were convoyed between ports, or from deep-water rendezvous through the submarine areas'. Captain Smith said he had often noticed 'straggling lines of ships, who had all left on the same tide. They were much more vulnerable to torpedo attack than a compact squadron.' The only thing against convoy, Captain Smith thought, would be 'port congestion'. Admiral Tupper commanding the Northern Patrol forwarded the letter, saying, 'I recommend its trial.' But the docket in the Admiralty was marked merely, 'Noted' and 'Submit no action necessary' and 'the writer has a great deal to learn'. An imploring letter of 6 November 1916 from the shipowner Donald MacLeod, recommending CONVOY in capital letters, received the same cool notations from Admiral Oliver, the Chief of Staff and Captain Richard Webb, Director of Trade Division.

While the documents circulated in Whitehall and staff officers found ever more convincing reasons against convoy and ever more dampening comments to write on dockets, the carnage at sea went on. The 2617-ton steamer *Brantingham* left Archangel on 2 October and was never seen again; her Master and crew of twenty-three were lost. The Germans announced that she had been torpedoed on the 4th. The 3871-ton *Rappahannock* sailed from

Halifax on 17 October and was never heard of again. She was '*spurlos versenkt*' – sunk without trace – on 26 October, seventy miles from Scillies. Neither her Master nor any of the thirty-seven men on board survived. The 4072-ton *North Wales* disappeared towards the end of October. A boat was washed ashore at Penzance a month later and several bodies identified, but everybody on board was dead. The 5204-ton steamer *Marina*, bound from Glasgow to the United States, was torpedoed off the Fastnet Rock on 28 October. Of the 108 on board, eighteen were drowned. One of the surviving passengers, an American, said, 'They did not give warning, nor did they warn us either when the submarine came round to fire on the port side, while we were in the lifeboats and almost beside the sinking ship. I guess that is not playing the game.'

By October 1916, public dissatisfaction that the game was not going well for the Admiralty, which had rumbled on and off in the press all year, began to gather some momentum again. It was known that ships were being sunk at sea, although the numbers seemed minute compared with the thousands of weekly arrivals and departures. But U-boats were not being announced as sunk nearly often enough. The public wanted blood. German destroyers were raiding into the Channel. The German Navy seemed always to be launching new, fresh warships in a blaze of publicity. German Zeppelins were bombing English towns and villages, killing English civilians.

Meanwhile, what was the Admiralty doing? Not much, it seemed. The Admiralty appeared stick-in-the-mud and stay-at-home, devoid of dash and initiative, lacking the fresh breath of free salt air which sea-time would have given it. There had been no fleet action since Jutland and even that had certainly not satisfied public expectations; indeed as first announced the results suggested a defeat. Even on the best construction of events at Jutland, it had clearly not been the final, apocalyptic crushing of German sea power which the nation had confidently expected.

By October 1916 Admiral Sir John Jellicoe, C-in-C of the Grand Fleet, in his northern fastness at Scapa Flow, had become perturbed about the trend of sinkings by U-boats. His main concern until then had been, of course, the conduct and operations of the Grand Fleet. He had not considered the problems of anti-submarine warfare except where they affected his fleet. But by October he and his staff had come to realize that the centre of gravity of the war at sea was shifting. Conflicts between fleets of dreadnoughts in the North Sea were becoming more and more unlikely. Far more dangerous now was the rate of losses of ships to U-boats.

On 29 October Jellicoe sent a memorandum to the First Lord, Arthur Balfour, on what he called 'the submarine menace'. He began in sober and sombre vein. 'The very serious and ever-increasing menace of the enemy's submarine attack on trade is by far the most pressing question at the present time.' In Jellicoe's opinion, this attack would have such an effect upon food imports and other necessities for the Allies that it might by the early summer of 1917 force the country into accepting peace terms which, as Jellicoe delicately expressed it, 'the military position on the Continent would not justify and which would fall far short of our desires'. Not to be mealy-mouthed about it, Britain would lose the war.

Jellicoe pointed out that previous methods of sinking submarines were not meeting with the same success (they had never been successful anyway, although Jellicoe did not say that). This was because of the increased size and operational range of the U-boats, their greater use of the torpedo (which meant they came much less often to the surface), and their very much more powerful gun armament (which made them more than a match for small patrol craft). Also, the enemy had rumbled various methods such as Q ships for attacking U-boats.

Jellicoe called for new methods and new weapons. He was not, he said, putting forward 'concrete proposals' but calling for a committee to be formed 'whose one and only aim should be the production in the shortest possible time and not later than the spring of 1917, of methods for overcoming the most serious menace with which the Empire has ever been faced'. He proposed that the committee should take particular notice of the suggestions and inventions of *younger* officers.

Amongst the safety measures Jellicoe suggested was the re-routing of ships from the dangerous zones into what he called 'safe areas'. He did not suggest convoy, although he did come very close to it. 'The destroyer,' he wrote, 'although very effective in confined waters, and when present in large numbers, is ineffective for offence in open waters . . .' but '. . . is, of course, very efficient defensively as a screen to individual ships, or to a large number of ships. . . .'

As a measure of his concern Jellicoe made a final suggestion which anybody who knew him would have thought temperamentally impossible only a few months earlier: he proposed the demobilizing of a whole battle squadron of battleships, so that their destroyer screen could be used in the attack against submarines. If any further proof were needed of the gravity of the situation, this almost heretical proposal provided it.

Jellicoe's memo was not the first consideration of the U-boat problem in the Navy, but Jellicoe appears to have been the first 'big name' to draw such attention to it. His memo was like the first touch to a long fuse. In its own way it was one of the most important and far-reaching documents that Jellicoe ever wrote. Balfour was profoundly impressed and showed it to Asquith, the Prime Minister, suggesting that Jellicoe be invited to attend a meeting of the War Cabinet on 2 November 1916.

Jellicoe travelled down specially from Scapa to be there. Also present were the First Sea Lord, Admiral Sir Henry Jackson, Admiral Sir Henry Oliver, Bonar Law, Walter Runciman, the President of the Board of Trade, and Lloyd George, who later called that meeting 'the beginning of the story of the amazing and incomprehensible difficulties encountered in inducing the

Admiralty even to try the convoy system'. That meeting, he said, was 'the first effort made to overcome their blind obstinacy'. Writing some years after the events, Lloyd George used strong language about the Admiralty which, as time has passed, has seemed more and more justified.

After some general discussion about submarine attacks by gunfire on merchant ships and the increasing losses of Allied and neutral ships due to submarines, it was stated that losses were not being made good by building new ships or by captured or interned enemy ships. Lloyd George and Bonar Law then raised the question of convoy. Jellicoe said he did not approve of convoys 'as they offered too big a target'. Oliver said that convoys were used in the Mediterranean, by the French and Italians as well as ourselves, but it had been found best not to send more than one ship at a time under escort. The French had tried to convoy more and had lost two or three ships.

Lloyd George then suggested convoys of a dozen ships escorted by, say, three warships. Jellicoe said he doubted whether merchant ships could keep together sufficiently to allow a few destroyers to screen them. 'It was different with warships,' he said, 'which they could keep in a lock-up formation'. Mr Runciman, for his part, said that 'looking at the principle of convoy from the point of view of tonnage it was most wasteful'. There was no advantage in speed, as a convoy must go at the speed of the slowest ship. In spite of the protests of Lloyd George and Bonar Law, the War Cabinet recorded that, for the above reasons, 'the system of convoys was not therefore generally accepted'.

Lloyd George later used some caustic but quite understandable invective about this meeting. Although Runciman had mentioned that convoys would be uneconomical because of loss of time, 'he did not mention the loss of time occasioned by ships being held up because there was submarine activity off the ports. Nor did he mention the loss of time by the ship having to steam considerable extra distances to keep out of the submarine danger zone. In effect,' Lloyd George wound up, 'his last argument meant that it were better for a ship to be at the bottom of the sea than arrive late, besides which, the more ships that failed to arrive, the less would be the congestion at the ports'. Against the overall picture of the Admiralty's stupidity over convoys, Lloyd George's sarcasm now seems, if anything, to have been too moderate.

Lloyd George asked Jellicoe if he had any plans against U-boats now working in the open seas. Jellicoe said he had not (in any case, he was, after all, only the C-in-C Grand Fleet with no special responsibility for the whole war against the U-boats). There were only armed merchant ships and these could not be effective against dived submarines which they could not see to fire at. Jellicoe suggested 'floating intelligence centres to direct shipping routes'.

According to Lloyd George, the reports of the First Sea Lord and of the President of the Board of Trade at every meeting in this period were 'models of unrelieved dejection'. He took as an example a memo to the Government written by what Lloyd George called 'the high admirals' in November 1916. This 'paralytic document penned by a trembling hand' reported that submarine attack on merchant vessels was 'the most formidable and embarrassing problem the Admiralty had to face. No conclusive answer has as yet been found to this form of warfare; perhaps no conclusive answer ever will be found. We must for the present be content with palliation.' That is, Lloyd George said, in one of the frequent medical metaphors he used to describe the convoy episode, 'we do not see how the patient's life can be saved but we can prolong his agony – perhaps ease it a little!'

The following day another meeting was held in the Admiralty to discuss the formation of a special department or division to investigate methods of defeating submarines. Jellicoe attended, and all four Sea Lords, with Oliver, Admiral Sir Arthur Knyvet Wilson, and several other officers. They briefly discussed existing methods of combating submarines. Convoy was not mentioned.

Jackson had wanted to ask Jellicoe to chair such a committee but decided it might embarrass their relationship. But in any case, there were other plans afoot for Jellicoe. Balfour had decided that change was needed at the Admiralty and, much impressed by Jellicoe's paper on the submarine menace, offered him the post of First Sea Lord, which Sir John duly took over on 5 December 1916. With him, Jellicoe brought Rear Admiral Alexander Duff, to be Director of the newly-formed Anti-Submarine Division.

It is quite possible that Jellicoe's perennial pessimism, which eventually came to overshadow his whole tenure of office as First Sea Lord and which certainly played a part in leading to his premature dismissal, was first aroused by the shocking figures he was shown when he arrived at the Admiralty. By December 1916, the country had lost 738 vessels, totalling over 2,300,000 tons, nearly a fifth of the tonnage with which Great Britain had entered the war. Most of the lost ships had been sunk by U-boats.

Under Jellicoe, the most vigorous anti-submarine campaign was put in train. But it was curiously hidebound. It presupposed no change in the system of routing merchant ships independently. Defence was still piecemeal, and directed at defined portions of the sea rather than the ships which sailed on them. Special patrolling groups, with improved and faster designs of coastal motor boats were established at bases in Portsmouth and Plymouth. The system of air patrols was expanded, with improved and longer-ranged aircraft and airships capable of bombing. Improved designs of hydrophones and depth-charges were put in hand, although these would not bear fruit for some time. Plans were made for British submarines to hunt down their German opposite numbers, on the excellent principle of setting a thief to catch a thief. But none of this would show results for some time.

Merchantmen were already being armed, but the programme was greatly augmented. Out-going and in-going merchantmen were routed into 'safe channels' which would lead them to 'safe areas'. The number and variety of

Q ships was vastly increased. These were mostly tramp steamers, or even sailing ships such as schooners, armed with 6- or 12-pounder guns (later increased to 4-inch and 4.7-inch guns). Some of the latest Q ships had depth-charges and torpedoes.

Over 180 Q ships were fitted out, with about thirty at sea at any given time. Up to March 1917 they sank seven U-boats, but after that they only sank another four, as the enemy became aware of their secret. Q ships continued to go to sea until the end of the war, although they only sank one U-boat after September 1917. Some twenty-seven Q ships themselves were lost.

Everything, in fact, was tried or put in hand *except* convoy.

Chapter Four

At sea, the killing went on. On 7 December 1916, the tanker *Conch* owned by the Anglo-Saxon Petroleum Company was torpedoed whilst making her way down Channel. It was a bright moonlit night and *Conch*, with 7000 tons of benzine on board, burned like a giant torch. The explosion blew the after-tank tops off and showered the bridge and superstructure with blazing oil, killing the Master and everybody there. The only officers to survive were three engineers who, when they discovered the scene on deck, kept the engines going, hoping to prevent blazing oil collecting round the ship.

With her upperdecks burning like a furnace, *Conch* steamed on down Channel, trailing a great column of flame and smoke behind her. The Chief Engineer, two other engineers and some of the surviving Chinese crew jumped or fell into the water and were picked up by following trawlers and a destroyer. About half the Chinese survived. *Conch* herself steamed onwards, unmanned but still blazing furiously, until she foundered next morning.

The 2600-ton steamer *Lux* left New York on 20 January 1917 and then the 'great silence' fell on her. The bodies of her Chief Officer and her Chief Engineer were washed ashore near Cork in February. Nothing else is known. On 26 January, the 5076-ton steamer *Ava* left Birkenhead for Dakar and Rangoon with a cargo of coal and general; she disappeared without trace and nothing more was ever heard of the ninety-two officers and men on board. Many masters who did survive were taken on board the U-boat which had sunk them. Several masters found other unfortunates already on board. When Mr Bertram Edmonds, Master of the 7316-ton *Baycraig*, torpedoed without warning off Malta in December 1916, arrived on board UC-22 the U-boat captain waved a revolver which had been thrown overboard in Mr Edmonds's overcoat and said, 'You remember Captain Fryatt?'

For ship after ship, the experience was the same: the suspicious hull on the horizon, the conning tower, the stream of bubbles, the gunfire, or the torpedo without warning, and the hasty rush for the boats. Officers, crew,

Chinese, lascars, sometimes terrified women and children, the wounded, the sick, the burned, the brave and the cowards – for everybody the choice of lifeboat meant literally the difference between life and death. Some boats were picked up at once. Others drifted for days and were recovered with not a soul on board still alive. Many boats simply disappeared for ever.

Meanwhile, opinion in the Admiralty was, if anything, actually hardening against convoy. In January 1917 the official staff view was put forward in a pamphlet which stated, quite definitely and emphatically, that convoy was not a sound method of defending trade:

> Whenever possible, vessels should sail singly, escorted as considered nec-
> essary. The system of several ships sailing together in a convoy is not
> recommended in any area where submarine attack is a possibility. It is evident
> that the larger the number of ships forming the convoy, the greater is the
> chance of a submarine being enabled to attack successfully, the greater the
> difficulty of the escort in preventing such an attack. In the case of defensively
> armed merchant vessels, it is preferable that they should sail singly rather than
> that they should be formed into a convoy with several other vessels. A
> submarine could remain at a distance and fire her torpedo into the middle of a
> convoy with every chance of success. A defensively armed merchant vessel of
> good speed should rarely, if ever, be captured. If the submarine comes to the
> surface to overtake and attack with her gun the merchant vessel's gun will
> nearly always make the submarine dive, in which case the preponderance of
> speed will allow of the merchant ship escaping.

It would be difficult to find, even in the long record of Admiralty bur-eaucracy, a more stupid document and one which more pigheadedly ignored all the lessons of past naval history. It was all the more dangerous because it was not obviously the work of a lunatic. It sounded a reasonable measured judgement, taken after all the circumstances had been brought to account. Nor was it the product of a single deranged mind. As far as can be judged, it represented collective opinion in the Admiralty at the time. The Director of the Trade Division had recently minuted: 'The question of convoy has frequently been gone into, but experience so far has not justified its existence outside the Mediterranean.' And the Director of Operations minuted on the same papers that 'convoy was a matter of expediency rather than principle and if sufficient destroyers were available they might be employed on convoy duties in the Mediterranean'. Admiral Duff thought of the difficulties in the way of introducing convoy rather than of the possible benefits of introducing it, 'differences of speed [between ships in the convoy], loss of the safety afforded by zigzagging [evidently he did not consider that a whole convoy could zigzag as one] and the inevitable tendency of merchant ships to straggle at night, are *some* of the reasons against an organized system of convoy'.

Admiral Oliver, the Chief of Staff, set out on paper some of the difficulties of introducing convoy. These were the official Admiralty objections to convoy; like the fabulous hydra of ancient mythology, they had many heads – and, like hydra's heads, fresh objections grew as soon as one was removed. It was not possible, in the Admiralty's and Oliver's view, to establish the firm and comprehensive control over shipping which convoy would require. Merchant-ship masters, especially *tramp*-steamer masters which would make up a high proportion of every convoy, could not keep proper station upon one another, nor could their quartermasters steer a straight enough course. Convoys could not be assembled in neutral ports. There were not nearly enough escorts to convoy the enormous numbers of ships which entered and sailed from British ports (some 5000 per week, it was calculated). Much time would be wasted while a convoy was being assembled, time in which individual ships could have sailed and carried on earning their keep. When many ships in one convoy arrived at a port, the unloading facilities of that port would be overloaded – whilst lying idle at other times because all the ships would be at sea together, in convoy. Convoys would have to go at the speed of the slowest ship, or slower, to allow a margin for manoeuvring, thus depriving the faster ships of the defence of speed. A convoy would conveniently concentrate all the targets a U-boat needed into one space, instead of dispersing them at a safe distance.

All these objections, apart from the difficulty of assembling convoys in neutral ports (and even that was to be largely removed with the entry of the United States into the war), were utterly groundless and, moreover, went in the face of all the Royal Navy's experience in the past. However, Jellicoe minuted on the paper that the whole question must be borne in mind and brought up again later if need be.

On 31 January 1917, the German government announced that unrestricted submarine warfare would begin from the next day. Any ship was then liable to be sunk without warning, at sight, anywhere in the war zone. The forty-six U-boats then at sea were given *carte blanche* to open a new submarine offensive which, the German government believed, held out the real prospect of forcing Great Britain to come to the negotiating table.

This belief was not hopeful conjecture, but cold calculation. It could be traced in the lines of graphs, in columns of figures. Great Britain had entered the war with about 11 million tons of shipping. The U-boats sank 368,521 tons of shipping in January 1917, the last month of restricted warfare. They could be expected to double this figure at least, to nearly 750,000 tons of shipping a month. At that rate, Great Britain would lose up to 40 per cent of her remaining shipping tonnage in about six months.

And so, it seemed, it was going to be. The shipping losses soon began to accumulate at a catastrophic speed. In the first week of unrestricted warfare, thirty-five ships were lost in the Western Approaches and the English Channel alone. The total figure climbed to 500,500 tons in February, to 556,000 tons in March, and to a horrifying 870,000 tons in April. There were then over seventy U-boats at sea, and for a few weeks they really were winning the war. One in four of the ships going to sea was not returning. Neutral shipping was being frightened off. The war insurance scheme was running at a heavy loss. Furthermore, some of the astuter minds in the Admiralty were beginning to see that the loss of one ship was cumulative on the war effort. It was not just the loss of the current cargo, when the ship was sunk, but the loss of all the future loads which that ship would have been able to carry.

However, the Admiralty could see no solutions except to increase the numbers of surface patrols, to continue to sail ships singly on 'safe routes', to mine more U-boat entrance ports and transit areas.

The 'safe routes' used a complicated system, of four 'approach areas' for in-coming steamers, each area in the form of a cone, with apexes at Falmouth (for approach route A), Berehaven (route B), Inistrahull (C) and Kirkwall (D). Generally speaking, route A was for all vessels from the south Atlantic and the Mediterranean, bound for London, the Channel and east coast ports; route B took vessels from the North Atlantic for Bristol, London and the Channel, and from the South Atlantic for Bristol and the Mersey; route C was for all vessels from the North Atlantic for the Clyde, Belfast, the Irish Sea and Liverpool; route D was for North Atlantic vessels for all NE coast ports, as far south as the Humber. When each vessel reached the apex of its cone, it was then routed along the coast to its destination. Out-going traffic followed the system in reverse.

On wall-charts it looked an admirable scheme. But the approach areas covered some 10,000 square miles *each*, and were far too big to be patrolled by the ships available. In practice the so-called 'safe routes' were lethal. The presence of more escorts and their increased activity actually drew the U-boats' attention, betraying the existence of a 'safe route'. Lloyd George thought them death traps. 'In fact,' he wrote, 'by this egregrious plan our ships were in effect often shepherded into the abattoir where the slaughterers lay in wait for them.'

The effect on the Admiralty of those thirty-five vessels lost in the first week was, according to Lloyd George, 'to stun and not to stimulate'. Again, he summoned up an extended medical metaphor: 'They were like doctors who, whilst they are unable to arrest the ravages of disease which is gradually weakening the resistance of a patient despite all their efforts, are suddenly confronted with a new, unexpected and grave complication. They go about with gloomy mien and despondent hearts. Their reports are full of despair. It is clear that they think the case is now hopeless. All the same, their only advice is to persist in the application of the same treatment.'

To Lloyd George, as an admitted layman in naval affairs, convoy seemed obvious and necessary. Surely, at least it was worth a try. Yet he could also see the massed ranks of prejudice and opposition to convoy in the Admiralty. He was sensitive enough to perceive that it was not now just a matter of naval tactics. Personalities were also involved. Many experienced and distinguished sailors had privately and publicly declared themselves against convoy, and had staked their professional reputations on the belief that 'convoy was impracticable and dangerous to convoyers and convoyed alike'.

Years later, Lloyd George asked himself, what *should* he and the other members of the War Cabinet have done? Ultimately, if they really believed that Jellicoe and the other 'high admirals' were endangering the country then surely they should have sacked them. But that was not politically feasible or practicable. For one thing, Jellicoe had recently been appointed First Sea Lord precisely because his predecessors had not been tackling the submarine problem energetically or successfully enough. He must be given a fair chance. Lloyd George therefore decided that 'it was worth spending some time and patience in winning over Jellicoe to the views held by Bonar Law, the Shipping Controller, Sir Maurice Hankey and myself. We could not take too long over the process for our ships were being destroyed at an alarming rate.'

Meanwhile Lloyd George urged the First Lord, Sir Edward Carson, who was himself in favour of convoy, to insist on convoy being tried. But Carson had a good and fairly close relationship with Jellicoe and the other Sea Lords. He was reluctant to go against his professional advisers. Lloyd George could not ask Carson to press Jellicoe too hard at the War Cabinet meetings. Carson, a skilled legal debater and cross-examiner, would very probably get the best of the argument, but at the likely cost of the resignation of the entire Board of Admiralty – which for Lloyd George, already engaged head to head with the Army, would have been a Pyrrhic victory indeed. It was an age when it was virtually impossible to remove a senior officer unless he chose to go, yet senior officers flourished the threat of their resignations rather as heroes of the Trojan war brandished their swords. As Lloyd George said, it all needed time and patience.

Lloyd George decided to invite Jellicoe, Carson and Duff to an informal meeting, a working breakfast, at 10 Downing Street on 13 February 1917, to discuss the whole situation. Beforehand, Sir Maurice Hankey prepared and circulated a paper in which he rehearsed the arguments for and against convoy, and the existing system of independent routings. Although Hankey admitted he was 'not intimately acquainted with the existing system', his paper was a marvellously succinct and impeccably reasoned argument for convoy and against the existing system. In one sentence, Hankey summed up the greatest weakness of the existing system: 'the attack on trade routes is a "soft thing" for the submarine, with a constant stream of isolated merchant ships almost devoid of offensive power, to choose from'.

In an admirable restatement of naval principles of warfare, behind which one can hear the ghostly applause of generations of naval officers of the seventeenth and eighteenth centuries, Sir Maurice wrote that the convoy system, 'if practicable, appears to offer certain very distinct advantages'.

The enemy can never know the day nor the hour when the convoy will come, nor the route it will take. The most dangerous and contracted passages can be passed at night. Routes can be selected as far as possible in waters so deep that submarine mines cannot be laid. The convoy can be preceded by minesweepers or by vessels fitted with paravanes. The most valuable ships can be placed in the safest parts of the convoy. Neutrals and other unarmed vessels can be placed under the protection of armed vessels. The enemy submarines, instead of attacking a defenceless prey, will know that a fight is inevitable in which he may be worsted. All hope of successful surface attack will have to be dismissed at once.

The adoption of the convoy system would appear to offer great opportunities for mutual support by the merchant vessels themselves, apart from the defence provided by their escorts. Instead of meeting one small gun on board one ship the enemy might be under fire from, say, ten guns, distributed amongst twenty ships. Each merchant ship might have depth-charges, and explosive charges in addition might be towed between pairs of ships, to be exploded electrically. One or two ships with paravanes might save a line of a dozen ships from the mine danger. Special salvage ships might accompany the convoy to salve those ships which were mined or torpedoed without sinking immediately and in any event to save the crews.

'Perhaps,' Sir Maurice concluded in a postscript which he may have thought would have had the most force for his particular readers, 'the best commentary on the convoy system is that it is invariably adopted for our main fleets and for our transports.'

But it was no use. Jellicoe and Duff both read the paper before the meeting. They agreed with much of it. As a statement of strategic principles it was well nigh faultless. It was a brilliant paper. *But* . . . as a blueprint on which practical action could be taken, it had disadvantages. For a start, and in Jellicoe's opinion this was quite damning, it did not solve the problem of providing more escort vessels to start the convoy system, bearing in mind the huge number of weekly sailings in and out of British ports.

The meeting broke up after two hours, with no firm agreement or commitment except that Jellicoe did agree to convene a meeting as soon as possible of merchant-ship captains, to get their opinions on whether they as practical seamen thought the convoy system workable. That meeting took place on 23 February and, according to one naval officer Captain Bertram H. Smith who was present, 'it was fully representative and included captains of every class of ship from the large passenger liner through to smaller passenger ships, the cargo liner and other intermediate types to the ordinary tramp'. It was 'a meeting between professionals of the same service, that is – the sea'.

Jellicoe himself took the chair. He put the case 'dispassionately and impartially'. He explained what station-keeping involved, the apparatus necessary, and he asked the captains for their views. It is impossible now to judge how the audience were subconsciously influenced by their chairman and the stated purpose of the meeting, how far they tended to say what perhaps they might have been expected to say, but the captains were 'unanimously of the opinion that as things were it could not be done'.

Lloyd George, however, was never convinced. He was surprised at the time, and particularly sarcastic when writing years later. He remained convinced that the meeting had been entirely composed of passenger-liner captains and their view 'was simply the arrogant sense of superiority which induces the uniformed chauffeur of a Rolls-Royce to look down on the driver of what is contemptuously stigmatized as a "tin Lizzie" '.

It is easy, with hindsight, to mock the 'high admirals' of 1917 for their blindness and stupidity. But it does seem nothing short of incredible that the advantages of convoy did not make themselves clearer much earlier, and especially when they were being demonstrated every day. The Dutch trade was still being convoyed smoothly and without much incident. In February 1917, another important route was put under convoy.

Since the beginning of the war there had been a steady carriage of coal across to France and, recently, an equally steady decline, month by month, through sinkings. France required some 2 million tons of coal a month, or certainly a minimum of $1\frac{3}{4}$ million tons per month. But in 1916 the monthly totals had declined to between $1\frac{1}{2}$ and $1\frac{1}{4}$ million, and in December a French naval officer, Commander Vandier, came across to point out the seriousness of the situation.

It was discovered there was no lack of coal. There was plenty, but it was being held up in the ports. The tonnage lost to submarine attack was actually far less than the loss of tonnage in ships held back from sailing because of the reports of submarines. In other words, the threat of submarine attack was as effective in disrupting trade as the attack itself. (So much for the argument that convoy caused delays while ships assembled.) It was found that there had been a virtual blockade of the coal trade for between 30 and 40 per cent of the total days in November and December 1916.

When the system was further examined, it was found that existing dangers were being unnecessarily increased by stupid routeing; for example, ships from Newcastle were sailing through the dangerous area of the Dover Straits bound for Bordeaux, while colliers from Bristol, Glasgow and the Channel ports were sailing through the Straits in the opposite direction, bound for Dunkirk.

The routeings were rationalized and convoy for the French coal trade was introduced on 7 February 1917, although the actual word 'convoy', evidently thought emotive and provocative, was not used. They were called 'controlled sailings'. Otherwise, it was feared, the enemy would sink all neutrals at sight.

Whatever they were called, they were in fact convoys and they sailed on four main routes: Route A from Mount's Bay to Brest; Route B from

Weymouth to Cherbourg; C from Weymouth to Le Havre; and D from Folkestone and Dover to Calais and Boulogne. Crossings took place about every twenty-four hours. Ships sailed in rough station-keeping formation, keeping in touch with each other and visible to their escorts, which were almost always only armed trawlers. So the naval forces involved were minute compared with the total scale of the war at sea: eleven armed trawlers convoyed the Mount's Bay to Brest route, for example, and another fifteen handled the Weymouth routes.

Yet they worked. The convoy formation, with the trawlers in close company, had a dramatic effect on losses. Some 1500 ships were convoyed in March 1917. Three were lost. In the quarter ending April 1917, some thirty armed trawlers had convoyed over 4000 individual Channel crossings, for the loss of eight ships. From then until the end of the war, on only two occasions was more than one ship lost from the same convoy. On both occasions the convoy was scattered at the time, because of bad weather.

The French coal convoys showed, yet again, how puzzlingly difficult a convoy was for a U-boat to attack. The ships were extraordinarily hard to find, because a convoy was not that much more visible than a single ship. If a U-boat captain did chance on a convoy he was generally restricted to only one shot before the assembly of ships swept over and past him. By November 1918, 39,352 ships of the French coal trade had been convoyed. They carried 32,500 tons of coal. Fifty-three ships were lost, or 0.13 per cent.

Once again, the figures were ignored or shelved. Meanwhile at sea the blood-letting went on, like some great national haemorrhage in which the country's strength was bleeding away into the water. Seven hundred lives were lost from merchant ships in March 1917, and over 100 ships were sunk, sixty-two without warning. The killing began on the first day of the month with the loss, torpedoed without warning, of the 11,483-ton *Drina* and fifteen of her crew. On the 3rd, the 5197-ton *Sagamore* was sunk, costing fifty-two lives including her Master. On the 17th it was the 6446-ton *Anthony* with fifty-five lives, and in the four days between the 19th and the 23rd eight vessels were sunk, including the 3597-ton *Stuart*, with twenty lives. On 25th March alone, five ships were sunk, one of them being *Queen Eugenie* (4358 tons) with the Master and thirty-four of his crew.

On Monday 19 March 1917 the 5900-ton Union-Castle liner *Alnwick Castle* was torpedoed some 300 miles SW of the Bishop Rock. It was just after six in the morning and still dark but all six of the ship's boats got safely away. The Master, Captain Benjamin Chave, was the last to leave:

The forecastle was now [6.30 a.m.] just dipping, though the ship maintained an upright position without list. The people in my boat were clamouring for me to come, as they were alarmed by the danger of the ship plunging. The purser informed me that everyone was out of the ship, and I then took Mr Carnaby from his post, and we went down to No. 1 boat and pulled away.

At a safe distance we waited to see the end of the *Alnwick Castle*. Then we observed the submarine quietly emerge from the sea, end on to the ship, with a gun trained on her. She showed no periscope – just a conning tower and a gun as she lay there – silent and sinister. In about ten minutes the *Alnwick Castle* plunged bow first below the surface, her whistle gave one blast and the main topmast broke off; there was a smothered roar and a cloud of dirt, and we were left in our boats, 139 people, 300 miles from land. The submarine lay between the boats, but whether she spoke any of them I do not know. She proceeded NE after a steamer which was homeward bound, about four miles away, and soon after we saw a tall column of water, and knew that she had found another victim.

Benjamin Chave's account of the ordeal in the life-boat continued, like a saga from Hakluyt:

. . . I found only three men who could help me to steer, and one of these subsequently became delirious, leaving only three of us. . . . We spent the whole of Tuesday fighting the sea, struggling with oars to assist the sea-anchor to head the boat up to the waves, constantly soaked with cold spray and pierced with the bitter wind, which was now from the north. . . . I served out water twice daily, one dipper between two men, which made a portion about equal to one-third of a condensed milk tin. . . . Most of the men were now helpless, and several were raving in delirium. The foreman cattleman, W. Kitcher, died, and was buried. Soon after dark the sea became confused and angry; I furled the tiny reefed sail and put out the sea-anchor. At 8 p.m. we were swamped by a breaking sea, and I thought all was over. A moan of despair rose in the darkness, but I shouted to them to bale, bale, bale, and assured them the boat could not sink. How they found the balers and the bucket in the dark, I do not know, but they managed to free the boat while I shifted the sea-anchor to the stern, and made a tiny bit of sail, and got her away before the wind. . . . Several of the men collapsed, and others temporarily lost their reason, and one of these became pugnacious and climbed about the boat, uttering complaints and threats. The horrors of that night, together with the physical suffering, are beyond my power of description. . . . No one could now eat biscuits, it was impossible to swallow anything solid, our throats were afire, our lips furred, our limbs numbed, our hands were white and bloodless. During the afternoon, Friday, March 23rd, another fireman, named Tride, died, and my Steward, Buckley, died, also a cattleman whose only name I could get was Peter, collapsed and died about noon. . . .

But that afternoon, they were picked up by the French steamer *Venezia*. Chave and his men were too weak to help themselves. The twenty-four survivors were hoisted out with ropes, one by one, leaving four corpses in the boat.

There was one other significant loss that month, on the 27th, when the 2891-ton *Thrace* was torpedoed and sunk off Brest. She was carrying iron ore from Bilbao to Ardrossan and was actually in a convoy of twelve ships, escorted by a French destroyer and two trawlers, steaming by night and anchoring by day. The convoy system had recently been introduced for the valuable iron-ore trade from northern Spain.

Clearly, the U-boat had just one shot, for the other eleven ships were untouched. There were only two survivors from *Thrace*'s crew of thirty-eight, one of them a fifteen-year-old cadet named Dove, who lashed himself to an upturned lifeboat and stayed there, while seven others slipped off and drowned. He was actually interrogated by the captain of a U-boat which surfaced close to him. They called him an English swine and threatened to shoot him. 'Shoot away,' said Dove, 'and be damned to you.' The U-boat captain replied that shooting was too good for him. Dove was picked up by a fishing-boat next day, after thirteen hours in the water.

While Benjamin Chave and his fellow survivors, some of whom were still raving and delirious, were being fed brandy, hot soup and gallons of water to quench their seemingly insatiable thirst, while young Dove was being pumped for the details of his incredible story (he was reported to be an abnormally shy boy), while all the other soaked, exhausted, dehydrated and frost-bitten survivors were being led or carried ashore at ports all round the United Kingdom – there were no new developments towards convoy.

Jellicoe, whose personal pessimism about the way the war at sea was developing seemed to deepen with every passing day, reported regularly to the War Cabinet, but his bulletins consisted almost entirely of accounts of individual actions between single ships and U-boats. He had no new strategic initiative to announce, no radical shift of opinion. When, that same month of March, the War Cabinet asked Jellicoe about convoy, he said the matter was still being considered.

However, there is nothing so irresistible as an idea whose time has come and, by March 1917, the time for convoy was almost at hand. The first crack in the Admiralty's united opposition to convoy came early in April 1917 with the unexpected discovery (unexpected, that is, by the Admiralty) that the weekly figures of ships' arrivals and departures from British ports were grossly misleading. Had anybody in any of the Admiralty departments paused to consider it seriously, that figure of some 5000 shipping movements every week must have appeared ridiculous. That enormous total included all the movements, sailings, and repeated calls of small coasters and short-haul trading vessels of 300 tons and upwards which could not conceivably have been concerned in any system of ocean convoy.

The 5000 figure had never been accurately computed, because the necessary computing arrangements did not exist. All the extra sailings and departures were lumped together and the total bandied about and widely promulgated by the Admiralty in a very understandable and praiseworthy attempt to confuse the enemy, by making him think that losses to U-boats were only a pin-prick on Great Britain's merchant marine.

In fact, the Admiralty were only deceiving themselves. The enemy knew the true position well enough. The Admiralty forgot the origins of that huge total, which became lost in the wastes of the Admiralty's bureaucratic system and actually came to believe that 5000 ocean-going ships called and sailed from the United Kingdom every week. That figure, if true, would have meant that the country was still importing, in 1917, some 200 million tons of imports every year – or about four times the amount imported every year before the war!

The first serious misgivings about the 5000 figure seem to have been aroused by Commander R. G. H. Henderson, the officer in the Admiralty responsible for organizing the French coal-trade 'controlled sailings'. He began to search for information about the volume of trade and its points of origin and found that no Admiralty department had any accurate figures, or any means of obtaining them. The information was eventually supplied from Mr Norman Leslie at the Ministry of Shipping. A check was made to see if the Admiralty figures were reliable guides as to the number of vessels to be convoyed and hence the number of escorts needed.

The awful suspicion began to dawn, which was soon confirmed, that the Admiralty figures had no basis in fact whatsoever. With the help of the Ministry and an extensive card index of ship sailings and arrivals, exhaustive returns were produced in a few days. The evidence of the card index was checked many times and in many ways, but the answer was always the same. The suspicion became certainty that the Admiralty collectively had made a supreme ass of itself. Daily arrivals in the United Kingdom and the Channel Islands of ocean-going vessels averaged about twenty a day. Out-going vessels were, naturally, about the same number.

There was yet another unpleasant fact for the Admiralty to digest. At the end of April 1917, the country still possessed 3200 steamers – some 5 million tons of shipping – which appeared comfortably adequate. But of those, 1900 were engaged on war work, leaving only 1300 to carry food and raw materials for the country. At that time, ten ships were being lost every day. Out of every 100 ocean-going steamers leaving the country, twenty-five, or *one in four*, were failing to return.

Now it was possible to see how dangerously complacent the Admiralty had been. As long as it was believed that 2500 ships arrived and another 2500 left our ports every week, the loss of, say, fifty large British, neutral and Allied steamers in a week did seem unimportant. Against the true figures of only 120 to 140 sailings a week, those sinkings suddenly leaped into their true and deadly focus.

When Lloyd George heard of this colossal blunder, he behaved in his usual intolerable (to the Admiralty) manner. 'What an amazing miscalculation!' he crowed. 'The blunder on which their policy was based was an arithmetical mix-up which would not have been perpetrated by an ordinary clerk in a shipping office. A moment's reflection would have told them that nothing approaching 2500 deep sea vessels could be concluding voyages to this country every week.'

The true figure of about 140 ships a week also removed a serious mental block in the Admiralty's thinking about escorts. It was widely believed that the ratio of escorts to ships in a convoy should be at least one to one. It had therefore been estimated, for i..stance, that a minimum of seventy destroyers (in addition to those already engaged in submarine-hunting) would be needed to implement a full convoy system. But now, only twenty or thirty destroyers would be required, and some of these could be found at once.

But they were not found at once. By the beginning of April 1917 the Dutch and French coastal trades were both successfully under convoy. But pre-liminary moves towards a general system were still being opposed by many senior naval officers. On 3 April 1917, a conference assembled at Longhope in the Orkneys to consider how the heavy losses then being sustained on the Scandinavian route could be reduced. With the Dutch and French examples before them, the conference unanimously recommended convoy for the Scandinavian route.

The proposal was not greeted with unanimous approval. Admiral Pears, at Invergordon, recommended that convoys should be kept small, with only four or five ships at a time. Admiral Hamilton, at Rosyth, generally supported the recommendations but added that convoy arrangements could not be kept secret and that sooner or later the enemy would attack a convoy in strength. In Admiral Stuart Nicholson, at Grimsby, the pre-war Navy reared its unlovely, reactionary head; he was in favour of 'individual escort by single trawler of the more valuable ships, the rest proceeding independently, and destroyers being used to patrol the route'.

Admiral Beatty, the C-in-C Grand Fleet, strongly supported convoy and had been impatient at the Admiralty's tardiness in introducing it. He believed that this business of 'patrolling vast spaces of ocean' was not practical and that the Admiralty's policy of *defensive* patrolling by trawlers and *offensive* patrolling by destroyers was simply wrong in principle. Cer-tainly, it was not sinking U-boats. There were seventy destroyers, eight at Queenstown, forty-one at Plymouth, twenty-one at Portsmouth, and in the first three months of unrestricted submarine warfare they had not between them sunk a single U-boat. In Beatty's opinion, the cruisers, the destroyers, sloops, P boats, and armed trawlers – the whole lot them – should stop patrolling and start escorting merchantmen.

Beatty endorsed the recommendations of the Longhope conference:

It is necessary to decide the relative urgency of (1) protecting and patrolling the coast and (2) protecting the traffic along the coast. At first sight it would seem that these two objects are similar, and that if the coast is patrolled and protected, traffic should be able to proceed safely along it. Experience has shown, however, that this is not the case; patrols have given little if any security

to shipping during the war; submarines attack vessels close to the coast and
mines are continually being laid off the shore. Escorts have, however, proved
an effectual protection and a sytem of escorts does, to a large extent, fulfil the
conditions of a patrol, the escorting vessels being placed in the best position
for meeting and attacking hostile submarines. It is manifestly impracticable to
provide an escort for each individual vessel, the only alternative is to introduce
a system of convoys. . . .

The Longhope conference recommendations reached the Admiralty on 11
April 1917. Duff took the line that an effective convoy escort needed two
escorts to every ship in the convoy. Otherwise, submarines would make
mince-meat of insufficiently guarded convoys passing regularly over the
same route. However, he was prepared to sanction convoy on the Scandinavian route because of what he thought were two special factors: the ships
would all have much the same speed, and the Scandinavian nights were short
in the summer. Jellicoe ordered the system to be tried, and results reported
fortnightly.

So, with Admiralty misgivings, the Scandinavian convoys began. Some
twenty destroyers from the Humber, Tyne, Rosyth and Cromarty flotillas
were allotted as escorts, with between fifty and seventy armed trawlers from
patrol areas between Orkney and the Humber. Ships from east coast ports
were convoyed up to Lerwick, in the Shetlands, which became the central
'staging post'. Eastbound convoys, which were at first restricted to nine
ships, were escorted across the North Sea by destroyers and armed patrol
vessels to the Norwegian coast, where the ships dispersed to their destinations. The escort waited at a rendezvous for a westbound convoy which
was escorted across to Lerwick. Southbound convoys for the east coast ports
left Lerwick every day, westbound convoys for the Scottish ports about once
a week.

The first convoys in both directions sailed on 29 April 1917. There were
normally about six or seven ships in a convoy, escorted by an average of two
destroyers and four or five auxiliary patrol vessels (normally gunboats, armed
yachts or trawlers). But convoy numbers were soon increased to between
twenty and fifty ships. Twenty-five convoys sailed in May 1917, and the
number of ships convoyed rose to 300 easterly and 200 westerly. One ship
was lost between Lerwick and Bergen in May. Five ships, four of them
between Lerwick and the Humber, were lost in June, out of a total of 1871
ships convoyed, or 0.3 per cent.

On 6 April 1917 America entered the war. On the 9th Rear-Admiral
William Sims US Navy arrived in Britain to act as liaison officer between his
navy and the Admiralty. On Sim's first visit, Jellicoe showed him the true
figures of current shipping losses. Sims was horrified and appalled. The
figures published were not actually false, but they certainly were misleading
and Sims, like everybody else, had believed that the Allies were slowly but

surely winning the war. Jellicoe's figures showed that, far from winning, the Allies were on their way to losing, and within a measurable period of time.

Jellicoe hoped for the maximum amount of assistance in the way of escorts from the US Navy and may deliberately have painted as black a picture as he could. Their conversation had a dramatic effect upon Sims. The losses were some three or four times as bad as those published, so bad that according to Sims's own account of their meeting, years later, Jellicoe said, 'It is impossible for us to go on with the war if losses like this continue.' When Sims asked what was being done about it, Jellicoe replied, 'Everything we can'. Sims said it looked as though the Germans were winning the war. Jellicoe said, 'They will win, unless we can stop these losses – and stop them soon.' Sims then asked if there was no solution to the problem. Jellicoe said, 'Absolutely none that we can see now.'

Jellicoe's own recollections of this meeting, also written down years later, are not so unrelievedly gloomy. He claimed he gave Sims enough information to realize the full danger. His reply to Sims's question about a solution had been, 'The counter measures being devised could not be immediately successful as time was required for their production. I then urged him to do his best to obtain small fast craft from the United States.' Sims conveyed the true gravity of the position to Washington and the first six US destroyers arrived in Queenstown, Ireland, on 4 May 1917.

The Admiralty's unsteady shuffle towards convoy, the deliberations, the conferences, the re-assessments, the re-castings of plans, the introduction of new weapons, the advent of more destroyers, all took time. Meanwhile the country's life blood continued to gush into the sea. In the first fortnight of April 1917, the U-boats sank 419,621 tons of British, Allied and neutral shipping. On one day, 20 April, 27,704 tons were lost. The next day, the loss was 29,705 tons. The total cost in April was 881,027 tons and 997 lives.

On 8 April, the 5597-ton *Torrington* was torpedoed without warning 150 miles SW of the Scillies. The Master, Mr A. Starkey, and the twenty men in his lifeboat were taken on board the U-boat. Mr Starkey himself was taken below. His men were left on deck while the U-boat submerged and the men drowned. The other boat, commanded by the mate, was never seen again and thus all *Torrington*'s thirty-four men except the Master were lost.

In the first week of April, twenty-three vessels were sunk, the worst loss being 122 lives in the 9239-ton *City of Paris*. In the second week, twenty-eight ships were sunk, in the third, fifty-eight. Valuable ships were given special escort but even this was no guarantee of safety. Two ambulance ships, *Lanfranc* and *Donegal*, were torpedoed within an hour of each other on the evening of 17 April, on passage from Le Havre to Southampton. *Lanfranc* carried 234 wounded British and 167 wounded German prisoners and was escorted by the destroyer *Badger* and the sloop P. 37. Both escorts came alongside in heavy seas to take off survivors, but four British, fifteen German wounded and five of the crew were lost.

Donegal was escorted by two destroyers, *Liffey* and *Jackal*, which also came alongside and took off the wounded, though twenty-six were drowned, with eleven of the crew. One of *Donegal*'s survivors was a fireman, John Priest, who had been a survivor of the liner *Titanic* when she sank on her maiden voyage in 1912. He was in the liner *Olympic* when she collided with the cruiser *Hawke*. He was wounded but was again a survivor of the armed merchant cruiser *Alcantara* when she foundered after her action with the German raider *Greif* in February 1916. He survived when the *Britannic* was mined and sunk in the Mediterranean in November 1916. He was taken with head injuries on board *Jackal*. 'Good old Navy,' was all he said.

Chapter Five

It is impossible at this distance of time to retrace all the twists and turns of Admiralty policies and attitudes towards convoy in the last few months leading up to its introduction. Some of those most closely involved were later to use the pruning knife on documents with what Winston Churchill later called 'no timid hand'. But in any account of the events, the personality of Sir John Jellicoe is central. As First Sea Lord, he was the professional head of the Navy. As Jack Jellicoe, he had the respect and affection of the whole Navy. He had, so to speak, been groomed for his position for years before the war, when Lord Fisher had chosen him, and planned and schemed for him, to be in command of the fleet when Armageddon should come. He was cautious by nature, conservative by upbringing and training. The Royal Navy before 1914 was one of the most conservative societies in history, and Jellicoe was very much a man of that service and that time.

The threat of Armageddon, when it came, was not at Jutland but in the shipping losses of 1917. Jellicoe had planned and trained for a Jutland. He had made no such preparations for a prolonged war against trade. Towards convoy, he was curiously neutral. He certainly did not press its case forward, as the one sure way of saving the situation. On the other hand, he did not oppose it. He seemed content to let events prove or disprove, whilst he himself withheld judgement. His writings show that to the end of his life Jellicoe thought of convoy as a *defensive* measure. He never seemed to grasp that convoy also took the initiative away from the attacking U-boat. It certainly was a superb defensive measure; but it was also the most effective offensive tactic against submarines.

Jellicoe disliked and distrusted most politicians. War Cabinet meetings bored and fatigued him. Politically he was no match for Lloyd George, who consistently outmanoeuvred him. But Jellicoe did not learn from his experience, as many other senior naval officers have done before and since. Most politicians knew very little about the Navy and its affairs. But that did not mean they had nothing useful to contribute. The eye of the innocent often saw the obvious which was hidden to the *cognoscenti*.

Lloyd George raised the subject of convoy in War Cabinet on 23 April 1917. Jellicoe said the matter was still under consideration. Although the Scandinavian system had not yet been properly instituted, convoys with escorts had been assembled and dispatched already under Beatty's aegis. They had not been wholly successful, but that depended on which way one looked at them. Most of the ships had arrived, but two had been sunk.

Lloyd George complained later, and was quite justified, that this news, and indeed any news of any losses for some time after convoy had been introduced was told to him with a 'We told you so' expression. 'The fact that the [Norwegian] experiment was not a systematic convoy,' he wrote, 'was imperfectly organized and was therefore not given a fair chance, was not taken into account. It was not a success and the Admirals "had told us so".'

On the same day, 23 April, Jellicoe submitted a memorandum which did not put convoy forward as a new or even as a possible solution. Jellicoe's suggested remedy for the continual drain on shipping was: more destroyers should be built; the United States should be asked to send more ships; and more merchant shipping should be built, either small ships which would make lesser targets, or very large ships for which it would be worthwhile providing an escort. Jellicoe admitted the failure of the policy of mining the Heligoland Bight to prevent submarines leaving. He put this down to ineffective mines. Otherwise, with the very large number of mines laid in the last four months, it was scarcely credible that the U-boats had not suffered heavier losses. But they had not so suffered, so the mines must be faulty. New patterns of mine had been developed and ordered. But they would not be available in numbers until July 1917.

Meanwhile, Jellicoe intended to combat the U-boats with the means already at his disposal, 'by bombs dropped from aircraft, by depth-charges dropped from patrol vessels, by paravane attack, by heavy shell in the nature of depth-charges fired by patrol vessels'. The only immediate remedy he could see was the provision of more destroyers and patrol boats from the United States. It was to be more of the same, although it had already become clear that surface vessels were at a tremendous disadvantage against submarines, which they could not see. Their enemy might be three miles away, or he might be actually under their keel, and they had no means of knowing. Otherwise, they could, like whalehunters, only pursue their prey when they saw it, harrowing and harrassing the mammal until it had to surface for air. This was a markedly inefficient method against submarines. By March 1917, there had been thousands of offensive patrols by destroyers, and no less than 142 actions between destroyers and U-boats. But only six U-boats had been sunk in all these encounters.

The War Cabinet discussed convoy again on 25 April. Lloyd George said he would visit the Admiralty on the 30th. Afterwards, he claimed that the threat of this visit had an electric effect upon the Admiralty, galvanizing them into deciding to introduce convoy. The Admiralty and the Admirals strenuously denied any such thing.

Both sides overstated their case. Lloyd George came to the Admiralty to discuss a number of matters, not just anti-submarine warfare, and of the possible anti-submarine methods convoy was only one (although by far the most important and effective one). But it was naive of the Admirals, on their part, to insist that the impending visit of the Prime Minister had little or no effect. It *must* have helped to concentrate minds wonderfully.

At any rate, by the time Lloyd George did arrive, much had happened. It must have been on the evening of 25 April 1917 that Duff came to Jellicoe's room in the Admiralty and said that the shipping losses had convinced him that a general system of convoy simply had to be given a try. Jellicoe agreed that Duff should draw up a minute making out this recommendation in detail.

But Jellicoe appeared still unconvinced at heart. On the 25th he told Admiral Hamilton, C-in-C at Rosyth (in a letter actually written during the War Cabinet meeting):

> I am wasting my time at a War Cabinet meeting and have an opportunity of writing to you which does not occur during any other portion of the day!! I am rather afraid the convoy system on East Coast [this was the Scandinavian system] will fail for lack of destroyers, but as you know we are trying it. There are no destroyers at all to carry it out on Western Approaches, but some day I may be able to carry it out, and the arrangements for doing so are being prepared.

On 27th April Jellicoe sent a memorandum to the First Lord which was, in a sense, the last message from the old pre-convoy world, the last despondent account before the end of an era. It was even more gloomy, written in even more sombre language, than any of its predecessors. 'I feel it my duty,' Jellicoe wrote, 'to place before you my considered opinion that the time has arrived when it is necessary to bring home more fully to the government the very serious nature of the naval position with which we are now confronted. I fear that the War Cabinet is not as yet fully impressed with the gravity of the situation.'

Jellicoe admitted that all he himself had done was to appoint committees to look into the rate at which ships could be built to replace losses, and the extent to which shipping could be reduced without starving the country. But, he said, 'this kind of administrative action does nothing to grapple with the vital difficulties of the situation'.

Forecasts of shipping losses, Jellicoe said, were 'utterly useless'. Losses depended upon a number of problematical factors, ranging from the skill of the U-boat captains to the rate at which merchant ships could be armed, from

the number of torpedoes a U-boat could carry to the number of patrol vessels
we could put to sea, from the weather to the effect of labour strikes on the
delivery dates of new weapons. He said he had urged 'time after time' the
absolute necessity of reducing the number of lines of communication which
the Navy was called upon to safeguard.

He certainly did not mince his words:

> The real fact of the matter is this. We are carrying on the war at sea at the
> present time as if we had the absolute command of the sea, whereas we have
> not such a command or anything approaching it. It is quite true that we are
> masters of the situation so far as surface ships are concerned, but it must be
> realized – and realized at once – that this will be quite useless if the enemy's
> submarines paralyse, as they do now, our lines of communication. History has
> shown from time to time the fatal results of basing naval and military strategy
> on an insecure line of communications. Disaster is certain to follow, *and our
> present policy is heading for disaster.*

But what did Jellicoe himself suggest should be done? First: withdraw the
whole of the Allied force from Salonika. Second: realize that we could not
continue to bring fresh troops to this country unless they were convoyed in
ships carrying other essentials, such as food from the colonies. The Navy
could not provide the necessary troopships. Third: the policy of importing
native labour must stop. Last: 'the import of everything that is not essential to
the life of the country is ruthlessly and immediately stopped'.

It is hard to believe that Jellicoe thought any solution was possible. He
used the word 'convoy' but only in the sense of 'convey'. He was urging the
government to return to a consideration of basic strategy in sea communications, but his suggested remedies were only palliatives, really only a
prolonged and desperate effort to avoid a final catastrophe. Jellicoe's memo
was the nadir of the depression, the darkest hour before the dawn.

The First Lord did not present the memo to the War Cabinet until 1 May.
By that time, dawn was breaking. Duff's memo of the 26th had been written.
It was a seminal document in the history of the country's wars at sea. It was so
detailed, and contained so many considered points and tabulated conclusions, that it suggested that Duff, or somebody, must have been working on it
for some time beforehand.

Duff's memo was a proposal for the convoy of *all* vessels (except those
above fifteen knots) – British, Allied and neutral – from north and south
Atlantic ports to the United Kingdom. Vessels would be convoyed by
men-of-war or by merchant Q ships from 'certain Convoy Depots' and
escorted to a longitude clear of the danger zone, there to be met by an escort
of destroyers and 'convoyed into a port of refuge'. From there they would be
taken by other escorts to their destination. The convoy depots would be at
Gibraltar, Dakar, Louisburg in Canada, and Newport News.

Duff worked out that an average of twenty-six vessels per day would require to be escorted through the danger zone. He proposed that convoys should leave every four days from Gibraltar, each with about twenty-eight vessels; every five days, with about eighteen vessels from Dakar; every three days, with between sixteen and twenty vessels, from Louisburg; and every three days, with eighteen vessels from Newport News. He calculated that these convoys would require a total of forty-five escorts to take them through the danger zone.

At times it is difficult to believe that Duff was the sole author of the memorandum, the views expressed in it are so at variance with his previous statements. For instance, the same officer who commented on the Longhope conference that an effective convoy needed two escorts to every ship in the convoy was now, apparently, of the opinion:

> the larger the convoy passing through any given danger zone, provided it is moderately protected, the less the loss to the Merchant Services; that is, for instance, were it feasible to escort the entire volume of trade which normally enters the United Kingdom *per diem* in one large group, the submarine as now working would be limited to one attack, which, with a Destroyer escort, would result in negligible losses compared with those now being experienced.

This, for Duff, was an astounding statement, the Admiralty equivalent of the light on the road to Damascus.

Jellicoe approved Duff's memo the next day, 27 April. A trial system was agreed, for one convoy homeward bound from Gibraltar and another from Hampton Roads, Virginia. So, when Lloyd George visited the Admiralty on the 30th, Jellicoe was able to tell him that a convoy system was on trial, and the visit passed off pleasantly enough.

On 28 April the Admiralty signalled the Senior Naval Officer Gibraltar to inform him that it was proposed to start convoys for British and Allied vessels from Gibraltar and that the first convoy would sail in about ten days' time. The convoy was not to exceed twenty vessels, and the SNO was not to include in it ships which could do more than 11 knots, because the mean speed of the convoy was not expected to be more than 7 knots. The SNO was ordered to prepare to fit each ship with a portable telephone line from the fore-bridge to the engine-room plates, to issue fog-buoy casks for station-keeping and to nominate signal ratings RNVR, one for each merchant ship, for taking and repeating signals. On 4 May, the Admiralty told the SNO to start assembling ships for the first convoy on 7 May.

Meanwhile, Captain H. C. Lockey, who was to be the convoy commodore, and who was specially given the rank of Commodore Second Class, sailed from Devonport on 2 May with the Q ships *Mavis* (Acting Commodore A. St V. Keyes) and *Rule* (Lieutenant Langton-Jones) arriving in Gibraltar on 7 May. A convoy of sixteen ships had been assembled and a conference of their masters was held on the same day, during which the masters were briefed on signalling, station-keeping, keeping down funnel smoke – all the advice and cautions and warnings which innumerable masters were to receive at countless similar such conferences in that war and the next.

The convoy sailed in three columns after dark on 10 May. The columns were led independently to a rendezvous at Jermias anchorage, where the assembly was not carried out very successfully in the dark. However, the convoy finally formed up in its correct cruising order at about 3 p.m. on 11 May. The two wing columns contained five ships each and the centre column of six ships was led by Commodore Lockey himself in the *Clan Gordon*, his ship also being the guide of the fleet. Columns were 6 cables (1200 yards) apart, ships 3 cables (600 yards) apart. Three armed yachts from Gibraltar accompanied the convoy through the submarine danger zone as far as 11° W. The route was one of two, chosen at the last moment by SNO Gibraltar.

The convoy was met by a flying boat from the Scillies in the Western Approaches and by destroyers from Devonport. They should have met at 8 a.m. on 18 May but the convoy was actually some twenty miles west of its rendezvous and the meeting did not take place until 4 p.m. that day. The port column of five ships bound for western ports in the UK was detached south of the Scillies, escorted by two destroyers, and dispersed off the Smalls on 20 May. The other two columns put into Plymouth on 20 May and sailed again that evening. Off Portland the four destroyers were relieved by twenty-four drifters from Poole and the convoy went on up Channel in three divisions, each escorted by eight drifters. The ships arrived in the Downs on 22nd May and dispersed to their respective destinations. No enemy submarines had been encountered and the convoy had actually made its passage two days faster than if the ships had been routed by any of the independent routes.

Station-keeping, the point on which the Admiralty had been so doubtful, was extremely good. The average distance between ships in column was estimated to be about 5 cables. The masters said that they had had much more sleep on passage than they had had for months. Relieved of the responsibilities of looking out for the enemy, they could devote themselves to station-keeping and navigation. Some of the lower-powered ships had had difficulty in maintaining their claimed speed at sea. One 'seven-knot' vessel twice had to be allowed to cut corners so as to keep the rendezvous with the destroyers. But, in general, that first convoy from Gibraltar could be called a success.

However, it was not seen as such across the Atlantic. The Admiralty accepted in principle a scheme for convoy in the Atlantic at the beginning of May 1917. On 3 May they asked the US Navy Department to send a trial convoy of sixteen to twenty British or Allied ships, all under 12 knots' speed, escorted by those first six American destroyers which were just about to sail for Queenstown. But the Navy Department in Washington had the gravest doubts and misgivings. They cabled to the Admiralty their opinion that it was far safer to arm merchant vessels defensively. The US Navy was willing to help in an experimental scheme for North Atlantic convoy, but they remained very strongly opposed to the principle. From the British Embassy, Commodore Guy Gaunt reported that the Navy Department were very strongly against the convoy scheme, 'Admiral Benson particularly so.' Gaunt summed up the American position, 'from first to last they were most courteous and evidently very anxious to fall in with the Admiralty's views, but honestly thought the scheme of so many merchant ships travelling together was not a sound one'. 'The Navy Department,' he wrote, 'does not consider it advisable to attempt the character of convoy outlined. In large groups of ships under convoy, fog, gales, inexperience of personnel, and general tension on merchant vessels make the hazards of the attempt great and the probability of a scattering of the convoy very strong.'

The US Navy still held the almost atavistic belief that bigger convoys meant bigger risks. As a concession, they suggested smaller convoys, of four ships, each group being convoyed by two destroyers. The Admiralty accepted the offer but then changed their minds on 22 May. The upshot was that the first experimental Atlantic convoy sailed from Hampton Roads on 24 May 1917. It consisted of twelve ships, with an average speed of 9 knots. Considering the volume of debate, pro and con, and all the doubts and misgivings by so many senior officers, the ocean escort was small – one cruiser, HMS *Roxburgh* (Captain F. A. Whitehead RN).

Two ships, *Ravenshoe*, loaded with sugar, and *Highbury*, with nitrate, soon found 9 knots too much for them and had to drop out. Whitehead sent them back to Halifax, but *Highbury* was torpedoed and sunk on the way. With the remaining ten ships disposed in three columns, Whitehead took the convoy onward, practising zigzagging whenever possible. On the afternoon of 4 June, the convoy formation was changed to a front of five ships, i.e. in five columns of only two ships each, by bringing up the rear ships of the wing columns. At 11.55 a.m. on 5 June, after crossing the 20° W meridian, the whole convoy and escort began zigzagging as one. The escort of eight destroyers from Devonport was met on the evening of 6 June. At 6 p.m. *Roxburgh* altered course for Plymouth, with two destroyers. The other six destroyers, reinforced by trawlers and by aircraft, took the convoy on towards the Channel. Ships for the west coast were detached off the Smalls on 8 June, the rest reaching St Helens, Isle of Wight, on 9 June.

Although there had been bad weather and fog on the way, Captain Whitehead reported that 'the convoy were attentive to signals, kept good station, and zigzagged in a satisfactory manner'. He was, he said, prepared to escort as many as thirty ships in convoy, instead of just twelve. The idea of merchant-ship masters being able to *zigzag*, in *any* fashion, came as a great surprise to many naval officers. But it was one more piece of evidence that the chief obstacles to convoy were mental ones.

Because of a critical and worsening oil-fuel shortage at home, four more convoys, largely consisting of tankers, were authorized and left Hampton Roads on 4, 12, 19 and 25 June, with twelve, eleven, eighteen and twenty ships respectively. One tanker, the *Wabasha* was torpedoed and some 2000 tons of oil were lost, but the ship eventually reached harbour. She was the only casualty in any of the convoys. It seemed that her convoy had been found by a U-boat but the convoy formation had restricted it to one 'browning' shot, fired at a venture. The rest of *Wabasha*'s column, and the rest of the convoy, with all the ships in the other three convoys, steamed safely onwards.

Thus, by the end of May 1917 the Scandinavian, the Dutch, the French coal and the Spanish ore routes, were all under convoy. The first Gibraltar convoy had arrived safely. Having approved convoy in principle and seen these examples working, there was everything to be said for the Admiralty introducing wholesale convoy as quickly as possible, before the enemy realized what was happening. Convoy, *now*, was strongly urged by some officers in the Admiralty and in the Ministry of Shipping.

But the only action taken was to hold a seemingly interminable series of more meetings. A second Gibraltar convoy did not leave until as late as 26 July. In the meantime, on 15 May a preliminary conference was held at the Admiralty to decide on the appointment of an Atlantic Trade Convoy Committee to draw up the complete organization for the ocean convoys. This was in fact a committee to decide about another committee.

The committee was appointed on 17 May; it consisted of four naval officers, Captain H. W. Longden, Fleet-Paymaster H. W. E. Manisty, Commander J. S. Wilde, and Lieutenant G. E. Burton, and, from the Ministry of Shipping, Mr Norman Leslie. They reported on 6 June, with detailed proposals for organizing staff in the Admiralty, and in the convoy assembly ports, at home and abroad. They had proposals for equipping merchant ships with signalling apparatus and personnel, voice-pipes, and detailed instructions for convoy escorts, commodore and individual masters.

The report was, in its way, a complete blueprint for convoy. It suggested eight homeward-bound and eight outward convoys every eight days. Assembly ports for the homeward convoys were to be New York, Hampton Roads, Dakar and Gibraltar. New York would handle ships from its own docks, Boston and Portland, to be joined at sea by ships from Cape Breton in summer or Halifax in winter. Hampton Roads would handle ships from American ports south of New York, from Panama, the Gulf and the Caribbean. Dakar would service vessels from south America, south and west Africa, Australia and the Far East. Gibraltar would be the rendezvous for ships homeward-bound from the Mediterranean.

The plan was for two convoys, average size twenty ships, speeds between 12 and 8¼ knots, to sail from each of these ports every eight days. Ships of 12 knots were thought fast enough to take their chance alone. Ships below 8 knots also had to take their chance: it was thought such lame ducks would unduly delay a convoy. One concession was allowed: the Gibraltar convoys were 7 knots, because of the large number of old and slow ships in the coal and ore traffic.

The committee paid special attention to the question of escorts. The Atlantic convoys were to be escorted by a cruiser, or an armed merchant cruiser, from its sailing port to a rendezvous outside the 'danger zone', where they would be met by destroyers, sloops, or P boats who would convoy them to their dispersal point, where a coastal escort would meet them. The committee recommended that out-going and in-coming convoys should be escorted, but for some time only in-coming ships were escorted.

For outward convoys, the committee proposed four convoys, each sailing twice during an eight-day cycle. Ships for the north Atlantic trade would sail from Liverpool and the Clyde; a second convoy system would take traffic from the Bristol Channel to the north and south Atlantic ports; a third would take all east coast ships bound for the Atlantic, assembling at a port in the Channel; Gibraltar convoys would sail every four days, from a port in the south or west.

This programme would obviously require a large number of escorts. The committee considered that fourteen flotillas, each with six ships, would be needed: two based on Gibraltar, three each on Lough Swilly, Queenstown, Portland and Plymouth, for a total of eighty-four destroyers or similar ships, plus fifty-two cruisers or armed merchant ships for the ocean escort.

On 6 June, Jellicoe reported to the Cabinet on the success of the Gibraltar convoy, and said that the Admiralty hoped to start a system of weekly convoys of oilers and provision ships in the immediate future. Duff formally approved the report of the committee on convoy on 11th June, Jellicoe on 14th and Carson, First Lord of the Admiralty, on 15th. For a time it did seem that matters were really moving.

But, in fact, progress towards convoy was still terribly slow. By the end of June 1917, only those four Hampton Roads convoys had sailed, and those had only been authorized because they carried oil fuel. Outward-bound ships from the UK were still unconvoyed. No general system had been introduced for in-coming ships. There were no convoys at all in the south Atlantic or in the Mediterranean.

The Admiralty, led by Jellicoe, still seemed reluctant to put its own decisions into effect. There was no added urgency, no extra weight put behind the preparations, no extra escorts provided. Convoy had been agreed, certainly, but the feeling still persisted in the corridors of the Admiralty that it was something of a last desperate throw. Many officers still looked over their shoulders at the old system of route patrolling.

On 25 June the Admiralty said in a circular that it 'approved generally' of the committee's recommendations. But the letter was approved rather than the spirit. The recommendations would be put into effect 'as the necessary vessels for escort and convoy duties became available'. It was estimated that

fourteen ocean escorts and ninety anti-submarine escorts would be required
for a partial convoy system; for a full system those figures rose to fifty and 170.
But nothing particular was done to make those vessels available more
quickly.

Three main questions weighed most heavily in the balance when deciding
whether, and when, to introduce convoy: the number of ships to be escorted,
the number of escorts available, and America's entry into the war. America's
entry made more escorts available, and simplified problems of assembling
convoys in hitherto neutral ports. But the decision to introduce convoy was
made before American ships could have any influence on the situation. The
new statistics had revealed the true number of ships to be escorted. So the
only real problem seemed to be the number of escorts.

There was no shortage of escorts in early 1917. The only blockages were
mental ones. There were available, and ready to start on convoy duties, 350
destroyers and sixty sloops, with sixty old cruisers and twenty-four old
battleships. This was a truly staggering total of *very nearly 500 ships*. But large
numbers of destroyers and cruisers were still used in patrolling empty ocean
wastes, or escorting single troopships.

Meanwhile, in the space of time between decision and actual im-
plementation, the losses continued. In May 1917 the number of U-boats at sea
had fallen to forty, spending 535 days on patrol (the equivalent figures for
April were fifty and 660) but they sank a total of nearly 595,000 tons of
British, Allied and neutral shipping. Only six U-boats were sunk in the
month, and only one by a destroyer – UC-26 rammed by *Milne* on 9 May. Two
were sunk by torpedoes from Allied submarines, one by the Q ship *Glen*, one
by German mines, and one, most significantly for the future, by a Curtiss
flying boat on anti-submarine air patrol from Felixstowe. Six U-boats, sunk
in these ways, seemed a very poor return for all the patrolling.

However, by the end of May 1917 the Germans themselves were beginning
to have doubts about the long-term success of their unrestricted U-boat
campaign. In February the German government had confidently believed
that Great Britain was heading towards an overwhelming defeat through
losses at sea. But by June they were discouraging hopes expressed in German
newspapers that the war might be over by the autumn because Britain would
have to sue for peace after her trading position had become impossible. By
the end of June, the German government had virtually conceded that the
submarine campaign would not win the war as they had hoped and had
forecast.

In June, the shipping losses rose again to over 680,000 tons. The
Germans would have been even more encouraged had they known of an
operation off the Orkneys and Shetlands between 15 and 25 June. It was a
return to, or rather, a continuation of, the old methods which one would have
thought had been discredited.

Destroyers and submarines were stationed in various areas, stretching from NW of Stornoway, round to the north of the Shetlands and eastward down into the North Sea. The destroyers and submarines were so placed in successive areas that (it was hoped) U-boats transitting to and from their patrols would be forced to dive in the areas patrolled by destroyers, and thus be on the surface with their batteries depleted when they reached the adjacent areas patrolled by submarines.

Four flotilla leaders, with some fifty destroyers in all, and seventeen submarines took part. U-boats were sighted on sixty-one occasions and attacked twelve times. None were sunk. Meanwhile, six U-boats left the Fastnet area and were relieved by another four from Germany. One attack could and should have been successful; on the afternoon of 16 June, in the Fair Isle Channel, one of a new large steam-driven class of submarine, K.7, fired a salvo of four torpedoes at U-95. The third torpedo hit, but did not explode.

Once again, the rate of U-boat sinking was abysmal. Only four were sunk in June 1917: two off Ireland, one by another Q ship, *Pargust*, and the second rammed and sunk by a merchantman. Two were sunk in the English Channel, one by depth charges from the trawler *Sea King*, the other by gunfire from a French destroyer. No patrolling destroyer sank a U-boat. But, the official verdict on the operation in the north was that 'the Admiralty, whilst admitting that the operation was disappointing in its results, agreed that it ought to be repeated as soon as possible in order to give it a fair trial'!

Chapter Six

The Admiralty's general attitude towards convoy in that summer of 1917 is well summed up by the historian Arthur Marder:

> The Admiralty no longer objected to convoy in principle and were prepared to see a fair trial made. But their hearts were not in it. They regarded convoy as the last shot in their lockers, were sceptical of its success, and had a lingering preference for a trade protection system based on patrolling.

Lloyd George was more brutally direct:

> The High Admirals had at last been persuaded by the 'Convoyers' not perhaps to take action, but to try action. But there was a reluctance and a tardiness in their movements. They acted as men whose doubts were by no means removed, and who therefore proceed with excessive caution and with an ill-concealed expectation that their forebodings will be justified by the experience. When anything went wrong with convoyed ships, it was reported with an 'I told you so' air to the War Cabinet. I can find no minute where the First Sea Lord reported the unquestionable success of the system in cases where it was fairly tried.

After discussing the success of the first Hampton Roads convoy, Lloyd George went on: 'The Gibraltar convoy was equally successful. But these disappointing successes simply irritated the Admirals into sullen recalcitrance.'

There is evidence of Admiralty reluctance from several quarters. Manisty, who knew Jellicoe very well, wrote: 'I am not certain now, but I believe my feeling at the time was that J.R.J. did not seem confident as to the success of the system, but that he believed it to be the only chance, and that he was prepared to take the responsibility of the decision, and to support the scheme to the full, as he did.' Duff still had misgivings about practical details: 'Where the [escorts] are to come from Heaven knows, but a recent visit to the War Council showed me very clearly that they will look on Convoy as the only salvation to a very critical position, and great pressure will be brought to extend the system at once.'

Even the very word 'convoy' was taboo. After the war, during a discussion of a paper read at the RUSI, Admiral George Ballard had a revealing anecdote of his experience as Senior Naval Officer, Malta. His Chief of Staff had sent a signal, 'Transport So-and-so has left, convoyed by three destroyers'. Back came the answer: 'You are not to convoy.' Baffled, and perplexed, his Chief of Staff showed the reply to Ballard, who said, 'Do not say anything about a convoy, say an escort, and see what they say.' Next day a signal was sent: 'Transport So-and-so was escorted by three destroyers'. That was all right, and not a word was said.

References to convoy were deleted or amended in contexts which fudged the truth. Captain K. G. B. Dewar, who prepared weekly appreciations of the naval situation, and particularly the submarine campaign, in the Operations Division, wrote later about convoy:

> Remarks favourable to it were deleted from the Weekly Appreciations and the suggestion (made in July 1917) that outward-bound ships should be placed under convoy as quickly as possible was crossed out, with a note in the margin to say that 'these ships were being sunk because patrols had been withdrawn to provide escorts for the homeward convoys'. Not only was this statement incorrect, but it showed a simple faith in the system of patrolled routes along which our ships had been shepherded like sheep to the slaughter.

In such an atmosphere at the Admiralty, the regular North Atlantic convoy system began in July 1917. The first regular convoy from Hampton Roads (HH6) sailed on 2 July. It was the last 'mixed' convoy, containing ships bound for both east- and west-coast UK ports. Thereafter, convoys sailed every four days, alternately to east and west ports. The next, HH7, with west-coast vessels, sailed on 7 July.

Ships from Canadian ports assembled at Sydney, Cape Breton, from where the convoys sailed every eight days; the first, HS1, on 10 July, was escorted by the cruiser *Highflyer*. Ships from ports north of Philadelphia assembled at New York and sailed in convoys every eight days, the first, HN1, on 14 July.

In July 1917, 162 ships sailed in eight convoys from Hampton Roads; forty-five ships sailed in three convoys from Sydney; and thirty-seven ships in two convoys from New York. Of these 244 ships, two were sunk, and one of those, the steamer *Whitehall*, was lost from a Sydney convoy whilst sailing independently, having strayed from the convoy a day earlier.

Escorts were provided by seven cruisers, *Berwick*, *Roxburgh*, *Antrim*, *Drake*, *Cumberland*, *Isis* and *Highflyer* from the North American and West Indies

Squadron, augmented by four armed merchant cruisers, *Virginian*, *Alman-zara*, *Kildona Castle* and *Victorian* from the 10th Cruiser Squadron, and by five 'Commissioned Escort Ships', *Carrigan Head*, *Cambrian III* (renamed *Bostonian*), *Knight Templar*, *Sachem* and *Discoverer*.

These escort ships were merchant ships, carrying their cargo in the normal way and navigated by their masters, but fitted with three or four 6-inch guns, complemented by thirty gunnery ratings, and with a retired flag officer embarked as commodore. They flew the White Ensign, and their admiral's flag, while they were with their convoy.

HMS *Sachem*, a typical escort ship, commissioned at Liverpool on 5 June 1917. She was a Furness Withy steamer, used as a cattle boat, with a speed of 10½ knots. She was to carry three 6-inch guns, on central mountings, with a range of 12,000 yards, but as a man-of-war she was unprepossessing, as her Commodore reported: 'her poor speed, bad steering qualities, patched boilers twenty-six years old, narrow beam of 46 feet, compared to length of 445 feet which made her roll and list abnormally giving a most unsteady gun platform, was scarcely what was required in a ship whose function was to protect a convoy and drive off and engage well-found enemy raiders'.

On commissioning day, *Sachem* 'hoisted flag, and hauled it down at sunset; the mercantile crew refused to sign on'. There were delays because of submarine reports and the trade route was closed for days. On 13 June 'trade route open. Five firemen, one quartermaster, one boy, bolted'. Finally, the ship sailed on the 14th and, despite one boiler giving out on the 23rd, reached Hampton Roads on the 27th.

The Commodore's diary and account gives a clear picture of some of the early difficulties of convoy. *Sachem* went to load at Newport News on 28 June, and by 8 July was almost ready to sail. 'Held a conference at Norfolk, 11 masters present, detailed the *Remuera* (Capt. Green) from New Zealand as guide; four more ships joined later; loading very slow. It was suspected that the black labour men were being threatened and financed by pro-Germans; they said if they worked overtime they would be set on and maltreated by white men.'

The convoy (HH8) sailed on the 11th, *Sachem* casting off 'from Sewell's Point in a heavy thunderstorm at 1 p.m. while still coaling, the ship being in a state of chaos, and full of flies and mosquitoes. Convoy of fifteen ships formed, and proceeding at 7½ knots by 6 p.m. Required considerable patience, both in signals and in station-keeping. The Master was of no assistance, telling me that trying to combine a man-of-war and a merchant ship was impossible. The leading signalman had a fondness for chewing gum, and the RNVR signal ratings were inexperienced.'

However, the convoy practised zigzagging and altering course together, carried out target gunnery firings, 'sound signals etc.'. Two ships broke down. There were 'continuous SOS calls' on the radio. Six destroyers joined as escort on the 25th. The next day was misty, two rescue tugs joined, and there were reports of sinkings. On the 27th, two submarines were sighted close to the rendezvous and the convoy altered course.

The melancholy 'stream of SOS calls' of the 24th translated themselves into 'continuous wreckage, hatches, ladders, skylights, boats, casks, coconut oil etc. all day, showing the depredations the submarines had committed. It was a mournful sight. Two kite balloons and a seaplane circling round us.' But the convoy arrived without loss in the Thames on 29 July, and as *Remuera* passed off Gravesend 'Capt. Green signalled: "All on board wish me to express their many thanks and deep gratitude for bringing the *Remuera* into safety." '

In his account of a later convoy, HH23 which sailed with twenty ships from Hampton Roads on 8 September 1917, this officer gives a graphic description of some of the difficulties caused by eccentric merchantmen. This time it was the SS *Hermione*, which had already stopped for four hours to repair her steering gear and straggled more by the time a gale blew up on the 20th. 'The *Hermione* gave considerable trouble for the next forty-two hours on account of the Master steering a course of his own, giving most contradictory positions by wireless, not knowing the rendezvous we referred to, as he had not troubled to note it when ordered to, and being most careless in his code messages. After fixing him to a course, which we had to make to him *en clair*, he signalled his position at 8 a.m. on the 22nd 31 miles to the SSE of us, our speed the same; at noon he made his position 30 miles NE of us; taking the latter as probably correct, I altered her course so as to intercept ours, and we met a few hours later. The Master could give no reason for what he did; in fact, he said he had taken no notes of what he had done.'

The convoy arrived without loss in the Mersey on 28 September. Of the twenty ships 'eight carried steel, metals, and munitions, two sugar, one sulphur, two nitrates, four oil, three wheat, and ten of the above carried wheat, barley and flour in addition to the cargoes mentioned'. All these commodities were the very stuff of war.

With HH31, homeward bound in November, *Sachem* had more problems. *Mascanomo* joined late, with no code tables, and had to have every signal made in plain language. *Cantal* and *Rockefeller* had no signalmen. A case of Asiatic cholera was reported on board *Gordon Castle*. In *Sachem* herself, a 'consignment of eggs on board all rotten' and the ship broke down, refusing to answer her helm for two hours (she always did carry 7 degrees of port helm even under normal conditions). *Cantal* misread a signal and headed off to Halifax. *Sachem* had to stop the convoy and go after her. She paid no attention to any other flags or signals and eventually *Sachem* fired a shot across her bows. On rejoining, *Kalibia* 'who was out of her position, tried to cut into it across our bows, during which process her helm jammed, and we had to go full speed astern to avoid ramming her, only missing her by 20 yards, the excuse the Master gave being "the cook had fallen down the hatchway and the steering gear had jammed".' *Sachem* was in collision and then torpedoed in December. Very badly damaged, she was towed in and paid off.

By mid July 1917, four homeward-bound convoys were sailing every eight days, two from Hampton Roads and one each from New York and Sydney. The convoys were met at sea by destroyers and escorted in, convoys going south-about Ireland by the 2nd and 4th Flotillas at Devonport, north-about convoys by 14th and 15th Flotillas (both Grand Fleet flotillas) and sloops, from Buncrana in Ireland. There were twenty-eight US destroyers operating with the Royal Navy by the end of June and thirty-seven by the end of July.

From the very beginning the American ships made what Admiral Bayly called 'all the difference'; the longer the convoy system went on and the more convoys were organized, the more important the American ships became. Rear Admiral Sims proved to be an unobtrusively influential figure from the time he first arrived in the United Kingdom. He had already impressed his masters in Washington with the urgency of Jellicoe's arguments, and when he went to Queenstown in overall command of the American ships based there, he quickly established a close personal and professional *rapport* with Admiral Sir Lewis Bayly, the C-in-C, Coast of Ireland.

Bayly was not the easiest of men to deal with, and, as late as March 1917, he was still firmly advocating the old system of patrolling a few, heavily guarded routes, rather than convoy. But such was Sims's standing that when Bayly went on one week's leave on 18 June, the Admiralty agreed that Sims should take command of both British and American ships at Queenstown. At that time Sims had under his command twenty-four American destroyers, and five British, some seventeen sloops, eight minesweepers, four torpedo boats and ten Q ships – sixty-eight ships in all.

It sounded a large force but, with ships away for necessary rest and refitting, and the minesweepers constantly engaged, it was nothing like big enough to patrol the vast areas of sea in Bayly's command. Sims soon became a keen advocate of convoy. It had taken him a little time to accustom himself to the situation and he had first called for more ships for patrolling, because that was the recognized tactic when he arrived, but by June 1917 he had come to see that convoy was the only solution.

Soon after he took over, Sims was asked to provide destroyers to escort three troop convoys, bringing the first American troops over to Europe. Sims knew that his ships were already hard-pressed and that demands for destroyers would deplete them even further, to the point where he would not be able to maintain an effective patrol system. He also knew that the naval authorities at home were doubtful about convoy. Nevertheless, the proper course of action in his view was to send across the Atlantic every available destroyer and anti-submarine escort, to join in convoy duties as soon as possible.

'The success of the convoys so far brought in,' Sims wrote in June, 'shows that the system will defeat the submarines if applied generally, and in time.

. . . The present campaign is not succeeding.' And 'it would seem suicidal,' as Sims told Daniels, Secretary of the Navy, 'if the convoy system as proposed by the British Admiralty is not put into immediate operation and applied to all merchant vessels thus forcing submarines to encounter anti-submarine craft in order to attack shipping.' By 2 July, he was 'happy to see that our government has now expressed its willingness to help out with convoy'.

The numbers of ships available for convoy escort did slowly increase, despite hesitations. At a War Cabinet meeting of 13 July, Lloyd George *ordered* the Admiralty to look into the possibilities of rearranging the dispositions of destroyer flotillas in home waters, so as to make more destroyers available for convoy escort. Jellicoe wrote a memorandum next day which showed that none of the 218 modern and seventy-six old destroyers engaged in trade protection, screening the Grand Fleet, or patrolling the Dover Straits, could be diverted to convoy duties. However in July 1917 there were sixty-four destroyers, eleven sloops and sixteen P boats, ninety-one ships in all, available for convoy escort. By November this figure had climbed to 170: 102 destroyers, twenty-four sloops and forty-four P boats.

By the end of August 1917, the North Atlantic convoy system was in full swing. During the month eight convoys sailed from Hampton Roads, with 158 ships; five from Sydney, with sixty-seven ships; and four from New York, with forty-nine ships. The first HX convoy from Halifax, with six ships, sailed on 22 August. In the same month the convoy system was extended to ships from Gibraltar and the south Atlantic. A homeward-bound convoy (HG) sailed from Gibraltar on 26 July. Seven more with 119 ships sailed in August. Two HL convoys sailed from Sierra Leone, the first on 11 August, with eleven ships. The first two HD Dakar convoys sailed with thirty ships, the first on 22 August.

Of this total of 440 ships in convoy, ten were sunk. One of them collided with a U-boat, and five were sunk after parting from their convoy and sailing independently, or after a convoy had been broken up by bad weather. In other words, only four ships out of more than 400 were lost from the ranks of a properly conducted formation-keeping convoy.

Amongst the first people to notice this success were the U-boat captains. It very soon became clear to them that the easy days were over, when they had been able to lie some 200 miles off Fastnet and pick off a stream of tame, on-coming targets until their torpedoes were exhausted. The U-boats left their waiting positions out in the Atlantic and began to come much closer inshore, looking for targets amongst out-going unconvoyed ships. Thus, while the rate of losses amongst in-coming ships in convoy dropped remarkably, the losses of outward-bound, independently routed, ships began to rise.

This reversal was also noticed in the Admiralty. Until then, the losses had been largely of in-coming ships converging upon certain known routes, not in possession of the latest information about submarine movements, and nearly always fully loaded, and therefore much more valuable. Now the losses were of outward-bound ships, often in ballast. Nevertheless, it was seen at a series of conferences between the Admiralty, the War Cabinet, the Ministry of Shipping and representatives of the shipping industry on 12, 13 and 20 July that a system of convoy applied only to in-coming ships would not be enough.

Losses in June had climbed to 685,000 tons, well above the May figure of 595,000, and the figures for July were still rising (eventually they would be 550,000). Sir Norman Hill, for the Ministry, warned that in spite of new construction the reserves of ocean-going shipping were still being expended faster than they were being replaced. He prophesied that there would be a complete breakdown unless the current losses in the approach areas were reduced.

By the end of August almost the only ships that were being sunk were outward bound. Admiral Duff advised outward-bound convoys, but for an unexpected reason – 'to give as many ships as possible experience of sailing in Convoy before the bad weather sets in'. The inference is that Admiral Duff had still not properly hoisted in the truth that, without convoy, many of those ships would not still be afloat to experience any bad weather.

On 11 August telegrams were sent to all the shipping intelligence and routeing officers in ports in the United Kingdom and northern France that ships were no longer to be dispatched independently but sent to selected assembly ports for convoy. From Channel and east-coast ports, slow (7–10 knot) vessels assembled at Falmouth, fast (10 knots and upwards) at Devenport. For the west coast, fast tonnage for America and the South Atlantic sailed from Queenstown, slow vessels for the Mediterranean at Milford, and ships from Liverpool and Glasgow bound for America and the south Atlantic rendezvoused at Lamlash, on the Ilse of Arran.

Early on there was a disaster. The defences of Lamlash were incomplete and ships sailed from Buncrana. On 7 August, the steamers came out in single file, to form up some 20 miles from the shore. Two U-boats were waiting, and two merchantmen, *Devonian* and *Roscommon*, were sunk. The armed merchant cruiser *Virginian* was badly damaged.

The first outward convoy, with nine ships, had sailed from Milford on 13 August. Four more convoys sailed that month from Milford, with a total of seventy-seven ships. Outward convoys started from Queenstown on the 21st; three convoys sailed with eighteen ships. Twenty ships in two convoys sailed from Falmouth starting on the 18th. The first of three convoys, with thirty-four ships, sailed from Buncrana on the 17th. Apart from the two ships lost on the 21st, the only loss was the steamer *Assyria* torpedoed off Lamlash on the 28th; 193 other ships arrived safely in convoy.

The month of September 1917, the first full month of both inward- and outward- bound convoys, marked a turning-point in the war at sea in the

Atlantic approaches to the British Isles. The first three outward convoys, of a monthly total of thirty-seven, sailed from Milford, Devonport and Buncrana on 1 September. During the month there were thirty-three homeward-bound convoys. The convoy system was roughly in balance, with 470 ships outward- and 482 homeward-bound. Seven ships were lost from homeward convoys (three of them were torpedoed as stragglers). No ships at all were torpedoed from outward convoys.

By the end of September, ocean escorts had to be provided for eight Atlantic convoy systems: four inward, from Hampton Roads, New York, Halifax and Sydney; and four outward, from Queenstown, Buncrana, Devonport and Falmouth. By the 30th, there were forty-three ships on ocean escort duty: twelve cruisers, nine light cruisers (seven of them American), fifteen armed merchant cruisers, and seven commissioned escort ships. Convoys from Gibraltar were normally escorted by eight Q ships, replaced later by American light cruisers, gunboats, armed yachts and revenue cutters.

The destroyers were concentrated at Buncrana, where there were twenty-seven of the 2nd Flotilla and three Grand Fleet destroyers; Queenstown, with thirty-six American destroyers; and Devonport, with thirty-six de-stroyers of 4th Flotilla. There were also numerous sloops, torpedo boats, submarines (at Buncrana), and minesweepers. Although the latest and fastest destroyers still went to the Grand Fleet, there was a steady shift of destroyer resources to the ocean-escort bases.

Movements of convoys, in and out, were co-ordinated by adjusting the intervals between the sailings of fast and slow convoys and the intervals between any two convoys of a given system. Even so, the organization of the escorts needed a great deal of skill and expertise. Outward-bound convoys were escorted through the danger zone out to 17 degrees W where the escorting destroyers left, normally after dusk, and the convoy dispersed, each ship making its way independently to its destination. The escorts then steamed through the night, sometimes 60 or 100 miles, to meet an in-coming convoy. At daylight the destroyers spread out in a 'scouting' line, looking for their charges, who were almost always late at the rendezvous. Having sighted and picked up their convoy, the destroyers escorted it to its dispersal points: in the North Channel, if north-about round Ireland; off the Smalls (or, if submarines had been reported, off the Skerries) for south-about convoys. Ships for Channel, east-coast and French ports normally dispersed off St Catherine's Point, Isle of Wight.

The destroyers soon came to know the eccentricities of their charges. Lt Cdr Joseph Taussig USN, commanding USS *Wadsworth*, one of the Queenstown destroyers, knew how to 'prod the laggards': 'If a ship lagged too far astern, I would have the *Wadsworth* pass between that ship and the convoy. This often had the desired result. The smoke would begin to pour out of the stack, and slowly but surely this "doing our utmost" ship would regain position. I often wondered in those cases what took place between master and engineer officer on the one hand, and the engineer and fireman on the other hand.'

There were other difficulties, as one escort commander had in getting an Italian tramp merchant ship to understand a message. He tried international flag hoist, semaphore, radio, and megaphone; all to no avail. Finally he ran close aboard and shouted through the megaphone: 'You blank, blank, blankety blank, when I hoist Flag X you head *south* blank blank quick, savvy?' and without a moment's hesitation came the answer: 'All right, Sir!'

Convoy meant, of course, a great deal of extra work in the Admiralty. It was very probable that this very knowledge that convoy would surely mean extra work for an already desperately hard-worked organization contributed greatly to the opposition to convoy. Furthermore, like all great bureaucratic masses, the Admiralty was extremely sensitive to anything which it considered an alien implant. Convoy would mean the coming of new departments and possibly the lessening of the importance of old. It would bring in new faces and might reduce the influence of old ones, especially those who had opposed convoy most vigorously.

There was another point. When merchant ships sailed independently, the Admiralty merely issued routeing instructions. The rest was left to individual masters. The Admiralty neither took, nor felt, the slightest responsibility for the subsequent fate of the ships. The loss of a single warship, or of any ship under Admiralty control, was always the subject of searching and exhaustive enquiries. But the loss of thousands of tons of merchant shiping, as at the height of the U-boat offensive in April 1917, each day amounting to a serious naval defeat at sea, caused not the least ripple of departmental concern in the Admiralty. The ships might go down. But there was nobody in the Admiralty who was departmentally responsible for their loss. Convoy brought the responsibility for *all* ships lost at sea back, where it belonged, on to the desks of the Admiralty.

The extent to which the Admiralty assumed responsibility for merchant shipping was shown even by the titles eventually given to the Convoy Section, which was first set up on 25 June 1917, as part of the Trade Division of the Naval Staff. The section was headed by Fleet Paymaster H. W. E. Manisty, who was Organizing Manager of Convoys ('not,' as Lloyd George scornfully pointed out, ' "Director", as is customary for heads of important departments; but he was given neither room nor a staff, and had to go round and "scrounge" for these as best he could'.) In fact, Manisty did have a staff of ten, later increased to fifteen. His function was, simply, to manage the convoy system, responsible for providing and allocating escorts, controlling convoyed ships from their assembly ports to their destinations, assigning convoy routes, ordering diversions and (rarely) dispersals, laying down passage routes as decided from the latest intelligence information. In September 1917 the Section became part of the newly set up Mercantile

Movements Divisions, responsible to Captain Whitehead, the Director of Mercantile Movements. With this officer, with this title, the Admiralty moved back to the responsibilities it had held in the eighteenth century.

The Convoy Section at the Admiralty worked very closely with their opposite numbers in the Convoy Section at the Ministry of Shipping, under Norman Leslie. The Ministry was responsible for what might be called the domestic aspects of convoyed ships – their destinations, employment, which cargoes they should carry, the bunkering of all ships requiring escort.

The Ministry set up a simple but effective arrangement for providing up-to-date, accurate information on the probable composition of ships needing convoy at any given day from any given port. The card index which had been so valuable before was continued and augmented. Ships' cards, which were in alphabetical order, were taken out and arranged according to routes and destinations, so that it was possible on any day to see the names and the total numbers of the ships in any port, or on passage to any given destination.

For example, all the ships in New York, or Liverpool or in Dakar were represented by cards in a 'New York', 'Liverpool' or 'Dakar' pack. Cards were added to the packs as ships arrived, and taken out when ships left. The position of a card, nearer the front or the back of the pack, showed which ships had been in that port longest. Similar packs, one for each convoy, showed the names of the ships in the convoy and their destinations. The remaining cards for that route were of ships proceeding independently.

The heart of the Convoy Section was the chart-room where a large wall-chart, some 6 feet by 9, displayed the convoy situation in home waters. The position of each convoy was plotted, and its onward track represented by a thread of red silk. Coloured flags showed the last reported positions of U-boats: a red flag for 'today', a blue for 'yesterday', and a grey for 'the day before yesterday'. The chart showed up any danger lying in a convoy's path at once and a convoy could be diverted by wireless. One signal to the commodore was enough to direct the convoy out of danger in a way which would have been impossible for a similar number of individual ships.

The convoy system, coupled with strategically placed minefields off their home bases, began to force U-boat commanders to give away very much more information about their positions and movements. As the convoys seemed to empty the seas of targets, so the U-boats had to traverse much greater distances and communicate more with each other and with their bases, to obtain information about targets. At the same time, fresh mines were always being laid in the swept channels from Wilhelmshaven and other U-boat bases. Incoming U-boats signalled their tonnage claimed sunk and their estimated time of arrival at the end of the swept channel, so that they could be met by sweepers.

All this increased signal traffic gave more opportunities for interceptions. Most of the vital information for the chart room came from Room 40, the

Admiralty's secret intelligence and deciphering centre, although for a long time Room 40 feared that its secret information might be compromised and strictly guarded access to it. It was not until May 1917 that information from Room 40 intercepts was made available to the chart-room and then, for the first time in the war, the latest information about U-boats could be plotted on the chart and when convoys began, seen side by side with movements of merchant ships.

Convoy was not, of course, an infallible tactic for all occasions. In July 1917 Jellicoe wrote to Admiral Browning, that the politicians 'expect the convoys will prevent any loss at all. I have warned them from the very start that we may quite easily have a very big disaster one day with a convoy. . . .'

The two most likely possibilities for a convoy disaster were, first, that one or more U-boats might penetrate the screen and sink most of the ships inside (this never happened to any convoy during the war); or, much more likely, that a convoy might be attacked by superior surface force which eliminated the escort and then went on to destroy the merchant ships. In October 1917, off the coast of Norway, there was just such a disaster. It was afterwards known as the *Mary Rose* convoy.

The Scandinavian convoys had always faced special problems, of geography and of security. Their passages were very short, compared to the Atlantic convoys, but they were in the submarine danger zone for almost the whole time and at risk of attack from surface ships as well as U-boats. Many of the ships were neutrals, and they sailed from neutral ports. Ships and ports were close to Germany and there was always the risk of a security leak. When Scandinavian convoys were first suggested, several officers commanding patrol areas had pointed out that the enemy would learn about the convoys from their consuls and neutral captains, and would make every effort to attack them. However, the Scandinavian convoys continued (perhaps surprisingly) to sail very successfully and with very few losses, until October 1917, when the Admiralty became aware through intelligence and signal traffic that something was afoot in the North Sea.

Admiral Beatty, at Scapa Flow, was informed, although he was not given all the information that was available. By 15 October, Beatty had sent no less than forty-two ships to sea: three cruisers, twenty-seven light cruisers, and twelve destroyers, on several patrol lines off the southern coast of Norway and in the central area of the North Sea, but all well south of the Scandinavian convoy routes.

An east-bound convoy left Lerwick on the 15th, escorted by two Grand Fleet destroyers *Mary Rose* (Lt Cdr Charles Fox) and *Strongbow* (Lt Cdr Edward Brooke) and two armed trawlers, *Elise* and *P. Fannon*. Just before noon on the 16th, *Mary Rose* went on ahead to collect a west-bound convoy assembling in the Bergen Leads near Marsten. Fox ordered Brooke to take the east-bound ships on, disperse them off the coast, and then come back and meet him at sea.

Mary Rose sailed from Marsten on the afternoon of the 16th, with a mixed convoy of twelve ships: two British, one Belgian, one Danish, five Norwegian, and three Swedish. By dusk *Mary Rose* had drawn some way ahead of her convoy, and when *Strongbow* rejoined after dark neither ship could contact the other. Brooke called up Fox several times during the night but got no answer. *Strongbow* took up her station on the convoy's port quarter. The ships were then spread out in loose formation to the N and NW of *Strongbow*.

At 6 a.m., half an hour after dawn on 17 October, the convoy was about 65 miles east of Lerwick. *Mary Rose* was some six or seven miles ahead, *Strongbow* had moved up to the convoy's port bow. There was a heavy swell and the wind was freshening from the SW. Visibility was fair, out to about two miles. Neither Fox nor Brooke knew that cruiser and light cruiser forces were out, nor that there was a general state of alert in the North Sea. So, when *Strongbow*'s lookouts sighted, a few minutes after six, two strange vessels two points before the port beam and on a converging course, Brooke ordered his signalman to challenge them by small searchlight.

At first, Brooke thought they were British cruisers (they had in fact been disguised to resemble cruisers of the *Cleopatra* class). But when the newcomers ignored two challenges and the leading ship answered the third with the meaningless group 'AN', Brooke realized they were German. By then they were closing at high speed. At 6.15 a.m., as *Strongbow*'s ship's company were going to action stations, the nearest ship opened fire, range about 3000 yards.

The rumours had been true. An enemy operation *was* under way. Two 3800-ton 34-knot German cruisers *Bremse* and *Brummer*, both armed with four 5.9-inch guns, had steamed at high speed straight through all the patrol lines. It was known in Room 40 that the call-signs of these two ships had moved north from Wilhelmshaven. It was known that they had sailed. But as it was also known they were both fitted for mine-laying, nobody connected them with any possible sortie against the Scandinavian convoys.

Scheer had decided to attack the convoys, which U-boats had reported as getting larger in size and sailing more often. It would lessen pressure on U-boats further south if the British were forced to strengthen the escorts of the Scandinavian convoys. But, by another of those communications failures which bedevilled the Navy at sea throughout the Great War, Beatty was not informed that the two ships had sailed. His ships were still at sea, searching for they knew not what, but which was thought to be a mine-layer and some destroyers emerging from the Kattegat.

Before *Strongbow*'s ship's company could reach their action stations and clear away guns and torpedo tubes, an 'unequal and disastrous engagement' had already begun. *Strongbow* suffered several hits. The first salvo severed a main steam pipe below, and many men were scalded to death. The upper deck was swept by a murderously effective fire, which mowed down almost everybody in an exposed position.

Brooke himself was hit in the leg by a shell splinter from the second salvo. He ordered confidential documents to be destroyed, and only when he was assured this had been done did he order the remnants of his ship's company to abandon ship. *Strongbow* was then heavily on fire forward. However, two torpedoes were fired at the enemy, before the ship was abandoned at about 7.30. She floated for some time and finally sank, on an even keel, at about 9.40. Her two torpedoes, both of which missed, were the only retaliation.

Brooke was carried, very badly wounded, down to the upper deck and placed in a Carley float which was launched over the side. Despite the action of the nearest German ship, which fired on the Carley float and on *Strongbow*'s motor-boat, Brooke, three of his officers, and forty-one of his men, were later picked up by the trawler *Elise* and survived. They brought away one of *Strongbow*'s ensigns, leaving another flying until she sank. Meanwhile Fox, who was some way ahead of the convoy, had heard the gunfire astern of him on his port quarter. Believing it was *Strongbow* engaging a U-boat, he turned back. Even at full speed, it was some time before *Mary Rose* sighted the enemy. Her range and deflection transmitters were not working properly but she opened with the forward gun in local control shortly after 7.15, range about 3000 yards.

The German cruisers seemed by then more preoccupied in destroying the merchant ships and *Mary Rose* had closed to within 2000 yards' range before she was hit. At that moment Fox ordered the helm hard a starboard and *Mary Rose* wheeled away to the southward. For a short while it seemed she might draw the attackers away from the convoy, by sacrificing herself. After their initial hesitation, the German gunners could hardly miss at that range and began to hit rapidly and repeatedly. *Mary Rose*'s upper deck was quickly reduced to the same shambles as *Strongbow*'s. Soon, her midships gun was the only one still firing. Fox came down from the bridge to encourage the gun's crew. 'God bless my heart, lads,' he said, 'get her going again, we're not done yet!'

But *Mary Rose*'s day was done. The nearest enemy ship had closed to within 200 yards and shortly after 7.30, *Mary Rose* was hit in the forward magazine and blew up. Fox was seen in the water, but he was not picked up. Two of *Mary Rose*'s officers and eight of her men were rescued by a lifeboat from one of the ships sunk in the convoy. They were the only survivors.

Having disposed of the escort, *Bremse* and *Brummer* set about the convoy (it seems that one of the cruisers was already attacking the merchant ships while the other was dealing with the destroyers). In about forty-five minutes' brisk and efficient shelling, they sank nine ships. Only the British *Bencleuch* and *City of Cork*, and the Belgian *Londonies*, escaped. After firing at some of the lifeboats, *Bremse* and *Brummer* made for home at about 8.20.

Their raid had been a brilliant success. They had steamed for 500 miles through waters patrolled by a total of some eighty ships, inflicted a terrible disaster upon a convoy and its escort, and returned safe home. Either *Mary Rose* or *Strongbow* tried to send an 'enemy in sight' signal but the transmission was weak and was possibly jammed by *Brummer*. The exchange was not noticed by any British ship or shore station and it was 4 p.m. that day before Beatty heard about the raid, after the destroyers *Marmion* and *Obedient* had fallen in with *Elise*, bringing home some of the survivors. Beatty redisposed his patrols, but it was too late. *Bremse* and *Brummer* were home and dry.

The *Mary Rose* convoy aroused a *furore* in the neutral Scandinavian press, which seemed divided about which was more reprehensible, 'British Slackness' or 'German Brutality'. It also caused a great deal of concern in the Admiralty. The actual tonnage lost, 10,248, was less than on several days which had gone unremarked in April 1917. But this tonnage had been in convoy, escorted by HM Ships, under the direct responsibility of the Admiralty. A thorough and exhaustive inquiry was carried out.

It was seen that the convoy system had limitations. It was still undoubtedly the best defence against U-boats, but in the face of a superior surface force, huddling together might only make the attackers' task easier. A better plan would be to scatter. Beatty also told destroyer flotilla commanders to impress upon all destroyer officers the paramount importance of being ready for action at a moment's notice. Every vessel sighted should be treated as hostile, until proved otherwise. It seems remarkable that it should have been thought necessary to stress such caution after three years of war.

Further, Beatty went on, destroyers 'while using their utmost endeavours to damage the enemy' were not to engage superior forces. They were to use their speed to maintain a safe distance from the enemy. Their most important duty was to report the presence and position of the enemy vessels at once.

Such was the comment and criticism of the *Mary Rose* convoy at home, that Sir Eric Geddes, the First Lord, felt impelled to mention it to the House of Commons on 1 November 1917. After describing the action briefly, he explained why the raiders had not been intercepted. The area of the North Sea, he reminded the House, was 140,000 square miles. The area of vision of a light cruiser, with its attendant destroyers, at night was five miles. 'Five square miles in 140,000!' the First Lord exclaimed. This physical limitation, and the fact that both destroyers were badly damaged before they could signal and the one trawler fitted with wireless had dropped back to escort a straggler whose cargo had shifted, accounted for the delay before the C-in-C heard of the action. With that, the House seemed content.

In the long term, the *Mary Rose* incident had surprisingly little effect. The usual westbound convoy sailed from Norway on 19 October, two days later, and the next eastbound convoy sailed from Lerwick only a day late. Shipping was held up for a time but the order was soon relaxed and the Scandinavian convoy system continued with clockwork regularity, almost like a peace-time ferry service.

But German light cruisers might always try another sortie. The four or five cruisers normally waiting for convoys at Liverpool, Glasgow and Plymouth were ordered to be at twenty-four hours' notice for sea at all times.

Henceforward, Beatty's staff were kept informed of the daily position and destination of every convoy east of 25 degrees W, which was taken to be the limit that raiding cruisers could attack convoys.

The ocean escorts, the aged cruisers, the armed merchant ships, the commissioned escort vessels, were really effective only in shepherding a convoy across the ocean. In the danger zones, they were hardly capable of attacking a U-boat and sinking it. In fact, they were often as vulnerable as the ships they escorted. The old cruiser *Drake* was torpedoed, and later capsized, on 2 October 1917. The ocean escorts *Bostonian*, on the 10th, and *Orama*, on the 19th, were both torpedoed and sunk whilst in convoy.

But the difference between a surface and a submerged attack, and an ocean escort's effectiveness in controlling her convoy and diverting it away from danger in the open sea, was well-shown by the almost miraculous escape of a twenty-five-ship convoy, homeward bound from Dakar, escorted by the armed merchant cruiser *Marmora* (Captain Woodward). On 14 November, some 150 miles west of Madeira, *Marmora*'s lookouts sighted a U-boat (actually the large U-151) at six miles. Captain Woodward had time to order the convoy to steam away. Although U-151's periscope was actually sighted again only thirty yards from *Marmora*'s side, no ship was lost.

By October 1917 the convoy system was in full operation, not just to Scandinavia but to the north and south Atlantic. Every sixteen days, eighteen convoys bound for Great Britain or France were met by the escorts of eighteen outward-bound convoys. Some 400 to 500 ships a month were being escorted in and out. By the end of that month, it can now be seen, the critically dangerous stage of the war at sea in the Atlantic was past, although sinkings continued to exceed replacements by new building for some time. The October shipping losses (459,000 tons) were up on the September figures (345,000 tons) but about half of the increase was due to sinkings in the Mediterranean where there were still no regular convoy systems. The overall trend of shipping losses was downwards.

This trend was not due to the number of U-boats sunk; the rate of sinkings of U-boats did not begin to exceed the rate of commissioning of new U-boats until the last three months of 1917. The success was due to convoy. By then, ninety-nine homeward convoys had arrived, with 1502 ships. Ten ships, or 0.7 per cent, had been lost while in convoy. Another fourteen ships were torpedoed, after they had been separated from their convoys by bad weather, or because they had straggled or 'run' from their convoy. In October, seventy-seven outward convoys sailed, with 1052 ships, of which only 0.6 per cent were lost. The overall loss rate from convoys was 1.2 per cent, or just over one ship in a hundred – compared with some twenty-five ships in every hundred in the blackest days of April 1917. In October 1917 the ratio of losses of convoyed ships to independently routed ships was 1 to 12½. In six months, convoy had transformed the situation. Convoy did not win the war in 1917. But it did prevent the war from being lost in 1917.

Chapter Seven

Convoy was a success, but a success almost totally unappreciated by almost all those who were enjoying it. In the Admiralty, old habits of thought died very hard indeed. Convoy was still thought of as being defensive, and therefore not to be encouraged. Convoy was constantly judged by the number of U-boats it sank, not by the number of merchantmen it delivered safe from U-boat attack.

In fact, during the first six months of convoy, the escorts sank four U-boats, quite as many as did patrolling destroyers, with only a fraction of their number of ships. The Grand Fleet and its destroyers remained, in what Lloyd George derisively called their 'cold storage' at Scapa Flow, in readiness to counter another sortie by the German High Seas Fleet, or the threat of a possible invasion. While either of these two possibilities became more and more remote, U-boats on their way to their patrol areas actually transited past the entrances to Scapa Flow, entirely unmolested by any of the Grand Fleet destroyers. However, another intensive submarine hunt in the North Sea was organized in October 1917, in which three U-boats were sunk on mine barrages.

Bremse and *Brummer* had shown that convoys were vulnerable to surface attacks. The autumn nights were drawing in to winter. Admiral Scheer still had his bases close to the convoy routes. All the factors which had contributed to the *Mary Rose* disaster still favoured him, but it was December before he tried again.

The fate of the *Mary Rose* convoy had suggested that intervals between Scandinavian convoys should be lengthened (in other words, that larger convoys at longer intervals were safer) and that the route should be shortened if possible. Methil in Fife was a better-equipped port than Lerwick and was a more natural departure point for convoys to Denmark and Sweden. It was suggested that the Scandinavian convoys should sail from there, although Admiral Beatty did warn the Admiralty that sailings from

Methil would take the convoys that much nearer the German bases. The real solution would be to absorb the Scandinavian convoys into the general Atlantic convoy system, bringing them under the protection of the ocean cruiser escort as well as their own close escort. It was also thought that one contributing factor in the *Mary Rose* disaster was the practice of expecting the same ships to escort convoys both east- and west-bound. But the various organizational changes were still under consideration when, in December 1917, Scheer made his next move against the convoys.

At 2 p.m. on 10 December, the two destroyers *Garry* and *Ouse* sailed from Lerwick with a convoy of six ships southward down the east coast of Scotland, bound for Blyth in Northumberland. By noon on the 11th, convoy and escort were off Aberdeen. By teatime they were about 45 miles off Fifeness, still steering south.

Earlier that same day the German 2nd Flotilla, of eight of the latest and heaviest destroyers, escorted by the light cruiser *Emden*, sailed from the Elbe and by that afternoon were off the north-eastern shoals of the Dogger Bank, where the flotilla split up: one Half Flotilla (3rd) steamed north, the other (4th) steamed WSW towards the coast near Newcastle.

About an hour later the commander of the 4th Half Flotilla intercepted radio signals which caused him to think, mistakenly, that a convoy had just left the Firth of Forth. He turned his ships north to ambush it.

The night was particularly dark, with heavy showers of rain. The Danish *Peter Willemoes* and the Swedish *Nike* had straggled from the convoy; in poor visibility, *Garry* and *Ouse* did not try to round them up, thinking they were both making for Blyth independently. By eleven that night the rest of the convoy and the escort were off the Longstone, with the German force some miles to the east, and closing. At about half-past midnight, the four German destroyers chanced upon the solitary *Peter Willemoes* and sank her with torpedoes, some 25 miles to the east of the swept war channel. At that time, the convoy and escort were only some 30 miles to the south, off Coquet Island.

The Germans could easily have overtaken the convoy had they picked up survivors from *Peter Willemoes* and interrogated them. But they did not do so. At about 4 a.m. they came across the other straggler *Nike* and torpedoed her. Again, they picked up no survivors and got no intelligence. But as they were steaming away, they encountered four more small vessels, all trawlers, one of which they sank with gunfire. After searching for a little longer, the German ships broke off. By dawn they were out of sight of land, on their way home. The rest of the convoy arrived safely. *Peter Willemoes* and *Nike* had acted as the perfect sacrificial decoys.

If details of this action had been reported quickly and accurately it is just possible, though still unlikely, that the correct deduction of an enemy surface force could have been made. But the trawlers which escaped reported a submarine. Shore stations which heard gunfire thought it was a long way off, probably from *Garry* and *Ouse*, and concluded that the convoy could be in no danger. But even if all the facts had been known, it is doubtful if the disaster could have been averted which fell on another Scandinavian convoy.

On 11 December an eastbound convoy of six ships – one British, two Norwegian, two Swedish and one Danish – sailed from Lerwick, escorted by the destroyers *Pellew* and *Partridge* and by four trawlers, *Livingstone*, *Tokio*, *Commander Fullerton*, and *Lord Alverstone*. The convoy was due to arrive in the Leads off Marsten in the early afternoon of 12 December, having passed through designated rendezvous points, the first 15 miles S of Lerwick, the second 25 miles SW of Bjorne Fjord.

Meanwhile, precautions were taken to safeguard the convoy. The 3rd Light Cruiser Squadron, of *Chatham*, *Yarmouth* and *Birkenhead*, with four destroyers, sailed from Rosyth at 5 p.m. of the 11th, with orders to sweep eastward to the Norwegian coast and then south across the mouth of the Skagerrak, returning after dark on the 12th. At 10 p.m. on the 11th the 2nd Cruiser Squadron, of *Shannon* and *Minotaur*, with four destroyers, sailed from Scapa, with orders to contact the westbound convoy on the morning of the 12th, then steam eastward and cover the eastbound convoy, which would be crossing during the day. This protection did seem adequate, and there was no hint of added danger.

Shortly before noon on 12 December the eastbound convoy was approaching its second rendezvous, some 25 miles off the Norwegian coast. *Pellew* and *Partridge* were ahead of the convoy, with the trawlers disposed ahead and on either flank. There was a strong northwesterly wind blowing, gusting force 6 to 7, kicking up a heavy sea on a long swell. Both destroyers' lookouts sighted strange ships to the northward at about the same time. *Partridge* challenged by searchlight but her light was defective; it was some ten minutes before the challenge was properly made and, of course, wrongly answered.

During those ten minutes – a very long time in a naval action – the strangers continued to close the convoy. They were some five miles off by the time *Partridge* had signalled the news of the wrong challenge response to *Pellew*. The senior escort officer, Lt Cdr J. R. C. Cavendish in *Pellew*, ordered the convoy to scatter while *Pellew* steamed across the convoy's bows to reach the exposed northern flank. *Partridge* followed. Just before opening fire, her captain Lt Cdr R. H. Ransome made a signal to the C-in-C informing him that the convoy escort was in contact with an enemy force, size and composition unknown. Neither Cavendish nor Ransome knew that a cruiser force was at sea, so they could only signal the C-in-C direct.

Meanwhile Cavendish hoped that *Pellew* and *Partridge* would be able to engage the enemy hotly enough to allow the convoy to escape. But three of the enemy steamed parallel to the British destroyers, while the fourth slipped round them to attack the merchant ships.

The British ships were in the leeward position and their gun crews were blinded by the spray from the storming NW wind. The sea was so rough that if they tried to increase speed, their upper decks were washed down from end to end, and the enemy ships could only be properly seen from the crest of the waves; in the troughs only the mastheads and funnel tops were visible.

As so often happened in both world wars, the German initial ranging and gun-handling were excellent. The German ships opened with rapid and accurate salvoes. Their shooting was magnificent. One of their first salvoes hit *Partridge* in the engine-room forward, severing a main steam pipe. The compartment filled with scalding steam which killed everyone in it almost instantly. The ship at once lost way and came to a stop, beam on to wind and waves, wallowing 30 or 40 degrees each way in the tremendous swell. *Partridge*'s Engineer Commander P. L. Butt and his chief engine-room artificer tried repeatedly to get into the engine-room but were driven back by the clouds of steam.

A few moments later, *Partridge* was hit a second time aft, by a shell which blew her aftermost gun over the side. Almost at the same time a torpedo struck her forward. *Partridge* was now finished. She settled by the bows while great waves washed over her upper deck. Ransome gave the order to abandon ship and, for some reason, told the engine-room to make sure the ship went quickly. Butt now forced his way into the engine-room, still pitch-dark and steam-filled, to open the starboard condenser door, admitting the full rush of the sea into the compartment.

A second torpedo hit *Partridge* forward and she was now going fast, but Lieutenants A. A. D. Grey and L. J. B. Walters still manned the after torpedo tubes and actually fired one torpedo, which hit a German destroyer without exploding. Grey, though seriously wounded in the thigh, and Walters then climbed into a boat which capsized before it had gone far and threw them both in the water. The pair reached a raft but Grey could see that Walters was almost done. As there was only room for one, he put Walters on the raft and then swam towards a German destroyer which picked him up. From her deck he saw the detonation of a third torpedo which finally sank *Partridge*.

Pellew nearly suffered the same fate. She too was hit in the engine-room, lost way and eventually stopped. Luckily, she was hidden by a heavy rain-squall and the German destroyers turned away to complete the demolition of the convoy. Within an hour all six merchant ships and all four trawlers had been sunk. *Pellew* was the only survivor, limping slowly towards Norway on one boiler-room.

Partridge's enemy-reporting signal had been taken in by *Shannon*, about sixty miles to the west. At about a quarter past twelve *Shannon* intercepted another signal, part of which was jammed by German interference. But enough of the text was clear: 'Enemy destroyers at T [off the Norwegian coast] rendezvous.' Captain Molteno in *Shannon* sent his accompanying destroyers on at full speed and followed himself at 20 knots.

The signals had also been received by Beatty at Scapa Flow, who ordered the 3rd Light Cruiser Squadron to sweep towards the enemy's reported position. The destroyer *Rival* had also taken in *Partridge*'s signal and reported it to Captain Woollcombe, the senior officer of the 3rd Light Cruiser Squadron in *Birkenhead*. Woollcombe had acted promptly and turned his ships northwards at once. He was already some twenty miles on towards the enemy by the time he received the C-in-C's signal. Now, at last, it seemed that retribution was at hand. The right forces were in the right position, with the right information, in time.

But chance intervened, as it so often did, to rob the Navy. Had the German ships returned as they had set out, via Heligoland, Woollcombe's ships could hardly have missed them. But as the weather deteriorated further, the German commander had decided to make for the Skagerrak and return by the calmer waters of the Baltic. The German ships steered more easterly than southerly and crossed astern of Woollcombe's ships after dark, probably about five o'clock that evening. They were not sighted and got clear away.

Molteno's destroyers had arrived at the scene of the disaster at about two o'clock and picked up several boat- and raft-loads of survivors. *Pellew* went first to the Norwegian coast and was then escorted across to Rosyth, arriving on 15 December.

The destruction of *Pellew*'s convoy aroused an even greater furore than the *Mary Rose*. There was some extremely hostile comment in the press and critical questions in the House of Commons. (Although convoy had been a forgotten science in January 1917, by December the fate of individual convoys was causing deep concern to Parliament). The First Lord Sir Eric Geddes exerted himself to reassure members. He also pressed for an investigation, in a somewhat tactless manner.

Geddes ordered Beatty to submit the name of the officers who would serve on the enquiry. Beatty resented the implication that he would 'pack the court' with officers sympathetic to himself. He demanded an apology and (eventually) got it. Geddes compounded the offence by altering the wording of Jellicoe's signal concerning the enquiry to a much more offensive form. Jellicoe was ill in bed at the time and only discovered Geddes' amendments when a furious Beatty later showed them to him at Rosyth.

Three admirals, Sturdee, de Robeck and Goodenough, sat on the enquiry. Beatty took full responsibility for the strength of the convoy escort, though not for the timing of the convoy's sailing, which was the Admiralty's responsibility. It was Molteno's conduct and handling of his ships which caused most concern. Jellicoe later wrote that 'it was not clear why the protecting cruisers *Minotaur* and *Shannon* were not present at the time of the attack'. Beatty showed Jellicoe the orders he had given the cruisers and it seemed to Jellicoe that the cruisers 'should have been there at the time of the attack unless something had prevented them carrying out the orders'. 'We do have the most cursed luck,' said Beatty. 'The *Shannon* and *Minotaur* should have been alongside the convoy exactly at twelve o'clock after sighting the westbound convoy. Why they were not I do not know yet.'

The enquiry found that the main difficulty lay in having the same ships trying to cover both westbound and eastbound convoys. There were only enough destroyers to have one escort at sea at a time. The covering forces were, in a sense, trying to be in two places at once and consequently were never in the right place at the right time. The solution lay in having larger convoys, with one stronger close support force at sea.

The enquiry recommended that the Admiralty take over responsibility for routeing and diverting convoys as well as for sailing them. Scandinavian convoys should continue, but sailing every three days instead of daily, so that only one convoy was at sea at a time, steaming northward to the latitude of Aberdeen before turning eastward for Norway (the port of departure was still to be Methil, although it was closer to German bases.) The C-in-C would still provide covering forces, and a battle squadron was to be regularly allocated for convoy escort duties. That a Grand Fleet battle squadron should be set aside for *convoy* duties was the most significant indication of the importance convoys had assumed.

By December 1917 convoy had also been accepted in the Mediterranean. There, the introduction of convoy had been hampered by all the same difficulties and prejudices as in home waters, with the additional complication that three Allied nations, Great Britain, France and Italy, were involved in the area and co-operation between them was never achieved fully. In some cases and in some places co-operation was non-existent.

In the Mediterranean, there was an even greater imbalance than at home between the number of U-boats sunk and the total tonnage of shipping sunk by the U-boats. Only three U-boats were destroyed in the Mediterranean between June and December 1916. In the same period 256 vessels of 666,131 tons were sunk. Of these, 62 per cent, or ninety-six vessels of 415,471 tons, were British. At that time the Germans had an average of about sixteen U-boats at a time operating in the Mediterranean. One of them, U-35, with a particularly aggressive and successful captain, Korvetten-Kapitan von Arnauld de la Perriere, sank over forty ships in one patrol in June and July 1916, and another fifty ships in about three weeks of August. (This was two thirds of the total Allied tonnage sunk in all theatres of the war for that month, and it was all done with one four-inch gun.)

For trade defence purposes, the Mediterranean was split into no less than nine patrol zones, which caused considerable fragmentation of Allied forces. The British controlled a zone in the western Mediterranean, from Gibraltar to the longitude of Oran, a central zone around Malta, roughly bounded by Tripoli, Sicily, Crete and Tobruk, and another zone touching it, which stretched east to Port Said. The Italians controlled two zones one on either side of their coast-line, and one on the African coast, and showed almost no interest in defence outside those areas. The French controlled the rest.

Specially valuable ships continued to have special escorts and steamed along patrolled routes, but there were occasional breakdowns in the organization, caused by lack of communication, when ships crossed from one Allied zone into another and lost their escort. In February 1917, the Italian troopship *Minas*, for example, was torpedoed on her way to Salonica and sunk with the loss of 870 lives because Admiral Ballard at Malta was not informed the ship would need an escort when she entered the British zone.

From January 1917 the British tried another method. Fixed patrol routes were abandoned for much of the Mediterranean (although they were still used by ships of other nationalities) in favour of 'dispersed routes': each ship sailed independently on a prescribed track laid down for that specific vessel. But the losses continued: fifty ships of 101,000 tons in February, thirty-six ships of 72,000 tons in March, when the losses in the western basin of the Mediterranean had climbed so high that the British were forced to stop routeing ships inshore along the Algerian coast and divert them instead northwards along the coast of Spain. Ships westbound from Malta steamed in large zigzags, each pattern different, so that a U-boat who sank one ship could not simply wait on that route for the next target to arrive.

It was all rather like a children's garden game of 'catch me if you can' in which the U-boats had all the advantages of concealment and surprise. Ominously, von Arnauld had yet another supremely successful cruise in March and April, sinking 65,000 tons of shipping, 47,000 tons west of Gibraltar in the entrances to the Straits. In April 1917, there were twenty-eight U-boats operating in the Mediterranean, who spent 290 days at sea. They sank the staggering number of ninety-four ships, totalling 234,170 tons, which was about a quarter of all the Allied tonnage lost that month in all theatres of the war. Not one U-boat was sunk in retaliation.

Troopships were still given special escort but even this did not save them. On 15 April 1917 the *Arcadian*, carrying over 1000 troops from Salonica to Alexandria, was torpedoed and sunk in the southern Aegean, with the loss of 277 lives. The same day, another troopship, *Cameronian* carrying 2630 officers and men from Marseilles to Egypt, was torpedoed when halfway between Sicily and Greece, with the loss of another 200 lives. Good discipline and good boat-drill in both ships, and the speedy arrival of destroyers and other ships on the scene, kept the casualty figures down.

Despite reproving signals, Admiral Ballard at Malta introduced convoy, it seems on his own initiative, in May 1917. Until then, ships had been escorted individually from Alexandria to Suva Bay in Crete and then brought on with a fresh escort. From 22 May Ballard introduced through convoys of five or six ships, with an escort of four armed trawlers, from Alexandria to Malta, and almost daily convoys in the opposite direction. West of Malta, between

Bizerta and Gibraltar, ships followed the coast of north Africa, with
protection given by the French navy. Very important ships were still given an
escort and routed independently. By 16 July, some 275 ships had been
convoyed and only two of them lost. But general convoy was still some way off
in the future. It still did not occur to anybody on the staff that if convoys of
three or four ships were successful, convoys of many more ships could be
tried.

An interesting comparison was provided by the Italian navy who began to
assemble supply ships running between Gibraltar and the Italian coast in
convoys of four ships at a time. Ships of over 12 knots still proceeded
independently. This system soon began to convoy some 190 ships a month.
The escorts allocated for convoy were one cruiser and eleven armed
merchant cruisers. Most convoys sailed escorted only by one armed merchant cruiser. But the system cut losses from the start. For instance, only one
steamer was torpedoed on the route between Gibraltar and Naples during
the whole of July 1917.

That month a general system of convoy was introduced for homeward
bound ships from Gibraltar. Ships with particularly valuable cargoes, liners,
troop transports and ships faster than 11 knots were still excluded, but all
tramp steamers, colliers and iron-ore ships were convoyed, with immediately
beneficial results. The first convoy sailed at 8 p.m. on 26 July, with thirteen
vessels. The ocean escort consisted only of one Q ship, though the convoy
was escorted through the first and very dangerous part of its journey as far as
the meridian of St Vincent, by two sloops, an armed boarding vessel and two
torpedo boats from Gibraltar. Submarines were reported on the convoy's
track but it reached the UK without mishap except to a French steamer,
which rammed one of the escorting sloops and then sank.

Another convoy of eight ships sailed on 31 July, and a third of twenty-three
ships (including three bound for America, which separated once through the
danger zone) on 4 August. From then on, the convoy system swung into
action regularly, dispatching one convoy every four days. Seven convoys
sailed in August with a total of 117 ships, of which one sank in the 4 August
convoy after colliding with a submerged U-boat. In September another seven
homeward convoys sailed, with 134 ships, of which two were sunk – both
stragglers, which dropped behind on their first day out and were torpedoed
60 miles astern of their convoy. Just as convoy was the safest course of action
for a merchant ship, so straggling was the most dangerous.

In the summer of 1917 some progress was made in improving Allied naval
co-operation. A naval conference at Corfu in April agreed that ships should
use coastal and neutral territorial waters as far as possible, and navigate at
night as far as practicable whenever submarines were reported in the area.
The French method of fixed patrol routes would be used on coastal journeys,
but the British system of independent ships dispersed on unpatrolled routes
and carrying out large zigzags, would be used for the open sea. Valuable

ships (though, it was stressed, not more than two or three at a time) would still be escorted.

Both the British and the French wanted to have overall control. A compromise was reached at another naval conference in Paris in July. A British C-in-C would fly his flag ashore in Malta, where he would frame policies for controlling, escorting and navigating merchant ships. A French C-in-C afloat would have control of all patrol-force operations. Like all compromises everything depended upon personalities, and these were not always harmoniously inclined. For instance, the French forbade the Italian coastal convoys to navigate in Spanish waters. The Italians took no notice whatsoever.

On 20 June Vice-Admiral Sir Rosslyn Wemyss, the C-in-C East Indies, was appointed C-in-C Mediterranean but never took up the appointment. He went home to discuss the general situation and later became Deputy First Sea Lord and then First Sea Lord in succession to Jellicoe in December. Meanwhile the Ministry of Shipping put in hand some research into shipping statistics for the Mediterranean, which were at first as scanty as they had once been for the Atlantic.

One of the first problems was another (there had been several) coal crisis in Italy. The Ministry proposed that liners on their way to India and the Far East, which were sailing only half loaded, should carry coal to Egypt, leaving the colliers free to take coal to Italy instead. The Ministry asked for a convoy system to take the liners through to Suez, and the colliers from Gibraltar to north Italy, which would amount to some 200 ships a month.

At a meeting on 14 August, Jellicoe turned these proposals down, causing some considerable resentment at the Ministry. For instance, the figure of 372 escorts, just to escort the liners through, was freely bandied about. The Ministry, thinking the Navy had very little idea of the delays and loss under the existing method of patrolling and routeing in the Mediterranean, were at their wits end to meet ever-growing appeals for shipping from all quarters.

On 26 August Vice-Admiral Sir Somerset Gough-Calthorpe was appointed C-in-C instead of Wemyss. He was another of those who had strong reservations about convoy. He thought it a defensive method, no more than a deterrent and not a 'reliable safeguard', which would become less effective as the enemy grew more expert in attack. He looked forward to 'an increased and increasing offensive which should in time enable us to dispense altogether with the need for these methods of defence'. Such were the stupid and reactionary statements Gough-Calthorpe was still making as late as November 1917.

In September the C-in-C at Malta signalled that he was ready to start a system of through Mediterranean convoys, provided the interval between convoys was at least ten days. A delighted Ministry of Shipping agreed on an interval of sixteen days, to ease the escort situation and because it was thought that thirty-two days was long enough to turn ships round in the United Kingdom.

The plan was for convoys to sail alternately from Liverpool with west-coast ships, and from Devonport with ships from London. In practice there were always three times as many ships for the Far East from Liverpool, and eventually the London ships had to sail with an Atlantic convoy and peel off southwards to Gibraltar where they would wait and join the next Liverpool convoy.

The first outward convoy OE1 sailed from Liverpool on 3 October, with eleven ships all capable of a good 10 knots. All went well until the convoy was off Crete when one ship, *Pera*, was torpedoed and sunk. The following day *Collegian* was sunk off the coast of Egypt. This was very discouraging, but there was worse to come. Whilst OE1 had been forming up, homeward-bound ships had been ordered to assemble at Perim and proceed up the Red Sea in formation under a commodore. This was the nucleus of the first homeward convoy, HE1, which sailed from Port Said on 16 November with six ships.

HE1 had a hard time of it, losing *Clan MacCorquodale* off Crete, *Kohist* off Malta and *Karema* off north Africa. This was such a blow to confidence that convoys were almost discontinued there and then. But OE3 and 4 arrived in Egypt without loss. HE2 lost one of fourteen ships, but she managed to struggle into Malta. HE3 and 4 were successful, each with fifteen ships; so was OE5, with thirteen ships. OE6 and HE5 both lost one ship, and at once a clamour started up, the Parliamentary Secretary to the Ministry pressing to have convoys stopped. Luckily, convoy had had just enough time to prove itself. Sir Aubrey Brocklebank, in charge of Indian shipping, said categorically that convoy was already saving so much shipping that if it were discontinued his department would not be able to carry on.

This saving in shipping was as unexpected as it was enormous. Since March 1916 ships from the Far East had been routed round the Cape of Good Hope. Ships from Karachi and Bombay had also had to use this route since April 1917. This diversion added immensely to the length of the voyage and hence drastically reduced the effective working lives of the ships. Once through Mediterranean convoys were introduced it was found that so much time was saved that ninety ships could now carry the same cargo as 130 ships had done before.

Convoy brought all manner of unexpected benefits. For example, in April 1918 there were extensive movements of troops in the Mediterranean. It was found that by using the HE convoy system as far as Sardinia for ships carrying motor vehicles, artillery and horses, and sailing all the troopships in one separate convoy, a complete division could be moved from Egypt to Marseilles in one quarter of the time it would have taken when ships sailed under escort one or two at a time.

Convoy escorts were normally destroyers, or sloops, or armed boarding steamers. Sometimes they had some odd convoys to escort. An officer in the sloop *Lychnis* reported that his 'most fantastic convoy from Genoa to Gibraltar consisted of my sloop as a fast escort (14½ knots!), a United States yacht, an Italian armed merchantman, a French trawler and a Portuguese trawler'.

Sometimes alertness and vigilance in the escorts paid off. *Lychnis* was escorting two troopships, *Manitou* and *Kandy*, assisted by an armed boarding steamer, when on 17 June 1918, towards Cape Bon,

> U-64 sighted the other three vessels but somehow did not notice the sloop. The German captain's plan was to torpedo the two troopships and when they had sunk, to engage the escort with gunfire. He knew that his submarine was faster than the armed boarding steamer and that his 4.1-gun would outrange her 12-pounders. Unfortunately for him the convoy zigzagged at the moment of firing. The torpedo intended for the *Manitou* missed and that for the *Kandy* hit her stern, causing the minimum of damage. The submarine kept her periscope up to observe the effect of the shots and met us bow to bow. Two depth-charges brought her to the surface to be finished off by gunfire and to yield five prisoners, the Captain, Navigating Officer and three men.

At about this time the first of the *Kil* class long-range patrol gunboats was introduced into service. These ships were capable of about 14 knots and an endurance of 4000 miles so that they could escort a convoy right through from Egypt to the United Kingdom. The officer in *Lychnis*, however, regarded them with mixed feelings:

> These vessels carried a 4-inch gun and had sufficient endurance to take a convoy from England to Egypt without coaling, but they were even slower than we. Each normally carried an RNR Lieutenant, one RNVR Lieutenant as navigator, and two RNR Midshipmen.
>
> We heard tales that these gunboats were so unpopular that their crews habitually deserted on arrival in England. It was said that they were coaled and stored by shore labour and then a new crew put on board who painted over the coal dust before sailing. My experience of them was that they seemed quite uninterested in any convoy. One night one of them steered away and we chased her. We went close alongside, signalled with a shaded lamp and hailed, but got no response. As they were showing a light we fired a rifle at it, whereupon they woke up and tried to ram us but we dodged and went back to the convoy. About half an hour later she and her sister, who ought to have been on the other side of the convoy, came up from astern of us, one each side, and started to close in. They got very close but my nerve was better than theirs and they finally sheered off.

This incident occurred shortly before Armistice Day, by which time, *pace Lychnis*' outraged feelings, the long-range escorts had proved their worth. From the time long-ranged escort was begun, in June 1918, seventeen convoys passed through, with 225 ships. The only vessel to be torpedoed was *City of Adelaide* from HE17, leaving Port Said on 17 August 1918. She was a special case. There was an epidemic of influenza on board, she could not maintain the convoy speed and was straggling 30 miles astern of the convoy when she was attacked.

Escorts for Mediterranean convoys were provided by the British, French, Italians and Japanese. In theory, escorts should have changed as a convoy passed from one national zone to another. In practice, the great majority of the escorts were British. The French agreed to pool their escorts and some convoys did have Anglo-French escorts, but Gough-Calthorpe never had any direct control over French ships. The Italians went their way throughout, never agreed to pool escorts, and in practice co-operated very little. Although the convoys were vital to their national economy and war effort, the Italians were preoccupied with fear of invasion in the Adriatic.

With Gibraltar convoys running regularly from the end of July, homeward convoys from Dakar began on 11 August – belatedly, for several steamers were sunk by gunfire off the Azores which could have been saved if convoy had been introduced earlier. At first Dakar convoys sailed every four days. But this was changed to eight days for slower ships. Faster ships, of 10 knots or more, went to Sierra Leone where the convoy also left every eight days. The first Sierra Leone convoy (HL1) sailed on 22 September.

Speed was a critical factor in convoys. It was shown that nothing under about 20 knots was guaranteed safety outside convoy. There was a great deal of juggling around of convoys, with ships of different speeds. The New York convoys' speed was reduced on 13 October to the more realistic (because of inferior coal and poor stokers) 9½ knots. By contrast a fast convoy was introduced from Halifax, of 12½ knots, beginning with HX1, of five Canadian troopships and seven cargo boats, on 5 September.

Thus by October 1917 all homeward Allied and neutral shipping bound for UK or French Atlantic ports was in convoy. Naval staffs had been very reluctant to include neutral shipping in convoy for fear of security leaks, but it was at last realized that the loss of a neutral ship carrying cargo for the Allies was exactly the same as the loss of an Allied ship. If neutrals were forbidden convoys and the protection given in them, they might refuse to trade.

The protection given by a convoy was real enough and the figures continued to demonstrate again and again the dangers of straggling. For example, sixty-two sugar ships sailed from Newport News between 2 July and 10 October 1917. Ten sailed independently, of which one was sunk. Of the fifty-two in convoy, one also was sunk, when she had been separated from her convoy by bad weather. Similarly, 115 wheat ships sailed between the same dates. Of the eighteen independent sailers, four were sunk. Of the other ninety-seven in convoy, only one sunk, yet *again* after being separated from her convoy. A ship sailing independently or straggling stood ten times the chance of being sunk as a ship in convoy formation.

Convoy gave the Admiralty real control over the country's shipping for the first time in over a century. In the days of patrolling, ships were held up for days or even weeks when U-boat danger was reported. But, apart from closing the Suez Canal for ships homeward bound for the United Kingdom, the Admiralty had done nothing more to interfere with the peace-time pattern of ship movements around the coast. Decisions were left to individual masters and shipping lines, and nothing was done to impress upon them that the less ships were moved about in the danger zone the better.

For all practical purposes ships had been left to their own devices. In the first six months of 1917, for instance, large steamers discharged cargoes at London or Middlesbrough and then moved to Liverpool, Glasgow or Manchester for loading. Royal Mail boats loaded at Liverpool and called at La Pallice and Lisbon for cargo and passengers, both outward- and homeward-bound. Coastal voyages were shortened, bunkering facilities increased, and everything was done to impress upon ship-owners and masters that they *must* avoid unnecessary movement, especially in the danger areas of the Channel and the Irish Sea.

Even when ships were sunk, convoy saved enormous numbers of lives. From April to August 1917, about thirty ships a month, or 135 in all, were sunk 50 miles or more from land. Many ships were sunk 200 or 300 miles from land and the crew members who did get away from their ships sometimes spent days at sea before being picked up (if they were picked up at all), by which time many men had perished of thirst or exposure. But from September to December 1917 only six ships were sunk more than 50 miles from land (and four of those were in September). Survivors from the rest of the ships were rarely more than 10 or 20 miles offshore and many were picked up after a few hours, or half a day at most. Furthermore, U-boats were not able to take so many masters or chief engineers of torpedoed ships prisoner; this was a tremendous boost to the morale of the merchant marine.

As the morale of the merchantmen went up, so the morale of the U-boats captains and crews went down. Looking through a periscope, a convoy made a curiously formidable sight. Those ordered ranks of ships, grey or mottled or streaked and patched with camouflage, looked uncomfortably like a disciplined body, a *fleet* in fact, advancing purposefully upon their enemy. They might alter course at any time, with different turning circles, but all obeying a common directive. There was no easy way into a convoy, and the larger the convoy the more threatening it looked. Any attack on it was bound to provoke a counter-attack. Eventually the U-boats were reduced to 'browning' shots, where the U-boat achieved a firing position and then fired a salvo hopefully, with the chance of hitting one ship.

Convoy escorts were run on a comparative shoestring up to the end of the war in the Mediterranean. Much more appealing to the traditional type of naval mind was an enterprise such as the Otranto Barrage. Submarine hunting in the North Sea could be compared with greyhound-coursing, in which surface ships were used as gaze-hounds to run down their prey no

matter how it jinked and swerved. In the Mediterranean a closer analogy
would be estuary fishing; just as salmon could be caught in nets, so it was
believed that U-boats could be caught in larger and longer nets.

The Otranto Barrage was much more than a net. It was a theatre of war on
its own. It stretched for some 45 miles, across towards Albania from the heel
of Italy, and its purpose was to prevent U-boats escaping from their bases in
the Adriatic into the Mediterranean, or, if they did succeed in escaping,
prevent them returning. The fixed barrage was begun in April 1917 and more
or less completed by September. It had a deep minefield, 1150-foot nets,
which stretched down for 33 feet, and themselves carried more mines. The
Barrage was a rare example of Allied co-operation; the Italians laid and
maintained the barrage, the mines were French, and the nets British.

The fixed barrage was supported by a mobile barrage force, of destroyers
with depth-charges, trawlers and drifters fitted with hydrophones, flotillas of
submarines, sloops flying kite balloons, American sub-chasers, torpedo
boats, MLs and one yacht. The total number of warships was some 300 and to
provide them the convoys were stripped to their minimum escort, convoys of
thirty ships often being escorted by one sloop and two trawlers. There were
also lines of fixed hydrophones laid out under water, constant patrols along
the length of the barrage, and air patrols (there were some seventy British
aircraft, bombers, fighters and seaplanes, with Italian and French aircraft
support, based at Taranto and Otranto).

There is no evidence that U-boats were unduly bothered by the Barrage.
They continued to make their passages more or less at will. The barrage
forces sank two U-boats. The net itself claimed one. In the same period the
much-depleted and often-disparaged convoy escorts sank eight out of the
twelve U-boats sunk in the Mediterranean during 1917 and 1918.

One of those U-boats, destroyed while attacking a convoy, was UB-68,
sunk by the gunfire of SS *Queensland* on 4 October 1918. The U-boat
commander survived, with his crew, and has left a very good description of
the effect of introducing convoy:

> The Oceans at once became bare and empty; for long periods at a time the
> U-boats, operating individually, would see nothing at all; then suddenly up
> would loom a huge concourse of ships, thirty or fifty or more of them,
> surrounded by a strong escort of warships of all types. The solitary U-boat,
> which most probably had sighted the convoy purely by chance, would then
> attack, thrusting again and again and persisting, if the commander had strong
> nerves, for perhaps several days and nights, until the physical exhaustion of
> both commander and crew called a halt. The lone U-boat might well sink one
> or two of the ships, or even several; but that was but a poor percentage of the
> whole. The convoy would steam on. In most cases no other German U-boat
> would catch sight of it, and it would reach Britain, bringing a rich cargo of
> foodstuffs and raw materials safely to port.

That U-boat commander, who became a prisoner-of-war, was Karl Doenitz.

Chapter Eight

In 1918 the Allied convoy escorts, aided by Allied aircraft, won a smashing victory over the U-boats. It was a war-winning victory, which received very little publicity, at the time or afterwards. Those who took part in it were hardly aware that they were winning. Those who directed it often doubted their own success, and several times actually considered abandoning the very tactic of convoy which was bringing victory about.

It was the widest-ranging campaign of the war by far, fought across thousands of square miles of sea, from the coast of Palestine to the eastern New England shoreline of the United States, and from the Norwegian Sea down to the south Atlantic. It was an international undertaking, carried out by the Royal Navy, greatly assisted by the United States Navy in the Atlantic, and by the United States, French, Japanese and Italian navies in the Mediterranean.

It was a battle fought with a low priority for weapons, without a proper means of locating the enemy in his natural element, and with only about 5 per cent of the naval forces available. Even that 5 per cent consisted mostly of the older ships and aircraft; the newer destroyers and aircraft, the very ones most suitable for convoy escort, were almost always allocated to patrolling and to escorting warships.

It was a battle fought very largely by men who were not professional men of war – by reserve officers who commanded the small ships, by the masters of merchantmen, by trawler skippers, and by a great host of temporary reserve officers and men who kept watches, manned the guns, flew the aircraft and balloons – the signallers, ground crews, stokers and sick berth attendants.

Above all, it was a gradual battle, with nothing much to show, day by day, and very little scope for headlines. There were no dramatic advances or glorious retreats. There was no 'Big Push'. There were no maps in *The Times* to record progress, sap by sap, yard by yard. The only real indication lay in the dull, obscure, and to many naval officers virtually unintelligible, columns of figures provided by Geddes's statisticians which showed, month by month, that the total tonnage of shipping lost *was* dropping, that new construction *was* climbing and, eventually, *did* surpass the losses.

There were more figures available than ever before in the Royal Navy's history. One of the suggestions Lloyd George had made on his historic visit to the Admiralty on 30 April 1917 was that there should be a department of statistics in the Admiralty. Lieut Col George Beharrell, a railwayman like Geddes, came to the Admiralty from the War Office as Director of Statistics in May 1917. By September his department was producing its figures, which were treated with reserve, amounting almost to ridicule, by many naval officers.

That certain kind, almost that certain social class, of naval officer who would chuckle at statistics would also resist the idea of convoy for so long. It is easy to lie with statistics, but used judiciously and sceptically, statistics can be of real war-winning value. This, some naval officers simply could not see. Admiral Oliver, in particular, was more concerned than most with providing the statisticians with their raw material and with generally easing the newcomers into their new jobs in the Admiralty. Oliver was a most able and intelligent officer, but he had the opinions and outlook typical of his generation of naval officer, and he tended to ridicule statistics. He drew disparaging comparisons between railways and the Navy. What was 'well enough' in a railway or 'in Life Assurance' was not suitable for the Navy.

To keep the statisticians out of their way and occupied, Oliver's staff used to 'make up data mixed with weather conditions and the phases of the moon'. In a few months, Oliver said, 'wonderful graphs arrived but you cannot run war like a railway; you must look ahead not back'. 'Unfortunately,' Oliver thought, quite wrongly, 'worrying about what happened last month does not help the present or the future and wastes a great deal of time'. Oliver's extremely stupid point of view only shows that even one of the best officers of his generation could make an ass of himself.

By January 1918 it was possible to examine quantitatively the effect of convoy on the war. The figures had all been collected and tabled, the graphs drawn. Whichever material was studied, whatever coordinates chosen and graphs plotted, the conclusions were always the same: losses were down, delays were reduced, and though this was not so obvious, convoy escorts were sinking more U-boats. On 15 January Beharrell produced a General Review of the U-boat situation which, in its own way, was a most remarkable document. It was a statistical forecast, supported by figures and formulae, of how to win a war at sea, although it was not seen as such at the time.

The main conclusion was that, in the period from February 1917, when unrestricted U-boat warfare began, until December 1917, attacks by U-boats had declined by some 35 per cent. There had been 138 attacks in February, sinking sixty-five ships; 217 in April, the worst month, with 124 ships lost; but had declined to 126 attacks and sixty-seven ships lost in December (having

To: South Dublin Book Store

Intransit Item

Branch: South Dublin Mobiles
Date: 7/05/2024   Time: 1:54 PI

Item: Convoy : the defence of sea
        trade 1890-1990
        07181216351001

From: South Dublin Mobiles
To: South Dublin Book Store

Instruction: Please process item

CIVICA

been as low as forty-three ships lost in November). Examining the figures more closely showed that the most dramatic drop in losses (some 90 per cent in the last five months compared with the first five) was in home waters and in particular the Atlantic traffic in the Western Approaches i.e. among the very ships which were now being convoyed.

Convoy removed the initiative, for the first time, from the U-boat com- manders and forced a strategic necessity upon them. They had to alter their tactics, and change their scene of operations. From 200 to 300 miles in the Atlantic, they now moved closer inshore, where they discovered a weakness in the defences: ships were still unescorted (although the seas were as extensively patrolled as ever) whilst steaming between the port of departure and the convoy assembly point, or between the point of convoy dispersal and the port of destination. Ships along the east coast were not convoyed for some time, and the U-boats moved into the southern part of the North Sea. There was also a successful mine barrier across the Dover Straits, which forced U-boats to go north-about around Scotland to reach their patrol areas.

The longer passage times, with the consequent shorter time on patrol, the scarcity of targets, the long and fruitless waits between sightings, the increased number and explosive power of depth-charges, the fear of minefields, and, above all, the growing skill of the convoy escorts, at last began to affect the morale of the U-boat crews. Submarine warfare has always depended upon the mettle of submariners, and the skill, daring and leadership of the individual U-boat commander was very important; a staggering 60 per cent of shipping sunk was accounted for by only 20 per cent of the U-boats. Too much should not be read into the statements made by U-boat prisoners-of-war to their interrogators, but late in the war dilution of experienced personnel by recruits and the increasing ordeal of every patrol did provide evidence that U-boat crew morale was, if not cracking, at least creaking.

Convoys could still be attacked by powerful surface forces. The Scandina- vian convoys, which in 1918 were running every four days instead of daily and were twice as large as before, were particularly vulnerable. Battleships, cruisers and destroyers from the Grand Fleet were detached in support, although Beatty realized how dangerous it was to rely on intelligence to get wind of a German attack before it reached a convoy. A German force of capital ships could slip out and destroy convoy and support force before the Grand Fleet, although it had moved from Scapa down to Rosyth, could sally out. But the Scandinavian convoys were considered so important that these known risks were accepted.

In April 1918 Scheer made another move, which happened to coincide with the Zeebrugge Raid on the 23rd. Although the Raid did wind up tension by several notches, it also diverted attention away from the rest of the North Sea. Scheer concealed his plans with great care and skill, cutting out radio traffic and assembling his ships, on the 22nd, as though they were about to sail on exercises.

The same day a convoy of thirty-four ships, escorted by the armed boarding steamer *Duke of Cornwall* and the destroyers *Lark* and *Llewellyn*, left Selbjorns Fiord in Norway bound for Methil. The 2nd Battle Cruiser Squadron and the 7th Light Cruiser Squadron met the convoy at sea and accompanied it southward.

Scheer sailed at 5 a.m. the next day, with a formidable force. Hipper commanding the battle cruisers, led the way with the 1st Scouting Group, the 2nd Scouting Group of light cruisers, and a destroyer flotilla, with orders to attack the convoy and its covering force. Scheer followed, with the 1st, 3rd and 4th Squadrons of dreadnoughts, the 4th Scouting Group of light cruisers and four destroyer flotillas. A British submarine J.6 actually sighted some of Scheer's ships but thought they were British and made no report. It seemed that Scheer had set the stage for a successful *coup* which, coupled with the German advance on land which had begun in March, would be a tremendous setback for the Allies.

But the battle cruiser *Moltke* suffered a serious main machinery defect which caused her at one time to come to a stop. Hipper sent her back to join Scheer and then turned back himself. This change in plan meant signalling which was at once picked up by British direction-finders. The Grand Fleet, of thirty-one battleships, four battle cruisers, two cruisers, twenty-four light cruisers, and eighty-five destroyers sailed that afternoon.

Scheer ordered the battleship *Oldenburg* to take *Moltke* in tow, and told Hipper to carry on with his attack on the convoy. But the chance had gone. The convoy was already nearing the Scottish coast, and nothing now could prevent it reaching Methil early on the morning of 24 April. Hipper's ships were searching an empty sea. Scheer ordered his force to return to harbour. The British submarine E.42 hit *Moltke* with one torpedo on the way back. This, the very last sortie of the High Seas Fleet in the war, was over. Although the Scandinavian convoys sailed regularly and Scheer should have been able to plan his attack precisely, he had in fact arrived in between convoys. A day earlier, and he would have caught the westbound convoy. A day *later*, and he would have had the next eastbound convoy.

As the convoy system forced U-boats to operate further inshore towards the end of 1917, the air offensive and the introduction of convoy on the east coast forced them back out again into the Western Approaches. When they attacked convoys at all, they did so far out to sea beyond the reach of air cover (in a forerunner of events in the Second World War). They continued to attack stragglers and small ships, which made up most of the independent sailings. To try and preserve their advantages of speed, surprise and secrecy they began to make more and more attacks at night, when they were safe from all observation except from airships and balloons. Using ominous tactics, in view of what was to happen in the next war at sea, the U-boats began to make many more attacks on the surface. In 1918, over half the U-boat attacks in the Mediterranean and just under half in Home Waters were made at night and on the surface. Towards the very end of the war, the proportion of night attacks was rising to nearly two-thirds. By then, U-boats had also taken the first tentative steps towards operating in pairs and in groups. The lessons of U-boat tactics in the Second World War were there to be read in the first.

At the outbreak of war, the Royal Navy Air Service had a nucleus of just under 800 men, seven non-rigid airships and about 100 seaplanes and aeroplanes. When the first U-boat campaign began early in 1915, the Admiralty initiated a great expansion of the RNAS for anti-submarine operations. The need was realized for long-range aircraft, although they were to be used, just as destroyers were on the surface, for patrolling, for hunting U-boats in transit and coastal areas, and in the Western Approaches.

Lord Fisher, as First Sea Lord, authorized the building of one of the first and somewhat primitive airships, the SS1. 'At last I think I've hit on a SUBMARINE DESTROYER!' he wrote jubilantly to Jellicoe on 28 February. 'The keel is being laid today and finished in three weeks and at work in the Dover Straits. Cost of first vessel, £5000! I won't tell you any more at present! I got it through yesterday in twenty minutes! It will make your mouth water and your sleep easy at Scapa!' The SS1 'destroyer' was in fact the fuselage of a BE2C fighter slung underneath a balloon. It stayed aloft for about eight hours, and by the end of the year there were nine of them (Fisher's memory was at fault when he said he ordered thirty-eight). The SS1s were stationed at Folkestone, Eastbourne, the French side of the Dover straits, with four in Wales and Northern Ireland.

The SS1s were followed by larger, longer-ranged types, the Coastal 'C' class in 1916 and in 1917 the 'North Seas', which were splendid long-distance airships, 262 feet long, 60 feet in diameter, able to carry a payload of 8500 pounds. They had an endurance of twenty-one hours at 48 knots, which throttling-back could extend to sixty hours.

As air support developed, and coastal convoys were introduced, airships and seaplanes were ideal for convoy air cover. They provide air escort for the French coal convoys, for convoys through the North Channel, across the Irish Sea between Larne and Stranraer, and on the Folkestone to Boulogne route. By the end of the war there were more than ninety airfields, airship or seaplane stations, or balloon stations, around the coastline from Scapa Flow to the Scillies and from Aberdeen to Kent. They were supported by an extensive network of radio direction-finding stations. An airship transmitted every hour, giving a bearing of itself to the D/F stations, and so its position could be plotted. In 1917, airships sighted U-boats on thirty-two occasions and made eighteen attacks. They sank no U-boat but their deterrent effect was enormous. Significantly, by the end of 1917, when the RNAS had some 180 airships and kite balloons, only one ship had been lost from any convoy with an airship escort.

Large seaplanes were also used for anti-submarine patrolling and convoy escort. Their design and operational tactics made enormous strides during the war. The leading spirit for much of the research and design of aircraft which were, in effect, the ancestors of the flying boats of the Second World War, was John C. Porte. He had been a naval pilot but had been invalided before the war and had gone to America to work for the Curtiss Co. He returned to England at the beginning of the war and rejoined the Navy. He persuaded the Admiralty to buy the two Curtiss aircraft in which he had been planning to make a transatlantic flight attempt.

Twelve more of these flying boats, designated H.4s, were ordered early in 1915 and another fifty by the end of that year. The H.4 had several disadvantages. It was underpowered, and its hull was not seaworthy enough for conditions in the North Sea. Porte, who had become station commander of the base at Felixstowe, took an H.4's wings and tail assembly and fitted them to a hull of his own design. This original Porte 1 machine became the Felixstowe (so named after the air station) F.1 prototype. Porte designed another prototype, the F.2, from a Curtiss H.12, a larger version of the H.4 (and known as the 'Large America', the H.4 being the 'Small America'). The F.2 went into production as the Felixstowe F2A, of which over a hundred were accepted into service, and it became one of the most successful warplanes of the First World War.

The F2A carried two pilots and had an armament of between four and seven Lewis guns and two 230-pound bombs. It had a long range, being capable of nine-hour patrols, and was a first class operational aircraft with high manoeuvrability and a robust air-frame. Its only weakness was in its fuel supply. F2As were sometimes forced to ditch, facing their crews with long and uncomfortable surface trips back to base (from which some crews never survived).

The Large Americas and later the Felixstowes carried out the evocatively named 'Spider's Web' system of patrols in the North Sea which began in May 1917. The spider's web was an octagonal pattern of patrol routes, some 60 miles across and covering some 4000 square miles of the North Sea, using the North Hinder Light vessel as a central 'hub' or starting point. Four flying boats could patrol the whole web in about five hours. The U-boats, who also used North Hinder Light as a navigational reference point, could traverse the 'web' in about ten hours on the surface. The first patrol was on 7 May and the first U-boat destroyed was UC-36, very probably bombed and sunk by a Large America on 20 May about 10 miles east of the North Hinder Light vessel.

Besides the routine Spider's Web patrols, flying boats were also available to respond to emergency calls, wherever intelligence reported the presence of a U-boat. The normal height for patrol was 1000 feet; in reasonable weather this gave visibility out to a distance of some 36 sea-miles. For convoy, aircraft usually flew at 600 feet. Other webs were maintained over the English Channel, the Bristol Channel and St George's Channel. But there was a gap in the coverage, off southern Ireland. Seaplane bases were proposed for Queenstown and Berehaven, but Vice-Admiral Bayly, who was 'decidedly lukewarm about aircraft', opposed them, on the grounds that his ships were better employed in hunting submarines than in looking for aircrews whose unreliable aeroplanes had ditched in the sea.

Like the airships, the flying boats had a greater effect on U-boats as deterrents than as destroyers. (UC-36, which never returned to harbour, was not confirmed as destroyed on 20 May, although she may well have eventually sunk from the after-effects of the attack.) By the end of 1917 there were seventy-five airships, twenty-three aeroplanes and 291 seaplanes and flying boats operating against submarines and, during the year, had averaged 4000 hours per month on operational flying.

Although they did not sink a single U-boat in 1918, aircraft gave convoys invaluable help by forcing U-boats in the path of the convoy to submerge, which at once reduced their speed and manoeuvrability, and prevented them taking up an attacking position. Even where an aircraft could not itself attack, a wise U-boat always dived, because an aircraft could report a U-boat's position accurately enough to bring a surface escort (which *could* attack with depth-charges) to the scene in a very short time.

The figures show the efficiency of this deterrent. In 1918 U-boats made only six attacks against convoys with air escort. Only two attacks were successful and three ships were sunk. Only five ships were sunk from any convoy with air escort during the whole war. As the U-boat commanders became increasingly nervous and wary of air attack, so the aircraft had to fly longer and further between sightings. In 1917 aircraft flew 1,526,000 hours, sighted U-boats on 169 occasions and made 106 attacks; but in 1918, although the flying hours trebled to 4,801,000, the sightings only increased to 192 and the attacks to 131.

During the last six months of the war the air effort available for anti-submarine operations had risen to 190 aeroplanes, 300 seaplanes and flying boats, and seventy-five airships. Of these, 150, 110 and fifty-two respectively were normally available on any one day. They sighted twenty-eight U-boats, and attacked nineteen. They flew 14,000 hours a month on anti-submarine operations – a figure not achieved again until the summer of 1943.

The Admiralty were responsible for the provision and allocation of maritime aircraft for all but six months of the war. In April 1918, these tasks became the responsibility of the new Air Ministry, although the Admiralty was still responsible for the operations of maritime aircraft, and of airships. The Air Ministry was more committed to the employment of aircraft on long-range bombing of German factories, railways and military installations – in fact, to a kind of long-range economic blockade.

Convoy was not, of course, infallible. It protected most ships for most of the time, but occasionally a very determined and skilful U-boat commander, or more than one such U-boat commander, brought off a striking success. Unfortunately such *coups* were then treated post-war, as 'mysteries' or 'controversies'. There was criticism that ships were sunk even while heavily escorted. The loss of the great 32,300-ton liner *Justicia*, for example, whilst in convoy off the coast of northern Ireland in July 1918, was even taken to demonstrate the futility of convoy as a whole.

Justicia was launched as the Holland-Amerika Liner *Statendam* at Harland and Wolff, Belfast, on 19 July 1914, and lay in a basin until 1917, after America had entered the war, when she was taken up for trooping by the Admiralty with a Cunard name but under the management of the White Star line. She sailed on her first trooping trip to America on 13 April 1917 and she sailed independently until August 1917 when she was one of six ships in the first fast homeward convoy HX1 from Halifax which sailed on the 21st, escorted by the armed merchant cruiser *Arlanza*.

On 19 July 1918, exactly four years after her launch, *Justicia* (Captain Hugh F. David) was one of seven ships in the fast outward-bound 'Liverpool Express' convoy OLX39. The ships were in four columns, 1000 yards apart, with three columns of two ships each, and a single ship in the fourth column. *Justicia*, flying the convoy commodore's pennant, led the starboard inboard column. There was an escort of no less than nine destroyers, three in line abreast some six miles ahead, and the remaining six as close escort disposed around the convoy, ahead and on both beams.

The visibility was about eight miles, the wind force 4, south-westerly. The convoy was making 13½ knots and zigzagging, but was practically on its mean course of N 22° W when, at 3.30 in the afternoon, with no prior warning or sighting of either submarine periscope or torpedo wake, *Justicia* was hit in the engine-room port side by a single torpedo, fired from UB-64 (von Schrader) which had penetrated the screen from the port side.

Justicia began to lose way and haul out of line. The six close-escort destroyers, *Pigeon*, *Nicator*, *Marne*, *Martial*, *Milbrook* and *Mystic*, converged on an area astern of the convoy and dropped twenty-two depth-charges. Two destroyers then remained with *Justicia*, who had slowed to about 3 knots. At 4.18 p.m. a periscope was sighted 1 mile astern of *Justicia* and the destroyers dropped another pattern of seven depth-charges. By 5.30 a tug, *Coringa*, had arrived and begun to take *Justicia* in tow.

But von Schrader had still not given up and shortly afterwards UB-64 fired two more torpedoes from the port side, which were seen but missed. The escorts counter-attacked with another eleven depth-charges. By 9 p.m. *Justicia* was successfully in tow and making for Lough Swilly, when von Schrader attacked for the third time, from the starboard beam. His single torpedo was seen and deflected off its course by a round fired from a howitzer. Once more the destroyers countered with eight depth-charges.

At 9.30 *Justicia* was in tow and making a good 3 knots. It was a calm night and it seemed *Justicia* had a good chance of reaching safety. But von Schrader had followed and at 5. 30 a.m. on 20 July he made another attack with one torpedo from the port side, which missed. The escorts were running out of depth-charges; only four were dropped but one seems at last to have done some damage to UB-64. Oil fuel tanks had been ruptured and the U-boat was leaving an oil slick behind it. Von Schrader radioed for help.

More ships had come out to join *Justicia* and by 7 a.m., she was escorted by twelve destroyers, two sloops, two yachts and eight trawlers. But this tremendous concourse of shipping was not enough to prevent U-54 (von Ruckteschell) making an attack. Von Ruckteschell had not actually heard von Schrader's call for assistance, but had sighted *Justicia* on his own. He attacked at 10.15 and hit *Justicia* port side, in Nos. 3 and 5 holds with two torpedoes. U-54 partly surfaced after firing, and her conning tower was seen a short distance off *Justicia*'s port quarter. The destroyers raced to the spot and once more the sea boiled and spouted with the detonations of thirty-three depth-charges. But U-54 survived.

After a running battle of nearly twenty hours, the end had come for *Justicia*. At 1.35 p.m. she rolled over to port and sank. She was then quite close to land, only some 20 miles NW of Skerryvore. A third engineer, Mr Evans, and fifteen men were lost, but more than 700 survivors were picked up by the destroyers.

Meanwhile a third U-boat, UB-124 (Wutzdorff), had heard von Shrader's signal and had closed the last position given. That afternoon, at about 5.55 p.m., the destroyers *Marne*, *Pigeon* and *Milbrook* (ironically, three of *Justicia*'s original escort), sighted a U-boat on the surface, and steered for it at full speed. The U-boat dived, whereupon *Marne* attacked with two depth charges and *Milbrook* with one. No results could be seen, and as a British submarine was patrolling that area and none of the three destroyers had any depth-charges left, they steamed away to the south-westward at 20 knots.

However, the excitement was not over. At 6.25 the U-boat was sighted again on the surface, bearing NE about 7 miles away. Unknown to the destroyers, *Marne*'s second depth-charge, dropped at about 6.05 p.m., had damaged UB-124's batteries and forced her to the surface. The three destroyers opened fire; *Milbrook* had a hit with her third round, *Pigeon* with her second, and *Marne* with her twelfth. The U-boat's bows tilted up until the submarine was vertical in the water and she sank stern first out of sight.

The destroyers picked up Wutzdorff and thirty-one of his ship's company, who had abandoned the submarine. Unfortunately for Wutzdorff's reputation, he had left his First Lieutenant and Engineer Officer on board to scuttle the submarine, and both men went down with her.

By the end of the war in November 1918, about 90 per cent of all coastal and ocean-going shipping was in convoy. The French, Dutch and Scandinavian trades were in convoy. There were several convoy systems in the Mediterranean: for instance, from Gibraltar to Genoa, Alexandria to Bizerta, and from Port Said to Syracuse. There were also homeward bound HE 10-knot convoys from Port Said every sixteen days, through to west- or east-coast ports and outward-bound OE 10-knot convoys from Liverpool through to Port Said, also every sixteen days. There were so many Atlantic convoy systems it is better to show them in a table:

ATLANTIC CONVOYS IN LATE 1918

Homeward

From	Code	Frequency	Speed (knots)
Hampton Roads	HH	every 8 days to east and west coasts alternately	8
Sydney, Cape Breton	HS	every 8 days to east and west coasts alternately	8
New York	HN	every 8 days to east coast	9½
New York	HX	every 8 days to west coast	13
Quebec	HC	every 8 days to east and west coasts alternately	11½
New York	HB	every 8 days to Bay of Biscay ports	8
Sierra Leone	HL	every 8 days to either coast	10
Dakar	HD	every 8 days to either coast	8
Gibraltar	HG	every 4 days to east and west coasts alternately	7

Outward

From	Code	Frequency	Speed (knots)
Lamlash	OB	every 8 days	8
Liverpool	OLB	every 8 days, northward	about 8
Liverpool	OLX	every 8 days, northward	about 13
Liverpool	OL	every 8 days, southward	about 10 to 11½
Milford	OM	every 4 days	7½
Falmouth	OF	every 8 days	7½
Devonport	OD	about every 3 days	8 to 10
Southend	OC	every 16 days	11½

Convoy life had a flavour of its own. In the First World War, just as in the Second, those who sailed in convoys and took part in the battle of the Atlantic could think of nothing else. Those who were not in it, could not imagine what it was like. It was a battle against the weather much more than the enemy, against the idiosyncrasies of individual merchant ships and the vagaries of ship's companies, with ratings who might be excellent, or who might or might not re-join the ship in time for sailing.

By March 1918, the convoy commodore who had sailed in *Sachem* earlier in the war was serving in the commissioned escort ship *Naneric*, a twenty-two-year-old ship whose Chief Engineer 'despaired of getting more than 10½ knots out of her'. The first voyage was outward-bound to Halifax and the account gives a vivid picture of convoy life. During a gale on 17 March,

> the wind blew with terrific force, the foremost wireless mast was carried away at 2 a.m., two lifeboats were stove in, the 800 tons of coal ballast took charge and gave the ship a list of 15 to 20 degrees, steerage way was unable to be maintained, the main injection pipe was continually being rolled out of the water, the vacuum was lost, the feed pumps refused to take the water, at the same time the bilge pumps got choked with coal and dirt in the lee bilges, and the ship stopped with a heavy list to starboard, rolling, straining, and labouring heavily in the submarine danger zone. Fires were drawn, and the ship remained wallowing in the trough of the sea twelve hours, her forefoot being lifted and crashed down again, causing her to quiver and shake as if every moment would be her last. The wind registered 10 to 12, and, owing to the state of the ship, cooking was impossible. My cabin on the boat deck, which I expected to be blown bodily away, stood the test well.

By the 22nd, the situation was

> very confused sea; speed 3¾ knots. The petty officers and men fell in to express their grievances regarding the ship, accommodation inadequate and unfinished, water dripping on them day and night, no baths, no hot meals, cooking galleys for fifty with 115 on board, insufficient light, heating arrangements useless, always leaking, and discomforts (apart from the weather) extreme.

On 20 August, the writer arrived in Norfolk, Virginia, to organize HH67 homeward-bound convoy from Hampton Roads to the Thames. The following morning he lectured to thirty-two masters, British, American, French, Italian, Norwegian and Brazilian, with a Dane expected to arrive at any time. The convoy sailed at 6 a.m. on the 22nd, on a lovely summer's morning. After passing the swept channel, the thirty-four ships (one or two had dropped out, others had arrived) formed into nine columns at noon.

The writer records in dry, sardonic tones the events of the passage. On the 23rd a U-boat was sighted 70 miles ahead and directly in their track. Two days later one ship 'opened fire at 4 a.m. at what she took for the wake of a submarine. Asked Jones, my steward, whether my whites were not too dirty to wear tomorrow; he promptly replied: "Not for this ship, sir; they would have been for the *Agamemnon*." '

From 29 August to 6 September, there were 'strong N to NE winds and a rough sea, bringing our speed as low as 5 knots. Eggs rotten; butter rancid.' On the 3rd, one ship opened fire on what she thought was a conning tower 'but which proved to be a bell-buoy adrift with a framework round the bell'.

The writer gives thumb-nail sketches of some of the men who served in his ship. Today, they are striking evidence of the sort of men who fought the

convoys through. There was A. Lumsden, Leading Seaman Gunlayer, 2nd
Class, of the Royal Fleet Reserve, one of the crew of the 4-inch gun of the
oil-tanker *Mirlo*, sunk off Cape Hatteras. A torpedo struck the ship on the
starboard side close to the boiler-room:

> The bulkhead was fractured before the stokehold, and the gasoline from the
> tank there had a free run into it, the ship immediately becoming a roaring
> furnace. One lifeboat capsized owing to the ship still going ahead and the boat
> getting broadside on, the falls still remaining hooked. Four hands out of
> fourteen were pinned under the boat and drowned, the others scrambling on
> to her as she detached herself and drifted away. The ship then broke in half
> and the oil began to spread over the sea, burning furiously. The men,
> expecting to be burnt, jumped overboard and swam for it. The good swimmers
> were all drowned, five in number, but the bad ones returned to the boat, and by
> dint of using their hands, kept the boat in the channel between the two fires,
> which had widened as the two parts of the ship drifted apart and eventually
> sank. Coastguardsmen came out and rescued them after they had been six
> hours in the boat.

Lumsden had also served in the Dardanelles and won the DSM for services in
a volunteer whaler's crew who cut out an armed Turkish ship at Mitylene.
He was in the SS *Philadelphia* when she was torpedoed and sunk 100 miles
west of the Scillies. He was dragged down with his gun but escaped because
the wheat cargo in the hold swelled and burst the hatches, throwing him clear
of the ship and the propellers.

Ordinary Seaman Charles Marmion, also from *Mirlo*, had 'joined for
hostilities only and at the commencement of the war served in France in the
Border Regiment, was shot through the head, the bullet entering the back of
the skull and coming out through the forehead. He remained for three days
with German wounded in a German dug-out before our line advanced
sufficiently to admit of him being removed. After leaving hospital he was
discharged and later joined the Navy'. After *Mirlo* was hit, 'he was told to get
into the port lifeboat which he did, and when the boat capsized, he, with nine
others, succeeded in getting clear from underneath her, scrambled on to her
bottom, and, the falls becoming detached, drifted clear of the ship which was
then burning furiously. . . . At this moment one of the ratings on board the
boat who was a good swimmer, began to shriek and scream, went off his
head, and jumped overboard, followed by the others'. Marmion, who had
injured a rib in the first explosion, found he could not swim properly and
returned to the boat. Four other bad swimmers did the same. But the man
who broke down, and all the other good swimmers, were burned or drowned.

Another member of *Naneric*'s crew was John Day, a trimmer, Merchant
Marine Reserve, 'who had served in the Liverpool Regiment at Ypres,
Neuve Chapelle, and on the Somme Front, where he was gassed by a shell
and wounded by shrapnel below the knee. He was discharged from the Army

and rejoined the merchant service, which he first made acquaintance with at the early age of twelve-and-a-half years. He was now twenty, having joined the Army at seventeen.'

Naneric's last convoy was HH75, which sailed from Norfolk on 25 October 1918 with twelve ships, British, Norwegian, Italian, Brazilian and American. Two more ships joined off Bermuda. On passage on 4 November they heard of the Armistice on the Italian front, and Nantes wireless and the Azores signalled NO SUBMARINES. On the 7th there was a gale and two ships lost lifeboats over the side, but at midnight on the 8th they were still able to signal Valentia 'Convoy on time'. On the 11th, they 'intercepted wireless message to all patrols that hostilities had ceased from 7 a.m.'.

Next day they received from Poldhur, the message of King George V:

Now that the last and most formidable of our enemies has acknowledged the triumph of the Allied arms, on behalf of right and justice, I wish to express my praise and thankfulness to the officers, men and women of the Royal Navy and marines, with their comrades of the Fleet Auxiliaries and Mercantile Marine, who for more than four years have kept open the seas, protected our shores, and given us safety ever since that fateful 4 August 1914. I have remained steadfast in my confidence that whether fortune smiled or frowned, the Royal Navy would once more prove the sure shield of the British Empire in the hour of trial. Never in its history has the Royal Navy, with God's help, done greater things for us nor better sustained its old glories and the chivalry of the seas. With full and grateful hearts, the peoples of the British Empire salute the White, the Red and the Blue Ensigns, and those who have given their lives for the Flag. I am proud to have served in the Navy. I am prouder still to be its head on this memorable day.

The last entry of *Naneric*'s last voyage, for 14 November, was: 'Arrived in the Downs.'

Chapter Nine

So, when it was all over, when the last convoy (very probably HH77, sailed homeward bound from Norfolk, Virginia, on 10 November 1918) had dispersed and all the ships had switched on their lights again and gone their separate ways, when the last escorts had returned to harbour, when all the trawler skippers and their crews had landed their guns and ammunition on the nearest available jetty and gone back to their proper business of fishing, when it was finally all over, it only remained to look at the figures.

They told a remarkable story, to anybody who was prepared to listen. Convoy had not defeated the U-boats, in the sense of sinking a great many of them (although the escorts did sink their fair share), but it certainly defeated their campaign. It could even be argued that the sinking of U-boats did not in the end matter very much. What counted was the safe and timely arrival of the merchant ships.

Whichever convoy system is chosen, and however the figures are dissected and examined, they still reveal the truly astonishing success of convoy. From January 1918 until the end of the war, 16,102 ships sailed in east-coast convoys; thirty-five were sunk, for a loss rate (the percentage of ships sunk of the total which sailed) of 0.2 per cent. On the Scandinavian convoys, in the same period, 4230 were convoyed, fifteen sunk, for a loss rate of 0.4 per cent. Over the whole period of Scandinavian convoys, 7653 ships sailed, fifty-five were sunk, for a loss rate of 0.7 per cent.

The loss rate in the Mediterranean was generally higher; of 11,509 ships convoyed, 136 were sunk, for a loss rate of 1.2 per cent. As more and more figures are amalgamated from different convoy systems, they seem to build to a tremendous climax of success. Of the 16,070 ships sailed in ocean convoys, U-boats sank ninety-six, a loss rate of 0.6 per cent. Of the 67,888 ships in the Dutch, French, Scandinavian, and home-waters coastal convoys, U-boats sank 161, or 0.2 per cent. Of the grand total of nearly 95,000 ships convoyed including Mediterranean local convoys, 393 ships were sunk, for a loss rate of 0.4 per cent.

The figures become even more striking when they are compared with those for ships sailing independently. From February 1917 until October 1918, 83,958 ships were convoyed in Atlantic and home waters, of which 260 were sunk (loss rate 0.3 per cent). From November 1917 (no earlier figures are available) until October 1918, 48,861 ships sailed independently, of which 1497 were sunk (loss rate 3.1 per cent). The total number of ships lost was 1757, of which 85 per cent were sailing independently.

This victory at sea certainly did not come about because of the numbers of U-boats sunk. Of the 178 U-boats sunk during the war, certainly the highest number (sixty-nine) were sunk in the ten months of 1918, compared with sixty-three in the whole of 1917 and forty-six in 1914–16. But in October 1918 the U-boat arm was as numerous and as formidable as ever. Eighty U-boats were built in the ten months to October 1918 compared with ninety-four in 1917, 108 in 1916, fifty-two in 1915 and only ten in 1914 (Germany entered the war with twenty-eight U-boats). 344 U-boats were built during the war but no less than 226 were building when the war ended, and another 212 projected.

The U-boats were as active at the end of the war as at any time during it. From January to October 1918, there was an average of 172 U-boats in commission; 123 were operational *Frontbootes*, of which an average of forty-five were at sea on any given day. The equivalent figures for 1917 were 163, 129 and ninety-three; for 1916, 103, seventy-one, and nineteen. The numbers of U-boats actually sunk did not begin to exceed the numbers of new U-boats commissioning until the last months of the war.

A statistic not often quoted was the number of casualties the war at sea incurred. These, taken over the four years of the war, eventually amounted to the same losses as a major battle on the Western Front. In the merchant navy and fishing fleet, 15,313 men, or $5\frac{1}{2}$ per cent of the total involved, were killed, with an unknown number permanently disabled or weakened through exposure and wounds. By comparison, 22,811 naval officers and ratings, or 4 per cent of the Navy's personnel, were killed or died of wounds. (Of those, some 6000, or over a quarter, were killed or died of wounds at Jutland.)

Naval officers in previous centuries had never troubled to find out how and why convoys were so successful. They just knew they were, and used them. But in 1917 a Commander Rollo Appleyard RNVR, M.Inst.CE, always an obscure and now an almost totally forgotten figure in naval history, sat down in the Admiralty to calculate quantitatively how and why convoys worked. Using ships' logs, eye-witness accounts, diagrams of U-boat attacks, diagrams of convoy formations, columns, and escort dispositions, and with an accurate knowledge of the capabilities of merchant ships, escorts, U-boats and their torpedoes, Appleyard made an analysis, the first in naval history, of the principles of convoy attack and defence.

Appleyard conceded that there were innumerable attacking options open to a U-boat, and there were also an infinite number of variations of convoy formation, numbers of ships, their speeds, weather conditions and sea states.

All these would affect convoy attack and defence. However, he decided that the way in which a U-boat attacked, the courses it steered, the angles it bore from its target, the areas of sea which it traversed in making its attack, could all be examined quantitatively. Once they were known, the formation, course and speed of a convoy could be varied from the opening move of the attack. In other words, there were certain immutable 'safe' things a convoy could do. By having ships in the right formation, by steering the right courses and keeping the right distances from each other, a convoy could defeat a U-boat's attack or at least make it more difficult. Once these 'cardinal' (as Appleyard called them) angles, paths and areas had been found, he could go on to examine the problems of where to station the escorts most efficiently, for the later stages of defence.

Although a U-boat had innumerable attacking options, and it was impossible to devise a single formula to deal with them all, Appleyard did show that quite a lot could be done by making certain basic assumptions. There was, for instance, what Appleyard called a 'close area' in which a U-boat must be lying in order to make a successful torpedo attack. A U-boat could be in this close area either by already being ahead of the convoy, and allowing the convoy to run towards and over it, or by sighting the convoy from the beam or even astern, hauling round out of visibility range on the surface, and diving again somewhere in the close area for its attack. The close area would be on the bows for a fast convoy. For a slow convoy it could extend to the beam and even for some away abaft the beam.

Appleyard chose six factors, or quantities, which when co-ordinated decided the chances of an attack from a U-boat approaching along any bearing abaft the convoy's beam. They were convoy speed, U-boat speed, torpedo speed, radius of visibility, torpedo range, and the endurance of the U-boat. For a given convoy speed, visibility range and U-boat speed, an angle which Appleyard called a 'danger angle' could be calculated, within which a U-boat attack *must* come if it came at all.

Once this danger angle had been calculated for a given convoy, the shape of the formation of the rear of that convoy could be altered, for its own protection. The flanks of the convoy should taper away, to correspond with the danger angle.

Appleyard even designed a simple hand-held protractor for determining the danger angle. The danger angle also governed the width the escorts should be apart, by continuing the danger-angle lines to the points where they cut the circle of visibility on either side of the convoy and measuring the distance between those points. In short, the danger angles were more acute and escorts could be closer together for a fast convoy, with danger angles more obtuse and escorts further apart with a slower convoy.

Appleyard's next step was to assume that a U-boat had overcome the difficulties of making its approach and was trying to take up a position for a successful torpedo attack. His task was to try and define, actually to draw out

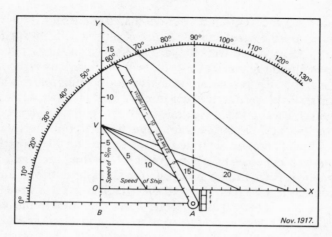

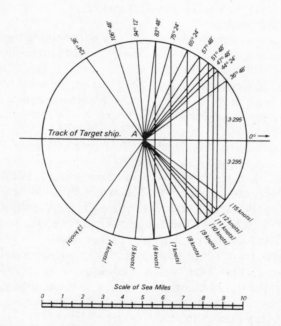

A Convoy at A is proceeding in the direction of the arrow. Visibility 5½ sea miles. A Submarine, approaching from about astern, tries to take up a position somewhere near the beam at Torpedo-range of 1 Mile. The Submarine cannot proceed for more than 1 Hour.
The Diagram shows the Danger Angles and the Widths of Screens corresponding to various speeds of Convoy.

Two diagrams from Captain R. Appleyard's *Elements of Convoy Defence* on a piece of paper, the shape and extent of that 'close area' within which the U-boat must be to have a reasonable chance of hitting with a torpedo.

These close areas varied with the size and speed of the target ship, the torpedo's speed, and the chances of a hit or miss at various torpedo ranges and firing bearings. By providing an algebraic formula for combining all these quantities, Appleyard arrived at a method of drawing the close areas for various attacks. He was also able to draw the 'broad path of slow approach' of the U-boat as it closed the target ship. Thus he arrived at the total area of close attack which had to be defended.

Appleyard drew balloon-shaped diagrams, illustrating the attack areas for different convoy speeds, from 6 knots up to 18 knots, and for varying lengths of ship, from 400 to 600 feet. To find the attack area for a whole convoy, diagrams were drawn, to port and starboard, for each ship in the convoy, so that their individual attack areas just overlapped, and a line was then drawn around the outermost attack areas. The area within this line was the attack area for the whole convoy and the task of the escorts was to deny the U-boats access to this combined area.

Next, Appleyard examined the effects of a target changing course during an attack. He analysed errors in the U-boat captain's estimate of his target's speed, distance, and course, to arrive at a method of finding the amount by which a torpedo missed its mark for a given change of target course, towards or away from, the torpedo track. In short, he obtained an estimate of the best course of action for a merchant ship's master to take, for a given range and bearing of a U-boat.

Appleyard particularly investigated the defensive value of zigzagging. He analysed the patterns of zigzags used by convoys and showed what the average turns and lengths of zigzag paths usually were. He then examined each zigzag pattern with reference to several factors: the time required by the U-boat to get torpedoes ready to fire, the time the target ship spent steaming along one leg of a zigzag, and the relationship between the number of times the U-boat captain looked through his periscope, the intervals between each look, and the number of zigzags the target ship made during the same time.

Appleyard found that there was, or should be, a very close relationship between the type of zigzag being used, and the behaviour of the escorts. He examined the amount of turn in particular zigzags and how far they decided whether a torpedo would hit or miss. He showed that for a zigzag to be really effective the U-boat captain must be denied the chance of long periscope looks at his target when the U-boat was in, or just nearing, torpedo range. This was where the escorts played a crucial part. A convoy zigzag and the movements of the escorts had to be developed as a connected plan, and not allowed to happen haphazardly, in a series of disconnected evolutions.

When a U-boat captain was allowed plenty of time to look whilst making his attack, then zigzagging was not likely to prevent him hitting. Appleyard had in fact arrived at a mathematical explanation for one of the reasons why

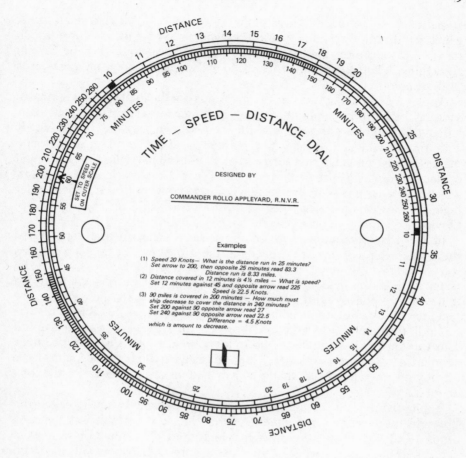

Captain Appleyard's 'Time-Speed-Distance' dial

independent ships were so vulnerable even when zigzagging. There simply were no escorts to distract the U-boat captain. If a convoy was zigzagging, and at the same time the escorts were restricting the U-boat captain's vision, thus adding the chance of further error in his calculations of torpedo angle, then a zigzag had a 50 per cent chance of making a torpedo miss, at least for shots wide of the beam.

Appleyard also looked at the zigzag 'bights', to decide what sort of turn gave the best tactical value. A ship could either make a sharp turn with 'a sting in it' and then steam for a comparatively long and vulnerable time on a straight course, or make its zigzagging in several co-ordinated small turns, which would not give much protection when a U-boat was within torpedo range. Furthermore, too much time and distance could not be lost in zigzagging. The convoy had, after all, to make reasonable progress towards its destination.

Appleyard found that the critical factor was not the total amount of turn in a zigzag, but just that amount of turn whilst the U-boat captain was actually looking through his periscope and the crew were getting the torpedo ready and firing it. A small turn at a critical point in the attack could cause a torpedo to miss, whilst a much larger turn earlier would still have allowed the U-boat captain to adjust his firing data and make a successful attack. Appleyard saw a useful defensive possibility in a ship doing a 'constant weave', being under helm the whole time. But this was only for a single independent ship. Obviously it could not be applied to convoys.

In the early days of convoy, the columns used to steam further apart. When there were ships of different speeds in the same convoy, the slower ships were placed in the inner columns and steered a straight course, whilst the faster ships in the flank columns zigzagged. But Appleyard recommended that, for any convoy with escorts, the merchantmen should get as close together as possible and manoeuvre together as nearly as possible so that, as he said, 'the convoy as a whole shall present an aggressive front to give full effect to the ramming menace and to leave no easy paths of entrance for a submarine'. Appleyard was merely describing what the U-boat captains were already discovering at sea, that a convoy had an unexpectedly hostile look about it.

Appleyard then examined the relationships between what he called the 'torpedo track area', a refinement of the close area, which was the area around and including the convoy in which the U-boat must be to make a successful hit, and the work of the close escorts. There was only a certain amount an escort could do, only a certain finite physical distance an escort could actually cover, during the time of a U-boat attack. Therefore Appleyard argued that the number of escorts required by a convoy should be governed not by the number of ships in the convoy but by the total area of sea enclosed by drawing imaginary lines connecting all the outermost ships.

In other words, the important factor was the convoy's size, expressed not in ships but in area. Doubling the number of ships in a convoy would not double its perimeter length and therefore a convoy twice as large would not require twice the number of escorts. Big convoys were best.

The torpedo track area, as Appleyard defined it, was found by drawing a diagram which combined the separate torpedo track areas of all the ships in the convoy, having first selected the right diagram for the speed of the convoy and the sizes of the ships in it. These superimposed areas formed, as Appleyard said, 'a somewhat complex web', but the escorts were only concerned with the outside edge of the web, and this could be simplified into a series of curves and tangents.

To arrive at the correct shape of torpedo track area for a given convoy, Appleyard designed a 'Convoy Board', divided into squares, with a scale and a protractor. To form up a convoy and to make out the torpedo track area which would decide the positions of the close escorts, one first prepared or procured a Convoy Board. The danger angle was calculated and then set out on the Board from any point on the central line of the convoy's advance and extending out on either side of the line of advance. This angle decided the shape of the rear of the convoy. Depending upon the number of ships, the stations were filled in, leaving, say, two cables between lines and two, three, or four cables between columns, depending upon the size of ships, the weather and the sea state. The rear and flanks of the convoy sloped away aft at the danger angle. This would shorten the flanks and add to the security of the rearmost ships of columns, but Appleyard warned that the sloping sides should not be carried so far as to produce a 'tail' of stragglers. The convoy had to be kept compact, to allow the escorts to take the shortest possible paths around it.

The positions of the escorts also depended upon their own speed, their armament and their signalling capacities. In general their primary object was to make the U-boat submerge and stay submerged. Figures showed that about 41 per cent of the U-boat approaches were made from ahead. U-boats approached from forward of the beam in 18 per cent of attacks, and from abaft the beam in 25 per cent of attacks. About 3 per cent of approaches were from astern, the remaining 13 per cent of approaches being from directions unknown.

For a fast convoy, the advanced escorts could form a screen of moderate width. For a slow convoy, the escorts had to be disposed all round the convoy. For large ships and fast convoys the close escort had to be extended further ahead than for small ships and slow convoys. The stern close escorts had to be brought nearer to the rearmost ships for fast convoys than for slow, and nearer also for small ships than for large.

'In theory,' Appleyard concluded, 'retaliation is not defence except in so far as it constitutes a menace. The main requirement is to place escorts to guard the front and flanks. Nevertheless, whatever may be written on the subject of disposition, if a destroyer is available for purposes of retaliation, it will go where it can retaliate for the zest for attack is the inspiration of all true defence.' As always, Appleyard supported his recommendations with data, laid out step by step, with diagrams and tables and algebraic formulae. It was like an account of the Trojan War, written by Euclid.

Appleyard published his conclusions in June 1918, in a treatise called 'The Elements of Convoy Defence in Submarine Warfare', with two supplements, an 'Escort Supplement' and an 'Evasion Supplement'. But Appleyard's fastidious logic, his mandarin language and choice of phrase, his formulae making elegant algebraic arabesques across the pages, did not recommend themselves to naval officers of the 1920s and 1930s. His 'Elements', a truly priceless record, bought with so much blood and treasure, should have been the best-thumbed book in the Navy.

But it was ignored. The 'Elements' and its two 'Supplements' formed part of a Technical History series which were officially classified as Confidential Books. 'CBS' were kept locked up in a safe except when actually in use. They were the responsibility of one nominated CB officer on board. Periodically, and when CB officers were relieved, the CBS were mustered page by page. Court-martials were held, careers were broken, when CBS went missing.

Thus, ironically, by treating these documents as priceless, which indeed they were, the Navy deprived them of their intended audience, making it almost impossible for anybody at all to read them and quite impossible for them to reach the readership they deserved. Finally, in 1939, they were declared obsolete and ordered to be destroyed, although copies do still survive in libraries. But it seems that enough of the lessons in Appleyard's 'Elements' were not read by enough of the officers responsible for planning convoy defence when the time came in the Second World War. Just as the cure for scurvy was discovered, forgotten and re-discovered at the cost of thousands of sailors' lives, so the lessons of convoy had to be re-learned at an even greater cost.

There were many and complex reasons for the neglect of convoy theory and practice between the wars. After such an experience, after such a narrow escape from defeat at sea, one would have expected the Navy to ensure, and the country to insist, that it was never likely to happen again. But it was not so. A peace-time shortage of money dogged the armed services almost until the outbreak of war. The 'Ten Year Rule', which assumed that there would be no major war for at least ten years, and which was re-affirmed every year, naturally encouraged complacency and conservatism, and inhibited discussion and innovation.

The Royal Navy still believed in battleships. The Navy also believed that Jutland had been somehow fumbled. There would be another Jutland in the next war – and this time there would be no fumbling. The battleships would see to that. The sheer massive presence of the battleships, laid out in impressive lines at reviews, steaming imposingly into newsreel shots or on magazine covers, seemed to stun the reasoning processes of very many naval officers. When thought was given to naval tactics, by some malignant fate, it was always the wrong lessons which were remembered: for instance, the great efficiency of aircraft in locating mines by reconnaissance was forgotten, but the laying of the expensive and virtually useless northern mine barrage was remembered.

With the belief in battleships went a mistrust of air power. The absorption of the Royal Naval Air Service into the new, independent Royal Air Force on 1 April 1918 had absolutely disastrous results for naval air. Many of the best and brightest air-minded naval officers transferred to the RAF, leaving the

American seaman rescued from a torpedoed tanker, 1942.
The photograph was captioned 'The price of petrol'

(*Above*) officers on the turret of a be-garlanded U-boat putting out to sea,
April 1917. (*Below*) gunnery practice on a First World War U-boat

(*Above*) zero non-rigid airship escorting a First World War convoy over the
North Sea. Semaphore signals are being made from its gondola. (*Below*)
Justicia sinking, 20 July 1918

(*Above*) the popular idea before 1914 of the fate of hostile submarines in the next war: *Hermione* running down B3. (*Below*) an American TB destroyer passing a bag containing written orders to one of the ships of a convoy while at sea

(*Above*) U-boat rendezvous in the Mediterranean during the First World War, with a small submarine of the UB type alongside U-35. The figure on the right in British military uniform is Captain Wilson, King's Messenger, taken prisoner by U-35. (*Below*) depth-charges exploding. Viewed from the airship R29 at 1000 feet off Scotland in September 1916

(*Above*) Convoy conference before the sailing of an east-coast convoy, 1941. (*Below*) John Waters, mate of the tanker *Empire Unity*, at sea again after being torpedoed twice

Rescue

(*Above*) ammunition ship exploding when hit in an Arctic convoy. This photograph was taken from the deck of a MAC ship, and the heads of some of its crew are seen silhouetted in the foreground. (*Below*) a mine-laying U-boat, U-118, on the surface and under attack by Avengers from USS *Bogue* in June 1943. She was sunk and seventeen survivors rescued

Navy with very few officers, and no senior officers, who had any previous experience of air. A naval officer who volunteered to join the air branch was certainly not improving his career prospects. Aircrew, rather like sub-mariners, were regarded as 'not quite the thing'.

The Fleet Air Arm was known as the 'Fleet Air Arm of the RAF'; it was always the orphan Annie of the air service. Just as a naval officer was less likely to be promoted if he took to the air, so an RAF officer was doing himself no good if he went to sea. The naval air service tended to get the least able aviators, and certainly got lower-performance aircraft. Design and produc-tion of naval aircraft lay with the RAF. Even when the Admiralty did give thought to the question of naval aircraft, they tended to think upon traditional lines: their first priority in 1919, naturally enough, was an aircraft for *gunnery spotting*.

Those who wanted to learn a lesson from the past had no text to use. A really determined reader could dig out Appleyard's work. But there was no equivalent for the air. After the RNAS disappeared it was decided that events in the air belonged to the RAF. The official histories of the war at sea from 1914–18 were written as though nothing interesting or significant had ever happened above masthead height. But the histories of the war in the air did not appear until the 1930s, the last volume not until 1937, by which time decisions on rearmament had already been taken.

The Navy's motto for the 1930s, as far as aircraft were concerned, was well put by Captain Bernard Acworth, a respected and widely-read commentator on naval affairs between the wars: 'In peace-time, it may be frankly admitted, seaplanes available for picnics, shooting parties, or as substitutes for cap-tain's galleys when lying at anchor far from shore, would be fun.' It was forgotten that only five ships had been lost from convoys which had an air escort.

Thus when war broke out again no properly designed and equipped aircraft were available for convoy escort. No effective depth-charge had been developed. No major oceanic convoy exercise was held between the wars. Fleet exercises were devoted to the handling and manoeuvres of the battle fleet. Convoy-passage exercises, when they were held, were designed more to give destroyers practice in operating their Asdic, which was generally thought to have made the submarine impotent. There were theoretical convoy exercises ashore, on the tactical floor, but no policy for tactical convoy formations was laid down, no evasive measures devised, no moves to distract or sink attacking submarines rehearsed.

The success of Asdic was greatly overrated. It was entirely forgotten that U-boats between 1914 and 1918 had made many attacks on the surface and at night, acting in fact as submersible torpedo boats, when Asdic could not have detected them. The success of submarines in exercises, whenever they were allowed to take full evasive action, was discounted. Much more reassuring results were taken from exercises at sea off Portland, the home of anti-

submarine warfare, with fast, fully-worked up destroyers with highly-trained
Asdic ratings, operating for an afternoon or at most a few days, against
submarines which were known to be there and whose whereabouts could be
quite accurately forecast. Nobody considered that results with slower,
smaller, and fewer escorts, with less well-trained Asdic crews, in the
Atlantic, after days and days of watch-keeping – in war conditions, in fact –
were likely to be much less comforting.

Coupled with the pre-war failure in the air was a failure on the surface. No
proper convoy escort design was developed. A convoy sloop was approved in
1933 and some, later called escort vessels, were built. In a debate on convoy
sloops on 15 March 1935, Lord Stanley, the Parliamentary Secretary to the
Admiralty, was presumably reflecting the official policy of the Admiralty
when he said that he could assure the house that

the convoy system would not be introduced at once on the outbreak of war . . .
the convoy system has very great disadvantages, and it certainly would not be
welcomed by the trading community until conditions had become so intolerable that they were prepared to make the necessary sacrifices. In the first place,
you get delay at each end. You would get delay while the ships assembled at the
starting-point to be taken up by their convoy. You would get delay by the ships
arriving at the same port at the same time. You would also have the difficulty of
the faster ship having to go at the same pace as the slower one. Therefore, the
convoy system will only be introduced when the balance of advantage is in its
favour, and when sinkings are so great that the country no longer feels justified
in allowing ships to sail by themselves, but feels that for the protection of their
crews the convoy system is necessary.

To hear this stupid and ignorant politician speak, one would have thought
the war had never been fought and won. Here were all the old arguments
against convoy, which should have been discredited for ever, appearing once
again, fresh and newly-minted.

While drowned ghosts in their thousands from the graveyards of the
Atlantic groaned and gesticulated from the gallery, another member asked:

Am I to understand the Noble Lord to suggest that the Admiralty would wait
before instituting the convoy system until so many ships had been sunk that the
country could not stand it any longer? Surely, they are not going to wait until
such conditions arise as occurred on 17 April 1917, when thirty-four ships were
sunk in one night. Are they going to let us get to that pitch before they start the
convoy system?

'Certainly not,' protested the Parliamentary Secretary to the Admiralty. But
his ignorance, his stupidity, his blind indifference to the lessons of the past,
were all immaculate. 'But you will not introduce it in the first place. . . . You
will not know in the first place whether the ships are going to be in any great

danger. . . . It may be that it will be safer for them to sail by themselves. . . . They will be a smaller target . . . The enemy ships would not know quite where they were to be found. . . .'

Chapter Ten

'The previous war,' wrote Winston Churchill, 'had proved the sovereign merits of convoy.' That was true. But, once again, not everybody was wholeheartedly in favour of convoy when the Second World War broke out. Before the war was many weeks old, Churchill himself as First Lord of the Admiralty became concerned about what he called 'the immense slowing down of trade' caused by convoy and and was minuting the First Sea Lord and others, frankly admitting: 'I had not appreciated this aspect, but in the war we must learn it from day to day. We must secretly loosen up the convoy system (while boasting about it publicly), especially on the outer routes.' Then, as though he wished to prove conclusively that *still* he had not properly grasped the *real* sovereign merits of convoy, Mr Churchill went on: 'If we could only combine it with a large effective destroyer force, sweeping the Western Approaches as a matter of course instead of providing focal points on which convoys could be directed, we should have more freedom.'

The Admiralty had in fact made many preparations for war, including convoy. The Admiralty assumed control of merchant shipping some time before war was declared. Liaison with the merchant navy had already been established. A Shipping Defence Advisory Committee, on which the Admiralty and shipowners were represented, was formed in 1937 and had met regularly ever since. Churchill himself attended the first war-time meeting, on 11th September 1939, when, as he sombrely told the meeting, the country had already lost 11,000 tons of shipping a day in the first five days of war.

The Admiralty also had contingency plans for a ship-building programme of convoy escorts, and for taking up the largest and newest trawlers and fitting them with guns and Asdics. Commanders-in-chief were empowered to order merchant ships into convoys in their commands. The Admiralty intended to introduce convoy, without any of the prolonged debate of the previous war. But the exact time of introducing convoy would depend upon circumstances: upon the severity of U-boat attacks, the number of escorts actually available, whether surface raiders had begun to inflict heavy losses, in fact, upon the general climate of the war at the time. Where there was a shortage of escorts, ships would be evasively routed. In any case, U-boats were not expected to operate much outside the immediate area of the Western Approaches.

In the event, the Donaldson liner *Athenia* was torpedoed without warning and sank, with the loss of 112 lives, including twenty-eight American citizens, off Ireland on the very first night of the war. The Germans later claimed that the U-boat commander responsible had exceeded his instructions. But the effect at the time was to concentrate the Admiralty's mind wonderfully. Convoy was introduced at once for ships between 9 and 14.9 knots speed.

The very first convoy, of eight ships bound from Gibraltar to Cape Town, sailed on 2 September, the day before war was declared. On the 5th, a convoy of eleven troop transports sailed from the Clyde for Gibraltar, escorted by the battleship *Ramillies* and eight destroyers.

But these were special operations. The first regular convoy cycle began on 6 September, up and down the east coast, northwards (coded FN) and southwards (SN) between the Thames and the Firth of Forth, one convoy in each direction sailing every second day. The escorts for these convoys were largely provided by the Rosyth Escort Force.

Outward-bound Atlantic convoys, coded OA, OB and OG, began on 7 September. OA convoys assembled at Southend and were met in the Downs by escorts of Western Approaches Command. Convoys then went on down Channel, picking up ships from Southampton, Plymouth and Falmouth on the way. Ships from Plymouth and Falmouth had to rendezvous six miles south of the Lizard and, so as to preserve radio silence, had to be in this position at daybreak on the given day. This required accurate fixing of the convoy's progress down Channel from the air. 'Positions' given for convoys sometimes varied enormously; one was found to be near the town hall, Reading, another in the Place de la Concorde, Paris.

From the Lizard the convoy was taken over by relief escorts, the original escort returning to Plymouth. The ocean escort, normally two destroyers, accompanied the convoy for another day and a half, by which time it would expect to have reached about 12°30′ W. There, the escort left at dark and steamed on to meet an in-coming homeward-bound convoy, at about 15° W.

Meeting a convoy was always fraught with difficulties. The convoy could be delayed or diverted for any number of reasons, and a convoy was only permitted to break silence to report its position if it was likely to be more than six hours early, or three hours late, at the rendezvous. Aircraft of 15 Group RAF Coastal Command, based at Plymouth, assisted these meets by reporting convoy positions to the shore authorities who relayed them to the escorts. (Aircraft and escorts had to withdraw to a distance of twenty miles from a convoy before reporting its position.)

OB convoys, which averaged about eighteen a month until June 1940, after which they sailed every second day, assembled and sailed from Liverpool, also escorted by ships of Western Approaches Command. Bristol Channel ships, normally escorted by trawlers, came out from Milford Haven to join the convoys off the Smalls. OBs were also escorted to about 12½° W, where the escorts left to join an in-coming HX convoy, while the OB went on unescorted for another twenty-four hours before dispersing. Southbound ships for Gibraltar parted from OA or OB convoys off the Scillies and formed their own OG convoys, with an ocean escort. They were met by anti-submarine vessels off the Straits of Gibraltar.

As a more comprehensive convoy system began to swing into action, some familiar names from the previous war came into prominence again. The first homeward (SL) convoy from Freetown, Sierra Leone, sailed on 14 September; the first homeward Halifax (HX) convoy on the 16th; a fast Halifax convoy (HSF) on the 19th; the first homeward (SG) Gibraltar convoy on the 26th. By 7 October, some 161,000 men, 24,000 vehicles and 140,000 tons of stores of the British Expeditionary Force had been convoyed across to France without loss, just as their fathers and their equipment had been convoyed a generation earlier.

To add to the uncanny resemblances to the opening of the previous war, another Canadian convoy, consisting of five liners carrying 7450 men of the First Canadian Division, crossed the Atlantic in December 1939. On their way over, the Canadians had a narrow escape from what could have been one of the worst maritime disasters in history. As a security precaution, the routeing authorities in Liverpool had not been told of the in-coming convoy's movements. One night, the darkened liner *Samaria* passed right through the convoy, actually striking the wireless masts of the carrier *Furious*, escorting the convoy.

The troopers were in line ahead and if *Furious* had collided with *Samaria*, the liners following astern would also have crashed into her. Lieut Cdr C. A. Jenkins, *Furious*'s navigating officer, realized next morning that '*Furious* had been even luckier than that' – for 'after striking the wireless masts on our *starboard* side, she [*Samaria*] had struck a glancing blow on the *port* side of our next astern [*Aquitania*] and passed close down the *starboard* side of the third and fourth ships in the line'.

As in the previous war, convoys began to impose their own patterns of safety on events from their first day. By December 1939, 5756 ships had sailed in convoy. U-boats sank four of them. But it had never been intended to include in convoys ships which could go better than 15 knots, or could not make the minimum convoy speed of 9 knots. These ships were allocated their own routes and sailed independently. These, the U-boats found much easier targets, sinking forty-six.

One would have expected that the old notions of 'guarding the sea-lanes', of seeking submarines by patrolling for them, would have been thoroughly and permanently discredited years before 1939. But in some quarters in the

Admiralty, and especially in the First Lord's office, vestigial remains of pre-1914 thinking still lingered on. The old atavistic belief still held that convoy was, in some way, *defensive*. Therefore, it was much better to use ships *offensively*. Mr Churchill could not have his 'large effective destroyer force sweeping the Western Approaches'. But he could and did use the Navy's few and precious aircraft carriers with what he called 'some freedom in helping bring in the unarmed, unorganized and unconvoyed traffic which was then approaching our shores in large numbers'. In practice, this meant that the carriers were used as a form of anti-submarine cavalry, to lunge about the ocean on would-be punitive expeditions, to search for and sink U-boats wherever they had been reported.

The policy was quite useless and ultimately disastrous. *Ark Royal* was narrowly missed on 14 September by U-39, whilst hunting U-boats off the Hebrides. The destroyers *Faulknor*, *Foxhound* and *Firedrake* from *Ark*'s escort at once sank the U-boat and captured her crew. But it had been a very close shave, and there was worse to come on the evening of the 17th, when another carrier, *Courageous*, was attacked in much the same circumstances by U-29.

Courageous and her escort of four destroyers were hunting for U-boats in the Western Approaches off Ireland. Two of the destroyers had been detached to stand by a merchant ship which had been attacked earlier in the day. *Courageous* altered course to fly on some of her aircraft and, in doing so, crossed in front of U-29's periscope. U-29's patrol was, in fact, almost completed and she was on her way to intercept a convoy reported by another U-boat.

Courageous was hit port-side by two torpedoes from U-29's salvo of three. 'There were two explosions, a split second apart, the like of which I had never imagined possible,' wrote Sub-Lieutenant Charles Lamb, who had just landed his Swordfish (the last aircraft ever to land on *Courageous*). 'If the core of the earth exploded, and the universe split from pole to pole, it could sound no worse. . . . In the sudden deathly silence which followed I knew the ship had died.' *Courageous* turned over and sank in fifteen minutes, with the loss of 519 of her people, including her commanding officer, Captain W. T. Makeig-Jones, who stayed on his bridge, saluting the flag, as his ship went down.

Mr Churchill bore philosophically the loss of what he called this 'very necessary ship at this time'. He thanked Admiral Sir Dudley Pound, the First Sea Lord, for coming to break the news to him personally and said, 'We can't expect to carry on a war like this without that sort of thing happening from time to time. I have seen lots of it before.' The whole episode of *Courageous* had been, he said, 'a risk which it was quite right to run'.

Here Mr Churchill was, very surprisingly for someone with such tremendous experience of the Navy and naval affairs, utterly wrong. It was *not* a risk which it had been right to run. It had been an anachronistic return to the bad old days of patrolling. But at least one lesson was learned. Carriers were not employed on these sorties again (though other ships were).

Thus the picture which Churchill painted to the House of Commons on 26 September was a comparatively bright one. Losses to U-boats had dropped to 9000 tons in the previous six days, compared to the 65,000 tons lost in the first seven days of the war. The convoys were steaming all over the oceans. Troops had been brought safely across. The enemy's shipping had been swept from the seas. More and more merchant ships were being armed. The British onslaught on the U-boats was only just beginning, but the hunting forces were getting stronger every day. Mr Churchill said that six or seven U-boats, 'as a safe figure', had been sunk; this was one-tenth of the U-boat force with which Germany had begun the war.

His speech, as Mr Churchill said, was extremely well received by the House, and by the country. It was, in fact, rather too well received by the country. Later, in 1940, convoy escort commanders on the east-coast routes to and from the Firth of Forth reported that a number of merchant-ship masters were being slack about station-keeping and general convoy discipline 'because of a belief that the enemy attack had been "broken" ', which was certainly not true.

Although Mr Churchill was slightly but excusably exaggerating (the 'safe figure' of U-boats sunk was actually only two at the time), by the end of 1939 the picture was broadly as encouraging as he had claimed. Nine U-boats had then been sunk, which was a sixth of the enemy's force. Merchant ship losses were 114, of which twelve were sunk in convoy and five as stragglers from convoys, totalling 421,156 tons. Mines, and especially magnetic mines, were then sinking more ships than the U-boats.

In spite of *Courageous*'s fate, in spite of the ominous figures already beginning to show the great dangers of sailing independently, the notion of patrolling simply would not die away. Mr Churchill himself gave it another fresh impetus on 20 November when he minuted to Admiral Pound:

> Nothing can be more important in the anti-submarine war than to try to obtain an independent flotilla which could work like a cavalry division on the approaches, without worrying about the traffic or U-boat sinkings, but could systematically search large areas over a wide front. In this way these areas would become untenable to U-boats, and many other advantages would flow from this manoeuvre.

The passage has several revealing key phrases: 'independent flotilla', 'like a cavalry division', 'without worrying about the traffic or the U-boat sinkings', 'systematically search large areas'. Here was the old, stupid, 1914 view that U-boats could be hunted down by packs of destroyers acting like waterborne Galway Blazers, freshly regenerated, still refusing to learn from bitter experience, still unrepentant.

As a result of this thinking, many destroyers and sloops were sent off to search fruitlessly for submarines, whilst the convoys they should have been escorting were guarded only by a single ship. Sometimes, even these remaining escorts were diverted from their convoys to join these wild-goose chases. By acting in this manner they would be behaving *offensively*. Remaining with their convoys was merely to remain on the *defensive*.

Yet all the evidence was precisely to the contrary. Even so early in the war, it was the convoy escorts who were sinking the U-boats. On 30 January 1940, U-55 attacked OA80 in the Channel. Bad weather had broken up the convoy and the only escort still with it was the sloop *Fowey*, but she, assisted by the destroyer *Whitshed* and a Sunderland of 228 Squadron RAF sank the U-boat, in the first joint surface-ship/aircraft sinking of a U-boat in the war. On 5 February, when U-41 attacked OB84 off the coast of southern Ireland, the destroyer *Antelope* was the only escort present, but she smartly counter-attacked and sank the U-boat. On 25 February, when U-63 attacked the Norwegian convoy HN14 in the North Sea, the destroyers *Escort*, *Inglefield* and *Imogen*, with the submarine *Narwhal*, combined to sink it.

By contrast, U-25 attacked an OG convoy off the mouth of the Tagus on 3 February and sank the 6800-ton steamer *Armanistan*, when the convoy escort had been called away to search for a non-existent submarine in the Channel. In the same month of February, a hunting group of destroyers formed by C-in-C Rosyth especially to find and sink U-boats in the North Sea had no success at all.

Meanwhile, the figures of sinkings remorselessly demonstrated the perils of sailing out of convoy. In January 1940, U-boats sank forty ships, of 111,263 tons; in February, forty-five ships, of 169,566 tons. But only four ships in January and three in February were lost in convoy. The rest were all stragglers or independently routed. U-boats sank twenty-two ships in the North Sea. *All* were sailing independently. No less than twelve were sunk in an area where ships converged upon a passage through the northern end of the east-coast mine barrier. This was a state of affairs similar to the First War, where U-boats could lie in wait, knowing their targets would steam by, one by one.

In March 1940 U-boats sank twenty-three ships, of 62,781 tons, but by the end of the month they had withdrawn from the Western Approaches and the coasts of Britain, to concentrate for the coming campaign in Norway. In April, U-boats sank only seven ships, of 32,467 tons; in May, thirteen ships, of 55,580 tons. The Admiralty then estimated that nineteen U-boats had been destroyed and forty-three were in commission. The actual figures were twenty-two destroyed, and fifty-two in commission. By the fall of France in June 1940, U-boats had sunk over 200 British, Allied and neutral ships sailing independently. But of the thousands of ships which had sailed in convoy, the U-boats sank only eight. Convoy escorts sank eight U-boats. Clearly this was an unfavourable rate of exchange for the U-boat command.

Early in 1940 the Luftwaffe began to attack the northbound (FN) and southbound (FS) east-coast convoys which sailed between the Thames and Methil every other day. These convoys of necessity followed a fixed navigational route, through a channel only a few hundred yards wide, between shoals and minefields (it was actually called 'The Tramlines'), marked by light buoys every five miles. Although the channel was swept as often as possible by minesweepers it could never be guaranteed clear.

The convoys were large, for that time, often consisting of sixty ships, spread out in two ragged columns over a distance of as much as 20 miles. 'Camp followers' often attached themselves to a convoy, joining and leaving at all times and in any sort of order. Often there were only two escorts, from the Rosyth Escort Force, one at the head and the other bringing up the rear. In the frequent poor visibility, or at night, much could happen in the middle of a convoy, quite unknown to the escorts. A ship could be mined and sunk, and her survivors picked up by the next astern, without either escort having the slightest inkling of the incident until the convoy reached its destination.

Besides the dangers of mines, there were the hazards of collisions and groundings and, later in 1940, attacks by E-boats, which would lie in wait off certain well-known buoys along the route, glide in to attack, and slip away again. Aircraft suddenly materialized out of the murk overhead, dropped their bombs, and vanished again before a round could be fired at them.

Yet the old principles of convoy and the safeguards it provided still remained. It was slack discipline which led to losses. 'In all cases of losses of ships between Tyne and Southend whilst in convoy,' the C-in-C Rosyth reported to the Admiralty in January 1940, 'the cause has been inattention to orders.' Occasionally the merchant-ship masters were their own worst enemies. Some thought that the enemy's strength had been 'broken', and almost all of them were of an extremely independent frame of mind, unenthusiastic about the convoy system (although noticeably more of them became 'camp followers' as the Luftwaffe attacks intensified). In any case, these men knew the east coast like the backs of their horny hands. They resented being chivvied and chased about (as they thought) by cheeky destroyer and sloop captains, those impatient young shavers, still wet behind the ears.

A fine piece of sustained invective in the report of one east-coast escort commander to the C-in-C put the position very well:

I put it on record as a curiosity of the war that it took four hours and four separate visits alongside one ship to make her Master carry out a perfectly simple manoeuvre needed for the greater safety of himself and those following him in the line during the rest of the day. Apparently he had his own ideas about convoy tactics and if ordered to go to port determined to go to starboard, and if ordered to haul out and move ahead, he decided that the order was bunkum and made no move to touch his engine-room telegraph.

Some air cover for east-coast convoys was provided by Nos. 11 and 12 Groups, Fighter Command, but in the early days the fighters responded only to radio calls for help when a convoy was already under attack. The fighters thus almost always arrived too late, often having had little idea of the convoy's position when they set out. Aircraft recognition was a constant problem. The understandable response of the men in the ships was to fire at an aircraft first and look up the identification book later. Pilots were always complaining of being fired on by those they had come to help. The ships retorted that the fighters often appeared very suddenly, very low over the convoy, and without having made the proper recognition signals. In February 1940, Fighter Command instituted some standing patrols over some of the two north-bound and two southbound convoys normally at sea at any given time. What was really needed was good ship/air radio communication and actual control of the fighters from the convoy. But this was still a long way in the future.

As the number of sunken ships increased, wrecks became a particular hazard. In shallow waters, the masts and funnels often stood up out of the water and the position could be marked by a green-painted buoy showing a green flashing light at night. Later in the war, some areas such as the region off the Wash from Sheringham up to Hull became what the escorts called 'a Piccadilly Circus' of winking lights. But the precise position of many ships was not known and these unmarked wrecks were a real danger.

With the normal poor visibility often becoming thick fog, with mines, E-boats, the Luftwaffe, wrecks, shoals, collisions, groundings, and the constant anxiety of navigating along a narrow channel off a generally featureless coast-line, life for the east-coast convoys and their escorts was hard and dangerous. But there were so many east-coast convoys during the war that they were seldom 'news'. Occasionally a particular incident, such as the shooting down of a Heinkel III by the corvette *Guillemot* in March 1941, was pictured in the press (actually in the *Sphere*) but in general the work of the Rosyth Escort Force and the ships they escorted was not well publicized.

On 8 January 1940, Bernard Stubbs broadcast for the BBC an account of a trip with an east-coast escort:

You may remember that last month the Nazis were claiming that they had won control of the North Sea. They said that the British Navy had lost its command and that the merchant ships had fled to port. Well, I've just come back from the North Sea. I spent eight days in a British warship escorting about a score of merchant ships from Scotland to a southern port and then another lot of ships back again, and I saw nothing whatever of this Nazi control of the North Sea.

I was in the senior ship of the escort and most of our time was spent zigzagging backwards and forwards at the head of the convoy, keeping a close watch for mines and submarines. The other ships covered the flanks and the rear. One blessing we had last week was tolerably good weather. One night I kept the middle watch on the bridge with the officer of the watch, well wrapped up in warm woolly clothing which some kind soul had sent the Navy.

It was a night of stars and stillness, broken only by the sound of water lapping round the bows, with a faint breeze, and the distant engines. As we talked in the low confidential tones one instinctively uses in the darkness at sea, I became aware of the tense, silent watchfulness on the bridge. Occasionally a sharp-eyed lookout would report something, a darkened ship perhaps, an almost imperceptible shape, and the guns would be ready and trained on it. Every little thing is watched, queried, investigated, because it is only by this constant vigilance that our ships are so well protected.

At the end of our voyage we passed an outward bound ship who signalled to us, 'Well done.' We were a bit puzzled by this, but when we were alongside a messenger came aboard with the glad news that our captain had been awarded the DSO for what was officially described as 'Faithful devotion to the hazardous duty of escorting and protecting other ships from the violence of the enemy'.

Memories of the merchant navy tended to grow kinder over the years. Commander William Donald, *Guillemot*'s captain when she shot down the Heinkel, wrote many years later:

I think a great deal about those trips, and especially so in winter time. I remember so vividly the two lines of ships, butting along steadily through the darkness, come hell or high water, for five and a half years – until the light of victory dawned.

Even more vividly do I remember, with admiration and humble pride, such men as the Chief Engineer of one of those ships. We fished him out of the water with two others only, from a crew of twenty; their ship had been mined, and it sank almost before the sound of the explosion had died away. Aged over sixty, with a broken leg and other injuries, his only thought was to get back to sea again.

'I'll be back soon,' he said, as we put him ashore at Rosyth, 'they'll no' get me down.'

They'll no' get me down. . . .

As the enemy overran the Low Countries and advanced in France in the summer of 1940, the number of convoy escorts was reduced even further to provide 'flotillas in the narrow seas', in Mr Churchill's phrase, to guard against the threat of invasion. Meanwhile, the First Lord said, 'losses in the Western Approaches must be accepted. . . .' This was clearly the correct disposition of forces while the invasion threat was real. The best convoy system in the world was futile if the Germans invaded and occupied the United Kingdom.

The shortage of escorts led to an unexpected return to a system of patrolled routes when, on 15 June, it was decided to evacuate that part of the British Expeditionary Force (which had not already been lifted from the beaches of Dunkirk) from the ports of Cherbourg, St Malo, Brest, St Nazaire and La Pallice. Admiral Sir William James, C-in-C Portsmouth, decided he did not have enough flotilla vessels for convoy so arranged for a continuous flow of troopships, transports and store ships, all sailing independently, whilst warships patrolled the routes. Admiral Sir Martin Dunbar-Nasmith, c-in-c Plymouth, had no flotilla vessels at all, and he too routed all ships independently.

Conditions were ripe for a massacre. But the U-boats made no attacks and the Luftwaffe was held at bay, except at St Nazaire on 17 June, when the bombing and sinking of *Lancastria*, with the loss of 3000 lives, showed what might have been.

Once the enemy was ensconced on the French coast, every ship in the Channel had to run the gauntlet of attack by dive-bombers and E-boats. The Master of the 1800-ton steamer *Paris* vividly described his ship's fate, whilst sailing down Channel in a convoy on 2 June 1940:

At 4.15 p.m. I went up on the bridge and sent one of the officers down for some rest. I had no sooner done so than the sound of an aeroplane was heard. I saw it at once almost right overhead, slightly to port. It was diving at us in a vertical dive at terrific speed. I knew instantly that this time we were going to be hit, and said to the Second Officer, 'He's got us this time.' First we were machine-gunned, the bullets falling into the water just alongside the starboard quarter, splashing the sea like a shoal of flying fish diving together. Then came the screaming of the bombs, followed by the explosions as the first bomb burst. This bomb struck the port side of our vessel abaft the amidships, piercing her side.

The second bomb went down the after-cross bunker trunkway, and must have exploded deep down. It evidently blew out the ship's side to starboard, because she took a sudden heavy list of about 15 degrees to starboard, and I knew then that there would be great difficulty in lowering the port lifeboats. The explosion was terrific. The whole ship shivered and trembled violently. The fore stay and foretopmast stay carried away and the foremast shook and swung aft.

I felt instinctively that the poor old ship had been punished too severely. This bomb must have burst the main steam-pipes or boilers and set ship and bunkers on fire. I came to the conclusion that most of the watch in the stokehold must have been killed instantly. I tried the telegraph and the speaking-tube to the engine-room, but they evidently had been shattered and I could not get any reply.

When the plane made the vertical dive, the gun crew got into position and were just going to fire when the concussion caused by the first or second bomb blew them away from the gun and they could not use it at all.

The engines were still going round, but slowing down gradually. A third bomb fell in the water close alongside on the starboard side, and again the ship shivered violently. The fourth bomb fell in the sea about sixty feet away on the starboard quarter. I was informed that a fifth bomb also fell in the water, but I did not actually see this, and it may be that I lost count of them. The attack, from the time we sighted the plane till it was all over, did not last more than fifteen or twenty seconds.

As the *Paris* heeled further over to starboard, almost hidden in dense clouds of smoke, the Master and his crew took to the boats and were later picked up by the convoy escort. According to *Paris*'s Master, the escort captain 'felt the loss of the ship in his convoy very keenly – undoubtedly a conscientious officer with that manly fellow-feeling for those in misfortune that is met in its full and genuine form only at sea'.

One officer particularly concerned about air attacks in the Channel was Vice-Admiral Sir Max Horton, Flag Officer Submarines. He was indignant at Fighter Command's attitude that their role was the defence of Britain and not the defence of ships, and alarmed by the lack of any coordination between the Navy and Fighter Command. In his view, the Air was 'fighting a war of its own' and their 'divided control' was sure to end in disaster.

Horton was especially incensed by the fate of convoy OA178, on 4 July 1940. It was, in his opinion, 'a disgraceful episode' and

> a blatant indication of the complete absence of co-operation by Air Force and perils of divided responsibility – this convoy coming down Channel was attacked by relays of bombers off Portland between 1 and 2 p.m. – six at a time for two hours – some ten ships sunk, fired or damaged. At midnight – E-boats torpedoed two more of the wretched convoy. Yesterday [6th] they were bombed again – two ships in Portland Harbour also damaged – a total of fourteen or fifteen ships with valuable cargoes! No fighters and no escort worth talking about. With our system there is nobody to appeal to if the Air doesn't turn up – it is a criminally inefficient system. . . .

The ships were not quite as completely undefended as Admiral Horton described them. One of the escorts for OA178 was the auxiliary anti-aircraft ship HMS *Foylebank* who put up a spirited defence, with the convoy, and later at anchor in Portland Harbour, where Acting Leading Seaman Jack Hantle fought the starboard 20 mm pompom with such gallantry he was later awarded a posthumous Victoria Cross.

Charles Gardner of the BBC accompanied one convoy down Channel and thrilled his listeners with a first-hand eye-witness account, just as it took place, of a Stuka attack on 14 July:

> Well, now the Germans are dive-bombing a convoy out at sea. There are one, two, three, four, five six seven German dive-bombers, Junkers 87s – there's one going down on its target now [sound of heavy explosion] – no – there, he's missed the ships! He hasn't hit a single ship! There are about ten ships in the convoy, but he hasn't hit a single one! I'm looking round now: I can hear machine-gun fire, but I can't see our Spitfires – they must be somewhere there. Oh, here's one coming down now! There's one coming down in flames! Somebody's hit a German and he's coming down with a long streak . . . he's coming down completely out of control! A long streak of smoke! Oh, the man's baled out by parachute! The pilot's baled out by parachute! He's a Junkers 87

and he's going *slap* into the sea ... and there he goes ... *smash*! A terrific column of water, and there was a Junkers 87. There was only one man got out by parachute, so presumably there was only a crew of one in it. There's one definitely down in this battle and there's a fight going on – you can hear the little rattles of machine-gun bullets [sound of explosion] ... that was a bomb, as you may imagine. Here come – there's one Spitfire, there's a little burst – there's another bomb dropping. Yes, it dropped – oh it missed the convoy – it hasn't hit the convoy in all this! The sky is absolutely patterned now with bursts of anti-aircraft fire and the sea is covered with smoke where the bombs have burst. But as far as I can see there's not one single ship hit, and there is definitely one German machine down ... and I'm looking across the sea now ... I can see a little white dot of parachute as the German pilot is floating down towards the spot where his machine crashed with such a big fountain of water about two minutes ago. Well, now, everything is peaceful again for the moment. The Germans who came over in about twenty dive-bombers delivered their attack on the convoy, and I think they've made off as quickly as they can. Oh, yes – I can see one, two, three, four five six seven eight nine, *ten* Germans haring back towards France now for all they can go!

The Channel convoys (coded CW for westbound, CE for eastbound) were normally quite large, of between twenty and thirty ships, and always very slow, never much more than 5 knots. Making their way so close to the enemy coast-line, they were very vulnerable to attacks by aircraft which had only a few minutes' flying time from their bases in France. Although losses to mines at that time were, in fact, even greater than those to aircraft, the near-vertical descents of the Stukas, and that famous screaming noise as they plummeted downwards, had a very disconcerting effect upon morale.

Despite Spitfire and Hurricane air cover, the convoy CW7 came under heavy attack on 20 July. The destroyer *Brazen* was hit and so badly damaged she sank whilst under tow off Dover. However, the convoy escort commander reported that the 'conduct of the convoy was excellent throughout the action'. The next westbound convoy, CW8, came under even heavier attack, on 25 July. The fighter escort was overwhelmed and five merchant ships were bombed and sunk. Next day, three more ships were sunk by E-boats and only eleven of that convoy eventually reached their destinations.

Later in the year, the Channel convoys were subjected to long-range bombardment by heavy guns on the French coast. The ships of CE9, off Cap Griz Nez on 20 August, could not at first believe they were actually being shelled; they had seen how 'extremely frightened' the Luftwaffe were of Fighter Command and thought the shell bursts were 'bombs dropped from a great height'.

However, Bernard Stubbs of the BBC was in no doubt:

At the moment we can see two bright flashes, three flashes, from the other side of the Channel and three great puffs of smoke, and now a fourth. .... At any

moment now the shells will be arriving on this side. . . . Four columns of
smoke going up on the far side, as the convoy goes past us here. And there's
the [sound of explosion] and the second [explosion]. Just a very short way in
front of us, we can see, a tremendous column of water goes up. There's a third
bomb to come down now, or rather [sound of heavy explosion] . . . one more to
come [explosion]. And there it is. All those completely wide of the convoy, as
they've all been so far. As they steam past us slowly here. You heard those
explosions and a great swirl of water goes up. A cloud of smoke and spray in the
air still. The extraordinary thing is, you see the flash right over on the far side
of the coast and the little column of smoke goes up from it and then wait for the
explosion over this side. The bombardment is absolutely terrific from the far
side. . . . We've heard lots of rumours about shells being fired from the French
coast. This time they certainly were. . . .

The most important cargo carried by the Channel convoys, in this war as in
previous wars, was coal. The ports and towns along the south coast needed
about 40,000 tons of coal a week. There was no way of carrying such
quantities, other than in ships. But many seamen in those convoys thought
their lives were being unnecessarily hazarded. A representative of the Short
Sea Trade Section of the Ministry of Shipping sailed with CWII in September 1940 and reported that every member of the crew in his ship 'said he
would not sail in the convoy again, risking lives just for household coal which
the sailors thought could go by rail, or north-about'.

As the U-boats and the Luftwaffe made more and more use of bases and
airfields in France, and while Irish ports stayed closed to the Allies, most
ships were routed north-about. Convoys stopped using the route south of
Ireland and sailed through the North Channel into the northwest
approaches. OA178 was the last outward-bound convoy to go through the
Channel. East-coast ships outward-bound were routed round the north of
Scotland in WN and EN convoys which started in July and August 1940, sailing
from Methil to the Clyde, and back again. They were large convoys, escorted
by two or three armed trawlers from the Belfast Trawler Force.

Convoy WN4, escorted by the trawlers *Arab* and *Man-o-War*, was attacked
by aircraft off the north coast of Scotland in the early hours of 3 August. One
ship was set on fire and two others damaged. The escort commander,
Lieutenant Richard Stannard RNR, in *Arab*, was not at all pleased by the
convoy's performance under attack. He wrote next day to the Flag Officer in
Charge Belfast listing 'the great disadvantages *Man-o-War* and myself were
in. (1) Forty-two ships to escort. (2) Only one ship opened fire. (3) Thirteen
ships were fitted with twelve-pounder AA armament. (4) *Man-o-War* and
Arab opened fire immediately, the former with Oerlikon and the latter with
Lewis guns and French automatic rifles.'

Stannard complained, justifiably, that only one merchantman had opened
fire: 'It should be made clear to all Masters of ships that any plane at night at
short range should be deemed an enemy plane notwithstanding the lights the

plane shows. This plane was showing a red light on each wing and fired coloured lights which did not deceive us but did deceive most of the convoy.'

Stannard took *Arab* alongside the burning ship *Statira* (which he considered should never have been abandoned) and fought the fire. 'Blazing oil barrels were exploding a few feet away while the shell plating was red hot. The paint was burnt off my bows with the heat. There was a chance her magazine might blow up.'

Stannard commended his crew 'who experienced constant air attacks in Norway and the east coast and who are well broke in now. The only complaint is they cannot hit back. I am sure they could do better and be of far more use than most merchant ships fitted with HA [High Angle] who do not use them.'

Stannard spoke from experience. A few days later, on 16 August, the *London Gazette* published the citation for his Victoria Cross, awarded for his great gallantry at Namsos in April and May, when he and his crew had helped put out a fire on a burning jetty, survived thirty-one air attacks spread over five days and, though many of them were wounded and frost-bitten, shot down a Heinkel whilst on their way home. For the episode with WN4, Stannard was mentioned in dispatches in December 1940.

Apart from armed trawlers, convoys were also defended by destroyers, many of them *Hunt* Class, MLs, Motor Gunboats (MGBS), and Motor Anti-Submarine Boats (MASBIs), and, especially in the Channel, by balloons and kites flown from ships in the convoy. These were excellent deterrents against air attack, although kites could not often be flown, because of the weather. The balloon ships were manned by the Mobile Balloon Barrage Flotilla and by No. 952 Balloon Barrage Squadron RAF. CE8 had seven balloon ships from Portsmouth. Two ships of the Mobile Balloon Barrage Flotilla, *Pinguin and Gatinaiss*, sailed with CE9.

The Senior Officer of the Mobile Balloon Barrage, Lt Cdr Garth Owles, had a poor opinion of MASBIs which, he said, 'are a menace to the convoy and to themselves'. He criticized their 'inability to do slow speed', their 'perpetual booming roar', 'the broad white wake they leave because of their speed' and said 'their frequent appearances were bad for the nerves'. However, the senior officer of CE8's escort, Cdr Grant, had a better opinion of Owles's efforts. According to him, 'the balloon ships kept station very well and at all times the convoy was well covered by the barrage'. Grant noticed that the balloon ships encouraged good station-keeping, 'keeping all ships well closed up as naturally they would be keen to keep in its protection'.

Despite their escorts of destroyers and motor craft, their kites and balloons, their own guns which were being fitted in increasing numbers (to be manned by men of the Channel Guard), the best defence for convoys, and particularly the Channel convoys, was fighter cover. Obviously Fighter Command could not provide continuous cover for every convoy all the time and certainly liaison in the early days was as bad as Horton described it. But it improved and Fighter Command did their best, despite their professional reluctance to delegate any form of 'control' over their fighters. The solution was escort vessels fitted with radar and with good ship/fighter radio communication to summon fighter assistance and then actually to direct them on to their targets.

Fighter Command resisted this idea, and claimed it was unworkable. But by December 1940 trials towards this end had started, held jointly by the c-in-c Rosyth and No. 14 Group Fighter Command. But still the ships were permitted only to *inform* the fighter pilots, not in any way to *direct* them. This was more than a difference in semantics. Nevertheless, it was one more step in the Navy's and the RAF's slow, groping progress towards a joint strategy and a combined policy for the protection of ships at sea. At its least, it was still a great deal more co-operation than the Kriegsmarine and the Luftwaffe ever achieved.

German successes on land meant that they too now had to run convoys along the length of the continental coast-line, from Norway down to the Biscay ports. These now came under attack by Allied aircraft and coastal forces, and to a lesser extent by submarines (whose first target priority remained, until 1943, enemy warships). Ironically, the Germans introduced convoy as a matter of course and not as an option for discussion.

Ironically, too, by August 1940 the Germans had demonstrated in the waters off southern Norway that aircraft were the natural predators of submarines. They made excellent use of aircraft to sight submarines and summon up surface vessels to attack them. Occasionally the aircraft themselves made successful attacks, using an airborne depth-charge. The aircraft were often slow, ponderous seaplanes and their crews were not specially trained for anti-submarine work. Yet these tactics took a terrible toll of Allied submarines: *Thistle*, *Tarpon*, and *Sterlet* in April, *Seal* and the Polish *Orzel* in May, the Dutch *0.13* in June. The worst months were July and August when *Shark*, *Salmon*, *Thames*, *Narwhal* and *Spearfish* were all lost.

Individual British airmen seemed to recognize instinctively the vital importance of convoy work. *The Times* of 18 June 1940 published a letter written by a young bomber pilot, to be sent to his mother if he was killed or reported missing:

Though I feel no premonition at all, events are moving rapidly, and I have instructed that this letter be forwarded to you should I fail to return from one of the raids which we shall shortly be called upon to undertake. You must hope on for a month, but at the end of that time you must accept the fact that I have handed my task over to the extremely capable hands of my comrades of the Royal Air Force, as so many splendid fellows have already done.

First, it will comfort you to know that my role in this war has been of the greatest importance. Our patrols far out over the North Sea have helped to keep the trade routes clear for our convoys and supply ships, and on one occasion our information was instrumental in saving the lives of the men in a crippled lighthouse relief ship. Though it will be difficult for you, you will disappoint me if you do not at least try to accept the facts dispassionately, for I shall have done my duty to the utmost of my ability. No man can do more, and no one calling himself a man could do less.

This was the temper of the young men of the summer of 1940. They would need every ounce of spirit and tenacity in the new phase of the Battle of the Atlantic which was to open after the fall of France.

Chapter Eleven

Early in the summer of 1940, a destroyer was shepherding the ships of her convoy together when she noticed an unfamiliar-looking, chunky little warship approaching, evidently intending to join her.

Pretending to be astonished, the destroyer signalled: 'What are you?'

'*Periwinkle*,' was the reply.

'Can I stick a pin in you?'

'No, I am a pale blue flower, not a shell-fish.'

'Then I shall come over and fertilize you.'

As a result of this fertilization, so the same story goes, there were eventually 144 *Flower* class corvettes, literally from *Abelia* to *Zinnia*, of which *Periwinkle* was one of the very first. They were 925 tons, 205 feet long, 33 feet in the beam, a complement of eighty-five officers and men, armed with one 4-inch gun, a 20-mm pompom, and depth-charges. They had their disadvantages: a very primitive form of Asdic and, at first, no radar; they rolled, as the saying went, 'on wet grass'; and at their maximum speed of about 16 knots, at full chat, they could not catch a surfaced U-boat on both diesels. They demanded a great deal of physical and mental stamina and resilience of their crews; as they used to say, 'the man who invented corvettes was a genius; the only trouble is he didn't invent the men to go in them'. Later in the war, another twenty-five Modified *Flowers* were built, a little longer at 208 feet, a little bigger at 980 tons, more men (109), but essentially the same. An officer who served in them described one as 'something like an overgrown trawler. But she'd have to do more than a trawler's work.' In fact, these small but famous vessels, with their delightful garden names, like *Bittersweet* and *Marigold* and *Heartsease* and *Honeysuckle*, bore the brunt of the battle of the Atlantic for more than five years. They actually had their first success as early as 1 July 1940 when *Gladiolus*, assisted by a Sunderland of 10 Squadron RAF, sank U-26 (Korvetten-Kapitan Scheringer) whilst it was attacking a convoy off the south-west of Ireland.

By July 1940 there was a very serious shortage of escorts. The evacuation of the BEF and French troops from Dunkirk had cost six destroyers sunk and another nineteen damaged, some so badly they would be out of commission for months. There were about ninety destroyers in home waters, and nearly half of them were under repair. Of the destroyers which were operational, most were concentrated in the narrow seas, against the threat of invasion. Destroyers kept on being added to the strength in those waters in such numbers as to suggest that Mr Churchill, now Prime Minister, was taking the most pessimistic view: that the Germans would be able to invade the United Kingdom virtually overnight, with overwhelming force, with prior intelligence unable to give warning and existing air and sea power unable to resist effectively. Meanwhile convoys were sailing with only one or two escorts, and even those few escorts were likely to be called away to search for U-boats.

The results of this policy soon showed in the figures of sinkings (one of the features of the war against shipping was that successes and failures appeared at once, in the weekly statistics). The losses began to climb again: in June 1940, 140 ships of 585,496 tons; in July, 105 ships of 386,913 tons; in August, ninety-two ships of 397,229 tons; and in September, 100 ships of 448,621. Of these, 211 ships, of well over a million tons, were sunk by U-boats although there were only a few at sea during this period.

On 4 August, Mr Churchill minuted his concern to the First Lord, now Mr A. V. Alexander, and the First Sea Lord: 'The repeated severe losses in the North-Western Approaches are most grievous, and I wish to feel assured that they are being grappled with the same intense energy that marked the Admiralty treatment of the magnetic mine. There seems to have been a great falling-off in the control of these Approaches. No doubt this is largely due to the shortage of destroyers through invasion precautions. . . .' Mr Churchill wished to know the strength of destroyers, corvettes, Asdic trawlers, and aircraft. He suggested a move from Plymouth to the Clyde for the Command. 'Anyhow, we cannot go on like this. . . .'

The Allies certainly could not go on like this. The overall figures were quite depressing enough, but there were specific aspects of the situation which were even more appalling. The 289,000 tons of shipping lost to U-boats in June 1940 were sunk by only six operational boats, who were disposing of their targets at the rate of roughly one ship every twenty-four hours. Doenitz, the Commodore U-boats, issued a new standing order that month: 'In the first place attack, and keep on attacking, do not let yourself be shaken off. If your boat is temporarily driven off or forced to submerge, follow in the general direction of the convoy. Endeavour to regain contact and once again – attack.'

On 15 August, Hitler proclaimed a total blockade of all waters around Great Britain, and warned neutrals to keep their ships out of the war zone. The last week of August was the worst of the whole war for shipping losses –

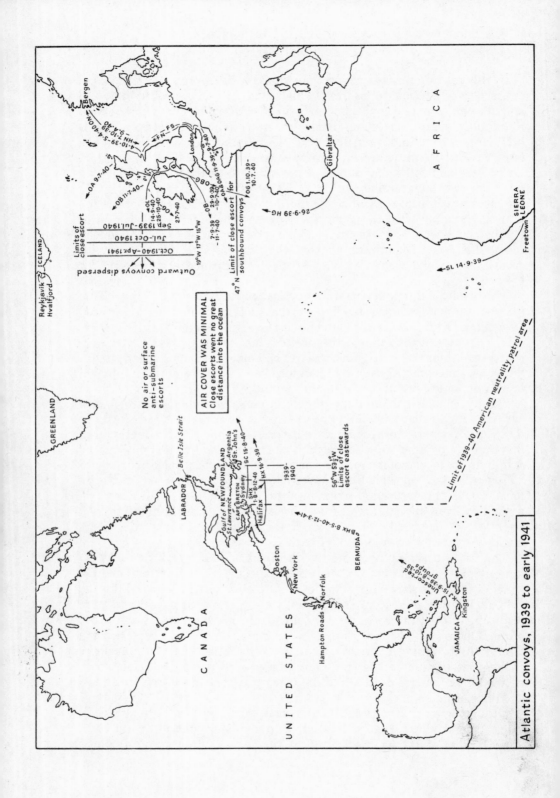

Atlantic convoys, 1939 to early 1941

Labels and annotations visible on the map:

Bergen
HN 4·10·39—5·4·40
HN 7·9·40
FN · FS
London
0980
OA 9·7·40
OB 11·7·40
9·1·40
9·0
27·7·40
29·9·39—9·11·39
OA 6·11·39—10·7·40
OB 10·7·40
14·9·40
25·10·40
7·9·39—11·7·40
OG 1·10·39—10·7·40
HG 26·9·39
SL 14·9·39
Reykjavik
Hvalfjord
ICELAND
GREENLAND
SIERRA LEONE
Freetown
AFRICA
Gibraltar

Limits of close escort
Sep. 1939—Jul. 1940
Jul.—Oct. 1940
Oct. 1940—Apr. 1941
Outward convoys dispersed
19°W 17°W 15°W
47°N Limit of close escort for southbound convoys

No air or surface anti-submarine escorts

AIR COVER WAS MINIMAL
Close escorts went no great distance into the ocean

LABRADOR
Belle Isle Strait
Gulf of NEWFOUNDLAND
St. Lawrence
Argentia
St. John's
SC 15·8·40
CAPE BRETON I.
Sydney
SHX 1·8·12·40
HX 16·9·39
Halifax
1939—1940
56°W 53½°W
Limits of close escort eastwards

Boston
New York
Norfolk
Hampton Roads
BERMUDA
OBHX B·5·40—12·3·41

CANADA
UNITED STATES

Limit of 1939–40 American neutrality patrol area

JAMAICA
Kingston
unescorted
X·1·39—18·10·39
9 groups

over 110,000 tons. This was what the U-boat arm called '*Die glückliche Zeit*', 'the happy time'. On the other hand, no U-boats were sunk anywhere in June or September. After *Gladiolus*'s success, the only other sinking was of U-51, by the submarine *Cachalot* on patrol in the bay of Biscay on 20 August (although U-25 was lost to mines, and U-122 and U-102 by unknown causes, in July and August).

The U-boats' 'happy time' lasted from about August 1940 until the end of the year. This was the heyday of the 'aces'. Men like Gunther Prien, Otto Kretschmer, Joachim Schepke, Vaddi Schultz, Engelbert Endrass, Heinrich Bleichrodt and Fritz Frauenheim were submariners of great experience. Many of them had been in the Navy for years before the war. As in the First War, it was the quality of the individual U-boat captains which mattered and most of the sinkings were the handiwork of a very few men. They began with orthodox submerged attacks but, enlightened by information from the German B-Dienst decoding service, and encouraged by Doenitz to try methods he had pioneered himself, the 'aces' soon began to attack convoys on the surface, by night, using their U-boats as submersible torpedo boats. Trimmed down, their small conning towers were difficult to see and, with their high surface speed, they were almost impossible for a corvette to catch. Using such tactics, one particularly successful U-boat commander, Gunther Prien – the man who had taken U-47 into Scapa Flow in October 1939 and sunk the battleship *Royal Oak* – returned to Wilhelmshaven in July 1940, having sunk 67,000 tons of shipping.

Prien was known as the 'Bull of Scapa'. Many of the 'aces' had lucky emblems on the sides of their conning towers, just as bomber crews had on their fuselages later in the war. Heinrich Bleichrodt had a black cat, with an arched back, on U-48. Erich Topp's U-57 had two red devils, each carrying a lighted torch. One of the most famous symbols of all was a pair of gilt-painted horseshoes, on U-99, commanded by Korvetten-Kapitan Otto Kretschmer. His first command had been the small coastal Type IIB U-23, in which he did nine patrols, from September 1939 until March 1940. In June he commissioned the larger Type VIIB U-99. The type VII A, B and C U-boats of about 700 tons, with five torpedo tubes, a surfaced speed of nearly 18 knots, dived speed of 10 knots, an endurance of some 9000 miles, and a crew of forty-four, were some of the most successful operational submarines of all time and of any navy.

Kretschmer's seven patrols in U-99 with their successes and set-backs, represent the archetypal U-boat career of that stage in the war. U-99 sailed first from Kiel on 17 June, was bombed by an aircraft, and returned to Wilhelmshaven, after a stay at Bergen in Norway. By 5 July, U-99 was on patrol again in the south-western approaches. Kretschmer sank two ships sailing independently and then, on 8 July, attacked a convoy, sinking the 5758-ton *Humber Arm*.

However, a destroyer escort counter-attacked, inflicting an experience upon Kretschmer and his crew they never forgot, and certainly made the crew for ever afterwards uneasy in the presence of a convoy, U-99 was driven down to 350 feet, kept submerged for over nineteen hours, and survived a total of 127 depth-charges.

On 24 July, U-99 sailed again, this time from Lorient in northern France. Once again, Kretschmer ran up a string of successes against lone ships – *Auckland Star* on the 28th, *Clan Menzies* on the 19th and *Jamaica Progress* on the 30th. On the 31st he attacked a convoy and sank *Jersey City* before being counter-attacked by a destroyer and forced down by an aircraft. Trying to regain position on the convoy, Kretschmer was again forced down by a Sunderland, which attacked with bombs. Kretschmer surfaced forty minutes later and was again attacked by a Sunderland and forced to dive. When he surfaced an hour later, the convoy had gone.

Kretschmer was well aware of what had happened: the Sunderland had been primarily concerned with keeping him down, whilst the convoy escaped. The whole episode had been a classical exhibition of convoy tactics. The single ships had been picked off, one by one. But the convoy had passed on, with the loss of one ship.

On 2 August Kretschmer caught up with the convoy again, at a time when the escort had just left to join an in-coming convoy. That night, Kretschmer attacked on the surface, for the first time, twisting and turning inside the convoy's ranks as the ships made their emergency turns in their attempts to escape him. Kretschmer torpedoed two tankers, *Lucerna* and *Alexia*, which both blew up in spectacular fashion, but did not sink. With no torpedoes left, U-99 returned to Lorient on 8 August, flying seven horseshoe victory-pennants, having sunk an estimated 65,000 tons of shipping during the patrol.

The returning U-boat was greeted by bands playing and crowds applauding. It was a time for cheering and champagne, for radio interviews and newspaper pictures. Kretschmer was awarded the Knights Cross. He and his crew had quite forgotten that their last convoy success was achieved at a time when the escorts had withdrawn, as they had to do at about 12–15°W. This was only about 200 miles west of Ireland. But in July the convoy dispersal point was moved to 17°W and, in October, to 19°W.

From mid-August until the beginning of September four U-boats from Wilhelmshaven and five from Lorient attacked independently routed ships and, aided by the B-Dienst Service, in-coming and outward-bound convoys over a wide sea area from the Hebrides to the North Channel and off Rockall. U-57 (Topp) sank two ships from OB202 on 24 August. U-37 (Korvetten-Kapitan Oehrn) sank one ship and the sloop *Penzance* from SC1 during the night of the 24th–25th. U-48 (Bleichrodt) and U-124 (Schultz) both attacked HX65 on the 25th and each sank two ships. SC1 lost another ship to U-28 (Korvetten-Kapitan Kunhke) on the 27th. Joachim Schepke, one of the foremost aces, in U-100 sank two ships and torpedoed a third in HX66 on the

29th and another two ships from OA204, all on the 29th. HX66 was attacked again by U-32 (Korvetten-Kapitan Jenisch) on the 30th and lost another three ships. On the 30th and 31st OB205 was attacked by U-59 (Korvetten-Kapitan Matz), U-60 (Kapitan-Leutnant Schee), and U-38 (Korvetten-Kapitan Liebe) and lost one ship sunk and another three damaged. With sinkings by U-101 (Frauenheim), over 100,000 tons of merchant shipping and the sloop *Penzance* were sunk and a further 37,000 tons of shipping damaged, in this disastrous period for the Allies.

The B-Dienst decrypting service enabled Doenitz to bring off the first 'wolf pack' success against a convoy in September. Signals from the fifty-three ship slow homeward convoy SC2 were decoded on 30 August, giving away the time and place of the meeting with its escort on 6 September. On 2 September U-124 (Schultz), U-65 (Korvetten-Kapitan Von Stock-hausen), U-101 (Frauenheim) and Prien in U-47 – all four of them 'aces' – were deployed in a patrol line to intercept the convoy. By the 6th, when the leading ships were first sighted by von Stockhausen, the convoy had been joined by its escort of two sloops, *Lowestoft* (with the senior officer, Cdr A. M. Knapp) and *Scarborough*, the destroyer *Westcott* and the Canadian destroyer *Skeena*, the corvette *Periwinkle*, and two anti-submarine trawlers, *Apollo* and *Berkshire*.

Skeena and *Periwinkle* successfully drove off von Stockhausen but he returned on the night of the 6th–7th and led Prien to the scene, who sank three ships in quick succession. Sunderlands forced the U-boats down at daybreak but U-65 and U-47 attacked again in the late evening of the 8th, when Prien sank another ship. U-28 (Kuhnke) sank a fifth ship from the convoy before dawn on the 9th, but Kretschmer was driven off after daylight and failed to attack. But five ships, of 20,943 tons, had been lost from SC2.

By September 1940 westbound convoys were normally escorted as far as 17°W, after which the ships steamed on in convoy as far as possible, but unescorted, into the area known as 'the Gap', where every merchant ship was vulnerable – how vulnerable was demonstrated by a particularly shocking incident on 17 September.

The 11,000-ton City Line passenger ship *City of Benares* (Captain Landles Nicoll) had sailed from Liverpool on 13 September, in convoy, of which she was the Commodore's ship. She had some 400 passengers on board, and nearly 100 children on their way across the Atlantic under the Children's Overseas Resettlement Scheme. Under this scheme, chaired by Sir Geof-frey Shakespeare MP, Bart., Under Secretary for the Dominions, people in the Dominions offered homes to British children for the duration of the war.

The scheme began in July 1940 and prospered at first: 1530 children were sent to Canada, 577 to Australia, 202 to New Zealand and 353 to South Africa. Another 838 children were unofficially sent to the United States by the American Committee in London. But in August 1940 the Dutch ship *Vollendam* was torpedoed and sunk off the north coast of Ireland. However, the 321 children on board were saved.

City of Benares was five days out, still in convoy but now unescorted, when she was torpedoed at about ten o'clock at night by Bleichrodt in U-48. The ship was in 21° 15′W, or about 600 miles from land. There was a full gale blowing and a very heavy sea running. Another ship *Marina* was torpedoed shortly afterwards. In the darkness and rough seas, some boats capsized. Over 300 of the passengers in *City of Benares* were drowned. The Commodore, Rear Admiral E. J. G. Mackinnon DSO, was amongst those lost.

The drama and perils of a torpedoing at sea were well captured, by a young Irish girl who survived, in a broadcast made on 27 September:

> We had been five days at sea when we were torpedoed. I was sitting knitting when there was a tremendous explosion and I understand the torpedo went through the quarters where there were about ninety-seven children. We went to our posts and got into the lifeboat all right, but when our lifeboat was lowered it landed on top of another one filled with children. There was a hole knocked in the bottom of our boat, and we were left up to our waists in water. We were like that for eighteen to twenty hours and had to keep on changing from one side of the boat to the other to save it from turning turtle. One of my legs was wrapped round an iron bar to keep me from falling overboard and as a result I've lost every bit of skin on my knee but it saved me. Some of the others tied themselves in. We started off with thirty people in the boat and ended up with fourteen. On the morning after we were torpedoed seven of the people in our boat had died. Their bodies, which floated about in the water inside the boat, had to be thrown overboard. One child was on board, named Colin. He was wonderful, and I am thankful to say he got through. Once an upturned boat with four people clinging to it floated by but we couldn't do anything to help them. Although some tins of corned beef and condensed milk were on board and although we were grateful for it, it wasn't much good. Our mouths were swollen up with salt water so that we could hardly eat. Then at last we caught sight of a British destroyer. We cut out a sail with a penknife and one of the officers held it up. He was the only person in our boat strong enough to hold it. We were taken on board the destroyer and I really must pay tribute to the officers and crew. They were marvellous to us. They gave up their bunks, provided us with hot baths, clothes and excellent food, and everything possible was done for us.

The stories from *City of Benares* show vividly how chance often decided whether a man survived or not. Go in the lifeboat on the starboard side, and live. Or choose the port boat, which was never seen again. 'Passengers are the amateurs of marine warfare,' said Eric Davis, one of the *City of Benares*'s survivors. 'They are inexpert. They do not know what to do at a time when professional seamanship is the only quality that counts, and in spite of all that they were magnificent. There is no routine method of dealing with a bitter gale and a rough sea. What would you do if there were a dozen women in the water, and boats and rafts were being dashed about?'

As Mr Davis said, the passengers were magnificent. One boat had forty-six survivors in it, including six children and two of the 'escorts' sent along to look after them, Miss Mary Cornish and Father Sullivan, and thirty-two lascar seamen. Under the excellent leadership of Mr Cooper, the Fourth Officer, that boat sailed for 8 days, whilst Miss Cornish told the boys Bulldog Drummond stories and all that she could remember of *The Thirty-nine Steps*, before being sighted by a patrolling Sunderland which directed the destroyer *Anthony* to the rescue. With seven children from another boat, in the end only thirteen children and four of their escorts survived. There were no more Children's Overseas Resettlement ships.

City of Benares shocked people at home in a way which the hundreds of other ships sunk by that time of the war failed to do:

> We were a cosmopolitan company [said Mr Davis]. That torpedo did not merely strike at an English ship. It was a blow to all that was free and hopeful in Europe. My cabin companion was a Hungarian journalist whose wit and learning made the journey more stimulating than any I had ever undertaken. At table there sat with me a French aviator with great achievements to his name, and a Czech who had escaped from greater Germany. There were on board Dutch and Germans and Austrians and Poles, all of whom believed, as we believed, that freedom to think and to act and to bring up young children in security and safety are fundamental to a good world order.

Meanwhile, Kretschmer was still at sea, still picking off independents with a sniper's care (the Norwegian *Hird* on 15 September, the *Crown Arun* on the 17th) and he took part in another U-boat attack on the homeward-bound 8-knot convoy HX72 of thirty-seven ships (from the forty-one which had started out from Halifax). The ocean escort was the armed merchant cruiser *Jervis Bay*, which left the convoy according to plan at dusk on 20 September. It was most unfortunate for the convoy that it was then sighted by Prien, who only had one torpedo left after his exertions against SC2, and was far to the west reporting the weather.

The U-boats were gaining in confidence and in co-ordination with every attack. Prien shadowed the convoy for some hours and as a result of his reports Doenitz summoned U-29 (Schuhart), U-43 (Korvetten-Kapitan Ambrosius), von Stockhausen, Bleichrodt (fresh from *City of Benares*), and Endrass, who had once been Prien's First Lieutenant, in his own boat, U-46. Kretschmer arrived on the scene before any of them, and sank one ship, and damaged two others which he and Prien finished off between them with torpedoes and gunfire. Bleichrodt also attacked and sank another ship from the convoy on the 21st, before it met the escort group, which consisted of *Lowestoft* (Knapp), the destroyer *Shikari*, and the corvettes *Calendula*, *Heartsease* and *La Malouine* (which had a part-French crew).

Knapp disposed his escorts ahead and on each side of the convoy. He and his group already had a plan to follow in the event of an attack. Escorts were to search outwards, fan-wise, on the engaged side of the convoy to a distance of 5 miles, firing star-shell away from the convoy as they went. If they found nothing, they were to turn inwards, forming up 1 mile apart, and conduct an Asdic sweep back in towards the convoy's flank.

But, as Knapp's report later made clear, all this was much easer said than done. With a large convoy and a small escort it was often very difficult and sometimes actually impossible to find out quickly that the convoy had been attacked, and if so, on which side the attack had taken place. It was discovered that a torpedo exploding by no means always made the colossal noise or threw up the great plume of spray and smoke which everybody imagined.

From the reports, it seems that Knapp and his escort were out-numbered and out-classed. Kretschmer stalked the convoy, sank *Invershannon* leading the seventh column of ships, saw a destroyer astern at once turn at right angles to the convoy's course (obviously following Knapp's search and counter-attack plan) and fire star-shells. Kretschmer slipped further into the convoy to evade the lights and torpedoed another ship, *Elmbank*, almost at once.

But the main and most devastating attack was delivered by Schepke in U-100, who reached the convoy on the evening of the 21st. He hung on to the convoy for four hours, attacking several times and eventually sinking seven ships, of no less than 50,340 tons, without being attacked himself.

The convoy eventually scattered of its own accord late on the 21st. When the events on the night were analysed, some disturbing aspects of Schepke's tactics came to light. Convoys always sailed, when possible, in a large number of columns, each column containing a small number of ships. A long straggling convoy was more vulnerable than a convoy spread out over a broad front which would, with luck, march quickly over a U-boat, leaving it at best only one shot. HX72 had nine columns, numbered 1 to 9, No. 1 column being on the port hand, in the usual convention, 9 on the starboard. Ships were also individually numbered, according to their positions in their columns. Thus, ship No. 43 was in the fourth column, third ship; No. 53 likewise was the third ship, in the fifth column.

Knapp noticed that at least three of the ships sunk were torpedoed very close together, each was the second ship in a column, and they were hit within a few minutes. 'The one really remarkable fact,' he reported, 'is that three ships, *Torinia* (42), *Canonesa* (52) and *Dalcairn* (62) were torpedoed well down inside the convoy at 22.11, 22.17, and 22.26. It seems most unlikely that a submarine would keep station inside the convoy in the vicinity of 72 and take deliberate aim at the ships on her beam but results indicate that this is what happened.'

Schepke had kept inside the convoy, picking off ships as they went along. The sinkings were so close together and so unexpected that the suspicions of other ships were aroused. There were even suggestions of a 'fifth-column' or 'spy traitor' ship, fitted with submerged torpedo tubes, in column 7 which had been firing at ships to port of her!

At first it was difficult for Admiralty staff officers to credit what was happening. Captain George Creasy, Director of Anti-Submarine Division, analysed one of Kretschmer's attacks: '. . . the times at which torpedoes hit, and the position of his targets in the various columns of the convoy, convinced me that not only was Kretschmer's U-boat on the surface, but that he must have passed diagonally right through the convoy. This was something new. . . . I considered that the manoeuvre was so risky that he had done it by mistake. . . . But it was a deliberate tactic, carefully thought out and brilliantly executed.' Doenitz himself had fully described these surfaced tactics in a book published before the war. Nevertheless they caught the Admiralty utterly by surprise.

The battles in and around HX72 highlighted several other disquieting aspects of convoy warfare at that time. The merchant ships grumbled incessantly about unnecessary signalling by warships (this was an old complaint, going back to the days of sail). They also complained that, at this stage of the war, escorts were things they only read about in the newspapers. When escorts did arrive, they sometimes had a derisive welcome: 'Look at that, they've sent us a lifeboat and a raft!' was one reaction when one corvette and one trawler arrived to escort one convoy.

But the men-of-war also had legitimate grounds for complaint. *Calendula* said that HX72 was the worst convoy for showing lights he had ever escorted. The positions of U-boat sightings reported by merchantmen were sometimes so far in error (one by *Torinia* was 32 miles out) that they were counterproductive, taking the escorts away from a position where a submarine might actually be. Knapp insisted that there were no excuses for such gross navigational inaccuracies. On the night of *Torinia*'s report his own star-sights were excellent and dawn sights the next day showed that his dead-reckoning position was only 3 miles in error.

Knapp also complained justifiably about the master of *Canonesa*. The ship did eventually sink, but the Master had apparently walked off his bridge without checking that everybody was in the boats, or that all secret and confidential documents had been ditched; some were left, still open, on the bridge.

Survivors were always a tremendous problem. Particular ships were normally detailed to pick up survivors, but it remained a matter for individual masters whether or not they actually did stop to pick them up. The escorts' first priority was, of course, counter-attack, and an escort captain frequently had to decide between his own humane instincts and the overriding possibility that by stopping he might be jeopardizing even more lives. In HX72, for instance, it is quite possible that Schepke slipped into the convoy whilst *Shikari* had dropped astern to pick up survivors. In his report, Knapp suggested special ships, fitted for rescue purposes, should sail with convoys.

Kretschmer's own standing orders for U-99 give an insight into a successful U-boat commander's tactical thinking. He attached paramount importance to keeping a good lookout, not just on the surface of the sea, but also in the air. Aircraft he recognized as a deadly menace to U-boats (a fact not yet appreciated by most of the RAF or even by all of the Royal Navy). Single ships not wearing neutral flags or the Red Cross should be sunk by gunfire, to save torpedoes. Survivors were to be assisted were possible. Kretschmer reminded his own crew that they themselves would expect to be picked up.

Kretschmer was most revealing on convoys, and methods of attacking them. Daylight was for shadowing, attacks being normally too dangerous, and for working ahead into a favourable position for an attack by nightfall. Attacks should be made from the dark side when there was a moon, from the windward side, to cut down spray and wind blowing into lookouts' faces, when there was no moon. One torpedo for one ship – not salvoes; this meant getting inside the escort and firing at close range.

In view of what was to come, some of Kretschmer's instructions have an ironic flavour. During an attack 'we must not under any but the most desperate of circumstances submerge. As a general rule I alone must decide when to dive.' Kretschmer knew that a surfaced U-boat had great speed and manoeuvrability, and was virtually invisible. Dived, a U-boat at once became much slower, much less manoeuvrable, and had greatly restricted vision. Above all, it became detectable by Asdic.

October 1940 was the happiest of the 'happy time'. In that month the U-boats sank sixty-three ships, of over 352,000 tons. In one week leading up to Trafalgar Day they sank twenty-seven British merchant ships, of 137,000 tons. This amounted to a major naval defeat. Although the actions have no name or battle honour, many of the ships were sunk in Lat. 57°N and Long. 12°W, or about 250 miles from the north-western tip of Ireland, most aptly called the Bloody Foreland.

The slow convoy SC7 sailed from Sydney, Cape Breton, on 5 October with over thirty ships (the number varied, with stragglers and late-joiners) escorted by the Canadian armed yacht *Elk* and the sloop *Scarborough* (Cdr N. V. Dickinson). The commodore was Vice Admiral L. D. I. MacKinnon, in the 2962-ton *Assyrian*, leading the centre of the nine columns. *Elk* left on 7 October, leaving *Scarborough* as the sole ocean escort. The weather was fine and clear and although the convoy made plenty of smoke, it was still unmolested by the 16th when the escort was strengthened by the sloop *Fowey* (Lt Cdr R. Aubrey) and the corvette *Bluebell* (Lt Cdr R. E. Sherwood RNR). However, four ships had already straggled. One of them, *Trevisa* was sunk by U-124 that day. Another, the Greek *Aenos*, was sunk by U-38 on the 18th. (A third re-joined the convoy, and a fourth, *Eaglescliffe Hall*, pressed on independently and eventually reached the Clyde safely.)

On the 17th the convoy was sighted by Bleichrodt in U-48. He reported the convoy, but instead of shadowing, closed at once and at about 5 a.m. that morning sank two ships, *Scoresby* and *Languedoc*. U-48 was sighted, bombed and forced deep by a Sunderland, and then stalked for several hours by *Scarborough*. Dickinson spent most of the day searching for U-48 and at one time actually sighted the U-boat on the surface and gave chase. But U-48 escaped and *Scarborough* was left many miles astern of her convoy. She never regained contact, and thus one of the convoy's few escorts was absent for the whole of the actions to come. With hindsight, Dickinson might have been better advised to have merely driven Bleichrodt off and rejoined promptly.

Meanwhile, Doenitz had ordered Frauenheim, Endrass, Moehle (in U-123), Kretschmer and Schepke to form a patrol line ahead of the convoy. But soon after midnight on the 18th, the escort was strengthened by another sloop, *Leith* (Cdr R. C. Allen), and another corvette, *Heartsease* (Lt Cdr E. J. North RNR). None of these escorts formed an 'escort group'; the ships had not previously exercised together and the captains were not used to each other's tactics.

The next attack, at about 1 a.m. on the 18th, was actually by Liebe in U-38, who torpedoed *Carsbreck*. But the ship did not sink and *Heartsease* was detached to stand by her. So, a second escort was removed from the convoy screen.

The main attack on SC7 opened shortly after 8 p.m. on the 18th, when Endrass in U-46 approached from the port side of the convoy and torpedoed the 2000-ton Swedish ship *Convallaria*. At that time *Fowey* was about 5 miles astern of the convoy, as ordered by Allen who was the senior officer, searching for any shadowing U-boats. *Bluebell* was also in the station given her by Allen, on the convoy's starboard flank, while *Leith* was ahead of the convoy. Endrass had therefore struck at an undefended point.

Leith crossed to the port side and searched for some miles at right angles to the convoy's course. *Fowey*, some way astern, headed for the port side but stopped to pick up *Convallaria*'s survivors, hoping they would provide him with some information. Again, with hindsight, it would have been better had Aubrey hardened his heart and gone on. In the next six hours, until the last attack at about 3 a.m. on the 19th, the convoy lost another fifteen ships, whilst *Leith*, *Fowey* and *Bluebell* were all out of position, astern or on the flank of the convoy picking up survivors.

All five U-boats attacked. Kretschmer made one of his deadly diagonal slashes through the convoy ranks and sank six ships. Frauenheim sank three ships and torpedoed another two. Moehle sank two, Schepke sank one and shared two with Moehle. Endrass sank his second.

For the convoy it was a catastrophe. *Fiscus*, 4815 tons with a cargo of steel, disintegrated in one violent explosion and sank with all hands. *Shekatika*, 5458 tons, also loaded with steel, survived one torpedo but was sunk, whilst abandoned, by a second. Another ship carrying steel, the 6000-ton Greek *Thalia*, also sank with all hands. The 5555-ton *Sedgepool* floated long enough for some of her crew to get away but then turned her hull vertically and literally nose-dived out of their horrified sight. The Commodore's ship *Assyria* actually sighted a surfaced U-boat at about 10.30 and chased it for forty minutes before having to give up. She too was sunk in the early hours of the 19th. The Greek *Niritos* with a cargo of sulphur, which had straggled, survived and re-joined, was now torpedoed and sunk.

Leith also sighted a surfaced U-boat at about the same time as *Assyria*. *Leith* had run through the convoy and was then astern of it. After *Leith* had opened fire with star-shell, the U-boat dived. *Leith* got an Asdic echo almost at once and ran it down from 2 mile's range to 800 yards but then lost contact. *Bluebell* also joined in the hunt. But Cdr Allen decided the U-boat had escaped and *Bluebell* was ordered to pick up survivors.

By midnight, *Bluebell* had survivors from the Swedish *Gunborg*, from *Niritos* and *Empire Miniver*. *Fowey* had survivors from *Convallaria*, *Shekatika* and the Dutch *Boekolo* (who had been torpedoed whilst stopping to try and pick up survivors from *Beatus*). But although the escorts had many survivors, the convoy's ships were unguarded as *Creekirk*, the Dutch *Soesterberg*, *Empire Brigade*, *Clintonia* and the Norwegian *Sneffjeld* were all sunk, and *Blairspey* was torpedoed three times (but survived). In all, SC7 lost twenty-one ships of 79,592 tons, with *Carsbreck* and *Blairspey* badly damaged but reaching home.

By early on 20 October, the remnants of SC7 were steaming eastwards, into a rising gale. *Leith* rounded up the Norwegian *Inger Elisabeth* and the British *Corinthic*, and also found *Heartsease*, still escorting *Carsbreck*. *Fowey* meanwhile had shepherded together eight ships of SC7, but by daybreak on the 20th had lost them all again except the *Botusk*. *Scarborough* was still some 80 miles to the north-west in the rear. *Bluebell*, with four times as many survivors on board as her crew, steamed back to the Clyde, arriving on the 20th without sighting another ship.

At noon on the 20th *Leith*, having also lost touch, was quite alone. She had survivors on board from *Assyrian*, *Empire Brigade*, *Soesterberg* and from an Estonian ship called *Nora*, torpedoed from an earlier convoy. Cdr Allen signalled to C-in-C Western Approaches that he was heading for Liverpool to land survivors and that there were no ships in company.

That, in its own way, was a suitable epitaph for SC7. Although nobody could possibly criticize the humane purposes of the escorts in picking up so many survivors, arguably the convoy's better interests would have been served by staying closer to it. Certainly, Cdr Knapp's suggestion of special rescue ships had been underlined in the most dramatic manner possible.

Kretschmer, Frauenheim and Moehle had expended all their torpedoes and returned to harbour. But on the 19th Prien sighted another convoy far out to the west and reported it, bringing up Schepke, Endrass and Kuhnke (who had missed the action against SC7). The convoy was the fast (9-knot) homeward-bound Halifax convoy HX79 with forty-nine ships, disposed in nine columns.

Prien had found the convoy at its most vulnerable. The ocean escort, the armed merchant cruisers *Alaunia* and *Montclare*, had turned back the day before, and the escort group did not join until that evening, having just released the outward-bound convoy OB229. Although Prien was still shadowing and, towards evening, began to haul ahead to prepare for his attack, the other U-boats had still not taken up their attacking positions by the time the escort arrived.

The escort was unusually strong for October 1940: the destroyer *Whitehall* (with the senior officer, Lt Cdr Russell), a second destroyer *Sturdy*, the minesweeper *Jason*, corvettes *Arabis*, *Heliotrope*, *Hibiscus*, and *Coreopsis*, anti-submarine trawlers *Angle*, *Lady Elsa* and *Blackfly*, and the Dutch submarine O.14.

The main damage to HX79 was done by Prien, attacking from the starboard side, and by Endrass from the port side. Prien began, at 21.18, by sinking *Matheran* (in position 81), *Bilderdijk* (92) at 21.25, and *Uganda* (93) at 21.30. The convoy made an emergency turn to port, in poor visibility with drizzling rain, which brought Endrass into a firing position. *Shirak* (36) apparently did not take in the emergency signal and became separated. Endrass torpedoed her at 22.35, and she finally blew up with a tremendous detonation and flash of flame at 23.26.

Prien, having retired, re-loaded, and returned, set about the starboard side again, sinking *Caprella* (61) at 23.15 and *Sitala* (71) at 23.18, while Endrass began on the port side, with *Wandby* (26) at 23.22, *Ruperra* (45) at 23.23, and *La Estancia* at 23.40. In the fourth attack on the convoy, Endrass sank *Whitford Point* (42) at 01.24, and torpedoed *Athel Monarch* (75) at 01.25.

The O.14 was having a difficult time. The merchantman *Induna*, mistaking her for a U-boat, had made a very determined effort to ram her during Prien's second attack, and at 01.24, during Endrass's second attack, O.14 found herself narrowly missed by two torpedoes which passed a few feet astern.

The whole convoy was in confusion. Some of the escorts were picking up survivors, others firing star-shell and carrying out Asdic sweeps along the edges of the convoy. The *Sandanger* (95) missed one of the frequent emergency turns, became separated, and was attacked, but re-joined. By then, the whole starboard wing of the convoy had crumbled under Prien's repeated attacks. There was no ninth column left and even the eighth had dropped some distance astern. At 23.40 the Master of the *Janus* decided he had had enough, and bolted from the convoy. *Janus* was torpedoed and sunk at 04.20, some 24 miles WSW of the convoy. The last ship torpedoed was *Loch Lomond*, at 6.30 the next morning, although some torpedoed ships were still afloat (*Sitala* did not actually break up and sink until 7 a.m. on 22 October).

Later analysis showed that Prien had pressed in to very close range and picked off his targets one by one. Or it was thought possible that he had steamed parallel to the convoy for some distance and fired 90°-angled shots. Whichever method he had used, he had coolly fired, withdrawn to re-load, and pressed close in again. Endrass, to port, had fired salvoes of two torpedoes on at least two occasions, from a greater range than Prien, and 'browned' the convoy.

A jubilant German broadcast later claimed eight ships for Prien and nine for Endrass, for a total of over 110,000 tons sunk. It was not quite that bad, but it was still bad enough. HX79 had lost twelve ships of 75,069 tons, with the large 8995-ton tanker *Athel Monarch* torpedoed but surviving. Prien had sunk six, Endrass had hit seven (including *Athel Monarch*).

The U-boats were not alone. The Luftwaffe played an increasing part in the offensive against shipping from the summer of 1940 onwards. In August, the first squadron of long-range four-engined Focke Wulfe FW.200 Kondor bomber/reconnaissance aircraft began to operate from an airfield at Merignac, near Bordeaux. On 26 August, four Heinkel HE115 seaplanes of No. 506 Kustenfliegergruppe (Coastal Air Wing) flying from Stavanger attacked HX65 off Kinnaird Head, and torpedoed and sank the 11,445-ton *Remuera*. The same day, eight Junkers JU88s of the same group bombed the 5027-ton *Cape York* and damaged her so badly she was later abandoned and sank. The Kondors also moved up to Stavanger late in August, and aircraft sank fifteen ships of 53,283 tons in that month. On 26 October a Kondor of Kampfgeschwader 40, piloted by Leutnant Jope, bombed and hit the giant 42,348-ton liner *Empress of Britain* about 90 miles NW of Donegal Bay. Though badly damaged and on fire, the ship was taken in tow and might have reached port but on the 28th she was torpedoed by U-32 (Kapitan-Leutnant Hans Jenisch) and sank about 60 miles further north, off the Bloody Foreland.

In sharp contrast to the sinkings by the U-boats in August, September and October was the marked lack of success against the U-boats themselves. There were no more sinkings by escorts in July, after *Gladiolus* and 10 Squadron had dispatched U-26 on the 1st. No U-boats were sunk by escorts in August. No U-boats were sunk through any cause at all in September. The first success in October did not come until the end of the month, when the destroyers *Harvester* and *Highlander* revenged the *Empress of Britain* by sinking U-32 when Jenisch was attacking a convoy on the 30th.

The war around the convoys of 1941 bore a strong resemblance to the events of the previous war. It was still a contest between escort and submarine, taking place along many of the same convoy routes. Some convoys even had the same distinguishing serial letters, such as OB and HX. For the Allies, the new device of Asdic was being steadily improved although it did not have a reliable effective range of much more than a mile, except in ideal conditions; Asdic generally indicated a target's range and bearing, but only gave an estimation of depth, and its performance was affected by false echoes and by variations of temperature and density in the sea-water. For the Germans, the U-boats were larger, faster and better-armed than their predecessors of 1918 and they had the priceless advantage of wireless communications, to direct each other on to their targets. The Type VII U-boat, in particular, was proving a superb instrument for a war against commerce – arguably the best submarine for this purpose ever designed.

Chapter Twelve

'Every day when they met, those few who knew looked at one another,' wrote Mr Churchill of this stage of war at sea. 'One understands the diver deep below the surface of the sea, dependent from minute to minute upon his air-pipe. What would he feel if he could see a growing shoal of sharks biting at it? All the more where there was no possibility of his being hauled to the surface! For us there was no surface.' In the vivid phrases of this extended metaphor, Mr Churchill asked what could the sharks do to the air-pipe and how could the diver ward them off or destroy them?

In fact, there was a great deal that could be done. There was, first, the growing realization that the Atlantic battle was no place for half-measures and second-raters. The U-boats were among the most formidable opponents the Navy had ever encountered. Yet, as Commander Peter Gretton, himself an escort commander, wrote:

> For the first few years of the war, the Home and Mediterranean Fleets got all the best officers and it was considered somewhat unfashionable to be in the Western Approaches Command, which, as a result, received many of the failures from Scapa Flow, many retired officers and many incompetents. There were a few young lieutenants in their first commands and a very few more senior officers to support the reserves who were such splendid material, but the good regulars were desperately few.

There was a desperate need not only for better captains but for better crews and a thorough training for everyone. Pre-war anti-submarine warfare training had been carried out under the aegis of the shore establishment HMS *Osprey* at Portland. But after the fall of France and with the swelling number of small ships commissioning out of the building yards, training was moved to Scotland, to establishments at Dunoon, and at Campbeltown.

On 12 July 1940, Vice Admiral Gilbert ('Monkey') Stephenson, who had already served as a convoy commodore, commissioned HMS *Western Isles* (actually a large and extremely ugly Belgian passenger steamer anchored in Tobermory Bay) as Commodore Western Isles. There he and his staff carried out a short (normally two- to four-week) and very sharp 'work-up' course for all Asdic-fitted ships of frigate size and below.

Most of the ships were new from the builders, and almost all the crews had never been to sea before and hardly knew their bows from their stern. Under Monkey Stephenson's urging – and very violent urging it sometimes was – the officers and ships' companies learned to work their ships, fire their guns, put out fires, rescue survivors, and the rudiments of locating and tracking a submarine. Life at Tobermory was unpredictable and never dull. Monkey or his staff were likely to descend upon a ship at any hour of day or night, with some order or exercise which had never occurred to her ship's company before.

One famous story perfectly illustrates Monkey Stephenson's methods and his personality. Boarding a brand-new corvette for the first time, Admiral Stephenson suddenly seized his cap and flung it down upon the deck. 'That's a *bomb*!' he roared at the startled gangway staff. 'That's a *live* bomb! What are you going to do about it?' Whereupon an extremely quick-witted sailor at once stepped forward and swiftly kicked the admiral's gold-braided cap over the side into the water. Monkey glared bleakly at his floating cap for a few seconds. Then, 'That's a survivor!' he roared again. 'He's *drowning*! Jump over the side and rescue him!'

Another improvement was the escort group system, initiated by C-in-C Western Approaches in a signal of 12 October 1940. Encouraged by a forecast that sixty additional destroyers would be available to Western Approaches Command by 1 November (the actual number by that date was two), the first of eight groups sailed on 21 October. It consisted of two destroyers, two corvettes and a sloop. Many escort groups were groups only in name. The composition of the group constantly changed due to refits, boiler cleans, enemy losses, and diversions to other duties. Nevertheless it did provide some sort of corporate entity, some sense of belonging, similar to a destroyer flotilla. The escort commanders at least had a better chance of knowing each personally, of exercising together previously, of discussing tactics and plans over a glass of gin in harbour. The superbly drilled and deadly hunting groups which went to sea later in the war had their origins in these early groups of October 1940.

The convoy disasters of October spurred the Defence Committee to order more escort vessels to be taken from anti-invasion patrols and put back to their proper duty of convoy escort. It was also decided to press for an efficient radar set for escorts and for aircraft, for a radio-telephone link between aircraft and escorts, and for much more use of aerial depth-charges. It was also decided to try a system of routing convoys along narrow ocean channels, or 'tram lines'.

Bases in Iceland were also pressed forward. The first detachments of troops had arrived in Iceland in May, and were reinforced by Canadians in June. An anti-submarine boom was begun in Hvalfiord, just north of Reykjavik, which was to be the main naval base, in July. On 27 August the first Coastal Command base was established in Iceland, the first squadron flying obsolescent Fairey Battle aircraft. Coastal command was still very short of aircraft, of trained crews, proper anti-submarine weapons, and of suitable bases in the north-west of the United Kingdom. From a strength of 170 aircraft at the beginning of the war, Coastal Command had only risen to 226 aircraft by September 1940. Their first operational duty until well into 1941, remained anti-invasion patrols; anti-U-boat patrols in support of convoys were still well down the list of priorities.

Mr Churchill had foreseen the shortage of escorts. He knew that new construction would provide more ships in 1941. Meantime the country needed ships *now*, in 1940. On 15 May he sent a telegram to President Roosevelt asking for the loan of 'forty or fifty of your older destroyers to bridge the gap between what we have now and the large new construction we put in hand at the beginning of the war'. On 31 July he was urging 'Mr President, with great respect I must tell you that in the long history of the world this is a thing to do *now*.' The agreement was finally signed on 5 September 1940. In exchange for fifty destroyers, the United States was granted ninety-nine-year leases of naval and air bases in Newfoundland, Bermuda, the Bahamas, Jamaica, Antigua, St Lucia, Trinidad and British Guiana.

The destroyers were already being brought forward from reserve by the time the agreement was signed. The first British crews arrived to take over their new charges in October. Although Mr Churchill told the House of Commons there 'will be no delay in bringing the American destroyers into active service' and indeed forty of them were brought across the Atlantic by December 1940, the majority of the destroyers were not in service until the spring of 1941.

The *Town* class (they were renamed, with the names of towns common to the United Kingdom and the United States) were all four funnelled ships, dating from the 1914–18 war and kept in a state of preservation since. They aroused mixed feelings in this country (inspiring one film, with the significant title *The Gift Horse*). Admiral Tovey thought 'they were the worst destroyers I had ever seen . . . the price paid for them was scandalous'. But Admiral Cunningham thought them 'worth their weight in gold'. Admiral Vian merely commented that they were 'some sort of deterrent'.

Certainly the four-stackers had their idiosyncrasies. Their turning circle was as large as a battle cruiser's and their steering engines were operated by wires running in the open, down from the bridge, and along the upperdeck. They had handling quirks, giving their crews some exciting moments. On one occasion *Chesterfield* rammed *Churchill* in the stern, withdrew as though apologetically, and then rammed her again in the same spot. In what was known as the 'Newmarket Stakes', *Newmarket*'s main manoeuvring valve jammed open during a basin trial. She surged ahead into a dockyard wall carrying two neighbours with her. In all, twelve of the *Towns* were involved in collisions with friendly ships.

However, during 1941 the four-stackers made up between a fifth and a quarter of all the vessels available for convoy escort. Eventually they assisted in the destruction of five U-boats. Three of them were lost to enemy action. But perhaps their chief service to this country was political. In this sense they were priceless. They were visible symbols of a closer Anglo-American relationship, tokens of an unofficial alliance.

In July 1940, one of the first British-made war films of the Second World War opened at the New Gallery in Regent Street, in London's West End. Produced by Michael Balcon and directed by Pen Tennyson, it was called *Convoy* and starred Clive Brooks as the Captain of the cruiser *Apollo*, Judy Campbell as his wife, and John Clements as one of the officers, Lieutenant Cranford. There were also several excellent character cameo parts for which Ealing Studios became famous, such as Edward Chapman playing Captain Eckersley of the tramp steamer *Seaflower*, with Polish refugees on board, assuring his Mate (Edward Rigby) with some vehemence that he 'was not going to be chivvied about in convoy'.

The centre-piece of the film was an action in which Clive Brooks fought the convoy through against submarines and the attentions of a *Deutschland* class pocket battleship, while John Clements died a hero's death. The film crew made three trips to sea in actual convoys, and the location shots were very skilfully spliced into studio scenes. The critics were not over-impressed. Ivor Brown of the *Illustrated London News* called it 'Ealing plus deep-sea production with a certain monotony about so much bombardment'. But the film had a popular success and, only a few months later, something very like it actually happened.

The 12,000-ton German pocket battleship *Admiral Scheer* (Kapitan zur Sëe Theodor Krancke) sailed from the Baltic for the Kiel Canal on 23 October 1940. She took her final departure from Brunsbüttel on the 27th and sailed northwards, undetected by air reconnaissance or by intelligence. At that time air patrols were still concentrating upon anti-invasion searches and none of the North Sea patrols sighted *Scheer*. No regular search patrols were being flown from Iceland either and *Admiral Scheer* was still undetected when she passed through the Denmark Strait and into the open Atlantic on 31 October.

Nothing was seen or heard of *Scheer* until 5 November, when she caught and sank the independent British refrigerator ship *Mopan*, which did not broadcast a warning signal. Meanwhile, *Scheer*'s Arado reconnaissance seaplane had reported ships to the south. Shortly after three o'clock smoke was sighted on the southern horizon.

The homeward-bound convoy HX84 of thirty-eight ships, including ten loaded tankers, had sailed from Halifax on 28 October. The sole ocean escort was the 14,000-ton ex-Aberdeen and Commonwealth Line ship HMS *Jervis Bay*, which had been converted into an armed merchant cruiser, carrying seven 6-inch guns. By the afternoon of 5 November, the thirty-seven ships still with the convoy (the Polish *Morska Wola* had straggled, but did reach harbour safely in the end) were steaming in nine columns, with the Commodore's ship *Cornish City* leading the fifth column and *Jervis Bay* (Captain E. S. F. Fegen) in the centre of the convoy, between the fourth and fifth columns.

It was a fine late autumn afternoon, with a little sunshine, a smooth sea and good visibility. At about 3.40 p.m. the *Rangitiki*, leading the sixth column, reported smoke bearing NE. At 5 p.m. the *Empire Penguin*, leading the fourth column, signalled that she had sighted a ship bearing almost due north, heading towards the convoy. The ship had also been sighted from *Jervis Bay*, which signalled to the Admiralty six minutes later, giving the strange vessel's bearing, range, course and position. Fegen also warned the convoy to be prepared to scatter.

In the Standard Oil tanker *San Demetrio*, Second Officer Hawkins had just come off the afternoon watch and was walking aft to the gun when he 'sighted the topmast of a vessel on the port beam. Through binoculars I recognized it as a warship, and about five minutes afterwards the armed merchant cruiser *Jervis Bay* turned to port and opened fire. At the same time the scatter signal was given.'

Scheer had steadily closed the convoy and at 5.10 p.m. opened fire at a range of about 17,000 yards, her first two salvoes pitching in the middle of the convoy lanes. *Jervis Bay*'s guns, made when Queen Victoria was on the throne, had a problematical range of only about 10,000 yards, and it was thus most unlikely that *Jervis Bay* would ever get within range of the enemy. Nevertheless, Fegen hauled out of line and headed straight for *Scheer*, opening fire as *Jervis Bay* cleared the leading ship in the nearest column. Hawkins, watching from *San Demetrio*, said, 'I can only describe the way the *Jervis Bay* engaged that ship as magnificent. She just turned away and engaged the ship as though she was protecting a brood of little chickens from a cat coming over the fence.' Behind *Jervis Bay*, the convoy began to scatter to starboard under orders from the Commodore, laying a covering smoke screen from floats dropped as the ships retired.

The Chief Wireless Officer of *Rangitiki* was playing table tennis when the action began:

We'd won a set and were just on the final set when there were certain noises. The Second Officer looked out from the veranda cafe and said, 'Oh they're practising emergency night effects.' Well, when the next bang went off we realized it wasn't in fun. I beat the world speed record along 'A' deck and up to my wireless office. I got there and after a few minutes the Captain was on the phone and said we were being attacked by a raider of the *Graf Spee* type, and this was slung out [on W/T]. The only thing that I am regretting is that this particular set of ours not only reached England but also reached America, rather alarming our wives and babies, and that sort of thing. But anyway, it got out, after that, well, we saw flashes in the air and just kept them astern and ran away from them. Thanks to the *Jervis Bay*, which put up a jolly good scrap against absolutely impossible odds, well, I'm able to tell you this.

Admiral Scheer hit *Jervis Bay*, whose first salvoes fell well short, with her third or fourth salvo. From then on, it was not a fight but a massacre. *Jervis Bay* was hit first amidships, then on the bridge, setting it on fire, and shattering Fegen's right arm. *Jervis Bay*'s fire control, range-finder, steering gear and wireless were all put out of action. Fegen moved for a time to the after-bridge, and then returned to the remains of the fore-bridge. After that, as one of his officers said, 'We did not see him again'.

Jervis Bay was hit repeatedly on her superstructure, her hull was holed in several places, and major fires were raging below. However, her guns continued to fire for some time. Able Seaman Henry Lane, a London taxi-driver in civilian life, was serving one gun

which received a direct hit from the Nazi's heavy shells after the fight had been going on for half an hour or so. There was an ear-splitting crash, and the whole gun was blown out to sea. The entire crew was lifted bodily and thrown overboard. I was the only one to escape. The ship was by now practically a blazing inferno. The fires could have been put out, perhaps, but the engine-room had been hit and we could get no water. Ropes, cordite cases, and cordite itself were lying scattered about the deck, directly in the path of the flames. New fires that started among this stuff we did our best to stamp out. Burning ropes and blazing wood from the decks we had to throw overboard with our bare hands. Yet all the time those of our guns still in action continued to bang away at the raider. Our steering gear went, our decks were awash, but still our guns kept firing, knowing that the longer we could engage the enemy the better was the chance the convoy had of escaping.

In the midst of the action *Jervis Bay*'s ensign was shot away and, in an episode of pure Elizabethan drama worthy of Hakluyt, a sailor climbed the shattered flagstaff and nailed another in place which still flew as *Jervis Bay* went down. She was last seen by the convoy at about 7 p.m., burning but still afloat. She did not finally sink until almost 8 p.m., nearly three hours after *Scheer*'s first salvoes.

One passenger, a Dr Firth, had a good view of the action from *Rangitiki*:

We were in mid-Atlantic, with the convoy all around us and the *Jervis Bay* close on our port side. It was a perfect day, bright and sunny, with a lovely calm sea, so lovely that we were all saying, in a joking kind of way, that it ought to be a naval holiday. We had the usual submarine lookouts. I had done my watch in the afternoon. I was doing some work in the lounge just after five o'clock when I heard two sharp cracks.

I didn't bother very much, because the *Jervis Bay* had been doing a bit of anti-aircraft practice in the morning. But I went out on deck to have a look. Then I saw bursts in the water, between us and the *Jervis Bay*. I thought for a second it must be an air attack, though I couldn't think why. Then a steward standing beside me said, 'Good Lord, it's a naval action!' And then away beyond the convoy I saw the grey shape of the raider and I knew we were in for something. Then there were two more yellow flashes as the raider fired again.

By this time the *Jervis Bay* had got up speed and was drawing ahead and turning out to meet the enemy. She fired, but her shells fell short. All the time she was trying to get closer. People beside me were shouting, 'Go at him, boy!', 'Give it to him!', 'That's the stuff!' Then the raider fired again. This time she scored a hit. The *Jervis Bay* seemed to slow down, but she went on firing. Once, when there was a dark crimson flash from the raider, not at all like the yellow flashes of her early salvoes, we thought she had got it and one of the crew shouted, 'Good boy, he's hit the raider!' But from what we knew afterwards it couldn't have been.

Soon after that, there was a terrific explosion on the *Jervis Bay*. An enormous spout of flame, almost blue-crimson in colour, and a huge column of black smoke. We knew then it was a hopeless fight. It was only a matter of time. What had happened so far had seemed like an hour but it was only about ten minutes.

Then I turned to go below, where my wife and most of the others were. We'd had our instructions for an emergency. But before doing so I had a look over the other side. The convoy had been turning away from the raider with all the speed they could and some of the ships had dropped smoke screens. The wind was just right for these and they certainly helped to save the *Rangitiki* and some of the others.'

After *Jervis Bay*, *Admiral Scheer* turned to fire on *Rangitiki*:

We could hear the shell bursts uncomfortably close [said Dr Firth]. Suddenly there was one terrific bang and a thud which shook the whole ship. It was on the side we were so we all moved over to the port alleyway. We guessed it wouldn't be much use if the next one got us, but it might have given us just a bit of extra chance. This was the shell which splashed the bridge and left some of its bits on the deck. Then we waited for the next one. Those of us who had seen the *Jervis Bay* knew how good the enemy's gunnery was and there wasn't much doubt of what would happen. But the *next* shot didn't come! It was a strain just waiting. But we sang 'Roll out the barrel', and some other songs, and we got along all right. We could feel the engines throbbing. We knew that dusk was coming on and we hoped for the best. Every now and then some of us went on deck. We could see far astern of us the crimson glow of the shattered *Jervis Bay* and the flashes of firing from her and the raider and also from one or two other ships which were being attacked. We knew that we, like the other ships of the convoy, were still very much at the raider's mercy. She had twice our speed. But the darkness helped us and, as you know, nearly all of the convoy escaped.

There were three things that saved the convoy. The first was that the wind was just right for the smoke screens. The second was the fact that, still to be satisfactorily explained, why the raider attacked so late in the day. And the third was the courage of the men of the *Jervis Bay*. The action of the *Jervis Bay* was a most moving sight. After the first salvo, they *knew* what was in front of them. But they ran up their battle flag and went straight for the enemy. They were outranged, out-speeded, no armour, and guns only a little more than half the calibre of what they had to face. I am not ashamed to admit that for the next few days when I thought of that superb response to duty, in the face of certain destruction, I couldn't stop my eyes from filling with tears.

The precious delay caused by *Jervis Bay* saved the convoy, whose ships had scattered and were steaming separately south-east, south and west. *Scheer* steered east and then south to skirt the smoke-screen, but most of the ships escaped. In *Cornish City* the Commodore heard several heavy explosions and saw gun-flashes to the south, in the moonlight, until about 10.30 p.m.

In the end, *Scheer* sank the *Beaverford*, *Maidan*, *Trewellard*, *Kenbane Head*, and *Fresno City* from the convoy, totalling 33,331 tons. The Swedish *Vingaland* escaped but was bombed by aircraft, set on fire and abandoned three days later.

The tanker *San Demetrio* had been hit by *Scheer*'s earlier salvoes, set on fire and abandoned by her crew, who left in three lifeboats. Next day, the men in the lifeboat commanded by Mr Hawkins sighted a ship to leeward, on fire and drifting. They closed her and found she was their own *San Demetrio*, still afloat. They re-boarded her, put out most of the fires, raised steam, rigged emergency steering gear and, in a remarkable saga of the sea, took *San Demetrio* to the coast of Ireland under her own power; escorted by a warship, she eventually reached the Clyde.

Including *San Demetrio*, thirty-one ships of HX84 escaped, three of them returning to Canada and the rest reaching the United Kingdom. The Swedish *Stureholm* picked up sixty-eight of *Jervis Bay*'s survivors (of a total complement of 254 officers and men: from the Royal Navy and Royal Canadian Navy, some 'hostilities-only' men and some from the merchant navy). Three were already dead when they were picked up. Fegen went down with his ship.

Jervis Bay's heroic defence of her convoy thrilled the free world. It became one of the most famous sea stories of all time, told and re-told, celebrated in prose, verse and on film. 'There she rode, like a hero,' said Captain Olander of *Stureholm*. 'If ever a ship deserved a VC,' said *The Times*, 'that ship is surely the *Jervis Bay*.'

Fegen himself became the first and greatest convoy hero of the war. King

George VI himself decided to award him a posthumous Victoria Cross, which was announced on 19 November and published in the *London Gazette* on the 22nd. Tributes to him were sent from all over the world. One appeared in *The Times* on 19 November under the initials A.S.W.A., actually those of Captain Augustus Agar, himself a VC and Fegen's old captain in the cruiser *Emerald* in 1939: 'Deeds like his will live and shine so long as history is written, while those of us who live can only envy them the manner of their death.'

But the tribute which Fegen himself would most have appreciated also appeared in *The Times*:

> Sir, I avail myself of this opportunity to write to you after safe arrival in this country on behalf of myself and the crew of the Polish steamer *Puck*, the smallest of all which took part in the recent convoy from Canada, which was shelled by a German raider of the *Graf Spee* class on 5 November, to express our grateful thanks through the columns of *The Times* for the way in which the *Jervis Bay* defended us to the last. The fine example set to us by the British crew of this ship, who through their sacrifice saved a lot of valuable tonnage and very valuable cargo, filled us with deep admiration and made us their spiritual debtors. This fresh example of British valour on the high seas is sufficient to give renewed confidence in the British Navy and in British victory.
>
> On behalf of my crew and myself I should like to say how much we commiserate with the relatives and friends of the courageous crew of the *Jervis Bay* who lost their lives in this historic action, but who may be proud for the role they have played in the fight for freedom.
> I am, Sir, your obedient servant,
> J. Piekarski.

(*Puck* was in fact only 1065 tons, and her cargo was listed as '329 standards of spoolwood'.)

The Atlantic convoy schedules were seriously disrupted by *Admiral Scheer*'s attack on HX84. Two HX convoys were recalled to Halifax. Normal traffic was not resumed until 17 November when HX89 sailed. *Scheer* meanwhile headed for the south Atlantic, sinking the British *Port Hobart* off Bermuda on 24 November and *Tribesman* on 1 December. Although a number of warships tried to find her, the distances were too great; apart from a sighting by an aircraft from the cruiser *Glasgow* on 22 February 1941, Admiral Scheer was undetected. After a cruise of five months, she returned to Kiel on 1 April, having sunk *Jervis Bay* and sixteen ships of 99,059 tons. She had steamed 46,419 miles since leaving in October.

In spite of *Jervis Bay*'s heroic self-sacrifice, the subject of the employment of such armed merchant cruisers, whether they should patrol or convoy, was still under lively debate in November 1940. In a minute which, with hindsight, can only be read now with disbelief, Captain Cecil Harcourt, the Director of the Operations Division (Home) wrote on the 22nd: 'What is to be decided is which is the more important, (i), the offensive work of throttling the enemy's trade, for which the Northern and Western patrols are an essential order, or, (ii) the defensive task of escorting these SC convoys across the Atlantic?' Here, yet again, was the old discredited notion that convoys were *defensive*.

'It is considered,' Captain Harcourt blithely went on, 'that the offensive task is the more important, and that therefore the SC convoys should be run without ocean escort but with the Commodore's ship supplied with sufficient staff and cyphers to enable good communications to be maintained.' The matter actually went to the Vice Chief of Naval Staff, Admiral Tom Phillips, who ruled that two armed merchant cruisers should be transferred to escort duties with SC convoys.

Even the U-boat commanders themselves misunderstood important aspects of convoy warfare. Otto Kretschmer and the other aces were by now highly decorated officers. On 4 November, Kretschmer learned that he had been awarded Oak Leaves to his Knight's Cross, and he was to go to Berlin to receive them from the Führer's own hands.

In his brief conversation with Hitler, Kretschmer urged for more aerial reconnaissance of convoys, on a much wider scale. He suggested some means of homing U-boats on to convoys by means of a radio signal transmitted by the sighting aircraft. He said that if only workers in factories realized that the more U-boats they could build, the more night surface-attacks could be carried out, and the more wolf-packs could be formed, to wipe out convoys, or at least make the convoy system too expensive to maintain. At the moment, Kretschmer explained, 'the British obligingly gather their ships together in large numbers for us to attack. It saves us searching the high seas for lone ships.' This was a complete misreading of the principles of convoys. Convoys did *not* bring targets obligingly together for an attack, as Kretschmer himself was to find out.

Misunderstanding about convoy extended to the highest political levels, and not only on the Axis side. By November 1940 the numbers of ships sunk, both in and out of convoy, threatened to reduce Britain's imports to below the quantity needed to maintain the war effort. In working out their figures of losses, government statisticians always included ships as 'lost in convoy' all those which had started out in convoy, even though they were actually straggling at the time they were sunk. This might have been just a statistical quirk or idiosyncrasy. But it had a deadly effect upon opinion, as it appeared to show that convoys were less safe than they really were.

Armed with the latest figures of shipping losses, an executive body was set up to solve the threatened shortage of supplies. Professor Lindemann, later Lord Cherwell, the Prime Minister's chief scientific adviser, visited the Admiralty Trade Division to see how the situation could be improved. 'His recommendation, which horrified us,' wrote Cdr G. N. Brewer, Convoy Planning Officer in the Division at the time, 'was that ships of 12 knots and over should be sailed independently instead of the lower limit of 15 knots as hitherto. I used to pray at nights that he would be run over by a bus.'

Lindemann's object, which was commendable enough, was to reduce the 'delays due to convoy' by enabling slower, and therefore considerably more, ships to sail independently. But this decision flew in the face of all experience from the First World War. Ships sailing independently might indeed make individually quicker round voyages than ships in convoy – but only if they survived. However, the Cabinet decided that the upper speed limit should be reduced from 15 to 12 knots, by which time the figures had shown, once again and just as remorselessly, the dangers of sailing independently. On the Freetown route, for example, between November 1940 and May 1941, 15.4 per cent of independent ships were lost on the round trip compared with 5.5 per cent lost from convoys. On the Halifax route, in the same period, 13.8 per cent of independents were lost, but only 5.8 per cent in convoy. Once more the same lesson had to be learned.

Very bad weather in December 1940 subdued the U-boats, but convoy HX90 suffered five attacks by four U-boats on 1 and 2 December. The convoy originally had forty-one ships, in eleven columns, but two ships put back and nine were separated during a gale. Only thirty ships remained in nine columns by 1 December, when the sole ocean escort, the armed merchant cruiser HMS *Laconia*, left at 17.00.

Unfortunately the convoy was sighted by U-101 (Korvetten-Kapitan Mengersen) shortly after *Laconia* left and the first attack, by U-101, took place shortly after 8 p.m., in good visibility due to the Northern lights. Mengersen torpedoed two ships, *Appalachee* and *Loch Ranza*, just astern of her, but *Loch Ranza* survived. A third ship, *Ville d'Arlon*, straggled in the early hours of the 2nd and was lost.

Mengersen's sighting report summoned Prien, Kretschmer and Luth in U-43. From now onwards, HX90 suffered the classic pattern of wolf-pack attacks, with U-boats rising to attack, retiring to re-load, and attacking again, while surfaced U-boats slipped through the lanes of ships unmolested, because *Laconia* had left and the escort group had not yet joined.

The next on the scene was U-47. Prien attacked at 3.20 a.m. on the 2nd, sinking *Lady Glanely* and torpedoing the tanker *Conch* just astern of her. *Dunsley*, in the same column astern of *Conch*, actually saw U-47 on the surface and opened fire. U-47 fired back briefly before disappearing into the darkness.

At 5.15 Mengersen was back and in a series of swift attacks sank *Kavak*, and *Tasso* and put one torpedo into *Goodleigh*. U-101 was also sighted by *Penrose*. Meanwhile, Kretschmer had been searching for the convoy to the north. On the morning of the 2nd he sighted the armed merchant cruiser *Forfar*, on her way to join another convoy. Kretschmer had already sunk two other armed merchant cruisers, *Laurentic* and *Patroclus*, in quick succession in November. He had to fire four torpedoes at *Forfar*, over a period of an hour between 3.50 and 4.50 a.m. before she finally sank. Kretschmer later finished off *Conch* and *Goodleigh* (who received three torpedoes before sinking).

The sloop *Folkestone* joined at 12.30 on 2 December and the corvette *Gentian* at tea-time, having just left the outward-bound convoy OB251. Nevertheless, U-94 (Kapitan-Leutnant Kuppisch) attacked that afternoon and sank *Stirlingshire* and *Wilhelmina* from the starboard columns of the convoy.

While Prien, Mengersen and Kuppisch attended to HX90, Luth had found OB251, whose escort had left at 7 p.m. on the 1st. In one attack on the 2nd U-43 sank *Victor Ross*, a large tanker of 12,000 tons, and *Pacific President*. *Victoria City*, the Vice Commodore's ship from HX90, became separated from her convoy and was never seen again. Her independent route (allocated to every ship to follow should she ever become separated) would have taken her across the area where Luth was operating, and very probably *Victoria City* was sunk by U-43. But nothing more was ever heard from her.

Another escort, the destroyer *Viscount*, also from OB251, joined on the morning of 3 December. But HX90's troubles were not over. *W. Hendrik* had straggled two miles astern of the convoy, where Focke-Wulfe aircraft found her at 10 a.m. that morning and sank her with bombs. A total of eleven ships of nearly 60,000 tons were lost from HX90, plus *Forfar* of 16,000 tons, and also the two ships of 20,000 tons from OB251.

After HX90, the B-Dienst decoding system enabled Doenitz to direct Luth, Salman in U-52, Kuppisch and Kretschmer to search for the slow in-coming convoy SC13. But they failed to find it. Only *Argo*, one of the most enterprising and successful of the generally ineffective Italian U-boats which had joined the battle in the Atlantic, found and sank *Silverpine* from that convoy on 5 December. *Argo* (Korvetten-Kapitan Crepas) had also torpedoed the Canadian destroyer *Saguenay* in an attack on HG47 on 1 December.

On 18 December, in the south Atlantic, *Admiral Scheer* captured the British *Duquesa*, and allowed her to broadcast a radio signal reporting a raider. This was no oversight on Krancke's part, but a deliberate attempt to divert attention away from the north Atlantic where the cruiser *Admiral Hipper* (Kapitan zur Sëe Meisel) was beginning her first sortie.

Hipper had sailed before, in September, but engine defects had forced her to turn back. She had been sighted by photographic reconnaissance at Brunsbüttel on 29 November, but no significance had been paid to her presence and she sailed undetected the next day. After lurking for some time in the Norwegian Leads until bad weather stopped flying, she broke out through the Denmark Straits, still undetected, on the night of 6–7 December.

Unlike *Scheer*, who had been ordered to concentrate upon independently routed shipping, *Hipper*'s task was to attack convoys. She searched first along the Halifax route unsuccessfully and then turned south to the Sierra Leone route. In general, *Hipper*'s cruise was much less effective than *Scheer*'s. She was not so well served by the B-Dienst service, and the ship herself had a low endurance and seemed prone to defects.

After an entirely fruitless cruise, *Hipper* finally encountered a convoy some 700 miles west of Finisterre, on Christmas Eve. It was WS5A (the initials supposed to represent 'Winston Specials'), a fast troop convoy of twenty ships bound for the Middle East via the Cape of Good Hope, but also including five ships destined for Operation Excess in the Mediterranean (to pass supplies eastward from Gibraltar to Malta and the Piraeus.) The convoy was strongly escorted by the cruisers *Berwick*, *Bonaventure* and *Dunedin*, with two aircraft carriers, *Furious* and *Argus*, which had aircraft in packing cases, to be assembled at Takoradi and flown across Africa to Egypt.

Hipper shadowed all night and approached the convoy at dawn on Christmas Day. There was a brief engagement between *Hipper* and *Berwick* in which *Berwick* was slightly damaged by two hits. *Bonaventure* opened fire at 8.49 a.m. and expended a prodigious amount of her main armament ammunition, firing 438 rounds before she broke off at 9.56. *Hipper* also broke away and the action ceased, Meisel having decided the convoy was too strongly protected. One ship *Jumna* was sunk, with the loss of yet another convoy commodore, Rear Admiral H. B. Maltby. *Empire Trooper* and another ship were damaged.

The losses could have been much more serious. At one point, both *Furious* and *Argus* were steaming westwards together, in low visibility and totally unescorted, to look for *Hipper*. *Furious* had torpedoes but no Swordfish. *Argus* had two Swordfish and no torpedoes. So the Swordfish were flown to *Furious* where, with the ship's outfit of two Skuas, *Furious*'s Captain considered his ship ready to engage.

This opinion was not shared by *Argus*, who thought it very foolish to go looking for a heavy cruiser in thick weather, nor by *Furious*'s Navigating Officer: 'I knew the old ship too well to imagine that even she could rise to the occasion sufficiently to represent a battle cruiser in a gun action at close range,' he wrote. 'The difficulty was to ensure that one was really viewing the matter objectively and not being swayed by the conscious or subconscious thought that I myself was among the many who might be blown up at short notice if we made contact.' However, *Furious* pressed on for some three hours, in visibility never better than 300 or 400 yards, and to ever more discouraging hints from *Argus*, until the Admiralty finally signalled directly to abandon the operation. 'And so I live to tell the tale,' wrote Jenkins, 'one of anti-climax, I fear.' Meanwhile the convoy had scattered somewhat prematurely, and had difficulty in re-forming. It was as well for everybody concerned that the affair did end in anti-climax. *Hipper* herself returned to Brest on 27 December, the first major German warship to make use of a French port.

Chapter Thirteen

On 7 January 1941, reputedly at a time when Hermann Goering was away on a hunting trip, Hitler himself ordered a squadron of Focke-Wulfe FW200 Kondors of Kampfgeschwader 40, based at Bordeaux, to be placed under Doenitz's direct operational control. Doenitz had flown to Berlin on the 2nd, to put the case for joint submarine/air operations. He understood, better than anybody else on either side at that time, that just as aircraft were the natural predators of the U-boats so they could also be the most powerful and effective colleagues.

The big Kondors made a tentative start, but enough convoys were sighted to show what might be achieved as soon as U-boats and aircraft had perfected their homing and reporting techniques and began to cooperate properly together. On 11 January a FW200 reported a convoy outward bound for Gibraltar but the U-boats could not gain position and only one ship was sunk. Three days later, U-105 sighted an OB convoy and transmitted homing signals, but the two searching FW200s failed to run down the D/F bearings. But on the 15th the Italian U-boat *Torelli* (Cdr Langobardi) closed the convoy and sank three ships. Langobardi had recently been to sea with Kretschmer to gain experience and clearly had not wasted his time. Next day a FW200 again sighted the convoy and sank two ships with bombs. But the U-boats again could not get into position in time. However, two large passenger steamers, *Almeda Star* and *Oropesa*, were sunk sailing on their own. On 28 January five Kondors found a convoy and each sank or damaged two ships. Next day, a U-boat pack found SC19, which lost five ships.

By the end of the month, the Kondors had not achieved any marked success with U-boats, but they had themselves sunk fifteen ships totalling nearly 60,000 tons. The U-boats were having a comparatively unsuccessful time. A whole week would go by in which they made no attacks, or perhaps just one attack, against a convoy. They kept on sinking stragglers and independents, but their striking rate had dropped from eight ships a month for every U-boat at sea in October 1940 to only two ships per month per U-boat at sea in February 1941.

No German U-boats were sunk in December 1940 or in January or February 1941. The losses were born at this time by the Italians. *Tarantini* was ambushed and sunk by the British submarine *Thunderbolt* (ex *Thetis*) in the Bay of Biscay on 15 December. *Marcello* was surprised on the surface and sunk with depth-charges by a Sunderland of 210 Squadron west of Cape Wrath on 6 January. Next day, *Nani* was depth-charged and sunk whilst attacking a convoy in the north Atlantic by the corvette *Anemone*.

In the early months of 1941, convoys had to face attacks by U-boats, by aircraft and by surface raiders. *Scharnhorst* and *Gneisenau* were at sea, and *Admiral Hipper* sailed again on 1 February. One very unfortunate convoy, the homeward-bound Gibraltar HG53, was sighted by U-37 (Korvetten-Kapitan Clausen) south-west of St Vincent on the evening of 8 February. U-37 closed and sank two ships the next day, maintained contact and homed five Kondors of 2/KG40 in to attack at midday, when they sank five ships. Clausen claimed one more ship on the 10th and the following day, by which time the survivors of the convoy had scattered. *Admiral Hipper* caught and sank one straggler. In all, nine ships were sunk from the original sixteen in the convoy.

After her attack on HG53, *Admiral Hipper* made contact with the slow convoy SLS64, which was unescorted at the time. After stalking them through the night, *Hipper* sank seven of the nine ships in the convoy on 12 February, and badly damaged the remaining two. *Hipper* returned to Brest on 15 February and, eventually, to Kiel on 28 March.

At the end of February there was an ominous improvement in joint operations between U-boats and aircraft. It was set off by Prien, newly arrived on patrol in the Atlantic. Clearly, Prien was almost a genius as a U-boat commander, not only a brilliant shot himself but immensely successful at summoning up others to the attack. He sighted the convoy OB290 in the afternoon of 25 February and tried to close, but was driven off and forced to dive by a Sunderland. Towards dusk he approached again and made three attacks, sinking three ships and damaging a fourth.

U-47's homing signals led one Kondor of 1/KG40 to the scene at midday and another five during the afternoon. Between them they sank seven ships of 36,250 tons and damaged another four of 20,755 tons. This was a tremendous *coup* for KG40 and their greatest single success against a convoy. It should have removed, once and for all, any remaining doubts about the potential of joint U-boat/aircraft operations. But, luckily for the Allies, Goering returned from his hunting sortie and the long-standing animosity between him, as head of the Luftwaffe, and Admiral Raeder, as head of the Kriegsmarine, was resumed. By the end of February 1941, air operations over the Atlantic had once more become the responsibility of the German Air Force. The Atlantic air group commander and his staff were on good terms with Doenitz and his staff but they never achieved the close co-operation and

understanding which would have had an enormous effect upon the battle of
the Atlantic.

Perhaps it was the resumption of partial hostilities between the Luftwaffe
and the German Navy which saved OB292 from a disaster similar to OB290.
On 2 March a Kondor located the convoy and sank one ship from it. An
ambush of eight German and Italian U-boats was laid, but the convoy was not
found. A Kondor sighted the convoy again on the 4th, and another patrol
line, again of eight U-boats, was deployed. But their presence was betrayed
by W/T interception of their transmissions, and the convoy avoided the
ambush.

Meanwhile, the Royal Navy and the Royal Air Force were, slowly and
painfully, coming closer together, as both services began to take the full
measure of their opponents. Because of German air attacks on Plymouth,
the C-in-C Western Approaches and his staff moved headquarters to an old
fort at Egg Buckland. There, they not only spent a cold and uncomfortable
winter, but they were much more remote from the day-to-day happenings of
the port and had much less chance of meeting convoy commodores and
escort commanders.

On 7 February 1941, a new headquarters was opened in Liverpool, at
Derby House. Admiral Sir Percy Noble became C-in-C Western
Approaches Command on the 17th, while Admiral Dunbar-Nasmith remained as C-in-C Plymouth. Admiral Noble's brief from the Admiralty was
'to be directly responsible for the protection of trade, the routeing, and
control of the outward and home-bound ocean convoys and measures to
combat any attacks on convoys by U-boats or hostile aircraft within his
command'. Or, in other words, to ensure that the United Nations did not
lose the war.

From its very first days, Derby House was a much closer-knit community
than had ever been possible in Plymouth. There was the impression of many
and various threads in the battle being drawn together into one firm
controlling hand. Admiral Noble and his staff had close contact and daily
consultations with Air Vice-Marshal J. M. Robb, commanding 15 Group
Coastal Command, responsible for air operations in the north-west
approaches, and his staff. They were also in constant touch with the Atlantic
shipping control organization, with convoy commodores, escort-group commanders and captains of individual escorts, as well as masters of merchant
ships. All the main personalities of the Atlantic battle were to be found in and
around Derby House.

An operations-room was set up and a plot was kept, duplicating the Trade
Plot in the Admiralty, with a direct telephone linking the two. From the plot,
the Admiral, his staff and everyone concerned could oversee the whole huge
battleground, with all the convoys, ships, aircraft, and U-boats, plotted
up-to-date.

By February 1941, twelve escort groups had been formed, most of them consisting of five destroyers, and five sloops or corvettes, so that a convoy could normally expect an escort of at least six to eight ships (allowing for some ships refitting and boiler-cleaning). Trawlers provided additional escorts for many convoys, and the Home Fleet sometimes contributed a 'striking force' of three destroyers. The escort groups were based in Liverpool or on the Clyde, with another base at Londonderry being developed as quickly as possible.

At this stage, HX from Halifax and SC from Sydney, Cape Breton, convoys were still normally escorted by an armed merchant cruiser (AMC), with an occasional submarine in company to attack surface raiders. The AMCs parted company shortly after the convoy had rendezvoused with the escort group and proceeded at their best speed to their own base at Greenock.

Meeting in-coming convoys still depended a great deal upon the weather. Often a convoy arrived at the rendezvous with more stragglers than ships in company. However convoys were routed as far north as 62°N, which had been thought impracticable earlier in the war. This gave much more ocean room for diverting convoys away from danger, and of course it forced the U-boats, now patrolling as far as 22°W, to extend their patrol lines.

Outward-bound OB convoys for north America sailed on average twelve times a month. OG convoys sailed every ten days for Gibraltar and the Mediterranean, including ships for south African and south American ports.

Ships for OB convoys were brought from their assembly port by a local escort of trawlers and formed up at Oversay. Most were routed through the Minches, where the Loch Ewe section, of ships from the east coast, could join as the convoy passed. The destroyers normally topped up with fuel before leaving the Minches and escorted the convoy as far as possible before breaking off to refuel at Reykjavik. They then sailed to rendezvous with an in-coming HX or SC convoy. Corvettes could normally take a convoy out and transfer to another convoy coming in without refuelling.

OB convoys not going through the Minches steamed west and south-west from the North Channel, their destroyers topping up at Londonderry. The escorts normally transferred in about 18°W to an incoming SL from Sierra Leone or HG homeward bound from Gibraltar. All OB convoys at this time dispersed in about 20°W where, with no escorts present, there were golden chances for the U-boats.

The OG convoys were normally escorted by their groups to about 18°W, where all except one sloop left. That sloop took the convoy through to Gibraltar and returned with a homeward HG. Often an Ocean Boarding Vessel joined a convoy at the end of her patrol and, whenever possible, convoys were accompanied by a battleship or a cruiser.

Air cover for convoys was given by fighters as long as they were in range, with Ansons, Whitleys, Hudsons and Blenheims carrying out anti-submarine patrols in the north-western approaches. The standard long-range aircraft was the Sunderland flying boat which, though not particularly well-equipped for actually sinking U-boats, was invaluable in forcing them to dive.

At this stage the Irish Sea and the Minches were considered to be safe from U-boats, but ships were still very liable to be attacked by aircraft. All ships in the Irish Sea of more than 1000 tons were usually convoyed, with an escort of trawlers, backed up by an anti-aircraft ship. Ships sailing in waters liable to air attack still flew balloons or kites.

It was Gunther Prien who had located OB290; just as most of the best shooting chances seem to fall to the best shots, so it was he who sighted the next convoy late on 6 March. It was the outward-bound OB293, escorted by the destroyers *Wolverine* (Cdr J. M. Rowland) and *Verity*, and the corvettes *Arbutus* and *Camellia*. Prien sent off a sighting report and closed to attack, but was smartly driven off by Rowland and his team. Prien and the rest were to discover that, this time, they were opposed by an escort group well above the average.

Kretschmer was the first to sight the convoy after Prien's first report. Closing after midnight on 7 March, he and his bridge crew were disconcerted to find themselves bathed in the ghostly light of St Elmo's fire; they, the conning tower and the bridge aerials were all vividly outlined in fiery illumination. This was a very bad omen to superstitious sailors. It was supposed to mean that the ship would shortly be sunk.

But, by 1 a.m., Kretschmer had crossed the front of what he estimated was a very large convoy and briskly set to work, torpedoing the tanker *Athelbeach* and the giant 20,000-ton whale factory-ship *Terje Viken*. *Athelbeach*'s crew took to the boats as their ship went down. It seems that U-47 was on the surface somewhere in the convoy. Mr H. L. Jones, *Athelbeach*'s Second Mate, said later that a man in his lifeboat claimed that he saw a U-boat with 'U-41' clearly painted on the side. The U-boat captain spoke 'quite good English, with a definite accent'.

Terje Viken did not sink at once, in fact she floated as a wreck for another week and finally sank on the 14th. Kretschmer closed her the next day and saw destroyers picking up survivors. As U-99 dived, she was attacked by *Arbutus* and *Camellia* and had a very uncomfortable time. Lights went out, hull rivets started, the whole boat rocked and pitched under the impact of the detonations. In a very prolonged attack, Kretschmer's crew counted over 100 depth-charges.

But most of those charges were aimed at U-70 (Korvetten-Kapitan Matz) who had been next to attack. U-70 had suffered structural damage to the bridge from the weather, but Kretschmer actually sighted U-70 going into the attack on the morning of the 7th. Matz was himself an experienced and able commander and quickly torpedoed two ships in the convoy. But he was taken aback by the speed and ferocity of the counter-attack by *Arbutus* and *Camellia*. The very first attack caused a slight but persistent leak in the hull fitting for the hydrophone listening gear.

Joachim Matz later wrote an account of his U-boat's last hours. U-70 was at 300 feet, compensating for the water leaking in by puffing compressed air into the ballast tanks (a very risky procedure, as it made the submarine's bodily trim inherently unstable). But Matz hoped to keep quiet, and then softly and silently vanish away.

Meanwhile the attackers above had the initiative:

Then they came at us again! The grinding noise of the propellers became louder. The bearing remained static; and that meant the destroyer was coming straight at us. Then with our own ears we could clearly hear the rhythmic beat above our heads. . . . Twenty seconds of oppressive, absolute silence and then with a roar and a crash down came a pattern of charges helter-skelter all round us. The ship shuddered from stem to stern, shook herself; lockers sprang open, from here and there came the tinkle of splintered glass, but we suffered no serious damage, thank God.

Matz's only real concern was that leak which was getting worse. By 11.30, they had been dived for five hours, 'and the Chief Engineer was having difficulty in keeping the boat under control. The amount of water we had shipped was now becoming very noticeable.'

At 12.10 'Report from hydrophones: "Destroyer approaching." ' This time the attack aggravated the leak and drove the U-boat down to 460 feet. By going full ahead, with hydroplanes hard-a-rise and every available man running aft to bring the bows up, Matz caught and steadied her at 650-feet depth. But at once the U-boat began to rise, ever more quickly. Once again, Matz ordered full ahead, planes hard-a-*dive*, every man running forward to bring the bows *down*.

U-70 was now virtually uncontrollable and unstable, finding her own depth anywhere between 300 and 600 feet. All the compressed air had been used. The next lunge towards the bottom was prevented by the main motors, but when the U-boat began to rise again, this time there was no stopping her and she soared irresistibly up to the surface. Matz gave the order to abandon ship: 'In spite of my fears, we all got out safely. As I reached the deck, I saw the destroyer – in reality it turned out to be a corvette – close beside us. She was firing rather wildly. From the bridge a voice shouted in bad German: "Jump overboard, I'm going to fire!" And fire they did, though as far as I could see no one was hurt in those first few moments.'

The corvette lowered a boat, obviously hoping to board the U-boat, but Matz went back to take one last look and check that the main vents were open. 'The whole of the U-boat's stern was already under water. We jumped for it. When I was about 25 yards from her, she reared steeply up. Menacingly the stern pointed upwards at the heavens for a few seconds and then U-70 plunged for the last time to the bottom of the North Atlantic.' Twenty of the crew were lost, but the rest including Matz were picked up and became prisoners-of-war.

Prien meanwhile had been broadcasting details of the convoy's position, course and speed (Kretschmer heard one of his signals at 4.24 a.m. that morning). A fourth U-boat sighted the convoy. It was UA (the ex-Turkish submarine *Batiray*, taken over by the Germans) commanded by Fregatten-Kapitan Eckermann who prepared for his first attack that evening of the 7th. But *Wolverine* and *Verity* were too good for him and drove UA off with serious depth-charge damage.

Rowland and his team had now damaged U-99 and UA, and sunk U-70. Shortly after midnight on the 8th, they had a chance at the biggest prize of all. It is clear that U-47 was running on the surface, perhaps searching for the convoy. Possibly Prien was over-confident or his lookouts momentarily slack. Certainly the visibility was very poor, in a heavy rain-squall. But it was *Wolverine* who reacted first to the encounter. A lookout reported a shape fine on the port bow. The Asdic operator reported propeller noises close to, and, as it was all happening at once, Rowland himself on *Wolverine*'s bridge suddenly smelled the unmistakable whiff of diesel-engine exhaust fumes.

Wolverine turned on to the bearing and increased speed. *Verity*'s star-shell clearly illuminated a U-boat, which dived at once. Rowland and his men were not going to waste such a perfect attack datum point. They could actually still see the surface swirl of the U-boat's wake when *Wolverine* fired a full pattern of ten depth-charges and ran out, while *Verity* attacked. They took it in turns, one keeping Asdic contact, whilst the other worked the U-boat over with various patterns, sometimes three or four charges, sometimes a single charge.

But Prien was a tough and wily customer, as Rowland conceded. It was 4 a.m. and over three hours after the attack began, before there was any sign of success. 'Lo and behold,' said *Wolverine*'s Chief Bosun's Mate Boyer, 'there was a lovely oil trail. . . . We took up the trail and it was, "Tally ho" and the hunt was on again.'

Shortly after another attack at 5 a.m. there was 'a loud clattering sound, like crockery breaking' over the headphones. 'As the sub's air bubbles went down our starboard side, we wagged our tail and ten depth-charges went down in the middle of them.' At 5.19, U-47 surfaced and Prien must have seen *Wolverine* almost on top of him, for he dived again almost at once. The hours of darting about, of changing course and depth and speed, had exhausted U-47's batteries. Prien had nothing left, and U-47 was almost stationary as *Wolverine* ran overhead for the last time.

There was a tremendous underwater detonation, as though the depth-charges had counter-mined the torpedoes remaining in U-47. From *Wolverine*'s bridge they said they saw a deep orange glow, far under the sea, which lasted for several seconds. Some even claimed they saw orange flames licking on the surface for a time. U-47 was lost with all hands. Later, Kretschmer heard U-boat Headquarters calling Prien, asking him to report his position. A few hours' silence was not significant. U-47 might have gone deep.

Atmospheric conditions might prevent radio reception. But as the hours went by and Prien did not answer, it became clear that the Bull of Scapa had fought his last *corrida*.

Wolverine was justifiably pleased. The ship had been painted a shade of 'Mountbatten pink' for camouflage purposes and was known as *Barmaid's Blush*. The resident poet of the ship's newspaper, *The Ping-k 'Un*, burst into jubilant verse:

> If, My Lords, you would employ a
> Most efficient old destroyer
> And should want one that is clean
> > Send at once for *Wolverine*!
>
> If its crew must know their stuff,
> And can take it, calm or rough,
> One whose motto is '*Ich Dien*'
> > It MUST be the *Wolverine*!
>
> If the Huns are out in packs
> Pressing home their night attacks
> Or produce a second Prien
> > Whistle up the *Wolverine*!

Even the ship's captains who were sunk bore no hard feelings. Captain R. Dicks, of *Dunaff Head*, who was torpedoed on the 7th, later wrote that 'I have no suggestion to make regarding convoys; I am quite satisfied that everything possible is being done for us.' Captain H. MacLachlan, of *Delilion*, who was torpedoed but reached port eventually, complained of unnecessary signalling but, like many merchant-ship masters, produced a suggestion of real value: 'that an escort drop astern of the convoy every evening to check for lights showing'.

Only a week after Prien's death came confirmation that the U-boat's 'happy time' was finally over and that the escorts had new and formidable muscle. This was during the much-trumpeted German 'spring offensive' in the Atlantic. As so often in war, actual events did not bear out the hopeful slogan. On the evening of 15 March, south of Iceland on the 61st parallel, U-110 (Lemp) sighted the homeward-bound convoy HX112. It was a large, forty-one-ship, 8-knot convoy, steering SE, and escorted by the 5th Escort Group, the destroyers *Walker* (Cdr D. MacIntyre), *Vanoc* (Cdr J. G. W. Deneys), and *Volunteer*, assisted by *Sardonyx* and *Scimitar*, with two corvettes, *Bluebell* and *Hydrangea*.

Lemp's reporting signal summoned up some familiar names: Schepke in U-100, Kretschmer in U-99, Clausen in U-37, and Kentrat in U-74. Schepke attacked first on the night of the 15th–16th and torpedoed the large tanker *Erodona* (the convoy contained a large proportion of tankers), which, in Walker's words, burst into 'blinding flame, casting a ghastly glare over the heaving waters'. The detonation of the torpedo was 'the most appalling of all night disasters'. It shocked everybody on *Walker*'s bridge into silence. Yet, astonishingly, *Erodona* survived the attack and reached port.

Schepke might now have been expected to sink ships one by one until his torpedoes were gone. But he made one more attack and then was driven off just before dawn. So, too was Clausen, who tried to attack at about midday on the 16th, and was finally driven off by the evening, when MacIntyre and his fellow captains could have congratulated themselves that they had won the first rounds. *Erodona* was straggling astern, but the rest of the convoy was in good order.

But Kretschmer had found the convoy early on the 16th and had shadowed all day, despite the poor visibility and once, in the afternoon, losing contact altogether. That evening, he closed the convoy from the port side and slipped between the two escorts and into the centre of the convoy for one of the most accomplished surface attacks of his career. In the space of an hour he sank two Norwegian tankers *Ferm* and *Bedouin*, and torpedoed the British tanker *France Comte* (which survived), sank another British tanker *Venetia* and the steamer *JB White*. U-99 was clearly illuminated in the flames from the burning tankers (Kretschmer later said he felt as exposed as a man sunbathing on a beach), but he remained with the convoy keeping station in its centre lane for nearly fifteen minutes. Sinking a sixth ship, *Korsham*, as he went, Kretschmer withdrew astern of the convoy, all his torpedoes expended.

Meanwhile, MacIntyre was, in his own words, 'near to despair' and racked his brains 'to find some way to stop the holocaust'. He decided that his one hope was to put *Walker* on a gently curving course, whilst he looked out through binoculars on a steady bearing. He *might* sight the tell-tale white wake of a U-boat. Then he could give chase, and force the U-boat to dive.

It worked. MacIntyre sighted the thin line of a wake where none of the convoy or escorts were, ordered 30 knots and closed the position. The U-boat (actually U-100) dived in a hurry. *Walker* delivered a cracking pattern of ten charges as she crossed the spot where the last swirl had been seen. MacIntyre thought they could hardly have missed, especially as there was a final explosion and that 'orange' flash spread across the surface.

Walker and *Vanoc* now systematically hunted their target, dropping pattern after pattern, one destroyer holding contact while the other attacked. But it 'was a wily opponent and, dodging and twisting in the depths, he managed to escape destruction though heavily damaged'.

MacIntyre called off the attack when the water was so disturbed by explosions that the hydrophone operator was reporting 'echoes' all over the compass. He stopped to pick up the Master and thirty-seven of the crew of *JB White*, while *Vanoc* steamed round him to give some protection. MacIntyre had just decided it was time to 'head quietly back to where the U-boat had last been located and perhaps catch him licking his wounds on the surface', when he saw *Vanoc* increasing speed. Shortly afterwards she radioed, 'Have rammed and sunk U-boat'. She had had a contact on her Type 286 radar screen, identified it as a surfaced U-boat and headed straight for it.

U-100 had been badly damaged in the depth-charge attack and had had to surface almost under *Vanoc*'s nose – in fact, at 1.52 a.m., Deneys on *Vanoc*'s bridge had actually smelled diesel-oil fumes, while his Asdic operator reported 'noises of bubbling sounds' in his headphones. Some said later they heard Schepke roaring from the U-boat's bridge that the destroyer would pass safely astern. If so, he was badly mistaken. The destroyer's bows hit the U-boat almost at right angles, in the centre of the conning tower. To try and save damage to his own ship, Deneys had ordered main engines to stop at what he estimated was about five seconds before impact.

Even so, *Vanoc* hit U-100 with enough force to collapse the conning-tower plating, pinning Schepke to the periscope standard behind him and (again, some said) severing both his legs at the hip. The weight of the destroyer forced the submarine down, and the ship rode over the submarine's hull for some distance along its keel. Deneys had to manoeuvre his main engines furiously before he could disengage. Meanwhile, U-100's bows rose, tossing men off the casing and throwing Schepke, still alive, into the sea before the U-boat slid out of sight.

Vanoc stopped to examine herself for damage and to pick up survivors. There were six, five ratings and Korvetten-Kapitan Siegfried Flister, thirty-five years old, with fifteen years' service in the navy, who had been Gunnery Officer in *Scharnhorst* earlier in the war. He had transferred to the U-boat branch and was now a 'makee-learn' U-boat captain, on a war patrol with Schepke to gain experience.

While *Walker* covered *Vanoc* by circling round her, Able Seaman Back-house, *Walker*'s Asdic operator, reported a submarine contact, range and bearing placing it almost under *Vanoc*'s stern. MacIntyre could not believe it. The coincidence was too much. The 'echo' was obviously water turbulence, after all the excitement, or maybe even the hull of the stricken U-boat sinking into the ocean depths. But Backhouse insisted. The echo, indistinct at first, steadily hardened. Backhouse confirmed it as a genuine submarine contact.

There was no time for a precise, drilled attack. After a rough and ready calculation by mental arithmetic, *Walker* eventually sent down a pattern of six depth-charges, all that could be got ready in the time. *Walker* ran on, to get the sea-room to make another attack, 'but as we turned came the thrilling signal from *Vanoc* – "U-boat surfaced astern of me" '.

Kretschmer had been betrayed by his bridge staff. U-99's starboard lookout had failed to sight *Vanoc* until she was almost on top of him; when he heard the alarming report the startled officer-of-the-watch forgot all his training and, as a pure unthinking reflex action, gave the order to dive – in direct contravention of his Captain's standing orders. As it happened, neither *Vanoc* nor *Walker* had sighted U-99. But once she had dived, she was immediately detected by Asdic. Hence the sudden contact gained by Backhouse, and MacIntyre's disbelief.

Kretschmer doubted whether it had been necessary to dive, when he heard the story. He was given no opportunity to dwell upon the matter. The six charges burst on top of and around U-99 in what Kreschmer realized was the worst attack he had ever suffered. U-99 plunged to 700 feet, below the designed crushing depth, before pulling out of the dive. Both propellers seemed to have seized up. The hydroplanes were stiff, as though obstructed. It was as though the U-boat had been literally stunned by the shock.

Unable to manoeuvre, Kretschmer blew all main ballast tanks and the U-boat began at last to rise. Kretschmer hoped to catch a trim at about 300 feet, when he might have a chance to work out an evasion plan. But U-99 rose uncontrollably to the surface. *Vanoc* illuminated the target with a searchlight, while *Walker* opened fire with main and secondary armament. But with no flashless cordite and the quantities of tracer being fired, the guns' crews were almost totally blind for most of the time, and the firing was spectacular rather than effective.

However, it had its effect. A lamp on U-99 signalled 'We are sunking' and the action was over. MacIntyre hoped to lower a boat and board, but just as he was thinking about it, the U-boat's hull tipped up and vanished. MacIntyre kept *Walker* to windward of the swimming Germans, to drift down on them. *Walker* picked up forty men, the whole crew except Schroeder the Engineer Officer, who had gone below at the last to ensure all main vents were open.

'The last to come over the side was obviously the Captain,' wrote MacIntyre, 'as he swam to *Walker* still wearing his brass-bound cap. We were soon to find out that we had made indeed a notable capture, for the Captain was Otto Kretschmer, leading ace of the U-boat arm, holder of the Knight's Cross with Oak Leaves and top scorer in terms of tonnage sunk.'

Kretschmer, Matz, Flister, and the survivors of U-70, U-100 and U-99, all became prisoners-of-war. They were naturally of considerable interest to interrogators. Kretschmer, when told of U-47's demise, said he was very surprised to hear of the 'orange glow' and the 'orange flames' on the surface. Kretschmer himself was a great surprise to his captors. They knew he was an 'ace'. They knew his name and reputation from the German newspapers, quite apart from the intelligence reports. But he was not at all the arrogant, bombastic Nazi they had somehow come to expect.

Captain George Creasy, Director of the Anti-Submarine Division at the Admiralty, specially asked to meet Kretschmer:

I was anxious to judge for myself what manner of man a successful U-boat captain might be; to see for myself, if I could, the state of his nerves; to measure his judgement; gauge his reactions to his seniors and his juniors, the expected and the unexpected. In simple words, to 'size him up'.

. . . I saw a young and obviously self-confident naval commander who bore himself, in the difficult conditions of recent captivity, with self-respect, modesty and courtesy. His record stamped him as brave and quick-witted; his appearance and manners were those of an officer and a gentleman. When he left me [Creasy added] I sincerely hoped that there were not too many like him.

On 23 March, whilst escorting a convoy in the passage between Iceland and the Faeroes, the anti-submarine trawler *Visenda* surprised and sank U-551. So, in a disastrous month, five U-boats were lost, three of them commanded by aces. This was a quarter of the total U-boat operational strength at the time. On 19 March Doenitz gloomily noted in his war log, 'With certainty we can now count on only three boats in the north Atlantic.' There was, unknown to Doenitz, one even more ominous aspect of the U-boat losses in March 1941. U-100 was the first U-boat ever to have been lost as a direct result of radar contact. The tremendous tactical advantage the U-boats had enjoyed so far, of being able to manoeuvre almost as they wished undetected on the surface at night, was about to be removed.

While Siegfried Flister went on his way to a POW camp, his old ship with her sister *Gneisenau* was demonstrating some classical principles of convoy warfare. *Scharnhorst* (Kapitan zur Sëe Kurt Hoffman) and *Gneisenau* (Kapitan zur Sëe Otto Fein), flying the flag of Admiral Gunther Lutjens, sailed from Kiel to begin Operation BERLIN, an assault on Allied merchant shipping, on 22 January. Intelligence of their passing the Belt reached London on the 23rd and the Home Fleet under Admiral Sir John Tovey, the battleships *Nelson* and *Rodney*, the battle cruiser *Repulse*, eight cruisers and eleven destroyers, sailed from Scapa on the 25th.

The two ships, already known in England as 'Salmon' and 'Gluckstein', were not only well handled but lucky – especially *Scharnhorst*. They were briefly sighted by the cruiser *Naiad* on 28 January while they were steaming out into the Atlantic south-east of Iceland. They turned back to the north-east, but *Naiad* lost contact almost at once.

On 4 February the two broke out through the Denmark Strait, north of Iceland and on the 8th they were stalking the convoy HX106. But when Lutjens sighted the fighting tops of the battleship *Ramillies* escorting the convoy, he broke off. The mere sight of a capital ship had been enough; but without her, the convoy would have had no defence except to scatter.

On 22 February, about 500 miles east of Newfoundland, the two German battle cruisers came across members of a westbound convoy which had dispersed. With no escort of any kind, they were easy prey. Five ships of 25,784 tons were sunk in two hours' shelling, between 11 a.m. and 1 p.m.

As *Scharnhorst* and *Gneisenau*'s war cruise went on, the contrast between the apparent security of ships in convoy, and their utter helplessness once they were dispersed, was brutally demonstrated once again. A radio message from one of the ships slaughtered on 22 February had been transmitted, despite jamming, and Lutjens knew that he had been reported. He headed south and east for the Sierra Leone route, refuelling at a rendezvous with his tankers on the way.

At 9.20 a.m. on 7 March, about 350 miles NE of the Cape Verde Islands, *Scharnhorst* sighted the fore-top and bridge superstructure of a large warship, correctly identified as a battleship (actually, *Malaya*). *Scharnhorst* at once turned away and made a sighting report to Lutjens in *Gneisenau*, who increased speed, deciding that the battleship was very probably escorting a convoy. At 11.20 the masts of merchant ships were sighted to the south. It was SL67, of 12 ships, escorted by the destroyers *Faulknor* and *Forester*, and the corvette *Cecilia*.

The 11-inch guns of the raiders should have made short work of convoy and escort. But there was still the battleship. Lutjens knew that at least three U-boats were in the area, although he had no means of communicating directly with them. *Scharnhorst* and *Gneisenau* therefore shadowed the convoy from astern for most of that day, transmitting homing signals which brought U-124 and U-105 to the scene. The two U-boats attacked during the night. U-105 (Korvetten-Kapitan Schewe) sank one ship and U-124 (Korvetten-Kapitan Schulz) four, totalling nearly 30,000 tons, in a unique example of a co-ordinated convoy attack by capital ships and U-boats which was the more remarkable because all signals had to be relayed through U-boat headquarters in France.

Towards dawn the two battle cruisers steered to close the convoy and sighted it again to the SE at about noon. They were themselves sighted briefly by *Malaya*, and her Walrus reconnaissance aircraft also sighted and reported *Scharnhorst*. Once again, Lutjens broke off, without venturing an action, and for the second time the mere presence of a battleship prevented a massacre. Knowing that he must have been reported, Lutjens headed north and west again for the Halifax route.

On the way north, the independent Greek ship *Marathon* was sunk on the 9th, after her crew had been taken off. Lutjens was heading for the position off Newfoundland where he had had such success on 22 February. On 15 March, some way south of his destination, *Scharnhorst* and *Gneisenau* came upon six unescorted merchant ships from a dispersed westbound convoy. Next day, they found ten more, from another convoy, also dispersed and defenceless. In those two days, in an area between 40° and 46°N, and 43° to 46°W, *Scharnhorst* and *Gneisenau* sank or captured sixteen ships of over 82,000 tons – their greatest success of the war.

Late on the 16th, while *Gneisenau* was picking up survivors from the last ship, another battleship was sighted to the SE. It was *Rodney*, who had been escorting HX114. Once again *Gneisenau* broke off and slipped away. The two ships reached Brest on 23 March, having sunk or captured twenty-two ships of 115,622 tons during Operation BERLIN. Just as important, they had disrupted the Atlantic convoy cycle and tied up enormous numbers of Allied ships in a fruitless search for them.

This was the first and only such sortie against Atlantic shipping and it had been an almost complete success. The two battle cruisers had done exactly what they had been designed and intended to do. They had shown how much harm well-armed and well-handled ships could achieve, and how extremely difficult it was to bring them to action. The rendezvous with supply tankers, the refuellings and the transfers of prisoners had gone well. Two of the tankers, *Uckermark* and *Ermland*, actually took part in the scouting line which searched for ships on 15 March. Lutjens had had his necessary share of luck. His ships had been sighted several times, by aircraft from *Ark Royal* on 20 March and by Coastal Command aircraft the next day.

In Brest, *Scharnhorst* and *Gneisenau* were well within range of the RAF. In the months that followed they were constantly harassed by air attacks, while the seas off Brest were patrolled by submarines. Nevertheless their cruise had the most disturbing implications for the Allies. The heavy cruiser *Prinz Eugen* was in commission. The battleship *Bismarck* was doing her trials in the Baltic, with her sister ship *Tirpitz* to follow. The Allied staff mind boggled at the carnage these ships, with *Scharnhorst* and *Gneisenau*, could cause if they ever formed one force. But happily for the United Nations, in the event, as somebody said, Hitler preferred to expend his capital ships in 'penny packets'.

By the end of March 1941, the figures of British, Allied and neutral merchant ships lost through enemy action showed another crescendo in the war against commerce. The numbers of ships sunk climbed from seventy-six of 320,240 tons in January; to 139 of 529,706 tons in March; making a total of 317 ships, of 1,250,000 tons for the quarter. Of these, U-boats sank 101 ships of 566,000 tons; aircraft eight-eight ships of 280,000 tons; and warship raiders thirty-seven ships of 187,000 tons.

The Prime Minister had already in a sense defined the gravity of the battle. His Battle of the Atlantic Directive, issued on 6 March declared: 'We must take the offensive against the U-boat and the Focke-Wulfe wherever we can and whenever we can. The U-boat at sea must be hunted, the U-boat in the building yard or in dock must be bombed. The Focke-Wulfe and other bombers employed against our shipping must be attacked in the air and in their nests.'

The Directive gave extreme priority to fitting out ships to catapult fighters at sea. Coastal Command's main strength was to be concentrated in the North-western Approaches. The question of 'freeing from convoy' ships of between 13 and 12 knots was to be reexamined. The Admiralty was to have first claim on all short-range anti-aircraft guns. A new drive would be made to clear the back-log of damaged shipping now lying in the ports. Turn-round times were to be improved. There were proposals for greater interchangeability of labour at the docks, reducing congestion in the ports. A

Committee was to be formed, meeting daily, and attended by representatives of the Admiralty Transport Department, the Ministry of Shipping and the Ministry of Transport, to report on hitches.

These proposals were sound and necessary, except for the ancient and apparently indestructible fallacy of 'freeing' ships from convoy. But in the remaining months of 1941 to come, the Atlantic battle was going to need a great deal more than directives and committees.

Chapter Fourteen

Early in April 1941, *Wolverine*'s resident bard was able to burst into joyful verse again:

> If, without the slightest ripple
> Lurking deep there is a Hippel
> And the Asdic's chance is lean
>   What you want is *Wolverine*!

'Hippel' was Kapitan-Leutnant von Hippel, of U-76, sunk in a crisp, competent attack which showed that the convoy escorts were coming properly to grips with their enemies. But, as the escorts' growing success made matters more difficult for the U-boats, so the U-boats moved further and further into the Atlantic. Convoys were often diverted out of danger in time, but it was still vital to keep at least some escorts with a convoy until it had finally cleared the danger zone, whose limits were being moved steadily further west. In April SC26 was attacked in 21°W, in May HX126 in 40°W, both convoys before any escorts had reached them from the United Kingdom.

SC26 was a slow homeward-bound convoy of twenty-two ships, in seven columns, escorted by the armed merchant cruiser *Worcestershire*. It was sighted by von Hippel, south of Iceland, on 1 April and an ambush of eight U-boats, including U-46 (Endrass) and U-74 (Kentrat) was formed the next day. SC26 ran into it, and the first ship was sunk at 00.35 a.m. on the 3rd. It was a bright, clear night, with the Northern Lights shining and conditions perfect for the hunters. By morning six ships had been sunk. Three of them were in centre columns, which showed that U-boats had penetrated into the middle of the convoy, as in the days of Kretschmer and Prien. *Worcestershire* was hit by one torpedo from U-74 but eventually got home safely.

The convoy scattered almost involuntarily and one straggler, *Harpledon*, was sunk. By evening the convoy had mostly re-formed. But the U-boats had also re-grouped and sank another four ships, and damaged a fifth, *Thirlsby*, whose master said he could actually hear the 'screaming noise of the torpedo' which hit them. *Thirlsby* was attacked again by Heinkel He IIIs off the Butt of Lewis a week later, and again escaped.

One of the last ships to be sunk was *Athenic*, torpedoed by U-76 at about 7 p.m. on the 4th. U-76 retired to charge batteries overnight, surfacing at about 4.30 a.m. Von Hippel hoped to close the convoy and attack again at dawn, but by then SC26 had been joined by its escort of *Wolverine, Scarborough* and *Arbitus*, led by that wily old bird, John Rowland himself. U-76 was detected by *Wolverine* at 7.05 a.m. on the 5th. Rowland dropped only one charge but it was so shrewdly placed it did tremendous damage, preventing U-76 from manoeuvring freely.

Scarborough ran in again at 9.20 and fired a full pattern of ten charges which exploded so close, according to survivors, that it actually drove inwards one of the main welded seams in the U-boat's hull. Every instrument was destroyed, most of the auxiliary machinery and the main motors were put out of action, and U-76 came to the surface almost involuntarily. Friedrich von Hippel was only twenty-six years old, and regarded as one of the brightest and boldest sparks in the U-boat arm, but for him and his crew the war was almost over.

As U-76 wallowed in the sea, with waves breaking over and her crew abandoning her, *Arbitus* put out a boat with a boarding party who got down inside the U-boat, finding it half-flooded and already filling with chlorine gas. They had to leave quickly before it went down with them.

Some of U-76's survivors were taken on board *Arbitus*, amongst them Steurmannsmaat Carl Becker, who wrote in a letter to Frau Edith Becker, at home in Wiesbaden, an account of U-76's last moments:

> In a short time it would be daylight and we should be very fortunate to escape. Had our batteries been fully charged, it would perhaps have been possible. Astern of us the whole time was the sound of the destroyers' searching apparatus, *tsst*, so it continued for a long time and then she was above us and dropped three charges which caused comparatively little damage.
>
> Then she proceeded away and we breathed again, but after about forty minutes we heard the noise of the propellers of two destroyers and again the *tsst tsst tsst* which went through and through us, and it is quite definite that they find us. Then things begin to happen.
>
> Their depth charges are on us. The boat shook all over. Ten minutes later there was a hailstorm of depth charges. Everything in the boat was shattered, the depth gauges moved like blazes. The boat assumed a vertical position and all was over. I had my escape apparatus and crawled up the ladder to the conning tower.

On 28 April the homeward-bound HX121 was sighted by U-123 and five more U-boats were directed to the attack. U-123 was driven off, but the convoy lost three ships including two large tankers. But at 5.50 a.m. on the 29th the corvette *Gladiolus* sighted what seemed to be smoke and closed it at full speed. The target proved to be a U-boat flying a kite at a fair height. The U-boat dived, kite and all, but the Asdic picked it up and *Gladiolus* made two attacks with ten charges each time. There appeared one enormous air bubble and the remains of a small inflatable rubber float or raft. That was all the evidence of Korvetten-Kapitan Hoppe and the crew of U-65.

The remaining four U-boats formed another patrol line, but the convoy was diverted around it, although U-75 sank the large independent steamer *City of Nagpur* some way to the south on the 29th. But HX121 had been a disappointment to the U-boat command. This had been the first daylight wolf-pack attack upon a fully escorted convoy since the summer of 1940 (HX90, attacked in daylight on 2 December, was escorted only by one sloop), and it had failed. Clearly, this sort of attack was no longer feasible when a full escort was present.

Between 1 January and 1 April 1941 thirty new U-boats were commissioned (compared with twenty-two built in the previous quarter) and the total fleet rose from eighty-nine U-boats to 113. In April 195 ships of 687,901 tons were sunk by all forms of Axis action. But, of those, only ten, all from SC26 or HX121, were sunk whilst actually in convoy, although the U-boats sank a total of forty-three ships of 249,375 tons during the month. To put these figures in perspective: during the first three months of 1941, 687 ships sailed in HX convoys, 306 in SC convoys, and no less than 1282 in OB outward-bound convoys.

Arbutus had tried very hard to capture U-76. Her Captain, like all escort captains, had been impressed in the strongest terms by the staff with the absolute priority to be given to boarding and, if possible, capturing a U-boat. Even if the U-boat subsequently sank, the boarding party were to get as much information as possible from its interior. The greatest prize of all, of course, would be the capture of a complete U-boat, with all its codes, tables, cyphers and coding machines intact, with their current settings. In May 1941, through a combination of luck, skill, bravery and cunning, it was achieved.

The nucleus of seventeen ships of the outward-bound OB318 sailed from Liverpool on 2 May, being joined by another four ships from Milford Haven, five from the Clyde and finally twelve off Loch Ewe, which had already been convoyed around the north coast of Scotland from ports on the east coast. The escort, when the convoy finally took its departure, was a strong one: three destroyers, *Westcott*, *Newmarket* and *Campbeltown*, the sloop *Rochester*, five corvettes, *Primrose, Marigold, Nasturtium, Dianthus* and *Auricula*, and the anti-submarine trawler *Angle*. The Senior Officer of the 7th Escort Group was Cdr I. H. Bockett-Pugh in *Westcott*. The total number of ships was thirty-eight, of six nationalities; Commodore Mackenzie in *Colonial* leading the fourth column.

Three ships departed for Iceland on 7 May, the same day *Westcott* sighted an empty lifeboat (from the whale factory-ship *Terje Viken*, sunk on 7 March during Otto Kretschmer's last patrol). Meanwhile U-95 sighted and reported a convoy further to the west. The signal was intercepted and plotted; though it could not be deciphered, it was obviously a convoy-sighting report. The Admiralty Tracking Room decided that U-95 had sighted OB318 and ordered the convoy to make an operational turn to starboard to the latitude of 62°N. Unhappily, OB318 was now steering directly for U-94 (Kuppisch).

Kuppisch actually sighted OB318 on the evening of 7 May, at about the same time as it was joined by its relief escort from Iceland, the 3rd Escort Group, of the destroyers *Bulldog* (Senior Officer, Cdr A. J. Baker-Cresswell), *Amazon* and *Broadway*. Baker-Cresswell also had with him the armed merchant cruiser *Ranpura*, and some miles astern were another four ships for the convoy escorted by the corvettes *Aubrietia*, *Hollyhock* and *Nigella*, and the trawler *St Apollo* (all four also of the 3rd Escort Group). These joined the convoy at about 10 p.m. on the 7th.

Bockett-Pugh's destroyers were now short of fuel and had to go. *Rochester* and the five corvettes were to stay with the convoy for another twenty-four hours, and then leave to join the homeward-bound HX123. But their added strength meant that on the evening of the 7th, when the first attack developed, Baker-Cresswell had a considerable escort strength, which he deployed in the then standard formation. He himself in *Bulldog* led the starboard van, with *Amazon* to port. *Nasturtium*, *Auricula* and *Dianthus* formed the starboard side screen. *Angle*, *Primrose*, *Marigold* and another trawler *Daneman* which had re-joined the group after repairing defects, formed the port side. *Rochester* and *Broadway* brought up the rear. In the middle, between the fifth and sixth columns and 'sticking out like a haystack', was *Ranpura*.

The weather was fine, with visibility up to 10 miles, and Kuppisch could see his targets clearly silhouetted. At 9.15 p.m. he slipped in between *Broadway* and *Rochester* and with one salvo torpedoed *Eastern Star* and *Ixion*, who were both at the rear of their columns. *Eastern Star*, carrying a large quantity of whisky, sank burning furiously, but her survivors were taken off by *Daneman*. *Ixion* survived until the early hours of the 8th before sinking.

Rochester had actually sighted a periscope in the glare of the burning *Eastern Star*, and *Amazon*, coming down through the convoy, gained a firm contact. They were joined by *Bulldog*, and by midnight had carried out three bruising attacks on U-94. *Bulldog* and *Amazon* did not give up the search until 9.30 a.m. the next day, when they had expended eighty-nine charges and damaged, but not sunk, U-94.

When Baker-Cresswell re-joined at 4 p.m. on the 8th, he placed *Aubrietia* on the starboard wing, with *Broadway*, *Nigella*, *Bulldog* (in the centre), *Hollyhock* and *Amazon* stretched across the convoy's van. *Daneman* was on the port wing, and *St Apollo* brought up the rear. Baker-Cresswell released the remaining ships of the 7th Escort Group to join HX123.

Towards midday on the 9th, U-110 (Lemp) closed the convoy from the starboard side, and at 11.58 a.m. fired a salvo of three torpedoes, hitting *Esmond* (leading the starboard wing column) and *Bengore Head* (leading the seventh column). *Aubrietia*, the nearest escort, heard the noise of the torpedoes on her hydrophones and turned hard-a-starboard where, at 12.03, she sighted a periscope and almost at once gained a firm Asdic contact.

Although the Asdic went out of action immediately after the first contact, Lt Cdr Smith put in a quick attack by eye with a full pattern of ten charges at 12.06. The attack was probably out for depth and distance but, giving the U-boat no chance to recover, Smith ran out clear of the convoy, turned back, and made another attack with another full pattern at 12.23, set for depths from 150 to 385 feet. Smith thought he had probably fired too late, and headed for *Esmond* to pick up her survivors.

By now *Broadway* and *Bulldog* had both gained firm Asdic contacts and were just about to attack, when all eyes were caught by a sudden and violent water turbulence, almost directly between the ships. The patch of strange broken water, containing quite eerily large bubbles, spread very rapidly and then, before anybody could react or give an order, up popped a U-boat in the middle of it, with men already pouring out of her conning tower.

Baker-Cresswell 'saw red' and steered to ram, but when he saw the men appearing on the U-boat's upperdeck, he steered away again. It seemed that the U-boat sailors were manning their gun, and *Bulldog* opened fire with all weapons down to small arms. *Broadway* joined in and for a minute or so there was utter bedlam. Captain J. B. McCafferty, Master of *Esmond*, who had just been rescued with his entire crew of forty-nine officers and men, stood on *Aubrietia*'s bridge to watch the fun. 'My,' he remarked at one point, 'the Battle of Trafalgar must have been a snowball fight compared to this!'

Meanwhile, Lt Cdr Taylor was trying to bring *Broadway* alongside the U-boat so that he could drop two depth-charges set very shallow underneath her, to prevent her diving and to encourage her crew to abandon her. Baker-Cresswell, who was already having thoughts of capturing the U-boat, was afraid *Broadway* was going to ram and warned Taylor not to. Unfortunately the *Broadway* collided with U-110, the U-boat's starboard hydroplane slicing through the thin plating of *Broadway*'s port bow, holing her underwater, and tearing off her port propeller.

Baker-Cresswell detailed *Aubrietia* to pick up the German survivors who, when brought on board, were quickly taken below out of sight of what was happening. Lemp was not among them. Meanwhile, a boarding party of six sailors, a stoker and a telegraphist, led by Sub. Lt D. E. Balme, set out in *Bulldog*'s whaler.

Balme leaped on board, loaded revolver in hand. The submarine was deserted. Below, in the control room, he found the lights still burning; 'everything was lying around just as if one had arrived at someone's house after breakfast, before they had time to make the beds'. Methodically, Balme and his party began to strip the interior of anything movable: binoculars, sextants, books, logs, charts, diaries, pictures, tools, instruments, tables, cyphers and the Enigma coding machine, with that day's settings still on it. The telegraphist noted down the tuning positions of all the U-boat's radio sets in the wireless office. *Bulldog*'s Engineer Officer came over to try and start some machinery, without success. The whaler had to make several trips, loaded with treasures, back and forth, and *Broadway*'s larger American-type motor-boat was later sent to help. Everybody was vastly impressed by the quality of everything in U-110: food, clothing, equipment were all of the highest standard.

By now, Baker-Cresswell realized that there must be a good chance of saving this U-boat and, with all her survivors hustled below, of keeping any information gained from her secret from the Germans. While Balme and his party were in the U-boat, *Bulldog*, *Broadway* and *Aubrietia* patrolled round, dropping the occasional charge to discourage visitors. The visibility was worsening, but Baker-Cresswell knew that his group were conspicuous targets. They would be even more vulnerable when they began the tricky task of taking U-110 in tow.

Meanwhile there was the sound of several depth-charge explosions to the south. The convoy had made two 40 degree emergency turns to port and was steering SE instead of SW when U-201 (Korvetten-Kapitan Schnee) caught up from astern and attacked at 12.28. Schnee had first sighted OB318 at 8.30 that morning and had conferred with Lemp, the two U-boats lying side by side on the surface. They agreed that Lemp should attack first and Schnee half an hour later. This was what Schnee was now doing.

U-201's periscope was sighted by an alert lookout in *Ranpura*, but Schnee managed to close the convoy and fired a salvo of two torpedoes at 12.26, one of which hit *Empire Cloud*. Two minutes later he fired one torpedo from a stern tube which hit *Gregalia*.

Amazon, who was senior officer in *Bulldog*'s absence, *Nigella* and *St Apollo* began a prolonged counter-attack which lasted nearly five hours, used nearly 100 depth-charges and left a square mile of sea covered in oil (which must have come from U-201; all the sunk or sinking merchant ships were coal-burners). At one point *Bulldog* and *Broadway* got a firm Asdic contact while they were guarding U-110, and attacked; this was very probably U-201 as well. Schnee was a most determined and able U-boat captain, and he got U-201, though quite badly damaged, safely away to resume her patrol.

OB318's adventures were not over. A fourth U-boat, U-556 (Korvetten-Kapitan Wohlfarth) had received the sighting reports, closed the convoy early on the 10th, and torpedoed the one remaining ship of the starboard wing column, the 5000-ton *Aelybryn* (which survived and was towed home). The convoy made an emergency turn to port and then at 3.25 a.m. that morning dispersed, each ship making individually for her destination. But Wohlfarth had followed the convoy on the surface and sank two more ships,

Empire Caribou and the Belgian *Gand*, after dispersal. Two more ships from OB318 were lost: the Dutch *Berhala* sunk by U-38 on 24 May, and the Commodore's *Colonial* by U-107 on the 26th when she was only 100 miles from Freetown. Thus, though OB318 had been well-defended, the convoy actually lost eight ships of over 45,000 tons, with two more ships *Aelybryn* and *Empire Cloud* damaged but towed in.

Bulldog had U-110 in tow shortly after 4 p.m. on 9 May, although the U-boat's rudder was jammed over to port. The tow had to be broken for a submarine alarm, but it was picked up again by 6.50, and that evening Baker-Cresswell cautiously worked the towing speed up to 7½ knots. U-110 seemed a little further down by the stern, but was riding fairly easily. But wind and sea got up after midnight, and by 7 a.m. on the 10th *Bulldog* was hove to. At 10.50 U-110 suddenly put her bows up in the air, until they were nearly vertical, and then sank slowly out of sight.

After refuelling at Reykjavik, *Bulldog* steamed direct to Scapa Flow, reaching the anchorage on the afternoon of the 12th. When the men from the Admiralty came on board, they found two packing cases full of treasures beyond their wildest dreams. The First Sea Lord, Admiral Sir Dudley Pound, signalled Baker-Cresswell: 'Hearty congratulations, the petals of your flower are of rare beauty.' King George VI said simply it was perhaps the most important single event in the whole war at sea. Best of all, U-110's survivors were all convinced their ship had sunk just after they abandoned her.

The Government Code and Cypher School at Bletchley Park had broken into the 'Heimisch' naval Enigma keys, in general use by ships and shore authorities in home waters and the Baltic, and by the Atlantic U-boats, in the latter half of March 1941. By 10 May Ultra had read most of the traffic for April. But the delay was steadily getting shorter and May's traffic was read with an average delay of between three and seven days. The captures from U-110 provided the code books for the Kurzsignale, the short signals U-boats used to report convoys and weather information. These, including signals for 'officers only', could be read virtually currently (almost as soon as their intended recipients could read them) for June and July. The Heimisch-coded signals were read, except for very short 'black-out' periods, for the rest of the war.

But this precious information from U-110 was not processed in time to save HX126, which was attacked on 19 May by Kuppisch, who had assumed the mantle of Prien, in 41°W, further west than any other convoy, on the 20th. Kuppisch sank three ships in two attacks, Wohlfarth another three, and U-111, U-98 and U-93 sank a ship each, all before the convoy had been met by its escort. The convoy had scattered and four of the nine ships lost had been sunk after the convoy had broken up.

HX126's fate spurred on some important decisions about the strengths of convoy air and surface escorts. In April 1941 the first squadrons of the Coastal

Command Hudsons and Sunderlands had begun to operate from Iceland. After HX126, nine Lend–Lease long-range Catalina flying boats were transferred to the Canadian Air Force. Although there was still a 'gap' of some 300 miles in mid-ocean where there was no air cover, aircraft could now patrol up to 700 miles westwards from the United Kingdom, 400 miles southwards from Iceland and 600 miles eastwards from Canada.

After HX126 it seemed essential to escort convoys all the way across, in both directions. A Newfoundland Escort Force was formed with, by June 1941, thirty destroyers, nine sloops and twenty-four corvettes. A naval base was set up at St John's, and Iceland became a separate naval command. The Royal Canadian Navy supplied the ships for local escort in the waters off New-foundland and for the ocean escort for the first stage of the Atlantic passage, as far as the Mid Ocean Meeting Point (MOMP) in about 35°W, between Greenland and Iceland. There a British escort group which had sailed from Iceland would take over and escort the convoy to the Eastern Ocean Meeting Point (EastOMP) in 18°W, to be relieved by a Western Approaches Group from the United Kingdom, which would escort to the west coast of Scotland. There, ships for east coast ports would join a WN convoy at Loch Ewe and be convoyed round the north of Scotland.

Thus, a ship bound from Halifax to, say, Rosyth would go in an HX convoy under a local Canadian escort from Halifax to Cape Race, where a St John's Escort Group would rendezvous and escort to MOMP; there, an Iceland group would meet and escort to EastOMP, where a Western Approaches group would take over and escort to the Scottish coast. Finally, a group of anti-submarine trawlers or a sloop would take the ships round to the east coast.

It was a most complicated system, demanding good timing, good navigation and a dash of good luck. If there was any prolonged delay, if the escorts ran short of fuel, or for any reason failed to relieve on time, a convoy would be left unprotected. To help the escorts to their rendezvous, 'MEET' signals sent them by the convoy authorities were enlarged in the summer of 1941, to include information about a convoy's escort, route, the number of ships, the rendezvous position, the names of the Commodore and Vice Commodore and their ships, and the 'secret positions', which were varied for each convoy. The commodore and the ships in convoy reported their own positions by means of bearings and distances from these 'secret positions'.

HX129 sailed from Halifax on 27 May, the first homeward-bound convoy to have surface escort the whole way across the Atlantic. None of its ships was lost or damaged by the enemy. By then the U-boats had gone south, in search of easier pickings. In May 1941 U-boats sank fifty-eight ships of 325,492 tons, but more than half of those ships were sunk in the neighbourhood of Freetown, Sierra Leone, by a group of six U-boats sent by Doenitz at the beginning of the month.

Some of the U-boats were supplied with fuel from tankers operating

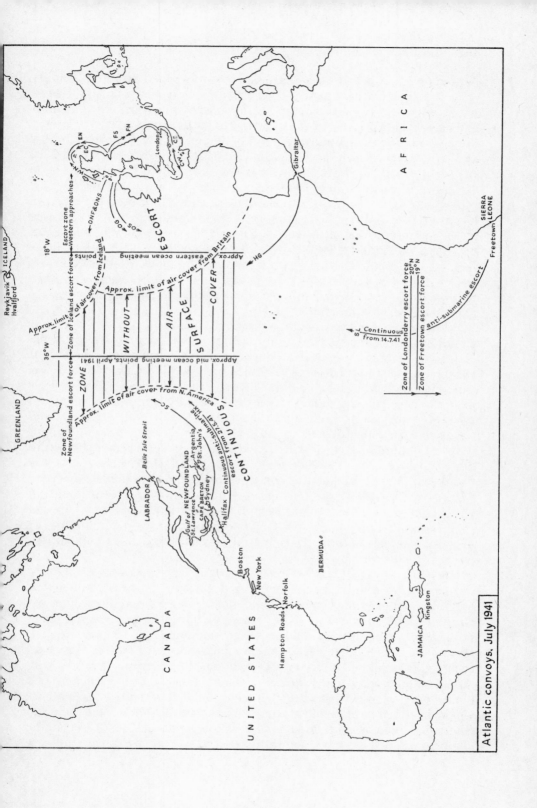

Atlantic convoys, July 1941

ICELAND
Reykjavik
Hvalfjord

GREENLAND

Escort zone — Western approaches
18° W

Escort zone — Western approaches
ONW
ON(F&ON)
OB
OG
OS
London
CW
CE

ESCORT

Approx. eastern ocean meeting points
eastern ocean meeting

Approx. limit of air cover from Britain

HG

Approx. limit of air cover from Iceland
Zone of Iceland escort forces

Approx. limit of air cover

SURFACE   COVER

Approx. limit of air cover from N. America

WITHOUT   AIR   ZONE

35° W
Approx. mid ocean meeting points, April 1941

Zone of Newfoundland escort force
Zone of

CONTINUOUS

Belle Isle Strait

LABRADOR

NEWFOUNDLAND
Gulf of
St. Lawrence
CAPE BRETON
St. John's
Sydney
Argentia, Continuous anti-submarine
escort from 23.5.41
Halifax   Continuous anti-submarine escort from 2.7.41
SC
HX

Boston
New York
Hampton Roads
Norfolk

CANADA

UNITED STATES

BERMUDA

JAMAICA
Kingston

AFRICA

SIERRA LEONE
Freetown

Gibraltar

Zone of Londonderry escort force
Zone of Freetown escort force
Continuous anti-submarine escort
20° N
19° N
Continuous from 14.7.41

between Freetown and the Canaries. Given this added range and endurance, in a generally 'soft' area of convoys with fine weather and dark tropical nights, the U-boats had some tremendous successes against independents, and against convoys SL67, SL68 and SL76 in particular. Korvetten-Kapitan Hessler, in U-107, sank fourteen ships of 86,699 tons on his patrol in May and June, the most successful single U-boat patrol of the Second World War. In June the total of U-boat sinkings was sixty-one ships of 310,143 tons.

Clearly it was high time the SL and OS convoys were also given escort throughout their voyages. The homeward-bound SL convoys were escorted by corvettes from Freetown to Lat. 19°N, where they were met by an escort provided from a force of fifteen sloops and ten ex-US coastguard cutters based at Londonderry, for the rest of the passage home. SL81, sailing on 14 July, was the first to have an escort right through. Outward, the OS convoys were escorted by the Londonderry groups down to 19°N, where they were relieved by the corvettes from Freetown, the Londonderry ships themselves going to refuel at Bathurst in the Gambia.

With these escort dispositions, the armed merchant cruisers could be withdrawn, from the Sierra Leone convoys in August 1941, and from the Halifax convoys in October. They had given tremendous service, at tremendous cost to themselves. Thirteen had been lost (and one more was sunk off Colombo in 1942) and their crews called themselves (not entirely jokingly) the 'suicide squads'. Most of the surviving armed merchant cruisers went back to the control of the Ministry of War Transport and reverted to trooping duties.

It was not until May 1941 that the old argument over whether ships were more effective as convoy escorts or as patrols searching for U-boats was finally laid to rest. An Admiralty study committee reported that ships were too scarce to be spared for searching expeditions. Convoy escorts should not be weakened until far greater strength became available. This would not prevent some Commanders-in-Chief forming 'hunter–killer groups' or using ships to patrol for U-boats, but the official policy, at least and at last, was that convoy was the answer.

Ironically, it was already becoming clear that convoy was not enough. At the current rate of sinkings, the merchant fleet would lose over 4 million tons by the end of 1941. The combined output of the British and Allied shipyards was about 1 million tons a year. We had already appealed to the United States for help but no new ships would arrive for another eighteen months. In 1941, Great Britain needed at least 36 million tons of dry cargo and not less than 720 cargoes of oil fuel, to feed the population and maintain war production. At the rate in mid-1941, only 28.5 million tons of dry cargo and 660 tanker-cargoes would have been landed by the end of the year, when there would be a deficit of 7 million tons of imports and 2 million tons of food. Shortages could be made good by withdrawals from stock but the remaining shipping would have to be used with the greatest economy. No new military operations involving any ocean passage could be contemplated. The outlook for 1942 was even more bleak unless the U-boats could be brought under control.

Not to beat about the bush, the U-boats were winning. The lines on the graphs did not meet safely. The totals did not add up to survival. In 1941, just as in 1917, the country's certain defeat was there in the figures.

On 18 June the Admiralty were allowed to raise the minimum speed for independently routed ships from 13 to 15 knots, thus at last reversing the Cabinet decision of November 1940, which the Admiralty had protested at the time. The Trade Division reported in May 1941 that although everything possible had been done to give these independents protection, they had still suffered many more losses than ships in convoy. The rate of loss of independently routed ships on the round voyage to and from Halifax was 13.8 per cent, for convoyed ships only 5.8 per cent. For ships on the round voyage to and from Freetown the difference was even more striking: 15.4 per cent rate of loss for independents, 5.5 per cent for convoyed ships. For ships too slow to be included in convoys the losses were described as 'tragic'; one in four on the homeward route had been sunk. Even where independents were capable of 15 knots, their loss rate was as high as ships in convoy. The only exceptions to the rules were the 'monsters', the giant liners like the *Queen Mary* which sailed alone. Their very high speed, of around 30 knots, was an adequate defence.

The other factor which averted defeat in the war against the U-boats was the information gained through Ultra, which enabled convoys to be evasively routed with great success. Sinkings by U-boats fell to twenty-two ships of 94,209 tons in July 1941, and twenty-three ships of only 80,310 tons in August.

The first Atlantic convoy to benefit directly from Ultra was HX133, which sailed with forty-nine ships from Halifax on 16 June. On 1 June Doenitz had begun to form the 'West' Group of U-boats, with four boats, adding to the group as more arrived. But by the 20th, when twenty U-boats were spread in a great arc across the central and north Atlantic, Doenitz was beginning to suspect (not for the last time) that there was a security leak; it seemed to him beyond coincidence that his U-boats were sighting no convoys.

The homeward-bound HX133 was sighted at 13.35 on the 23rd by U-203, who closed the convoy that night and sank one straggler. This was *Vigrid*, about whom there had already been suspicions of sabotage to prevent her sailing. Her engines had given constant trouble, causing her to straggle and bringing about her loss.

The outward-bound OB-336 had also been sighted the same day. This convoy should have been diverted, but human frailty frustrated the best-laid plans of the Admiralty and Ultra. The signal to alter course was received in the Commodore's ship *Harpagon*, not by the Petty Officer Telegraphist, who was sick, but by an inexperienced junior rating. He did not know how to decode it, was afraid to ask, put the signal in his pocket and said nothing about it for another twenty-seven hours. U-203 had lost contact with HX133 but chanced upon OB336 and sank two ships on the 24th.

Later the same day U-79 also found OB336 and directed U-71, U-371 and U-651 to the scene. Between them they sank two more ships. But the Admiralty Tracking Room decided, from Ultra intercepts, that HX133 was more seriously threatened; most of OB336's escort was ordered to join HX133, bringing its escort up to thirteen ships. In the five-day battle which began on 24 June, the escorts actually outnumbered the attacking U-boats. HX133 was attacked at 7 p.m. on the 24th, and again at about 11 p.m., and at midnight on the 26th, and there was a fifth attack at 00.30 on the 29th. Happily, although eight or nine U-boats were in contact at one time or another, every U-boat which made an attack subsequently lost contact and dropped astern. In all, from HX133, and from OB336 with its depleted escort, eleven ships of about 57,000 tons were sunk. Another two were damaged but managed to keep up with their convoy.

On 27 June *Gladiolus*, *Nasturtium* and *Celandine* sank U-556 in a very neat joint exercise. *Nasturtium* got the first clear, unmistakable Asdic contact at 7.35 that morning. But unfortunately she had no depth-charges left. So *Ottawa*, the senior officer, ordered *Gladiolus* to take over the attack. 'Have had good contact for two hours,' signalled *Nasturtium*, wistfully, 'I hope someone will pick it up before I leave.'

The next ship to join was *Celandine* who could get no Asdic contact at all. So *Nasturtium* led her, steaming over the target and indicating the time to fire by dipping a flag, and the place by turning with full rudder over the target, to make an easily visible aiming mark. Guided in this way, *Celandine* made four attacks, with twenty-four depth-charges. She never gained contact and kept making signals like, 'Hope you are not wasting my depth-charges.' *Nasturtium* would hasten to reassure her: 'You are doing fine, give him the works.'

At 11.07 *Celandine* dropped a full ten-charge pattern, although she still had no Asdic contact. 'It seems strange we cannot get anything,' she signalled. 'Wish you could see my recorder trace,' replied *Nasturtium*. At 12.17 there was a strong and pungent smell of oil, and a wide slick spread on the surface. In the middle of it a U-boat surfaced, and at 13.03 its crew abandoned ship. This was the end for Korvetten-Kapitan Wohlfarth and his crew. All but the Engineer Officer and three men were picked up. At no time during the attack had *Celandine* the slightest vestige of an Asdic contact.

Korvetten-Kapitan Lohrmeyer in U-651 had been one of the very few captains to attack from inside the convoy, as in the old days of Prien and Kretschmer. It brought about his downfall. U-651 collided with a merchant-man in the early hours of the 29th, was damaged and forced to surface. The smoke of its diesel exhaust, when the engines started, betrayed it.

At 5.30 that morning a small cloud of black smoke was sighted on the horizon from the bridge of the destroyer *Malcolm*. *Malcolm* closed at full speed, a very young Engine-Room Artificer 4th Class being so overcome with excitement at the telegraph order 'Full Ahead' he opened the main turbine throttle valve wide. *Malcolm* rapidly achieved a speed which nobody had previously thought possible. The upshot was that the small black cloud was seen to contain a conning tower.

The U-boat dived, but *Malcolm* had too good a datum point and made one accurate attack with a full pattern which blew U-651 to the surface. *Malcolm* opened fire. Although no hits were scored, Lohrmeyer and his crew abandoned ship. *Malcolm* picked up forty-four survivors. It would have been forty-five but another destroyer *Scimitar* which had assisted in the attack, darted in and snatched one survivor right off *Malcolm*'s scrambling net, saying, 'We must have one of those.' *Malcolm* protested vigorously but in fact the single prisoner, isolated from his comrades, gave very useful intelligence.

OB349 was the last OB convoy to sail, these outward convoys being redesignated ON. They sailed alternately Slow (7 knots) and Fast (9 knots), each on a six-day cycle, the Fast sailing two days after the Slow. ON1 sailed from Liverpool on 26 July 1941 and crossed the Atlantic with no enemy encounters of any kind. From April 1941, outward escort was given from Britain to Iceland, and from Iceland to 35°W, by four escort groups of Western Approaches Command, based at Greenock and Londonderry. To assist them, eleven Asdic-fitted minesweepers of the 1st and 6th Minesweeper Flotillas at Scapa were allocated to Western Approaches Command and the Home Fleet continued to supply four destroyers from Iceland.

The forty-nine ships of ON1 included two Catapult Aircraft Merchant (CAM) Ships, and a Rescue Ship, two specialized types of convoy vessel evolved during the war. The idea of a rescue ship, specially fitted and trained to pick up survivors, had been suggested during the First World War, though nothing much was done then or between the wars. It was very important indeed for morale in a convoy for there to be at least a chance that survivors would be picked up. Escorts often carried out this duty but there were many occasions when it was dangerous, and certainly not in the convoy's own best interests, for an escort to pick up survivors instead of concentrating upon a counter-attack. Nominating one ship, normally the last in a column, was also unsatisfactory. Everything then depended upon how good a seaman, or how good a Samaritan, her master was.

What was needed was a special vessel, seaworthy, handy, fairly fast, preferably with straight sides to make recoveries easier, and with ample accommodation below decks – it was found that for psychological reason survivors preferred to stay together in a large space – with easy and quick access to the upper deck.

The most promising ships for the purpose were former coastal passenger steamers, although their seaworthiness had to be proved and naturally they were not of long endurance. But they were handy, of about 1500 to 2000 tons, and had the essential speed (a 12-knot ship, for instance, would only have a margin of 3 or 4 knots over a fast convoy, and many rescues were made astern of a convoy, after which the rescue ship had to catch up, or become a straggler herself).

As time went on, rescue ships had many refinements: an operating theatre, medical staff, supplies of drugs, specially fitted rescue-boats, scrambling nets, boom nets which stuck out at right angles, for stopping rafts or boats drifting past, extra Carley floats and float-nets, to which men in the water could cling, extra clothing, books, games, toilet outfits. Rescue ships were armed, and were also fitted with H/F/D/F equipment, and 10-inch signalling lamps. To show who she was, when in company or engaged in rescue, a rescue ship flew a large green flag with a white diagonal bar.

At first it was planned, for administrative ease, to have rescue ships manned under the White Ensign. But the master and his men knew their own ship and their own way of doing things and it was found that merchant seamen were tremendously impressed and encouraged to be rescued by men of their own service. So the rescue ships continued to sail under the Red Ensign.

The first rescue ship, the Dutch *Hontestroom*, sailed on 11 January 1941 but she was found unsuitable. The first really successful rescue ship, the 1526-ton ex-Clyde Shipping Co.'s *Toward*, sailed on 24 January, 1941, and only four days later pulled off her first rescue, taking twelve survivors from the torpedoed *Baron Renfrew*.

Eventually there were twenty-nine rescue ships who covered 786 voyages, steamed 2,250,000 miles and rescued 4194 survivors. The record-holder was the ex-Pharaonic Mail Line Steamer *Zamalek*, with 665 survivors. But *Rathlin* recovered 634 survivors, *Perth* 455, and *Copeland* (who sailed with seventy-two convoys) 433. A typical rescue ship's record was *Melrose Abbey*'s. She covered forty-two convoys, steamed 123,000 miles, sent her rescue boat away fifty times, performed thirteen major operations at sea, and gave medical advice to other ships in over 600 cases. She rescued eighty-four survivors, and one dog. Six rescue ships, *Toward*, *Zaafaran*, *Walmer Castle*, *Stockport*, *St Sunniva* and *Pinto*, were lost to enemy action, some in appalling circumstances: *St Sunniva* was lost with all hands, *Walmer Castle* with eleven of her crew and twenty survivors, *Stockport* with sixty-four crew and ninety-one survivors.

CAM ships were a logical development from the Battle of the Atlantic Directive, which had called for fighters to be catapulted or otherwise launched in defence of convoys. Shore-based air power was vital for convoy defence. But there was still no substitute for a convoy's own organic air power, carried along inside the convoy and responsive to the convoy's immediate tactical situation.

The first attempt to provide this form of air cover was the old seaplane carrier *Pegasus* (formerly the *Ark Royal* of the First World War, renamed in 1934). She had three Fairey Fulmar fighters of 807 Squadron FAA embarked, and escorted nine convoys between December 1940 and July 1941. After

Pegasus, four Fighter Catapult Ships, *Patia*, *Springbank*, *Ariguani* and *Maplin*, were converted to fly one Fulmar of 804 Squadron.

Flying from a catapult ship demanded a peculiarly cold-blooded form of courage of the fighter pilot. Normally there was no diversion airfield. After being launched and carrying out his attack, the pilot had to bale out or ditch and wait to be picked up by a ship in the convoy or by an escort.

The fighters were intended to operate, not so much against the U-boats as their partners the long-range Focke-Wulfe Kondors. *Patia* was sunk, before embarking her fighter, in April 1941. *Springbank*, and *Ariguani* both had Fulmars embarked from May. But the first fighter catapult success, and a most heartening event it proved to be for all concerned, was pulled off by *Maplin*, whose Hurricane shot down a FW200C on 3 August 1941, in defence of SL81, homeward-bound from Sierra Leone.

The pilot was Lt R. W. H. Everett RNVR (who incidentally had piloted Gregalach to win the 1929 Grand National), who closed to within 1½ miles of his quarry before it noticed him: 'I fired five-second bursts all the way until I was 40 yards astern of the enemy. Another short burst at this range and my guns were empty. I noticed pieces flying off the starboard side of the Focke-Wulfe and it appeared to be alight inside the fuselage. I broke away to port at 30 yards. My windshield and hood were covered with oil and I quickly jumped to the conclusion that my engine oil system was badly hit.' But the oil was actually from the Kondor, which dived into the sea. 'My one idea was to get down while I still had charge of the situation. I made two rather half-hearted attempts to bale out, but the machine nosed down and caught me when half out. I changed my mind and decided to land in the sea near HMS *Wanderer* and did so. The ship sent a boat and I was extremely well looked after.' Everett was awarded the DSO.

Although Everett's was the only enemy shot down, fighter catapult ships made ten launches in anger. Five pilots were rescued; four and their Fulmars flew safely to shore; and one pilot was killed when he flew into a hillside in Ireland. Unfortunately Everett also lost his life in an accident whilst ferrying an aircraft from Liverpool to Belfast in January 1942.

The fighter catapult ships certainly deterred the Focke-Wulfes. Every launch drove off the intruder even if he were not shot down. The catapult ships were in service until June 1942, by which time they had long been superseded by the CAM ships. These, unlike the fighter catapult ships, wore the Red Ensigh and continued to ply their normal trade as merchantmen whilst performing as CAM ships.

Except for *Michael E*, one of the earliest CAM ships, which had a naval pilot and a Sea Hurricane of 804 Squadron, the pilots and aircraft of the CAM ships were from the RAF. Sixty pilots, all volunteers, and from every type of job in Fighter Command, formed the Merchant Ship Fighter Unit in April 1941. The first CO was Sq Ldr Louis Strange DSO, MC, DFC and Bar. The unit in each ship consisted of the pilot, four aircrew, naval ratings for catapult

maintenance, and a naval Fighter Direction Officer to guide the pilot on to
his target by radio-telephone from the ship.

Empire Rainbow, the first CAM ship to be ready, was followed by thirty-four
more. The catapult was a steel runway 85 feet long. The trolley carrying the
fighter was driven along the track by a bank of cordite rockets for some 60
feet; by this distance, using 30-degree flaps and 6¼ pounds' boost, a perfect
take-off could be made without any loss of height at all. In many cases the
fighter climbed directly off the trolley, with an airspeed of well over
80 m.p.h.

The first catapult launch took place on 31 May 1941, and the first action
between a CAM ship fighter and a Focke-Wulfe in November. Between May
1941 and August 1943 CAM ships sailed on 170 round convoy voyages, in the
Atlantic, Arctic and to Gibraltar. Only eight launches were made in anger,
but they had a high batting average: six enemy aircraft were destroyed and
three damaged. *Empire Morn*, the only CAM ship to make two operational
launches, destroyed three enemy aircraft. Twelve CAM ships were lost while
sailing with convoys.

In August there were twenty U-boats waiting for targets south-west of
Iceland, but no pack attacks took place during the month. Convoys were
sighted, but each time were evasively routed by Ultra. Concerned by the lack
of success, Doenitz moved the U-boats eastwards, nearer Ireland. But
Coastal Command was waiting, and on 27 August a Hudson of 269 Squadron
piloted by Sq Ldr J. H. Thompson brought off a truly marvellous *coup* by
attacking and forcing U-570 (Kapitan-Leutnant Rahmlow) to surrender.
U-570 was taken in, and on 19 September recommissioned as HMS *Graph*.

After such success, and two comparatively light months for U-boat
sinkings, there was a temptation by 1 September to think that the worst of the
Battle of the Atlantic was over. There were suggestions that aircraft should
be removed from Coastal Command and put back to bombing shore targets
on the Continent, suggestions the Admiralty had to resist with every
argument and persuasion at its command. There was, in fact, a second
'Battle of the Atlantic', the battle to obtain and keep long-range aircraft for
Coastal Command.

The Admiralty assessed Doenitz's strength at 184 U-boats, and his losses
to date at forty-four. Admiralty estimates were always realistic, and post-war
analysis showed that the actual figures were 198 U-boats, and forty-seven
lost. U-boats were entering service faster than they were being sunk. It was
estimated that Doenitz would have 229 U-boats; as it turned out, this was an
underestimate. In other words, the trend was upwards and there was
absolutely no cause for complacency. The September figures, fifty-three
ships sunk by U-boats, of 202,820 tons, showed that the lull was over.

Most of those losses were borne by a few convoys, the worst hit being SC42,
which lost sixteen ships of over 65,000 tons, and a tanker damaged but towed
home. The sixty-four-ship convoy, carrying half a million tons of cargo, left

Sydney on 30 August, escorted by the Canadian 24th Escort Group of the destroyer *Skeena* (Cdr Hibbard) and the corvettes *Alberni*, *Kenogami* and *Orillia*.

The 'Markgraf' group of U-boats, some fourteen of them, was spread out in a search line, each boat twenty miles apart, SW of Iceland. Their presence was known but not their position, due to delays in Ultra de-crypting (the U-boats had recently introduced a new cypher and new instructions). SC42 was diverted far to the north, rounding Cape Farewell at the southern tip of Greenland and keeping only some sixty miles off the Greenland coast.

The convoy might have escaped, but it was making a lot of smoke (which the Commodore, Rear Admiral Mackenzie complained was visible at 30 miles), which on 9 September was sighted by U-85, the northernmost boat of the pack. At 7 p.m. the convoy made another diversionary turn to the north-east, actually towards the coast of Greenland, but it was too late. U-85 closed and attacked. Although she failed (a straggler astern reported a periscope and torpedo tracks), her report brought another three U-boats to the scene. When the sun went down, and a brilliant moon rose, the U-boats went to work. The first ship sunk, with all hands, was *Muneric* just before 10 p.m. U-432 sank four ships, U-82 the CAM ship *Empire Hudson*, and U-652 torpedoed the tanker *Tahchee*. All four U-boats were inside the convoy. The Norwegian *Regin* fired on surfaced U-boats three times, and *Skeena* chased one U-boat up and down the convoy columns. *Skeena* did get an Asdic contact and carried out an attack but broke off to rescue survivors. At one time three of the escorts were astern of the convoy picking up survivors. By dawn, eight ships had been sunk.

Not all the losses need have been. *Kenogami* went alongside *Empire Hudson*, to find her confidential books still undestroyed, likewise her fighter aircraft and her radio direction-finding sets. *Kenogami* sent a party on board to destroy all this equipment. The general opinion in *Kenogami* was that *Empire Hudson* could have been salvaged. However, *Orillia* took *Tahchee* in tow and set off towards Reykjavik.

But this meant one escort less and, after U-432 had shadowed during the day, the U-boats closed in again at nightfall. Outnumbering the escort by more than two to one, they sank another seven ships. But the escorts also had a success. The Admiralty had ordered the two Canadian corvettes *Chambly* and *Moosejaw* to join SC42. Coming up astern of the convoy after dark on the 10th, they surprised U-501. They carried out one sharp and accurate attack at 9.40 p.m., which blew U-501 to the surface close to *Moosejaw*.

Moosejaw opened fire with her 4-inch gun which jammed after one round. She hit the U-boat a glancing blow and then ran alongside her for some distance, the U-boat still going ahead at a rate of knots. *Moosejaw*'s sailors were suddenly flabbergasted to find on their upperdeck a stranger, yelling at the top of his voice in what sounded like German! It was the U-boat commander, Korvetten-Kapitan Förster, who had leaped across from his conning tower to the corvette's decks and 'did not even get his feet wet in the process'!

Chambly's First Lieutenant actually boarded U-501. Although one of the crew told him the U-boat was about to blow up and the sea-cocks were all open, he went down into the control room. But the water was flooding in fast and the lights went out while he was standing there. He and his boarding party swam off to their boat, while the U-boat went down 'with a rush' behind them.

Förster, meanwhile, was explaining that 'he had felt impelled to get aboard *Moosejaw* at once in order to insist on the British rescuing his crew, otherwise they might be left to drown'. This did not convince his rescuers and 'succeeded in infuriating his own crew into a high state of blood pressure'. Six officers and thirty-one ratings of U-501 were rescued. Ten ratings drowned.

During the night the escort was strengthened by *Gladiolus*, the Canadian corvette *Wetaskiwin*, the Free French *Mimose* and the anti-submarine trawler *Buttermere*. At noon on the 11th the 2nd Escort Group arrived, of the destroyers *Douglas*, *Veteran*, *Saladin*, *Skate* and *Leamington*, from Iceland. This redressed the odds against the convoy and that evening *Veteran* and *Leamington* sighted and sank U-207 (which had sunk three ships the previous night). U-boats sank one or two cripples astern of SC42, but the main body of the convoy steamed into a protective fog bank and suffered no more losses.

The quality of the escort could make a tremendous difference to a convoy's fate, as two examples in September 1941 showed. HG72 set out from Gibraltar on the 10th, and was attacked by the Italian U-boats *Da Vinci*, *Morosini*, *Torelli* and *Malaspina*. But the escort of the destroyers *Faulknor* (Captain de Salis), *Avondale*, *Encounter*, *Nestor* and the sloop *Deptford*, held the ring so well and drove off their attackers so comprehensively that the convoy suffered no loss at all. The papers on that convoy were passed around the Admiralty departments as a perfect example of an escort in complete control of the situation.

The experience of SL87 later that month was quite different. This convoy of eleven ships from Freetown was escorted by the sloops *Gorleston* (Senior Officer) and *Bideford*, the corvette *Gardenia* and the Free French sloop *Commandant Duboc*. It was a case of highly experienced U-boat commanders against an inexpert and unorganised escort. On 21 September everything started to go wrong. *Gorleston* picked up a signal on 352 kilocycles at 5.30 a.m., but did not realize it was a U-boat transmitting. As a result the convoy ran directly into the path of U-68 (Fregatten-Kapitan Merten) who sank one ship to begin four days of attacks. U-107 (Hessler), U-103 (Winter) and U-67 (Muller-Stockheim) all made attacks, and by the 23rd the convoy had split into two groups and was in complete disarray.

No retaliation was taken by the escorts. At most times only one escort was with the convoy, the others being dispersed, to transmit W/T signals (which had to be made away from the convoy), to pick up survivors, to carry out 'dusk sweeps' or, in *Gorleston*'s case, to tow a damaged ship. *Gardenia* had to leave early. She had tried to refuel in Freetown but had been told by the tanker to wait her turn. Life in Freetown moved slowly, even during a war, *Gardenia*'s sailing time came near, and still she had not fuelled. Her captain did not insist, and *Gardenia* eventually sailed short of fuel.

The upshot, by 24 September, was seven ships (of the eleven) sunk, of 33,000 tons. A board of enquiry concluded that it was 'due to this lack of balance and leadership and to the fact that the Group were untrained and mixed, that the convoy was not afforded its maximum protection'. Admiral Noble minuted that 'arrangements have been made that the CO of *Gorleston* shall not in future act as the Senior Officer of an Escort Group'.

Another convoy to suffer heavily was HG73, which left Gibraltar homeward-bound on 17 September. In spite of a strong escort – the fighter catapult ship *Springbank*, a destroyer, two sloops and eight corvettes – the convoy lost nine ships of over 25,000 tons from its complement of twenty-five. The escorts were hampered by defects in their radar sets while the attackers were helped by some excellent air/U-boat co-operation. *Springbank*'s fighter did drive off one Kondor on the 24th, but the Kondors returned on the 26th and 27th to home U-boats on to their targets.

Amongst the ships sunk were *Springbank* and the Commodore's *Avoceta*. The Commodore, Rear Admiral Sir Kenelm Creighton, was a survivor:

> I was about to go to the upper bridge to see the Master and the Officer-of-the-Watch. A violent tremor went through *Avoceta*. She staggered like a stumbling horse and shuddered in to a lurching stop as a violent explosion came from the direction of the engine-room aft. My ears were buzzing from the crash of the exploding torpedo – I had no doubt but that that was what it was. My left arm was numb from being flung against the side of the bridge ladder. The vicious scream of escaping steam smothered some of the unearthly gargling sounds coming from the drowning and the tearing squeals of those trapped in the scalding agony of the engine-room. All these sounds darted into my ears during the two or three seconds before I picked myself up and stumbled across with Signalman Erskine to fire the distress rockets as an indication that we had been hit. As they whizzed up I glanced aft and saw the stern was already underwater and the dreadful noises were ceasing from that part of the ship. The escape of steam was easing now as *Avoceta* sat back on her haunches and the bows rose in an ever more crazy angle into the air. No boats could be lowered. There was complete pandemonium; the thunderous bangs and crashes of furniture and cargo being hurled about below decks all mingled with the ghastly shrieks of the sleeping people waking to their deaths. As the bows went higher so did the shrieks. I clung to a stanchion feeling sick and helpless as I had to look on while the children were swept out into the darkness below by the torrent of water which roared through the smoking room.
>
> Instinctively I must have blown up my lifebelt and I thrust my false teeth into my jacket pocket – thinking, I suppose, of other commodores who had been sunk and not been compensated for the loss of their teeth.

Almost completely deafened by the explosion, Admiral Creighton reached a raft, with the Master of *Avoceta* and six others. After three hours those who survived were picked up by the corvette *Periwinkle*.

The convoy commodores were a most gallant body of senior retired naval officers, some of them admirals, who on the outbreak of war wrote to the Admiralty asking (some demanded, some begged) to be employed afloat in any capacity, rank or rating whatsoever. There were some 159 convoy commodores RNR (junior, it was explained to them, to all captains RN), a third of them officers of the Merchant Navy or the RNR, but including officers of the Royal Norwegian and Royal Netherlands Navies.

Most of the commodores were comparatively elderly for active service and were going to sea after years ashore, growing vegetables, taking the dog for walks, acting as JPs or parish councillors. For them the convoy was curiously chastening as well as an exciting and exhausting experience. As young men they had dreamed of having huge fleets obedient to their every signal. As for huge fleets, they certainly did command unusually large numbers of ships (the biggest westbound convoy of the war had 187 ships). They soon learned that the preface word 'Please' worked wonders in the merchant service, and that every signal meant that some officer had to be rousted out from his well-earned watch below to answer it. They often had to refrain from making signals about bad station-keeping, and instead just allow for 'ebb and flow', on the 'Little Bo Peep' principle of leaving them alone and letting them come home.

A commodore had a harassing existence when a convoy formed up, with difficulties over late-comers, unnotified absentees, fogs, tides and collisions. Once every ship had found her proper place, and the convoy was clear of land, then there were problems of station-keeping, and making smoke, and stragglers, and showing lights, and garbage. No two ships were the same: some had anti-torpedo nets, some were fitted for making smoke, for oiling the escorts, and some with direction-finding sets.

The relationship between the commodore and the escort commander was crucial. The commodore was responsible for the good order and conduct of the ships in the convoy but the escort commander took control of all convoy operations. Thus a very senior admiral who had recently flown his flag on an important station as Commander-in-Chief could find himself subordinate to an officer many years and many ranks his junior. But normally it all worked very well.

Some convoy commodores lost much more than false teeth. Twenty-one of them died, among them Admiral Sir H. J. Studholme Brownrigg KBE, CB, DSO (lost in SS *Ville de Tamatave*, 24 January 1943) who was very probably the most senior naval officer on either side to be killed on active service.

Another casualty was Vice-Admiral Humphrey Hugh Smith DSO, who was killed in *Manchester Brigade* on 29 July 1940. For him, to be a convoy commodore was like being 'exhumed from a living grave'. 'A certain old yellow admiral,' as he described himself, 'who has been brought back to blue water by the convoy system, often looks at the ships ploughing along all round him and says to himself, "I hope this is not a beautiful dream, from which I shall awake to find myself only an urban district councillor."'

Chapter Fifteen

Just as the U-boats had had their 'aces', so the escorts produced their own maestros. The most formidable and successful was Commander (later Captain) F. J. Walker, who first entered upon the convoy warfare scene in 1941. He was a specialist in anti-submarine warfare, and known in the Navy as an authority, but ironically he had already been passed over for promotion before the war, for 'lack of leadership'. But for the war, he would eventually have retired into obscurity.

Even in the war, Walker's special gifts were not recognized and his talents took some time to emerge. In 1940, including the period of the Dunkirk evacuation, he was Staff Officer (Operations) to the Flag Officer, Dover, Vice Admiral Sir Bertram Ramsay (by a curiosity, another officer whose career had run into shallows before the war and who now took a fresh course).

Walker hankered after a sea command, and in March 1941 asked Captain George Creasy, Director of Anti-Submarine Warfare and old friend, to intercede for him. In September Walker went up to Liverpool to take command of the sloop *Stork*, as Senior Officer of the 36th Escort Group.

From Walker's first day on his bridge, it was clear that here was an unusually aggressive, exacting and thoughtful leader. Those long years of anti-submarine exercises off Portland before the war had left him with an almost intuitive knowledge of what an attacking and retreating submarine could do. This special flair, coupled with his insatiable desire to kill, and go on killing U-boats, made him a most formidable opponent.

Walker began to exercise his ships, drilling them as a team, always trying to cut down on signalling, always encouraging his subordinate captains to act on their own initiative. Always his first object was to destroy U-boats. For instance, his group exercised a form of counter-attack known as Operation Buttercup, which was later modified and used throughout Western Approaches Command, to force a U-boat to dive, where it immediately lost

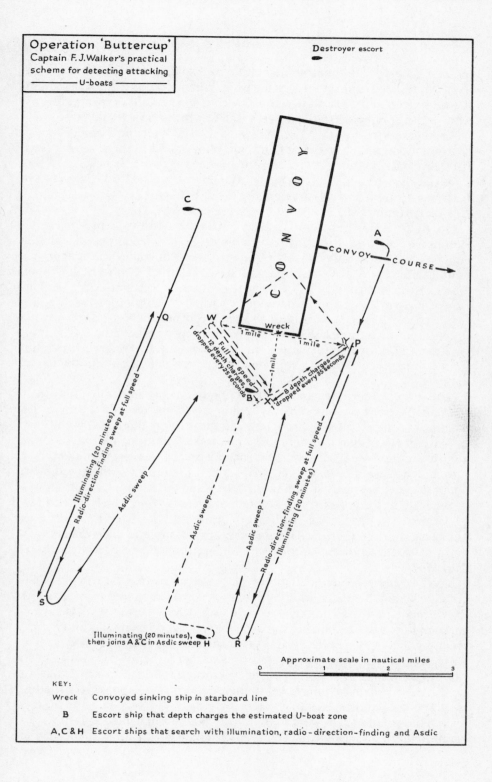

Operation 'Buttercup'
Captain F. J. Walker's practical
scheme for detecting attacking
—— U-boats ——

Destroyer escort

CONVOY

CONVOY COURSE

Wreck
1 mile   1 mile
1 mile

Full speed
12 depth charges
dropped every 25 seconds

8 depth charges
dropped every 35 seconds

Illuminating (20 minutes)
Radio-direction-finding sweep at full speed

Asdic sweep

Asdic sweep

Asdic sweep

Radio-direction-finding sweep at full speed
Illuminating (20 minutes)

Illuminating (20 minutes),
then joins A & C in Asdic sweep

Approximate scale in nautical miles
0   1   2   3

KEY:

Wreck   Convoyed sinking ship in starboard line

B   Escort ship that depth charges the estimated U-boat zone

A, C & H   Escort ships that search with illumination, radio-direction-finding and Asdic most of its speed and became detectable by Asdic. In Buttercup, the most likely routes of escape on the surface were illuminated, and the area around the torpedoed ship was plastered with depth-charges. The escorts meanwhile waited on the outskirts, to see which way the U-boat would bolt.

The composition of 36th Escort Group showed the typical proportion of RNR and RNVR captains to RN at that time. With *Stork* was the sloop *Deptford* (Lt Cdr H. R. White), and the corvettes *Vetch* (Lt Cdr H. J. Beverley RNR), *Rhododendron* (Lt Cdr L. A. Sayers RNR), *Pentstemon* (Lt Cdr J. Byron RNR), *Gardenia* (Lt J. Firth RNVR), *Convolvulus* (Lt R. S. Connell RNR), *Samphire* (Lt Cdr F. T. Renny RNR) and *Marigold* (Lt J. Renwick RNR).

On these fellow captains, Walker constantly impressed the object of Buttercup was to 'destroy any U-boat which has succeeded in attacking a convoy escorted at night by this Group'. Always, in conversation as in his written orders, Walker stressed the destruction of U-boats: 'I cannot emphasize too strongly that a U-boat sighted or otherwise detected is immediately to be attacked continuously without further orders, with guns, depth charges, and/or ram until she has been destroyed or until further orders are received.' Just as Nelson urged his captains that they could never go far wrong in laying their ship alongside an enemy, so Walker assured his Group, 'No officer will ever be blamed by me for getting on with the job in hand.'

The Group escorted a convoy out to Gibraltar in November 1941, by which time the Germans were already sending groups of U-boats into the Mediterranean; six passed through the Straits in September, and another six in November. Walker's group meanwhile were sent on patrols which were almost fruitless. *Marigold* gave the Group its first success off Gibraltar on 16 November, when she sank U-433 (Korvetten-Kapitan Ey), which had been about to attack a convoy steaming eastwards into the Mediterranean.

36th Escort Group's first UK-bound convoy was HG76 which sailed from Gibraltar on 14 December, with a strong escort: 36th Escort Group, less *Gardenia*; the destroyers *Exmoor*, *Blankney* and *Stanley*; the sloops *Black Swan* and *Fowey*; the corvettes *Carnation* and *Jonquil*, and the Free French *La Malouine*.

HG76's escort also included the auxiliary aircraft carrier *Audacity*, who had already begun to usher in a new era of convoy defence. She was the ex-German *Hannover*, a single-screw diesel-driven ship of 5537 tons, captured in February 1940 in the Mona Passage, between Dominica and Puerto Rico, by the cruiser *Dunedin* and the Canadian destroyer *Assiniboine*. She was towed to Jamaica as a prize after fires started by her own crew had been put out, and later steamed to Blyth in Northumberland for an extensive conversion. Her masts, derricks, funnel, upper bridge and superstructure were removed and replaced by a steel flight deck, 368 feet long and 60 feet wide. Her exhaust gases were led out to the side through ducts and she had a small combined bridge/flying control position flush with the flight deck. She had two hydraulically-retarded arrester wires, and a third, stout, unretarded wire known as the 'Jesus Christ wire'.

Audacity's captain was Cdr D. W. McKendrick, an old Swordfish pilot himself, who saw to it that the best accommodation was given to aircrew. The ship's original first-class cabins still remained and the young pilots were the only sub-lieutenants in the Navy to have their own cabins, with private bathrooms. Her first air group was eight pilots of 802 Squadron led by their CO, Lt Cdr J. M. Wintour, and six Grumman Martlet fighters, an American marque with a rugged airframe and undercarriage, specifically designed for deck landings. The ship had no hangar and the aircraft were stowed on deck, open to winds and rain and salt spray. All maintenance had also to be done in the open; at night, blue-shaded torches, held under a jacket, had to be used.

Audacity sailed with her first convoy, OG74 to Gibraltar, on 12 September 1941. It consisted of twenty-six ships, escorted by the sloop *Deptford*, the ocean-boarding vessel *Corinthian* and five corvettes. The convoy was sighted by U-124 on the 20th and U-201 was directed to the attack but at 6.15 p.m. she was sighted on the surface by one of *Audacity*'s Martlets, machine-gunned and forced to dive – an omen for the future. But U-124 (Korvetten-Kapitan Mohr) continued to shadow the convoy and sank *Empire Moat* and *Baltallin* that night.

The rescue ship *Walmer Castle* dropped astern to look for survivors. She was only small, at 906 tons, but she could make 15 knots and had a fully equipped sickbay and operating theatre. She rescued the entire crew of thirty from *Empire Moat* and twenty-eight from *Baltallin* but in doing so lost touch with the convoy. Two Martlets were flown off to search for her and three ships which had straggled. They sighted *Walmer Castle* and signalled to her the convoy's position, course and speed. Rescue ships had already been given a series of positions, through which the convoy would pass, to enable them to rejoin. But before she could do so, *Walmer Castle* was attacked by a Focke-Wulfe Kondor which killed her Master, Captain G. K. Clarke, and sank her with bombs and gunfire, with the loss of another ten officers and twenty men. *Deptford* and *Marigold* came back and picked up the rest.

Two Martlets were scrambled from *Audacity* when the radar echo of *Walmer Castle*'s attacker was detected. They could see *Walmer Castle* blazing when they arrived, but no sign of the Kondor. However, they were redirected to an echo twenty-six miles further west and Sub Lieutenants N. H. Patterson and G. R. P. Fletcher together shot down a second Focke-Wulfe. Its complete tailplane broke off after a thirty-five-round burst from Fletcher. A pair of white flying overalls was all that was recovered from it. This was the first Focke-Wulfe to be shot down by an escort carrier's aircraft. Clearly it must have come as a complete surprise for its pilot to meet a single-engined single-seat fighter more than 900 miles from land. But there were still three stragglers, *Lissa*, *Runa*, and *Rhineland*, which were all picked off and sunk by U-201 during the night of the 21st to 22nd.

Audacity took a seventy-ship convoy, HG74, back to the Clyde in October and on the 29th joined OG76, with twenty ships bound for Gibraltar. Once again the convoy was shadowed by Focke-Wulfes and there were several radar echoes on *Audacity*'s screen. Just before noon on 8 November the corvette *Cowslip* reported a Kondor astern of the convoy. Wintour, the squadron CO, and his wingman Sub Lt D. A. Hutchinson were scrambled and quickly found their target. Wintour made two attacks, from astern and from the quarter, setting the big aircraft on fire. Obviously thinking the Kondor was now harmless, Wintour ranged up alongside it, when the dorsal gunner opened fire. Wintour banked away but his Martlet was hit square amidships by a 7.9 mm cannon shell. The fighter radio net had been switched on to *Audacity*'s internal speakers, and Wintour's dying cry went right round the ship. Hutchinson attacked five times and expended 1080 rounds, finally shooting the Kondor down. *Bradford* found the wreckage of Wintour's Martlet and recovered his body. (His father, Captain Charles John Wintour, was also killed in action, leading the 4th Destroyer Flotilla in *Tipperary* at Jutland.)

Less than two hours later, another two Martlets were scrambled and Sub Lieutenants Brown and Lamb had an exciting game of hide-and-seek with two more Kondors, of which Brown shot down one:

> The enemy, making a turn inside the cloud, put his upper wing tip through the top. The pilot couldn't have known it, for the cabin was still in cloud. But to me it was a godsend. I followed his direction and waited.
>
> Sure enough, a few minutes later he broke out. No doubt he thought he had lost me. I was about 500 yards from him, and we were flying head on into each other. It was a perfect position for attack, and I opened fire immediately, holding it the whole way in. Our combined speeds were probably in the neighbourhood of 500 miles an hour, and there was little time. But I watched his windscreen disintegrating under the heavy 0.5 ammunition. Yet he held his course, and for a fraction of a second I thought he was going to ram me. The last burst from his forward-firing cannons was so close that the blast scorched the underside of my own aircraft. I shot upwards clear of him, and did a steep turn to see him dive into cloud.

Lamb, the other Martlet pilot, watched the Kondor go down and saw two of the crew climb out on to the wing.

In the next two days, at least six Kondors and the 'Störtebecker' Group of eight U-boats were searching for the convoys HG75 and SL91, the latter having been reported by the B-Dienst service. But neither convoy met a U-boat nor lost a ship.

After OG76, *Audacity* remained at Gibraltar for a month, before joining HG76, whose sailing had been postponed because of the indications of a number of U-boats in the area west of Gibraltar. In the fortnight beginning 26 November there were several attacks on U-boats by surface ships and by aircraft. Hudson aircraft of 233 Squadron, and Fairey Swordfish of 812 Squadron FAA had been disembarked from *Ark Royal*, which had been sunk in the Mediterranean earlier that month, and operated from Gibraltar.

In the second week of December many U-boats were known to be operating west of Gibraltar, and OG77 was approaching escorted by one group. Walker's 36th Group were temporarily diverted from patrols and reinforced OG77. The convoy had probably been reported by U-434 off Lisbon, but it arrived at Gibraltar on the 13th without loss.

HG76 was due to sail on the 15th but Gibraltar was so crowded after OG77's arrival that it left early, in the afternoon of the 14th. *Empire Barracuda* and four tankers, escorted by the destroyer *Wishart* and three corvettes, also sailed that evening, bound south for the Cape of Good Hope and the Near East.

There were thirty-two ships in nine columns in HG76, with an average speed of just over 7 knots. The Commodore was Vice-Admiral Sir Raymond Fitzmaurice, in *Spero*, leading the central fifth column. The Commodore later reported that 'there was never a dull moment' for HG76. The action began that first night, at 23.25 when a Swordfish of 812, flying some 6 miles on the starboard beam of the convoy, got a radar contact, range 3½ miles. It was a U-boat steering towards the convoy. The Swordfish attacked from astern and dropped three charges, set to 25 and 50 feet depth. The first two fell 80 feet ahead and the third 60 feet on the starboard bow as the U-boat took evasive action to port.

Walker, ahead of the convoy in *Stork*, heard the explosions and saw two calcium flares burning on the water ahead of the ship. But the Swordfish was not fitted with R/T, so Walker did not know until some time later that it was a U-boat. He carried out a search and ordered *Deptford* and *Rhododendron* to carry on until 4 a.m. the next morning, but nothing was seen. However the U-boat had certainly been closing the convoy and had been prevented from attacking.

Just after midnight an Admiralty signal warned HG76 that a U-boat had made a sighting report, either of the convoy or of *Wishart* and her tankers. At 1.35 a.m. the same Swordfish sighted another U-boat, some ten miles astern of the convoy. The aircraft had already dropped its charges, but it still forced the U-boat to dive and break off its approach.

Later that night it became clear that the U-boat report (actually by U-74) was of *Wishart* and her charges. At 3.25 U-77 sank *Empire Barracuda* with two torpedoes. The ship sank within ten minutes, but survivors were picked up by the corvette *Coltsfoot* and taken to Gibraltar. After this, the convoy went on its way without further incident.

At 5.37 a.m. another Swordfish of 812 Squadron sighted a U-boat some 24 miles south-west of Cape Trafalgar and dropped two charges set to 25 and 50 feet. The U-boat had already been dived for about six seconds. One charge fell on the forward edge of the swirl. There was no sign of a hit or damage, but once again a U-boat had been forced down.

There had been no replacements for *Audacity*'s unserviceable Martlets at Gibraltar, and she had sailed with only four embarked. Past experience showed that about that number were expended each trip. So flying had to be kept to a careful minimum. Aircraft were not flown off on anti-submarine patrols unless a U-boat had been seen, or there was a strong probability of a sighting. The Martlets' main objectives were still the Kondors, not the U-boats. It had been suggested that *Audacity* embark some of *Ark Royal*'s Swordfish for anti-submarine duties, but there was a shortage of observers and telegraphist–air-gunners, as well as a lack of suitable R/T sets. So the Swordfish were kept at Gibraltar for night patrols in the Straits (where a Swordfish did sink U-451 on 21 December).

Audacity's safest place was generally the centre of the convoy, although as she normally operated only two aircraft at a time, she was able to fly them off and recover them ahead of the convoy, while staying inside the escort screen. In poor visibility she dropped back to the rearmost ship of the centre column. At night, it was up to Cdr McKendrick to decide whether to stay inside the convoy or to zigzag outside it.

There was no flying on the 16th, and the Commodore took advantage of the lull to practise emergency turns, and altering course by visual and sound signals – rehearsal which would stand the convoy in good stead. During the night the Admiralty signalled that U-boats were assembling ahead of the convoy. This was the 'Seerauber' Group, of U-434, U-131, U-67, U-108 and U-107, who were directed towards the convoy following agents' reports from Spain. From now on, Kondors or U-boats or both would be in contact with HG76 for almost the whole time. Walker asked *Audacity* to fly off an anti-submarine search at dawn on the 17th. Flying would now go on virtually continuously, although *Audacity* only had three Martlets operational.

At 9.25 a.m. on the 17th a Martlet reported a U-boat on the convoy's port beam, range 22 miles. This was near enough for Walker, who at once headed for the position at full speed, telling *Blankney*, *Exmoor*, *Stanley* and *Pentstemon* to join him. *Blankney* arrived first and began an anti-submarine search, getting a doubtful contact and dropping six charges, until contact was lost. Walker, steaming hard to close the datum, heard *Blankney*'s signals about 'rattle effect', 'oil', 'several non-sub echoes here'.

It did not sound promising, but *Stork*, *Blankney* and *Exmoor* formed up in line abreast, 1.2 miles apart, and started an anti-submarine sweep to the westward. Walker was sure the U-boat had been shadowing on a westerly course and reasoned that although the U-boat Captain had been forced to dive he would surely want to press on to the west. Having swept 12 miles out, *Stork* altered course in two 90-degree turns to port and steered east on towards the convoy again, but covering now a fresh sweep of sea.

Meanwhile *Stanley* and *Pentstemon* had joined the hunt. At 10.49 *Pentstemon* got a firm Asdic contact, range 1100 yards, and made a deliberate attack, with ten charges set to 150 and 385 feet. After the explosions had died away,

Pentstemon got a poor contact astern, but this was lost at 11.10.

The U-boat was U-131, commanded by Fregatten-Kapitan Baumann, which had been ordered south to the Gibraltar area on 12 December. Baumann had first sighted HG76 on the 16th. He had come rather too close during the night and had dropped back astern, to shadow from a discreet distance. U-131 had dived at dawn, but at 9.20 Baumann decided to come up for a look around. This was fatal. He was sighted by the Martlet and, guessing that this would bring warships to the scene, Baumann dived to 250 feet and lay quiet.

Pentstemon's attack was very accurate. It caused severe damage and some flooding. The main motors were damaged and only usable at slow speed. The hydrophone went dead, and oil poured into the engine-room bilges. U-131 lay over at an angle of 40 degrees and began to sink deeper. The hull compressed under the enormous pressure, so that steel plates cracked with sharp reports, paint peeled off bulkheads, and locker doors jammed. Baumann managed to catch a trim, and then ordered main ballast tanks to be blown.

Meanwhile, *Stanley* and *Pentstemon* had set out to join Walker. At 12.47 *Stanley* reported an object on the horizon bearing 130°, and immediately afterwards, 'U-boat on the surface bearing 060°.' All ships altered course towards at full speed.

Twenty minutes later, the ships saw a Martlet diving at something on the surface. It was Fletcher attacking U-131, who replied with accurate 2-cm and 3.9-cm gunfire, hitting the Martlet's windscreen. The Martlet dived into the sea and Fletcher was killed.

By now the destroyers were within range and opened fire at 7 miles. The two Hunts, *Exmoor* and *Blankney*, had drawn ahead of the rest and *Exmoor*'s fire was particularly accurate. The U-131 returned a few rounds at *Blankney* before Baumann and his crew abandoned ship. They were all picked up by *Exmoor* and *Stanley*. This was first blood to the escorts.

That afternoon the Admiralty signalled that the convoy was still being shadowed by a U-boat. Course was altered at 10 p.m., and *Stanley* was stationed on the outer screen, on the port quarter. But the night was quiet and it was not until just after 9 a.m. on the 18th that *Stanley* reported a U-boat 6 miles away on her port quarter. Walker ordered *Blankney*, *Deptford* and *Exmoor* to assist.

Stanley headed for the U-boat, which dived when she was 3 miles off. *Stanley*'s Asdics were out of action and remained so, but when she was about a mile from the diving position, oil and the turbulence of a wake were seen to starboard. *Stanley* came down to 12 knots and began to mark out the spot by dropping single depth-charges in a square. She had completed three sides, dropping nineteen charges, when *Blankney* arrived and got a firm contact almost at once.

When the range had come down to 800 yards, *Blankney* increased speed to

18 knots and prepared to attack. But the U-boat took violent evasive action, strong Doppler effect being heard to port, with loud propeller noises. The U-boat passed down *Blankney*'s port side, only 50 yards away, but *Blankney* got off an attack, with six charges.

Blankney got a firm contact again at once, and passed ranges and bearings to *Stanley* who ran in and plastered the spot with fourteen charges set to explode deep. *Blankney* guessed the U-boat was hurt and decided to attack again before it could recover. At 9.42 *Blankney* fired six charges, with medium settings. Six minutes later, while the throwers were being reloaded, a U-boat surfaced 2000 yards away. Both destroyers opened fire on it and *Blankney*, increasing speed, steered to ram. The U-boat swung stern on, and *Blankney* hit it a glancing blow, damaging her own port side.

The U-boat was U-434, commanded by Korvetten-Kapitan Heyda, who had tried and failed to maintain contact with two earlier convoys. He had first sighted HG76 on thè 17th but lost it again in low visibility in the early hours of the 18th. Heyda had actually witnessed U-131's last fight and final fate, from a distance. Trying to pick up the convoy again he had sighted destroyers, apparently attacking, and dived. He had fired one torpedo which missed (which may have caused the noises heard by *Blankney*).

Stanley's deep pattern had exploded all around U-434 and done tremendous damage. A large amount of water flooded into the submarine, and Heyda decided to surface. *Blankney* lowered a whaler with a boarding party but scuttling charges exploded inside U-434 and the submarine sank. All but one officer and one sailor were picked up.

At 11 a.m. *Exmoor* and *Blankney* left for Gibraltar. They had assisted in the sinking of two U-boats and rendered the convoy priceless assistance.

During the forenoon, two Kondors were intercepted by Hutchinson and Lt D. C. E. F. Gibson. The guns in both Martlets jammed, but the Kondors were driven off. Gibson was the new squadron CO, having flown out to join at Gibraltar. (He was the only one of the five COs of 802 Squadron to survive the war; the other four were all killed in action with the Squadron.)

Audacity flew off dusk searches, but Walker thought they were flown too early. He was right – although they reported no U-boats, there certainly was at least one there. At 6.47 p.m. *Pentstemon*, on the convoy's port beam, sighted a U-boat at Red 60°, only 5 miles off. *Pentstemon* set off in pursuit, but the U-boat had the legs of her. Although she opened fire with 4-inch and later with star-shell, nothing more was seen, and when *Stanley* and *Convolvulus* arrived to help they found nothing either. However, the U-boat was still there, because at 8.49 p.m. *Pentstemon* heard torpedoes passing from port to starboard. The three ships illuminated the area, and dropped some depth-charges, and then set course to re-join the convoy.

But the U-boat had not finished. At 3.45 a.m. on the 19th *Stanley*, who was then astern of the convoy, signalled, 'U-boat in sight'. Walker had very little idea where *Stanley* was, and asked her to show her position by illuminating.

At 3.55 *Stanley* signalled 'Torpedoes passed from astern'. *Stanley* had signalled her numeral pendants twice by light, and at 4.15 a.m. *Stork* was just replying when *Stanley* was torpedoed, very probably on her port side, and blew up in a great sheet of flame several hundreds of feet high. Torpedoes were also reported passing astern of *Stork* herself and the merchant ship *Largo*, fourth ship in the fourth column.

Walker, always quick to learn a lesson, realized that the U-boat had almost certainly followed *Stanley* and *Pentstemon* back to the convoy, and made up his mind that he would always order escorts re-joining at night to use an indirect route. But meanwhile, there was a U-boat to deal with. Walker ordered 'Buttercup Astern' and headed for the position where he calculated it must be.

The U-boat was U-574 (Kapitan-Leutnant Gengelbach), which had left Kiel in November on her first war patrol. Gengelbach had first sighted HG76 on the morning of the 17th, and U-574 was the object sighted by *Stanley* on the horizon just before U-131 was sunk. Gengelbach had also witnessed U-131's last moments. He then dived and stayed down until dusk, surfacing at 6 p.m. when Gengelbach saw the convoy again, but again lost contact until the following evening. It was very probably U-574 which *Pentstemon* had sighted and chased on the 18th.

U-574 regained touch with HG76 at 2 a.m. on the 19th, when she approached from ahead, dived, and kept contact by hydrophone. At 4 a.m. Gengelbach could see nothing through his periscope and decided to surface. He found that he had miscalculated his position and was in fact very close to the convoy. He saw a number of ships pass to starboard of him, followed by two warships, *Stanley* and *Stork*. Gengelbach fired first at *Stork* and then a salvo of three torpedoes at *Stanley*, range about 1200 yards. As soon as he saw the great curtain of flame from *Stanley*, Gengelbach turned and retired at full speed. Five minutes later, he saw *Stork* pursuing from astern and dived. This gave Walker his chance.

Stork steamed in at 15 knots, dropping single charges until, at 4.24, less than ten minutes after *Stanley* was hit, she got an Asdic contact, range 700 yards. The movement of the target was very slight and Walker thought the U-boat was very probably waiting for a ship to stop and pick up *Stanley*'s survivors, thus giving her another target.

Stork's first attack was at 4.26 a.m. with five charges, set shallow to 50 feet because the U-boat could not have gained depth in the time. This 'fatefully accurate' attack did U-574 colossal damage, put both electric motors out of action, fractured a main pressure-hull rib and started a fire in the control-room, where Gengelbach and his Engineer Officer were engaged in a furious argument. The Engineer Officer said it was imperative to surface. Gengelbach refused, but as a concession ordered the crew to put on their lifejackets and escape apparatus.

The explosion of the depth-charges had knocked *Stork*'s own generator off the board and there was a short delay before contact was regained. In the meantime, the target began moving rapidly right as the range closed. *Stork* altered sharply to starboard and attacked with ten more charges, set to 50 and 140 feet. This attack too did great damage inside U-574 and made Gengelbach decide to surface. He ordered main ballast tanks to be blown.

Stork's dynamo again gave trouble and contact was lost once more. *Stork* opened the range, turned back, and for the third time got a clear hard Asdic contact, range 700 yards. Just as *Stork* was starting a third attack, very loud hydrophone effect was heard and a U-boat surfaced 200 yards ahead. Walker ordered full speed ahead to ram, and another ten-charge pattern was prepared, set to 50 and 150 feet.

The chase lasted eleven minutes, and Walker was later very surprised to see from the plot that *Stork* had turned through three complete circles. The U-boat was turning just inside *Stork*'s turning circle at a speed only 2 or 3 knots less than *Stork*'s best. Walker kept the target well illuminated with clusters of 'snowflake' and some rounds of 4-inch were fired from 'A' gun until the U-boat was so close the gun could not be depressed any further, 'after which the guns crew were reduced to fist shakings and roaring curses at an enemy who several times seemed to be a matter of a few feet away rather than yards. A burst of 0.5-inch machine-gun fire was let off when these could bear, but the prettiest shooting was made by my First Lieutenant Lieut G. T. S. Gray DSC RN, with a stripped Lewis gun from over the top of the bridge screen. He quickly reduced the conning tower to a mortuary.'

Eventually at 4.48 a.m. only just over thirty minutes after *Stanley* was sunk, *Stork* rammed U-574 just forward of the conning tower from an angle about 20° on her starboard quarter and rolled her over. U-574 hung on the bow for a few seconds, and again on the Asdic dome, then scraped aft 'where she was greeted by a ten-charge pattern at shallowest settings.'

Stork searched for *Stanley*'s survivors and heard what sounded like English from the water. Five men were picked up, but when they were found to be German the boats were hoisted and *Stork* set course for the wreck of *Stanley*. Considering the violence of the detonation, there seemed little chance of finding anybody alive, but in fact twenty-five men were picked up. At 5.28 a.m. *Stork* signalled, '*Stanley* sunk by U-boat. U-boat sunk by *Stork*.' *Samphire* picked up another thirteen Germans, and three from *Stanley*.

While *Stork* was thus pre-occupied, U-108 (Korvetten-Kapitan Scholz) closed the convoy from the port side and at 5.15 a.m. torpedoed *Ruckinge*, the leading ship in the port-hand column. *Finland*, the rear ship from the column, picked up one boat load of survivors and *Stork* another after daybreak. The ship did not sink and was boarded by a party from *Samphire* who found the ship listing 25 degrees and a bag full of confidential books lying on the upper deck. It had been thrown from the bridge but had not cleared the side because of the list. *Samphire* then shelled the wreck, and left it on fire and slowly sinking, watched at a respectful distance by a circling Kondor.

The Focke-Wulfe were especially active that day. Soon after 11 a.m. the same team of Brown and Lamb intercepted two Kondors, of which Brown shot down one, using the same head-on approach, and Lamb damaged and chased away the other. Brown's Kondor returned a very hot fire which, as he reported, 'destroyed the Pilot's hood, passing through where his neck should have been, fortunately he had got his neck near his boots just in time!' Walker, watching from *Stork*, noticed approvingly that 'the aircraft presently returned leaving a very dead Wulf'.

The convoy was now covered by 8/8ths cloud and for every interception it was necessary to have one Martlet above and the other below the cloud level. At 4 p.m. a Kondor was sighted ahead, very low on the horizon, evidently trying to evade *Audacity*'s radar. Sub Lieutenants J. W. Sleigh and H. E. Williams intercepted, and after some stern attacks, Sleigh tried a head-on approach and shot the Kondor down, but flew so close his Martlet struck the Kondor a glancing blow with the port mainplane. He landed with some of the Kondor's w/t aerial wire wrapped around the tail wheel.

A Martlet sighted another U-boat that afternoon. *Deptford*, *Marigold* and *Convolvulus* went to look but found nothing. The convoy was now in a highly sensitive state, and when these three ships returned they were mistaken for a U-boat. But after a flurry of snowflake and star-shell, the night passed peacefully.

The routine Focke-Wulfe arrived in the forenoon and was chased back into his cloud. In the afternoon, a Martlet sighted two U-boats ahead of the convoy which altered 80 degrees to starboard to steer NNE. Walker decided it was too late in the day, too far, and he had nothing fast enough, to make an attack. U-107 had kept in touch, and was summoning up U-108, U-67, U-567, U-751 and U-71. Martlets were dispatched to make the U-boats dive, which they did. But *Audacity*, which had previously stayed in the middle of the convoy, this night steamed 30 miles to starboard and zigzagged at 14 knots, escorted by *Rhododendron*.

At 9.10 a.m. on the 21st, during his morning patrol, Brown sighted two U-boats 25 miles astern of the convoy, with a plank out between them. He thought one had a hole in her port bow. Diving over them, Brown found that their oerlikons could not fire at an elevation greater than 70 degrees. Using this knowledge, he kept his height and bearing, and shot three men off the plank.

Walker decided that these U-boats must have collided during the night and were transferring the whole crew, or a working party, from one to the other. It was worth a try and he sent *Deptford*, *Pentstemon*, *Vetch* and *Samphire*. But the relief aircraft saw no U-boats and the escorts got no contacts.

There were more U-boat sightings that day. The escorts made sorties out to look for them and force them down. By now Walker realized that HG76 was likely to be shadowed continuously and attacked whichever route it took. So the best way home was the shortest. That afternoon a U-boat was sighted 12 miles ahead from *Stork*'s foretop and Walker wrote that 'the net of U-boats around us seemed at this stage to be growing uncomfortably close in spite of *Audacity*'s heroic efforts to keep them at arm's length'. Walker decided on a drastic alteration of course, after dark, coupled with a 'mock battle' using star-shell and depth-charges by *Deptford* and the other ships who were still coming up from astern after their unsuccessful search for the 'plank' U-boats.

McKendrick intended to zigzag clear of the convoy again that night and asked for an escort. But Walker had only four escorts with the convoy, and had to refuse. He suggested that *Audacity* take station to port, as the U-boats were expected to starboard. But McKendrick said that the convoy's alterations to port would inconvenience *Audacity*, and went off to starboard. 'I should have finally ordered her either on the port side or into the middle of the convoy,' Walker wrote, 'and I feel myself accordingly responsible. . . .'

The 'mock battle' went wrong. First, a merchant ship fired snowflake at dusk by accident, and when the 'battle' did begin several ships in the convoy let off snowflake. However, this probably made little difference. The U-boats were already in position and at 8.32 p.m. U-567 (Endrass) torpedoed *Annavore*, rear ship of the centre column. Loaded with 5000 tons of iron ore, she sank like a stone, with only four survivors.

Walker ordered 'Buttercup starboard', not realizing the attack was astern. The convoy was in the middle of a 90-degree turn to port at the time, but the turn was completed in good order.

An attack was meanwhile developing on the starboard side. *Finland*, leading the starboard column, saw a U-boat surfaced 200 yards away on the port bow. She missed ramming by 30 feet and the U-boat passed so close astern the 12-pounder gun could not be used for fear of hitting the next convoy ship astern.

The snowflake and star-shell clearly lit up *Audacity*, some 10 miles to starboard and zigzagging. Lt Gibson later said they expected the torpedo to come 'at dinner. It actually came with the coffee'. At 8.35 p.m. an Aircraft Fitter on the flight deck saw torpedo tracks approaching *Audacity* from the port side. He ran across the bridge, but before he could give the alarm the torpedo struck the engine-room. The single shaft stopped and the steering gear jammed. Two white rockets were fired. McKendrick ordered confidential books to be ditched and hands to go to abandon-ship stations. The 4-inch and 20-mm pompom guns were manned, and at least one pompom on the port side got off some rounds at the U-boat, which could be seen clearly in the light of star-shell (some said it was St Elmo's fire) about 500 yards on the port side, with *Convolvulus* and *Marigold* approaching beyond her.

Two more torpedo tracks were seen, and 'those so inclined,' said one survivor, 'including myself, lay down, then rose smartly into the air twice in succession as they hit us. One struck under the bridge and the other exploded in the Wardroom.' McKendrick then ordered abandon ship. The fore part of *Audacity* was virtually blown off and the ship began to sink by the bows, until the flight deck was almost vertical, with aircraft falling off and causing casualties amongst the swimmers in the sea.

Chief Yeoman of Signals T. Pearson was with the Captain. 'It was a quarter of an hour after everybody had gone before we left the ship. She broke in two and each piece came out and then sank and broke away. The stern portion seemed to stand on its fore end for a moment before it sank.' He could see the submarine on the port beam, almost 500 yards away as he helped the Captain prepare a small rubber dinghy.

Convolvulus, *Marigold* and *Pentstemon* picked up *Audacity*'s survivors, including Chief Yeoman Pearson, but McKendrick was not among them. He was reported to have been grabbed by sailors in *Pentstemon*'s whaler but slipped away and drowned. Pearson said that *Pentstemon*'s First Lieutenant went over the side to try and help him, but the Captain hit his head against the ship's side and disappeared.

The attacking U-boat was U-751, commanded by Kapitan-Leutnant Biegalk, who described the incident on Frankfurt Radio on 30 December:

The whole area was as light as day. Other U-boats must have been attacking. Ten or fifteen rockets hung over the U-boat as though spellbound. The destroyers nearby also started firing tracer-bullets and suddenly I saw in the light of the tracer-bullets and rockets a large aircraft carrier lying in front of us. Good God! What a chance! An opportunity such as a U-boat Commander does not find every day. The whole bridge was wildly enthusiastic.

Now I was in a favourable position for attack. I had to fire. I fired several torpedoes, and then came terrible tension while waiting to see if, or if not, one of them hits its mark. Then suddenly a fiery detonation aft. A hit aft! The ship described a semi-circle portside, and then stopped, unable to manoeuvre. Apparently my torpedo had smashed her screws. I turned a short distance off to load new torpedoes. Down below in the forward compartment there was a terrific crowding, since we had only left a few days before, and the forward compartment was full of provisions and all sorts of impossible things necessary for an operational cruise. My torpedo mate and torpedo crew worked like mad. We in the meantime were standing on the bridge, constantly watching the aircraft carrier, and were terribly excited lest the destroyer should approach and mess up this unique chance.

But apparently the destroyers were furiously busy, for way back on the horizon there were bangs and detonations, and tracer-bullets were being fired. Our comrades were doing their work. The torpedo tubes were reported clear for action, thank God. I made another attack approaching the ship at a crawling pace so that she could under no account hear me. The water was phosphorescing like mad, and I could only proceed very slowly so as not to be discovered by the aircraft carrier, which had stopped.

I came nearer and nearer. I didn't care any more. I had to get so near that my torpedoes could on no account miss. A gigantic shadow growing larger and larger all the time! I had approached so closely that no torpedo could possibly miss, and then I gave permission to fire. The torpedoes left their tubes. Seconds of great tension. There, hit forrard, 20 metres behind the stem. A great detonation, with a gigantic sheet of flame. A short time afterwards, another detonation, in the middle; again a great column of fire. . . . I turned off, and in doing so cast another glance at the aircraft carrier. The fore was already flooded and the deck was turning upwards. At that moment destroyers were reported starboard. They were dashing at top speed towards the aircraft carrier, which was wildly firing distress signals – great stars bursting in the air. I was able to get away from the pursuit. I got a rain of depth charges, but that was of no avail to the English – I escaped.

The 'rain of depth-charges' was very probably dropped by *Marigold*, on her way to pick up *Audacity*'s survivors, when she had a radar contact at 9.24 p.m., range 3500 yards. *Marigold* chased this contact for some time, firing star-shell but seeing nothing except the swirl of a wake, until the range had come down to 2000 yards, when star-shell revealed a U-boat dead ahead. *Marigold*, already at full speed, fired one round of 4-inch and, losing the radar contact at 1000 yards, attacked with a pattern of ten charges set to 100 and 225 feet. Contact was lost and not regained.

In the next two hours *Samphire*, *Deptford* and *Vetch* all had strong clear contacts and all three made attacks. *Samphire* and *Vetch* had nothing to show for their efforts but *Deptford* had more luck. Her U-boat was first detected by hydrophone and then sighted on the surface, closing the convoy, at about 10.30 p.m. It dived as soon as it was aware that it had been detected. *Deptford* attacked with ten charges, aimed by eye, opened the range to 1700 yards, regained firm contact and dropped a full pattern set to 150 and 385 feet. The U-boat had clearly gone deep and the third attack was made with five charges, set to 385 feet.

It was now time to re-join the convoy. *Deptford* dropped two final charges, set to 500 feet. There were no signs of oil of wreckage. But, eight minutes after the depth-charges had exploded, there was a loud double explosion under water, on the bearing. *Deptford* thought the U-boat was still moving after the last attack when she herself set off to re-join the convoy, at 1.05 a.m. on the 22nd.

In fact, Lt Cdr White and his ship's company had scored a notable success. The U-boat was U-567, lost with all hands, including her Captain, the ace Engelbert Endrass.

Deptford re-joined the convoy rather too enthusiastically, for at 5.17 a.m. that morning Walker was woken by an 'unusually ominous crash' and went on deck to find *Deptford*'s stem embedded one-third of the way into *Stork*'s quarterdeck. It had walked straight into *Stork*'s temporary prison, and 'two of the five Boche were pulped, literally into a bloody mess'.

At dawn on the 22nd Walker therefore found it 'difficult not to take a somewhat gloomy view'. *Stork* had no Asdics after her collision with U-574, and after her brush with *Deptford* had to shift depth-charges forward to lighten the stern. She could only make 9 to 10 knots. Likewise *Deptford* had no Asdics and could only do 11 knots. Most of the radar sets in the Group had broken down, and worst of all, '*Audacity* and her gallant aircraft had gone.' But the day was uneventful, with a Liberator escorting the convoy morning and afternoon. At 12.45 p.m., one Liberator sighted a U-boat 7 miles away and about 10 miles to port of the convoy. But the U-boat dived as soon as it saw the Liberator, and was completely submerged by the time the depth-charges arrived.

A Focke-Wulfe appeared during the day, was fired at by *Stork*, and then circled warily at a safe distance. A Liberator sighted two U-boats on the convoy's port bow and put them down. Clearly the convoy was still in great danger, and Walker decided that the 'one thing *not* to be done' was to continue on a steady course and wait to be attacked. The convoy made a large alteration of course, *Deptford* and *Jonquil* carried out a mock battle, and the night passed with no major incident except an attack by *Vetch* on a contact. The noise of the depth-charge explosions persuaded some of the crew of *Ogmore Castle* that they had been torpedoed and they abandoned ship. They slipped a boat, even though *Ogmore Castle* was still making 7½ knots. When the master discovered what had happened, the ship was stopped and a somewhat sheepish boatload of 'survivors' came back on board.

After another attack by the destroyer *Vanquisher* (coming to meet the convoy) on the 23rd, and a false alarm with star-shell by *Stork* on Christmas Eve, the rest of the voyage was uneventful and HG76 arrived in the UK on 27 December.

Considering the number of times the convoy was sighted by Kondors and the number of U-boats involved in operations in and around it, it was truly remarkable that more attacks were not made on HG76 and more ships lost. Walker and his fellow captains had fought a splendidly intelligent and successful ten-day battle. They had been on their guard and ready to counter-attack at all times, but they had not lashed out blindly just for the sake of it, when there was little chance of success. Several times they had put a U-boat down, while the convoy moved on. They had lost two of their charges, and one of their number, against four U-boats destroyed. Walker could not be blamed for the loss of *Audacity*, although he did reproach himself.

Nor were their opponents novices. Biegalk was a new name, but his attack on *Audacity*, through the ranks of the convoy and between the escorts, was as cool and daring as anything in the Battle of the Atlantic. Gengelbach was a most determined captain, who had gone down with his ship, while Endrass, of course, was one of Doenitz's aces.

But the really novel feature of HG76's voyage was the quality of the close air support. Kondors had not just been sighted, they had been shot down, or damaged, or chivvied away. U-boats had been rudely forced to dive whilst making their approaches, and harassed, and machine-gunned, and depth-charged. U-131's loss had been directly brought about by an aircraft sighting.

For Doenitz, the loss of four U-boats was bad enough, but he was quick to realize that the aircraft carrier was the 'worst feature', and he stressed the importance of sinking the aircraft carrier 'not only in this case but also in every future convoy action . . .'.

These truths about air power at sea might have been clear to Doenitz but they were not nearly so apparent to the Allies; indeed in certain circles of the RAF and the Prime Minister's scientific advisers, they were regarded as heresies. This was in spite of evidence already available in abundance by the autumn of 1941.

By that time, Operational Research Sections (ORS) had been set up in RAF Commands, including Coastal, consisting of scientists – 'boffins' in the service terminology – many of them very distinguished in their various fields and some who were Nobel Prize-winners, whose task it was to apply scientific methods to questions of strategy and tactics.

This was a much greater break with tradition that it appeared. As one of those ORS scientists, Professor Waddington, wrote, the service scientific departments until then had concentrated

> either on detailed technical problems as they arise, or on general technical questions, such as the improvement of the ballistic properties of guns, or of the speed and fighting power of aeroplanes. Yet the use of these weapons and the organization of the men who handle them are at least as much scientific problems as is their production. The waging of warfare represents a series of human operations carried out for more or less definitive ends. Seeing whether these operations actually yield the results expected from them should be a matter of direct scientific analysis.

The ORS boffins turned a bleak, critical eye on many aspects of operations. They were the enemies of wishful thinking. They concerned themselves, not with what men thought they had done, or deserved to have done, but what they had actually done. Some of their surveys showed up some surprising truths. A study of manpower, numbers of aircraft, flying hours, and maintenance routines, to find ways of using men and machines more efficiently, showed that aircraft unserviceability was often *greater* after a planned maintenance inspection and that in some circumstances aircraft were being inspected too *often*.

ORS examined the most effective means of camouflage for Coastal Command aircraft and established that they would be best painted white on their undersides – certainly they should not be left black, as they had come from Bomber Command. They studied attacks on U-boats and established that it was important to catch a U-boat on the surface; it was difficult, almost impossible, to drop depth-charges from the air close enough to hurt a U-boat once it had dived. U-boats almost always dived as soon as they sighted an aircraft, and every second thereafter dramatically improved their chances of escape. It was vital for the aircraft to get over its target fast.

ORS established that depth-charges should be set to explode shallow. With a lethal radius of some 20–30 feet, it was pointless to drop a depth-charge to explode at 100 feet. ORS could even calculate the number of U-boats which got away. From a graph of U-boats sighted they constructed the 'missing half' of the graph, to show the numbers of U-boats which must have been there but were not sighted.

A study of 'meets' between convoys and their escorting aircraft showed that some 75 per cent of aircraft met their convoys. The 'not met' rate, understandably, went up the further the convoys were from shore: from 8½ per cent 'not met' 100 miles from shore, to 40 per cent 'not met' over 600 miles from shore. ORS was able to analyse errors in convoy and aircraft navigation, and suggest improvements in 'homing transmissions'. Analysis of failures showed, interestingly, that 70 per cent of failures to meet were the fault of the ships, due to inadequate staffing, failure of signals from shore, use of wrong codes, etc.

ORS studied the use of binoculars in aircraft and the best positions for keeping a good look-out when airborne, the best heights to fly, and ways of improving efficiency of radar searches. They designed an improved bomb sight, and drew 'attack lethality' diagrams and Attack Cards, making it easier to assemble and study attack data. Where ORS scientists were trusted and received cooperation, they achieved valuable results, even though their conclusions sometimes went against the received opinions and prejudices of the command. For instance, when they examined a series of depth-charge attacks by aircraft on U-boats they found that pilots were 'aiming off' too much and thus exaggerating errors in line and range. They showed that there was nothing wrong with the depth-charges; the fault lay in the men aiming them. Furthermore, if improved depth-charges were to be designed, it would be much better to have a 'stick' of more and smaller charges rather than fewer and bigger ones.

By the time, late in 1941, ORS came to study convoy actions, it was already clear that some pre-war ideas about convoy were mistaken. Air cover for convoys, for example, was thought of as an adjunct to the surface escort and should be used in the same way, close to the convoy. But experience showed that it was impossible, and unnecessary, to give air cover to all the convoys all the time, and much better to concentrate air cover on convoys which appeared to be threatened. It was quite possible, from intelligence, Ultra de-crypts, and Admiralty Tracking-Room deductions, as well as considerations of convoy position, weather and recent events, to estimate which convoys were most threatened.

It was also clear how valuable aircraft were in preventing U-boats shadowing a convoy and assembling into packs. One aircraft in the sky, like a hawk above a covey of grouse, put them all down. It was more important for aircraft to disrupt the wolf packs than to patrol in the vicinity of the convoy. In other words, in many cases air patrols were being laid on too *close* to convoys.

Above all, ORS showed the enormous importance of long-range aircraft in convoy defence. This importance was not incalculable. On the contrary, it could be shown in quantitative terms, in graphs and formulae which would have delighted Rollo Appleyard. They were not matters of opinion but scientifically proven facts.

The effect of long-range aircraft could be demonstrated in terms of 'ships not sunk'. One would expect ship sinkings to be proportional to the product of U-boat density and convoy density: the more convoys and the more U-boats there were, the more ships would be sunk. But this was not so. Inside 300 miles from shore, where there was regular air cover, the density product (of U-boats × convoys) was 6.4, and the number of ships sunk for that product was seventeen. For 300–500 miles from shore, where there was occasional air cover, the density product fell to 3.2, but the number of ships sunk rose to forty-six. Finally, outside 500 miles, where air cover was very scarce, density product was 3.3 and the number of ships sunk was fifty-five.

Looking at these figures, it can be seen that the density of U-boats and convoys was almost twice as high (6.4) inside 300 miles from shore as it was over 500 miles from shore (3.3). Other things being equal, one would have expected the number of ships sunk to increase in the same ratio, and some 106 ships to be sunk within 300 miles of the coast. But the number of ships was actually only seventeen. The difference was due to air cover.

These figures were born out in practice. In October 1941, U-boats sank thirty-two ships of 156,554 tons, but none of those ships were sunk within 400 miles of a Coastal Command base. Between 400 and 600 miles from such bases, twelve ships were sunk. Beyond 600 miles, where there was little or no air cover, fourteen ships were sunk.

In January 1942, the argument for very-long-range aircraft in the Atlantic was put to the Prime Minister's anti-U-boat committee in a different way: 'Taking the average life of an aircraft at forty sorties, and adding in the ships saved by the actual sinking of U-boats, it was estimated that each aircraft in its life-time saved an average of sixteen ships.'

But all these arguments, backed by graphs and statistics, fell on deaf ears. The views of 'Bomber' Harris, supported by the Prime Minister's scientific adviser, Professor Lindemann, won the day, and delayed for about a year the transfer of the comparatively small number – between forty and eighty – VLR aircraft needed to win the Battle of the Atlantic. For the ships and men of the Atlantic, this was the worst decision of the whole war.

Chapter Sixteen

The Japanese attack on Pearl Harbor caught Hitler by surprise. But he at once abandoned his policy of trying not to provoke the United States. Germany declared war on 11 December 1941, formalizing a state of virtual war which had existed, at least in the Atlantic, for some months.

President Roosevelt had issued his first warning to the Axis as early as September 1939, when he announced the organization of a Neutrality Patrol, to report and track any belligerent air, surface or underwater naval forces approaching the United States or the West Indies. In January 1941 secret discussions began in Washington between the Chief of Naval Operations and the Army Chief of Staff, and a United Kingdom delegation representing the British Chiefs of Staff.

By March, these concluded with a staff agreement which was the basis for Anglo-American cooperation during the war. The plan was, first, a 'short of war' situation on the basis of lend–lease in the Atlantic; second, to dissuade Japan from further aggression in the Pacific; third, and most important, to provide for full Anglo-American cooperation if and when the Axis forced the United States into war. All these agreements rested on the one basic strategic agreement, that Hitler must be defeated first. In August 1941, in Placentia Bay, Newfoundland, President Roosevelt and Winston Churchill agreed on the Atlantic Charter, which was a broad statement of human rights in the free world, and presupposed 'the final destruction of Nazi tyranny'.

In 1941, the United States was becoming as involved in the war operationally as it had been politically. President Roosevelt, while maintaining that the USA was to do everything 'short of war', said that America would hold herself responsible for the defence of the western hemisphere. On 18 April, Admiral Ernest King USN, the C-in-C Atlantic Fleet, rather in the manner of a Renaissance Pope, set the limit of the western hemisphere at 26° W, or about 50 miles east of Reykjavik, and including the whole of Greenland, the Gulf of St Lawrence, the Bahamas, the Caribbean and the Azores.

That same month of April 1941, an American Central Atlantic Neutrality Patrol, with a task group including an aircraft-carrier division, began to operate from the newly opened American base at Bermuda (which, with Argentia on Placentia Bay, was not actually part of the fifty destroyers deal with Britain but a gift). In April and May three battleships and the carrier *Yorktown* were transferred from the Pacific to the Atlantic.

Individual American ships became involved in incidents. On 10 April the destroyer *Niblack*, on passage to Iceland, depth-charged a suspected submarine contact. On 21 May, an American merchant ship, the *Robin Moor*, was sunk by U-69. The U-boat captain, Jost Metzler, claimed after the war that he thought the ship was a Q-ship, that he saw what looked like aircraft in packing cases on her upper deck, and when she was boarded, she proved to be carrying contraband; and therefore she was quite properly sunk under prize rules. He claimed that U-69 (nicknamed by the crew '*La Vache qui rit*'), towed the lifeboats for some distance towards safety. (The survivors actually sailed for hundreds of miles before being picked up.)

Meanwhile, Hitler was still chary of provoking the United States. On 20 June, U-203 sighted the battleship *Texas* inside the 'operational area' declared by Germany and shadowed her for several hours. When U-203 reported, her Captain was told that attacks on US ships were forbidden even inside the 'operational area'.

But American involvement became deeper with every month. On 1 June, the US Coastguard started a South Greenland Patrol. The American occupation of Iceland began on 1 July. US marines relieved British forces, and were themselves reinforced later by units of the US Army. On 19 July the Atlantic Fleet formed a Task Force for the defence of Iceland. American Catalinas and Mariners began to operate from Hvalfjord.

On 1 September a task group was formed to patrol the Denmark Strait, and all American vessels were ordered to darken ship east of Cape Breton. On the 4th the destroyer *Greer*, on passage to Iceland, picked up a signal from a British aircraft that there was a U-boat some 10 miles ahead. *Greer* detected the submarine and tracked it for three hours. The aircraft dropped depth-charges, and the U-boat, U-652, fired torpedoes. *Greer* evaded the topedoes, and counter-attacked with depth-charges. From then on, the United States was engaged in an undeclared but *de facto* naval war with Germany in the Atlantic.

In September American groups took over the escort of fast HX and ON convoys between Newfoundland and Iceland. Their first was HX150 which sailed from Halifax with fifty ships under local Canadian escort on 16 September. Next day the convoy was met, about 150 miles south of Argentia, by an American group of five destroyers under Captain Morton L. Deyo and convoyed to Mid Ocean Meeting Point (MOMP) in about 22° W, where a British group took over. The American ships then went to Hvalfjord to refuel. The first westbound convoy with American escort was ON18, met at

MOMP on 24 September by five American destroyers under Captain F. D. Kirtland, and escorted to their dispersal point off the Newfoundland coast. This unabashed, outright escort of convoy by American ships was justified by the explanation that the vessels were being convoyed between two American bases (Argentia and Hvalfjord, Iceland), and 'shipping of any other nationalities might join'.

By 10 October 1941 the situation had settled down. Slow SC eastbound convoys from Sydney were escorted by Canadian destroyers and corvettes, which then brought slow ONS convoys back. US escorts took HX and ON convoys between Newfoundland, MOMP and Iceland, and back, relieving from, or turning over to, British Groups at MOMP, when convoy control passed from the American Operations Department (OPNAV) to the Admiralty. The point of change-over was known as the 'Chop' line.

Regular convoy escort was bound to lead to blood. On the night of 14–15 October, SC48 was sighted by U-553 about 400 miles south of Iceland. The convoy had sailed with fifty ships but very bad weather had caused eleven ships, including that of the convoy Commodore, to straggle. It was escorted by four corvettes, *Gladiolus*, the Canadians *Wetaskiwin* and *Baddeck*, and the Free French *Mimose*, joined later by the Canadian destroyer *Columbia*.

Two ships were sunk that night and a third later in the day. By the afternoon of the 16th, five U-boats were in contact, but the escort was reinforced by four US destroyers summoned from ON24, as well as the destroyer *Broadwater* and the Free French corvette *Alysse* from Reykjavik. The American destroyers kept rigid station, about 1000 yards from the convoy perimeter, and were discouraged from patrolling around at night. None was fitted with radar, and none obtained any Asdic contact during the night. But the U-boats sank six ships, and *Gladiolus* disappeared, without trace and with all hands, torpedoed by a U-boat, probably U-553. U-568 torpedoed and damaged the USS *Kearny*, the first American warship damaged in the war. She eventually reached Hvalfjord escorted by *Greer*. Meanwhile on the 18th U-101 (Mengersen) torpedoed *Broadwater*, who was later abandoned and sunk.

There were lessons to be learned from SC48's experience, but they had not been promulgated through the US Navy by 31 October, when HX156 was attacked about 600 miles west of Iceland. Just after dawn one of the escorting destroyers, USS *Reuben James*, was hit port side by one torpedo fired from U-552 (Korvetten-Kapitan Topp). The torpedo evidently hit the forward magazine, for the ship blew up with tremendous loss of life. Of her company of about 160, no officers and only forty-five men were picked up. She was the first American warship lost to enemy action in the Second World War.

By November 1941, Hitler's war in Russia was going well enough to encourage him not to be so cautious towards the United States, and he permitted Doenitz to send U-boats closer to the North American coast-line, to operate south of Greenland, and in Newfoundland waters around Cape

Race and the Belle Isle Strait. One convoy, SC52, after clearing Cape Race, was diverted southward by OPNAV because of U-boats reported in its track. But it was then considered safer to the north west and the convoy was turned through 180 degrees and steered north.

However, on 1 November, SC52 was sighted by U-374, who called up other boats of the 'Raubritter' Group. Four ships were sunk on 3 November, and two more drove ashore in foggy weather. OPNAV then thought it safest to divert the convoy southwards again, through the Belle Isle Strait, and disperse. The Commodore's report on this convoy began: 'Sir, I beg to report that I have just returned to Sydney, CB, after a cruise round Newfoundland lasting a week, starting with thirty-five ships and returning with twenty-nine.'

As though in answer to Hitler's freeing of restrictions on Doenitz, the United States amended its Neutrality Act which forbade American merchant ships to carry goods to Great Britain or to be armed, even in their own defence. In November 1941, two amendments to the Act allowed American vessels to enter the war zone and to defend themselves against attack.

Hitler and Raeder had decided to send U-boats to operate off the American coastline on 12 December 1941, the day after war was declared. The operation was to be code-named '*Paukenschlag*', or 'Roll of drums'. But it took Doenitz some time to gather together enough U-boats. He was heavily committed in what he rightly called the 'trap' of the Mediterranean, where Hitler was pressing eagerly for victory in the desert. Hitler also had an obsession with Norway, which he constantly feared was about to be invaded by the Allies. He continually frustrated Doenitz by insisting that U-boats be diverted to operate in northern waters.

Twelve Type VIIC 500-ton U-boats of the 'Ziethen' Group arrived, one after the other, beginning on 8 January 1942, to operate off the Newfoundland Bank, and as far south as Nova Scotia. Five larger Type IX 1100-tonners arrived to start Paukenschleg on 11 January, nearly a month after the declaration of war.

The U-boats found a coastline still at peace. Lighthouses still flashed, buoys still winked, harbour lights shone into the night, as did bright lights and neon signs from buildings and hotels on sea-fronts. Along the Florida coast, for instance, it was considered that blackout would affect the vital tourist season, and no attempt was made to black out lights until April.

Offshore, ships still steamed along independently, lights blazing, radios squawking, keeping a casual, peace-time lookout. The Eastern Sea Frontier Command of the United States, which stretched from the Canadian border down to Jacksonville in Florida, had only a handful of Coast Guard cutters and some miscellaneous craft. The C-in-C, Admiral Adolphus Andrews, had no equivalent of Coastal Command aircraft under his own command. Patrols were carried out by a few US Army Air Force aircraft. The direction of these vital air patrols was therefore divided between the US Navy and the

US Army who were not always on the best of terms. There were no other preparations for the defence of coastal shipping. There was no evasive routeing, no zigzagging, and, above all, no convoys.

Scarcely believing their good luck, the U-boat commanders went to work, to begin the 'happy times' again. Hardegen, in U-123, sank the British steamer *Cyclops* about 300 miles east of Cape Cod on 12 January, and went on to sink another eight ships of 53,000 tons. 'It is a pity there were not . . . ten to twenty U-boats here last night, instead of one,' he wrote in his diary, off Cape Hatteras, North Carolina, on 19 January. 'I am sure all would have found ample targets. Altogether I saw about twenty steamships, some undarkened; also a few tramp steamers, all hugging the coast. Buoys and beacons in the area had dimmed lights which, however, were visible up to 2 or 3 miles.'

Besides Hardegen, Bleichrodt (now in U-109) sank five ships, of 33,700 tons, and U-130 and U-66 sank another eleven ships, totalling more than 70,000 tons. The U-boats normally lay offshore submerged during the day, surfaced and moved inshore to attack with guns or torpedoes by night. In January 1942 U-boats sank thirty-five ships, of more than 200,000 tons, in the Eastern Sea Frontier Command, off the Canadian coast and around Bermuda. Meanwhile they sank ten ships, of 63,000 tons, in the North Atlantic, only three of those ships from convoys.

This 'merry massacre' as the American historian S. E. Morison called it, continued. During February, in the same coastal areas of the United States, Canada and in the area of Bermuda, the U-boats sank forty-five ships, of more than 250,000 tons. A high proportion of the tonnage lost were tankers. Glutted by targets, U-boats eventually began to husband their torpedoes, letting ships obviously in ballast pass, and attacking only heavily laden ships or tankers. In March U-boats sank twenty-eight ships of nearly 160,000 tons in the Eastern Sea Frontier, and another fifteen of 92,000 tons in the Gulf of Mexico and the Caribbean.

While the actual date of the outbreak of war might have taken the US Navy by surprise, one would have expected them to have prepared contingency plans. They had had months of convoy experience on the North Atlantic. Also, they had the reports of Admiral R. L. Ghormley, who had led a mission of American officers to Britain in August 1940. Ghormley's task had been to find out, and to inform the President, whether the United Kingdom was going to survive, and when that became clear, to ascertain how best American naval and military force could be applied, and to exchange information.

Ghormley's party were given access to all information, apart from the method of sweeping British magnetic mines. Otherwise, all doors and files were opened to them. They were uniquely able to watch the progress of the war at sea, to learn its lessons, as though it were a demonstration of oceanic trade defence, played out for their benefit upon a gigantic stage. One would therefore have expected the Americans to have their own plans for convoy.

Astonishingly, this was not so. In defiance of all previous naval history, they tried patrolling. Admiral Andrews asked for fifteen destroyers and was given seven. But the patrols achieved nothing, and the destroyer *Jacob Jones* was torpedoed on 28 February off the Delaware Capes, with the loss of all her officers and most of her crew.

They even tried Q ships. A Boston trawler called *Wave*, renamed *Eagle*, and two small steamships, *Carolyn* and *Evelyn*, renamed *Atik* and *Asterion*, were armed with guns, fitted with depth-charges and sonar gear. None of them sank a U-boat, and *Atik* herself was attacked and shelled by Hardegen's U-123 on 27 March and sunk with all hands.

They tried everything, it seemed, except convoy and escort. Meanwhile, the Admiralty grew increasingly alarmed by the American failure to institute convoy. Some officers thought such behaviour quite incomprehensible, in view of American knowledge of events in the Atlantic. The huge losses off the North American coast were especially galling for the Admiralty because many of the ships had already been laboriously but successfully convoyed across the Atlantic, only to be sunk beyond Admiralty jurisdiction. Likewise, many of the losses were fully-loaded tankers, sunk before they could be taken into convoy.

The Royal Navy did its best to help. Pound, remembering the fifty US destroyers and the continuing help with Atlantic convoy escort by the Americans, offered to loan twenty-five anti-submarine trawlers. In February, the British Mission in Washington suggested the transferring of ten corvettes. Most of all, they pressed the idea of convoy. In March, Pound advised Admiral King, now Commander in Chief of the US Navy (Cominch), that convoy should be introduced as a matter of urgency and that even convoys with weak escorts were better than none. Winston Churchill telegraphed to Harry Hopkins, the President's personal adviser, that he was most deeply concerned by the immense sinkings of tankers west of the 40th Meridian and in the Caribbean. Roosevelt's reply, evidently reflecting the advice of King, suggested the opening-out of the convoy cycle, more restraint on British imports, and more bombing of submarine bases.

King's own answer to Pound was that he was giving convoy continuous consideration, but felt that convoys 'would invite trouble' unless adequately escorted. There simply were not enough escorts, in his view, to start convoys. And, thought King, 'Inadequately escorted convoys were worse than none.' This opinion was, of course, in direct contradiction of previous experience in both World Wars in which King himself served.

It was true that the US Navy lacked ships, men and aircraft. But they also lacked the will to introduce convoy. When Cdr G. N. Brewer of the Trade Division, commented on the American unwillingness to start convoys until they had enough escorts, one of Admiral Ghormley's mission replied that Brewer 'must realize that the US Navy did not enjoy the respect of the American public as was the case with the Royal Navy and the British. If an

American ship was sunk even in a weakly escorted convoy there would be an outcry for someone in the Navy office to be hung.'

The personality of King himself must have played a part. He was a bitter Anglophobe. He was a most able and dedicated officer, who eventually wore himself out in his country's service. But he was not about to take advice from Limeys. Possibly his antipathy dated from the First War, when he had served with the US Fleet at Scapa and had noted the undoubtedly junior status of the US Navy compared with the Royal Navy. No doubt he had decided that nothing similar would ever happen when *he* reached the top of his profession.

One especially intrepid British officer, Cdr Rodger Winn of the Operational Intelligence Centre in the Admiralty, was sent across to the States early in 1942 to discuss with the Americans the setting-up of their equivalent to OIC and also, as an additional brief, to press the case for convoy. Winn was able to show from his own OIC experience that it was quite possible to forecast the movement and intentions of U-boats – using intelligence information, de-crypted signals, and a lot of intuition – with enough accuracy and certainty to be able to dispose anti-submarine forces and re-route convoys safely.

Though sceptical at first, the Americans were eventually convinced. But on convoy, they were still capable of the most callous stupidity. Rear Admiral Richard D. Edwards, King's deputy chief of staff, and as confirmed an Anglophobe as his master, told Winn that the Americans were determined to learn their own lessons and they had plenty of ships to learn them with. Taking his courage in both hands, Winn retorted, 'The trouble is, Admiral, it's not only your bloody ships you are losing; a lot of them are ours!' Edwards admitted Winn had a point.

At sea, the U-boats were extending their operations, under clear skies, in warm weather and calm waters, with no escorts or much opposition of any kind. On 16 February three U-boats began Operation 'Neuland', with simultaneous attacks on the oil-terminal ports of Aruba, Curaçao, and Maracaibo in the south Caribbean. On the 19th, U-161 entered the harbour of Port of Spain, Trinidad, and sank two freighters. On 10 March, U-161 sank two more ships inside Port Castries, in the island of St Lucia. By 18 March, five U-boats had sunk some 110,000 tons of shipping, much of it tankers, and damaged another 60,000 tons.

No U-boats were sunk by US forces in January and February 1942. On 1 March, off Newfoundland, U-656 was sunk by a Hudson of the US squadron VP82. On the 15th, another aircraft of the same squadron sank U-503 while searching for the in-coming convoy ON72 off the Grand Bank. On 14 April, whilst on passage off Norfolk Virginia, the destroyer *Roper* detected the surfaced U-85 with radar, evaded a torpedo, and then sank the U-boat with gunfire and depth-charges. It was the first U-boat of the war to be sunk by an American warship.

On 1 April, a system was introduced whereby ships passed up and down the American coastline in a series of hops. Ships steamed during daylight hours as close to shore as navigationally possible, stopping for the night in a sheltered harbour or a protected anchorage. The Atlantic coast of America north of Cape Hatteras does divide conveniently into approximately 120-mile stretches between harbours, roughly a day's steaming apart. South of Cape Henry, net-protected anchorages were provided.

This system, called by Admiral Andrews the 'Bucket Brigade', was not convoy. The US Navy still believed that convoy without escorts was worse than no convoy at all. The American admirals still had a fundamental misunderstanding of the workings and benefits of convoy. On average, some 120 to 130 ships worked the 'Bucket Brigade' every day. Only some twenty-eight surface vessels were available to escort them. These could have been used for convoy escort. But, said the Eastern Frontier war diary, 'should these ships be used on such duty, the harbour entrances and coastwise lanes would be practically stripped of protection.' Here was the old fallacy that it was the sea-*lanes*, and not the ships, which needed protection. Just as on every other occasion in the past, the fallacy was quickly shown up by the figures. Another twenty-three ships, of 133,000 tons, were sunk in the Eastern Sea Frontier areas in April, the first full month of the 'Bucket Brigade', making a total of eighty-two ships, of over 490,000 tons, in that area since the beginning of 'Paukenschlag', and no less than 198 ships, of over 1,250,000 tons, lost along the coasts of north America, in the Gulf of Mexico, and in the Caribbean during the same period.

But there were signs that the truth was at last beginning to prevail. In response to Pound's message of 19 March, Admiral King set up an informal board, with representatives from Cominch and the commanders of the sea areas concerned, to plan for extended convoy operations. The board's recommendations, made on 27 March, were accepted by King on 2 April. Here was the germ of the Interlocking Convoy System, which came to spread like a great tree from south America to Halifax, with branches and roots, feeding in or taking out ships, to and from the Gulf of Mexico, Florida and the West Indies. A ship could steam virtually the whole length of north and south Americas, transferring from coastal to ocean and back to coastal convoys again.

Ocean convoys ran between Guantánamo in Cuba and Halifax (later to New York, which became the greatest shipping staging-post in the world). Coastal convoys ran between New York and Key West, Florida, the first sailing southbound from Hampton Roads on 14 May, the first northbound a day later. Traffic was so heavy it was estimated that one forty-five ship convoy, both ocean and coastal, would have to sail every three days, needing a minimum of thirty-one destroyers and forty-seven corvettes as escorts. On 16 April the HX Halifax to UK convoy cycle was opened out from six to seven days to allow two escort groups to transfer to the east coast of America.

Even so, the board's comments showed that they *still* had not properly grasped the significance of convoy. The board said, of the shortage of escorts: 'it should be borne in mind that effective convoying depends upon the escorts being in sufficient strength to permit their taking the offensive against attacking submarines without their withdrawal for this purpose resulting in unduly exposing the convoy to other submarines while they are on this mission. Any protection less than this simply results in the convoy's becoming a convenient target for submarines. . . .' The notions that convoy was defensive, and that it increased a submarine's target, seemed quite indestructable.

The 'Bucket Brigade' was continued between New York and Hampton Roads, where there was good air cover en route. But convoys on the rest of the coast-line began to show results at once. From twenty-three in April, the number of ships sunk in the Eastern Sea Frontier area sank to five in May, rose to thirteen in June, fell to three in July, to zero in August, and for the rest of the year.

As convoys made sinkings more difficult in the north, so the U-boats transferred their main effort to the Caribbean and the Gulf of Mexico where, between May and September 1942, they sank over 250 ships of more than a million tons. Convoys began there in July with four new routes: Halifax to the Dutch West Indies; the Panama Canal to Guantánamo; Trinidad to Key West; and Trinidad to the Panama Canal. In September the Trinidad to Key West convoys ended at Guantánamo, and became one of the feeder branches of the Interlocking System. By then, 746 ships had sailed along the route in thirty-four convoys. Only fifteen ships had been lost to enemy action.

Convoy gave similarly dramatic improvements all over the Caribbean. From August to November 1942, 1360 ships arrived at Port of Spain, Trinidad, or the Gulf of Paria, and 1462 left; of those, 1354 ships sailed in 119 convoys. Fifty-three were sunk, but only eleven of them whilst in convoy.

By the end of August 1942 the Interlocking Convoy System was taking firm shape. Its pivot was New York, whence the Atlantic convoys took their departure and where they made their final westward landfall. Two main coastal convoys, from Key West to New York and back, and from Guantánamo to New York and back, sailed every four or five days, timing their arrivals so as to arrive in New York just before the next UK-bound convoy sailed. The 'feeder' convoys, from the Gulf of Mexico, from Panama, from Aruba, from Trinidad and (later) from Recife in Brazil, normally sailed every ten days, thus connecting with alternate main coastal convoys.

Between 1 July and 7 December 1942, 527 convoys, with 9064 ships, sailed along the Interlocking System. Of these, thirty-nine ships, or less than ½ a per cent, were lost to enemy action. Compared with the bloodbath earlier in the year in the same waters, it was a quite astounding improvement. Yet, the opinion of some US naval officers was still that 'the navy does not like convoys. It is a purely defensive form of warfare, and although the develop-

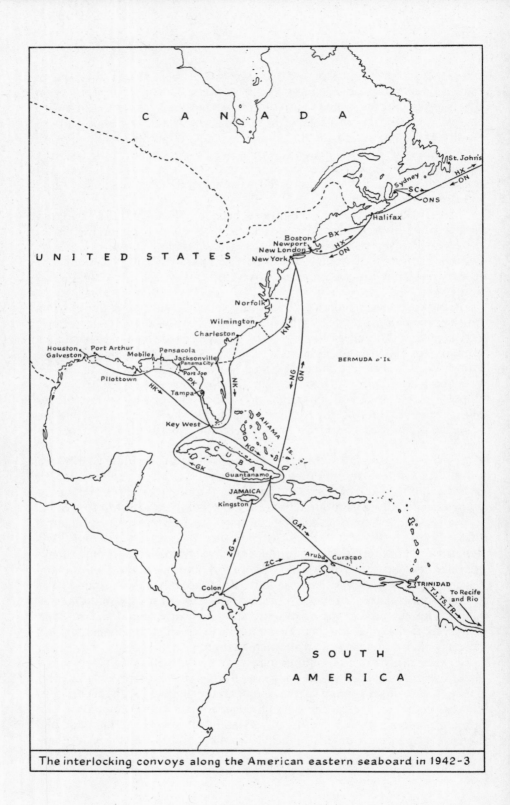

The interlocking convoys along the American eastern seaboard in 1942-3

(*Above*) U-boat captain's view of an unsuspecting merchant ship about to be torpedoed. (*Below*) one of the most famous convoy posters of the war, with a bitter ironical caption. Specially redrawn by the artist, Captain Jack Broome, who says, 'It is worth emphasizing how hopeless straggling was. Escorts couldn't cope. The only chap who enjoyed it was the U-boat fielding longstop.'

AN EXTRAORDINARY GENERAL MEETING OF
THE STRAGGLER'S CLUB

(*Above*) U-boat officers of the First World War. Second from right is Korvetten-Kapitan Otto Hersing, of the U-21. (*Below*) Captain F. J. Walker, the most successful of the escort commanders of the Second World War

(*Above*) Admiral Karl Doenitz, Befehlshaber der U-boote
(Head of the U-boat Arm) and (*below*) Admiral Sir Max
Horton KCB, DSO, C-in-C Western Approaches

(*Above*) U-38 leaves for patrol early in the Second World War, and (*below*) the
company of U-48, commanded by Bleichrodt, on their return to Kiel after
the battle of convoys SC7 and HX79

U-744 (*above*) entering Brest in early 1944 after a successful Atlantic patrol, and (*below*) blown to the surface a few weeks later by Canadian and British ships. A boat is arriving to take off survivors

(*Above*) An Atlantic convoy safely nears the British ports. This photograph, probably of SC105, was taken by a Flying Fortress of Coastal Command in 1942. (*Below*) a sadder end for a British merchantman, breaking up after attack by a U-boat in the First World War

Second World War air cover. (*Above*) *Tracker*'s Avengers of 846 Squadron
escort a Gibraltar convoy in 1944, with *Biter* in the background. (*Below*)
Fighter Catapult Ship *Springbank*, with Fairey Fulmar of 804 Squadron
embarked

Air cover for the 1980s. (*Above*) *Invincible* with Sea Harrier above the flight deck and Sea King helicopter near by. (*Below*) Loading torpedoes on to a Lynx helicopter on the frigate *Arrow*

ment of the Interlocking System has speeded shipment of strategic war materials, it is still, and by necessity always will be, slower than allowing vessels to sail independently. Thus, insofar as enemy submarine warfare forces us to use the convoy system, we unwittingly play into his hands by consuming more shipping days than would otherwise be necessary.' It seems hardly credible that any American naval officer could express such views, late in 1942, when that year's wounds were still fresh.

While the majority of U-boats were thus engaged off the American coast-line, life was much more peaceful on the North Atlantic convoy routes. Losses in May 1942 had dropped to eight ships, of 42,475 tons, although the U-boats had developed a disconcerting new tactic of going for the escorts. In particular, Korvetten-Kapitan Zimmermann in U-136 sank the corvette *Arbutus* from ONS63 on 5 February, and the Canadian corvette *Spikenard* from SC67 on the 11th.

In February 1942 a system of Through escorts was introduced, from WestOMP across to about 7° W where trawlers relieved the escort. This gave much greater flexibility in convoy routeing. Convoys maintained the 'Great Circle' route as far as possible, but had often been diverted to keep the rendezvous with MOMP. Now, they could be redirected to any preferred route without having to worry about the 'Meet'.

A new system of fourteen escort groups came into force, seven British, three American and four Canadian. The British and Canadian groups aimed at a strength of three destroyers and seven corvettes, thus giving convoys an average protection of two destroyers and five corvettes. The new system was introduced with HX176 and ON68 late in February.

The destroyers used in these groups had to be 'long-leggers', until oiling at sea was achieved. Some of the 'short-leggers' underwent a process of 'duo-boilerization', to increase their endurance. Whenever the U-boat situation allowed, destroyers escorting slow ON convoys would sail late, to overtake, and thus save a day's fuel. Similarly, they might leave a homeward-bound convoy early. American and Canadian groups used Londonderry as their base in the UK; British groups used Argentia as a stop-over base. However, nothing could be done about the destroyers' ages. Somebody calculated at this time that the combined ages of the destroyers in the Western Approaches Command totalled 1409 years. 'This dates back to AD 533.'

On the tactical front, equipment introduced in 1942 had uncomfortable implications for the U-boats. On 27 March, U-587 was returning from operations off the east coast of America when it heard and then sighted the fast troopship convoy WS17. Its contact report was detected by High Frequency Direction Finding (H/F D/F) equipment, which was just being fitted in surface escorts. The destroyer *Leamington* was first on the scene, ran past, returned, sighted U-587 (which had just transmitted a second report), and attacked. The destroyers *Aldenham*, *Grove* and *Volunteer* assisted, and sank the U-boat; the first success due to H/F D/F.

In April, there was an even more disquieting incident for the U-boats. The action was once again by Walker's 36th Escort Group, escorting the Gibraltar convoy OG82. On the night of 14–15 April, when the Admiralty had already warned Walker of a U-boat's presence near the convoy, OG82 was some 450 miles NW of Finisterre, steering SSE, at about 8 knots. The corvette *Vetch* (Lt Cdr Beverley) was scouting ahead of the convoy, with *Pentstemon* in the normal screening position ahead, *Convolvulus* to port, and *Gardenia* to starboard, with Walker himself bringing up the rear in *Stork* (at sea for the first time since the damage suffered with HG76).

At 9.45 p.m. *Vetch* was doing a wide zigzag ahead of the port-hand column when she obtained a contact on her Type 271 10-cm radar set to the NE, roughly on the convoy's port beam. *Vetch* closed the contact. Beverley at first thought it was *Pentstemon* but, to make sure, he illuminated the target with star-shell at 9.57 p.m. It was a U-boat, on the surface and heading into the convoy.

The U-boat, actually U-252 (Korvetten-Kapitan Lercher), was returning from landing an agent in Iceland and had been directed on to the convoy. In fact, Lercher had been just as surprised by the encounter and turned away, firing two torpedoes from the stern tubes as he went. The nearest torpedo passed less than 40 feet from *Vetch*'s port side.

Beverley had signalled, 'Submarine 1 mile away', but Walker was still uncertain where *Vetch* was. Nor was Beverley's next signal, 'Submarine has dived', any more informative. But *Vetch* had fired a burst of tracer at the U-boat, which gave Walker a datum point, and he steered towards it.

As *Stork* came up to join *Vetch*, U-252 surfaced about a mile away and a chase began. As usual, the U-boat just about had the legs of a corvette. Both ships opened fire, and *Stork* expended over 100 rounds. *Vetch* actually claimed four hits but this was not possible because, at 10.30, Lercher decided to dive. This was a grave mistake. He and his crew now had only minutes to live.

The slight loss of speed on diving allowed *Vetch* to get closer, and she released the first pattern only three minutes after U-252 dived. *Stork* gained an immediate firm Asdic contact and carried out an attack which, while 'no perfect drill-book attack', seemed to stun the U-boat and reduce it to dead slow. It never picked up speed again.

In the next twenty minutes, *Stork* and *Vetch* made four attacks, with a total of fifty charges. Leading Seaman Kelly, *Stork*'s Asdic operator, then heard the typical sound of a U-boat blowing tanks. Above, Walker waited, to see what would happen.

Nothing appeared, so *Stork* ran in again. This time the U-boat took the attack 'where the chicken took the axe'. *Vetch*'s final charges must have broken up completely whatever remained of U-252. 'I was tolerably certain that the Boche had been pole-axed,' wrote Walker, 'as indeed he had.

Wreckage boiled to the surface and in high delight I had a boat lowered to investigate.'

The gruesome evidence was all around. The 10-inch signal projector, sweeping the surface of the sea from side to side, revealed a revolting mixture of oil, shattered wood, blood and human remains, though nothing as complete as a whole corpse. The whaler's crew retrieved from this appalling soup a sheepskin coat, and leather trousers made in Stuttgart; a box, containing a compass tool outfit; half a wooden base-plate tallied *Sternfinder*; a numbered locker lid; chunks of a black cork-like substance; a pencilled chit, possibly from a trouser pocket, headed U-252; and a human heart and lungs, complete but penetrated by splinters, suggesting that 'the unlucky man must have been blown practically inside out'.

Also in 'high delight', Walker signalled his ships to 'splice the mainbrace'. It had been another of Walker's characteristic attacks, reaching a successful conclusion from very sparse initial data. But from such little information, Walker had summed up the situation, detached himself and one other escort to attack, while the rest remained to protect the convoy, and sunk the U-boat – all in much less than an hour. But most ominous of all for the U-boats, the attack showed what could be done by surface escorts equipped with good radar. The old happy times, when a U-boat could steal in on a convoy, trimmed down on the surface and at high speed, were gone. The radar-equipped surface escort could now do to U-boats near the convoy what the air escorts had been already achieving out in the deep field.

On 5 July 1942 a Mark 8 Wellington of 172 Squadron RAF sank U-502 in the Bay of Biscay. This was the first success for an aircraft fitted with a Leigh Light, a very brilliant searchlight with a flat but broad beam carried under the fuselage of a bomber. It was developed on the private initiative of Wing Cdr Leigh, a First World War pilot, in the face of some considerable official apathy. The 22-million-candlepower light, which had its own generator, was fitted in a retractable turret, in the belly of the aircraft, which also had 1½-metre ASV radar.

When the radar operator obtained a U-boat contact, he guided the pilot towards it, until he lost the contact in the 'sea clutter' on his set, which was normally at the range of about a mile. The light was lowered and switched on, turning night into day. If all had gone well, it illuminated the U-boat dead ahead, where depth-charges could be dropped from a height of about 50 feet. The method immediately made the U-boats more cautious, and by August 1942 few U-boats surfaced at night. Of course, once they began to surface by day instead, they became better visual targets.

There were other weapon developments. The escorts had found disadvantages in attacking U-boats with depth charges thrown over the astern. It was difficult to steer the ship accurately so that the stern passed directly over the target. More important was the problem of the 'blind time' which elapsed after the U-boat had left the Asdic beam ahead of the escort, while the escort passed over it and the depth-charges sank towards their target. For a U-boat at a range of 450 yards and a depth of 300 feet, this 'blind time' was as long as two minutes, time enough for a skilled U-boat commander to evade the attack.

It would be better to attack the U-boat whilst it was still ahead of the escort and held in the Asdic beam. Ahead-throwing mortars were developed, code-named 'Hedgehog', which threw twenty-four projectiles each with 31 pounds of TNT, fitted with contact fuses and sinking at a rate of 22 feet per second. Ships were fitted with Hedgehog from January 1942, and forty-eight U-boats were sunk with this weapon during the war.

However, Hedgehog did not explode unless it actually hit its target. So the effect of near-misses, both in damaging the U-boat and in lowering the morale of its crew, was lost. In February 1942, the design of a much heavier, three-barrelled 'Squid' mortar began. Squid was first fitted in the corvette *Hadleigh Castle* and went into full production in 1943.

From June 1942 it became possible for tankers in convoys to refuel the escorts. This was a tremendous step forward. Trials had begun with RFA *Rapidol* in a Gibraltar-bound convoy early in 1941 but there was a shortage of tankers, special equipment had to be made and fitted, and the crews trained in refuelling techniques. But once refuelling became commonplace, it simplified convoy organization enormously. Escort groups no longer had to be sent out to overtake convoys at rendezvous which might or might not be kept, and groups no longer had to return without having met their convoy because they were short of fuel. Convoys could now use more southerly and shorter routes because escorts no longer had to fuel halfway across in Iceland.

In 1942 the Operational Research Sections began to investigate several aspects of convoy operations. A statistical analysis of losses of merchant vessels in convoy during the previous two years found that a convoy with nine escorts suffered, on the average, some 25 per cent less losses than a convoy with only six escorts. From the number of convoys run every year, the average size of those convoys, and the number of escort vessels in use, it could be calculated that every extra escort put into service could be expected to save between two and three merchant vessels a year. Thus, provided the war lasted a year or more longer (a *very* reasonable assumption in 1942), it was better to build more escorts and less merchant vessels. However, there were practical difficulties in changing over shipyards from building merchant ships to warships.

The value of an escort could be defined even more strictly, and mathematically. For Doenitz, the critical equation of the war at sea was the exchange rate, of U-boats sunk against Allied ships sunk. In 1941 the total sinkings were 1,967,000 tons, for a loss of thirty-six German U-boats. That was 54,000 tons of shipping per U-boat lost. The average number of U-boats at sea was about twenty-five, so that each U-boat was sinking some 6000 tons per month. Until the end of 1942, the exchange rate was still eight ships, or 45,000 tons, per U-boat lost, and the ships sunk per U-boat per month about 4000 tons. From January to April 1943, the results continued at about 28,000 tons per U-boat lost, or about 3000 tons per U-boat per month. Then came the change: from 15 April to the end of the year, after the coming of sufficient very-long-range aircraft and the victory of the escorts in May, only 5000 tons were sunk per U-boat lost, or 2500 tons per U-boat per month, an exchange rate so poor that it amounted to a defeat for the U-boats.

The number of U-boats sunk by the escorts was proportional to the number of U-boats present and the number of escorts. Thus:

K (U-boat sunk) $\propto U$ (U-boats present) $\times E$ (escorts present).

Similarly, the convoy losses (L) were proportional to the number of U-boats attacking, divided by the number of escorts present:

$$L \propto \frac{U}{E}.$$

Dividing the top equation by the second, to arrive at Doenitz's critical exchange rate of U-boats sunk per ships sunk,

$$\frac{K}{L} \propto \frac{UE}{\dfrac{U}{E}} = UE \times \frac{E}{U} = E^2.$$

Thus, the number of U-boats sunk per ship lost in convoy is proportional to the *square* of the number of escorts, when those escorts are employed as convoy escorts. Six escorts were therefore not twice but *four times* as effective as three escorts. But this square rule did not apply when escorts were employed on other duties such as patrolling. It also applied equally to aircraft and submarines, but again, only while they were being used as convoy escorts.

In the autumn of 1942, ORS began to examine the implications of varying convoy sizes. Later, Professor Blackett wrote that he bitterly regretted that this had not been done before. Losses of merchant ships, he calculated, could have been reduced by 20 per cent, from 5 million tons to 4 million, or about 200 ships, in the space of a year.

At that time, the general opinion was that large convoys were dangerous. 'It stood to reason' that the larger the convoy the bigger and more vulnerable the target. 'Common sense dictated' that a larger convoy was putting more eggs in one basket. The average size of convoy then was set at about forty ships, with about six escorts. Convoys of more than sixty ships were actually forbidden.

The rule of thumb was that the number of escorts required for a convoy was three, plus the number of ships in the convoy divided by ten. Thus, a

convoy of twenty ships needed three escorts, plus another two, making five; a
convoy of thirty ships three plus three, making six; and so on. But there was a
basic inconsistency in these Admiralty rules. For example, three convoys
each of twenty ships would need five escorts per convoy, or fifteen escorts. By
the same rule, a single convoy of the same sixty ships, would need only nine
escorts. How could the same number of ships need *more* escorts in smaller
convoys, if smaller convoys really were safer?

As so often, when the figures were closely examined some surprising
results appeared. In the previous two years large convoys had suffered
relatively less losses than small. Convoys with an average of thirty-two ships
had an average loss of 2.5 per cent. But convoys with an average of 54 ships
had suffered only losses of 1.1 per cent. Thus larger convoys appeared to be
more than twice as safe as smaller convoys, and there were very strong
grounds for believing that convoys got safer the larger they were.

The scientists in ORS, by that time called the Directorate of Naval
Operational Research (DNOR), were sure their figures and conclusions were
correct. But there must be a practical explanation, to convince the Sea
Lords. Intense research, analysis and discussion, very much assisted by the
personal accounts of U-boat POWs, established some revealing facts: that the
chance of a convoy being sighted by a U-boat was the same, or very nearly the
same, for a large convoy as for a small; that the chances of a U-boat
penetrating the escort screen depended upon the number of escort vessels
for each mile of convoy perimeter; and that when a U-boat did penetrate the
screen, the number of merchant ships it then sank was the same for both
large and small convoys. With a given number of escorts and a given number
of U-boats, and other things being equal, the same absolute number of
merchant ships would be sunk whatever the size of the convoy. But the
percentage of ships sunk would be in inverse proportion to the size of the
convoy. The best tactic was to reduce the number of U-boat sightings by
reducing the number of convoys, but increasing their size so as to sail the
same total number of ships.

A larger convoy did not, in fact, need a proportionately larger number of
escorts. The area covered by a convoy increases as the square of the radius
from its centre, but the perimeter increases only in proportion to the length
of the radius. If the escorts are set at a distance of about 4000 yards from the
convoy, the perimeter of an eighty-ship convoy is only about one-seventh
longer than that of a forty-ship convoy. Therefore, seven escorts could
protect the convoy of eighty ships just as effectively as six escorts could
protect the convoy of forty.

These arguments were illustrated in one very apt comparison between a
submarine and a man out duck-shooting: 'if a flock of eighty duck fly over
him, he will not be able to shoot down any more than if a flock of only forty
birds fly over; for he will be able to fire only the same number of shots in both
cases. He will not have time to re-load. Neither is the submarine able to

return to base, re-load, and re-attack, after it has fired its store of torpedoes.'

After what Blackett called 'some weeks of earnest argument' DNOR won the day. Changes were made to Admiralty orders about convoy sizes in the spring of 1943. Running much larger convoys made it possible to transfer escorts from the Atlantic in due course to support the invasion of Normandy in 1944. That summer the Admiralty gave tremendous publicity to the safe arrival in this country of a convoy of 187 ships.

Another important training step was taken in 1942 with the establishment of a Western Approaches Tactical School. Its purposes were to examine and evaluate U-boat attacks on shipping, to evolve the best doctrine of counter-attack, and to teach the appropriate methods and counter-moves. Cdr Gilbert Roberts, who had retired because of ill-health, was recalled to run the School. He took over the top floor of Derby House in Liverpool, where he and his staff, which consisted mostly of very young Wrens, laid out a tactical floor, with models, and chalk and canvas, and bits of string. In fact, they created a facsimile of a stretch of ocean, about 20 miles square, on which convoy actions could be fought, in the form of 'games'.

The games were made as realistic as possible by, for instance, arranging to restrict a player's vision of events, just as poor visibility would restrict him at sea. Incidents were injected – signals, sightings, radar reports, helm orders, U-boat attacks, sinkings. The Wrens ran the games (and discreetly assisted the players). It was a primitive forerunner of the sophisticated electronic and computerized tactical trainers of today.

Although Western Approaches Command Instructions (WACIs) was a very bulky book indeed, overflowing with ever-multiplying amendments, each obsolescent almost before it was promulgated, Roberts discovered that there was no great quantity of hard fact and firm policy on counter-measures. It was his job to study such sources as reports of proceedings, survivors' accounts, interrogations of POWs, Asdic traces made during attacks and, above all, to chat informally to returning escort commanders about their tactics.

Roberts asked escort commanders what they did when a U-boat was detected or a ship was sunk. He heard a great deal of talk about 'going to action stations', 'carrying out Asdic sweeps' and 'increasing speed' but found that – apart from such men as Walker with his 'Buttercup' – counter-attacks might amount to no more than plunging about the ocean on the outskirts of the convoy, hoping to pick up an Asdic contact.

Roberts evolved counter-attack plans with famous 'fruity' code-names, such as RASPBERRY, PINEAPPLE and GOOSEBERRY, and taught them to the escort and group commanders when they came to the School for their tactical courses. Now, escorts could move about their convoys with an increased sense of purpose and the assurance of knowing what the others were doing. Most important, these plans worked at sea. Roberts was always avid for the latest gossip from sea, eager to hear how his brainchildren were performing and always ready to amend in the light of experience. It was very gratifying for him to have former pupils returning, with the glad news that such-and-such a U-boat had been caught with such-and-such a counter-attack.

Roberts was a subtle opponent. For instance, he evolved a plan for countering a shadowing U-boat. On sighting the U-boat the escorts should not attack at once, but wait until it dived and then plot its intended course around to the rear of the convoy, where one or more of the escorts would be waiting.

In November Admiral Sir Max Horton took over the Western Approaches Command from Sir Percy Noble. One of his first moves was to undergo Roberts's course in full. Max Horton was, of course, one of the most successful and distinguished submariners the Royal Navy ever had. He was a superbly apt choice for the Western Approaches, on the principle of setting a thief to catch a thief. Doenitz was a most able and formidable opponent, but Horton was to beat him, fair and square. But when Horton took the part of the U-boat on Roberts's tactical floor he was firmly nailed five times running and was not at all pleased to discover that his antagonist on each occasion had been an eighteen-year-old Wren plotter.

Roberts was no respecter of persons and never minced his words when commenting on dockets containing convoy reports of proceedings:

> Narrative is brimful of failures to report, [he noted on one (actually of ONS102)] dud reports, quaint signals, accidental lights, partial illumination by snowflake rockets for protracted periods, errors in identification etc. and all by the convoy. . . . I note in each torpedoing that one or more often two escorts who were astern and in the exit line of the U-boat, immediately went to pick up survivors, for which they are commended. Valuable lives were saved by one, while the other protected her, and the U-boat retired to re-load. It may be callous but this is not my idea of the duty prescribed for an escort vessel. It is all in the book. An untidy voyage. No information for me in it.

When convoys were introduced along the American coast, the U-boats naturally moved back to the mid-Atlantic, except for some places such as the coast of Trinidad where the pickings were still easy for the time being. The U-boats began to operate in the 'Greenland gap', where air cover was non-existent or very spasmodic, and in other 'black pits', east of the Azores and the Canaries, where again there was no air cover and 'milch cow' U-boats could operate undisturbed. Doenitz's new plan was for the U-boats to locate a convoy before it reached the Greenland air gap, attack whilst the convoy was crossing the gap, and withdraw at the eastern end, when the air cover returned.

In spite of the improvements in weapons and tactics on the Allied side, and the numbers of new escorts coming off the slipways, the U-boats by this time had a most important advantage. A fourth 'wheel' added to the Enigma coding machine on 1 February 1942 brought about a decoding 'blackout' for most of the year, until Ultra were in December 1942 once again able to break the U-boat codes. The German cryptographers had a success too; the B-Dienst decoding service succeeded in cracking the Admiralty Naval Cypher No. 3 in February, which carried the bulk of signal traffic concerning the north Atlantic convoys. The B-Dienst service was able to read most of this traffic until June 1943, with one short 'blackout' in December 1942 and January 1943.

This German success in de-crypting coincided with a dramatic increase in the numbers of U-boats at sea, which climbed from twenty-two in January 1942, to sixty-one in May, to eighty-six in August, soaring to over 100 in October. The main onslaught began again in August and September 1942, when U-boats located twenty-one out of sixty-three convoys that sailed, attacked seven of them, and sank forty-three of their ships.

The U-boats resumed determined attacks in daylight, in a way which they had not done for the previous ten months. In August a German home service broadcast said, 'Young U-boat commanders were attacking the enemy for the first time.' On 1 and 2 August twelve U-boats formed the 'Pirat' patrol line to search for ON115, of forty-one ships, whose escort, the Canadian Group C3, had already driven off repeated attacks on 30 and 31 July, while the destroyer *Skeena* and the corvette *Wetaskiwin* had sunk U-588. Topp, in U-552, sighted the convoy on the 2nd, and his report brought up another five U-boats. The convoy lost three ships, but once again the Canadian escort drove off more attacks before the U-boats broke off in poor visibility on the 3rd.

From ON115, most of the U-boats taking part formed a new 'Steinbrinck' Group of eight U-boats east of the Newfoundland Bank where, on the 5th, U-593 sighted SC94, thirty-six ships escorted by another Canadian group. This group, C1, consisted of the Canadian destroyer *Assiniboine* (Lt Cdr J. H. Stubbs RCN), and the corvettes *Chilliwack* and *Orillia*, with the British corvettes *Primrose*, *Nasturtium* and *Dianthus*.

U-593 (Korvetten-Kapitan Kelbling) attacked at once and picked off a straggler before being driven off by gunfire. Next day, most of the escorts were in action, *Chilliwack* and *Primrose* damaging and driving off U-595 with gunfire and depth-charges, and depth-charges from *Dianthus* forcing U-454 to break off. At 6.36 p.m. that day, *Assiniboine* sighted U-210 on the surface in very foggy weather and tracked it by radar.

When *Assiniboine* closed to finish the engagement, U-210 replied with gunfire and started to wriggle away on the surface. The U-boat actually turned well inside the destroyer's turning circle and *Assiniboine* had to go full astern on the inboard screw to help her round. Meanwhile the U-boat Captain, Korvetten-Kapitan Lemcke, could be seen on his conning tower, bending to give orders down the voice-pipe. Shortly, he was seen to leave the bridge and in the few seconds the U-boat was on a steady course before

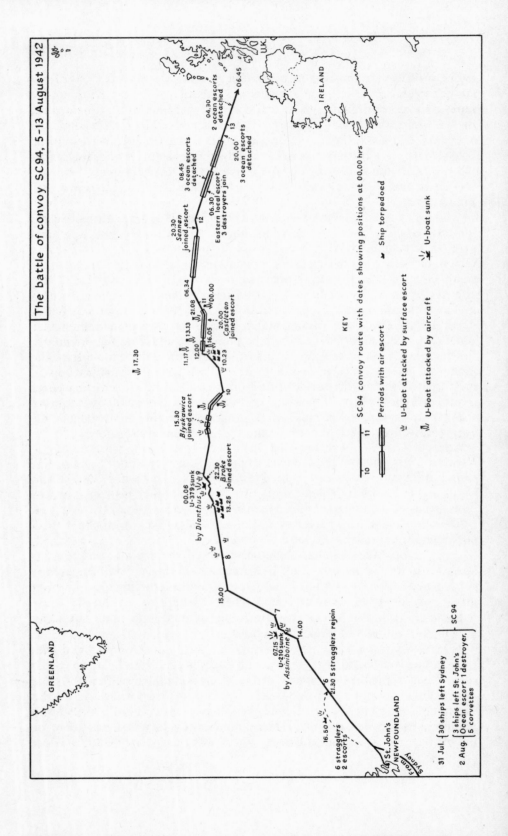

The battle of convoy SC94, 5–13 August 1942

GREENLAND

NEWFOUNDLAND

St. John's

from Sydney

IRELAND

U.K.

15.00

14.00

07.15
U-210 sunk
by Assiniboine

21.30 5 stragglers rejoin

16.50

6 stragglers
2 escorts

00.06
U-379 sunk
by Dianthus

13.25
Broke
joined escort

22.30

15.30
Blyskawica
joined escort

17.30

11.17
12.00

10.23

13.13
21.08
06.34

00.00

16.05

20.00
Castleton
joined escort

20.30
Sennen
joined escort

06.30
Eastern local escort
3 destroyers join

08.45
3 ocean escorts
detached

04.30
2 ocean escorts
detached

20.00
3 ocean escorts
detached

06.45

KEY

——— SC94 convoy route with dates showing positions at 00.00 hrs

⬛ Periods with air escort

Ship torpedoed

U-boat attacked by surface escort

U-boat attacked by aircraft

U-boat sunk

| 10 | 11 |

SC94 {
31 Jul. 30 ships left Sydney
2 Aug. 3 ships left St. John's
Ocean escort 1 destroyer,
5 corvettes
}

diving, *Assiniboine* rammed it just abaft the conning tower.

U-210 surfaced again and its guns were manned, spraying *Assiniboine*'s upper deck with incendiary machine-gun bullets. *Assiniboine*'s bridge was set on fire, one rating killed, and one officer and twelve ratings wounded. *Assiniboine* rammed the U-boat again, then fired a shallow pattern of depth-charges and one 4.7-inch round from 'Y' turret as she passed. The U-boat sank by the bow in about two minutes.

Dianthus, in *Assiniboine*'s words, 'appeared out of the fog just in time to see him go. The yell that went up from both ships must have frightened U-boats for about 10 miles in the vicinity.' *Assiniboine* picked up ten survivors, *Dianthus* twenty-eight. Six were later transferred to *Assiniboine*, shouting '*Heil Hitler*' at the tops of their voices.

The night of 6–7 August was also a busy one, *Dianthus* making six depth-charge attacks on contacts between 11 p.m. and 12.30 a.m. But the respite won was only temporary. At 1.25 p.m. on the 8th, U-176 and U-379 attacked almost together and sank five of the convoy – *Trehata*, *Kelso*, *Anneberg*, *Mount Kassion* and *Kaimaku*, which blew up with a tremendous detonation which turned the whole ship into a sheet of flame, followed a few moments later, as the remains of the ship sank, by a colossal underwater explosion.

At this, the crews of *Empire Moonbeam*, *Empire Antelope* and *Radchurch* abandoned ship. Those of the two *Empires* eventually returned, but the crew of *Radchurch* refused. The ship was last seen adrift, with just her Master on board, and she was later torpedoed and sunk by U-176.

Korvetten-Kapitan Kettner, of U-379, was obviously a confident commander in the old style. Later on the 8th, he approached SC94 again. His conning tower was sighted at 7.10 p.m. by the Coxswain of *Dianthus*, who happened to be on deck aft. U-379 dived, or anyway disappeared, before anything could be done but at 8.45 two U-boats were sighted ahead. *Dianthus* fired twelve rounds of high explosive at 12,000 yards. At 8.50 both boats dived but no contact was found. Kettner closed the convoy for a third time at 11.08, when *Dianthus*'s signalman on the bridge sighted a dark object and eight rounds of star-shell were fired at it. In the mist the U-boat dived again and at 11.39 *Dianthus*, at last, got a good Asdic contact, range 2500 yards and fired five charges.

U-379 surfaced two minutes later and at 11.50 *Dianthus* rammed it, riding over the hull and then dropped six more charges. *Dianthus* actually rammed the U-boat four times, fired seven rounds of 4-inch, 100 rounds of 20-mm pompom, and several belts of Hotchkiss, as well as illuminating the target by searchlight and snowflake. U-379 sank stern first just after midnight on the 9th. 'Those nineteen minutes,' wrote *Dianthus*'s captain, 'between the surfacing and sinking of the U-boat can be described as very lively and gave our crew the opportunity for which during the whole commission they strived so hard.' Five survivors were picked up. *Dianthus* left a Carley float for any others, not wanting to stay longer in the area.

The sinking U-boat had damaged *Dianthus*'s fo'c'sle and she had to drop out, but the destroyers *Broke* and the Polish *Blyskawica* joined during the night, and air cover also arrived the next day. But on that forenoon of the 10th, U-660 and U-438 sank another four ships in quick succession, making eleven lost from sc94.

From August 1942 onwards there were some tremendous battles in and around convoys. SL118, homeward-bound from Sierra Leone with thirty-four ships, was attacked by four U-boats of the eight in the 'Blucher' Group on 17 and 18 August. Four ships were lost and the armed merchant cruiser *Cheshire* torpedoed. The air and surface escorts counter-attacked twenty times, escorts dropping depth-charges eight times, and Liberators three times. U-333 was damaged, and the rest driven off.

Four days later, from the 22nd, ON122's thirty-six ships were attacked over a period of days by seven U-boats of the 'Lohs' Group. The convoy lost four ships but the escort group B6, of the destroyer *Viscount*, with the Norwegian corvettes *Potentilla*, *Eglantin*, *Montbretia* and *Acanthus* put up a vigorous defence; they carried out no fewer than thirty depth-charge and two Hedgehog attacks, damaging U-605 and U-256 (which was attacked again by aircraft in the Bay of Biscay and put out of action for over a year).

The fatal lack of radar in the surface escorts was demonstrated in September when thirteen U-boats of the 'Vorwarts' Group lay in wait for ON127. This convoy had thirty-two ships, escorted by the Canadian group C4 (destroyers *St Croix*, *Ottawa*, corvettes *Amherst*, *Arvida* and *Sherbrooke*, and the British corvette *Celandine*). ON127 was first sighted by U-584 on 5 September, but contact was lost in the night and not regained until midday on the 10th when the convoy was out of air cover.

In a three-day battle, in which for the only time in 1942 and 1943 every U-boat taking part (thirteen in this case) fired torpedoes, *Ottawa* and seven merchant ships of 50,000 tons were sunk, and four other ships damaged. The escorts' radar was unserviceable at all the crucial times, and no U-boat was sunk, but U-659 was damaged on the 11th.

The last four months of 1942, when there were over 100 boats at sea, were some of the most successful of the war for the U-boat Command, from the technical point of view. With some quick and accurate sighting and reporting amongst themselves, and very ably assisted by timely intelligence from the B-Dienst Service, the U-boats prospered. Forming and re-forming in groups, named for such carnivores as Leopard, Panther and Puma, they seemed free to go from one convoy to the next.

sc104 was located by several U-boats and attacked over a period of nearly a week in October, losing seven ships. Ten U-boats attacked SL125 off Madeira and sank thirteen ships in a seven-day battle. sc107 was attacked by seven U-boats in November and lost fifteen ships. ON144 fought a four-day battle with a U-boat pack of six, lost six ships and the corvette *Montbretia*, who was hit twice while going at full speed and went down without stopping, with her Captain and forty-six of her people. HX212 lost twelve ships, and ONS154 another thirteen in a fierce battle at the end of the year.

But the escorts were not idle. *Viscount* sank U-163, and *Fame* blew U-353 to the surface and sank it by ramming, both whilst escorting SC104. *Fame* picked up thirty-eight survivors, including the U-boat's Captain who apparently had little faith in his hydrophones. He had actually been in his bunk at the time of the attack, under the impression that he was shadowing the convoy from a safe distance!

The Norwegian corvette *Potentilla* sank U-184 whilst escorting ONI44 and, in spite of the six ships lost from that convoy, the escorts thought the 'U-boats showed little fight. On many occasions they turned away and dived when they realized the escorts were after them.' HX217, which sailed in November, was escorted by British, Polish and Norwegian ships, supported by British, Canadian and American aircraft and lost only two out of thirty-three ships, one torpedoed from outside the screen and the other by an undetected U-boat. But this was because of scarcity of U-boats. Fifteen of them were summoned to the scene, though not all made successful approaches. But there were thirteen U-boat detections in the night of 7–8 December, and two Liberators of 120 Squadron, B-Bravo and M-Mike, made eight sightings and five sightings respectively next day. Certainly, the performances of individual U-boats varied greatly. Mengersen, now in U-607, and Topp in U-552 scored consistently. But other U-boats do not seem to figure in the sinkings tallies at all.

Most encouraging for the Allies were the figures of U-boats sunk by aircraft. From the sinking of U-582 by aircraft of 269 Squadron, south of Iceland on 5 October, aircraft went on to sink another fifteen U-boats in the Atlantic areas by the end of the year.

Nevertheless the state of the battle in the Atlantic towards the end of 1942 was in rough balance, but with the advantage already beginning to tilt again towards the U-boats. In fact, the situation had all the appearances of becoming as grave for the Allies as at any time in the war. Mr Churchill had recently formed a Cabinet Anti-U-boat Committee, on which the Navy, the RAF, Ministers, scientists and the United States were all represented, to give, as he said, the same impulse to anti-U-boat warfare as had been applied to the Battle of the Atlantic and night anti-aircraft defence.

At the Committee's first meeting on 4 November 1942, Mr Churchill estimated that there were 243 U-boats operational, that new boats were being produced at the rate of twenty to thirty a month, and that the Allies had sunk or captured 159, with a probable forty-four more, since the outset of the war. (In fact the Germans had lost 135 U-boats, the Italians fifty-three, and the number of operational U-boats at that time was about 200, with another 170 doing trials or training crews.) These figures clearly showed the Allies were not sinking more than about a third of the monthly output of new U-boats.

On 18 November the same Committee took the vital decision to provide more long-range aircraft for the Battle of the Atlantic. Thirty Halifaxes were to be transferred to Coastal Command. The Wellingtons would be replaced by more modern aircraft, with Leigh lights and, later, with improved radar. The RAF also agreed to meet the Admiralty's requirement for air patrols in the Bay of Biscay.

It was a momentous decision, and taken not a moment too soon. By the end of 1942 the U-boats had sunk 1160 ships of 6,266,215 tons, out of a total of 1664 ships of 7,790,697 tons. Some 7 million tons of new shipping had been built during the year, meaning an overall loss of nearly a million tons. Another crisis in the Atlantic battle was looming.

Chapter Seventeen

'Have sunk one steamship for certain and one tanker (probable) in Square 8852,' signalled Korvetten-Kapitan H. O. Schultze, of U-432, to BdU. 'Set one tanker on fire on 15 October. My present position is Square 8967. Have 69 cubic metres of fuel oil left. Have two [air] and one [electric] torpedoes left. Wind south-west, force 3 to 4. Pressure 996 millibars. Temperature 21 degrees [above freezing].'

This lengthy signal was only one of dozens which BdU (Befehlshaber der U-boote, Head of the U-boat Arm) received, and sent, every day. The Atlantic U-boats were the most talkative opponents in the whole history of naval warfare. Every U-boat outward-bound from the French ports had to report by signal when it cleared the Bay of Biscay; U-boats from Norway or the Baltic had to signal when they crossed 60°N. Unless a U-boat had sailed for a specific task or for a particularly remote area, its patrol destination and operational orders, decided in the light of the latest tactical situation, were signalled to it at sea. U-boats were not allowed to deviate from these orders without asking for and receiving permission. No U-boat could leave its patrol and begin its homeward passage without receiving permission.

Every time a U-boat made a signal, it had to include its present position. If it failed to do so, or if it made no signals for several days, BdU would order it to report. When U-boats were to replenish from a 'milch cow', BdU signalled the fuelling rendezvous, indicated which U-boats were to refuel, in which order and at what time, and now much fuel each U-boat was to receive. When replenishment was finished, the 'milch-cow' U-boat confirmed that the orders had been carried out, or not, and reported how much fuel and stores it had remaining.

In addition to deciding U-boats' patrol areas, and how long U-boats should remain on patrol, BdU also ordered the forming and re-forming of the patrol lines of U-boats. Every U-boat commander was addressed, *by name*, and told which line to join and which place in the line to occupy. BdU provided the latest information about expected convoys, and whenever a convoy was sighted BdU decided which U-boats should attack, in what order, in which direction and even at what time. Any U-boat sighting and shadowing a convoy was required to transmit medium-frequency homing signals for other U-boats in the vicinity and to send detailed descriptions to BdU on high frequency. When reception was bad, BdU nominated U-boats to relay signals to those in contact.

The U-boats never realized the great dangers to themselves, and the enormous benefits to the Allies, of all this signalling. These long and frequent messages were God's gift to H/F D/F operators, providing accurate bearings and often, by their strength, a good estimate of range. Time and time again, escorts ran down a H/F D/F bearing and found a U-boat at the end of it. Two or more simultaneous H/F D/F bearings from different escorts gave an accurate position fix. Some U-boat commanders returning off patrol commented on the curious coincidence that a W/T transmission was so often followed by an attack, and suggested there might be some connection. But BdU could conceive of no such thing. Any U-boat commander who insisted was regarded as something of a crank.

This colossal signal traffic, continuing almost ceaselessly day and night, provided the Allied de-crypting service with a priceless mass of raw material which, when decoded over a considerable length of time, gave the Admiralty staff in the Tracking-Room an almost uncanny familiarity with their opponents. In time they came to know BdU's foibles, the characters and likely responses of the staff, even the personalities and professional standings of individual U-boat captains.

The intelligence opportunities were almost limitless. Since U-boats were required to transmit so regularly, any U-boat which failed to report after a long time could confidently be assumed sunk. From the fuel reports and its calculated daily consumption, the type of U-boat could be fairly judged. From the reports of torpedoes remaining, it could be seen which U-boats had attacked and when. Even the weather reports provided an invaluable meteorological service.

Allied Special Intelligence had taken a giant step forward on 13 December 1942 when the German 'Shark' code, using a fourth wheel on the Enigma machine, introduced the previous February, at last yielded to the effects of Ultra. By the end of 1943 some Shark traffic was being read quickly enough to be of immediate operational use. But during the first five months of the year, at a time when several crucial convoy battles were being fought, there were some frequent and occasionally lengthy delays. From about June onwards, with the co-operation and assistance of US Navy cryptographers, Shark traffic was read faster and almost continuously; from August 1943, until the end of the war, Shark signals were read the same day, virtually as a matter of course.

The Allied cryptographers were much more flexible in their thinking than their German counterparts. After reading such large quantities of German traffic, and especially the 'For officers' eyes only' signals, Allied crypto-graphers had conclusive proof early in 1943 that the German B-Dienst Service must have broken into the Naval Cypher No. 3. On 10 April 1943 the Admiralty brought forward preparations (begun as early as April 1941) to update and render more secure its cyphers. These improvements came into force in June 1943. Meantime the Germans, particularly Doenitz himself, simply could not believe that 'Shark' had been compromised. Certainly they often suspected that something was amiss; but their suspicions were always directed elsewhere – at careless talk amongst naval personnel, Allied use of radar and direction finding, the machinations of French agents of the American SIS, bad luck, or acts of God. The Enigma machine, they were confident, must be inviolate. As Doenitz wrote in his memoirs: 'Our cyphers were checked and re-checked, to make sure they were unbreakable: and on each occasion the head of the Naval Intelligence Service at Naval High Command adhered to his opinion that it would be impossible for the enemy to decipher them.'

Just as there were Allied advances in cryptography, so there were new resources actually at sea. Ever since *Audacity*'s success in 1941 it had been realized that a convoy's best air defence was its own, so that – like Mary's little lamb – everywhere the convoy went, the air cover was sure to go. A convoy did not need the full pomp and panoply of a fleet carrier. What was needed was a small, 'cheap and cheerful' vessel, a 'Woolworth' carrier in fact.

These small carriers (14,000 tons, as opposed to a fleet carrier's 30,000 tons) were almost all built in the United States, where the conversion of the first American escort carrier USS *Long Island* began in January 1941. She was ready by June. In May the conversion of SS *Mormacland* to HMS *Archer* began, and she was finished in November. Five further C-3 merchant ship hulls were allocated for carrier conversion. One became USS *Charger*, and re-mained in the States for training. The others were commissioned as HMS *Avenger, Biter, Dasher* and *Tracker*.

The British and American views of what was required of an escort carrier were very different. The Americans tended to make provision for more men to handle and to repair aircraft. But the Admiralty had much stricter standards of ship stability and fire-fighting and damage control precautions (and was much criticized by the Americans for excessive caution). *Avenger* was torpedoed in November 1942, whilst escorting a convoy for the 'Torch' landings in North Africa, and sank after an internal petrol explosion. On 27 March 1943, *Dasher* blew up in the Clyde and sank with the loss of 378 lives, also after a petrol explosion. The Admiralty caution seemed to have been well justified. Escort carriers had to spend months in British yards, under-going major alterations and additions, before they were passed for oper-ational service.

In December 1941, after Pearl Harbor, the Americans began a huge escort-carrier building programme, with the conversion of four fleet-oilers to become carriers of the *Santee* class. Twenty C-3 hulls were allocated for conversion, ten becoming the US *Bogue* class and ten the British *Attacker* class. These were 14,000-ton ships, with a speed of about 17 knots, normally carrying a complement of sixteen fighters and twelve torpedo-bombers. Twenty more C-3 hulls were allocated for conversion in April 1942. These became the British *Ruler* class. In the end, thirty-eight C-3 hulls were turned over to the Royal Navy, for conversion to escort carriers.

1943 saw the first appearance of a new type of convoy escort which was given the Nelsonian name of 'frigate'. They were larger, faster, more heavily armed than the hard-pressed corvettes they reinforced and, to a certain extent, replaced. The *River* class frigates, of which there were eventually no less than sixty-five, were 1370-ton vessels, over 300 feet long, with three 4-inch guns and several close-range anti-aircraft guns, improved radar, Asdics and H/F D/F, increased depth-charge stowages and Hedgehog, manned by a crew of 140. They had two shafts, powered by turbines, to give a top speed of about 20 knots.

In April 1943 the first of the *Captain* class of frigates began to operate from Londonderry. These were ex-US Navy *Evart* and *Buckley* class converted destroyer-escorts provided under lease–lend. There were eventually thirty-two *Evarts*, of 1140 tons, and forty-six *Buckleys*, bigger at 1400 tons. Both classes had three 3-inch guns, and a great array of radar and anti-submarine weapons; both had crews of over 200 men, and could do well over 20 knots. Later additions were the *Colony* class frigates, at 1430 tons, and the numerous *Bay* and *Loch* class frigates, both developed from the *Rivers*.

All these extra escorts meant that many more Support Groups could be formed. This concept was developed from the Escort Group in 1942, and Captain Walker was one of its first and certainly its finest exponent. Normally, a Support Group consisted of about ten escorts, a mix of frigates, sloops and corvettes, sometimes with an oiler attached. Support groups were not required to stay with one particular convoy. They could detach and go to support another, wherever the danger seemed greatest.

Nobody welcomed the Support Groups more warmly than Mr Churchill: 'We were now strong enough to form independent flotilla groups to act like cavalry divisions,' he wrote, 'apart from all escort duties. This I had long desired to see.' The significant phrase 'cavalry divisions' showed that the Prime Minister's thinking was still veering dangerously near the old heresy of 'hunting groups', to plunge about the ocean searching for submarines.

In fact, Support Groups were *not* 'apart from all escort duties'. Escort duty was still their prime function. The convoy could change, but the purpose was the same. The great tactical advantage of a Support Group was that its ships could afford to stay with a contact and hunt it to death. Experience had shown that, generally, the first three attacks knocked out a U-boat. But if they did not, the next three often had little effect. From the seventh attack onward, it then became a matter of wearing the U-boat out. Previously, if the first attacks were not successful, a convoy escort had to re-join her convoy and be content with driving off or putting the U-boat down. The safe and timely arrival of the merchant ships remained the escort's paramount concern. But a Support Group could remain on the spot and hunt a target to destruction, for however long it took, using two or more ships, one directing, others attacking, passing the contact from one to another, until they wore out the U-boat captain's patience or his judgement. Then, they could move in to the kill.

Ironically, no sooner had the first Support Group been formed than it had to disband because its ships were required for Operation Torch, the landings in North Africa in November 1942 which were the first major joint Anglo-US undertakings of the war. They simply had to succeed. Everything else, even the Battle of the Atlantic, had to take second place. The diversion of escorts, escort carriers and the shipping needed to transport the troops and their supplies to North Africa temporarily tilted the balance in the Atlantic towards the U-boats.

It was a 'Torch' convoy which suffered the first convoy disaster of 1943, an unfortunate affair showing how easy it still was for convoy defence to go wrong. An unfortunate routeing decision, defects in radar and H/F D/F equipment, a de-crypting blackout at a critical time, all coupled with lack of air cover, gave the U-boats the chances they needed.

Convoy TM1, of nine tankers, sailed from Trinidad for Gibraltar on 28 December 1942. BdU did not know of its sailing or its route, but very probably learned from agents in Trinidad that tankers were loading for Gibraltar. The Escort Group was B5, under Cdr Boyle in the destroyer *Havelock*, with three corvettes, *Pimpernel*, *Saxifrage* and *Godetia*. *Havelock*'s H/F D/F was not working properly, and there were also defects in the corvettes' radar sets.

However, TM1 proceeded without incident until about 4.30 p.m. on 3 January, when, quite by chance, it was sighted by U-514 on passage to the West Indies. The convoy, reported by U-514 as 'about ten ships with destroyers, course 070°, speed 9 knots' was then in mid ocean, about equidistant from Trinidad and the Cape Verde Islands.

U-514 was ordered to 'stick at it without fail' and given permission to attack. Later, he was told to report at two- to four-hour intervals, to assist U-125 to find the convoy from about 250 miles to the east. Korvetten-Kapitan Auffermann in U-514 closed the convoy after dark, and at 9.45 p.m. sank *British Vigilance*. He was not attacked by the escorts although U-514 was sighted on the surface, passing through the convoy columns from ahead, and some merchant ships fired at it with oerlikons.

The Special Intelligence information was patchy. It was known that the 'Delphin' Group of six U-boats, which had been patrolling between Madeira and the Azores since 29 December, hoping to pick up 'Torch' convoys, had been ordered on 2 January to sweep southward. But there was no more intelligence from noon on the 3rd until the morning of the 9th, and a critical period from noon on the 3rd to noon on the 5th stayed blank. At 2.05 p.m. on the 3rd, the convoy was ordered to alter course after dark and steer well southward of its original route, but the Escort Commander decided to stay to the north, where he expected to find better weather for refuelling the escorts. It was a most unfortunate decision.

Meanwhile the U-boats had lost touch. U-514's W/T was defective, and U-125 never gained contact. BdU expressed displeasure and ordered all U-boats to avoid a repetition of this state of affairs. 'Delphin' Group's southward sweep was cancelled and they were told to proceed south-east, at full speed, to find TMI. At 8.35 p.m. on the 3rd U-182, outward-bound for the south Atlantic, happened to sight a Gibraltar to New York convoy, GUF3, about 400 miles west of Madeira. U-182 was depth-charged and lost contact. BdU still thought GUF3 a better prospect, but the convoy was too fast and escaped to the west before the U-boats could be redisposed into its path.

After getting further reports from U-514 and U-125, BdU decided to turn back to TMI; seemingly acting almost entirely on intuition, BdU ordered the 'Delphin' boats at 5.54 p.m. on the 5th to form a new 'reconnaissance line' for 7 January, 180 miles long, about 650 miles W by S of the Canaries and about the same distance NE of the last reported position of TMI.

Hunch or not, it worked. The southerly route ordered on the 3rd would have taken TMI 120 miles clear of the U-boat line. As it was, TMI was sighted by U-381, the third boat from the northern end of the line, at 3 p.m. on the 8th. At once, BdU ordered four more U-boats, U-511 and U-522, outward-bound for the south Atlantic, and U-128 and U-134, homeward bound from patrols in the St Paul Rocks area, to join the line.

The main battle took place on the night of the 8th–9th. U-571 attacked and was driven off by *Pimpernel*. U-381 lost contact, but U-436 torpedoed *Oltenia II* and *Albert L. Ellsworth*, was depth-charged by *Havelock* and withdrew for repairs. U-536 sighted flares from the convoy, claimed three hits at 11 p.m. on the 8th, another hit in a second attack at 5.30 the next morning, followed almost at once by three hits on 'overlapping tankers'. These were *Norvik*, *Minister Wedel* and *Empire Lytton* (actually torpedoed twice). U-571 attacked three tankers at 7 a.m. that morning but was depth-charged and damaged by *Havelock*. During the day U-181, U-620, U-381 and U-134 made attacks and were all driven off.

There was something of a lull on 10 January, although U-436 finished off *Albert L. Ellsworth* and U-511 sank *William Wilberforce*, an independent north of the convoy. The U-boats were back in contact again on the evening of the 10th, and U-522, having missed with a salvo of four torpedoes, then sank *British Dominion*. BdU was still signalling 'the last tankers must also fall' but a Sunderland arrived early on the 11th and by 9.30 had forced U-511 to dive. The U-boats were called off that evening. The remaining two tankers of TMI reached Gibraltar without mishap on 14 January. Seven valuable tankers had been lost.

BdU had certainly wiped the Admiralty Tracking-Room's eye. As Lt Cdr Beesly, who worked in the Operational Intelligence Centre, wrote years later: 'TMI was but one example of the unending battle of wits between BdU and the Tracking-Room. We lost some and we won some. This was one we definitely lost.' BdU was well aware of it, describing the escort as 'oldish gunboats and corvettes; it was inexperienced and not very tough. Despite very good hydrophone and Asdic conditions in very calm weather and smooth sea they did not succeed in damaging a single boat seriously let alone destroy any.'

Not every U-boat commander would have agreed with that. Korvetten-Kapitan Schendel of U-134, broadcasting in English from Zeesen on 1 February, described a surfaced attack he made at about 2.30 p.m. on 9 January, when he claimed three hits on a tanker (actually *Vanja*, which was not hit) but was counter-attacked and heavily depth-charged. The charges came 'pouring down', he said, and 'during the next minutes nearly everything on board went wrong'. Many of U-134's crew thought 'the end had come.' But the boat survived and Schendel could only praise the 'masterwork' of the German shipyards.

Largely because of the almost incessant bad weather, January 1943 was a comparatively light month for losses: the U-boats sank thirty-seven ships of 203,128 tons, of a total of fifty ships, of more than a quarter of a million tons, from all causes. But in February the losses to U-boats rose to sixty-three ships of 359,328 tons, in a series of large-scale attacks on convoys.

The experience of SC118 showed what could happen if there was a break in Special Intelligence, if the escort were not thoroughly rehearsed as a group, and if the escort commander made any kind of misjudgement, such as placing his ships mostly to leeward of the convoy, on a night when the U-boats themselves would attack from down wind.

SC118 was a convoy for the most part ably handled and defended. Had the Escort Group not been 'a scratch team', the Admiralty said, 'it might have been one of the highlights of the U-boat war'. The first shadowing U-boat was firmly sunk. Air cover duly arrived, and the surface escort was reinforced. Counter-attacks were going satisfactorily, and the H/F D/F on the rescue ship *Toward* was giving splendid results. Nevertheless, at a time when the escort had been increased to twelve ships, the U-boats regained the initiative.

It all began with a survivor from the tanker *Cordelia*, a straggler from HX224 (which lost only three ships in all). This man was picked up by U-632, which had sunk his ship, and told his captors that another large convoy was to follow his own along the same route.

There were at that time some sixty U-boats north of 50°N, but most of them were not well placed to attack SC118. The Special Intelligence situation was also unusually bad. Intelligence for the period from 29 January to 1–2 February had not been received, and important details of the 'Pfeil' Group of U-boats, who were the best placed to attack sc118, were not available until the 7th. The only evasive routeing possible was to alter the convoy's course southward, to evade the 'Haudegan' Group, of twenty-one U-boats, off Cape Farewell, who were still somewhat scattered after chasing a convoy south of Greenland.

Five 'Haudegan' boats took part in the attacks on sc118. A smaller 'Jaguar' Group, from Newfoundland, provided three boats. Another batch of nineteen U-boats patrolling west of Iceland in about 25°W had dispersed. Seven of these, with two more outward-bound U-boats, formed the 'Pfeil' Group, which was placed along the route of HX224, hoping that the promised second convoy would duly follow.

Convoy sc118 sailed from New York on 24 January with sixty-four ships, and B2 Escort Group (the 'scratch team'), of the destroyers *Vanessa* (Lt Cdr Proudfoot), *Vimy* (Lt Cdr Stannard VC), and *Beverley*, and the corvettes *Campanula*, *Mignonette*, *Abelia* and the Free French *Lobelia*, the US Coast Guard cutter *Bibb*, and *Toward*.

The first sighting was by U-187, of the 'Pfeil' Group, at 9.49 a.m. on 4 February. The rest of the Group, with three 'Jaguar' boats and the five 'Haudegan' boats, were exhorted by BdU: 'Convoy is probably destined for Murmansk, at 'em! Operate ruthlessly, to relieve the Eastern Front!'

U-187's signal was detected by H/F D/F in *Toward* and in *Bibb*, and shortly afterwards the U-boat itself was sighted by *Beverley*, still on the surface about 7 miles ahead of the convoy. This was careless of U-187's Commander, Korvetten-Kapitan Ralph Münnich, and fulfilled the worst forebodings of his crew. Münnich had just married a young and very beautiful wife, whom he had first met at the famous White Horse Inn on the Wolfgangsee. He had taken the inn's white horse as the emblem of U-187 and Frau Münnich had knitted forty-five woollen white horses, one for every man on board. Poor Münnich, described as 'well-intentioned but irresolute', was in the most unfortunate position for a captain of having a veteran ship's company who were much more experienced submariners than he was himself.

Beverley and *Vimy* together closed the U-boat at full speed as it dived, and dropped smoke floats to mark the datum position. Then they began to carry out four measured depth-charge and Hedgehog attacks, the last of which, at about 1.40 p.m. that afternoon, was so close it stove in the port side of U-187's control-room and caused a fracture 4 feet long by ⅛ inch wide in the pressure hull aft. Münnich ordered all main ballast tanks to be blown, and U-187 reached the surface, listing badly and sinking by the stern, in time for most of her crew to jump overboard. *Vimy* got off a few rounds from her 'B' gun, one of which actually hit the U-boat's hull up forward, as several feet of its length rose into the air, before sliding stern first out of sight.

The two destroyers stopped to pick up survivors, *Vimy* signalling to

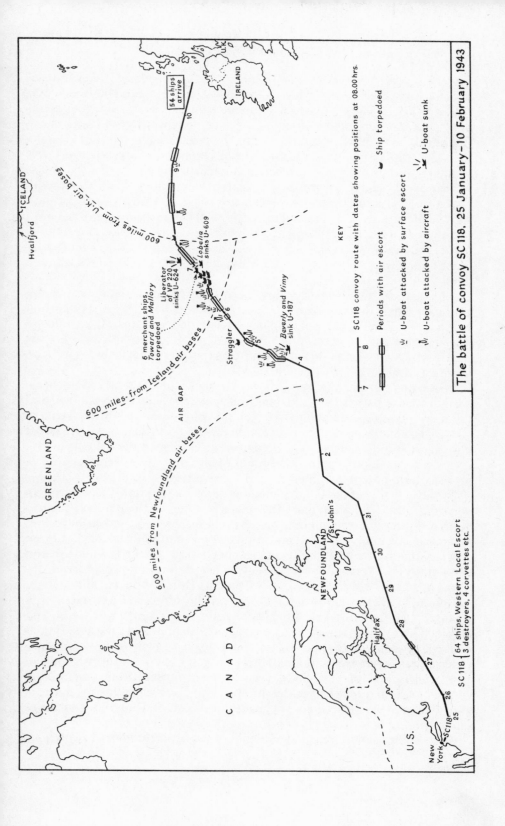

The battle of convoy SC 118, 25 January–10 February 1943

GREENLAND

ICELAND

Hvalfjord

ICELAND

IRELAND

54 ships arrive

600 miles from U.K. air bases

10

9

8

Lobelia sinks U-609

Liberator of VP 220 sinks U-624

6 merchant ships, Toward and Mallory torpedoed

Straggler

7

6

5

Beverly and Vimy sink U-187

4

600 miles from Iceland air bases

AIR GAP

600 miles from Newfoundland air bases

3

2

1

31

30

29

28

27

26

25

NEWFOUNDLAND

St. John's

Halifax

CANADA

U.S.

New York

SC 118

SC 118 { 64 ships, Western Local Escort
{ 3 destroyers, 4 corvettes etc.

KEY

7 ——— 8   SC 118 convoy route with dates showing positions at 08.00 hrs.

——□—□——   Periods with air escort

↘   U-boat attacked by surface escort   ⊢•   Ship torpedoed

↘   U-boat attacked by aircraft   ↘   U-boat sunk

Beverley, 'Don't be greedy, leave us a few!' Münnich, his Engineer Officer, and the forty-five woolly white horses were lost but everybody else was rescued. The striking difference in morale between the two antagonists was perhaps a measure of the changing balance of power in the battle of the Atlantic. U-187's crew had said of Münnich, 'If that man is to be our Captain, then the U-boat is bound to be lost.' Richard Stannard, who was to get a DSO to add to his VC, made just one brief, triumphant signal to *Vanessa*; 'Got him!' 'That was all,' said Stannard later, relishing the memory. 'He understood!'

While *Vimy* and *Beverley* had been disposing of U-187, U-402 had also sighted the convoy. It was joined that afternoon by four more U-boats, one of them U-609 (Korvetten-Kapitan Rudloff), which was driven off, like the others, but regained contact that night. U-609 became SC118's most persistent shadower, staying in contact with only short breaks for the next three days.

BdU had still not properly summed up the situation, and was further confused when the convoy made a large emergency turn to starboard at 7.48 p.m. But the three port columns misunderstood the Commodore's sound signals and stood on to the north on the original course. As the convoy thus inadvertently split into two, it gave the reporting U-boats the impression there was a fast and a slow section.

U-609 was still in contact and, during the forenoon of the 5th, five U-boats tried to attack. A sixth, U-262, claimed one hit but in fact no ship was lost until 1 p.m. in the afternoon when U-413, the first of the 'Jaguar' Group boats to take part, sank the straggling *West Portal*. As various U-boats were driven off or began to report defects, BdU became restive, pressed the U-boats to give the enemy no respite, warned them not to lose the convoy again, and once more exhorted them to 'remember the Eastern Front'.

By the morning of the 6th, the missing 'rump' of the convoy had joined up correctly, and it did seem that the U-boats had missed their golden chance. SC118 was now about 720 miles south-west of Iceland, and 820 miles west of Londonderry, and the very-long-range air escort duly arrived. Eleven U-boats reported aircraft, and four of them were attacked by bombs and cannon. By the evening, several U-boats had been forced down or driven off. U-465 had been badly damaged, and withdrew. Even U-609 had lost contact.

Another straggler, *Polyktor*, was lost on the 6th, sunk by U-266, who reported that he had taken the Master and Chief Engineer prisoner, and obtained some information on the convoy's formation and progress. But, in general, it seemed that the escort could begin to feel quietly confident, especially as they were reinforced by the arrivals of the US destroyers *Babbitt* and *Schenk*, and the US Coast Guard cutter *Ingham* from Iceland. By contrast, BdU had received no fresh reports and was signalling his displeasure that more U-boats had not made more use of Rudloff's consistent shadowing reports.

At 5.30 p.m. that evening, U-438 made contact again, followed half an hour later by the persistent U-609, and by U-262 and U-456. These four, with U-267 who was damaged by depth-charges, and U-624, hunted and depth-charged for four hours, were all driven off or lost contact. But through the night the U-boats, in spite of their set-backs, regained the initiative.

When Captain Roberts came to study SC118's reports of proceedings and survivors' accounts, he bitterly criticized Proudfoot for placing most of his escorts on the convoy's bow, when the wind was astern and U-boats were known to like attacking downwind. As so often in convoy actions, one particularly able and bold U-boat captain could turn a battle. During the night of the 6th–7th, at least three U-boats slipped in to the convoy's ranks from astern. The convoy lost eight ships that night, including *Toward*. Six of them were lost in two attacks before dawn by U-402 (Korvetten-Kapitan Freiherr Siegfried von Forstner).

Of a company of seventy-two officers and men and two medical cases embarked in *Toward*, only one officer and fifteen men survived. Just over an hour later, at about 4 a.m., the American troopship *Henry R. Mallory* sank with even greater loss of life. She had actually stayed afloat for ninety minutes after the torpedo hit, but no general alarm was sounded, no orders were given from the bridge for lifeboats to be launched, and men abandoned ship in a state of near-panic and almost complete confusion: only half the lifeboats were launched, all dangerously overloaded. Of the 384 US soldiers and sailors, seventy-seven crew and thirty-four gunners of the Naval Armed Guard on board, less than 200 survived.

U-262 and U-614 had also sunk a ship each during the night but, on the convoy's credit side, the Free French corvette *Lobelia*, commanded by the very able Lt Cdr de V. De Morsier, detected U-609 at about 4.30 a.m. that morning. Rudloff's long trail was over. *Lobelia* sank U-609 with all hands in one brisk, deadly attack.

Nevertheless BdU sensed that his boats had done well, and at 7.45 ordered repeated attacks, despite the air cover. He advised them to get ahead of the convoy. 'The Broad formation,' said BdU, was 'the most favourable for submerged as well as surface attack'. The U-boats did their best. At least eleven of them were still able to attack, although some were now short of torpedoes. U-456 and U-402, joined later by U-438, all made contact at some time during the day. Von Forstner pursued the convoy all day, and was driven off or forced down no less than seven times.

Another U-boat in contact was U-624, who transmitted a long signal just after 5 p.m. recounting experiences the night before. The signal was its last. Shortly after 6 o'clock, U-624 was slow in diving, after being sighted on the surface by Liberator 'J' of 220 Squadron, who dropped three depth-charges close on the U-boat's port bow. U-624 was seen to 'sink bodily on a more or less even keel. The depth-charge scum and explosion eddies faded away slowly, giving place to a large patch of bubbles and underwater disturbances which persisted gradually increasing in intensity'. Forty minutes later, when the aircraft finally flew away, there was some wreckage – light brown cylinders, some wooden debris, and one black box – over which the seabirds were swooping for dead fish.

BdU sent a special signal of commendation to von Forstner and urged him to stay in contact. This von Forstner did. While the U-boats one by one lost contact and dropped away, he closed SC118 again during the night of the 7th–8th and sank one final ship, *Newton Ash*, just after 1 a.m. That day U-135, U-89 and U-614 all reported being forced to dive by aircraft. U-135 said he had been 'surprised' and damaged; the boat was down by the stern and leaving an oil trace. In the evening, when SC188 was 450 miles north-west of London-derry, even von Forstner abandoned the chase and headed south-west to meet the supply U-boat. As late as 9.30 on the 9th, BdU was still urging all boats to search at high speed on zigzagging courses until dawn. But nobody complied.

Of nineteen U-boats which had made contact with the convoy, three were sunk and four badly damaged. They had sunk ten ships, and *Toward*. BdU seems to have been displeased, although his U-boats had not been favourably placed to attack when the convoy was first sighted and some of them had been some time on patrol. BdU sent congratulatory signals to U-402, U-609 and U-262 but to nobody else.

For much of February 1943, convoys and U-boats had to battle against some of the worst weather of the whole war at sea. From November 1942 through the winter to April 1943 there was a succession of fierce westerly and north-westerly gales in the north Atlantic. Both sides had as hard a fight against the sea as they had against each other.

Convoy warfare was as much a contest between decrypting resources as between ships and weapons. The B-Dienst Service struggled to give BdU the information to deploy U-boats ahead of a convoy in time, while Ultra battled just as hard to give the Admiralty Tracking-Room enough warning to divert a convoy around danger. For most of February this contest was evenly balanced. Of the homeward-bound convoys, HX223 lost one ship only, HX224 two and a straggler. HX225 was not located by the U-boats, and nor was HX226. HX227 lost one ship, HX228 four. SC119 and 120 were unscathed.

Of the outward-bound convoys, ONS165 lost one ship and one straggler, while the destroyers *Fame* and *Viscount* sank a U-boat each; and ON167, though sighted by chance, lost only two ships. But the fate of the convoy between these two, ON166, showed what timely advice from the B-Dienst Service, coupled with lack of air cover in the infamous 'gap', could do to a convoy, however ably defended.

ON166 was comparatively large, a convoy of sixty-three vessels, escorted by the American A3 Escort Group, under Captain P. R. Heineman USN, with ships of mixed nationalities: the two American US Coast Guard cutters *Spencer* and *Campbell*, the RN corvette *Dianthus*, and four Canadian corvettes, *Chilliwack*, *Rosthern*, *Trillium* and *Dauphin*, and, joining later, the Polish destroyer *Burza*. Meanwhile, B-Dienst reports enabled BdU to deploy two groups, totalling sixteen U-boats, ahead of the convoy.

The weather was so bad, with constant north-westerly gales, that ONI66 averaged only 4 knots for the first four days. When U-604 sighted the first ships on the 20th, there were no fewer than nine stragglers. Nevertheless the convoy was in good heart and were immensely cheered the following evening, the 21st, when *Spencer*, on her way with *Dianthus* to assist a Liberator attacking a U-boat on the port beam of the convoy, sighted another U-boat on the surface. *Spencer* attacked with gunfire and then with depth-charges. She had to leave too early, in Heineman's opinion, but this proved to be the end of U-225.

But that night the convoy passed out of range of air cover and a five-day battle began, which stretched over more than 1000 miles of sea. Seventeen U-boats were in contact at one time or another and, although Heineman's ships determinedly fought them off, sank no less than fourteen ships, of more than 85,000 tons. Against that, *Campbell* and *Burza* attacked U-606 on 22 February, *Campbell* finally sinking the U-boat by ramming and gunfire, after which *Campbell* herself was left helpless and had to be taken in tow by *Burza*. Among the ships lost was the rescue ship *Stockport*, torpedoed like *Toward* whilst re-joining the convoy from astern (very like a straggler).

The fate of U-606, like that of U-187, showed once again that to the victor went all the spoils. Heineman's multi-national escort group was nicknamed, with perhaps excusable American hyperbole, 'Heineman's Harriers' and Ricky Heineman himself was later promoted Captain and became Commander of the Anti-Submarine Warfare Unit of the Atlantic Fleet. Cdr James Hirshfield, of *Campbell*, wounded in the action, won a Navy Cross.

Kapitan-Leutnant Paul Döhler of U-606 was described by survivors as weak and inefficient. He tried to compensate for his weakness and inefficiency by imposing a draconian discipline, sentencing men guilty of stealing a packet of cigarettes (though admittedly petty theft was a particularly undesirable offence in the confined living conditions of a U-boat) to prison or transfer to the Russian Front. His First Lieutenant, by contrast, ruled with a rod of fear and tyranny, but in the agony of battle his was the nerve which broke. During *Burza*'s attack U-606 plunged at one time out of control, while the First Lieutenant ran panic-stricken through the boat and tried to open a hatch aft, although U-606 was at the time some 650 feet deep.

After the storm of *Campbell*'s gunfire had died away and it was clear that U-606 was sinking, there were surrealist scenes on the U-boat's casing. The First Lieutenant and the Engineer Officer stood regaling themselves with sausage and taking swigs from a bottle of champagne. Campbell took five ratings off and *Burza* rescued three officers and four ratings. Before being rescued, a petty officer repaid old scores by striking the First Lieutenant in the face, saying, 'I have been waiting a long time to do that.' He then jumped into the sea whilst another survivor was heard to ask, 'What had I done wrong in my life that I should be sent to such a boat?'

Allied interrogators were constantly on the lookout for signs that the morale of U-boat crews was cracking. Great importance was attached to prisoner-of-war statements that 'they had had enough' or that 'they were glad the war was over for them'. Perhaps not enough weight was given to a prisoner-of-war's understandable wish to say what evidently pleased his captors. Certainly, combat weeded out the weaklings, like Ralph Münnich and Paul Döhler, and their crews. Certainly, some U-boat captains exhibited the classical symptoms of the battle-shy: reporting torpedo failures, blaming their equipment, finding constant defects making it necessary to return early off patrol, insisting on exaggerated and unsubstantiated claims of sinkings, while generally showing 'a married man's' regard for personal safety. Many U-boat captains had a strong, and quite justifiable, fear of air attack. But in general morale in the U-boat arm remained extraordinarily good until the very end (indeed, in May 1945, some surrendering U-boat crews said they were expecting to continue the war – against the Russians).

On 1 March 1943 an Atlantic Convoy Conference opened in Washington, attended by representatives from the United States, Great Britain and Canada. The British contingent, led by Admiral Sir Percy Noble, were taken aback to discover that Admiral King proposed to withdraw American escorts entirely from the North Atlantic convoy routes. It seemed that he disliked escort groups of mixed nationalities and wished American ships to operate exclusively on the more southerly convoy routes, from America to North Africa and the Mediterranean (where US troops were then operating).

Apparently Admiral King had been much impressed by the melancholy events which surrounded the fate of the Arctic convoy PQ17, scattered by the direct intervention of the Admiralty and subsequently losing many ships. After that experience, which involved American ships, Admiral King did not want American and British ships to operate closely together again, and in particular he wished to avoid any future Admiralty interference. It seems strange that Admiral King should take this one example as a base for his decision and ignore the many occasions on which British and American ships had worked together in excellent harmony, and the thousands of American lives which must have been saved through the same direct intervention by the same British Admiralty to divert convoys containing American ships out of danger.

To compensate for the escorts removed from the Atlantic the US Navy agreed to take over the escort of the newly instituted fast CU and UC tanker convoys between Curaçao in the Dutch West Indies and the United Kingdom, and to provide one support group including an escort carrier USS *Bogue*, and five destroyers, to begin operations later in March.

Increased shipping of US troops and supplies to the UK meant new convoy cycles. ON convoys were reduced to a six-day cycle by the end of March, and to a five-day by mid April. ONS convoys were renumbered, beginning with

ONSI, in March, with an eight-day cycle from the start of April. HX convoys were to have a six-day cycle during April, then reducing to five days, SC convoys an eight-day cycle from the beginning of April. It was estimated that these cycles would require fourteen escort groups but in the event only twelve, seven British and five Canadian, were available. The one American Group (Heineman's) was to be released later in March, as well as American ships employed on the 'Shuttle' service to and from Ireland. Ships bound for Iceland now had to go to the UK for onward routeing in UR convoys, which sailed in an eight-day cycle, to fit the sailings and arrivals of ONS and SC convoys.

While the US Navy withdrew from the burden of the north Atlantic, so the Royal Canadian Navy began to play an even greater part. The Canadians now took responsibility for convoys west of the CHOP line, which was shifted as far as 47°W. In May 1943 North-west Atlantic Command was set up, with a Canadian admiral as C-in-C, based in Halifax which became the terminal port for ONS and SC convoys.

The Conference discussed the crucial question of long-range aircraft. The number of long-range aircraft based in Newfoundland was to be increased to four squadrons. But this went nowhere near dealing with the Greenland 'gap' which was still draining away ships every month. At Casablanca the Combined Chiefs of Staff had recommended that eighty very-long-range (VLR) aircraft should be allocated to cover the 'gap'. In Washington, the Canadians said that they had trained crews but still had no VLR aircraft for them to fly. It was agreed that twenty Liberators should be transferred, but they could not be available at once. It seemed that the US Navy, which had some seventy VLR Liberators mainly on reconnaissance duties in the Pacific, was not prepared to transfer any to the Atlantic. If necessary, the US Navy insisted, the US Army Air Force should give up some of its Liberators presently engaged in bombing Germany.

Behind all this wrangling and lack of cooperation lay the anti-British feelings of Admiral King. It is now clear that (it must be said) the stupid Anglophobia of this pig-headed man nearly lost the battle of the Atlantic. For want of a few score VLR aircraft in the spring of 1943 the Allies came very close to defeat. At the end of March President Roosevelt himself enquired where the VLR Liberators were being employed, at a time when there were horrific shipping losses in the Atlantic. It was established that not a single VLR Liberator was operating at any Allied air base west of Iceland. Thereafter seventy-five USAAF, sixty USN and 120 allocated to Britain, a total of 225 Liberators in all, were promised for the Atlantic. The first twenty were operational by the end of March.

They were only just in time. While the Conference had been debating, while the VLR Liberators were still withheld from the Atlantic, a series of great convoy battles was fought which, for a time, seriously shook the Allied faith in the convoy system. These convoy battles, were, of course, a godsend for German propaganda, coming so soon after the disaster at Stalingrad.

On 1 March there were nearly seventy U-boats at sea in the north Atlantic – more than ever before. The number grew until, on the 22nd, Admiral Sir Dudley Pound was informing the Anti-U-boat-Warfare Committee that 'we could no longer rely on evading the U-boat packs, and, hence, we shall have to fight the convoys through them'. On the 30th, after some of the worst convoy losses of the war, Pound told the Committee that although exceptionally bad weather, defects in the escorts and less air cover were partly responsible, a state had been reached where the 'Atlantic is now becoming so saturated by U-boats that the practice of evasion is rapidly becoming impossible'.

There was also a setback in Special Intelligence that month. One of the main ways of breaking into the four-wheel Enigma 'Shark' U-boat codes was through a code-book the U-boats used for short weather reports. A copy of this from U-559, sunk north of Port Said on 30 October, had enabled Ultra to break through in December 1942. On 10 March 1943, the Germans brought in a new book and Ultra faced a blackout similar to February 1942. Despite the most pessimistic forecasts, Ultra had broken back in nine days – a marvellous achievement, although not enough to forestall yet another convoy disaster.

By contrast, the B-Dienst Service was enjoying a consistently successful spell and on 3 March de-crypted part of the routeing instructions for the fifty-nine-ship SC121. Forewarned, BdU was able to deploy two groups, the 'Westmark' of seventeen U-boats, and the 'Ostmark' of nine, in the convoy's path. It was a 'Westmark' boat, U-405, which sighted SC121 on 6 March, in such heavy seas and bad weather that several ships were straggling.

The escort group was Heineman's Harriers, of *Spencer*, the US destroyer *Greer*, the corvettes *Rosthern*, *Trillium*, and *Dianthus*, with the rescue ship *Melrose Abbey*. Heineman was a very aggressive but evidently a somewhat unlucky escort commander. He and his ships had had only the barest minimum time of a few hours in harbour for repairs and recuperation after their experience with ON166. His crews were tired and the ships suffered from Asdic, radar, W/T and H/F D/F defects, because of a lack of time for maintenance and the appalling weather conditions.

The battle opened on the night of 6–7 March and lasted for five days. Seventeen U-boats in all were involved, who pursued the convoy night and day in bitter cold and extraordinarily bad weather, through a Force 10 gale, with blinding snow blizzards, and frequent storms of hail and rain. The escort was reinforced by *Bibb*, *Ingham* and *Babbitt* from Iceland on the 9th, and by the corvettes *Mallow* and *Campion* on the 10th, with air cover from 120 Squadron RAF Liberators from the 9th. Many U-boats were driven off but they still sank thirteen ships, of nearly 60,000 tons, before they broke off on the 11th. One of the ships sunk was the Commodore's, MV *Bonneville*; the Commodore himself, Captain H. C. Birnie DSO RD RNR, was lost. No

U-boats were sunk.

Meanwhile, far to the south and east, another battle around the next eastbound convoy, HX228, was taking shape. 'Shark' de-crypts for 5–7 March had revealed that the 'Raubgraf' Group of U-boats was waiting in the convoy's track, and it was therefore diverted in plenty of time to a much more southerly course. But this information was itself de-crypted by the B-Dienst Service, who thus obtained HX228's new course, and its estimated position for 8 March. Thirteen U-boats of the 'Neuland' Group spread out to look for it.

The new course very nearly saved HX228. The sixty-ship convoy was sighted at midday on 10 March by U-336, the most southerly boat in the line, but U-336 was located by H/F D/F and soon driven off. The convoy was defended by a very experienced escort group, B3, under Cdr A. A. Tait, in the destroyer *Harvester*, with another destroyer *Escapade*, the Polish destroyers *Garland* and *Burza*, the RN corvettes *Narcissus* and *Orchis*, and three Free French corvettes *Aconit*, *Roselys*, and *Renoncule*. From 5 to 14 March the convoy was also reinforced by the 6th Support Group, of the carrier *Bogue* and the US destroyers *Belknap* and *Osmond-Ingram*.

The main battle took place on the night of the 10th–11th. The new shadower was U-444 (Kapitan-Leutnant Langer) who torpedoed one ship himself and brought up five other U-boats. U-221, commanded by Kapitan-Leutnant Trojer, an up-and-coming ace, sank two ships and torpedoed a third. Trojer said that he 'fired two torpedoes at two large overlapping merchant ships. First torpedo hit. Ship disintegrated completely in flames and a vast cloud of smoke. Hundreds of steel plates flew like sheets of paper through the air. A great deal of ammunition exploded. Shortly afterwards scored another hit on a freighter, which also exploded. From bows to bridge the ship was underwater. Heavy debris crashed against my periscope which now became difficult to turn. The whole boat re-echoed with bangs and crashes.'

Trojer came so near his next target he had to go astern to avoid it and the detonation of his torpedo caused his periscope to go 'completely black' whilst heavy fragments of the ship rained down, making a noise as though the U-boat itself was being shelled.

Korvetten-Kapitan Deetz in U-757 put two torpedoes into a Norwegian ammunition ship, *Brant County*, which blew up, as the convoy commodore described it, 'with a tremendous explosion throwing debris hundreds of feet into the air – the scene was quite indescribable'. The detonation was so violent that U-757 was itself damaged.

Three U-boats that night fired salvoes of the new FAT (*Flachen Absuchender* or *Feder Apparat Torpedo*) pattern running torpedoes. These could be fired from a target's beam and, when they had run the estimated range, they turned on to the target's estimated course and 'weaved' either side of it. None of the FAT salvoes hit this first time.

U-444 did hit and sink one ship but in withdrawing was sighted by *Harvester* and forced to dive. *Harvester* attacked with depth-charges and blew the U-boat to the surface where, after some violent manoeuvring, *Harvester* rammed it. Destroyer and U-boat were locked together for some minutes, with the destroyer's port propeller entangled in the U-boat's hydroplanes. U-444 made off, quite badly damaged, but was found an hour later by *Aconit* (Lt Cdr Levasseur) and dispatched by ramming.

Harvester, meanwhile, steamed on one shaft to rejoin the convoy. But the next morning the starboard engine broke down also and the destroyer lay immobile until shortly before noon when U-432 hit her with two torpedoes. *Harvester* broke in two, her fore part standing out of the water for some time before it sank. Tait and most of his ship's company were lost. But, once again, *Aconit* came up to take revenge. She located U-432, damaged it with depth-charges, and finished it off on the surface with gunfire and ramming.

Attacks by four or five more U-boats were repulsed on the 11th, and the last shadower, U-590, was driven off on the 12th. Thus the convoy lost four ships and one escort, but two U-boats were sunk. *Bogue* had less effect on the battle than might have been expected. She remained inside the body of the convoy, because of the great danger of U-boat attacks, and her freedom of movement for flying off and landing aircraft seems to have been seriously restricted. The weather prevented flying for most of the time.

The same 'Shark' de-crypts of 5–7 March affected the courses of the next two eastbound convoys, SC122 and HX229, both of which were routed to the south instead of taking the intended north-easterly course, up past the coast of Newfoundland. But in the event these diversions were not enough to prevent the biggest single convoy disaster of the war. BdU was about to demonstrate what could be done if there was adequate advance intelligence warning, coupled with enough U-boats favourably placed to take advantage of it.

SC122 sailed from New York on 5 March. Several ships had joined and left by the 12th, when its ocean escort arrived, but its final shape was fifty ships (one, *Clarissa Radcliffe*, already a straggler) in thirteen columns. The ocean escort was B5 Escort Group, under Cdr R. C. Boyle DSO, in the destroyer *Havelock*, with the frigate *Swale*, the corvettes *Buttercup*, *Godetia*, *Lavender*, *Pimpernel* and *Saxifrage*, the US destroyer *Upshur*, and the trawler *Campobello*. The rescue ship was *Zamalek*.

HX229 sailed from New York on 8 March, with forty ships in eleven columns. The ocean escort which met it on the 14th, was B4 Escort Group. This was a weakened group whose leader, Cdr E. C. L. Day, had to stay in St John's whilst his ship, the destroyer *Highlander*, completed repairs to her Asdic dome. Command devolved on Lt Cdr G. J. Luther, in the destroyer *Volunteer*. Luther actually belonged to B5 but was a newcomer; he had made only one Atlantic convoy crossing previously and had never commanded an escort group before. With him, he had the destroyers *Beverley*, *Witherington* and *Mansfield*, and the corvettes *Anemone* and *Pennywort* (who actually joined on the 15th). There was no rescue ship.

Such was the pressure of ships building up in New York, all waiting for convoy, a third convoy, HX229A, sailed on the 9th, with thirty-nine ships, escorted by the 40th Escort Group, of four sloops and two frigates. This convoy was routed to the north, and became a source of confusion to BdU.

By the afternoon of the 14th or the forenoon of the 15th, BdU had details of the new southerly routes of SC122 and HX229. A re-organized 'Raubgraf' Group of eight U-boats, which had just searched unsuccessfully for ONS169, was formed to the north-east in SC122's path. A much larger 'Sturmer' Group of eighteen U-boats, formed from those who had operated against SC121 and some new arrivals, was drawn up further away, also in SC122's expected path. A third 'Draenger' Group, of eleven boats, which had just operated against HX228, lay to the east in wait for HX229.

With a westerly gale behind them, the ships of SC122 were well past to the east before the 'Raubgraf' boats took up position to intercept HX229, to the south and astern of SC122, was also ahead of schedule; although a 'Raubgraf' boat, U-91, did sight a destroyer (in the outer screen of HX229) steering north-east on the evening of 15th, the convoy might have steamed clear. But at 7.25 next morning, the 16th, HX229 was sighted and reported by U-653. This was not from any of these three groups, but a boat which had withdrawn for repairs after sinking a straggler from ONI70 on the 12th, and happened to be there. Immediately BdU ordered the whole 'Raubgraf' Group to get 'up and at 'em!'.

Six 'Raubgraf' U-boats and U-653 made contact with HX229 or stragglers that afternoon. The first to attack was U-603 which sank the Norwegian *Elin K* that evening. The next was U-758, which sank *Zaanland* and torpedoed *James Ogelthorpe*, later finished off by U-91. The convoy lost another ship, *William Eustis*, to U-435 in the early hours of the next morning, the 17th, and then U-600 (Kapitan-Leutnant Zurmühlen) hit three ships with one FAT salvo at about 5 a.m. He sank the 12,000-ton tanker *Southern Princess* and crippled *Nariva* and *Irenée du Pont*, both finished off by the scavenging U-91, who had also accounted for *Henry Luckenbach* an hour earlier.

In that one night HX229 had lost eight ships. The U-boats' task was certainly made easier when two of the escorts dropped astern to pick up survivors. The first boats from the 'Stuermer' Group arrived on the scene on the morning of the 17th. One of them took a shot at *Volunteer*, but missed. The U-boats reported a 'weak escort' but after an attack on a destroyer U-228 was depth-charged and damaged by *Beverley* early on the 17th.

As usual, much of the damage was done by a few of the U-boats. Away to the NE Kapitan-Leutnant Manfred Kinzel in U-338, of the 'Stuermer' Group, sighted SC122 in the moonlight at about 2 a.m. on the 17th. He reported it and then moved straight into the attack, passing between the two leading escorts and firing five torpedoes, four of which hit and sank

Kingsbury, King Gruffydd, Alderamin and *Fort Cedar Lake*. Kinzel pursued the convoy and sank his fifth ship, *Granville*, that afternoon.

At dawn on the 17th came the air cover, at the unprecedented ranges of 1000 miles (HX229) and 900 miles (SC122) from base. By noon two U-boats had been attacked and forced down.

BdU was still trying to find out the true situation. He knew that HX229 was following SC122 but believed that the reports he had been getting from the 'Raubgraf' boats were of attacks on SC122. U-338's report, from much further north, followed by another report of smoke by U-439, puzzled BdU so much that he called off the 'Stuermer' boats. But then another 'Stuermer' boat, U-527, also reported smoke in the same area and BdU told them all to resume.

HX229, which had been catching up SC122, was pulling the U-boats after it, until SC122, HX229, and several U-boats were all very close together. A comparatively small area of the Atlantic was occupied by a great mass of merchant shipping, all wallowing about in heavy seas and in a following wind, surrounded by the 'Raubgraf' boats coming up from astern to the west and by the 'Stuermer' boats approaching from the north-east and east, whilst the 'Draenger' boats still lay in wait to the south-east.

Two 'Stuermer' boats, U-631 and U-384, were still in contact during the forenoon of the 17th. They sank two more ships from HX229, *Coracero* and *Terkoelei*, just after 1 p.m. that afternoon. They were counter-attacked, the convoy began to draw away, and there were no more attacks that day. U-600 and U-134 shadowed, were put down by aircraft, and run over by convoy at about tea-time so they lost contact. U-221, the nearest of the 'Draenger' boats, was bombed by aircraft at about 7 p.m. before Trojer had sighted the convoy, and he did not find it until the next day.

17 March continued to be a busy day. Five 'Stuermer' boats had seemingly passed astern of SC122 whilst approaching HX229. Another six boats were still searching; at 1.45 p.m. U-305 sighted SC122 but was at once driven down. U-439 also found the convoy but was kept down for four hours. Both convoys had suffered, but their losses would have been much higher without air cover.

By the evening BdU had made up his mind that there *were* two convoys present after all and he ordered six 'Stuermer' boats and the northern half of the 'Draenger' line to operate against HX229. The weather had deteriorated; in a rising gale with heavy snow showers, *Godetia* and *Upshur* counter-attacked U-338 for four hours after *Granville* had been sunk. (Kinzel was a persistent opponent: he was damaged in this attack, but tried again, was depth-charged and damaged by *Lavender* on the 18th, then depth-charged and damaged a third time by a Sunderland on the 19th before he finally gave up.) Late in the evening of the 17th, U-305, which had been attacked three times already that day by aircraft, closed SC122 and sank *Port Auckland* and *Zouave*.

On the morning of the 18th, HX229 had five escorts: *Volunteer, Beverley*,

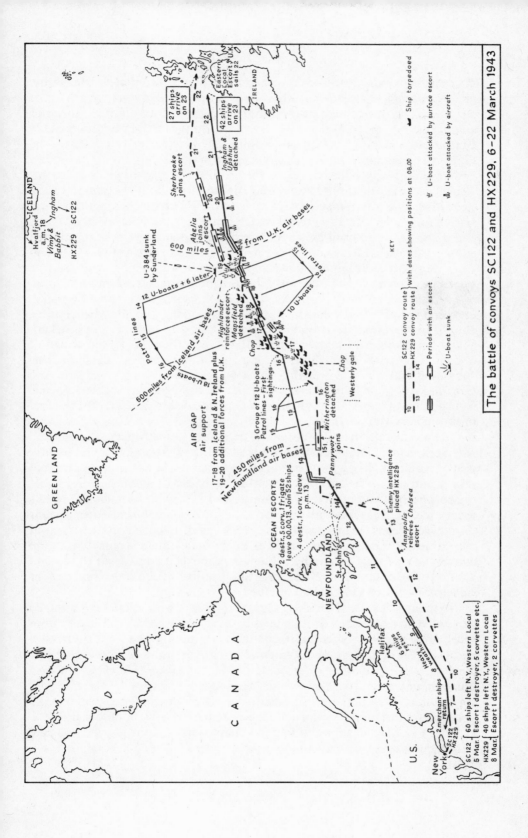

The battle of convoys SC122 and HX229, 6–22 March 1943

KEY

	SC122 convoy route	with dates showing positions at 08.00
	HX229 convoy route	
	Periods with air escort
	U-boat sunk

◗ Ship torpedoed
✠ U-boat attacked by surface escort
✠ U-boat attacked by aircraft

GREENLAND

ICELAND

Hvalfjord a.m. 18
Vimy & Babbit   Ingham
HX229   SC122

U-384 sunk by Sunderland

12 U-boats + 6 later

Patrol lines

18 U-boats

AIR GAP
Air support
17–18 from Iceland & N.Ireland plus
19–20 additional forces from U.K.

600 miles from Iceland air bases

600 miles   from U.K. air bases

Patrol lines

10 U-boats

Chop

Chop

Chop
Westerly gale

3 Group of 12 U-boats
Patrol lines – First sightings

450 miles from Newfoundland air bases

Enemy intelligence placed HX229

Annapolis relieves Chelsea escort

OCEAN ESCORTS
2 dest.,5 corv.,1 frigate
leave 00.00,13. Join 52 ships
4 destr.,1 corv. leave
p.m. 13

Witherington detached

Pennywort joins

Magsfield detached

Highlander reinforces escort

Abelia joins escort

Sherbrooke joins escort

Ingham & Upshur detached

27 ships arrive on 23

42 ships arrive on 23

Eastern Local Escort sails 22

IRELAND

NEWFOUNDLAND

St.John's

CANADA

Halifax
6 ships return

Heavy weather

New York

2 merchant ships return
SC122
HX229

U.S.

SC122 { 60 ships left N.Y., Western Local
5 Mar. { Escort 1 destroyer, 5 corvettes etc.
HX229 { 40 ships left N.Y., Western Local
8 Mar. { Escort 1 destroyer, 2 corvettes

Anemone and *Pennywort*, and *Witherington*, which had to detach later in the day. *Mansfield* had already left, short of fuel. Five escorts was better than the convoy had had for much of the time, when the escorts for one reason or another had dropped to three or even two, and for one period, none at all. But the worst was over. *Highlander*, with Cdr Day on board joined on the 18th, and more reinforcements were on their way.

The only really effective opponent on the 18th was Kapitan-Leutnant Trojer in U-221, who found HX229 and attacked it at about 3.30 p.m. He sank two ships, but was himself attacked by aircraft, broke off his patrol and started for home. Others were not so determined. U-134 attacked at 6.50 p.m. and then shadowed until he was driven off. U-610 and U-439 both reported counter-attacks and gave up. U-441 made several attempts between 3.30 and 5 a.m. the next morning but achieved nothing. At least seven other U-boats stayed in touch until the forenoon of the 19th, but there were no more attacks.

The last casualty in convoy was the Greek *Carras*, torpedoed by U-666 early on the 19th and finished off by U-333. Late on the 18th, the Master of the American *Matthew Luckenbach* decided that, as a 15-knot ship in a 9-knot convoy, he would do better alone and against orders he forged ahead of HX229. 'Romping', though much less usual, was just as dangerous as straggling and the ship was duly sunk by U-527 and U-523 next day. And *Clarissa Radcliffe*, who had been a straggler for days, was never seen or heard from again: very possibly she was the independent ship which U-663 claimed to sink at about 2 p.m. on the 18th.

Late on the 19th the action began to peter out. It finally ended on the 20th when BdU had decided that air cover was too heavy. At 9.34 a.m. on the 19th, U-384 was attacked by a Sunderland of 201 Squadron about 40 miles astern of HX229, and sunk – the only U-boat sunk in the battle around HX229 and SC122. HX229's escorts had made eleven attacks and damaged five U-boats. SC112's escort had made seven attacks and damaged two U-boats. Aircraft flew thirty-two sorties, made twenty-five sightings of U-boats, and carried out fifteen attacks. Some thirty-eight U-boats in all made contact with the convoys at one time or another. They sank thirteen ships from HX229 and another nine from SC122, for a total tonnage lost of 146,000. The trawler *Campobello* was also lost in bad weather.

German propaganda claimed a great victory – with reason. Coming so soon after the maulings experienced by SC121 and ONI66, and losses from several other convoys such as HX228, the loss of twenty-two ships from SC122 and HX229 sent a surge of alarm around the Admiralty. In some quarters, convoy itself began to be questioned, and there was talk of a return to independent routeing. Looking at the shocking figures, it certainly did appear that if the enemy had accurate enough intelligence, and enough U-boats to saturate the ocean and make evasive routeing impractical, as the First Sea Lord said, then sending merchant ships in convoy really was like herding animals into an abattoir.

In the first ten days of March, forty-one ships had been lost, in the next ten days another fifty-four, making a total loss of more than half a million tons. Nearly two-thirds of those ships had been sunk whilst in convoy. (Only seven U-boats had been sunk around convoys in the same period.) The total sunk by U-boats in March was 108 ships, of 627,377 tons; in all, from all causes, 120 ships were lost that month, 693,000 tons, the worst figures since November 1942.

The Admiralty appreciation was that 'the Germans never came so near to disrupting communication between the New World and the Old as in the first twenty days of March 1943'. 'It appeared possible,' wrote the Naval Staff, 'that we should not be able to continue convoy as an effective system of defence.' But convoy was the foundation stone of Allied naval strategy. It seemed unthinkable that convoy could fail. Yet that very possibility was apparently being considered.

Contemplation of these failures overlooked important successes: HX229A had passed far to the north with only one loss, a tanker wrecked on an iceberg; HX230 lost one ship, a straggler; SC123, with the services of USS *Bogue* and her group, and ONS1 were completely unscathed.

Significantly, the mood of general alarm and despondency about convoy was not shared by the Operational Intelligence Centre, who rubbed their minds daily against BdU and the U-boat's staff. OIC could sense the under-lying unease in BdU's signals, the ever-increasing fear of air attack, about which U-boat captains were constantly complaining, BdU's reluctance to reprove, his readiness to encourage, in his signals to U-boats at sea. OIC saw that BdU was acting not like a victor, but like someone losing his power to control events and knowing it.

In truth, no principles of convoy had been touched. Nothing of import-ance had changed. HX229 had had a weak escort, with an inexperienced commander, and no rescue ship. Even so, several of their attacks might have been successful; with a little more luck, a little more time, and one or two more ships in the right place, those near-misses would have been kills. The action had taken place when there was a blackout on 'Shark' traffic, while BdU had been fully informed by B-Dienst. BdU had had no less than twenty-nine U-boats well-placed at the start and was able to call on another ten. Even so, most of the damage was done by no more than four U-boats.

From the moment the aircraft arrived, the battle began to swing away from the U-boats. As with SC122 and HX229, so with the main struggle over the whole Atlantic. When the VLR aircraft made their appearance, the weather seemed to improve, the skies began to clear, the tide turned. It all happened in a matter of a few weeks.

Chapter Eighteen

Convoy ONS5 took departure from the United Kingdom, outward bound for Halifax, on 21 April 1943, with forty-three ships of nine nationalities: British, American, Panamanian, Greek, Dutch, Danish, Norwegian, Yugoslavian and Polish (although the Pole dropped out with engine trouble and returned after a few hours). The Commodore was Captain J. K. Brook RNR, in the Norwegian *Rena*, leading the sixth column (of twelve). The convoy also had two escort oilers, *British Lady* and *Argon*, and two trawlers, *Northern Gem* and *Northern Spray*, fitted out as rescue ships. The ocean escort, which joined off Oversay on the 22nd, was the very experienced B7 Escort Group led by Cdr Gretton in the destroyer *Duncan*, with the frigate *Tay* (Lt Cdr R. E. Sherwood RNR), and the corvettes *Sunflower* (Lt Cdr J. Plomer RCNVR), *Snowflake* (Lt H. G. Chesterman RNR), *Loosestrife* (Lt H. A. Stonehouse RNR), and *Pink* (Lt R. Atkinson RNR).

It had been a very stormy April. Spring had certainly not yet come to the north Atlantic. The convoy had been routed far north to avoid U-boats, a decision of very doubtful value because the convoy was at one time virtually hove to for two days off Greenland, which gave the U-boats more time to get into position.

The convoy speed was officially 7½ knots, but many of the ships were lightly loaded or in ballast and rolled prodigiously, making station-keeping very difficult, and for long periods the convoy was making only 1 or 2 knots, with several ships almost hove to. On the 26th a moderate gale blew from the west-north-west, dead in the convoy's teeth. The Norwegian *Bornholm* and the Dutch *Berkel* collided, and at one time Gretton could see no less than eight sets of 'two red lights vertical', the signal that a ship was not under command. *Bornholm* had to divert, alone, to Iceland. The same day the destroyer *Vidette* (Lt R. Hart RN) joined with three ships from Iceland.

Early on the 28th a radio transmission classified as coming from a U-boat was picked up to the south-east. U-650 sighted the convoy later that morning and began to shadow, diving from time to time because of aircraft. At noon *Duncan* detected a U-boat transmitting from dead ahead of the convoy and apparently quite close. It was, as Gretton said, 'clear that we were in for a heavy attack – again that horrible sinking feeling appeared'.

There was very little information about preliminary U-boat dispositions. Special Intelligence was available for 20–26 April, but then nothing more until 5 May. So it had not been possible to choose an evasive route. It was known that the 'Amsel', 'Specht' and 'Star' U-boat groups were in the general area of Newfoundland but little more.

BdU had made his preparations. On 22 April the 'Amsel' Group of eleven U-boats was patrolling east of Newfoundland. To the north-east, the 'Specht' Group of seventeen U-boats had been in position since the 21st. The 'Star' Group, of another fourteen boats, was further to the east and north, placed to catch convoys such as ONS5. A northbound convoy, very probably SC128, was sighted on 2 May and the 'Specht' and 'Star' boats were ordered to attack it. But the U-boats had a task to keep contact, in spite of BdU urging them, 'Do not hold back . . . something can and must be achieved by thirty-one boats.' However, even with thirty-one boats, the convoy disappeared out of sight, with no losses.

Meanwhile B7 Group had been beating off a succession of attacks. U-386 and U-378 came up on U-650's report, but *Duncan* and the others drove them off. U-386 was damaged by *Sunflower*'s depth-charges; U-650 and U-532 attacked *Duncan* and *Snowflake*, were counter-attacked and depth-charged; U-528 was damaged by a US Catalina. On the 29th the convoy suffered its first loss, the American *McKeesport* torpedoed at 5.35 a.m. by U-258. She sank some hours later, all her crew except one being taken off by *Northern Gem*.

C-in-C Western Approaches ordered the 3rd Support Group of the destroyers *Offa*, *Oribi*, *Penn* and *Panther* to reinforce ONS5. The first of them, *Oribi* (who had been escorting SC127) joined late on the 29th. By that time the weather had worsened again and the convoy was battling into a full gale. Some of the battered ships separated from the main body. The weather eased on the 30th but the visibility deteriorated. *Oribi* tried to fuel but, as Gretton said, 'Unfortunately she was new to the game, the weather got worse during the operation, and she made such a mess of the oiler's gear that no one else could fuel that day.' This was particularly galling for Gretton whose own *Duncan* was, by all accounts, the 'shortest-legged' of all short-legged pre-war destroyers.

The 30th of April was a quiet day, except for the weather, which blew another gale towards dusk. That night U-192, attempting to close the convoy, was detected by H/F D/F and driven off by *Sunflower* and *Snowflake*, two 'chummy' ships, sometimes called *Sunflake* and *Snowflower*, whose captains had worked up an almost telepathic *rapport*.

The U-boat lull continued on 1 May, while the weather got worse still, the wind, in Gretton's words, 'blowing like the bells of hell'. By now the convoy had virtually come to a stop, ships were hove to as best they could manage, but as they lost power to keep station, they began to fan out, miles from one another, and in no sort of convoy formation. Two ships turned right round, ran before the wind and never re-joined.

The convoy had made only about 20 miles in twenty-four hours. By 2 May, when the weather improved slightly, ONS5 had lost all cohesion. Its ships were scattered over a distance of 30 miles. One or two aircraft had continued to fly in spite of the weather, and a Liberator from Iceland helped Gretton round up his ships. But a small group of five stragglers, with *Pink* accompanying them, were still some miles astern.

The 3rd Support Group, of the destroyer *Offa* (Captain J. G. McCoy), with the Home Fleet destroyers *Impulsive*, *Penn* and *Panther*, joined on the evening of the 2nd, in such poor visibility *Duncan* had to home them in with radio signals. Although Captain McCoy was senior to Gretton, the convoy Escort Commander still remained in overall charge. As Gretton said, 'It might have been embarrassing to give instructions to a vastly senior officer, but I made "requests" and he complied with them in the most friendly way, and these unusual but necessary command arrangements worked quite admirably throughout the operation.'

Gretton, already concerned again about his fuel state, tried to refuel during a lull in the storm. But the tanker had to twist and turn to avoid ice floes and packs of small growlers. By the time they were clear of the ice, the weather was back to its normal full gale and *Duncan* could not fuel. However, the situation was marginally more cheerful towards the end of the 2nd. The destroyers had joined. The convoy had been rounded up, except for *Pink*'s little party in rear and one or two stragglers. In Gretton's view, 'I think the weather, the aircraft and, I hope, the performance of the escorts all persuaded him [BdU] that ONS5 should be left alone.'

Unfortunately, BdU had by no means given up. On 3 May, the 'Amsel' Group was augmented by a further thirteen U-boats and was then divided into four smaller Groups, coded 'Amsel 1', '2', '3', and '4', each of six boats, spread out in a vast semi-circle east of Newfoundland. The 'Specht' and 'Star' groups were ordered to form reconnaissance lines to the north of the 'Amsel' groups, and by 2.50 p.m. they were steering 205° at 4 knots, searching for the expected convoy.

For the convoy it had been another quiet night, although the wind went on blowing hard and the ships still crawled dead into its teeth. By morning, *Duncan* was so low on fuel she had only enough to reach Newfoundland at economical speed. For Gretton it was a terrible dilemma: 'On the one hand, the enemy was still in touch, and I did not want to leave my group at such a time. On the other hand, the weather forecast was very bad indeed and I did not like the idea of running out of fuel altogether and having to be towed, possibly at a very inconvenient phase of the operation.'

The weather was too bad for boat-work or for transfer by jackstay. Gretton decided he had to go and turned over command of the group to Sherwood in *Tay*. Sherwood was an extremely able officer and led the group very well, but that did not prevent those in *Duncan* being 'most depressed because we felt we left the group in the lurch and were thoroughly ashamed of ourselves, although there was really no one to blame except the staff who had decided in the 1920s the endurance of such destroyers'.

Duncan was not the only escort to leave for lack of fuel. *Impulsive* had to sail for Iceland late on the 3rd, and *Penn* and *Panther* to return to St John's on the morning of the 4th. *Oribi* and *Offa* would have to follow on the 5th if they could not refuel. More reinforcements were called up: the 1st Support Group of the sloop *Pelican* (Cdr G. N. Brewer) with the frigates *Wear*, *Jed* and *Spey*, and the US Coast Guard cutter *Sennen*, left St John's on 4 May.

BdU was also reorganizing his forces. From about 2 p.m. on the 4th onwards, U-boats began to report sighting destroyers on southerly or south-westerly courses. These were the forward screen of ONS5. BdU decided to abandon the search for a north- or north-east-bound convoy and look for a south-west-bound convoy instead. At 4 p.m. he ordered the twenty-seven U-boats of the 'Specht' and 'Star' groups to form a new 'Fink' patrol line and expect a convoy from 5 May onwards.

The first blood went to the air escorts. As the convoy steamed towards the waiting U-boats, Cansos (Canadian Catalina flying boats) of No. 5 Squadron RCAF sighted U-438 and then U-630, the most westerly boats of the Group. U-438 was damaged, and U-630 sunk by an accurate straddle of four depth-charges dropped by Catalina 9747, captained by Sq. Ldr B. H. Moffit, at about 6 p.m. on the 4th, 2 miles astern of the convoy.

Less than half an hour later, ONS5 crossed the centre of the U-boat line and was reported by U-628. BdU at once ordered his boats to concentrate upon this report, telling them, 'You are better placed than you ever were before.' U-614 was ordered to join the 'Fink' Group, and BdU urged everybody, 'I am certain you will fight with everything you've got. Don't overestimate your opponent, but strike him dead!'

By 8.30 that evening U-707 was definitely in contact, and BdU ordered in 'Amsel 1' and '2', making forty U-boats in all directed against ONS5. The main battle now opened, with U-boats reporting ships sunk and torpedoed, while the escorts counter-attacked.

ONS5 was defended by *Tay*, *Vidette*, *Sunflower* and *Snowflake*, *Loosestrife*, *Offa* and *Oribi*. *Pink* was still astern. So too was *Northern Gem*, bringing up another party of stragglers. Seven ships were torpedoed that night, although not all sank at once. Four of the casualties were from No. 1 and 2 columns on the convoy's easterly port wing. A fifth ship from No. 1 column, torpedoed later that day, was then one of *Pink*'s little flock.

Six U-boats were in contact at various times during the night, but most of them were roughly handled by the escorts. *Vidette* made an accurate attack on U-270 and damaged it. *Tay*, *Offa* and *Oribi* made attacks in succession.

U-648, U-168 and U-732 were depth-charged and retired, because of damage or fuel shortage. U-662, U-514 and U-707 were also depth-charged and attacked by gunfire on the surface. U-413 reported that he had been depth-charged by two corvettes which had pretended to be damaged and had then rounded on him (clearly a joint *Snowflake/Sunflower* enterprise).

At dawn on the 5th, four U-boats were still in contact although one, U-270, had been damaged and U-260, damaged in an earlier counter-attack, was driven off. BdU signalled to the remainder to make full use of daylight hours for submerged attack. Boats were to be as far ahead as possible by nightfall, when, said BdU 'the drum roll must be timed to begin. Make haste. Otherwise, as there are forty of you, there'll be nothing of the convoy left. The battles cannot last long as the sea space left is short, so use every chance to the full with all your might.'

There were not forty of them, or even thirty-nine, but thirty-eight. During the forenoon *Pink* obtained a very firm Asdic contact on U-192, which had been sniffing round their small band, by then some 80 miles astern of the main body. The echoes were, Atkinson said, 'by far the clearest and sharpest I have heard', and *Pink* dropped three charges. U-192 went deeper and very quiet. The second attack shook U-192 'like a rag doll in a puppy's mouth'. U-192 tried to creep away on an opposite course, but *Pink* heard and attacked three times more. Each time *Pink* lost contact, but after a pause, regained that marvellous rock-solid echo. After the third attack, a submarine could be heard blowing tanks, and three huge bubbles broke surface. 'It was green and white,' one of *Pink*'s crew said, 'like shallow water, and it looked as if some giant soda-water syphon had been shaken up and exploded.' U-192 did not reach the surface and was lost with all hands.

That forenoon no less than seven U-boats reported ONS5 or its escorts. All tried to attack but were forced to break off. U-638 reported at 9.50 a.m., 'Enemy in sight', the last BdU heard, for U-638 was sunk by *Loosestrife* at 11.30 that evening.

Eleven U-boats were still in contact that afternoon, and another attack from the convoy's starboard wing developed in the evening. Another three ships were sunk in the space of half an hour, shared by U-584 and U-266. In gathering mist and falling darkness, the escorts braced themselves for a long defence of the convoy. But unknown to them, the convoy had suffered its last loss, and the battle was to be one of counter-attack.

Nine U-boats were in contact at dusk, and eight boats reported some contact during the night. At one point *Tay* could see seven U-boats close to her on the surface. *Sunflower* detected four U-boats in succession and damaged one, U-267, with gunfire. *Loosestrife* surprised U-638 attacking on the surface in poor visibility, drove it down and briskly sank it with depth-charges. *Vidette* drove three U-boats off, one after the other. U-531 had sent his last convoy report at 1.58 p.m. on the 5th. Shortly after midnight he was located by *Oribi*'s radar, forced down and at 2.52 a.m. was sunk.

At about 3 a.m., U-125 reported being rammed (actually by *Oribi*), and BdU ordered four U-boats to its assistance. U-223 reported at 7 a.m. that it had found at the site of the ramming only a destroyer, which had forced it to dive and then depth-charged enthusiastically for the next three hours. In fact, *Vidette* had come across the disabled U-125 shortly after 4 a.m. and dispatched it.

The 1st Support Group, led by Cdr Brewer in *Pelican*, had been approaching ONS5 during the night. 'From nightfall the radio loudspeaker on my bridge was alive with reports from the convoy escorts,' wrote Captain Brewer later. ' "Have detected U-boat on the surface"; "U-boat has dived"; "Am attacking with depth charges"; from another "U-boat has exploded on the surface astern of me"; from another "Have rammed U-boat" and so on. This was music in my ears.'

But Brewer soon had his own part to play. At about 4 a.m. *Pelican* was in contact with the convoy at about 10 miles. At the same time 'a small bleep appeared on our radar screen two miles on our starboard beam'. Plotting showed that it was travelling at 9 knots away from the convoy – 'probably a U-boat that had found things too hot for it'. Soon *Pelican* heard hydrophone effect and then came 'the unmistakable smell of diesel exhaust fumes'. The U-boat was sighted through the mist at only 200 yards, with men clearly visible on the conning tower. They sighted *Pelican* at about the same time – 'it must have been a ghastly shock' – and dived. *Pelican* made two attacks and heard 'the clear sounds of the U-boat breaking up' after the second. That was U-438, the sixth U-boat sunk around ONS5.

That morning of 6 May, *Spey* found U-634 on the surface and hit it three times with gunfire, afterwards attacking and damaging it with depth-charges. This was actually the twenty-fourth attempted U-boat attack made *after* the last merchant ship had been sunk. At 11.46 all U-boats were ordered to break off. Twelve boats of Amsel 1 and 2 were to steer south, the rest to withdraw to the east. U-631 then piped up for the first time, to report that it had all its torpedoes left. BdU forebore to reply.

In all, twelve merchant ships had been sunk. Of forty U-boats all but four made some sort of signal during the battle. Six were sunk and two more (U-659 and U-439) lost in collision. Five U-boats reported severe damage, and twelve more reported lesser action damage. The escorts had made some forty attacks, and on twenty occasions U-boats had signalled that they were being driven off or forced to dive. There were as many U-boats as there were ships, and three and a half times as many U-boats as there were escorts.

The actions around ONS5 had been a resounding tactical victory for the escorts especially in their use of radar on the night of 5–6 May. BdU was well aware of it: 'In fog period fifteen U-boats were depth-charged, of which six U-boats were surprised in fog by destroyers and shelled. Without a remedy against location the boats were in a hopeless position. Loss of six boats in so short an operation is very high and considered serious'.

The battle of ONS5 was, as Gretton wrote, 'probably the most stirring of convoy history'. He himself had reached St John's with only 4 per cent fuel remaining in *Duncan*'s tanks, after she had been assisted by the wind shifting in her favour and by an unexpected favourable current. As for himself, 'I shall never cease to regret that I did not risk the weather and stay with them until the end. This decision has haunted me ever since. It was entirely correct and based on common sense.' Yet Gretton could not shake off the conviction that he 'had missed the "golden moment" which comes but once in a lifetime'. Gretton need not have reproached himself. Other moments were to come – and soon.

Many U-boats had approached ONS5 on the surface, hoping to close in poor visibility whilst the escorts were blind – on the tactics of three years before. But times had changed. Almost all the escorts and many of the aircraft were fitted with radar. It was now the U-boats which were blind.

The escort commander now had much greater choice of weapon and flexibility of method for his counter-attacks. He could use depth-charges or Hedgehog. With H/F D/F he could send a ship to run down the bearing, put the U-boat down and keep it down, whilst the convoy made a large alteration of course. With plentiful air cover and good R/T communication between surface and aircraft, he could ask an aircraft to investigate and attack a contact. Sometimes, the first indication of an aircraft's arrival was the water columns of its depth-charge explosions rising on the horizon. Radar, on the surface and in the air, was a constant shield around a convoy.

The convoys which came immediately after ONS5 also had the benefit of air support from escort carriers. But the U-boats had never been stronger. By 10 May the highest number of U-boats ever known was at sea. OIC estimated the figure at 128, most of them fresh on patrol, ninety-eight of them having sailed in April and most of those in the last half of the month. An estimated sixty U-boats were operating in the north Atlantic.

Shark de-crypts revealed some of the U-boat movements, and convoy HX237 was diverted. But the B-Dienst Service discovered the evasion, and BdU took the twelve U-boats from the 'Amsel 1' and '2' groups which had not been in action against ONS5, and set up a new 'Rhein' Group to lie in wait for HX237. This forty-six-ship convoy was escorted by C2 Group of eight escorts led by Captain Chevasse in the destroyer *Broadway*.

HX237 was first found by U-359 on 9 May, but the U-boat was driven off without attacking. The U-boats formed an ambush line ahead. When HX237 reached it the convoy had already been reinforced by the 5th Support Group, including the escort carrier *Biter*, which had embarked 811 Squadron, of nine Swordfish and three Martlets. By this time only one Martlet was left and it was the Swordfish who 'punched a hole' in the U-boat line by forcing down the nearest, U-454, so that it could not attack. Next day, U-403 was in contact, shadowing the tail-end rescue ship. The U-boat was sighted and harassed by a Swordfish. During the ONS5 actions, BdU had told his U-boats to 'stay on the surface and fire when aircraft appear'. U-403 took the Swordfish under fire and drove it off, but was then forced to dive by approaching destroyers and lost contact.

The 'Amsel' boats had now fallen too far behind, so BdU formed another 'Drossel' Group of eight boats coming up from the east. One of these, U-436, sighted HX237 on the evening of 11 May and one straggler was sunk, by U-403 and U-456. U-230 shot one Swordfish down.

There was some excellent cooperation between joint arms whilst defending the convoy. U-89, for example, was sunk on the 12th by *Broadway*, assisted by the frigate *Lagan* and a Swordfish from *Biter*. Next day, U-456 was very badly damaged by a Mark XXIV mine dropped from a Liberator of 210 Squadron, and then sunk by *Pathfinder* who was directed to the spot by a Swordfish. The same day two convoy stragglers were sunk, but once again a combined enterprise accounted for a U-boat, this time U-753: a Sunderland of 423 Squadron RCAF assisted *Lagan* and the corvette *Drumheller*, who destroyed the U-boat. The convoy close escort meanwhile drove off any remaining U-boats, and on the 14th BdU broke off the operation as hopeless. The score for HX237 was therefore three U-boats (all from the 'Drossel' Group) sunk, for three merchantmen (all stragglers) sunk.

Another battle had been taking place to the south, around the twenty-six-ship convoy SC129, which was escorted by B2 Group of nine escorts, led by Cdr D. MacIntyre in the destroyer *Hesperus*. This convoy had been evasively routed to the south but B-Dienst had decoded the manoeuvres and BdU had formed two more groups, 'Elbe 1', of twelve U-boats, and 'Elbe 2' of thirteen, mostly boats which had operated against ONS5.

An 'Elbe 2' boat, U-504, reported SC129 on the evening of 11 May. U-504 was driven off but one of the few remaining 'aces' at sea, von Forstner in U-402, attacked just before dusk and sank two ships. That night, U-383 and U-359 were repulsed by the destroyer *Whitehall* and the corvette *Clematis*, but U-223 was much more determined. Undeterred by a depth-charge attack from *Hesperus* which blew the U-boat to the surface, its commander Korvetten-Kapitan Wachter fired a salvo of five torpedoes at *Hesperus*. They missed. *Hesperus* replied with a clutch of depth-charges set to explode just below the U-boat, opened fire with main armament, and rammed – though MacIntyre was careful to take most of the way off his ship before the moment of impact. U-223 did not sink, was not disabled, and Wachter made his escape in the darkness.

The U-boats still made the fatal error of talking too much. Next morning *Hesperus* ran down a H/F D/F bearing of U-186, which had been shadowing the convoy, and sank it. Eleven other U-boats reported contact during the day, were all betrayed by H/F D/F and by nightfall had all been driven off, without sinking any ships. The 5th Escort Group had been steaming at full speed to reinforce SC129, and *Biter*'s first Swordfish were over the convoy early on 13 May. That afternoon Liberators from 86 Squadron RAF also arrived, and on the 14th sank U-266 (one of those which had attacked ONS5) astern of the convoy. Thus the score for SC129 was two ships (both sunk by von Forstner) for two U-boats.

This very poor exchange rate for BdU was to get even worse. On 11 and 12 May BdU formed three groups (romantically called after rivers, 'Isar', 'Lech' and 'Inn'), each of four U-boats to await ONS7 south-east of Cape Farewell. This forty-ship convoy, escorted by B5 Group, of the frigate *Swale*, five other escorts, and the rescue ship *Copeland*, was actually sighted on the night of the 11th–12th by U-640 on passage to join another group. U-640's captain Kap. Lt Nagle was most persistent, keeping in touch for three days and bringing up five other U-boats of the 'Iller' Group. But then U-640 was bombed and sunk by an American Catalina of VP84 Squadron for its pains, and the others lost contact.

To restore the situation, BdU formed two more much larger groups, 'Donau 1' of eleven and 'Donau 2' of twelve U-boats, and at last found a victim. On the night of the 16th–17th U-657 of the 'Donau 1' Group sank *Aymeric*, but was then swiftly counter-attacked and sunk by *Swale*. Two more boats on passage, U-646 and U-273, were sunk on 17 and 19 May by Hudsons from 269 Squadron RAF in Iceland. Four U-boats were lost around ONS7 – in exchange for one 5196-ton ship.

The B-Dienst Service was still providing information about convoy routes. The unsuccessful boats from ONS7 were moved south to intercept the forty-five-ship convoy HX238. But the convoy was not even sighted, although twenty-two U-boats of the 'Donau' groups and another eight of the 'Oder' Group were deployed to look for it.

The next eastbound convoy was SC130, a slow convoy of forty-five ships, escorted by Gretton's B7 Group, with *Duncan*, *Tay*, *Vidette*, *Snowflake* and *Sunflower*, *Pink*, *Loosestrife* and, for a time, the Canadian *Kitchener*, with the rescue ship *Zamalek* and two trawlers.

When joining the convoy and exchanging documents with the Commodore, Captain Forsythe, the Escort Commander included a note to say he had an especially pressing engagement with a Wren and the necessary witnesses at St Peter's, Cadogan Square, two days after the convoy was due to arrive. The Commodore replied that he had a golf match that same day and he would do his best.

On the night of the 19th the convoy was sighted by U-304 and reported. But three of the escorts and *Zamalek* had H/F D/F, the transmission was detected and plotted, and the convoy made a sharp turn away. Gretton practised the technique, when U-boats were detected by H/F D/F, of turning the convoy away whilst giving details of the U-boat's position to an attacking aircraft.

Excellent air cover was provided by Liberators of 120 Squadron RAF. One sank U-954 on the 19th as it was closing the convoy, and some five other U-boats were forced to dive. *Tay* depth-charged and badly damaged U-952, and *Snowflake* was disappointed not to sink U-381 on her own. The periscope was actually sighted in the middle of the depth-charge pattern. But *Duncan* came up and finished off the U-boat with Hedgehogs.

At noon the escort was reinforced by the 1st Escort Group, of *Wear*, *Jed*, *Spey* and *Sennen* who surprised two U-boats as they came up from astern of the convoy. U-209 dived and fired torpedoes at the frigates but was sunk by *Jed* and *Sennen*. For the rest of the day, escorts and aircraft co-operated to drive off all pursuers except U-92 which made one unsuccessful attack. Just before nightfall *Jed* and *Spey* drove off the last shadower. BdU broke off the operation in the morning. It was the end of the story for the U-boats – but not for the Liberators. One of them sank U-258 that day.

Both the Escort Commander and the Convoy Commodore kept their engagements. Not one ship had been lost from SC130 – but four U-boats had been sunk. This was another appalling reverse for BdU. More U-boats were now being sunk than merchant ships during the average convoy's passage.

From the twenty-one U-boats remaining, BdU formed the 'Moser' group on 19 May to operate against HX239 which, once again, had been forecast by B-Dienst Service. But the Shark de-crypts revealed this plan, and HX239 made a large evasive diversion to the south. Instead, the outward-bound convoy ONI84 reached the 'Moser' line. But this convoy had the services of the 6th Support Group, with the carrier *Bogue*, whose Avengers first attacked and damaged U-231 and then pushed the rest of the U-boats' heads down while the convoy passed by. U-305 reported ONI84 at midday on 22 May and the nearest, most southerly, boats from the 'Moser' line were directed to it. But *Bogue*'s Avengers once more drove them down, and although U-468 beat off an Avenger attack with gunfire, two Avengers sank U-569. The convoy lost no ships.

Meanwhile, to the south, U-218's hydrophones detected the propeller noises of the forty-two-ship HX239, which was escorted by B3 Group, led by Cdr Evans in the destroyer *Keppel*, with another destroyer *Escapade*, the frigate *Towey*, corvettes *Orchis* and *Narcissus*, and the Free French *Roselys*, *Lobelia* and *Renoncule*. The defence was also strengthened by the 4th Escort Group, under Captain Scott-Moncrieff, with the carrier *Archer* and four destroyers *Milne*, *Matchless*, *Eclipse* and *Fury*.

Archer's aircraft did for HX239 what *Bogue*'s had just done for ONI84, forcing a gap in the U-boat line. U-468 beat off an attacking Swordfish, but on 23 May U-752 was hit whilst diving by rockets from another Swordfish. The crippled U-boat successfully defended itself against the Swordfish and a Martlet fighter, but then had to scuttle when *Keppel* and *Escapade* came up. This was the first success of rockets in an anti-submarine role. HX239, like ONI84, suffered no loss at all. Thus four convoys – SC130, HX238, ONI84 and HX239, with a total of 161 ships – had passed without any loss, while their surface and air escorts between them had sunk six U-boats.

U-752 was the thirty-fourth U-boat sunk from all causes in May 1943. The total for the month eventually rose to forty-one, twenty-eight of them sunk by air or surface convoy escorts. U-752 seemed to be the breaking-point for BdU, who appeared numbed by such catastrophic losses. On 24 May BdU decided to halt, temporarily, the offensive against the convoys in the north Atlantic. The U-boats were withdrawn. Those with enough fuel were sent south to operate against the routes from the USA to Gibraltar, where BdU hoped opposition would be less fierce. The fifteen U-boats that were lower on fuel, were left in the north Atlantic, spread out over a wide area and instructed to transmit frequently. They were to make up in loquacity what they lacked in numbers to suggest that U-boats were still there, and in force. Doenitz meanwhile prophesied that the U-boats would be back in time, with new and better weapons, to fight another day.

The position at the end of May was that U-boats had sunk fifty ships of 264,852 tons in the month. This was a drop on April figures, and a big decrease on March. And no ship had been lost in an Atlantic convoy since *Aymeric* on the 17th. In the three weeks after the battle around ONS5, the 468 ships of eleven convoys (HX236, ONS6, ONI82, HX238, ONI83, SCI30, ONI84, HX239, SCI31, ONS8 and HX240) had all passed across without loss. Six ships were lost from three other convoys (HX237, SCI29 and ONS7), but another 106 ships in these convoys were unharmed. No ship was lost from any convoy at any time when it had air cover.

For the U-boats this was, in a word, defeat, as Doenitz recognized. 'Wolf-pack operations against convoys in the north Atlantic,' he wrote, 'the main theatre of operations and at the same time the theatre in which air cover was strongest, were no longer possible.' Unless the 'fighting power' of the U-boats could be 'radically' increased, 'we had lost the battle of the Atlantic.'

The series of great convoy actions of April and May 1943 had no particular names, except the convoys' own designation letters and numbers, no famous landmarks or head stones to hang legends on. They were fought over hundreds of miles of ocean wastes only identified by degrees of latitude and longitude. The winners were men in small ships, none over 2000 tons and many much less, who fought in appalling weather, almost constantly at action stations, living on bully beef and ship's biscuits when hot food was a memory, with not a stitch of dry clothing for days on end. They were supported by aircrews who flew for hours on end but who had to be ready to attack instantly, after a long period of boredom. The retreat of the Atlantic U-boats in May 1943 was a smashing victory for the Allies, as important a strategic victory as Midway in the west and Stalingrad in the east.

In the summer of 1943 an almost eerie calm descended upon the convoy routes of the north Atlantic. The weather was good after the tremendous and seemingly interminable gales of the spring. As tranquil day followed tranquil day, under a hotter sun, men on watch looked at each other in a wild surmise. There were thirty-two ocean convoys in June, with 1181 ships. Not one was attacked, and not one was lost. The cycle for SC and ONS convoys was changed to eleven days, with alternate seven- and eight-day cycles for HX and

ON convoys. In good weather, ONS11 of thirty-six ships reached Halifax in only fourteen days; the fast ON189, of fifty-four ships, arrived in Halifax in twelve days, New York in fifteen. ON190, with eighty-seven ships, was the largest ON convoy so far to sail.

July was another good month. There were no attacks on HX, SC or ON convoys. From the thirty-two ocean convoys in the month, containing 1367 ships, not one ship was lost. On the coastal routes around the United Kingdom, there were 141 convoys, of 3195 ships, again without loss. The OS convoys to Sierra Leone and the OG convoys to Gibraltar sailed on a twenty-day cycle in conjunction with KMS convoys from the UK to North Africa. Two convoys were attacked and two ships torpedoed, but both reached harbour.

There were no attacks on HX, SC and ON convoys in August. Of thirty-two ocean convoys, and 1209 ships, three ships were lost. OS53 had one ship sunk and another damaged by aircraft.

If the U-boats had expected an easier time and more plentiful targets to the south they were soon disappointed. This was a halcyon period for the American CVE escort carriers, each with a normal complement of twelve Avenger torpedo-bomber aircraft and six Grumman Wildcat fighters embarked. A CVE group commander cooperated with a convoy escort commander but could act independently and was not subject to the escort commander's orders. With his screen of four or five destroyers he had a free hand to range about the ocean wherever targets presented themselves, hunting down U-boats wherever H/F D/F or Ultra indicated. He could transfer his group to another convoy if that seemed to need extra support.

As time passed and they grew more proficient the CVE groups moved away from the practice of staying with a convoy and became more and more free-ranging, finally becoming virtually independent hunter – killer groups (almost the only occasion, thanks to information supplied by Ultra, that such groups were successful). But the CVE group was always required to return to a threatened convoy before U-boats could attack it. Convoy defence was still the primary consideration.

A CVE normally flew continuous patrols from before dawn until after sunset, with two sections, each of one Avenger and one Wildcat in the air, flying out at heights of between 5000 and 7000 feet to ranges of about 150 miles. On hearing of a U-boat concentration the CVE group would head for the centre of the area, adjusting speed to bring the group at daylight outside the area but within effective aircraft range. During the day the group would proceed through the centre of the area at full speed, searching out to a distance of about 100 miles on each side. It was hard work, with long hours; in one patrol the USS *Core* spent thirty-three days at sea, flying about twelve sorties a day, racking up 1200 Avenger flying hours and 450 Wildcat hours.

When a U-boat was sighted, the Avenger pilot would direct the Wildcat on a strafing run, and as the U-boat dived the Avenger would drop its load of four Torpex 350-pound bombs or, latterly, the deadly little homing torpedo FIDO. Once an attack was under way, at least four more aircraft were flown off as a striking force. U-boat crews who had already suffered the shattering experience of being blown to the surface and were abandoning ship would be further discouraged to see sometimes as many as eight aircraft flying round their U-boat when they reached the casing.

The CVE group methods were wonderfully efficient. In the last six months of 1943 operating in the calmer waters, lighter winds and generally better weather of the 'horse latitudes', the American CVEs *Bogue*, *Core*, *Card*, *Santee* and *Rock Island* sank twenty U-boats. The top scorer was USS *Card* and her group, with seven kills. In mid-July, *Core* and *Santee* enjoyed a purple patch, taking it in turns to sink one U-boat a day for four days.

Sometimes BdU hurried his U-boats on to their fates by mistaken tactics. In June, for example, the outward-bound U-758 fought an outstanding but misleading fight against eight aircraft from *Bogue* with its newly-fitted four-barrelled 20-mm gun. BdU then ordered U-boats to stay on the surface and fight it out. This merely increased their rate of losses, and by August BdU was signalling to U-boat captains: 'Do not report too much bad news, so as not to depress the other boats; every radio message goes the rounds of the crew in every boat.'

Convoy ONS9, which sailed on 28 May 1943, included the odd-looking 7950-ton grain ship *Empire MacAlpine*, whose merchantman's hull was fitted with a flat deck on top. A small superstructure with a signalling mast and a bridge was set over on the starboard side. She was the first Merchant Aircraft Carrier, or MAC ship, which could give a convoy its own integral air support, comparatively cheaply and conveniently. Ironically, the idea could have been implemented within a few months of the start of the war.

Early in 1942 it was clear to the Admiralty that the American escort carriers would not be coming forward as planned. Cdr Brewer, in the Trade Division, explained the problem, one evening quite by chance, to Sir Douglas Thomson, a director of the Ben Line, who said: 'I have often wondered why with ships that carry grain which can be poured down a chute and sucked out the same way it should not be possible to do away with masts and derricks. You can then have a flat-top deck to operate aircraft.'

This struck Brewer at once as a simply excellent idea. But, of course, there was official opposition. The Naval Air Division thought a 12-knot ship was too slow to operate aircraft, the Director of Naval Construction that it would take a year or more to design such a ship. When Mr John Lamb, Marine Superintendent of the Anglo Saxon Oil Company, suggested that tankers, too, could be given flight decks, there were concerted objections from the Admiralty and the Ministry of War Transport, that it would be dangerous to have aircraft taking off and landing on a thin steel flight-deck above thousands of tons of inflammable oil.

But the final and conclusive contribution was from Sir James Lithgow,

Director of Merchant Ship Building, who took an envelope out of his pocket and addressed the meeting, in Brewer's words, 'roughly thuswise: "Here is the sketch design. I have two ships about to be built at Burntisland which can be converted without undue delay in their coming into service. I am prepared to do this provided I am not interfered with by the Admiralty."' An order to convert two grain ships was issued in the spring of 1942, increased to six grain ships and six tankers in October.

The 'grainers', of which six were eventually converted to MAC ships, had flight-decks 422 feet by 62 feet, a hangar, a lift, and carried four Swordfish. The tankers, of which there were thirteen (nine of them from the Anglo Saxon Oil Co.), had flight decks 460 feet long, but had no lift or hangar, and three Swordfish embarked. Both types had a safety barrier and arrester wires. The first MAC tanker *Rapana* sailed with ONS17 in August 1943.

In all, over ninety Swordfish operated from MAC ships, all based at Maydown in northern Ireland, where there was an operational pool formed from 836, 840 and 860 (Royal Netherlands Navy) Squadrons. The flight decks were so short that a fully-loaded Swordfish, with rockets and/or depth-charges needed RATOG (Rocket Assisted Take-off Gear) to get airborne.

MAC ships spent 4447 days at sea, escorting 217 convoys, of which only two lost any ships whilst a MAC ship was in company. The Swordfish flew 4177 sorties, racked up 9,016 flying hours, and made twelve attacks on U-boats, without actually sinking one. Over 100 Swordfish were lost or damaged; six pilots, five observers, and eight air-gunners were lost.

As Brewer had prophesied, lack of windspeed was seldom a problem in the Atlantic. *Empire Macrae*, a 'grainer', was once seen steaming downwind in a Force 10 gale, in the opposite direction to a somewhat scattered convoy, whilst her Swordfish landed on over her bows.

Convoys normally had two MAC ships in company, although some had as many as four. The MAC ships still flew the Red Ensign (two of the later tankers flew the Dutch ensign), and carried up to 80 per cent of their usual cargoes. The Swordfish were the first Navy aircraft to land on civilian ships. The aircrew, an air staff officer, and a small maintenance team, were embarked for the passage. Relations between RN and merchant navy were excellent. It was, in any case, very good for any convoy's morale to see 'their' Swordfish taking off and landing from one of 'their' ships operating in its special 'box' in the sixth or seventh column. Some Swordfish were even supposed to have had 'Merchant Navy' painted on their fuselages.

By the end of 1944, the convoy situation had improved so greatly that most of the MAC ships were being reverted to trade, and several had been used as 'ferry' ships to bring aircraft to the United Kingdom from the United States. The last operational sortie from a MAC ship was from *Empire Mackay* on 28 June 1945.

Experience in the war had shown that in general it was best to search for

U-boats in and around the convoys; that was where escorts and aircraft were most effective. But special circumstances sometimes gave special results. Since the summer of 1942 Coastal Command had conducted an intermittent offensive against U-boats on transit through the Bay of Biscay from their bases in northern France to their patrol areas. With the lull in the north Atlantic in the summer of 1943, more attention could be paid to the Bay of Biscay and some Escort Groups, including Captain Walker's, were diverted to operate there.

The Bay was a special killing-ground of U-boats, where the battle swung to and fro as one side or another gained a temporary tactical or technological advantage. Wellingtons equipped with an early form of radar and Leigh lights damaged three U-boats in the Bay in June 1942 and actually sank two in July. BdU, suspecting the existence of some form of new locating device, fitted U-boats with a rudimentary detector. The 'Bay offensive' came to a pause in October 1942, began again in January, only to pause again when U-boats were fitted with a still primitive but more effective radar detector named 'Metox'.

In March Coastal Command were equipped with aircraft with the new 10-cm radar sets, and the Bay offensive began again in earnest. U-376 was sunk by aircraft in April, but the circumstances of this loss and reports from other U-boats which had been attacked and damaged on passage in the Bay convinced Doenitz that the Allies had some mysterious form of detection gear. He ordered U-boats to submerge at night, and to surface in daylight to recharge their batteries. If they were attacked they were to stay on the surface and fight back. This was the same advice he had given to U-boats in the Atlantic and it was just as wrong in the Bay. In May 1943 six U-boats were sunk in the Bay and several others so damaged they had to turn back.

The U-boats were given very meagre air cover, due to the long-standing vendetta between Doenitz and Goering, whilst the Allies devoted more and more aircraft to the Bay, in support of escorts, and in attacks of their own. In June, Walker's ships sank two U-boats. In July US Liberators and Catalinas joined the RAF's Wellingtons, Halifaxes and Sunderlands. Together, using radar, depth-charges, Leigh lights, rockets and magnetic anomaly detectors (which picked up the magnetic disturbance of a submarine's steel hull in the sea), they sank sixteen U-boats during the month, nine of them inside a week.

In August the Luftwaffe began to give reluctant air cover to the U-boats and to use glide bombs against the escorts. The U-boats transitted further to the south, where they were safer from radar detection under the shadow of the Pyrenees. Again the Bay offensive slackened. Some idea of the scale of the activity may be gained from the figures: between 14 June and 21 September the Bay offensive involved 576 ship-days and 3981 Coastal Command sorties.

Doenitz then made another error in deciding that it was Metox which was betraying his U-boats and ordering it to be removed. In November 1943 the

Bay offensive began again, and thirty-two U-boats were sunk there between May and December. During that same period 258 U-boats entered and 247 left the Bay, on transit to and from the French ports, so the percentage of U-boats sunk was not unduly high. From May to December, 183 U-boats were sunk in areas other than the Bay of Biscay.

Thus the Bay offensive by no means proved that it was better to leave the convoys, so as to go out and hunt for U-boats. But energetic sea and air searches, coupled with useful Special Intelligence, did cause BdU enough losses to have a very powerful psychological effect upon the Germans, who did not discover until much later how or why they were losing so many U-boats. By then another offensive had come and gone around the Atlantic convoys – the theatre of war at sea which both the Allies and Doenitz knew was the really decisive one.

Chapter Nineteen

The main battle, as everyone knew very well, had to be in the north Atlantic. Sooner or later, the U-boats must return there in force, or confess the war at sea as lost. After the summer lull, a fresh offensive opened around the convoys in September 1943.

The U-boats had some new weapons, although no new ideas. Many U-boats had much heavier anti-aircraft armament of up to eight 20-mm guns. They were fitted with a new Telefunken Fu.MB7 'Naxos' search receiver to pick up 10-cm radar transmission, just as Metox had done for 1½-metre radar. U-boats also had an Asdic decoy, known as the '*Pillenwerfer*' or '*Bolde*' (short for '*Lugenbold*', meaning a 'habitual liar'). This was a canister of chemicals which emitted a considerable stream of bubbles on contact with sea-water. The froth and turbulence of the *Pillenwerfer* gave a firm Asdic contact, whilst the U-boat slipped away. Above all, the U-boats had a new weapon on which BdU pinned great hopes. It was the 3300-pound Zaunkönig T-5 acoustic torpedo, known to the Allies by the acronym GNAT (German Naval Acoustic Torpedo). It had a sound basic tactical purpose: to enable the U-boat to draw aside and disable an escort, and then deal with the merchant-men at leisure. It was principally an anti-escort weapon.

None of these new measures was quite as effective as the Germans hoped. To fit a U-boat with heavy armament was itself an admission of failure. A U-boat's one strategic talent was its ability to dive. To stay on the surface as a 'flak' ship was an abuse of that talent. Naxos was not as sensitive as Metox had been and, in its early models, was non-directional; it gave an indication that 10-cm radar pulses were present, but was not much of a guide as to where and how far off. The GNAT had a modest range of 6000 yards and a very modest speed, for a torpedo, of 24 knots. A target moving at more than 25 knots, or less than 7 knots (when the acoustic listening gear could not pick up the sound of the propeller), was generally immune. The GNAT also had a tendency to explode behind its target, in the turbulent water of the wake.

The GNAT made its operational debut in September against convoys ON202 and ONS18. BdU had formed a new patrol line, of five U-boats which had just refuelled from the 'milch-cow' U-460 and another fifteen which had made the passage out through the Bay unscathed, code-named the 'Leuthen' Group. They were deployed south-east of Iceland, and warned to expect the convoys on 20 September. However, a Liberator of 10 Squadron RCAF sank U-341, one of the more southerly boats in the line on the 19th, before the main battle began.

The Shark de-crypts were being read almost continually on a daily basis, and the two convoys were diverted to the northward. ON202 had thirty-eight ships, escorted by C2 Group, of the Canadian destroyer *Gatineau* (Cdr P. W. Burnett) and the destroyer *Icarus*, the frigate *Lagan*, the corvettes *Polyanthus* and the Canadians *Drumheller* and *Kamloops*. ONS18, about 120 miles ahead of ON202, had twenty-seven ships escorted by B3 Group, of the destroyers *Keppel* (Cdr M. J. Evans) and *Escapade*, frigate *Towey*, the corvettes *Orchis* and *Narcissus* and the Free French *Roselys*, *Lobelia* and *Renoncule*, and the trawler *Northern Foam*. ONS18 included the MAC ship *Empire MacAlpine*. When it was realized that ONS18 was threatened, the Canadian 9th Escort Group, of the frigate *Itchen*, destroyers *St Croix* and *St Francis*, and corvettes *Chambly*, *Sackville* and *Morden*, was ordered to reinforce it.

The convoy ran over the first U-boat of the 'Leuthen' line in the early hours of the 20th. *Roselys* depth-charged one contact but *Escapade* suffered a very serious accident on deck, when a Hedgehog exploded prematurely, causing twenty-one casualties.

Some 30 miles to the north-east, U-270 had sighted and reported ON202. The transmission was detected by H/F D/F, and *Lagan* ran down the bearing. U-270 counter-attacked with a GNAT which blew off *Lagan*'s astern and killed twenty-nine of her company. *Gatineau* drove off U-270, and *Polyanthus* attacked another shadower, U-238. But the U-boat was not shaken off and three hours later slipped past and torpedoed two ships, one of which sank and the other was later finished off by U-645. Both *Gatineau* and *Polyanthus* had GNAT torpedoes fired at them, by U-645 and U-402 respectively, but both missed.

At dawn the air escort of Liberators of 120 Squadron from Iceland arrived overhead. U-338 signalled to other U-boats, in accordance with the prearranged plan: 'U-boats stay on the surface for defence.' It was not good advice, especially for U-338 itself, which was sighted by a Liberator just after 10 a.m. U-338 dived, and was sunk by a FIDO homing torpedo.

By midday on the 20th the faster ON202 had virtually caught ONS18 up and the two convoys were so close together that C-in-C Western Approaches ordered them to amalgamate, under Cdr Evans in *Keppel*. Unfortunately his signal was received in a very badly mutilated form, with the course to steer undecipherable. But the two convoys continued to close each other haphazardly, and by the afternoon the sixty-three merchant ships and twenty-one escorts (including the 9th Escort Group which had just joined from astern) all, as Cdr Evans described them, 'gyrated majestically about the ocean, never appearing to get much closer, and watched appreciatively by a growing swarm of U-boats'.

By the evening, the swarm had grown to eight U-boats and the convoy and its escorts had a busy night. U-386 sighted the convoy, but was detected by H/F D/F. *Keppel* and *Roselys* ran it down, and although *Keppel* actually saw 'a yard and a half' of the U-boat's periscope only a few feet off her starboard beam, U-386 survived the depth-charging. At about 8 p.m. *St Croix* was hit by a GNAT fired by U-305, and sunk by another from the same U-boat an hour later. *Itchen* came up to take off survivors and a GNAT exploded in her wake.

During the night of the 20th–21st the U-boats, in a phrase, tried to blast their way into the convoy, firing GNATs at any escort which approached. U-229 missed *Icarus* with one GNAT, and in manoeuvring violently to avoid, *Icarus* collided slightly with *Drumheller*, doing no damage. (*Drumheller* somewhat plaintively signalled, 'Having no U-boats?') U-260 missed *Narcissus*, but U-952 sank *Polyanthus* with a GNAT. *Itchen* took off her survivors. U-229, U-641, U-270, U-377 and U-584 all fired at escorts, but their GNATs all missed, or detonated in the wakes.

By dawn on the 21st, both convoys were shrouded in thick fog. *Renoncule* and *Roselys* drove off the one remaining shadower, U-377. The fog lifted for a few minutes, long enough for *Empire MacAlpine* to fly off a Swordfish, but the visibility closed down again almost to nothing. The Swordfish was lucky to land on again; it was regarded on board as nothing less than a miracle. When the fog lifted again for a short time that afternoon, Cdr Evans was surprised to see both convoys close together, with ONS18 neatly in station to starboard of ON202, a 'masterly manoeuvre', as Evans called it, which must have been 'organized by a Higher Authority'.

U-584 found the convoys towards the evening and once again, eight U-boats were soon in position for another hectic night. *Roselys* and *Renoncule* both drove off a U-boat. U-584 tried to hit *Chambly* with a GNAT, failed, and was in turn damaged by return gunfire. *Northern Foam* tried to ram U-952 and almost succeeded. Towards dawn the Free French were in action again: *Roselys*, *Lobelia* and *Renoncule* all attacked U-boats and drove them off. Finally, *Keppel* herself steamed down a H/F D/F bearing astern of the convoy, surprised U-229 on the surface, and rammed and sunk it.

The fog persisted until well into the afternoon of 22 September. When it lifted *Empire MacAlpine* was able to fly off her Swordfish and all around the convoys Evans saw 'the air was filled with Liberators'. The U-boats now tried the tactic of staying on the surface and shooting their way towards the convoy with their anti-aircraft armament. Some U-boats defended themselves adequately against aircraft, but U-377 and U-270 were both damaged.

After dark the U-boats resorted to GNATs again. U-952 missed *Renoncule* but shortly afterwards there was a tragedy. *Morden* sighted U-666 ahead of the convoy and ran in to attack. U-666 retaliated with two GNATs, one of which exploded astern of *Morden*. But the second ran on and hit *Itchen*. She blew up and sank with tremendous loss of life. She had on board survivors from *St Croix* and *Polyanthus*. Only three men survived from the three ships' companies.

Evans partly blamed himself. Earlier that day, he had formed up ONS18 astern of ON202, trying to reduce the convoys' overall width, and so avoid detection. But in so doing, he had of course increased the convoys' depth to some 6 or 7 miles, and made them harder to defend.

As usual, one or two U-boats did most of the damage. In the confusion after *Itchen*'s destruction, U-238 (Kapitan-Leutnant Hepp) who had torpedoed two ships on the 20th, now penetrated the convoy and sank three ships with one FAT salvo. U-952 was the only other boat to score, sinking one ship and hitting another with a torpedo which did not explode. The Liberators came back with the sun, and several U-boats had to defend themselves against air attack again. U-422 was damaged. That morning, the 23rd, BdU called off the operation.

In five days, nineteen U-boats had made contact with the convoys, a very high percentage of the total involved. They had sunk three escorts (*Lagan* was towed home) and six merchantmen, of 36,422 tons. It was a major success, the best the U-boats had achieved for some time. But it was not quite as much as they claimed. Understandably, the U-boat captains tended to overestimate. Their claim was ten escorts and eight ships sunk, for twenty-four T-5s fired. BdU, misled by these reports, considered the action 'very satisfactory' (although three U-boats had been lost and two more seriously damaged).

The Admiralty had been expecting the Zaunkönig T-5 for some time. Now that it had appeared, some antidote had to be found. From knowledge of broadly similar acoustic torpedoes designed by the British, from POWs goaded or trapped into indiscreet remarks about the weapon's performance, and from a study of the torpedo's behaviour during attacks, a decoy was devised, called the 'Foxer'. It was basically two pieces of steel which clapped together, making a loud rattling noise when towed behind a ship.

The early Foxers were so loud (they could be heard clearly from inside a U-boat) they defeated the towing vessel's own Asdic operator, and they could not be towed above 15 knots, making them unpopular with escort commanders. But a later model introduced in February 1944 could be towed at 20 knots, which removed the most important disadvantage.

By that time it was clear that the Zaunkönig T-5 was not the war-winning weapon BdU had hoped. Reports of the GNAT attacks were studied in the Admiralty, and by Roberts and his staff at the Tactical School. It seemed there was a common factor: U-boats equipped with T-5s actually waited until they knew they had been detected, either by seeing the escort alter course towards, or by sighting star-shell above, or hearing a sudden increase in propeller revolutions on the hydrophones, before they dived. It was as though they wanted to beckon their enemy towards them and make sure he ran upon their weapon.

It was clear, too, that the T-5 had a maximum listening range and, very probably, was sensitive only in an arc to either side of perhaps 30 degrees (a correct guess, as it turned out). Furthermore, like all torpedoes, it would be fired ahead of its target. From such facts and assumptions Roberts devised the 'Step-Aside' technique.

The trick was to make a large alteration of course, of the right amount and at the right time, to evade the torpedo. On sighting or detecting a U-boat on one bow, the escort turned towards the U-boat and then swung past its bearing until the U-boat was broad on the *other* bow (an alteration of about 150 degrees), steam on this new course for about a mile, and then turn back towards the U-boat, which would be detected again in a predictable time. The GNAT meanwhile would still be heading towards the place the escort would have been on its original course.

Roberts was soon getting reports from sea that the Step-Aside was working – one more indication that the new U-boat offensive was not succeeding. As September passed into October, the inescapable conclusions were that convoy life was getting safer and safer, whilst the lot of the U-boats was growing ever harder.

The 'Rossbach' Group, of twenty-one U-boats, spread out on 27 September to await ON203. The B-Dienst Service was not now so sharp as it had been (the British Naval Cypher No. 3 had been changed), whilst the Shark traffic was being read regularly (although an exact appreciation of U-boat whereabouts for ON203 was not possible because BdU had recently introduced a system of special reference points to define U-boats' locations in their signals). But quite enough was known to divert ON203 safely to the north, and it duly passed quietly beyond the northern end of the U-boat patrol line on 28 September. So, too, did ONS19 a day later.

The next eastbound convoy HX258 was safely diverted south of the U-boat line. Once the convoy had passed on, its air escort went back to the position of the U-boat line and began a most successful offensive which lasted some three days (long enough, in fact, for another convoy ONS204 to pass safely). Several U-boats were attacked and three were badly damaged. An American Lockheed Ventura of VB128 sank U-336 on 3 October, a Liberator of 120 Squadron sank U-279 on the 4th, and a rocket-firing Hudson of 269 Squadron sank U-389 on the 5th.

On 6 October, the seventeen surviving 'Rossbach' boats moved south to look for HX259 and SC143, which had both been reported by the B-Dienst Service. SC143, of thirty-nine ships, six escorts and a MAC ship, left Halifax on 28 September. HX259, forty-eight ships with nine escorts, left New York the same day. Both convoys were routed north, until 4 October. The problem of where to route the convoys next, in the light of latest intelligence, required nice judgement.

It was not wise to allow both convoys to continue northward. Both could be routed well to the south. Or one could go north, and the other south. If both went south, and the U-boats also moved south, it was very possible that the SC would be sighted first and the much more important HX convoy soon after. There was then the risk of another débâcle, as had happened to HX229 and SC122, when the U-boats had attacked one convoy first and then moved on to the other.

It was decided to route the SC to the north, where it would almost certainly be sighted, but to reinforce its escort strongly. Meanwhile, the HX should have a clear passage to the south. In other words, for the first time in a convoy action, the Admiralty felt that its escort forces were strong enough to accept battle deliberately.

SC143 carried on to the north, whilst HX259 was diverted southward on the 6th. SC143 was heavily reinforced by the 10th Escort Group from HX259, the 3rd Escort Group, and the frigate *Duckworth* from ONS19. Preparations were also made to give the convoy maximum air cover.

While these arrangements were being made, SC143 had got itself into a muddle, when one of the Commodore's signals was misunderstood on the 6th. The convoy was not properly re-formed until about 3 p.m. on the 7th, by which time the first U-boats were in contact. By the evening eight U-boats were closing the convoy. But the escorts made numerous sweeps during the night, running down H/F D/F bearings, and attacking when they had the chance. The Polish destroyer *Orkan*, from 10th Escort Group, followed the H/F D/F bearing provided by the destroyer *Musketeer* and attacked U-758 at the end of it. A GNAT exploded in *Orkan*'s wake.

At one point, 10th Escort Group put on a splendid 'fire-work display', with star-shell, searchlights and depth-charges, some 35 miles astern of the convoy, which misled a number of U-boats. But shortly after 6 a.m. on the 8th, U-378, which had already been driven off once by aircraft, returned and sank *Orkan* with a GNAT.

Aircraft made mysteriously few U-boat sightings that day but they did not waste their chances. Liberators of 86 and 120 Squadrons and a Sunderland of 423 Squadron RCAF sank U-419, U-643, and U-610, and damaged U-762. Later, there appeared a large German flying boat, one of the six-engined Blohm & Voss BV.222s, used for the first time in the Atlantic. It sighted SC143 and broadcast homing signals but no U-boat picked them up. U-91 did close the convoy that evening and fired a T-5 at a destroyer, which missed.

SC143 had another unexpected visitor: a Leigh-light Wellington which stayed with the convoy after dark, for the first time ever. But after the aircraft had left, towards morning, U-645 came upon a scattered group of ships and sank the merchant ship *Yorkman* – the convoy's only casualty. Later that day, a disappointed BdU called off the operation. Two convoys had crossed over, for the loss of one 5612-ton ship and one escort. Three U-boats had been sunk and others damaged. The Admiralty's decision to accept battle had been amply justified. It certainly made a very welcome change.

Though disappointed, BdU was undeterred for the time being. Ten days later the 'Schlieffen' Group of twelve U-boats was formed after convoy ON206 was reported by U-844, on the evening of 15 October. ONS20 was sighted by U-964 early the next day. ON206, of sixty-five ships, was escorted by B6 Group, under Cdr Currie in the destroyer *Fame*, with *Vanquisher* and the Norwegian corvettes *Rose* and *Potentilla*; it was reinforced on 13 October by *Duncan*, *Vidette*, *Sunflower*, *Loosestrife* and *Pink* of Cdr Gretton's B7 Group, this time acting in the role of support group. ONS20 (fifty-two ships) was escorted by the 4th Escort Group, led by Cdr Paramor in the destroyer *Bentinck*, with four more destroyers, *Byard*, *Berry*, *Drury* and *Bazely*.

Both convoys had very strong air escort, which proved decisive. The five-day battle opened when U-844 was driven off by *Duncan* and *Vanquisher* on the 15th. BdU had ordered U-boats to fight their way through to the convoys on the surface. They shot down one Liberator and badly damaged a second but paid a terrible price: Liberators of 59, 86 and 120 Squadrons, shared U-844, U-964 and U-470 between them, all on the 16th. One U-boat, U-426, closed the convoy that evening and sank *Essex Lance*.

There were several attempts to attack ON206 during the night of the 16th–17th, but *Duncan* and *Vidette* frustrated them all, and during the evening of the 17th two Liberators of 59 Squadron sank U-540 some way to the north of the convoy. By then, B7's ships were on their way to support ONS20, which was about 150 miles to the north-east of ON206. It was *Sunflower* (*Snowflake* was re-fitting) which got a radar contact at 3500 yards. The U-boat, U-631, dived but *Sunflower* got an Asdic contact almost at once and made two model attacks with depth-charges. The first blew U-631 to the surface, the second sank it.

Two U-boats had reported ONS20 during the day, but the 'Schlieffen' boats all complained they could make little headway against such strong air escort. One Sunderland of 423 Squadron RCAF was shot down, but at least two U-boats, U-448 and U-281, suffered several casualties amongst their gun-crews from aircraft gunfire. In one final flurry of action on the 17th, U-608 was depth-charged, and U-841 was sunk by *Byard*. BdU, once again disappointed, called off the U-boats on the 18th.

By mid October 1943 the convoy statistics were showing how formidably well convoys were being defended. Convoy after convoy was crossing the Atlantic without loss, whilst U-boats were being sunk around them by surface or air escorts, or by a combination of both. QN207, ONS21, HX263 and ON208 were completely untouched, although BdU had deployed a new 'Siegfried' Group of twenty-one fresh U-boats. ON207 had air cover from Iceland and from the escort carrier *Tracker*, sailing with the convoy; surface escort was C1 Group as close escort, with B7 Group in support and Captain Walker's 2nd Escort Group in the deep field.

Against this defence in depth, the U-boats were picked off one by one. A Liberator of 224 Squadron with *Duncan* and *Vidette* shared U-274 on 23 October. A Sunderland of 10 Squadron RCAF sank U-420 on the 26th. *Duncan, Vidette* and *Sunflower* jointly sank U-282 with Hedgehogs on the 28th. From the beginning of September until the end of October 1943, no less than 2468 merchant ships had sailed in sixty-four north Atlantic convoys. Only nine ships from those convoys were sunk. In the same period, surface ships had sunk five U-boats, aircraft operating around the convoys had sunk thirteen, and American carrier aircraft had sunk another six – twenty-five U-boats in all. It was another defeat for the U-boats, the second of the year. Like the first, it had taken place around the convoys.

What these hard-won victories involved for the ships concerned is well illustrated by the experience of B7 which had sailed from Londonderry to support ON206 in 12 October. By the time the Group steamed back up the Foyle on 5 November feeling, as Gretton said 'very pleased with itself', *Duncan* had been at sea for twenty-five days continuously, had steamed 6700 miles and had crossed the Atlantic five times: 'The track chart of our wanderings resembled the antics of a fly drying after a dip in a bottle of ink.' B7 Group had supported convoys ON206, ONS20, ON207, ON208 and HX263. It had sunk three U-boats and had not lost a ship whilst in company. *Duncan* had refuelled at sea six times and had also replenished stocks of depth-charges at sea.

Towards the end of October BdU began to comment upon air patrols apparently being flown from the Azores. These were the fruit of two years of negotiations between the British and Portugese governments. Portugal was Britain's oldest ally, but as long as the Germans seemed to be winning the war its dictator Dr Salazar had been afraid of provoking Hitler. He was also reluctant to allow American forces to land on the islands, and American insistence very nearly scuppered the negotiations. However, an agreement was signed on 18 August 1943, allowing the British to operate air bases on Fayal and Terceira in exchange for war materials and a guarantee against German retaliation.

The agreement came into effect on 8 October, and an expedition consisting of the escort carrier *Fencer* and escorting ships, with merchant ships, oilers and store-ships, arrived that day. The first Fortresses flew on to the islands on the 18th and began operations the following day. This filled in the last of the air 'gaps' (but only after four years of war) and meant that air cover could now be given to the whole Atlantic north of 30° N.

The opening of the Azores bases was particularly well-timed. After the setbacks in the Atlantic in September and October BdU moved the U-boats south to operate against the convoys running between the UK and Gibraltar and Sierra Leone. The convoy actions which followed had some new features, the most important being the quite astounding degree of coopera-tion belatedly given by the Luftwaffe who flew reconnaissance patrols, provided homing reports and, on one occasion, attacked a convoy with long-range Heinkel He.177 bombers armed with HS293 glider-bombs.

That occasion was a fierce battle around the northbound convoy SL139/ MKS30 between 18 and 21 November. BdU set up three lines, Schill 1, 2 and 3, with twenty-six U-boats to wait for the sixty-six-ship convoy, placing them in positions off the Portuguese coast indicated by Luftwaffe reports. But the methods of convoy defence which had been so effective in the north Atlantic worked just as well here. The convoy had a well-drilled close escort, the 40th Escort Group of seven ships, reinforced later by five ships of the 7th Escort Group, two more destroyers, and the 5th Escort Group of seven ships. Overhead flew Hudsons, Catalinas and Fortresses by day, and Leigh-light Wellingtons by night. Timely special intelligence had the convoy diverted to the westward.

Three U-boats were sunk, and one damaged. The convoy lost one straggler sunk and a second ship damaged. One Liberator and one Sunderland were shot down by U-boats. The convoy's anti-aircraft defences, greatly strengthened by the Canadian anti-aircraft ship *Prince Rupert*, who joined on the 21st, shot down three He.177s. But the sloop *Chanticleer* had her stern blown off by a GNAT

There was one revealing sequel. The operations around the convoy left Coastal Command short of Liberators. When an American Liberator squadron under Coastal control was asked for help, the squadron commander replied that his duty was 'an offensive mission against submarines'. What he called 'routine coverage of Gibraltar convoys' was a matter for Admiral King to decide. The old notion that convoys were 'defensive' seemed indestructible.

More convoy battles on the UK to Gibraltar route by the end of the year showed that the U-boats were being defeated again, and by the same well-tried tactics of convoy and escort. This was their third defeat of 1943 and, like the first two, it was won around and over the convoys.

As the Atlantic escorts were just about to gain their second victory of 1943 over the U-boats, there was another major turn towards the Allies in the Mediterranean. Italy was knocked out of the war, and Admiral Sir Andrew Cunningham, the C-in-C Mediterranean, was able to signal the Admiralty on 11 September, 'Be pleased to inform Their Lordships that the Italian battle fleet now lies at anchor under the guns of the fortress of Malta.' However, this did not mean that the war at sea in the Mediterranean was over. Convoy continued until September 1944.

But convoy had its own special flavour in the Mediterranean. There was never any debate over convoy, any question of independent routeing. Convoy was a fact of operational life in those waters, as it had been in Nelson's day. By Atlantic standards, the convoys were minute, but the size of their escorts was such as to make any Atlantic escort commander stare. There was no regular convoy cycle in the Atlantic sense. Both sides gathered together the ships they wanted to convoy, and the largest escort they could provide, and calculated the best moment to dispatch them.

Mediterranean convoys were always likely to lead to major fleet actions. The very first encounter between the Italian battle-fleet and the Mediterranean Fleet, off the Calabrian coast in July 1940, came about when the Italian navy was convoying troops to Benghazi while Cunningham's ships were covering two convoys, carrying civilian families, and the wives and children of servicemen, from Malta to Alexandria.

That action was inconclusive, as was the next, late in August, when the Mediterranean Fleet was again covering a convoy, this time to Malta. The Italian battle-fleet, which out-gunned and out-numbered Cunningham's ships, came within 90 miles, but a certain tactical timidity, strategic caution, and lack of air reconnaissance, caused the Italian Admiral to turn away and to lose a great opportunity.

Malta was the key to the Mediterranean campaign, not so much as a base for the heavy ships of the fleet (which, in any case, it soon ceased to be) but as the launching point for aircraft and submarines to attack Axis convoys. The main convoy routes of the two sides ran at right angles. The British ran ships to and from Gibraltar and Alexandria, through Malta, east and west. The Axis ran troop convoys, north and south, between Italy and north Africa. The nodal crossing-point was Malta.

Thus, while the Axis strove to neutralize Malta by sea and air, the Allies sought to keep Malta supplied, whilst lacking air cover in the central Mediterranean basin. Malta's fortunes and the progress of the land campaigns in North Africa were closely linked. If Malta had enough air and sea power to disrupt Axis supply convoys, then the Allied forces on land prospered and Malta's own situation became more secure. Conversely, if Malta lacked the capacity to interrupt Axis supplies, then the Allies were forced back on land, and Malta's position became even more dangerous.

Whenever possible, the occasion of a Malta convoy was used to pass reinforcements for the Mediterranean fleet from west to east. Some idea of the numbers of warships involved and the complex nature of the various interlocking operations necessary is given by Operation EXCESS, which took place in January 1941. The convoy MC4, of one 4000-ton ammunition ship, one 3000-ton ship carrying seed potatoes (equally vital for Malta's well-being) and twelve Hurricanes, and three ships destined for Piraeus sailed from Gibraltar, escorted by a cruiser and four destroyers. Cover as far as the Sicilian Channel was provided by Admiral Sir James Somerville's Force H (a task force formed to fill the naval vacuum in the western Mediterranean created by the capitulation of France), and including on this occasion the battleship *Malaya* and the battle cruiser *Renown*, the carrier *Ark Royal*, the cruiser *Sheffield*, and five destroyers. These all sailed on 7 January from Gibraltar.

Another force, of the cruisers *Gloucester* and *Southampton* with 500 troops for Malta embarked, and two destroyers, sailed from the Aegean to meet the convoy. Admiral Cunningham's main fleet, the battleships *Warspite* and *Valiant*, the carrier *Illustrious*, and eight destroyers sailed from Alexandria to cover the operations. The cruisers *Orion* and *Sydney*, with a tanker and four corvettes, formed another force which sailed from Suda Bay in Crete. Finally, a convoy of two merchant ships, convoy MW5½, set out from Alexandria escorted by the anti-aircraft cruiser *Calcutta* and two destroyers, bound for Malta.

The ships were opposed by the Luftwaffe's Fliegerkorps X, a crack anti-shipping unit, which had recently arrived in the Mediterranean to bolster the weak (in German eyes) high-level bombing of the Italian Air Force. The ships eventually reached Malta, but at the cost of *Illustrious* so badly damaged by dive-bombers she had eventually to sail to America for repairs; *Southampton* bombed and abandoned; and the gallant destroyer *Gallant* mined. The Italian torpedo-boat *Vega* was sunk by gunfire from the cruiser *Bonaventure*.

The presence of Fliegerkorps X, and the absence of *Illustrious* and, later, of her sister ship *Formidable* (also dive-bombed, damaged and withdrawn in March), meant there were no more Malta convoys until the SUBSTANCE operation in July. Six merchant ships were escorted from Gibraltar to Malta by Force H, of *Renown*, *Ark Royal*, the cruiser *Hermione*, and eight destroyers, backed up by the battleship *Nelson*, the cruisers *Arethusa*, *Edinburgh* and *Manchester*, the fast minelayer *Manxman*, and another eight destroyers, all from the Home Fleet. Meanwhile, the whole Mediterranean Fleet put to sea for diversionary operations from Alexandria. One ship was torpedoed by Italian aircraft but survived and all six eventually arrived in Malta. But *Manchester* was torpedoed, the destroyer *Fearless* sunk and *Firedrake* bombed.

In September another major operation took HALBERD of nine ships to Malta, escorted by the battleships *Prince of Wales* and *Rodney*, four cruisers, and twelve destroyers. The covering group was again Force H, with *Nelson*, *Ark Royal*, *Hermione* and six destroyers. The Italians put to sea, with two battleships, three heavy cruisers, two light cruisers and fourteen destroyers. Not for the first time, the presence of *Ark Royal*'s aircraft preyed on Italian minds and no fleet action took place. One ship was lost to Italian torpedo aircraft off the Tunisian coast near Cape Bon on 27 September, and *Nelson* was hit right on her stem by a torpedo travelling on an exactly opposite course.

The contrast between Atlantic and Mediterranean convoys was most clearly shown in what was later called the first Battle of Sirte in December 1941. At this stage of the war, when north Atlantic convoys of twenty or thirty ships were entrusted to a handful of corvettes and converted fishing trawlers, the single transport *Breconshire* left Alexandria on the 15th, carrying oil fuel for Malta. She had a close escort of two cruisers *Naiad* and *Euryalus*, under Rear Admiral Vian, the anti-aircraft cruiser *Carlisle*, and eight destroyers, to be reinforced on passage by the cruisers *Aurora* and *Penelope*, and two destroyers, four more destroyers under Captain Stokes, and later the cruiser *Neptune* and two destroyers: a total of six cruisers and sixteen destroyers. At the same time the Italians were passing convoy M42 of three ships to Tripoli, escorted by five destroyers, and a fourth ship escorted by a destroyer and a torpedo-boat. The convoy had a close covering force of a battleship, three cruisers and three destroyers. A distant covering force, with three battleships, two heavy cruisers, and ten destroyers was also at sea.

The two sides brushed just before dusk on 17 December. The Italians cautiously retreated on the threat of torpedo attack. Vian's ships survived some twenty air attacks during the day, and *Breconshire* safely reached Malta. But *Neptune* was lost in a minefield off Tripoli (there was only one survivor), *Aurora* was badly damaged, *Penelope* slightly damaged. The destroyer *Kandahar* had her stern blown off and eventually had to be sunk.

A second Battle of Sirte took place on 22 March 1942 around the Malta convoy MW10 of four ships, with a close escort of *Carlisle* and six destroyers, and a covering force of four cruisers and six destroyers, under Rear Admiral Vian. Brilliantly led by Vian, with judicious use of smokescreen, advancing as though to threaten, then retreating as though towards a trap, the covering force baffled and fought off two vastly superior Italian forces which included a battleship and three cruisers. Two destroyers were slightly damaged, the cruiser *Cleopatra* hit by one 15-inch shell, and other ships suffered slight splinter damage. The convoy survived unscathed but, as Captain E. W. Bush, commanding *Euryalus*, later wrote, 'had the roles been reversed it is difficult to imagine that anything of either convoy or escort would have survived.'

However, in the end only about a quarter of that convoy's cargo was safely discharged. Two of the ships were sunk before reaching Malta and the remaining two were bombed in port. By midsummer 1942 the situation of the people and garrison of Malta was desperate. In June two more convoys were sailed, HARPOON of six merchant ships from the west, and VIGOROUS of eleven from the east. Both convoys were fiercely attacked: VIGOROUS was threatened, as Vian described it, 'with all known forms of surface attack', including the battleships *Vittoria Veneto* and *Littorio*, and had to turn back to Alexandria. From the two convoys, only two HARPOON ships reached Malta, the cost of the two operations being the cruiser *Hermione*, the destroyers *Bedouin*, *Hasty*, *Airedale*, the Australian *Nestor* and the Polish *Kujawiak*, two minesweepers, and six merchant ships.

The War Cabinet now decided that these attempts to relieve Malta were simply draining away Allied strength without materially helping the island. A relief convoy for Malta had to be given priority over every other naval commitment. On 10 August 1942 the PEDESTAL convoy, of fourteen merchant ships including the tanker *Ohio*, steamed through the Straits of Gibraltar to begin one of the most spectacular naval actions of the whole war.

The covering force, under Vice-Admiral Sir Neville Syfret, had two battleships *Nelson* and *Rodney*, three aircraft carriers, *Victorious*, *Indomitable* and *Eagle*, with a fourth, *Furious*, carrying Spitfires for Malta, seven cruisers, and thirty-two destroyers.

The enemy knew of the convoy the moment it appeared in the Mediterranean. U-73, one of a line of U-boats deployed in its path, closed *Eagle* at about noon on the 11th and hit her with every torpedo of a salvo of four. She sank in some seven minutes with some 200 of her crew lost.

The nearer the convoy came to Sardinia, and to Malta, the more certain it was of being attacked from the air. The first attack of about thirty-five Junker Ju.88s took place that evening. It was repulsed by fighters from the fleet. A much more serious and sustained attack began at noon on the 12th. Over 100 aircraft – Ju.88s, Me.110 fighters, Savoia SM.79 bombers, Caproni fighter-bombers – took part over a period of two hours. None of them, nor an attack by torpedo-carrying SM.79s, achieved anything, but the merchantman *Deucalion* was later hit by Stuka dive-bombers and had to be sunk.

That evening the Italian U-boat *Cobalto* was depth-charged, forced to surface, rammed and sunk by the destroyer *Ithuriel*, but the Luftwaffe flying from bases in Sicily retaliated by sinking the destroyer *Foresight* and damaging *Indomitable* so badly her remaining aircraft had to be transferred to *Victorious*. At dusk the convoy was attacked by the Italian U-boats *Dessie* and *Axum*. It was *Axum* which fired a prodigious salvo, one of the most successful of the war, which hit three ships: the cruiser *Nigeria*, forcing her to return to Gibraltar; the anti-aircraft cruiser *Cairo*, causing her to be sunk; and the tanker *Ohio*, which caught fire but steamed on.

The capital ships had turned back as arranged when the convoy neared the Sicilian Narrows, leaving command of the convoy to Rear Admiral Burroughs in *Nigeria*. He now had to shift his flag to the destroyer *Ashanti*. As he was doing so, the convoy was attacked again by some eighty bombers, which sank two merchantmen and damaged a third. With the convoy in a state of confusion, the night sky lit by flashes, explosions and tracers and ships steering in all directions to avoid bombs, or torpedoes, or their next ahead, the U-boat *Alagi* compounded the chaos by putting a torpedo into the cruiser *Kenya*.

Rounding Cape Bon at about midnight, and still trying to restore itself to some kind of order, the convoy was attacked by German and Italian E-boats, lying in wait close inshore. Four merchantmen were sunk and the cruiser *Manchester* disabled and then scuttled (prematurely, a later court-martial decided).

From dawn on 13 August the bombing attacks increased. The ammunition ship *Wainamarama* disappeared in a gigantic sheet of flame, leaving a few survivors swimming in the sea. *Ohio* was damaged twice more. Another merchantman was sunk, and only three survivors reached Malta that evening. *Brisbane Star*, damaged in an air attack two days earlier, struggled in on the 14th. But the greatest prize was *Ohio*, with her 10,000 tons of priceless petrol and kerosene. She was towed in to Grand Harbour amid scenes of wild rejoicing on the 15th.

PEDESTAL had cost an aircraft carrier, two cruisers, a destroyer and nine merchant ships sunk; a second aircraft carrier, two cruisers and three merchantmen were damaged. Two U-boats were sunk and about forty Axis aircraft destroyed. However, Malta had only been reprieved, not relieved. Another convoy, STONEAGE, sailed in November 1942 from Port Said, unnoticed and now almost totally forgotten, although the cruiser *Arethusa* was badly damaged by aircraft and had to be towed through a gale to Alexandria. Not until convoy PORTCULLIS arrived in December 1942 was Malta finally relieved.

While Malta remained unconquered, every Axis convoy operation in the Mediterranean had to take notice of it. Except for a period in the spring of 1942, when constant bombing, coupled with the loss of several surface warships in previous months, reduced the island to comparative helplessness, Malta was like a constant lance in the Axis side. The failure to assault and capture Malta, when it was perfectly feasible to do so, was one of the Axis's greatest strategic errors of the war.

From Malta – as long as the island had the necessary resources – bombers and torpedo-bombers, surface warships and submarines sallied out to harry Axis convoys. The greatest disaster ever to befall an Italian convoy happened on the night of 8–9 November 1941. Assisted by Ultra, the cruisers *Aurora* and *Penelope* and the destroyers *Lance* and *Lively* (known collectively as Force K) intercepted a convoy of seven large store ships and tankers bound for north Africa and sank them all in a wild gunnery melée in the darkness. An escorting destroyer was also sunk by gunfire, and the submarine *Upholder* sank another.

Conversely, when the Axis did get a convoy across it had an immediate effect upon the land campaign. One large convoy, whose close escort included one battleship, with three more as distant cover, arrived unmolested in Tripoli on 5 January 1942. A second followed on the 22nd, when RAF Beauforts and a Swordfish together torpedoed the 13,000-ton liner *Victoria*; but another four large transports arrived in Tripoli on the 24th.

Rommel launched a careful attack, designed more to prevent the British advance. But somewhat to his surprise, his attack was a shattering success and the Eighth Army was rolled back past Benghazi to Gazala in very short order and remained there until May.

For Allied submarines, mines were the biggest danger in the shallow and restricted waters of the Mediterranean. Neither the Luftwaffe nor the Regia Aeronautica had any air arm which even remotely compared with Coastal Command, and aircraft were not in general a threat (although they did bomb and sink submarines alongside in Malta).

But British submarine captains, like the Atlantic U-boat commanders, found that an attack upon a defended convoy was their most dangerous undertaking. Lt Cdr Wanklyn, of *Upholder*, was one of the most daring and successful submarine commanders, but it was one particular exploit, an attack upon a convoy of four troopers bound for Libya in May 1941, which was picked out for his Victoria Cross. The Italian destroyer *Circe* was as fatal to Allied submarines as her name-sake had been to Ulysses and his men; she sank four submarines, under three different captains. *Union*, *Tempest*, *P.38*, *Utmost*, *P. 222*, *P.48*, *Tigris*, *Turbulent* and *Thunderbolt*, as well as *Upholder*, were among the British submarines all lost whilst attacking Axis convoys.

The Mediterranean convoys, for all their dramatic intensity and spectacular action, confirmed some old convoy principles. When all convoys are considered, not just those to and from Malta, but to and from the Aegean, and along the north African coast, the percentage of losses was high, at nearly three times the Atlantic convoy rate. But in general the convoys were only one-third the average Atlantic size.

In the footnotes to Mediterranean convoy history, one old fallacy was again exposed. On 20 March 1942, when the convoy and escort which was to lead to the second Battle of Sirte sailed from Alexandria, six *Hunt* class destroyers also sailed on a submarine-hunting expedition along the coast towards Tobruk. They were, in fact, a 'hunter–killer' group. They sank no U-boats, and U-652 sank *Heythrop* north of Bardia.

As late as December 1943, when the Admiralty was growing restless about the delays to be expected if convoy were introduced on all the routes in the Indian Ocean, where there was a chronic shortage of escorts, they recommended that what they considered 'relatively modest and local risks' should be accepted and convoys only run on routes 'actually or potentially threatened'. Escorts released from convoy should act 'as hunting groups in areas of known probability' of U-boat attack – in other words, as 'hunter –killer' groups. Unsurprisingly, eight independents were sunk in the Indian Ocean in January 1944, the highest tonnage loss in any theatre of the war for that month. Convoy was reintroduced in February on those routes where, to comply with the Admiralty's suggestion, it had been suspended. But in the meantime another ten independents were sunk.

The principle of convoy was most emphatically underlined in the Arctic, where convoys proved a triumph of sound tactics over an unsound strategy. For, whatever the political and moral justifications for the Allies to send supplies to Russia by sea round the North Cape after, in A. P. Herbert's words, Hitler 'leaped upon his largest friend' in June 1941, as naval undertakings the Arctic convoys were always basically unsound.

The merchant ships and their escorts had to make their ways to and from north Russian ports along a route often restricted by ice, and always within reach of enemy air, surface-ship and U-boat bases, where Allied heavy covering forces were unable to protect them. To the dangers of the enemy and the appalling violence of the Arctic weather were added the hostility of a suspicious and ungrateful ally.

Yet, in spite of their grim reputation, the Arctic convoys were in fact some of the safest of all. Convoy in the Arctic saved a great many ships which would have been sunk. From the first trial DERVISH convoy which sailed from Hvalfjord to Archangel in August 1941 until the last RA67 arrived in the Clyde on 31 May 1945, forty-two convoys sailed eastward to Russia, and thirty-six returned. Outward-bound, 813 ships sailed, of which thirty-three returned prematurely because of the weather, ice, or some other reason, and fifty-eight were sunk by U-boats, aircraft or surface-ship action. Homeward-bound, 717 ships sailed, eight returned prematurely, and twenty-six were lost to enemy action.

Of the fifty-eight outward ships lost, forty-three were from three convoys, PQ16, PQ17 and PQ18, which sailed in the perpetual daylight of the summer of 1942. Twenty-three were from PQ17, which actually lost only two ships whilst it was still a convoy before it was ordered to scatter. After the convoy had dispersed, the remnants formed small 'rump' convoys with whatever trawlers and corvettes of the escort were nearest. All but two of the thirteen ships in these 'rump' convoys reached harbour safely. The twenty-one remaining ships which proceeded independently had a melancholy fate: of these, nineteen were lost. Thus, the great majority of PQ17's casualties were not in convoy at all when they were lost.

Of the homeward-bound convoys, the greatest loss was suffered by QP13 (the convoys were lettered PQ out, after Cdr P. Q. Roberts RN in the Admiralty Trade Section, and QP homeward) in July 1942, when a navigational error led the convoy over a British minefield. Five ships and the minesweeper *Niger* were sunk.

After PQ18, Arctic convoys were suspended for a period. When they resumed they were lettered JW out and RA homeward. They were suspended again in the summer of 1943, but when they resumed, with an escort carrier normally included with each convoy, losses dropped away almost to nothing. Convoy after convoy crossed without loss. From the entire JW series of twenty-two convoys, from December 1942 until May 1945, five ships in all were lost. From the RA series, of twenty-one convoys over the same period, ten ships were lost by enemy action and one foundered.

The cost to the U-boats was very high: thirty-two were sunk in Arctic-convoy operations, a ratio not far from one U-boat for each of the thirty-nine merchant ships they sank. Of many achievements, the most astounding was by the escort carrier *Fencer*, whose Swordfish sank three U-boats in two days while defending RA59 in May 1944.

There were many outstandingly brave exploits by the convoy escorts. On New Year's Eve 1942, Convoy JW51B was threatened by the German heavy cruiser *Hipper*, the pocket battleship *Lutzow*, and six German destroyers. The convoy was defended by five destroyers, led by Captain Sherbrooke in

Onslow, and by all the theories of naval warfare should have been massacred. Sherbrooke himself lost an eye but won a Victoria Cross, and the convoy escaped unscathed. Of the fourteen merchant ships so ably defended, nine were American (a fact not stressed, or even mentioned, by Admiral King at the Washington convoy conference three months later). The destroyer *Achates* and the minesweeper *Bramble* were sunk, two of the eighteen British warships lost while escorting the Arctic convoys.

The Germans were slow to realize the effect of the supplies these convoys were delivering had on the Eastern Front; only one merchantman was lost from the first fourteen outward convoys. Much less excusably, after the war, the Soviet Union strongly disparaged the convoys, dismissing them as having had little or no effect upon the outcome of the war on land. Indeed, if the post war Russian 'statistics' of war-time production of tanks, aircraft and guns are to be believed, then the Soviet Union should in all equity have been sending convoys across the Arctic to the United Kingdom. In fact, about 4 million tons of cargo were delivered to Russian ports, including over 7000 aircraft, 5000 tanks, and huge quantities of other armaments and ammunition.

The great successes of the escorts around the convoys of 1943 gave rise to complacency, and some politicians persuaded themselves that the battle was won. This was very far from being the case. The U-boats remained aggressive and dangerous to the bitter end. U-2336 actually sank two ships off May Island in the Firth of Forth on the very last night of the war in Europe.

U-2336 was a Type XXIII U-boat, one of a new and small (230-ton) coastal class, with a crew of fourteen and two torpedo tubes. They were prefabricated, for speed and simplicity of building, and were stripped of everything but essentials. They were very difficult to catch (U-2336 actually got away undetected and returned to Kiel), and were only one of a number of new designs the Germans were developing.

In the final few months of the war, German production and German technical invention were still both increasing. In spite of all the bombing of factories and bases, U-boat production was higher in November 1944 than in any other month of the whole war. Few of the several new types of U-boats saw operations because, fortunately for the Allies, the war ended in time.

Amongst them were the large Atlantic Type XXI U-boats, of 1600 tons, with twenty torpedoes, a crew of fifty-seven, a range of over 15,000 miles, and a top submerged speed on trebly-enlarged batteries of over 17 knots (albeit for only an hour). U-boats with closed cycle diesel engines used compressed oxygen in bottles for combustion. In U-boats with Walter engines, hydrogen peroxide provided the oxygen in which kerosene was burned, and the resulting gas and steam (from the decomposition of the hydrogen peroxide) was passed through a turbine. The Walter boats were capable of very high underwater speeds of over 20 knots for very short periods.

New weapons included: the LUT (*Lageunabhangigertorpedo*) which could be pre-set before firing to follow a calculated course, independent of the target's true bearing at the time of firing; the Fa330 *Bachstelze* (Wagtail) rotary-wing kite, stored in two water-tight compartments on the upper decks of Type XI U-boats, which could take an observer up to 500 feet, useful in the Indian Ocean and south Atlantic, where ships were still routed independently; and 'Aphrodite' balloons, which released clouds of anti-radar metal foil when they reached height.

The device which had the most radical effect on the submarine campaign was the Schnorkel, a pre-war Dutch invention which the Germans developed and refined before they brought it into service early in 1944. It was in essence a breathing tube, made so that a U-boat could run its diesel engines whilst at or near periscope depth. A float valve prevented water entering the tube if the submarine lost depth. The engines exhausted up a subsidiary tube or against the back-pressure of the sea. The head of a Schnorkel tube made, of course, a very much smaller visual and radar target than a submarine's hull or conning tower. Though greatly restricting their mobility under diesel power, the Schnorkel enabled U-boats to penetrate areas under air and surface ship cover which would have been otherwise highly dangerous. Schnorkel-fitted U-boats achieved several successes, especially in waters around the United Kingdom, and it is fair to say that anti-submarine techniques had not fully come to grips with the Schnorkel-fitted U-boat by the end of the war.

Yet, in spite of these various devices and the massive building programme – there were forty-five U-boats at sea in the Atlantic when the war ended, twelve type XXIs ready for operations, and another *ninety-one* U-boats doing acceptance trials or training – it was still true to say that the battle against the U-boats *had* been won. They remained dangerous to the last, but they were never again the great strategic menace they had been in 1943.

Meanwhile, the convoys grew larger and safer, with almost continuous air cover and vastly increased numbers of escorts. There were eight support groups available for the Western Approaches in February 1944 and no less than twenty-one by November. The most successful remained Captain Walker's 2nd Escort Group who, in one patrol of twenty-seven days in January and February 1944, sank six U-boats, three of them within seventeen hours in support of SL147/MKS38, for the loss of *Woodpecker*, torpedoed by U-764. She finally capsized and sank off the Scillies after seven days in tow on 29 February.

One of the group's victims, on 19 February, was U-264, the first Schnorkel-fitted U-boat. Another was U-842, destroyed by a 'creeping attack', a tactic devised and perfected by Walker's group in 1943 for dealing with U-boats which had gone very deep. The escort in contact became the 'directing' ship and steered to point at the target and about 1000 yards astern of it. Behind her, and on one quarter, was the 'attacking ship'. Whilst the directing ship stayed in contact, steadily tapping away with her Asdic, the attacking ship waited for the signal. At some point the U-boat would be steering dead away from the directing ship. The attacking ship would overtake the directing ship, who would 'hand her' the target, and steam quietly ahead along the U-boat's track.

Conned by the directing ship, who was in an ideal position to detect any lateral evasion by the U-boat, the attacking ship would reach a distance ahead of the U-boat equal to the distance the U-boat would travel whilst the depth-charges were sinking through the water. Guided by a R/T message from the directing ship and from her own plot, the attacking ship would fire twenty-six depth charges in pairs, set to explode at 500 feet and 740 feet alternately, at ten-second intervals, whilst continuing to steam ahead of the U-boat.

The U-boat, meanwhile, could hear the directing ship's Asdic, but not the sound of the attacking ship, and would steer onwards, unsuspectingly, into a curtain of depth-charges. It was an extremely effective method against deep U-boats. A marker was often dropped with the tenth depth-charge. In one early 'creeping' attack on 24 June 1943, in the Bay of Biscay, a marker from *Wren* was found in the middle of the wreckage and human debris from U-449.

Allah, it is said, does not count against a man's life the time he spends hunting. Perhaps Allah did not include U-boats, for on 9 July 1944 Captain Walker died suddenly of a stroke brought on by heavy strain and overwork. Walker's biblically flavoured signals, his pungently written and vividly expressive reports, and above all his leadership in battle, passed into naval history. Admiral Sir Max Horton read his epitaph at his funeral service in Liverpool Cathedral, the 'parish church' of the Western Approaches: '. . . not dust nor the light weight of a stone, but all the sea of the Western Approaches shall be his tomb. His spirit returns unto God who gave it.' Captain Walker's body was buried at sea from the destroyer *Hesperus*. By chance two huge convoys were assembling in the Mersey at the time. Their crews, who knew very well what Walker had done for them, stood bareheaded and silent as *Hesperus*, with colours at half-mast, steamed past them on her way to sea.

In March 1944 the U-boats virtually abandoned all pack attacks, and contacts became extremely rare. The support groups had only six in the month, but sank them all. U-boat hunts were becoming much more protracted. On 29 February, the frigate *Gore, Garlies, Affleck* and *Gould* of the 1st Escort Group attacked U-358 with depth-charges and Hedgehogs. They held contact virtually continuously the next day, 1 March, but although they made one 'creeping attack' of 104 depth-charges which detonated like 'a marine convulsion', their enemy lay very deep, and very low, and stubborn. At last, the U-boat decided that evening to come up and fight it out. It actually hit and sank *Gould* with a GNAT, but then surfaced and was finished off with depth-charges and gunfire. The action had lasted thirty-eight hours, the longest continuous U-boat hunt of the war.

The U-boats slackened their activities in the Atlantic at a very fortunate time for the Allies, because many of the escorts were required to play their parts in the Invasion of Europe for which Western Approaches provided 162 ships of the British, Canadian, French, Norwegian, Belgian and Greek navies, including sixteen destroyers, fourteen sloops, forty-one frigates, seventy-one corvettes and twenty trawlers.

To provide these ships, the ONS and SC convoy cycles were discontinued, with the ONs and HXs on an alternate 7- and 8-day cycle, but sailing as fast (10 knots), medium (9 knots), or slow (8 knots). Convoy sizes increased. ON(S)233 sailed from Liverpool on 20 April 1944 with III ships, the first convoy to exceed the 'ton'. On 17 July HX(S)300, the largest convoy of the war, sailed from New York with 187 ships. The escort for this 'monster' was C5 Group, of a frigate and six corvettes. The convoy also included four MAC ships, eleven escort oilers and a rescue ship.

HX(S)300's route was arranged so as to avoid alterations of course. To relieve the task of the Commodore, Sir A. J. Tillard, as much as possible, eighty-eight ships for Loch Ewe and Oban were detached at 21° W, escorted by three corvettes. Another fast section of fourteen ships also left early, in the charge of one corvette. The convoy, with over a million tons of cargo, arrived without loss at an average speed of 7¾ knots – very good for a convoy open to ships of 8 knots. The average size of six consecutive HX convoys at this time was 119, and it was as well that the Atlantic was so quiescent.

The last enemy aircraft to threaten a trade convoy in the Atlantic approached SL165 on 7 August 1944, but nothing happened. As the time went by and it was realized that the danger from aircraft was past, the escort carriers were taken off the Atlantic routes, the last of them arriving in the Clyde with SL167, and used instead on the Russian convoys.

There were all manner of welcome developments that autumn. OS and SL convoys were routed south-about via the Cornish coast, instead of around the north of Ireland. This took four days off their journey time. The escort strength was reduced, first to one group of a sloop and two corvettes, and later to a single 'sheepdog' escort. But of course, every convoy escort was immediately reinforced at the least sign of danger, and while passing through known danger areas.

As the escorts engaged in the invasion of Europe returned to their 'proper' duties, ONSs and SCs were again run on a fifteen-day cycle. ONs and HXs reverted to 10-knot convoys sailing every five days, the first being ON256 from Liverpool on 28 September. By then, the swept channels south of Ireland had been widened, and HX306 was the first convoy since 1940 to be routed south of Ireland, dispersing off the Fastnet Rock on 15 September. The wheel had come full circle and after four years there were Channel convoys again.

Although the weather was particularly bad as the winter of 1944 came on, the main danger to convoys was indiscipline. Convoy after convoy was crossing without any attacks and merchant-ship masters became slap-dash about convoy discipline. It had to be impressed on them that the U-boat war was not over. As though to prove the point, U-boats began to operate with success in the Irish Sea in January 1945.

The final convoys to sail were ON305 of seventy-five ships from Liverpool on 27 May 1945, and SC177 of thirty-three ships from Halifax on the 26th, but some ships were detached in mid Atlantic to proceed independently from both convoys. Restrictions on darkening ships were removed from VE Day which, wrote one Senior Officer Escorts,

> did not pass entirely unheralded with ON301. To express our grateful appreciation and respect for the Allied Merchant Navies all naval escorts fired an eleven-gun salute, followed by a *feu de joie* consisting of five depth-charges. The firing of the gun salute and the dropping of the depth-charges were controlled by R/T and provided a spectacular and much-appreciated gesture of good will. The Commodore then ordered all merchant ships to fire four rockets as a salute to the Navy. This mutual demonstration of thankfulness and pride whilst a small thing compared to Moscow's 6480 guns or the noise outside Buckingham Palace, gave vent to our noisy exuberance in a most fitting manner.

Another escort commander wrote, in a manner strongly reminiscent of the feelings after the previous war:

> ... the sight of sixty-odd ships well formed in convoy and fully illuminated was a truly remarkable one and after 5½ years of complete darkness a little frightening to behold. However, we lighted up our pipes on the bridge and having 'cast away the works of darkness and put upon us the armour of light' we were soon readjusted to pursuing our lawful occasions for all the world to see.

Chapter Twenty

As the war at sea in the west ended, where convoy and escort had been the foundation of victory, so the war at sea in the east came to its final stages, where a failure to use convoy and escort properly was a major cause of defeat. Japan was a maritime nation, with one of the finest navies in the world. But neither her navy nor her government could accept that convoy was necessary until it was too late.

Japan should have learnt some lessons from the First World War, from the many Japanese destroyers sent to help the Allies, especially as convoy escorts in the Mediterranean. But in the 1920s and 1930s, the Japanese came to identify their main opponent as the United States. The Japanese navy's first task was to build and to maintain a first-line fleet capable of taking on and defeating the United States Pacific Fleet. Japanese submarines were to be used against an enemy's warships, not against commerce. The Japanese assumed that the Americans would use their submarines in the same way.

It was a matter of racial temperament. Convoy did not appeal to the samurai spirit. A few historians in the Japanese Naval War College lectured on anti-submarine warfare, but the students paid little attention. Outside the college, in the wider political and military world, commerce protection attracted almost no attention at all. The Japanese preferred to study fleet actions, such as their own victories over the Chinese at the Yalu in 1894 and over the Russians at Tsushima in 1905, the battles at Coronel, the Falkland Islands and, above all, at Jutland. Colourful and 'offensive' fighting, the clashes of great fleets at sea, appealed to the Japanese. Convoy, on the other hand, was thought hard and monotonous, which it almost always was, and 'defensive' which it certainly was not.

Japan's merchant shipping was always her weakness. Japan went to war for the rich resources, and especially the oil, of Indonesia, Malaya and the Philippines. But the related question, of how to transport those riches back to Japan, was curiously neglected. Before the war, merchant-shipping construction was cut down, in favour of warship construction. China and Russia were also seen as enemies, and total naval expenditure was cut in favour of expenditure on the army. So merchant shipping had a smaller share of a smaller budget. Furthermore, the Japanese Naval General Staff consistently underestimated the likely losses in merchant shipping.

Japan began the war with 2528 merchant ships, of 6,337,000 gross tonnage. Of these, 1528 ships (2,436,300 tons) were allocated for the supply of the civilian population, 519 ships (2,160,500 gross tons) for the army, and the smallest number, 482 ships of 1,740,200 gross tons, for the navy. It was estimated that shipping losses would be between 1,000,000 and 800,000 tons gross annually, but new construction would be some 600,000 tons gross. After the first phase of Japanese conquest had been completed, in April 1942, some 3,000,000 tons of shipping allocated to the army and navy were to have been returned to civilian use. The first phase was duly completed by April, but over-ambitious plans for further conquests, followed by some totally unexpected defeats, prevented the return of the merchant ships.

In the meantime, the Japanese neglected every aspect of commerce protection. No department of the navy was devoted to protecting commerce. While there were ten officers on the General Staff dealing with operations, mainly Combined Fleet operations, there were four staff officers to deal with 'rear-echelon' matters such as training and what was known as 'rear line defence', which included protection of shipping. There was one officer for anti-submarine warfare before the war. Another was appointed when war began; one was then responsible for mining and anti-aircraft defence, the second for commerce protection.

At the same time, every Japanese naval base, big or small, regarded its main functions as being the support and maintenance of the Combined Fleet. Shipping protection was almost totally ignored. At the large base at Yokosuka, for instance, which was responsible for the shipping and defences of some 600 miles of the eastern coast of Honshu, and the 700-mile route to and from Iwo Jima, the 'Staff Officer for Education' responsible for various training and educational establishments and facilities, also single-handedly looked after shipping protection, presumably in his spare time when his other duties allowed.

At sea, troopships were normally given escort, provided as necessary from the Combined Fleet. Although Japan was as dependent upon imported fuel and raw materials as the UK, there was no protection, no convoy, nothing at all, for merchant shipping. They were in fact encouraged to proceed independently, to increase the speed of 'circulation' of shipping. Regulations the control of merchant shipping in time of emergency actually did exist, but they were framed by individual area commanders, varied from area to area, and consequently confused rather than assisted merchant-ship masters.

In spite of their successes, by April 1942 the Japanese were suffering shipping losses. On the 10th, the First and Second Escort Groups were formed and a very limited form of convoy introduced. The First Escort Group consisted of ten old destroyers, two torpedo boats and five converted gunboats; their task was to escort merchant vessels along the 2500-mile route from Singapore to Moji, in Japan. The Second Escort Group had four old destroyers, two torpedo boats and one converted gunboat; their task was the care of merchant shipping along the 3000-mile route between Japan and the great naval base at Truk, in the Carolines. Unsurprisingly, with these forces, such convoys as were formed were small, of only a handful of ships and were organized according to the whims of local commanders.

By July 1942, the Japanese navy had suffered its first reverse in the Coral Sea and its first real catastrophe at Midway, while merchant-shipping losses, especially in the East China Sea, were rising. On the first day of the war the US navy had abandoned its pre-war policy of keeping its submarines for attacks on warships and had turned instead to an assault on merchant shipping. It was the American submarine fleet, not the surface fleet, which was to prove the Japanese merchant navy's most deadly opponent.

In response to the situation in the East China Sea, the First Convoy Escort Fleet was created in July 1942, under Admiral Nakajima, who had his headquarters outside the town of Takao, on the island of Formosa. Nakajima's task was to organize and escort convoys in the East China Sea, with his 'fleet' of eight old destroyers. Later, the convoys were extended to the Japan–Palusa route, and Nakajima's Fleet had staff officers appointed in Moji, Manila, Saigon and Singapore.

The First Convoy Escort Fleet, though undoubtedly a major step in the right direction, still had an antique air about it. Not only the ships but the men were 'over-age'. Nakajima himself was over sixty. His chief of staff, a rear-admiral, and his staff officers were all 'over-age' and many of them were reservists. The escort captains, too, were nearly all reserve officers; they were competent seamen, able to navigate and handle their ships, but they tended to be technically limited, and not particularly receptive to new tactical ideas.

The Convoy Fleet included almost no 'career' naval officers from Etajima, the equivalent of RN Dartmouth officers, and very few graduates from the naval academy. The younger, more able, 'high-flyers' amongst the officers much preferred more glamorous appointments in the Combined Fleet (in fact, this curiously resembled the position in the RN, vis-à-vis the Home Fleet and Western Approaches Command, commented upon in 1941 by Cdr Gretton).

The convoys mostly had only six or eight ships, escorted by one destroyer. Nevertheless Nakajima instituted a form of 'convoy conference', attended by the convoy commodore, the masters of the merchant ships, the escort commander and a representative from the First Convoy Escort Fleet. These all very quickly became convinced of convoy's effectiveness. So, too, did many of the merchantmen's crews and their owners. Unfortunately they met the same ignorance and indifference, shading into open hostility, from officers of the Combined Fleet. Warships of the main fleet often sailed to and from Japan by themselves when they could easily have escorted a convoy for much or at least part of its voyage. But the reply was always the same: convoy duty would interfere with their main task, which was 'the offensive'.

The pattern of Japanese conquests in the East imposed an awkward and inefficient shape on her main shipping routes. One route ran from Japan to the Philippines, to Singapore and ultimately to Burma, the other to New Guinea and Rabaul and eventually to Guadalcanal in the Solomon Islands. These routes were like the two sides of a huge triangle, with Japan herself at the apex. Normally ships sailed fully loaded out from Japan and in ballast, or only partly loaded, homeward. This was a grossly wasteful way of using merchant shipping but the Japanese were never able to recognize the need for, and to organize properly, the 'middle passage' across the base of the triangle.

In October 1942 convoy took another reluctant step forward with the creation of an independent division within the Naval General Staff, the 'Twelfth Division of the First Bureau', to take over the protection of shipping. The new division was headed by a captain, with three staff officers under him: one in charge of homeland defence; one for convoys and routeing, and anti-submarine operations in general; and a third in charge of the arming and signal equipment of merchantmen. At about the same time, there was also some attempt to standardize local instructions for the control of shipping, with the issue of a Naval General Staff directive called 'The doctrines concerning the protection of sea communications during the Greater East Asia War'.

The introduction of some form of convoy, however sketchy, with additions of captured shipping, and new construction, meant that Japan's merchant shipping was at its healthiest in August 1942. Some shipping was returned to civil purposes, so that civil shipping rose to over 3,000,000 gross tons. The overall tonnage available was only a few thousand tons less than at the beginning of the war, at 6,266,800 gross tons.

But that same month the struggle began for the vital strategic island of Guadalcanal, which lasted until January 1943. By then American submarines had sunk 139 ships of 560,000 tons since the beginning of the war, the tonnage for civil purposes had dropped to under 3,000,000, and Japan's merchant shipping was already in decline.

Throughout 1943, and especially in the latter months of the year, the Imperial Japanese Headquarters was increasingly hard-pressed to find the shipping to supply New Guinea and Rabaul from Palau and Truk; to bring petroleum, raw rubber, bauxite, steel and rice back to Japan from the resource areas in the south; and to take petroleum from Singapore and Balikpapan across to the fleet base at Truk.

'The news was bad from every direction,' wrote Major Y. Horie, the army liaison officer at First Convoy Fleet HQ on Formosa, 'there were shortages of ammunition in New Guinea; shortages of petroleum and gasoline in both Japan and Truk; insufficient bauxite at every plant; shortage of escort ships and shortage of ships to be escorted. Pleas (for more escort ships and anti-aircraft guns) came into Tokyo in an unending stream. An atmosphere of gloom closed in on Imperial Japanese headquarters. Such was the shortage of escorts,' Horie recorded, 'that on one occasion, thirty-two ships in Palau harbour waited ninety-five days for lack of one escort ship to travel back to the Japanese home ports with them!'

In March 1943 a Second Convoy Escort Fleet was formed, with its headquarters on Saipan, under a rear-admiral responsible for convoys from Yokohama to Saipan and Truk, Saipan to Yap and Palau, and from Truk to Palau. But, in fact, by July 1943 the Second 'Fleet' had only four destroyers and two torpedo boats (the First 'Fleet' at that time had twelve destroyers, five coast-defence ships, and three torpedo boats).

The coast-defence ships, or '*kaibo-kan*', were in fact escorts, but the name neatly sums up Japanese pre-war thinking. Four *Shumushu* class, of 1020 tons, with a speed of some 19 knots, were built between June 1940 and March 1941. Their depth-charge outfit steadily increased (another sign of the times) from an initial twelve, to twenty-four in May 1942, and to sixty in the autumn of 1943.

Fourteen of an improved *Etorufu* class were laid down between March 1943 and February 1944, and eight *Mikura* class between October 1943 and May 1944. Both were about 1000 tons, with a speed of 19 knots and carried up to 120 depth-charges. In 1943 the curve of Japanese escort production rose sharply. The first of a smaller 810-ton, 16-knot type was laid down in September 1943 and completed in February 1944. Some of this class were built in only three months, but they had radar, improved sonar and 120 depth-charges. The first of twenty-nine *Ukuru* class, 1020 tons and 19 knots, was laid down in June 1944. Some of these were built in four to five months, one of them in just 105 days.

But the Japanese did not have the will (or, eventually, the time) to carry the programme through. Only fifty-three 810-tonners were built, of 300 projected. Another 109 *Ukurus* were planned, but never laid down. Japanese thinking was still preoccupied with the offensive. They laid down twenty more aircraft carriers, and made the giant carrier *Shinano* out of a *Yamato* class battleship. From the materials used in these ships, designed purely for the offensive, they could have built hundreds more convoy escorts.

In June 1943 the Japanese Navy approved the building of forty frigates (of a total of 360 which the anti-submarine branch had asked for). But these were already much too late. The Japanese had yet to realize that even the losses they had already suffered were like breezes compared with the full hurricane which was about to overtake them. They did not use this providential period of comparative calm to remedy their neglect of anti-submarine warfare.

The Americans had been having trouble with torpedoes. Failures due to design faults in the torpedoes themselves were compounded by a long, bitter and entrenched struggle by bureaucrats to prove that the faults lay entirely with the submarine captains' failure to aim their salvoes properly. It had taken time to find that torpedoes with full warheads ran appreciably deeper than torpedoes with peace-time practice heads and, as the detonator was designed to explode at a certain depth beneath the target, there were many 'misses' when torpedoes ran under their targets and onwards.

The torpedoes had two detonator devices, one activated by the change in magnetic fields caused by the nearness of a ship's metal hull, and another activated by actual impact on the target's side. But in regions near the magnetic equator the magnetic device was prone to act prematurely, and many Japanese ships reported torpedo explosions close alongside. Meanwhile, the attacking submarine captains, hearing explosions at or very close to the calculated torpedo running times, and seeing columns of water and perhaps the target ship listing with the force of the explosion, believed they had scored hits.

The contact device was found to act reliably only when the torpedo struck at a glancing angle (thus penalizing the very captains who hit their targets squarely on). The fault was finally diagnosed after Lt Cdr L. R. Daspit, in *Tinosa* hit and stopped a large Japanese tanker west of Truk on 24 July 1943. With his quarry stationary, Daspit lined up his submarine and fired another nine torpedoes, each individually aimed and fired. All hit. None exploded. Daspit then had the presence of mind to bring back his remaining torpedo for examination.

The 'prematures' and the misfires (several Japanese ships arrived with unexploded torpedoes actually embedded in their sides) prompted a Japanese saying, 'A tanker cannot sink if it is torpedoed.' Curiously, this may have helped the Allies, because it made the average Japanese ship-master even more sceptical about the value of convoy and even more convinced he was better off on his own.

But towards the end of August the American torpedo defects were remedied and the shipping losses began to climb, so that the Japanese noticed them, from about the 20th onwards. Shipping losses for September 1943 were, at 172,082 gross tons, the highest for one month so far in the war.

At about the same time, the most realistic elements in the Japanese High Command understood that Japan was over-extended. She could not expect to defend the outer line of Rabaul, and the Bismarck archipelago for much longer. Amid much recrimination and loss of face, a retreat to the line of the Carolines, the Marianas and Western New Guinea was proposed, although the Combined Fleet continued to operate around Rabaul and the Solomon Islands as though nothing had happened to change the situation. It seemed that no extra resources would be given, no further attention paid, to the anti-submarine war.

The main obstacle, as in all navies, was a mental one. The anti-submarine warfare department (which was barely a department at all) had no influence on high, no friends at court. Everybody at the 'Red Bricks', the Navy Ministry and the Naval General Staff offices in red-brick buildings, was totally committed to the Combined Fleet.

It was time something was done. Shipping losses in November 1943 reached 265,068 tons gross and the total losses for 1943 were 305 ships, of 1,335,000 tons, to submarine attack, and another ninety-one ships, of 280,000 tons, to aircraft. The general trend of losses, especially to submarines, was rising rapidly: almost a half, 147 ships, of 651,235 tons, were lost to US submarines in the last four months of the year.

At last, on 15 November 1943, a Grand Escort Command Headquarters was set up, with a very senior admiral, Admiral Koshiro Oikawa, formerly Minister of the Navy, as C-in-C. The Japanese navy was reorganized into three main commands: the Combined Fleet, the China District Fleet, and the Combined Convoy Escort Fleet. Oikawa was responsible for the protection of shipping, convoy control and routeing, and anti-submarine warfare everywhere except between ports along the Chinese coast, and such local routes as between Truk and the Marshall Islands, and on the fringes of the Japanese empire, south of the Philippines and west of Singapore.

It was a huge task and very nearly impossible to achieve at that stage of the war. It was some time before Oikawa could gather together a full headquarters staff. At the beginning he had in his Fleet less than fifty ships of 800 tons or above, including four converted gunboats, and several destroyers which were so old they were judged incapable of making ocean-escort passages. His best ships were fifteen destroyers built in 1920–25, and only four of them had ever formed a proper escort group and worked together.

All the rest were individual ships, which had been administered by different commands at different bases. There was no common tactical anti-submarine doctrine, no equivalent of Gilbert Roberts's school, no common signalling or radio procedures. Most of the escort captains were from the merchant marine, competent seamen and navigators, but limited technically, and lacking fighting experience. None of them had the scope to act as an escort group commander.

There was a shortage of radar sets in escorts. Priority was given to the Combined Fleet. The first escorts were not fitted with radar, experimentally, until the spring of 1944, and radar was not in anything like general use until late in the year. There was also a shortage of skilled communications ratings. Those the escorts did have were conscripted into the army as soon as they had gained any experience. Much of the communications equipment fitted in escorts was obsolete.

The forces allocated to Oikawa also included four escort carriers and the 901st Air Group, for anti-submarine operations. The four escort carriers were actually under repair at the time, and a fifth, *Chuyo*, was sunk by a submarine on 4 December 1943, whilst in company with a small convoy. The first escort carrier did not join her first convoy until July 1944. None of them accompanied more than two convoys and one, *Kaiyo*, was used entirely for training pilots.

Lack of trained personnel was Oikawa's biggest problem. It was impossible to form an equivalent to Coastal Command overnight. The Japanese encountered, one after the other and in a very short space of time, all the problems the Allies had overcome years before. The pilots were so 'green' they not only had to be taught how to recognize and attack a submarine at sea, but in many cases how to fly on and off their carrier. The 901st, like the escorts, had to evolve a tactical doctrine. Furthermore, by January 1944, when the training programme had barely got under way, pilots were being taken away to operate with the Combined Fleet. And there was little communication between aircraft and escorts at sea.

But the main obstacle was Oikawa himself. He and his staff soon showed that they had joined the long line of naval officers who had learned nothing from the past. Faced with the two tremendous pressures, of keeping merchant ships moving, and the shortage of proper escorts, Oikawa should have instituted some sort of general convoy system immediately, with what escorts and aircraft he had, hoping and expecting to improve the loss rate as time went on.

Instead, Oikawa fell back on 'patrolled sea-lanes'. He proposed to safeguard shipping between Japan and Singapore by making the South China Sea, the Formosa Strait and the East China Sea into one vast, submarine-free lake, using Borneo, the Philippines, Formosa, and the Nansei Shoto islands, including Okinawa and the Ryukyus, as a gigantic barrier on the eastward side, filling in the gaps in the barrier with minefields and shore radar stations. Ships and planes would patrol the routes meanwhile. Similarly, convoys would sail along another 'patrolled belt' between Japan and the Marianas, being protected by radar stations on the Bonin and Volcano Islands, and by ships and planes at sea. Other patrolled routes would follow the coast of Japan, between Yokohama and Kobe, and northward from Yokohama, up the east coast of Honshu. The Sea of Japan and the Yellow Sea were still free of submarines.

Grand Escort Command began, without much enthusiasm, to put these plans into effect, but they were soon overtaken by events. Some mines were laid in the East China Sea, and the Formosa Strait, and a couple of radar stations were actually built, on Okinawa, before Japanese forces were overrun by Allied air superiority. Meanwhile, the Escort Command was under pressure from the High Command to free ships from such convoys as they were running, even though those convoys only had three or four ships in each.

While the Japanese still dallied over introducing general convoy, shocks fell upon them thick and fast. US submarines sank 240,840 tons of shipping in January 1944, and another 256,797 tons in February. Japanese naval confidence received a mortal blow when the US Fast Carrier Task Force attacked Truk on 17–18 February and sank another 200,000 tons, mostly tankers and store ships supporting the Combined Fleet.

Troop transports had always been convoyed, but even they were suffering heavy losses until, by the end of 1943, as Horie said, 'everyone aboard a transport or merchant had to be resigned to the likelihood of being sunk in his travels'. In the autumn of 1943 the Japanese carried out Operation TURTLE: the transfer of Second District Army consisting of seven divisions of the 2nd Army, and the 19th Army from Manchuria, China, Korea and the Japanese mainland to the Celebes, Morotai, Halmahera and Biak. According to Horie, 'about 40 per cent of our trooped transports were being lost to enemy action. One contingent loaded at Pusan, Korea, had the misfortune to have ships sunk three times en route – the first time near Okinawa, the second time off Formosa and the third time near New Guinea. Only about half their original strength remained when these troops finally were landed at New Guinea. And even then they were without weapons; many were minus shoes; and large numbers had become ill.'

In February 1944 a fast convoy taking troops from Korea to Saipan and Guam was attacked by the US submarine *Trout*, which sank one ship with over 4000 troops on board; more than half of them were drowned (although the escorts counter-attacked and sank *Trout*). On 3 February, the tankers *Goyo* Maru and *Ariake* Maru, escorted only by the frigate *Sado*, were sunk in the East China Sea en route to Japan. On the 19th, all five tankers in a bigger convoy, but again escorted only by one frigate, *Shumushu*, were sunk by the USS *Jack*. In both cases, the escort had been able to do little more than act as rescue ship, and it now occurred to some Japanese staff officers that larger convoys with more escorts would be more effective.

Meanwhile disasters continued. On 1 March, a large convoy of eight destroyers, seven transports, and a special service vessel left Rabaul with a complete infantry division of over 9000 men to reinforce the garrisons of Lae and Salamaua in New Guinea. Concealed under thick overcast that night, the convoy was sighted on 2 March in the Bismarck Sea, and aircraft of the USAAF and RAAF from Papua began a series of attacks which lasted intermittently for some thirty-six hours. By 4 March, the whole convoy had been sunk except for four of the destroyers, and over 3000 men had been drowned.

Later in the same month the US submarine *Sandlance* sank the light cruiser *Tatsuta* and two merchantmen from a convoy carrying reinforcements to the Marianas. In another attack, a large ship the *Mieke* Maru carrying the 29th Infantry Regiment from Pusan to Saipan was sunk just outside the Inland Sea with great loss of life. This incident finally forced the Naval General Staff to consider seriously the question of convoy. The General Staff demanded 'a study meeting before the Emperor concerning the convoy escort situation'. Oikawa's staff had the task of assembling the humiliating facts for the meeting. Clearly, loss of face for the Navy had much more effect on policy than the loss of ships.

And so, in March 1944, the Japanese finally instituted what they called 'a large convoy system' (to the Allies, accustomed to running convoys of seventy or eighty ships across the Atlantic, the Japanese convoys of only ten to twenty ships hardly seemed 'large'). An Escort of Convoy Headquarters was set up, with its own staff, despite misgivings about the ability of merchant masters to keep station (it was thought much too dangerous to have more than three columns of ships steaming abreast). Despite the fact that the Escort of Convoy staff officer for a particular convoy was only appointed shortly before the convoy sailed, despite the abysmal state of signalling within a convoy, despite the shortage of escorts and the sheer lack of convoy practice and expertise, despite everything, convoy at once began to save ships. It was soon clear that sinkings of independents were two and a half times those of convoyed ships. Further, the escorts were hitting back. US submarines lost more of their number to convoy escorts than to patrols, mines, aircraft, or indeed any other single cause.

The US submariners retaliated to this new challenge with wolf-pack tactics: three or four submarines, with picturesque nicknames based on their senior officer's name ('Blair's Blasters', the 'Mickey Finns', 'Wogan's Wolves', 'Coye's Coyotes', 'Clarey's Crushers') would operate together, to detect, follow and attack their targets, using good R/T communication between boats and excellent surface radar sets. The curve of Japanese shipping losses, which had begun to drop, started upward again.

In August US submarines moved to a base at Saipan, 3500 miles nearer the action than Pearl Harbor, and were able to stay much longer on patrol. Japanese convoys were soon forced to leave the eastern side of the East China Sea and hug the Chinese coast. The stretch of the East China Sea, from Luzon Strait across to Formosa and the Chinese coast, was named 'Convoy College', where the 'wolf-packs' were generally too much for the convoy escorts. Commander 'Red' Ramage, in *Parche*, for example, with *Steelhead* and *Hammerhead* in company, attacked a convoy in the Luzon Strait on 30–31 July and sank a tanker, two transports and two passenger–cargo ships, for a total score of 39,000 tons. Another pack under Cdr G. R. Donaho, with *Picudo*, *Redfish* and *Spadefish*, sank four ships out of one convoy and finished their patrols with a total of 64,456 tons sunk.

The Japanese themselves aggravated their own problems with a succession of further errors. The battle in the Philippine Sea in June 1944 had decimated Japanese carrier pilots and rendered the remaining fleet carriers virtually harmless. Instead of disbanding the First Mobile Fleet and concentrating their resources on convoys, the Japanese kept the carriers in commission for the final show-down at Leyte in October.

They went further. On 3 August 1944, Oikawa was appointed Chief of the Naval General Staff. Admiral Naokuni Nomura became C-in-C Grand Escort Command. But, at the same time, Grand Escort Command was amalgamated with the Combined Fleet. Any faint hopes of a successful campaign around the convoys now vanished. Even the 901st Naval Air Group, which had actually acquired a degree of expertise in radar operations against submarines, was thrown away as a reconnaissance unit for the Combined Fleet in an air battle with Halsey's Third Fleet, off Formosa in October. Grand Escort Command was defunct in everything but name, and the only question now remaining was how quickly US submarines could finish off the rest of Japan's merchant marine.

In October 1944, sixty-eight submarines sank 320,906 tons of Japanese shipping, the highest monthly total of the war. In November the figure dropped to 214,506 tons, and there began to be a noticeable shortage of targets. By the end of the year, the tonnage lost had risen to 545 ships, of 2,140,000 tons, nearly a third of them tankers. By the spring of 1945, Japan had been almost completely cut off from the southern resources area, but was still able to get supplies from Manchuria, across the Sea of Japan, which remained 'Hirohito's Lake'. Here, Japanese ships sailed on a peace-time basis, singly, with no escort, and with steaming lights burning.

In June, with Operation BARNEY, this last refuge was penetrated. 'Hydeman's Hellcats', a pack of nine submarines led by Cdr E. T. Hydeman in *Sea Dog*, fitted with an excellent 'FMS' device, which gave a visual presentation of underwater objects with enough accuracy to show mines, passed through the Tsushima Straits on the night of 6–7 June and, in eleven days, sank twenty-seven ships and the submarine I-122, for a total tonnage of 57,000 tons.

The Japanese desperate shortage of all kinds of shipping by that stage was demonstrated on 16 June, off Sourabaya, when two British submarines, *Thorough* and *Taciturn*, sighted the oddest-looking convoy of the war: one armed trawler, an old and visibly rusty ex-Dutch submarine with its forward gun removed, and a submarine chaser towing a large hulk 'which had several promenade decks and a roof overall'. *Taciturn* closed the convoy on the surface in shallow water and destroyed them all by gun-fire, except for the trawler which turned away, 'into *Thorough*'s arms' and was sunk by her.

When the end came, on 15 August 1945, Japan had lost 2345 ships, of 8,617,234 tons, of which 15 per cent (259 ships, of 1,284,946 tons) were tankers. The Japanese Navy lost 687 warships, of another 1,966,521 tons. In a much less well-known statistic, the Japanese merchant marine lost 108,000 officers and men, killed or missing, during the war.

After the war, there were plenty of such statistics for the Allies to digest. U-boats had sunk 2775 merchant ships, of 14,573,000 gross tons, out of a total of 4786 British, Allied and neutral merchant ships and fishing vessels, of 21,194,000 tons, lost from all causes – or nearly 60 per cent. Nearly 30,000

British seamen had been lost, killed or were missing, in those ships. But the
U-boat arm of the German navy had lost over 32,000 officers and men, in the
781 U-boats sunk from the total of 1175 built. The Italian Navy had lost
another eighty-five U-boats (they had sunk ninety-four ships, of 532,393
tons).

British and Allied merchantmen had completed over 300,000 Atlantic
voyages during the war. Examination of the raw figures showed (or rather,
confirmed) the influence of convoy. From the beginning of the war until June
1941, when end-to-end convoy escort was established, 79 per cent (643 ships)
were lost when sailing independently or as stragglers from convoys; 21 per
cent (169 ships) were lost from ocean convoys. Up to May 1943, when
end-to-end surface and air escort was established, 80 per cent (or 1992 ships)
were sunk as independents or stragglers, and 20 per cent (499 ships) from
ocean convoys. From May to September 1943, when the U-boats had
withdrawn from the Atlantic, nine ships were sunk from convoys. From
September 1943 until the end of the war, 37,500 ships sailed in ocean convoys,
of which fifty-six ships and one straggler were sunk. In coastal convoys,
another 57,300 ships sailed, of which thirty-seven and one straggler were
sunk.

Convoy was proved once again by far the most effective weapon for sinking
U-boats. From September 1939 until May 1943, 156 U-boats were sunk
(excluding the Mediterranean and the Indian Ocean) of which ninety-nine,
or 65 per cent, were sunk by convoy escorts and fifty-seven, or 35 per cent, by
all other means. From May to September 1943, when the U-boats withdrew,
thirty-three were sunk, all by convoy escorts. From September 1943 until the
end of the war, convoy escorts sank another 100 U-boats.

Convoy had also provided a safeguard against other forms of attack than
U-boats. Surface raiders sank 188 ships, of which only five were in convoy.
Seventy per cent of the losses due to mining were independents. Losses to
aircraft were more difficult to assess, but the best analysis suggested that 66
per cent of the ships lost to air attack were independents.

The hard clear light of post-war analysis showed up some uncomfortable
facts about other campaigns against the U-boats. The transit air patrols in the
Bay of Biscay sank one U-boat a month, on average. The northern transit
patrols, between Shetland and Iceland, sank eleven U-boats in three years.
Aircraft flew 1350 hours for each U-boat kill on transit air patrols, but only 360
hours for each U-boat killed whilst on convoy air escort. Convoy escort was
therefore once again shown to be nearly four times as effective as patrolling.

Mining absorbed a vast amount of resources in the war against the
U-boats. Offensive mine-laying, using 65,000 mines, sank nineteen U-boats.
Defensive mine-laying, with 136,000 mines, sank four U-boats and 'trap'
minefields, of 29,000 mines, sank three U-boats.

The bombing offensive against U-boat bases was found to have had very
little effect. Until 1943, when almost all the raids were by night, 15,000 tons of

bombs were dropped, and 198 aircraft were lost. One U-boat was damaged and delayed on patrol by two weeks. In 1944, after the invasion of Europe, when raids were carried out mostly by daylight, and had fighter escorts, sixty-two U-boats were destroyed, most of them in the shipyards at the very end of the war, when there was no aerial opposition (nevertheless, all these U-boats are included in losses due to bombing). The offensive against factories and bases producing U-boats cost 882 aircraft, and 33,000 tons of bombs dropped. Nevertheless, U-boat production actually reached its peak in June 1944.

Chapter Twenty-One

After the war, almost all navies suffered the usual post-war period of drastic decline, in numbers and in ships. Only the US navy seemed stable, or even to increase in power and influence. In the Royal Navy, the 257 destroyers, 542 sloops, corvettes and frigates, and the 1069 minesweepers and anti-submarine vessels in the Navy List at the end of the war, were rapidly whittled down: a few were re-fitted and modernized; some returned to civilian owners; more stayed in commission; but most were simply laid up, moored in creeks and estuaries all over the country, waiting for the knacker's yard. Of the fifty-two aircraft carriers, thirty-three escort carriers were returned to the United States under the terms of lend-lease. Of the five British-built escort carriers, three reverted to merchant-service use, *Nairana* was transferred to the Royal Netherlands Navy, and *Campania* was first an exhibition ship for the Festival of Britain in 1951 and then head-quarters ship for the British atomic test of 1952.

The nuclear bomb, first atomic and then hydrogen, seemed to overshadow every aspect of every navy, to make the very idea of planning for the future ludicrous. What ship could withstand those two awesome flashes which had immolated Hiroshima and Nagasaki? Who could use what conventional weapons when a hydrogen bomb would incinerate everything for miles around? Who could have any faith in convoy after watching the frigate *Plym*, a war-time convoy escort, vaporized into a handful of white-hot metal shards by the atomic explosion at Monte Bello on 3 October 1952? One such bomb would destroy a whole convoy and all its escorts. It appeared that ancient naval strategies were out-of-date and there was a new balance of power at sea, based on what Mr Churchill called 'the ownership of the means of mutual extermination'.

The other view was very well put by Mr Oliver Stanley MP, in a debate on defence in the House of Commons on 3 March 1949. In it he differed profoundly from some people outside who think that the advent of a new weapon, however powerful, means that everything we are discussing here has now become quite out of date, and that everything we are now doing in any of the three Services has become useless. Not only is that not my experience, but after every war we have to choose between the extremes; on the one side the Blimps who want to conduct the new war with the weapons of the last, and on the other the Boffins who say that new inventions have made everything else out of date. My experience from the beginning of the last war is that the true course lies between the two, and that there is just as much danger in listening too much to the one as in listening too much to the other.

Ironically, by threatening to make convoy impracticable, nuclear weapons did a great deal to ensure that convoy continued to be practised at sea. Clearly, the view that everything would soon vanish in one huge apocalyptic detonation was too pessimistic – and much too simplistic. Meanwhile the world was evidently a much more dangerous place than it had been in 1939. The Soviet Union, for instance, was building a colossal fleet of submarines, which would number some 300 boats by 1950. Naval staff in the west, outside what was already called the 'Iron Curtain', could reflect that Doenitz had begun in 1939 with only fifty U-boats. All those Soviet submarines could not possibly be needed to defend Russian shipping. Besides, at that date, Russia virtually had no world-wide shipping trade which needed protection. These submarines, largely designed and built with captured German expertise and technology, could only be used for offence.

The Soviet threat led to the formation of the North Atlantic Treaty Organization in 1949, which in itself, with the main convoy theatre embodied in its very title, ensured that convoy would never be neglected after the Second World War as it had been after the First. The first signatories of the Treaty, on 4 April 1949, were Belgium, Canada, Denmark, France, Iceland, Italy, Luxembourg, the Netherlands, Norway, Portugal, the United Kingdom and the United States. (Greece and Turkey acceded to the Treaty in 1952, the Federal Republic of Germany in 1955.)

Warships of some of the first signatory navies had already exercised together since the war but many of the earlier sorties were not much more than communications exercises (it was curious that, after six years of war, warships of various nationalities had learnt to communicate naturally and efficiently together but, as soon as peace broke out, communications exercises were necessary). But the coming of NATO meant that the various navies began to carry out strenuous, large-scale, annual maritime exercises in which convoy played a consistently major part.

This devotion to convoy continued in the absence of any practical application. None of the naval operations round the world, from Palestine in the 1940s to the Falklands in the 1980s, by way of Malaya, Korea, the Lebanon, Suez, Kuwait, Vietnam, required convoy. Korea, for instance,

involved the old naval arts of bombardment and blockade, together with
minesweeping, reconnaissance, amphibious landings, and close air support
– but not convoy.

Nevertheless escort groups were an important part of every fleet, and
convoy protection was an important part of every major exercise. For the first
time since the Napoleonic wars, at least in the Royal Navy, convoy warfare
was a respectable occupation for a young officer with ambitions, and the
torpedo-anti-submarine branch (TAS) more than held its own in the prestige
stakes for promotion. Frigates provided good commands and 'promotion
jobs'. Training was improved and refined, at Portland and in the joint
Navy–RAF anti-submarine school at Londonderry.

The statement accompanying the 1950–51 Naval Estimates stressed that
priority was to be given to the development of anti-submarine weapons for
ships and aircraft; shipbuilding effort was to be more concentrated upon new
anti-submarine frigates, converting existing vessels for submarine-hunting,
and designing cheaper, smaller and more numerous anti-submarine vessels;
new homing torpedoes and guided missiles were to be developed. The
cruiser *Cumberland* was already being converted as a trials ship for testing
new weapons and equipment.

The first large and really memorable NATO exercise was MAINBRACE, in
1952. NATO was still young, and some member nations were not always
prepared to subordinate their own national interests to NATO. But MAIN-
BRACE was a very good beginning, and served to interest the man-in-the-
street in NATO, especially in Denmark and Norway, two countries particularly concerned in preparation work, such as calling up reservists,
undertaking fresh training programmes, and completing work on military
installations.

Like all major exercises MAINBRACE had convoy serials in the programme,
and a convoy-defence phase. Many exercises included an actual convoy
passage across the Atlantic, or, as in RENDEZVOUS in 1953, across the
Mediterranean. RENDEZVOUS was under the general control of the C-in-C
Allied Forces Mediterranean (CINCAFMED), an office which was approved on
16 December 1952 and whose first occupant was the British C-in-C Med.,
Admiral the Earl Mountbatten of Burma.

The Mediterranean Fleet had just previously exercised with the Home
Fleet, with convoy exercises using the submarine depot ship *Forth* and two
Home Fleet Training Squadron carriers as 'the convoy'. Exercise RENDEZ-
VOUS was much more ambitious, starting in the western Mediterranean basin
and ending far to the east off the coast of Crete. It was run in three phases, by
the French, Italians, and Americans, with ships from the Greek, Turkish
and Royal navies, and aircraft from all six nations. Convoys, screened by
frigates, and supported by cruisers and destroyers, were attacked by submarines (under a Turkish admiral) and aircraft by day and night, and by
surface forces at night. However, the ten days of exercise serials, with a

carrier task force, minesweeping exercises, a cruiser bombardment, re-plenishment at sea, and an amphibious landing, also included 'a hunter –killer anti-submarine group'.

In Exercise MARINER, carried out in appalling weather in September and October 1953, between Cape Race and Hvalfjord, operating conditions were 'realistic': the cruiser *Swiftsure* and the destroyer *Diamond* collided; the American battleship *Iowa* and several destroyers suffered structural damage; and an aircraft broke adrift in the hanger of the carrier *Wasp* and damaged several others. But the presence of 'hunter–killer groups' showed, as in RENDEZVOUS, that the old heresies were only scotched, not killed.

Old hobby-horses were given another extensive airing in 1954, when the White Paper on defence assumed that both sides would use atomic weapons in a future war. After a heavy exchange of nuclear bombs, both sides would be 'broken-backed'. The emphasis in the White Paper was therefore on bombings and bombers, and announced the decision 'to build up in the Royal Air Force a force of modern bombers capable of using the atomic weapon to its fullest extent'.

In the House of Lords, a very distinguished sailor, Admiral of the Fleet Viscount Cunningham of Hyndhope, set himself in a speech on 16 March to refute some old fallacies. He did not, he said, accept that the 'bomber must always get through'. A bombing force may be a deterrent, but if it ever failed to deter, it will have failed utterly. 'We seemed to be in danger,' said Cunningham, 'of repeating the mistakes that we made at the beginning of the last war when – and I do not think this is in dispute – too little of our air effort was devoted to the defence of this country. . . .' Pointing out the dangers of relying too much on one retaliatory arm, ABC said it 'certainly would be a comforting thought to know that we were in a strong position to retaliate on the enemy; but it would be a much happier one if we could be reasonably sure that this country would not be brought into a condition of "broken-backness" by enemy attack.'

This overriding necessity for 'local' as well as 'strategic' air power, at sea, as well as over land continents, was well demonstrated the following year in the earliest SEATO exercise ANZEX ONE. The South-East Asia Treaty Organ-ization, of the United Kingdom, Australia, New Zealand, Pakistan, the United States, France, Thailand, and the Philippines came into being on 8 September 1954.

Two cruisers, *Newcastle* and the New Zealand *Black Prince*, three British and four Australian destroyers, and one Australian, three British and two New Zealand frigates, took part, as well as anti-submarine aircraft from the RAF at Singapore, the RAAF at Darwin, and the RNZAF from Fiji, three 'T' class submarines, and RFA tankers. The first serial began with a raider attack on a convoy as the Australian and New Zealand ships cleared the Torres Straits on 25 May, and there were more convoy exercises in the Java Sea from 2 to 7 June.

Later in June, in the South China Sea, *Black Prince* acted as a convoy raider, while Sunderland and Neptune aircraft patrolled as convoy escorts overhead. The exercise ships were always conscious of air cover, or the lack of it. Off the Malayan coast between Khota Bahru and Kuantan, in the very waters where Japanese aircraft sank *Prince of Wales* and *Repulse*, some officers in ANZEX ONE thought of those ships and imagined their survivors 'turning in their graves at the time' at the sight of more ships in the South China Sea, *still* without air cover.

As the years of peace passed on, and the war retreated further into the background, it was necessary to keep on stating and re-stating old truths. In December 1954, once again in the House of Lords, another very distinguished sailor, Admiral of the Fleet Lord Fraser of North Cape, commenting on the threat from the fleets and submarines of Russia (or whoever the enemy might be) said:

> It may be said that perhaps there ought to be new developments to safeguard our convoys. We have carried out, and are carrying out, many experiments, but, so far, nothing leads us to believe that there is any other method of protecting these convoys, which have to take to the sea in any weather for a fortnight, three weeks, or four weeks, than having naval ships in close attendance all the time, with the help, when necessary, of the Fleet Air Arm and the Royal Air Force. There is no other way known, and none is likely to be known in the near future, of protecting a convoy. . . .

At the time Lord Fraser was speaking, Russia was reported to have from 370 to 400 submarines, with about ninety building. The Royal Navy had eighty-two destroyers and 180 frigates, with a new programme of frigate-building getting under way. Some two dozen fleet destroyers of the war-time R, T, U, W and Z classes were 'fully converted' to Type 15 anti-submarine frigates by stripping down to the bare hull form and rebuilding. Another dozen of the war-time P, O, and T classes were 'limited conversions' to Type 16 fast anti-submarine frigates.

By the end of 1954, the first of several new classes of frigate had been launched: the Type 12 *Whitby* 1st Rate Frigates, of 2150 tons, 350 feet long, two shafts giving 31 knots, armed with two 4.5-inch guns, torpedo tubes and 'Limbo' three barrelled depth-charge ahead-throwing mortars; the Type 14 *Blackwood* 2nd Rate Utility Frigates, of 1180 tons, 300 feet long, single shaft giving 24½ knots, armed with two 40-mm bofors, and Limbo; the Type 41 *Leopard* class anti-aircraft frigates, designed for convoy protection, of 2300 tons, 320 feet long, two shafts giving 25 knots, armed with four 4.5-inch in two twin turrets, and Squid triple-barrelled depth-charge mortar; the Type 61 *Salisbury* class air-direction frigates, primarily for the direction of carrier-borne and shore-based aircraft, of 2170 tons, 320 feet long, two shafts giving 25 knots, armed with two 4.5-inch guns and Squid. *Ashanti*, the first of a new Type 81 *Tribal* class of general-purpose frigate was laid down in 1958: these were 2300 tons, 350 feet long, single shaft, with combined steam and gas turbine giving 28 knots, two 4.5-inch guns, and Limbo. They were also designed to carry one helicopter, the first class of frigate to do so.

In the debate on the Navy Estimates for 1956–7, the Hon George Ward MP, making his first speech as Parliamentary Secretary to the Admiralty, referred to 'the use of the helicopter for underwater warfare. It is proving very efficient at operating an Asdic set from the air, free from ship noises and practically free from effective retaliation by the submarine. We are exchanging ideas and information with the Americans, who share our confidence in the great possibilities of this method of anti-submarine defence. We are now planning to use the single-rotor S58.'

It was high time for the helicopter's debut. That year of 1956 was a very busy one for convoy exercises. In DAWN BREEZE in March, *Ark Royal* and *Bulwark* from the Home Fleet, and six submarines; French Neptune and Lancaster aircraft; a cruiser, a destroyer, a frigate and two submarines from the Royal Netherlands Navy; a destroyer, two frigates and two squadrons of Harpoon aircraft from Portugal; US navy attack aircraft; nine squadrons of Coastal Command aircraft, Lincolns, and Canberras from Bomber Command, had all participated in exercises to protect a carrier force and a convoy against air, surface and submarine attack.

Later in the month, in MONSOON, *Albion* and *Centaur*, the cruiser *Newfoundland*, five destroyers, three submarines, two Australian destroyers and three frigates, and two New Zealand frigates, with US aircraft from the Philippines, and the French carrier *Lafayette*, carried out convoy exercises in the largest Commonwealth maritime exercise ever held in the Far East. In April, in MEDFLEX DRAGON, convoy exercises took place over the whole Mediterranean, with 'Blue' forces protecting a number of convoys sailing from dispersed ports against the attacks of 'Orange' forces, after which convoy and escorts proceeded to Malta. There, a 'steam-past' and fly-past revealed the presence of one American general (SACEUR), two British, two American, three Italian and five French admirals, together with one Greek and one Turkish commodore.

On 1 May, American, Canadian and British ships and aircraft began a six-day exercise NEW BROOM V, in which a NATO 'merchant-ship' convoy, of US amphibious-force ships escorted by Canadian and American aircraft carriers and destroyers sailed from Norfolk, Virginia, to Gibraltar, being attacked by British and American submarines, which themselves were counter-attacked by Canadian and American hunter–killer groups, shore-based anti-submarine aircraft, and blimps from Weeksville, North Carolina. Two convoys made the return trip, subjected to the same attacks.

NATO exercises were growing bigger and more complicated. A series of SEA SPRAY, FISH PLAY II, STRIKE BACK, SEA WATCH (an anti-submarine and convoy exercise) and SHARP SQUALL II, involved over 300 ships and lasted from September of November 1957, stretching across the whole of the north

Atlantic. International cooperation was growing closer. Radar and sonar were becoming more accurate, longer ranged. Nevertheless, a decade after the end of the Second World War, there was a certain sameness about convoy exercises. Limbo, for example, though heavier and with longer range than Squid, was basically the same weapon. There was a limit to the number of ways in which convoy zigzags and evasive turns, escort-screening diagrams, anti-aircraft fire-concentration zones and underwater search patterns could be combined and permutated. To this somewhat stagnating scene, the helicopter therefore injected vital qualities of mobility and versatility.

Genuine helicopters (as opposed to autogyros, which are not capable of true vertical flight) made successful flights before the war, the Focke-Achgelis Fa.61 in 1938, Igor Sikorsky's VS-300 in 1939. During the war the German navy flew the Flettner F.1282 Kolibri (Hummingbird) and the Fa.223 Drache (Kite). A small rotary wing kite, the Fa330 Bach stelze (Wagtail), was used for spotting from U-boats.

The idea of using a helicopter to raise a spotter's height of eye appealed to the Admiralty who experimented with Sikorsky's YR.4A, later developed as the R4 Hoverfly. A platform was built on a tanker and the machine made one convoy trip to the UK. Trials were also carried out on the *Empire Mersey* of the US Pitcairn Autogyro. A provisional order for some 200 R4s was placed, but the project was dropped at the end of the war.

After the war, whilst the US army and navy pressed ahead with helicopter research and development, the Royal Navy still tended to regard 'choppers' as an interesting but noisy curiosity, somewhere between a toy and a circus trick: Lt Alan Bristow made the first-ever helicopter landing on a small ship, *Helmsdale*, in 1946, and Lt K. Reed delighted and astonished Their Majesties by landing a Hoverfly on the quarterdeck of *Vanguard* in February 1947.

The story of helicopters in the Navy properly began with the formation of 705 Squadron, equipped with Hoverflys, at Gosport in May 1947. In 1950 Westland began to build Sikorksy S.51s, renamed Dragonflys, under licence at their factory at Yeovil. These were much bigger machines, with a top speed of 95 m.p.h. and a range of about 250 miles. Fitted with a hydraulic winch, they inaugurated the first regular air-sea rescue service. Ship-borne trials were also carried out at sea in the Royal Fleet Auxiliary *Fort Duquesne* in 1951.

The Korean War gave helicopters the first real operational chance to show what versatile machines they were. The US army and navy used them for a score of different duties, for troop-carrying, spotting, fire support, evacuation of wounded, plane-guard astern of aircraft carriers, and air-sea rescue.

At the end of 1952, the United States supplied the United Kingdom with Sikorsky S.55s, to be renamed Whirlwinds, under the Mutual Aid Defence programme. In 1953 848 Squadron was formed with these Whirlwinds which went out to the Far East in the aircraft maintenance ship *Perseus* and gave valuable service ashore during the Malayan Emergency for the next three years.

The first RN anti-submarine helicopter squadron, 845, was formed with Whirlwind 22s in 1954. These had a top speed of 110 m.p.h. and a range of 400 miles. They carried a crew of two and were fitted with 'dipping sonar', lowered by a helicopter at the hover to 'listen' for submarines. A helicopter could thus extend the sonar range of its parent ship many times over, and several helicopters together could carry out a sonar sweep of a very large area. Exercises soon showed that helicopters with 'dunking' sonar added tremendous tactical flexibility and mobility to any anti-submarine operation.

At Suez in 1956, helicopters demonstrated another tactical role: Whirlwind 22s of 845 Squadron, and Whirlwinds and Bristol Sycamores of the Joint Experimental Helicopter Unit (the word 'Experimental' was dropped for the operation, so as to reassure the customers) operating from the light fleet carriers *Theseus* and *Ocean*, took nearly 500 men of 45 Commando Royal Marines, with some 20 tons of stores, ashore in ninety minutes.

The next Sikorsky 'import' was the Westland Wessex, which had first flown as the S-58 in 1954. Westland acquired a licence to build them in 1956 and deliveries to the Royal Navy began in 1960. In its anti-submarine role, the Wessex HAS Mark 1 had a range of nearly 500 miles, a top speed of 130 m.p.h., with a crew of one to three. It was fitted with a large dorsal radome, dipping sonar, two homing torpedoes, or four wire-guided missiles, rocket launchers or machine-guns. The first squadron, 815, formed at Culdrose in July 1961. Wessex were later embarked in the *County* class destroyers, such as *Devonshire*, and the assault ships *Fearless* and *Intrepid*. In its commando-carrying role, as the HU Mark 5, the Wessex was one of the best troop transports ever developed, and saw service all over the world.

Overshadowed by Sikorsky, the home-grown industry continued to produce helicopters, in hope rather than anger. Late in 1957, sea trials of the Fairey Ultra Light jet-powered helicopter were carried out in the frigate *Grenville*. The English Channel was very rough, but the helicopter landed and took off successfully some seventy times from a small platform, in winds up to 62 knots, with the ship pitching 10 to 12 feet and rolling up to 14 degrees to either side. In 1959, more trials were carried out on board the destroyer *Undaunted*, this time of the Saunders-Roe P.531. Nothing more was heard of the Fairey Ultra Light, but the P.531 eventually became the Westland Wasp.

With the marriage of the Wasp helicopter and the *Leander* class frigate, the helicopter came into its own in the Royal Navy. The *Leanders* were among the best small ships ever designed for the Navy. There were eventually twenty-six of these versatile 'all-singing, all-dancing' frigates, capable of anti-submarine, anti-aircraft and air direction roles. They were 2900 tons, 360 feet long, with a speed of 30 knots, armed with two 4.5-inch guns, Seacat anti-air missiles, Limbo and variable-depth sonar. The first of the class, *Leander* herself, was completed in March 1963, when the Wasp was already in production and being delivered to the Navy.

The Westland Wasp had a crew of two, a top speed of about 120 m.p.h. and a range of some 300 miles. It could carry the Mark 44 homing torpedo for anti-submarine work, or missiles. Although eventually it came to seem too small and too low-powered, in its day the Wasp was a game and willing little helicopter which gave every frigate captain his own air arm. It fulfilled all the requirements of what the Navy called its own 'organic' air power; it was versatile, controllable, and, above all, instantly available. Furthermore, the helicopter flight brought the air branch's equipment, methods, personnel and terminology intimately into the Navy's surface ships; never more would the Fleet Air Arm be a trade apart, known only in aircraft carriers and air stations.

Unknown to anybody at the time, the helicopter at sea was to perform a vital task for the Navy. Through all the vicissitudes of the 1960s and 1970s, the passing of the large carrier and the phasing out of fixed-wing flying, the sea-borne helicopter kept on maintaining the Navy's own air presence at sea, a continuity which was to prove a lifeline for the Navy.

Meanwhile, it was *still* necessary to state old truths about convoy. Admiral Sir George Creasy, C-in-C Portsmouth (and just about to become C-in-C Home Station) and NATO C-in-C of the Channel and southern North Sea, addressed the Commonwealth Naval Conference, Exercise FAIRLEAD, at Greenwich in the summer of 1957. In a thoughtful and wide-ranging speech, he confirmed his belief in NATO, his doubts that the experts could predict the future *quite* as accurately as they claimed, and his misgivings about the Russian submarine fleet, then estimated at over 500 boats. He wished he could be more confident of the ability of aircraft to detect modern submarines, and he had reservations about the 'hunter–killer group' concept. He had no doubt at all, he said, 'that in the last resort we shall rely, as we have so long relied, on convoy and escort to get our ships across the ocean. Convoys may well be very different in formation and tactics from those of the Second World War, but the principles remain unchanged.' But, his views and his opinions were entirely his own, Sir George said, 'and in case you may think that it is unduly conceited, let me remind you that it was the cackling of the geese that saved the Capitol in Rome!'

The convoy system was at that very moment undergoing one of its periodic attacks from bureaucrats. In October 1957, the Ministry of Transport circulated a paper considering the consequences, from the standpoint of the civilian shipping and port authorities in the United Kingdom, of ships sailing to and from NW Europe in 'monster' convoys of fifty to a hundred ships.

The Ministry decided that the convoy system 'greatly reduces the efficiency of the merchant fleet'; that 'if under independent sailings 100 ships are required to bring in a certain volume of cargo, a much greater number is required to move the same volume under convoy'; and that 'monster convoys' should be rejected because of the serious difficulties for the merchant shipping authorities caused by the 'loss of efficiency' and the 'lack of flexibility'. In the Ministry's view, such a system would be equivalent to 'putting out of action two-thirds of our merchant navy before the battle even begins', and would represent 'a major victory for an enemy' who successfully imposed it. Evidently, for the bureaucrats at the Ministry of Transport, the stories of convoy in two world wars were as the books destroyed by the Cumaean Sibyl: priceless, prophetic – and unread.

The Admiralty, hardly knowing whether to laugh or weep, but realizing that such crass inanities had to be answered, or the consequences might be grave (not, that is, for the bureaucrats, but for the country and not least for the men and women who had to go to sea in time of war) replied that actual war-time experiences showed that the Ministry's reasoning and conclusion were false. Peace-time British shipping was not 100 per cent efficient, and increased war-time attention to lading and routeing often meant an *increase* in efficiency; ships out of convoy were more often sunk, which was the ultimate inefficiency; it was the uncertainties and dangers of independent sailings which caused the most confusion and inefficiency in ports; the greatest problems of civilian authorities in handling cargoes in war-time arose, not from convoy, but from *not* convoying ships.

The Ministry, in talking of the 'greater number' (than the 100) to move the same cargo being 'the price exacted for the additional safety afforded by escorted convoy', showed that it had misunderstood the true value of convoy. Its statement could only be true if all independents completed their round voyages without being sunk, and their passage times were always shorter than if they were in convoy. In other words, the Ministry's reasoning suggested that ships were equally likely to complete their round voyages in all conditions, whether in war or peace, in convoy or out. But this simply was not the case. The figures from two wars contradicted it. Taking as their motto the words 'Truth does not win over error just on its merits. It, too has to be assiduously propagated,' the Admiralty believed they had won this particular exchange. But there would always be others.

Convoy, as a topic, did not figure very often or very large in any post-war White Paper on defence, as politician after politician charged with responsibility for defence affairs grappled (and some of them did not struggle long or hard) with the theory that the next war was bound to be short, sharp, and brutish, all over in a period of weeks, possibly even in days; there would be no opportunity to take a longer view of defence. Politicians seemed unable to grasp the point that an enemy, and especially one who was blatantly building up his submarine force over the years, might choose to attack merchant shipping, in the Atlantic, or round the Cape of Good Hope, in a campaign capable of an infinitely subtle range of variations, from threats, to outright blockade. The United Kingdom would then either have to form its shipping into convoys, and defend them; or, retaliate with nuclear weapons; or, submit.

The 1957 White Paper, for example, 'frankly recognized that there is at present no means of providing adequate protection for the people of this country against the consequences of an attack with nuclear weapons'. Thus, the role of Fighter Command for instance, was to be limited to the defence of the v bomber and Thor missile deterrent bases, and the air-defence force based in the United Kingdom would be 'substantially contracted'. Unsurprisingly, there was no mention of a possible role for Fighter Command in the defence of coastal shipping in convoy around the United Kingdom.

As for the Navy as a whole, the White Paper proclaimed that the 'role of naval forces in total war is uncertain'. Nuclear attack might bring the war to an end in a limited time, in which case naval forces would play no significant part. This, of course, was written under the shadow of the very recently detonated hydrogen bomb, but it still requires an effort of belief to realize that it was not scribbled by some raving lunatic on a lavatory wall but published in a government paper.

The crucial question of air cover for convoys was also very seldom debated at political level. How, where and by whom, convoys would be supported from the air had to be disentangled from the government of the day's general pronouncements on the Fleet Air Arm as a whole. By the beginning of the 1960s the long retreat from Empire was well under way (and nearing its end) but the Navy still had world-wide responsibilities, which normally included the deployment of an aircraft carrier, with its covering and supporting ships, east of Suez.

The Navy had three large carriers, *Ark Royal*, *Eagle*, and *Victorious*, the last and much-modernized survivor of the war-time *Illustrious* class. Of the smaller light-fleet carriers, *Hermes* was new and in her first commission; *Centaur* had been modernized, *Theseus* was in reserve; *Bulwark* and *Albion* were converted to 'commando carriers', to operate helicopters exclusively, with their fixed-wing facilities removed.

Front-line squadrons were equipped with the Supermarine Scimitar strike/fighter, armed with 30-mm guns, bombs, rockets and, later, missiles; the De Havilland Sea Vixen, successor to the Sea Venom all-weather fighter, armed with Firestreak missiles; and, later, the Blackburn Buccaneer fighter-bomber, 720 m.p.h., for low-level strike, and with a nuclear-bomb capability. Airborne early-warning radar was provided by modified Fairey Gannets. The first operational Buccaneer squadron commissioned in July 1962. The same year the Government announced that designs for a new large fleet carrier, known as CVA01, were in hand. It would take an estimated nine years to design, build and commission her.

Maybe the Navy should have exercised much stricter financial control over CVA01's design and requirements, because every department very naturally insisted on having the most of the very best. Maybe the Navy would have been wiser to have pressed instead for a larger number of smaller and cheaper carriers. Or maybe nothing could have saved CVA01. Amid suspicions that the government had made up its mind first and then found reasons to justify its decision, Mr Denis Healey, the Labour Defence Minister, announced in 1966 that the CVAOI project was cancelled.

The government argued that it had inherited a force of five carriers, which would reduce to three in a few years' time. Even if CVAOI were built, the carrier force would still be only three ships for the 1970s, at a cost of some £1400 million over ten years. This would give one carrier permanently stationed in the Far East, with another normally available at about fifteen days' notice.

The government believed that all the tasks for which they could conceive of carrier aircraft being required could be done more cheaply in other ways. Only one type of operation would be envisaged for which carriers and carrier-borne aircraft would be indispensable: a landing, or withdrawal, of troops against opposition armed with sophisticated weapons, outside the range of land-based air cover. The government thought it 'only realistic' to recognize that the country could not expect to undertake operations like this in the 1970s, unaided by our Allies (although the country did undertake just such an operation, in the Falklands, in the 1980s).

The government planned that aircraft operating from land-bases should take over the strike-reconnaissance and air-defence functions of the carrier on the reduced scale which the government thought would be all that was required after the mid 1970s. Helicopters would give close anti-submarine protection to ships, the helicopters flying from ships other than carriers. A surface-to-surface guided missile would be developed to give protection against surface ships. Airborne early-warning aircraft would continue to operate from carriers, and thereafter from land bases.

The Fleet Air Arm was to be 'carefully' run down, with the carriers operating as far as possible into the 1970s. Macdonell-Douglas Phantom all-weather strike fighters would be bought from the United States to replace the Sea Vixen. The Buccaneer Mark 2 would continue to enter service. The conversions of the two *Tiger* class cruisers to carry four anti-submarine helicopters each were to be completed. A new type of ship was planned to succeed them. A new class of Type 82 destroyer was to be ordered, to be equipped with the surface-to-air missile Sea Dart, and the Ikara anti-submarine rocket which delivered a homing torpedo at long range.

So, extrapolating from the statements in the White Paper, it seemed that any air cover for convoys, other than from helicopters flying from ships in the convoy itself, would have to be provided by the RAF, or the remnants of the fixed-wing Fleet Air Arm, if any still existed, flying from land bases spread throughout the world.

The decision to forsake carriers and to fly maritime air power from land bases seemed more extraordinary the more it was examined. Were land bases to be set up world-wide at the very time when naval bases were being closed and flag officers were hauling down their flags, for the last time, all

over the world? There was much talk of 'island bases'. Of two, in the Indian
Ocean, one had no fresh water and the other had its runway regularly flooded
by the sea in rough weather. Some heretics calculated that the cost of the
bases would be more than the carriers. Somebody suggested towing an old
carrier out and mooring it off an island as a base. But then somebody else
suggested commissioning the carrier and leaving the island where it was –
which brought the argument round in a hilarious circle.

It was, of course, perfectly feasible for shore-based aircraft to support
convoys. It depended where the convoys were. In the NATO Exercise EDEN
APPLE in November 1969 fifty ships from the United Kingdom, the United
States, Italy, Greece and France (although by then no longer formally a
member of NATO), under an Italian admiral, took part in a fortnight of air,
surface and anti-submarine exercises in the Mediterranean. The RAF flew
out stores and personnel from the squadrons of *Eagle* (then re-fitting at
home), and her aircraft flew from shore bases during the exercise, the
Buccaneers from Luqa, Malta, and the Sea Vixens and Gannets from an
Italian air base at Decimomannu in Sardinia. *Eagle*'s Wessex helicopters
were embarked in the RFAs *Olmeda* and *Tide Pool*. The whole episode was an
encouraging demonstration of the shore-based air support the RAF would
provide after the carrier force was phased out in the mid 1970s – although the
aircraft were actually from the Navy.

The NATO strategy concept of the 1970s was for a gradual escalation of
hostilities, with conventional weapons, up to general warfare with tactical
nuclear weapons. The concept was exercised on a major scale in NORTHERN
WEDDING in September 1971, when 180 ships from more than eight nations,
and the full range of NATO aircraft, from maritime long-range to strike
aircraft, took part in exercises stretching from the North Sea to the
Norwegian Sea, the Shetland–Faeroes Gap and the entrances to the Baltic.

The exercise plan supposed that an enemy ('Orange') nation had begun
harassing and boarding the fishing trawlers of the Allies ('Blue'). This, with
acts of sabotage ashore, led to the evacuation of 'Blue' shipping from ports,
the setting up of naval control shipping, and the institution of convoy, for
which thirty merchantmen were chartered.

The first convoy, of ten German naval auxiliaries, sailed from Cuxhaven to
Frederikshaven and back. The second, of ten vessels, sailed clockwise from
Rotterdam, across to East Anglia, up the east coast, and then to Stavanger;
the third sailed in the opposite direction, from Hartlepool Bay, south and
across to the Dutch coast, and then to Esbjerg in Denmark; the fourth,
nominated the most valuable and escorted by ships from the NATO Standing
Naval Force Atlantic (STANAVFORLANT) and the Royal Yacht *Britannia*,
sailed from Kristiansand and Stavanger to Invergordon and then to the Firth
of Forth. Meanwhile, far to the north, after a simulated threat to the NATO
Northern Flank, a strike group headed by *Ark Royal* made a high speed
transit to the Shetland–Faeroes Gap, opposed by 'Orange' forces.

The convoys had a busy exercise and their escorts were fully stretched. There were minefields to be cleared, or skirted, and attacks by submarines, aircraft and, off the German and Dutch coasts, by 'Orange' fast patrol boats. There were emergency turns, station-keeping and handling problems (the thirty chartered ships were all small coasters), but despite the frequent attacks and the many alarms and excursions, the convoy phases of the exercise had a calmness and a confidence, an almost 'olde worlde charm' about them. Other aspects of NORTHERN WEDDING might have given NATO planners furiously to think, but, as one captain said, 'Convoy still works.'

Later in 1971, in December, a joint Navy–RAF exercise dispelled any possible optimism about the RAF's ability to protect the fleet at sea. It was called HIGH WOOD and took place off the coast of northern Norway which, as cruel critics pointed out, was just about the only place in the world where the RAF could have provided enough aircraft for a realistic exercise.

As it was, the RAF found it hard going. Throughout the eleven days of the exercise they were bedevilled by shortage of aircraft and aircrews. Towards the end, the RAF's 'reaction time' to any reconnaissance sighting became so slow it was taking up to twelve hours for a strike to reach the position of the sighting, when the target could be as much as 300 miles away from the datum. The strike aircraft became increasingly disassociated from events at sea-level, which had changed entirely by the time they arrived. The weather was bad, strikes were thwarted by fog, and at one time all but three air stations in the United Kingdom were closed (at sea, where an aircraft carrier would have been operating, conditions were brilliantly clear for flying).

To use a homely metaphor, HIGH WOOD showed that in relying on the RAF for air cover at sea, the Navy was like a man who had to ring up a flunky to come out with an umbrella every time it looked like rain. Unfortunately, the flunky sometimes took twelve hours to arrive, by which time everybody would be soaked to the skin. Or, the flunky might find it raining so hard at his house he could not put a foot outside his door. If convoys really did have to rely wholly upon the RAF, then the prospect was grim. Fortunately, there were other alternatives.

Chapter Twenty-Two

Luckily for maritime nations such as the United Kingdom, the principle of convoy appears to be indestructible. Often derided as dangerously obsolete, ignored or criticized by ignorant politicians (it often seems that the cleverer the Defence Minister, the more stupid he is on naval affairs), convoy goes on surviving, with its theory handed down like some tribal lore, and its practical means assembled as though by some divinely surreptitious agency.

For the United Kingdom in the 1970s, the redeeming factor was the helicopter, and one helicopter in particular, the Westland Sea King. It is not so much a helicopter as a fully-integrated, all-weather, hunter-killer anti-submarine weapon system, with radar, sonar, automatic flight control system, a crew of four (two pilots, observer and sonar operator), armed with homing torpedoes or depth-charges. At 21,000 pounds, it is a large helicopter, with a cruising speed of about 130 m.p.h. and a range of nearly 800 miles. The first production model flew in 1969 and deliveries began in late 1970. Sea Kings from *Ark Royal* first performed very successfully in NORTHERN WEDDING, maintaining a constant anti-submarine guard round the strike force.

As the fixed-wing element of the Fleet Air Arm began to wither away, even though *Ark Royal*'s life was extended to the end of 1978, so the Sea King emerged as the Navy's major front-line aircraft. If fixed-wing flying was to cease, then clearly some ship (emphatically *not* a carrier) had to be designed to operate Sea Kings. The existing helicopter cruisers *Tiger* and *Blake* were hybrids, and with their huge hangars aft, had the awkward uncomfortable looks of all hybrids.

The new ship, also a cruiser, had to be designed from the outset to have enough flat surface to operate several Sea Kings in their anti-submarine role. So it was to be a through-deck cruiser. But it was also a *command* cruiser, able to exercise command and control of naval and maritime air forces. Finally, it was to make some contribution to area air defence, with missiles.

As it transpired, CVA01's cancellation was a blessing in disguise, although, to the Navy, it was very well disguised at the time. The cancellation concentrated minds wonderfully, to seek some other solution. Not that the new ship was a *carrier*, indeed anybody in the Ministry of Defence who seriously advocated carriers was running the gravest professional risk of, in MOD parlance, 'being drummed out of the Brownies'. The new ship was a through-deck command *cruiser*, and as a *cruiser* she survived a long campaign of committee battles, escaped a thousand paper ambushes, ran the gauntlet of Treasury hawks and a sustained hostile lobby by the RAF so brilliant as to be tantamount to back-stabbing.

The new ship, to be called *Invincible*, was ordered in April 1973, laid down in July, launched by HM The Queen in May 1977 and accepted into the Navy in March 1980. As the years went by, nobody dared mention she was looking more and more like a carrier. She was still officially a *cruiser*, with fourteen aircraft, twin Sea Dart surface-to-air missile mounting, gas turbines giving 28 knots, and a crew of nearly 1000 officers and men. At 16,000 tons, 678 feet long, she was the biggest new ship the Navy had had for over a quarter of a century. So, hardly believing its luck, the Navy emerged with a carrier and, more marvellous still, the promise of two more, *Illustrious* and *Indomitable* (renamed *Ark Royal*).

The Navy would still have been grateful for a cruiser that looked like a carrier. But two special pieces of equipment brought off the final miraculous metamorphosis. The first was the Sea Harrier Vertical or Short Take Off and Landing (V/STOL) aircraft, which had begun years before as a concept appropriately named the Flying Bedstead. Trials in *Ark Royal* in 1971 showed no deck-handling disadvantages, and the decision to go ahead with production was taken in 1975. The aircraft emerged as a genuine 650-knot fighter/reconnaissance/strike aircraft, armed with two 30-mm guns, Sidewinder air-to-air missiles, or Harpoon missiles for surface targets. *Invincible*'s normal aircraft complement would be nine Sea Kings and five Sea Harriers.

The second piece of equipment was the 'ski jump', a sloped deck which gave a loaded Sea Harrier a vital extra boost into the air, without any extra gear or machinery. The ski jump reduced the deck length needed for take-off by up to two-thirds at lower aircraft launch-weights, gave an aircraft an effective 30 knots excess speed at launch compared with a flat deck, increasing the pay-load by some 2000 pounds; and allowed the ship to launch aircraft at normal speeds, saving considerable amounts of fuel. It was one of those sublimely simple ideas which won £25,000 for its inventor and left everybody else kicking themselves for not thinking of it first.

With Sea Harriers, fixed-wing flying returned to the Fleet Air Arm. *Invincible*'s primary role was officially defined (with a distressing return to the 'hunter–killer' concept) as leading an anti-submarine-warfare Task Group, operating in such areas as the Greenland–Iceland–UK 'gap' which would be

a 'choke point' for hostile submarines on passage to and from the Atlantic. A
role in 'direct support of convoys carrying vital reinforcements or supplies to
Western Europe' was regarded as secondary.

At £175 million, *Invincible* was a costly ship. A cheaper alternative,
proposed by Vosper Thornycroft in 1975, was the so-called 'Harrier Carrier',
a return almost to the 'cheap and cheerful' concept of the war-time escort
carrier. The ship was basically the size of a large frigate, but with a greater
beam, of about 90 feet, a flight deck length of 420 feet, and a tonnage of
between 6000 and 8000. Ten aircraft, a mix of Sea Harriers and Sea Kings,
were to be housed in the hangar. The flight deck was tipped up by a 6-degree
ramp at the bows to give the ski-jump effect. The ship's complement would
be 250 officers and men, with a further 150 officers and men of the Air Group.
But no orders were placed for these ships.

The ships with *Invincible* in the Task Group are all types which emerged
during the 1970s: the Type 42 guided-missile destroyer, whose primary role
is to provide air defence for the Task Group, equipped with Sea Dart
air-defence missile, 4.5-inch rapid-fire gun, and Ship Torpedo Weapon
System (STWS), firing a homing torpedo, to provide quick-reaction defence
should a submarine have penetrated inside the cover of longer-range
systems. The first of this 3500-ton, 410-foot class, *Sheffield*, was completed in
1974.

In the same year the name ship of the *Amazon* class Type 21 general-
purpose frigates appeared: 2800 tons, 384 feet long, gas turbines and
controllable pitch propellers, Seacat close-range missile, Exocet surface-to-
surface missile, 4.5-inch rapid-fire gun, and STWS. The first of the *Broad-
sword* Type 22 frigates, designed for the anti-submarine role, with computer-
assisted sonar system and advanced sensor and communication equipment,
was completed in 1979: the first all-missile, all-metric ships, with Exocet, Sea
Wolf close-range air defence missile, six STWS tubes; 3550 tonnes, 131 metres
long.

All these ships carry the Lynx helicopter (the *Broadswords* carry two),
which is replacing the Wasp in small ships. The Lynx is an excellent little
multi-purpose, twin-engined helicopter, designed for the anti-submarine
role and to strike against surface ships. With a crew of two, pilot and
observer, it has a range of 370 miles, speed of 160 knots; it is armed with Sea
Skua air-to-surface missiles, or Mark 46 homing torpedoes, and Sea Spray
search radar system.

The problem of trade defence which these ships, and their counterparts in
the United States Navy and the other NATO navies, would face in time of war
is still huge, equally as large and formidable a task as at any time in the past.
Over 99½ per cent of the world's trade is still carried by ships. Every day of
the year, some 120 ocean-going ships arrive in western Europe and discharge
3 million tons of cargo. In September 1980, for instance, 29 million tons of
crude oil passed the Cape of Good Hope, bound for America and the West.

The minimum civilian and economic requirements of western Europe in time of war are estimated at 1000 shiploads every month. It is recognized that NATO land and air forces are unequal to those of the Warsaw Pact and would require quick reinforcement from the United States in time of war; those reinforcements would require an estimated 500 extra shiploads of stores, equipment, ammunition, fuel, and men.

In general, merchant ships are now larger (some three times the pre-war average), faster, and very much more specialized – with supertankers of 250,000 tons and over, defined as VLCCs (Very Large Crude Carriers), and over 350,000 tons, as ULCCs (Ultra Large Crude Carriers); RO-RO (Roll-On Roll-Off) ships, BO-RO (Bulk/oil/Ro-Ro) ships, OBO (oil/bulk/ore) ships, PROBO (product/oil bulk/ore) ships; LASH (Lighter Aboard Ship, carrying cargo barges) ships; ships carrying cryogenic cargoes in extremely cold liquid form, such as LNG (liquid natural gas: methane) ships and LPG (liquid petroleum gas: butane and propane) ships as well as PCC (Pure Car Carriers), capable of transporting up to 150,000 vehicles; and container ships of various specialized types.

Merchant fleets of the west have shrunk, in times of recession. The United Kingdom fleet has dwindled from 1600 ships of 50 million tons, as recently as 1975, down to only 970 ships of 29 million tons in 1982. By contrast the Soviet merchant marine has continued to expand, and Russia is now firmly in seventh place in the list of the world's carriers, with over 1500 ships of above 4000 gross registered tons, more than any other nation.

The Soviet merchant fleet clearly has a para-military function, containing as it does many more RO-RO ships, for instance, than any economic or commercial need could possibly require, as well as performing an invaluable intelligence and surveillance function world-wide. Such a large merchant fleet does, of course, make Soviet Russia more vulnerable in time of war. A great many ships would have to be defended. But defeat at sea for Russia would be serious, but not crippling. For the West, defeat at sea would be final.

The Russians may or may not introduce convoy (they certainly have the number of ships at sea to make it necessary) in time of hostilities, but the west undoubtedly would, or should. Convoy has not been used in earnest since 1945, but the means to introduce and control it are still maintained in good repair. The naval control of shipping, first voluntary and then compulsory, are necessary stages in the transition to war.

The precise stages, and especially the timing, of a real transition to a real war can only be imagined. Voluntary control of shipping could, of course, be introduced at any time in a state of political tension, the aim always being to cause the minimum disruption to trade, and to maintain the normal patterns and flows of merchant shipping for as long as possible. Voluntary control could vary from advice on routeing, for example, with warnings about possible hostile presences, to the offer of an actual escort by men-of-war.

But by that time, the transition to war would be in its final stages, the first of which would have been the signing of Queen's Order One. This is an initial response to threat, enabling the call-up of immediate reserves. Queen's Order Two initiates a more general state of emergency. Amongst other things, it enables the Navy to call up the Royal Naval Reserve and to enforce the compulsory control of shipping.

Compulsory control means virtual nationalization of shipping. NATO has a dormant command organization for the control of shipping, to be activated in time of war. The countries around the Pacific have their own agreement, a relic of the old agreements between the countries of the now-defunct SEATO, to carry out control of shipping in their respective areas. These command functions are regularly tested in 'paper' exercises. In March 1982, for instance, the NATO countries (minus Greece and Turkey), the nations of the 'old Commonwealth', with Brazil and Argentina, carried out a major exercise to test shipping control in areas of the world oceans beyond NATO.

At the local level, shipping control is directed by Naval Control of Shipping Officers, nominated beforehand and trained at the Naval Control of Shipping School in the Trade Defence Faculty of HMS *Vernon* at Portsmouth. These officers, coming from many walks of life, receive regular training, and exercises three or four times a year. In a time of threat they would travel out, as civilians, as 'consular shipping advisers' and the aim would be to have them at their posts 'before the balloon ascended'. Every effort is made to ensure that the same NCSOs go to the same ports, but often business or other reasons make this impossible. The United States has a more closely integrated system, in which parties of shipping control officers can be virtually certain they will be assigned to their own ports abroad. Naval officers already on the spot might have a dual appointment and take over as NCSOs until the nominated officer arrives. The Royal Naval Auxiliary Service (RNXS) provides the ratings for the Control of Shipping, the officers having RNR commissions.

Whilst the naval command decides the routes and numbers of convoys, and the times of sailings, the NCSO makes up the convoys, and deals with the problems of movements of ships in and out of his port. Meanwhile, the Civil Direction of Shipping, organized by officials of the Department of Transport, takes over the functions of the peace-time owners of the ships: allocating cargoes, turning ships round, loading and discharging, fuelling and manning.

There are NATO courses for convoy commodores, of whom there are presently between sixty and eighty: captains for ocean convoys, commanders for coastal convoys, but all recently retired officers with experience of command at sea.

The relationship between the Royal Navy and the merchant navy is crucial for any system of convoy. In this case, absence does *not* make the heart grow fonder. Essentially it is a matter of personalities, but differences are always liable to occur, caused by a great deal of ignorance on one side, and prejudice fuelled by inferiority complexes on the other. Relations are normally closer in war-time and more distant in peace-time; the men of both services got on extremely well together during the Falklands crisis, for example.

Many merchant navy officers have RNR commissions. The RN regularly sends its own officers on liaison voyages in merchantmen and holds regular courses for master mariners at *Vernon*, with briefings on naval problems and on defence matters particularly as it affects them. RN officers often entertain their brother officers in the sea service, but social visiting is even more difficult today than in the past. Tankers have always pumped quickly out or in, and be away; now container ships also load and unload in a very short space of time. In 1978 Commodore John Wacher, of the P&O, did a survey on RN/MN relationships and concluded that the two sides were tending to drift apart. He hoped it would not take another war to bring them together again.

Relations between the Royal and Merchant Navies were agreeably cordial, and showed a high degree of mutual respect and accord, during the operations to retake the Falkland Islands in the spring of 1982, when several stages of mobilization for war were actually carried out. The Falklands could not have been recaptured without the merchant navy. Some fifty-four ships (albeit a few of them foreign) were either chartered or requisitioned. Contingency plans for the assembly and dispatch of a Task Force, with its ancillary services, already existed in the Ministry of Defence. Shipowners were themselves taken aback by the accuracy of the Ministry's knowledge of the capabilities of their ships. They were astonished by the speed at which various types of ships were called up for service, and by the rapidity with which the dockyards carried out the numerous conversions, such as the fitting of helicopter pads in the *Queen Elizabeth 2*, and the preparation of a Roll-On-Roll-Off ship such as the *Atlantic Conveyor* to receive war stores. Such measures could be taken much further in future. *Atlantic Conveyor*'s replacement could be designed from the outset to have a helicopter pad (as many super-tankers already are). Many other kinds of ship could be built with decks already strengthened, to receive prefabricated helicopter pads quickly in times of emergency.

Since the war, the Soviet nation has become ostentatiously more aware of sea power. In 1964, the Russian navy began a tremendous metamorphosis, from what had been virtually a coastal defence force, to a 'blue-water' navy whose ships are now seen all over the world. In February 1956, Marshal Zhukov, one of the most successful of all Second World War generals, the man who never lost a battle, told the Twentieth Communist Party Congress that 'in a future war the struggle at sea will be of immeasurably greater importance than it was in the last war'. In 1957, the Russian Rear-Admiral Andreev wrote that 'the essence of the matter is that for the imperialist states the very possibility of conducting war depends upon the support of uninterrupted operation of sea and ocean communications'.

More recently, the Russians have come to see their navy as an important instrument of foreign policy. Admiral of the Fleet Sergei Gorshkov, the architect of the modern Russian navy, wrote that 'the role of the Navy is not limited to the execution of important missions in armed conflict. While representing a formidable force in war, it has always been a political weapon and an important support for diplomacy in peacetime owing to its inherent qualities . . . to exert pressure on potential enemies without direct employment of weaponry.'

With such views openly expressed, with the knowledge that the Russian Navy was completing a submarine every six weeks, and had laid down monster submarines of nearly 20,000 tons, there surely could be no doubt about Russian intentions. But, as always with Russian affairs, the matter is not so cut and dried. Soviet Russia is a collection of largely land-locked nations, a country of landsmen with a deep historical suspicion of the outside world – unsurprisingly, since it has been invaded from the land twice within the century.

Maritime nations, such as the United Kingdom, can see the chance the Russian Navy has to attack shipping. But where a British admiral sees opportunity a Russian sees risks, particularly the threat of the west's carrier battle groups and ballistic missile submarines (SSBNs). The Russians need their Navy to counter the threat of opposing carriers and submarines, and to protect their own SSBNs, which are now a vital and growing component in their strategic forces. Such other roles as attacking trade shipping, amphibious support of a land campaign, and mining of harbours and shipping routes, though very important, are secondary.

The Russians also face problems of distance and geography. To reach and attack Atlantic shipping, Russian ships in the Black Sea, the Baltic, and the Arctic must first pass through NATO-controlled 'choke-points' before beginning their long passages to their patrol areas. Similarly Russian aircraft have to pass through NATO-controlled airspace. The present generation of Russian strike aircraft, even with flight refuelling, can only just reach the South-West Approaches. North Atlantic shipping could be routed southwards, via the Azores, and so need air protection only on the last section northwards from the Azores.

Looking at the map of the northern hemisphere, and noticing the Russian geographical disadvantages, has lulled some NATO planners dangerously close to a 'Maginot Line' mentality – the belief that thousands of miles of sea can be physically sealed off, like keeping a neighbour's dog out of the garden, only on a larger scale. There are plans to throw a mine blockade across the Kola Inlet; to establish a 'barrier' of patrolling hunter–killer submarines in the 'choke-points'; and to provide hunter–killer groups, equipped with carriers, similarly to intercept submarines *en route*.

Historically, the omens for these measures are not encouraging. From Otranto in 1917 to Iceland in 1942, U-boats have generally ignored mine barriers. Submarines lying in wait for other submarines in transit generally stand as good a chance of being sunk as of sinking an opponent. A carrier group searching for a submarine might indeed find one, just as *Courageous* did, and suffer her fate. Experience shows that hunter–killers, in spite of the enormously increased range and sensitivity of modern sensors, would be more effective with or in support of convoys.

Even modern sensors can suffer breakdowns. Mistakes can be made, equipment be unreliable or defective. Often the finest sensor of all is the 'good old Mark One human eye-ball'. But the area where the hunter–killers would be called upon to operate has atrocious weather, with storms all year round and poor visibility. Radar might be an exact science, with straight or almost straight beams, but sonar is no such thing; the underwater world is full of vagaries and uncertainties, with layers of different density and temperature, inexplicable echoes and resonances, where sound and silence can be equally baffling.

With a policy defined as 'forward defence and flexible response', NATO navies would concentrate in the Norwegian Sea, in the hope of bringing the enemy to a decisive action in a battle for the sea lines of communication (SLOCs). NATO carrier and nuclear-submarine force would, it is hoped, necessarily attract the Soviet Navy and tie it down. If the battle was won, NATO navies would expect much less trouble in securing the SLOCs.

But if the battle was inconclusive, or even if it were conclusive in terms of the forces engaged, an enemy would surely have submarines at sea before the outset of hostilities and would not be prevented from carrying on a war against trade, like the French *guerre de course* of the Napoleonic wars, when – even after the strategic victory at Trafalgar – the Navy was still forced to run convoys as far as China and as late as 1815.

Just as the Russian navy could be expected to have submarines at sea before the start of hostilities, so it is to be hoped that the first of the NATO reinforcements (an estimated 1 million men and 12 million tons of supplies and equipment) would also be on their way. The intention is to run the reinforcement ships independently for as long as possible and as quickly as possible. A major staff survey carried out in 1978, which was subsequently exercised in TEAM WORK '80, concluded that if opposition was stiff enough to cause unacceptable losses then convoy would be introduced. 'Unacceptable losses' were put at 15 per cent. But this was just staff theory. There is no doubt that the appreciation of the threat would be drastically altered as soon as the first torpedo or missile hit the first merchant ship, and convoy would be introduced at once.

The convoys would fall into three main categories: those for 'Economic Shipping' carrying the food, fuel and raw materials that maintain the civilian populations of western Europe; 'Reinforcement Shipping', bringing the men and stores from the USA and Canada already earmarked for the defence of Europe; and 'Re-supply Shipping', for the military re-supply of Europe after the first stores have been used. Critics of convoy say that all three types are irrelevant in a thermonuclear war.

Certainly, a thermonuclear exchange which incinerated the whole of two continents would render any convoys at sea irrelevant. They would then be just collections of ships which had no meaningful destinations. But in any event short of a total cataclysm, and even some of the most serious might be followed by a so-called 'broken-backed period', life would still go on; ships would still sail and would have to be defended. For such defence, despite many appearances to the contrary, convoy is still the best option.

It could be argued that one hydrogen bomb dropped on a convoy would wipe out every ship. It would be politically and practically very unlikely that a bomb large enough would ever be directed at a convoy at sea. Tactical nuclear weapons, air-borne, or fired from submarines, and in the kiloton rather than the megaton range, are much more likely.

Against such weapons, ships are not wholly defenceless. Their very construction to withstand sea and storm, makes them much more resistant to blast and radiation than buildings ashore, and they can manoeuvre to avoid steaming through fall-out clouds, or use 'pre-wetting', by constantly hosing and spraying the outside of the ship, to minimize the effect of fall-out.

But a convoy's best defence against such weapons would be simply to spread out. Almost all modern merchantmen, and certainly all those which would be included in reinforcement convoys, have short-range radar and short-wave voice R/T equipment which would allow them to keep in station and in touch, without giving their presence away. A modern convoy could disperse to intervals of as much as 5 miles between ships and still remain a coherent entity. Such dispersal would give enormous protection. A forty-ship convoy, for instance, with five miles spacings between ships, could cover a sea area of 30 miles by 25 miles, 750 square miles, and still be a reasonably controllable unit. But it would require nine 5-megaton bombs, all exactly placed and detonated, before all its ships were certain to be sunk.

Increasing the space between ships also reduces dramatically the dangers of submarine attack, to the point where a submarine has to attack each ship, each time, individually. For instance, doubling the usual Second World War convoy ship interval of half a mile to one mile reduces the risk of loss to about a quarter, while only enlarging the defence perimeter to be covered by the escorts by a half. Increasing the spacing to two miles decreases the risk of loss to one-sixteenth, while increasing the convoy perimeter by only $2\frac{1}{2}$ times. To take the example of a 300-ship convoy with escorts placed 5 miles outside the convoy perimeter; at $\frac{1}{2}$-mile spacing between ships, the perimeter would be approximately 62 miles; at one-mile spacing, 93 miles; and at two-mile spacing, 157 miles.

A modern convoy would be much harder to 'lose', even in the wastes of the Atlantic. A timely diversion could take a Second World War convoy away from a waiting U-boat concentration, and it might never be seen by the enemy again. But radar satellites, advanced electronic surveillance methods, long-range maritime reconnaissance aircraft, and 'long-eared' nuclear sub-marines with much-enhanced long-range sonar capabilities, make convoys much easier to detect and hence much more vulnerable.

However, in practice, no detection system or collection of systems is 100 per cent effective. Satellites can be 'blinded' or destroyed. Shadowing aircraft can be shot down or at least chased away. Actual experience at sea has shown that bad weather and poor visibility, mechanical failures or enemy interference with satellites and aircraft, and the inherent uncertainties of sound propagation and detection at long ranges in the sea, can and do hinder detection. In fact, exercises have demonstrated again and again that it is not always possible to locate, identify and then track one's own forces satisfac-torily and consistently, even with the benefits of previously signalled pos-itions, radar, electronic surveillance methods, and other aids, let alone an enemy trying to evade detection.

Speed still gives excellent protection. Any speed over 20 knots is in itself a good defence even against modern nuclear high-speed submarines (SSNs). The ratio of submarine to convoy speed was 16:6 approximately in the Second World War (and to achieve that the U-boat had to surface). The modern ratio is about 30:17, with the SSN able to remain submerged. An SSN *should* be able to attack, withdraw and gain bearing, and attack again, until its torpedoes or missiles were exhausted. But here, apart from such practical limitations as that the submarine would be detectably noisy at 30 knots, whilst unable to hear anything itself, the ancient principle of convoy comes into play: to attack, the submarine must reveal its presence, and render it liable to counter-attack. The perils of being an independent or a straggler, however, still remain. A modern SSN can detect and, to a certain extent identify, independent merchant ships at ranges of over 100 miles.

The torpedo-firing submarine is only one threat. Convoys are also liable to attack by long-range maritime aircraft, armed with air-to-surface missiles; by strike air craft, armed with air-to-surface missiles, flying from a carrier (though this is much less likely by the Soviet Navy); from submarines such as the Soviet 'Echo' class, firing missiles, on aircraft or satellite information, from ranges of about 300 miles; and by submarines like the Soviet 'Charlie' class, firing missiles from about 30 miles.

But convoys also have a variety of defences. Air cover would be provided by fighters, either orthodox or V/STOL, flying from carriers, exactly as from the escort carriers of the Second World War, to shoot down shadowers and strike aircraft. But there will never be enough carriers, and it will be necessary to revive the MAC ship concept and give merchant ships their own air power with V/STOL aircraft embarked, flying from a specially streng-thened deck. The system would embark in three containers, one for the aircraft, another for the spare gear and tools, and a third as accommodation for the air and ground crew. Missile defence would be provided by electronic counter measures, to confuse in-coming missiles, or by direct anti-missile missile such as Sea Wolf, in the accompanying carrier and the anti-airwarfare (AAW) frigates in the convoy escorts. But, once again, the merchantmen could themselves be armed, in an exact comparison with the DEMS armed ships of the Second World War, with some system such as a light-weight Sea Wolf unit, embarked in containers, one for the missiles and launcher, a second for the control console. The carrier, if present, would act as control and command ship, in the centre of the convoy, with a MAC ship equipped with Sea Harrier in each column of the convoy. The outer columns to port and starboard would include the (DEMS) Sea Wolf-equipped merchantmen.

An unalerted submarine detection, that is to say, a detection 'out of the blue', around a convoy, with no fore-warning from long-range sensors or intelligence, remains today as difficult a task as it was in the Second World War, when the first knowledge of a submarine's presence was often the torpedoing of a ship. Recent exercises have shown how difficult this still is, a fact which has been used to discount the efficiency of surface escort and as an argument against convoy.

There will still be many casualties from convoys, and many of them are likely to be caused by submarines previously undetected. But there remains a great deal that can be done to protect convoys. Sighting reports transmitted to submarines at sea can be so jammed or interfered with that the would-be attacker receives only a garbled report or none at all. Modern sensors have very long ranges, indeed so long that some, such as those in maritime patrol aircraft, can be used 'to spread the assets' and protect more than one convoy at once. An attacking submarine may well be detected so far out that the attack and counter-attack may take hours to complete, as the submarine makes its run in from the deep field.

While the convoy, steaming as fast as possible, makes long-leg zigzags, and takes advantage of any available bad-weather cover, the attacking SSN has to approach through a sequence of long-range sonar 'ears': sound surveillance systems (SOSUS) on the sea-bed; sonobuoys monitored by maritime patrol aircraft; defending SSNs with their own sonar, and possibly using towed array systems; and advanced passive sonar ships positioned well clear of the convoy on the likeliest threatened side. SSNs or SSKs (hunter –killer submarines) will be ready to run down any detections made by aircraft or advanced passive sonar ships. Ships will use acoustic decoys, in the hope of confusing the attacking submarine's sonar, and forcing it to use radar or periscope and thus, at once, greatly increasing the chance of discovery. Electronic and other counter-measures meanwhile will seek to confuse the enemy's picture of his target, falsify his information, and avert his weapons.

Closer in, there will be heavy helicopters such as Sea Kings, embarked in the carrier, or equally well in the MAC ships, using the same container principle as the Sea Harriers, equipped with dipping sonar and anti-submarine weapons; frigates armed with Ikara, a rocket-propelled anti-submarine missile delivering homing torpedoes at long range; and light helicopters, operating from frigates, with depth charges or homing torpedoes. Lastly, the warships themselves will have STWS almost as a last resort.

Tactical nuclear weapons, in the form of nuclear depth-bombs, are likely to be used from the earliest stages of a war at sea, but by helicopters rather than frigates. A frigate will probably be unable to get 'astride' a fast and agile modern SSN in dropping or ahead-throwing range. Frigates are more likely to use homing torpedoes. Conceptually, what is required is a much cheaper 'intelligent depth-charge' analogous to the 'smart bomb' used by the USAAF in Vietnam, which can be dropped or lobbed on to its target and home itself onwards.

Convoy is only one, albeit a very important, counter-move against a Soviet threat. It is an essential part of the west's strategy of a flexible response. In the last five years there have been signs that the Soviet Navy has the capability to attack Atlantic shipping, and some evidence that they have been practising it in their exercises. Thus the protection of its shipping is still vital to the west, and without that ability the west's armoury is incomplete.

Short of a great, terminal nuclear holocaust, there are an infinite number of convincingly possible 'scenarios', in which the defence of trade becomes necessary for the survival of the west:

Imagine tension and unrest building up in the Soviet satellites as a result of economic stagnation and a shortage of commodities. The Conference for Security and Cooperation in Europe has sparked off a desire for more individual freedom in its member countries and they want to maintain their economic growth by trading with, indeed even joining, the EEC. To divert attention from its internal problems the Soviet leadership has been 'sabre rattling' against NATO, exhorting us to stop subversion of her satellites and pointing a finger at increases in NATO's real defence spending of 3 per cent. Russia realizes, however, that her influence over her allies will be precarious unless she can rapidly and substantially widen her economic base.

Moscow then informs NATO that there must be an end to the 'subversion' and states her intention to institute a blockade of Western Europe unless NATO agrees to the demilitarization of Germany, Denmark, Norway and the Low Countries. NATO is unable to apply conventional force against Russia and would indeed be hard pressed to defend her own territory. Therefore, unless the blockade can be broken, the only recourse is submission to Soviet demands or nuclear attack on Russia.

Faced with two such extreme remedies it would be impossible to convince the United States, and even a large section of European public opinion, that a full-scale nuclear exchange was preferable to bowing to the apparently limited Soviet demands. After all, no territory had been requested. The fact that in future we would have no bargaining position at all, that NATO would be

defunct, that the 'Finlandization' of Norway, Denmark, Germany and Bene-
lux would eventually follow and the EEC disintegrate would not immediately be
appreciated. The free world would be plunged into economic crisis and the
Soviets gain all they had aimed for.

In such circumstances, naval history suggests that convoy should be introduced at once, and in full, that large convoys are safer than small, and that the
larger the convoy the safer it is. Therefore, if it is calculated that 300 ships,
say, are required every fortnight, then a 300-ship convoy should sail every
fourteen days, accompanied by the strongest defence available: a carrier, if
possible, AAW and ASW frigates, MAC ships with Sea Harriers and Sea Kings,
individual DEMS ships armed with Sea Wolf, maritime patrol aircraft overhead, SSNs below and in the deep field, so that the convoy had cover above,
below, and on the surface of the sea. It should be accepted that the passage of
every such convoy is a major naval undertaking, comparable to a large fleet
action, and the enemy should simply be defied, to come on if he can.

Unfortunately, the political omens, at least in the United Kingdom, are
not encouraging. The 1981 White Paper on defence, produced by a Secretary
of State, Mr John Nott, who had never previously exhibited any knowledge of
or interest in defence matters, contained some alarming implications: an
apparent belief that the next war would be short and on Britain's front line,
meaning the central front in Europe; a concurrent ignorance that the ability
to protect shipping is an essential component of deterrence and, following
from that, an abandonment of the ancient strategy of convoy; a failure to
realize that Great Britain's contributions to the central front and to the
maritime forces of NATO are equally important; and, apparently the conviction that transatlantic reinforcement was irrelevant (so it was, though not in
the way the author of the White Paper intended: any success on the central
front would indeed become irrelevant if there were no means of reinforcing
it).

For the Navy, the most alarming aspects of the White Paper were the
proposed reductions in frigates, the vessels which could most readily act as
convoy escorts; and the reappearance of a 'Maginot-line' mentality, with a
concept of sheltering behind 'barriers', sealing the Greenland–Iceland–UK
gap.

More recently, there has been an even more disturbing event. Every new
naval generation firmly believes that its own new weapons make old truths
obsolete, and so an old and bloodstained heresy has recently been resur-
rected. It is now considered that the vastly improved ranges and sensitive-
ness of modern sensors makes the 'Defended Lane' viable. The concept is to
set up barriers in the north and behind them establish a 'Defended Lane'
down which independent ships would be 'fired'. Analysts have calculated
that although the rate of loss might be slightly higher in defended lanes than
in convoy, more ships can be 'fired' down the lane in a given time than can be

despatched in convoy and therefore more cargoes delivered in a given time.

All the old objections come to mind: that more cargoes might indeed be delivered than in convoy, provided the ships are not sunk; that defended lanes disperse escorts rather than concentrate them; that there simply are not enough escorts – no navy in history has ever had enough escorts – to defend 'defended lanes'; that air cover can be provided over a convoy, but not over a defended lane; and so on; and so on. But it would be wearisome to go on.

Defended lanes were tried out at sea in September 1981 in Exercise OCEAN SAFARI. Ten different merchant ships, varying from a 69,000-ton bulk carrier to a 3500-ton tramp steamer, were chartered by NATO. Basic convoy procedures were exercised in an area of the South-west Approaches and east Atlantic, down to the latitude of Lisbon. Convoys went from Lisbon to Falmouth and back again. The official conclusion was that 'defended lanes' were 'practicable'. They might well be introduced, until losses became intolerable at about 15 per cent.

So, an idea born in the 1880s, and many times discarded since, reappears as though fresh and new in the 1980s. Truly, as Karl Doenitz might well have said with von Schiller, '*Mit der Dummheit kämpfen Götter selbst vergebens*'. Against stupidity the Gods themselves battle in vain.

Sources and Bibliography

Chapter Sources

CHAPTER 1 (page 1)
The loss of *Pathfinder* is from 'Sunk', by Lt Cdr (E) E. O. Stallybrass RN, in the *Naval Review*, vol. LIX, no. 2, April 1971; Lord Fisher's Memo on 'The submarine and commerce' is in *Records*, by Admiral of the Fleet Lord Fisher, Hodder & Stoughton, 1919; Tirpitz's forecast of submarine warfare is from *My Memoirs*, vol. II, p. 392, and *The Times*, 24 December 1914; Admiral Wemyss's account and comments on the 'Canadian convoy' are from *The Life and Letters of Lord Wester Wemyss GCB: Admiral of the Fleet*, by Lady Wester Wemyss, Eyre & Spottiswoode, 1935, pp. 175–82; general details on the '*Lusitania*' are from *Lusitania*, by Colin Simpson, Longmans 1972.

CHAPTER 2 (page 17)
Sources on general nineteenth-century discussions for and against convoy are: Admiralty 'Memo on provisions to be made for the protection of trade', December 1874, Admiralty Records B2/A1/4/Dec. 1874; quote from Mahan, from *Brasseys Naval Annual*, 1906, p. 53; 'Naval intelligence and protection of commerce in war', by Captain John Colomb RMA, *Journal of RUSI*, 1881, pp. 553–78; 'The protection of commerce by patrolling the ocean highways and by convoy', Foreign Intelligence Committee (no. 75), May 1885; 'Convoys: are they any longer possible?', by Captain P. H. Colomb RN, *Journal of RUSI*, 1887, vol. 37, p. 297; quote from Sir Henry Holland, from *Parliamentary Papers*, 1887, vol. LVI, p. 10; Admiral Hornby's address, from *Journal of Chamber of Commerce*, 5 June 1888, see also his biography by Mrs Fred Egerton, *Admiral of the Fleet Sir Geoffrey Phipps Hornby GCB*, William Blackwood & Sons, 1896, p. 371; Professor J. K. Laughton, quoted from *Brasseys*, 1894, ch. XIII; 'Suggested lines of convoy in wartime, with a scheme of commerce protection', by Lt W. C. Crutchley RNR, and H. L. Swinburne Esq., *Journal of RUSI*, vol. 39, 1895; Colonel Sir H. M. Hozier, Lectures at Lloyd's, pamphlets in Admiralty Library, Earls Court, London; 'Commerce and war', by Cdr Carlyon Bellairs RN, *Brasseys*, 1904, ch. VII; 'The attack and defence of commerce', by James R. Thursfield, *Brasseys*, 1906, ch. IV; a discussion of the influence of the Colomb brothers, Mahan, Laughton, Admiral Sir Herbert Richmond, and Sir Julian Corbett, is in *The*

Education of a Navy: The Development of British Naval Strategic Thought 1867–1914, D. M. Schurmann, Cassell, 1965; 'British naval manoeuvres in 1906', by James R. Thursfield, *Brasseys*, 1907, ch. V; Churchill's speech at the Royal Academy, May 1912, from *Winston S. Churchill*, vol. II, *Young Statesman 1901–1914*, Randolph Churchill, Heinemann, 1974, p. 570; 'What is the influence of oversea commerce on the operations of war? etc.', by Cdr K. G. B. Dewar RN, *Journal of RUSI*, April 1913, and Cdr E. V. F. R. Dugmore RN, June 1913; also bearing on this period, *The Art of Naval Warfare*, by Admiral Sir Cyprian Bridge, Smith, Elder, 1907, and *Naval Policy: A Plea for the Study of War*, by Barfleur (Admiral Sir Reginald Custance), William Blackwood & Son, 1907.

CHAPTER 3 (page 32)
Anti-Submarine Developments and Experiments Prior to December 1916, Technical History no. 40, Naval Historical Section, Admiralty, 1919; Sir Percy Scott's letter, *The Times*, 5 June 1914; *The World Crisis*, vol. II, *1915*, by Winston Churchill, ch XIV, 'The first defeat of the U-boats', Thornton Butterworth, 1923; details of the Dutch convoys from *Miscellaneous Convoys*, Technical History no. 39, Naval Historical Section, Admiralty, 1919; Captain H. H. Smith's letter about convoy is in Public Record Office ADM 137/1322, as is Donald McLeod's letter; Jellicoe's memorandum to the First Lord, is in *The Jellicoe Papers*, vol. II, *1916–1935*, edited by A Temple Patterson, Navy Records Society, 1968, p. 90; Lloyd George's version of the convoy controversy is in *War Memoirs*, Nicholson and Watson, chs XL–XLII.

CHAPTER 4 (page 46)
The text of the official pamphlet on convoy, of January 1917, is from *History of the Great War, Naval Operations*, vol. V, by Henry Newbolt, Longmans, Green, 1931, p. 5; Sir Maurice Hankey's paper on convoy from Newbolt, pp. 10–14; details of the French coal trade from *Miscellaneous Convoys*, Technical History no. 39, Naval Historical Section, Admiralty, 1919; Admiral Sims's account of his meeting with Jellicoe is in *The Victory at Sea*, by Rear Admiral William Sowden Sims US Navy, John Murray, 1920, pp. 6–7; Captain Bertram H. Smith's account of the meeting between Jellicoe and merchant navy captains on 23 February 1917 is from *The Naval Review*, vol. XXIII, May 1935, p. 306.

CHAPTER 5 (page 61)
The most accessible sources for the introduction of convoy in 1917 are in: *From the Dreadnought to Scapa Flow*, vol. IV, *1917: Year of Crisis*, by Arthur J. Marder, Oxford University Press, 1969, especially ch. VI 'The introduction of mercantile convoy (December 1916–April 1917)' and ch. X 'The convoy system in operation (July 1917–December 1917)'; *History of the Great War, Naval Operations*, vol. V, by Henry Newbolt, especially ch. I 'The submarine campaign, April to August 1917', and ch. III 'The submarine campaign in home waters and the extension of the convoy system'; and the *Naval Review*, vol. V, 1917, 'The system of convoys for merchant shipping in 1917 and 1918, as seen by the ministry of shipping', 'HMS *Roxburgh*', and 'Slow convoys', all three anonymous. The text of Jellicoe's letter of 25 April to Hamilton is from *The Jellicoe Papers*, vol. II, p. 157; his memo of 27 April, p. 160. Duff's memo is from *The Submarine Peril*, by Admiral of the Fleet Earl Jellicoe, Cassell, 1934, pp. 124–8. Cdre Gaunt's comments on US opinion are from Public Record Office ADM 137/1322.

CHAPTER 6 (page 72)
The Admiralty's general attitude, *From the Dreadnought to Scapa Flow*, vol. IV, *1917: Year of Crisis* by Arthur J. Marder, Oxford University Press, 1969, p. 189; Lloyd George, from *War Memoirs*, Nicholson and Watson, vol. III, pp. 1164–7; Manisty's comment from ' "J.R.J.": some recollections: 1894–1934', by H. W. E. Manisty, *Naval Review*, vol. XXIV, no. 1, February 1936, p. 28; Duff's comment from his letter to Admiral Sir Alexander Bethell (C-in-C, Plymouth) 26 June 1917, from Duff MSS; Admiral Ballard's anecdote is from the discussion on C. V. Usborne's lecture 'The anti-submarine campaign in the Mediterranean subsequent to 1916', *Journal of RUSI*, vol. LXIX, p. 465; Dewar's comment from *The Navy from Within*, by Vice Admiral K. G. B. Dewar CBE, Victor Gollancz, 1939, p. 217; *Sachem*'s adventures from 'Slow convoys', *Naval Review*, vol. V, 1917, anonymous; Sims, from Marder, p. 258; Taussig's anecdotes from 'Destroyer experiences during the Great War', by Captain J. K. Taussig US Navy, *Proceedings of US Naval Institute*, Annapolis, 1923, pp. 237–9; details of the *'Mary Rose'* convoy from Public Record Office ADM 137/625 and 137/1947; Sir Eric Geddes's speech on the *Mary Rose* is from the Second Reading of the Consolidated Fund Bill, 1 November 1917, *Hansard*, 5th Series, vol. XCVIII, cols. 1663–90.

CHAPTER 7 (page 87)
Details of the 1917 attack on the Scandinavian convoys, from Public Record Office ADM 137/1325–6. General records of First World War convoys are in the ADM 137 series, in particular ADM 137/1327, 1328, and 1335–8 for 1917 Atlantic convoys, ADM 137/1528–33 for 1918 Atlantic convoys; general convoy policy in 1917, ADM 137/1322–4, in 1918 ADM 137/1534–6; Scandinavian convoys, in 1918, ADM 137/1537–8. Convoy records, ADM 137/2523–2664, Plans Division Records, ADM 137/2706–2714, Trade Division Records, ADM 137/2751–2775. Reports of losses of individual ships, ADM 137/3089–3830. *Lychnis*'s adventures and the comments about *Kil* Class gunboats are from 'Mediterranean convoys, 1918', by 'Yamew', *Naval Review*, vol. LIII, no. 3, July 1965, pp. 241–5; Doenitz's comment from *Memoirs: Ten Years and Twenty Days*, by Karl Doenitz, Weidenfeld & Nicholson, 1954, p. 4. General information in *The Atlantic Convoy System*, Technical History no. 14, *Scandinavian and East Coast Convoy Systems*, Technical History no. 8, and *Convoy Statistics and Diagrams*, Technical History no. 15, all by Naval Historical Section, Admiralty, 1919; 'Notes on the convoy system of naval warfare, thirteenth to twentieth centuries', Part II, 'First World War 1914–18', by D. W. Waters, Historical Section, Admiralty, March 1960 (unpublished).

CHAPTER 8 (page 101)
Lord Fisher's quote from *Fear God and Dread Nought*, vol. III by Arthur J. Marder, Cape, 1959, p. 161; *Naneric*'s adventures from the *Naval Review*, vol. V, 1917, pp. 111–31; the bibliography on the RNAS in general and on their convoy work in particular is surprisingly meagre: see *History of the Great War, The War in the Air*, vol. IV, by H. A. Jones, Oxford University Press, 1931, pp. 60–1; *Fly Navy: The History of Maritime Aviation*, by Brian Johnson, David & Charles, 1981, pp. 102–5; *Into Wind: A History of British Naval Flying*, by Hugh Popham, Hamish Hamilton, 1969, ch. VII 'Airships against submarines', and ch. VIII 'The spider's web'; *A Study of the Philosophy and Conduct of Maritime War 1815–1945*, by Lt Cdr D. W. Waters RN, FRHist.S, Historical

Section, Admiralty, February 1954, revised June 1957, in MS, pp. 20–25; also *My Airship Flights, 1915–1930*, by Captain George Meager AFC, William Kimber, 1970; *Story of a North Sea Air Station*, by C. F. Snowden Gamble, Oxford University Press, 1928; *Early Bird*, by Major W. G. Moore, Putnam, 1963; *In the RNAS*, by Harold Rosher, Chatto & Windus, 1916; *Fights and Flights*, by Charles Rumney Samson, Benn, 1930; *Naval Eight*, Signal Press, 1931.

CHAPTER 9 (page 114)
Between the wars: *A Study of the Philosophy and Conduct of Maritime War 1815–1945*, by Lt Cdr D. W. Waltas RN, FRHist.S, Historical Section, Admiralty, February 1954, revised June 1957, in MS, pp. 27–35; *From the Dardanelles to Oran*, by Arthur J. Marder, Oxford University Press, 1974, ch. II, 'The influence of history on sea power: the Royal Navy and the lessons of 1914–1918; 'The ten year rule', by Peter Silverman, *Journal of RUSI*, vol. CXVI, no. 661, March 1971; Lord Stanley's speech on convoy on 14 March 1935 is from Hansard, 5th Series, vol. CCIC, cols. 674–9. Cdr Rollo Appleyard's great work on convoy is in *The Elements of Convoy Defence in Submarine Warfare*, Technical History no. 16, and two Supplements, Technical History no. 17 *Escort Supplement*, and no. 18 *Evasion Supplement*, all published by Naval Historical Section, Admiralty, 1917–1919.

CHAPTER 10 (page 126)
Churchill's remarks about convoy are from his *The Second World War*, vol. I, *The Gathering Storm*, Cassell, 1948, 'sovereign merit' p. 378, Minute to First Sea Lord, of 9 September 1939, pp. 668–9; Jenkins's description of *Furious*'s near miss with *Samaria*, from his *Days of a Dogsbody*, Harrap, 1946, p. 211; Churchill's reaction to *Courageous*'s loss, from Churchill, pp. 387–8, and his Minute of 20 November 1939, p. 669; Sub Lt Lamb's account of *Courageous*, from *War in a Stringbag*, Cassell, 1977, p. 21. Descriptions of east-coast convoys are in *Stand By for Action*, by Cdr William Donald DSC and Bar, Kimber, 1956, Part 2, chs. III–IX; *East Coast Corvette*, by Nicholas Monsarrat, Cassell, 1945, reprinted in *Three Corvettes; Convoy Escort Commander*, by Vice Admiral Sir Peter Gretton KCB, DSO, OBE, DSC, Cassell, 1964, ch. 1. Reports of FN and FS convoys along east coast in Public Record Office ADM 199/6. Bernard Stubbs's BBC broadcast from 'Eight days of convoy duty', Imperial War Museum tape no. 2508. Cdr Donald's quote, from Donald, p. 106. Master of SS *Paris*'s account (though not named as such), from *Red Ensign: A History of Convoy*, by Owen Rutter, Robert Hale, 1942, pp. 187–8; Horton's comment from *Max Horton and the Western Approaches*, by Rear-Admiral W. S. Chalmers CBE, DSC, Hodder & Stoughton, 1954, letter of 7 July 1940, pp. 91–2. Charles Gardner's report on convoy attack, quoted in *Illustrated London News*, 20 July 1940, pp. 82–3. Robin Duff's broadcast of 22 August 1940, IWM tape no. 4933. Details of CE and CW convoys in ADM 199/42. WN and EN convoys and Lieut R. B. Stannard VC's report, in ADM 199/13. Details of Mobile Balloon Barrage units in ADM 199/42. Letter from an airman, from *The Times* of 18 June 1940 (by Flying Officer V. A. W. Rosewarne RAF), also published as *An Airman's Letter*, Putnam, 1940, actual extract from pp. 18–19.

CHAPTER 11 (page 142)
Periwinkle story from Public Record Office ADM 199/2165, Trade Division history of the Battle of the Atlantic 1939–1945. Churchill's Minute of 4 August 1940 from his

The Second World War, vol. II, *Their Finest Hour*, Cassell, 1948, p. 531; Kretschmer's career from *The Golden Horseshoe*, by Terence Robertson, Evans, 1955; reports and details of convoy HX72 from ADM 199/50, 51, 142, 144, and 1707; details of the Children's Overseas Resettlement Scheme from *Let Candles Be Brought In*, by Sir Geoffrey Shakespeare MP, Bart., Macdonald, 1949, ch. XIII; stories of *City of Benares* from Imperial War Museum tapes of Mary Cornish (no. 3390), Eric Davis (no. 2612), and a woman survivor (no. 3390), recorded 27 September 1940, and *Atlantic Ordeal: The Story of Mary Cornish*, by Elspeth Huxley, Chatto & Windus, 1941; reports and details of convoy SC7 from ADM 199/55, 58, 1707, and *Night of the U-Boats*, by Paul Lund and Harry Ludlam, Foulsham, 1973; details of convoy HX79, reports in ADM 199/50, 51, 58, 59, 142, 144, and in ADM 199/1489 'Analysis of submarine attacks on convoys and counter attacks by escorts, August 1940–December 1941'.

CHAPTER 12 (page 157)

Shark metaphor, from *The Second World War*, vol. II, *Their Finest Hour*, Cassell, 1948, by Winston S. Churchill, pp. 530–1; *Convoy Escort Commander*, by Vice Admiral Sir Peter Gretton KCB, DSO, OBE, DSC, Cassell, 1964, p. 107. Accounts of Admiral Stephenson and his work: *The Terror of Tobermory*, by Richard Baker, W. H. Allen, 1971; 'The Commodore', by Lt Cdr J. Ivester Lloyd DSC, in *Wavy Navy: By Some Who Served*, edited by J. Lennox Kerr and David James, Harrap, 1950; *Trawlers Go to War*, by Paul Lund and Harry Ludlam, W. Foulsham, 1971, ch. VIII. Fifty destroyers: Churchill, ch. XX, pp. 353–68, 'United States destroyers and West Indian bases'; *Fifty Ships that Saved the World*, by Philip Goodhart, Heinemann, 1965; *The Town Class Destroyers: The Story of the Four-Stackers*, Tactical & Staff Duties Division (Historical Section), Admiralty, 1949. An account of the cruise of *Admiral Scheer* is in *The Battleship Scheer*, by Admiral Theodor Krancke and H. J. Brennecke, William Kimber, 1956; reports on convoy HX84 are in Public Record Office ADM 199/50 and 51; honours and awards for *Jervis Bay* in ADM 1/17330; see also *The Jervis Bay*, by George Pollock, William Kimber, 1958; '*The Jervis Bay*' and other poems, by Lieut Michael Thwaite RNVR, Putnam, 1943; 'Personal tribute', by A.S.W.A., *The Times*, 19 November 1940; letter by J. Piekarski, *The Times*, 2 December 1940; 'Suicide – but magnificent', by Able Seaman Henry Lane, *Sunday Graphic*, 17 November 1940; *Ordeal by Sea: The New Zealand Shipping Company in the Second World War 1939–1945*, by Sydney D. Waters, New Zealand Shipping Co., London, 1949, ch. III; Chief Wireless Officer of *Rangitiki*, and Dr Firth's account, from Imperial War Museum tapes nos. 3425 and 3588, recorded on 17 and 20 November 1940; Second Officer Hawkins, of *San Demetrio*, from IWM tape no. 3425, recorded 17 November 1940; see also *The Saga of San Demetrio*, by F. Tennyson Jesse, HMSO, 1942, and *San Demetrio*, by Calum MacNeil, Angus & Robertson, 1957. Minute by Captain Harcourt, from ADM 199/6, p. 101. Kretschmer's comment on convoy from *Golden Horseshoe*, by Terence Robertson, Evans, 1955, ch. IX. Cdr Brewer's comment on Lindemann, from 'The melody lingers on, III', *Naval Review*, vol. LXII, no. 2, April 1974, p. 141. Loss of *Forfar*, from ADM 1/11216, and of *Patroclus* and *Laurentic*, from ADM 1/11215, see also *The Golden Horseshoe*; analysis of events around convoy HX90 from ADM 199/1489. Report on convoy WS5A from ADM 199/1136. Jenkins's account from his *Days of a Dogsbody*, Harrap, 1946, p. 232.

CHAPTER 13 (page 170)
General situation in February 1941, from Public Record Office ADM 199/2165, Trade
Division history of the Battle of the Atlantic, pp. 5–7. Accounts of convoy OB293,
from ADM 199/1707, 199/1141; *The Golden Horshoe*, by Terence Robertson, Evans
Bros., 1955; Joachim Matz's account of U-70's last moments from *The Hunters and the
Hunted*, by Jochen Brennecke, Burke, 1958, ch. VI. 'Barmaid's Blush', from *Stand By
to Ram*, by Lieut Guy Morgan RNVR, Crosby Lockwood, 1943; reports of convoy HX112
from ADM 199/718, 1144, 1179 and 1708, *Vanoc's* Report of Proceedings, in ADM 1/11065,
sinkings of U-99 and U-100 from *The Golden Horseshoe* and from *U-boat Killer*, by
Captain Donald MacIntyre, Weidenfeld & Nicolson, 1956; *Scharnhorst* and *Gneise-
nau*'s cruise from 'The Scharnhorst–Gneisenau team at its peak', by Lieut Cdr
Peter Handel-Mazzetti, edited by Philip Lundeberg, United States Naval Institute
Proceedings, August 1956, pp. 852–60; also from *Battleship Scharnhorst*, by Albert
Vulliez and Jacques Mordal, translated by George Malcolm, Hutchinson, 1958, chs.
VII–IX.

CHAPTER 14 (page 185)
Reports of convoy SC26 from Public Record Office ADM 199/55, 56, 1141, 1144, 1489
and 1983; ADM 237/29 for Steurmannsmaat Carl Becker's letter; reports on convoy
HX121 from ADM 199/718, 1144, 1489 and 1984; reports of convoy OB318 from ADM
199/1489, report of Operation PRIMROSE, the capture of U-110, from ADM 1/11133, and
from *The Secret Capture*, by Captain S. W. Roskill, Collins, 1959 (including excellent
summary of the convoy system in 1941 in general). Reports on convoys HX133 and
OB336 from ADM 199/1489. General history of rescue ships from *The Rescue Ships*, by
Vice Admiral B. B. Schofield CB, CBE, and Lt Cdr L. F. Martyn RNVR, Blackwoods,
1968; 'Convoy rescue ships', by Sir John McNee DSO, FRCP, D.SC, FRS(E), MD, *Journal
of the Royal Naval Medical Service*, vol. XXXI, 1945; and from ADM 199/2165, Trade
Division history. Information about CAM ships from *The Giant Killers* (Cam ships) by
Kenneth Poolman, William Kimber, 1960, and *The Catafighters and Merchant Aircraft
Carriers*, by Kenneth Poolman, William Kimber, 1970. Lieut Everett's account from
Fleet Air Arm, HMSO, 1943, p. 80. Reports of convoys SC42 and 44 from ADM 199/1489
and ADM 237/219. Rear Admiral Sir Kenelm Creighton's experience from his *Convoy
Commodore*, William Kimber, 1956. General information from 'Commodores of
ocean convoy', by Rear Admiral Sir Errol Manners KBE, *Naval Review*, vol. XXXIV, no.
2, May 1946, pp. 127–9, with a list of convoy commodores, on pp. 131–3. Vice Admiral
H. H. Smith DSO, comment from 'Convoy', *Naval Review*, vol. XXIX, no. 2, May 1941,
p. 236.

CHAPTER 15 (page 206)
Walker's career, with particulars of convoy HG76, is in *Walker RN*, by Terence
Robertson, Evans, 1956, and in *Walker's Groups in the Western Approaches*, by Cdr
D. E. G. Wemyss DSO, DSC, Liverpool Daily Post & Echo, 1948. Sub. Lieut Brown's
success against the Kondor, from *Find, Fix and Strike*, by Terence Horsley, Eyre &
Spottiswoode, 1943, p. 96. Analysis of HG76 and Biegalk's account of his attack on
Audacity, from ADM 199/1489. *Audacity*'s history is in *Escort Carrier 1941–1945*, by
Kenneth Poolman, Ian Allan, 1973, ch. III, 'A Little Audacity'. Minutes of the board
of enquiry into *Audacity*'s loss, from ADM 1/11895. History of Operational Research,
from *OR in World War Two: Operational Research against the U-boat*, by Professor

C. H. Waddington CBE, MA, DSC., FRS, Elek, 1973; *Science at War*, by J. G. Crowther and R. Whiddington CBE, FRS, HMSO, 1947, vol. II, *Operational Research; Studies of War*, by P. M. S. Blackett, Oliver & Boyd, 1962; Memoir on Lord Blackett OM, CH, FRS, in *Naval Review*, vol. LXII, 1974, p. 300; 'Operational research: recollections of problems studied 1940–45', by Professor P. M. S. Blackett, *Brasseys Annual*, 1953, and in ADM 219, Naval Operational Research, Studies and Reports.

CHAPTER 16 (page 225)
American involvement in the war at sea, from *History of United States Naval Operations in World War II*, vol. I, *The Battle of the Atlantic September 1939–May 1943*, by Samuel Eliot Morison, Oxford University Press, 1948; the *Robin Moor*, from *The Laughing Cow*, by Jost Metzler, William Kimber, 1955, ch. XX, 'An annoying incident – the *Robin Moor*'. See also *The Second World War*, by Winston S. Churchill, vol. IV, *The Hinge of Fate*, Cassell, 1960, ch. VII, 'The U-boat paradise'. Brewer's anecdote from the *Naval Review*, vol. LXII, no. 2, May 1974, 'The melody lingers on', p. 142. Winn's experience in Washington from *Very Special Intelligence*, by Patrick Beesly, Hamish Hamilton, 1977, ch. VII, 'January–July 1942: Operation Paukenschlag and the great black-out', especially p. 109. Report of convoy OG82 from Public Record Office ADM 237/60, including Captain Walker's report of proceedings. E^2 law of convoy and other formulae, from the *Naval Review*, vol. LI, no. 4, October 1963, 'The science of Admiralty', by Lt Cdr D. W. Waters. History of the Tactical School, from *Captain Gilbert Roberts RN and the Anti-U-boat School*, by Mark Williams, Cassell, 1979, especially ch. VIII. 'Duck-shooting' metaphor, from *Science at War*, by J. G. Crowther and R. Whiddington CBE, FRS, HMSO, 1947, p. 101. Reports on convoy SC94 from ADM 199/1490, on ON115 from ADM 237/18, on SL118 from ADM 199/1490 and 237/230, on ON122, SC104, ON144 and HX217 all from ADM 199/1490. Convoy ON154, from ADM 199/1274 and 1706 and *The Convoy that Nearly Died: The Story of ONS154*, by Henry Revely, William Kimber, 1979.

CHAPTER 17 (page 249)
Format of U-432's signal from *British Intelligence in the Second World War*, vol. II, by F. H. Hinsley, HMSO, 1981, ch. XXVI, 'The war at sea from November 1942 to the summer of 1943', p. 550n. Churchill's 'cavalry divisions' remark from his *The Second World War*, vol. V, *Closing the Ring*, Cassell, 1960, p. 8. Reports of convoy TM1 from Public Record Office ADM 199/476, 477, 1491, ADM 223/16, 223/88, ch. XIII, and Patrick Beesly, *Very Special Intelligence*, ch. X, pp. 158–60. Convoy SC118, from ADM 199/579, 580, 1491, ADM 223/16, 223/88, ch. XIV. Stannard's account of *Vimy*'s sinking of U-187 from Imperial War Museum tape no. 5568. Convoy ON166 from ADM 199/583, 1402, 1705, ADM 223/16, 'The cruise of the *Campbell*', *Life*, 5 July 1943, 'Convoy commander' by Stan Smith, *For Men Only*, 1962. SC121, from ADM 199/580 and 1491. HX228 from ADM 199/575, 576 and 1491. HX229 from ADM 199/579, 580, and 1491, and ADM 223/16. SC122 from ADM 199/579, 580, 1491, and ADM 223/16. Both HX229 and SC122 in ADM 223/88, ch. XV; *The Critical Convoy Battles of March 1943: The Battles for HX229/SC122*, by Jurgen Rohwer, Ian Allan, 1977; *Convoy: The Battle for Convoys SC122 and HX229*, by Martin Middlebrook, Allen Lane, 1976. Convoy HX231, *Crisis Convoy: The Story of HX231*, by Vice Admiral Sir Peter Gretton KCB, DSO, CBE, DSC, Peter Davies, 1974.

CHAPTER 18 (page 272)

Convoy ONS5, from Public Record Office ADM 223/16, 223/88, ch. XVI, ADM 237/113 (reports and signals); *The Fiercest Battle: The Story of Convoy ONS5*, by Ronald Seth, Hutchinson, 1961; *Convoy Escort Commander*, by Vice Admiral Sir Peter Gretton KCB, DSO, OBE, DSC, Cassell, 1964, ch. XI, 'A long fight'; 'The Melody Lingers On' by Cdr G. N. Brewer, *Naval Review*, vol. LXII, no. 3, July 1974; operations of *Biter* and *Archer* in May 1943, well summarized in *Escort Carrier 1941–1945*, by Kenneth Poolman, Ian Allan, 1972, ch. VII, 'The North American run'; convoys HX237, SC129, HX238, HX239, ONI84, SC130, from ADM 199/577, 579, 580, 1491, 2019, 2020, and from ADM 199/2060, Monthly Anti-Submarine Reports, January to December 1943. Convoy SC130 also from Gretton, ch XII. Operations of American CVE groups in central Atlantic, *History of United States Naval Operations in World War II*, vol. X, *The Atlantic Battle Won, May 1943–May 1945*, by Samuel Eliot Morison, Oxford University Press, 1958. MAC ships, from *The Catafighters and Merchant Aircraft Carriers*, by Kenneth Poolman, William Kimber, 1970; vivid description of MAC operations, from aircrew point of view, in *Bring Back My Stringbag*, by Lord Kilbracken (Lt Cdr (A) John Godley DSC, RNVR), Peter Davies, 1979, chs. VI, VII and VIII.

CHAPTER 19 (page 288)

Convoys ONS18, ON202, SC143, from Public Record Office ADM 223/16 and 223/88. 'Step-aside technique' from *Captain Gilbert Roberts RN and the Anti-U-boat School*, by Mark Williams, Cassell, 1979, p. 133. Convoys SL139/MKS30 from ADM 223/88. Mediterranean convoys: operations EXCESS, SUBSTANCE, HALBERD, HARPOON and PEDESTAL, Dispatches, Supplement to *London Gazette*, 10 August 1948; ADM 223/31. Italian convoys; *The Battle for the Mediterranean*, by Donald MacIntyre, Batsford, 1964; *Pedestal: The Malta Convoy of August 1942*, by Peter C. Smith, William Kimber, 1970. Arctic convoys: Dispatches, Supplement to *London Gazette*, 17 October 1950; ADM 199/73, 77 and 327; from an extensive bibliography: *Convoy is to Scatter*, by Captain Jack Broome DSC, William Kimber, 1972; *The Kola Run: A Record of Arctic Convoys 1941–1945*, by Vice-Admiral Sir Ian Campbell KBE, CB, DSO, and Captain Donald MacIntyre DSO, DSC, Frederick Muller, 1958; *Russian Convoys 1941–45*, by Captain I. M. R. Campbell DSO, *Journal of RUSI*, vol. XCI, Feb.–Nov. 1946, pp. 227–40; *The Destruction of Convoy PQ17*, by David Irving, Cassell, 1968; *PQ17 Convoy to Hell: The Survivors' Story*, by Paul Lund and Harry Ludlam, Foulsham, 1968; *73 North: The Battle of the Barents Sea*, by Dudley Pope, Weidenfeld & Nicolson, 1958; *The Russian Convoys*, by B. B. Schofield, Batsford, 1964; *Arctic Victory: The Story of Convoy PQ18*, by Peter C. Smith, William Kimber, 1975.

CHAPTERS 20–22 (page 309–49)

'The Failure of the Japanese convoy escort', by Major Y. Horie, *Proceedings of United States Naval Institute*, October 1956; 'Why Japan's anti-submarine warfare failed', by Atsushi Oi, *Proc. USNI*, June 1952; 'Defended lanes v. convoys', by Desmond Wettern, *Navy International*, vol. LXXXVI, no. 12, December 1981; *Flashing Blades over the Sea: The Development and History of Helicopters in the Royal Navy*, by Lt Cdr J. M. Milne RN, Maritime Books, 1980; 'The heel of Achilles', by Cdr F. Barley RNVR and Lt Cdr D. W. Waters FRHist.S., RN, *Journal of RUSI*, August 1958; scenario of possible Atlantic war from 'Technology and trade protection: have recent changes in technology invalidated the convoy system?', by Commander Alan West DSC, *Naval*

Review, vol. LXVII, no. 3, July 1979; *The Third World War. August 1985*, by General Sir John Hackett and others, Sidgwick & Jackson, 1978; *Frigate* (1980), *Carrier* (1981), *Submarine* (1982), all by John Wingate, Weidenfeld & Nicolson.

Select bibliography

Unprinted Sources in Public Record Office
ADM 1/9501   Convoy policy 1938–43
ADM 116/1768–76   World War One convoys
ADM 116/5456   Battle of Atlantic: convoy protection and anti-U-boat measures
    1943–5
ADM 186/801–4   Naval staff histories. Convoy warfare and trade defence.
ADM 199/1–85, 159, 161, 210–20   Various convoy reports
ADM 199/1195–8   Enemy submarine attacks on British and US shipping
ADM 199/1489   Analysis of submarine attacks on convoys 1940–1
ADM 199/1490   Analysis of submarine attacks on convoys 1942
ADM 199/1491   Analysis of submarine attacks on convoys 1943–4
ADM 199/1266–76   Enemy submarine attacks on merchant shipping
ADM 199/1705–11   Attacks on convoys: Department of Anti-Submarine Warfare
    departmental records
ADM 199/1730   Trade protection 1939–45, and Italian submarines
ADM 199/1976–2031   Analysis of U-boat attacks
ADM 199/2032–56   U-boat incidents
ADM 199/2057–62   Monthly anti-submarine warfare reports 1939–1945
ADM 199/2099–2102   Atlantic convoy analyses and reports 1941–5
ADM 199/2105   Convoy protection. Trade Division, historical review.
ADM 199/2130–48   Survivors' reports: merchant vessels 1939–45
ADM 199/2165   Battle of Atlantic history. Trade Division. 1939–1945, including
    c-in-c Western Approaches report of proceedings
ADM 217 series   Convoys: Western Approaches Station records
ADM 223/88   Admiralty use of Special Intelligence in naval operations
ADM 237 series   Convoys: Operations Division records

BARLEY-WATERS MSS
Collection of papers on trade defence from 1870 to 1960, Naval Library, Ministry of
Defence.

DUFF MSS
Papers and correspondence regarding introduction of convoy in 1917, Admiral Sir
Alexander Duff's papers, National Maritime Museum.

Printed sources

ANONYMOUS, 'The control of shipping during the war', *Naval Review*, vol. VII, 1919

BEESLY, PATRICK, *Very Special Intelligence*, Hamish Hamilton, 1977

BEKKER, CAJUS, *Hitler's Naval War*, Macdonald & Jane's, 1974

BONE, DAVID W., *Merchantmen-at-Arms: the British Merchant Service in the War*, Chatto
& Windus, 1919

BRENNECKE, JOCHEN, *The Hunters and the Hunted*, Burke, 1958

British Vessels Lost at Sea, 1914–18, HMSO, 1919 (reprinted, Patrick Stephens, 1977)

British Vessels Lost at Sea, 1939–45, HMSO, 1947 (reprinted, Patrick Stephens, 1976)

BUSCH, HARALD, *U-boats at War*, Putnam, 1955

CHALMERS, Rear-Admiral W. S., CBE, DSC, *Max Horton and the Western Approaches*,
Hodder & Stoughton, 1954

CHATTERTON, E. KEBLE, *Fighting the U-Boats*, Hurst & Blackett, 1942
  Beating the U-Boats, Hurst & Blackett, 1943

CHURCHILL, WINSTON S., *The Second World War*, 6 vols., Cassell, 1948–54

COMPTON-HALL, RICHARD, *The Underwater War 1939–1945*, Blandford Press, 1982

CORBETT, Sir JULIAN S., and NEWBOLT, Sir HENRY, *History of the Great War, Naval
Operations*, 5 vols., Longmans, 1920–31

COSTELLO, JOHN, and HUGHES, TERRY, *The Battle of the Atlantic*, Collins, 1977

DEWAR, K. C. B., 'War on shipping, 1914–18', *Naval Review*, vol. XLVII, no. 1, January
1959

DOENITZ, Admiral KARL, *Memoirs: Ten Years and Twenty Days*, Weidenfeld &
Nicolson, 1959

FAYLE, C. ERNEST, *History of the Great War, Seaborne Trade*, 3 vols., John Murray,
1920–4

GAYER, Captain A., German Navy, 'Summary of German submarine operations in
the various theaters of war from 1914 to 1918', *Proceedings of the US Naval
Institute*, 1926, pp. 621–59

GIBSON, R. H., and PRENDERGAST, MAURICE, *The German Submarine War, 1914–1918*,
Constable, 1931

GRANT, ROBERT M., 'Known sunk – German submarine war losses, 1914–1918',
Proceedings of the US Naval Institute, January 1938, pp. 66–77
  U-Boats Destroyed, Putnam, 1964
  U-Boat Intelligence, 1914–1918, Putnam, 1969

GRETTON, Vice-Admiral Sir PETER, KCB, DSO, OBE, DSC, *Convoy Escort Commander*,
Cassell, 1964

HEZLET, Vice-Admiral Sir ARTHUR, KBE, CB, DSO, DSC, *The Submarine and Sea Power*,
Peter Davies, 1967
  Aircraft and Sea Power, Peter Davies, 1970
  The Electron and Sea Power, Peter Davies, 1975

HILL, ROGER, *Destroyer Captain*, William Kimber, 1975

HINSLEY, F. H., *British Intelligence in the Second World War*, vols. I and II, HMSO, 1979,
1981

HURD, Sir ARCHIBALD, *History of the Great War, The Merchant Navy*, 3 vols., John Murry, 1921–9

JAMESON, Rear-Admiral Sir WILLIAM, KBE, CB, *The Most Formidable Thing*, Hart-Davis, 1965

JELLICOE, Admiral of the Fleet Viscount, of Scapa, GCB, OM, GCVO, *The Crisis of the Naval War*, Cassell, 1920

JELLICOE, The Rt Hon the Earl, *The Submarine Peril*, Cassell, 1934

JOHNSON, BRIAN, *The Secret War*, British Broadcasting Corporation, 1978

MACINTYRE, Captain DONALD, DSO, DSC, *The Battle of the Atlantic*, Batsford, 1961
U-Boat Killer, Weidenfeld & Nicolson, 1956

MALLALIEU, J. P. W., *Very Ordinary Seaman*, Victor Gollanz, 1944

MARDER, ARTHUR J., *From the Dreadnought to Scapa Flow: The Royal Navy in the Fisher Era, 1904–1919*, 5 vols., Oxford University Press, 1961–70
From the Dardanelles to Oran: Studies of the Royal Navy in War and Peace 1915–1940, Oxford University Press, 1974

MONSARRAT, NICHOLAS, *Three Corvettes*, Cassell, 1945

MORISON, SAMUEL ELIOT, *History of United States Naval Operations in World War II; Volume I, The Battle of the Atlantic September 1939–May 1943*; Volume X, *The Atlantic Battle Won, May 1943–May 1945*; Oxford University Press, 1948 and 1955

NAVAL HISTORY BRANCH, *Defeat of the Enemy Attack on Shipping, 1939–45*, Admiralty, 1951

R.H.N., 'The defence of trade 1914–18', *Naval Review*, vol. LIV, no. 2, April 1966

PUTT, S. GORLEY, *Men Dressed as Seamen*, Christophers, 1943

RAYNER, D. A., *Escort*, William Kimber, 1955

ROHWER, J., and HUMMELCHEN, G., *Chronology of the War at Sea, 1939–1945*, 2 vols., ed. A. J. Watts, Ian Allan, 1972–4

ROSKILL, Captain S. W., CBE, DSC, MA, FRHist.S, RN, *History of the Second World War, The War at Sea 1939–1945*, 3 vols., HMSO, 1954–62
A Merchant Fleet in War 1939–1945 (Alfred Holt & Co.), Collins, 1962
Naval Policy between the Wars, vol. I, *The Period of Anglo-American Antagonism, 1919–1929*, vol. II, *The Period of Reluctant Rearmament 1930–1939*, Collins, 1968 and 1976
Hankey, Man of Secrets, 3 vols., Collins, 1970–5

RUTTER, OWEN, *Red Ensign: A History of Convoy*, Robert Hale, 1942

SCHAEFFER, HEINZ, *U-boat 977*, William Kimber, 1952

SCHULL, JOSEPH, *The Far Distant Ships*, Ministry of National Defence, Ottawa, 1950

WATERS, Lt Cdr D. W., 'The science of Admiralty', *Naval Review*, vols. LI–LII, in 6 parts, July 1963–October 1964
'Historical survey of trade defence since 1914', *Journal of RUSI*, August 1954

WATERS, SYDNEY D., *Ordeal by Sea: The New Zealand Shipping Company in the Second World War 1939–1945*, New Zealand Shipping Co., 1949

WERNER, HERBERT A., *Iron Coffins: A personal account of the German U-boat battles of World War II*, Arthur Barker, 1970

WINN, GODFREY, *P.Q.17*, Hutchinson, n.d.

WOON, BASIL, *Atlantic Front*, Peter Davies, 1941

Fiction

BUCHHEIM, LOTHAR-GUNTHER, *U-boat*, Collins, 1974
FORESTER, C. S., *The Good Shepherd*, Michael Joseph, 1955
   The Ship, Michael Joseph, 1943
HARLING, ROBERT, *The Steep Atlantick Stream*, Chatto & Windus, 1946
MONSARRAT, NICHOLAS, *The Cruel Sea*, Cassell, 1951
OTT, WOLFGANG, *Sharks and Little Fish*, Hutchinson, 1957

Index